Advertising

Advertising Titles from International Thomson Publishing

Jakacki, *IMC: An Integrated Marketing Communications Exercise* (1998, South-Western)

Jewler/Drewniany, *Creative Strategy in Advertising,* 6e (1998, Wadsworth)

Mueller, *International Advertising: Communicating Across Cultures* (1996, Wadsworth)

O'Guinn/Allen/Semenik, *Advertising* (1998, South-Western)

Sayre, *Ad Campaign Workbook* (1998, South-Western)

Sivulka, *Soap, Sex, and Cigarettes: A Cultural History of American Advertising* (1998, Wadsworth)

Woods, *Advertising and Marketing to the New Majority: A Case Study Approach* (1995, Wadsworth)

Advertising

Thomas C. O'Guinn
Professor of Advertising and Business Administration
Research Professor, Institute of Communications Research
University of Illinois, Urbana-Champaign

Chris T. Allen
Professor of Marketing
University of Cincinnati

Richard J. Semenik
Professor of Marketing
David Eccles School of Business
University of Utah–Salt Lake City

SOUTH-WESTERN College Publishing

An International Thomson Publishing Company

Editor-in-Chief: Valerie A. Ashton
Team Director: John Szilagyi
Acquisitions Editor: Dreis Van Landuyt
Develpmental Editors: Cinci Stowell and Mary Pommert, Custom Editorial Productions, Inc.
Production Editor: Judith O'Neill
Photo Editor: Jennifer Mayhall
Production: Lachina Publishing Services, Inc.
Cover and Internal Designer: Craig LaGesse Ramsdell
Manufacturing Coordinator: Sue Disselkamp
Marketing Manager: Steve Scoble
Advertising Permissions: Jennifer Mayhall and Naples Publication Services
Cover Illustration: Copyright 1997 Gordon Studer

1 2 3 4 5 VH 1 0 9 8 7

Printed in the United States of America

Library of Congress Cataloging-in-Publication Data

O'Guinn, Thomas C.
      Advertising / Thomas C. O'Guinn, Chris T. Allen, Richard J.
   Semenik
         p.   cm.
      Includes bibliographical references and index.
      ISBN 0-538-86908-9 (hardcover)
      1. Advertising.   I. Allen, Chris T.   II. Semenik, Richard J.
   III. Title.
   HF5821.034   1997
   659.1—dc21   96-46515
                                                                           CIP

I⑦P ®
International Thomson Publishing
South-Western College Publishing is an ITP Company. The ITP trademark is used under
license.

Brief Contents

Contents

4 Social, Ethical, and Regulatory Aspects of Advertising 79

Delta Air Lines: The Process of Integrated Marketing Communications 106

PART 2
The Planning: Analyzing the Advertising Environment 115

5 Advertising and Consumer Behavior 117

6 Market Segmentation, Positioning, and Product Differentiation 155

7 Advertising Research 183

8 The Advertising Plan 211

9 Advertising Planning: An International Perspective 235

PART 3
Preparing the Message 269

13 Art Direction and Production in Broadcast Advertising 345

Delta Air Lines: Preparing the Integrated Marketing Communications Message 370

PART 4
Placing the Message: Media and Supportive Communications 377

Preface

Advertising is a lot of things. It's democratic pop culture, capitalist tool, oppressor, liberator, art, and theater, all rolled into one. It's free speech, it's creative flow, it's information, and it helps business get things sold. Above all, it's fun. We expect that students who read our book will learn an awful lot about advertising—and have a good time doing it!

Like other aspects of business, though, good advertising is the result of hard work and careful planning. The truth is that creating good advertising is an enormous challenge. It was written by three people with lots of experience in both academic and professional settings. We worked hard to deliver a book that is both engaging and academically solid. Since the publishers are the ones who get the real dough, you can rest assured that writing this book was a labor of love.

As you will discover, this book copies no one, yet pays homage to many. It will seem familiar and comfortable to you in many ways, and different and confrontational in others. More than anything, this book attempts to be honest. It acknowledges the complexity of human communication and consumer behavior, while still having a point of view. It tells you what the cutting-edge thinking is on various topics and what we're fairly certain about in the way of good advertising practices, but it also quickly admits that on certain issues no one really has a clue about a definitive "right way."

In terms of content and features, this book is loaded, simultaneously attuned to the vanguard and mindful of accepted wisdom. We pay particular attention to integrated marketing communication and to new media options like advertising on the World Wide Web. We have tried to guard against immediate outdating by underlying these discussions of new media with principles and perspectives that will endure after the specific examples are obsolete. We have also tried our best to make life easier for the overworked advertising professor by offering a wide variety of ancillary materials, all written and coordinated by the authors, that will assist in teaching from the book and fully engaging students on this fascinating topic.

Students will like this book. It's current, and it has an edge. We spent considerable time researching students' and instructors' likes and dislikes with existing advertising textbooks. The text was written and the examples were chosen to facilitate an effective meeting place for student and teacher.

From Chapter 1 to Chapter 20, Advertising Is *With-It!*

Advertising and its support package were written for use in all introductory advertising classes taught anywhere in the university: business and journalism schools, as well as mass communication and advertising departments. We recognize that many other fine textbooks are available for use in the introductory advertising class. Here are four good reasons why you'll want to get *with it* and take a close look at *Advertising:*

Compelling Fundamentals.

We fully expect our book to set the standard for coverage of new media topics. It is loaded with features and insights and commonsense perspectives about the new media. Hey, we got lucky. We were at the right place at the right time to build these issues into our very first edition of *Advertising.* Competitive books will have no choice but to follow our lead.

That said, the real strength of this book is in its treatment of the fundamentals of advertising. One cannot appreciate the role of the new media today, or in the next millennium, without a solid understanding of the fundamentals. If you doubt our commitment to the fundamentals, take a good look at Chapters 2 through 9. Here we present compelling coverage of the key issues involved in preparing a sound advertising plan. Chapter 2 begins this process by providing students with a perspective on the structure of the advertising industry. In Chapters 3 and 4, students will gain further insights by studying the evolution of modern-day advertising along with the social, ethical, and regulatory aspects of advertising. Chapter 5 provides a comprehensive treatment of how analysis of consumer behavior serves as the basis for sound advertising plans, and Chapter 6 establishes advertising's key role in executing coherent marketing strategies. The role of marketing and advertising research in laying the foundation for the plan is considered in Chapter 7, and the essentials of ad planning are consolidated and spelled out in Chapter 8. Notice that we don't wait until the end of the book to bring international considerations into our thinking about ad plans. Global topics are integrated throughout the text, because today's students must possess a global view. In addition, we incorporate the international chapter into the heart of the book in Chapter 9. Chapters 10 to 20 cover the full array of issues that must be attended to in executing an advertising plan, from message development to media planning and evaluation.

So *yes,* we have the new media covered in this first edition of *Advertising.* But *no,* the new media coverage does not come at the expense of full coverage of the fundamentals of advertising.

Balanced New Media Coverage.

If you have been waiting for an advertising text that will allow you to explore the possibilities of the new media in your introductory advertising class, your wait is over. Where other books now in their third or fourth editions struggle to come to terms with the new media that now animate our industry, our book has new media at its foundation, providing coverage of advertising on the Internet and the World Wide Web at a depth and breadth not attempted elsewhere. Every chapter contains a feature headed *New Media,* which furnishes contemporary examples of how the new media are affecting various aspects of advertising practice. And every chapter contains *Web Sightings,* application activities designed to bring the chapter ads into real time and the concept of new media to life. Every chapter ends with *Internet Exercises* that can be pursued via the Internet to help students learn about advertising generally, and the Internet specifically. In-depth consideration of new media vehicles is provided in Part 4 of the book: Chapter 16 discusses the major new media options and offers a frank assessment of what value they offer marketers today and for the future. Chapter 17 is all about advertising and marketing on the Internet and reviews many technical considerations for working in this new medium. Chapter 17 is the first of its kind among basic advertising texts. As we have already suggested, we fully expect that our book—a text *with it* all—will set the standard for coverage of new media topics.

Integrated IMC Coverage. Isn't it odd the way some authors treat integrated marketing communication (IMC) as if it were something disconnected from advertising? They seem to suggest that the two are naturally incompatible and in conflict. It's as though we might want to do one (mass media advertising), or the other (IMC), but certainly not both. We reject this disabling mind-set about advertising and IMC.

To create effective advertising for the next millennium, students must appreciate the full range of communication tools available to them. We make this point as our concluding premise in Chapter 1, and return to it over and over again throughout the book. Part 4 picks up on this general theme and presents a comprehensive treatment of the tools available to carry one's message to the consumer. While we give thorough consideration to traditional media, we also provide in-depth coverage of event sponsorship (Chapter 16), the wide array of possibilities in the area of sales promotion (Chapter 18), and the supportive role for PR and corporate advertising (Chapter 20). Is the direct marketing chapter in your old advertising book up to the standard of ours (Chapter 19)? Note also that throughout Part 4 we provide constant reminders of the coordination challenges that must be managed if our advertising and promotions are to speak to the customer *in a single voice.*

And the coverage doesn't stop there. Another unique feature of *Advertising* is the end-of-part case study that we developed in conjunction with Delta Air Lines. We went inside Delta and saw firsthand how this successful airline has practiced IMC for years. We worked with their agency, BBDO South, in securing current IMC campaign materials and discussed the role of the agency and the role of the client in the preparation of campaigns. The resulting Delta case illustrates the full array of considerations involved in implementing integrated marketing communication, including interactive communications and Web site development via Delta's *SkyLinks* site at www.delta-air.com. This comprehensive case study is offered in four installments, one at the end of each part in the text. As you will see, Delta provided us with all the planning, strategy, and implementation information for its "Cincinnati Instead" IMC campaign. We track the evolution of this campaign from its inception through its multimedia execution. This unique and comprehensive case vividly illustrates what it means to speak to the customer with multiple tools, but *in a single voice.* A complement to our text, *IMC: An Integrated Marketing Communications Exercise* by Bernard Jakacki, is also available to take students through the creation and management of an IMC program.

Student Engagement and Learning. You will find that this book provides a sophisticated examination of advertising fundamentals in lively, concise language. We don't beat around the bush, and we're not shy about challenging a few conventions. In addition, the book features an attractive internal design and hundreds of illustrations to support the text. Reading this book will be an engaging experience for new students of advertising.

We sincerely want this to be a learning experience as well. The markers of our commitment to student learning are easily identified throughout the book. Every chapter begins with a statement of the learning objectives for that chapter. (For a quick appreciation of the coverage provided by this book, take a pass through it and read the learning objectives on the first page of each chapter.) Chapters are organized to deliver content that is responsive to each learning objective, and the chapter summaries are written to reflect what the chapter has offered with respect to each learning objective.

We also believe that students must be challenged to go beyond their reading to think about the issues raised in the book. Thus, you will note that the Questions for Review and Critical Thinking sections at the end of each chapter demand thoughtful analysis rather than mere regurgitation, and the Experiential Exercises will help students put their learning to use in ways that will help them take more away from the course than just textbook learning. Complete use of this text and its ancillary materials will yield a dramatic and engaging learning experience for students of all ages who are studying advertising for the first time.

If you think about these four reasons, and give our book a serious look, we believe you will be excited by the possibilities of using it in your classes. Go ahead, try it. *Advertising* really is fun, and it's *with-it*.

A Closer Look at Some First Edition Features

How the Text Is Organized

Advertising is divided into four major parts: the process of advertising (Part 1), the planning of advertising (Part 2), preparing the advertising message (Part 3), and placing the advertising message (Part 4). Throughout the book, students are given both the client's and the agency's perspective on advertising practices. Two outstanding supplementary videos, created and filmed exclusively for *Advertising,* give students additional insights into the client's and the agency's view of advertising. These two videos are discussed in detail on page xxxiv.

Now, let us call your attention to some important chapter highlights:

Chapter Highlights

Chapter 1: Advertising as a Process. Chapter 1 quickly sets the stage for what's to come. Departing from decades-old communication models, the chapter presents advertising as mass-mediated communication. Students learn that advertising is both a communications process and a business process, and they're shown why this is so. The book's seamless IMC coverage begins right here, with students introduced to the terminology and concept of coordinating and integrating promotional efforts to achieve advertising synergy and to speak to consumers *in a single voice.* It's a great beginning.

Chapter 2: The Structure of the Advertising Industry. In this chapter, students read about six trends that are transforming the advertising industry today and the seismic changes the industry is experiencing in the 1990s. Students will see who the participants in the ad industry are today and the role each plays in the formulation and execution of ad campaigns. They will also learn how agencies are compensated for their services, including the trend toward fee-based compensation.

Chapter 3: The Evolution of Advertising. This chapter puts advertising in a historical context for students and provides numerous ads from the "good old days" to emphasize the historical concepts presented. Students will study the history of advertising through ten eras, seeing how advertising has changed and evolved, and how it is forged out of its social setting. Students will read about the Preindustrialization Era (pre-1800); the Era of Industrialization (1800 to 1875); the P. T. Barnum Era (1875 to 1918); the 1920s (1918 to 1929); the Struggle (1929 to 1941); War, Paranoia, and Economic Growth (1941 to 1960); Peace, Love, and the Creative Revolution (1960 to 1972); the 1970s (1973 to 1980); the Republican Era (1980 to 1993); and the Present Era. Definitely an entertaining chapter, at the same time it gives students a necessary and important perspective on advertising before launching into advertising planning concepts and issues.

Chapter 4: Social, Ethical, and Regulatory Aspects of Advertising. Advertising is dynamic and controversial. In this chapter, students will examine a variety of issues concerning advertising's effects on societal well-being. Is advertising intrusive, manipulative, and deceptive? Does it waste resources, promote materialism, and perpetuate stereotypes? Or does it inform, give exposure to important issues, and raise the standard of living? After debating the social merits of advertising, students will explore the ethical considerations that underlie the development of campaigns and learn about the regulatory agencies that set guidelines for advertisers. Lastly, students are introduced to the concept of self-regulation and why advertisers must practice it.

Chapter 5: Advertising and Consumer Behavior.

This chapter on consumer behavior begins Part 2 of the text. It describes consumer behavior, explaining it from two different perspectives. The first portrays consumers as systematic decision makers who seek to maximize the benefits they derive from their purchases. The second portrays consumers as active interpreters of advertising, whose membership in various cultures, subcultures, societies, and communities significantly affects their interpretations and responses to advertising. Student, shown the validity of both perspectives, learn that, like all human behavior, the behavior of consumers is complex, multifaceted, and often symbolic. Understanding buyer behavior is a tremendous challenge to advertisers, who should not settle for easy answers if they want, really want, good relationships with their customers.

Chapter 6: Market Segmentation, Positioning, and Product Differentiation.

Using the highly successful "Brain Freeze" ad campaign for the 7-Eleven slush drink, the Slurpee, students are introduced to the sequence of activities often referred to as STP marketing—segmenting, targeting and positioning. The remainder of the chapter is devoted to detailed analysis of how organizations develop market segmentation, positioning, and product differentiation strategies. The critical and difficult role of ad campaigns in successfully executing these strategies is emphasized over and over. Numerous references to real-world campaigns keep the narrative fresh and fast moving.

Chapter 7: Advertising Research.

This meaty and substantive chapter begins with the story of the Goodyear Aquatred tire, one of the most successful new tire introductions of all time, thanks to extensive and rigorous ad testing before and during the tire's release. This chapter covers the methods used in developmental research, the procedures used for pretesting messages prior to the launch of a campaign, the methods used to track the effectiveness of ads during and after a launch, and the many sources of secondary data that can aid the ad-planning effort. The accompanying Advertisng Education Foundation video on research and advertising brings these concepts to life. If students don't understand the importance of advertising research and testing after reading this chapter, well, then . . . they didn't read the chapter!

Chapter 8: The Advertising Plan.

The launch of Windows 95 by Microsoft® may have been the largest and most publicized new-product launch in history. Through this opening vignette, students are shown the importance of constructing a sound ad plan before launching any campaign. After reading this chapter, students will be familiar with the basic components of an ad plan. They will understand two fundamental approaches for setting advertising objectives, the budgeting process, and the role of the ad agency in formulating an advertising plan. By the end of the chapter, students will understand the significance of the closing sentence of the Windows 95 vignette: An advertising plan is the culmination of the planning effort.

Chapter 9: Advertising Planning: An International Perspective.

While many books bury their international chapter at the end, we chose to place this chapter in the heart of the book. We think you'll find the chapter impressive in the number of international ads that are included and impressive in the way the fast-moving discussion unfolds: from a discussion of cultural barriers and overcoming them to an examination of the creative, media, and regulatory challenges that international advertising presents. The chapter ends with an insightful discussion of the differences between globalized and localized campaigns.

Chapter 10: Message Development. This chapter explores the concept of creativity and the role of creativity in message development from the refreshingly honest perspective that no one knows exactly how advertising creativity works. Students are introduced to the concept of "The Big Idea": a bold, powerful, and distinctive creative concept that is also perfectly executed. Then, nine message development objectives are presented along with the creative methods used to accomplish the objectives, including humor ads, slice-of-life ads, anxiety ads, sexual-appeal ads, slogan ads, and repetition ads. This chapter makes excellent use of visuals to dramatize the concepts presented.

Chapter 11: Copywriting. This chapter flows logically from the chapter on message development. In this chapter students learn about the copywriting process and the importance of good, hard-hitting copy in the development of print, radio, and television advertising. Guidelines for writing headlines, subheads, and body copy for print ads are given, as are guidelines for writing radio and television ad copy. The chapter closes with a discussion of the most common mistakes copywriters make and a discussion of the copy-approval process.

Chapter 12: Art Direction and Production in Print Advertising. In Chapter 12, students learn about the strategic and creative impact of illustration, design, and layout, and the production steps required to get to the final printed ad. The chapter opens with the story of RCA's strong reliance on print advertising in its successful image-repositioning campaign, "Changing Entertainment. Again." Numerous engaging full-color ads are included in this chapter to illustrate important design, illustration, and layout concepts.

Chapter 13: Art Direction and Production in Broadcast Advertising. In Chapter 13, students are introduced to what is often thought of as the most glamorous side of advertising: television advertising. Students learn about the role of the creative team and the many agency and production company participants involved in the direction and production processes. Students are given six creative guidelines for television ads with examples of each. Radio is not treated as a second-class citizen in this chapter but is given full treatment, including six guidelines for the production of creative and effective radio ads. This chapter is comprehensive and informative without getting bogged down in production details.

Chapter 14: Media Planning, Objectives, and Strategy. In this chapter, which begins Part 4, students see that a well-planned and creatively prepared campaign needs to be placed in media (and not just any media!) to reach a target audience and to stimulate demand. This chapter drives home the point that advertising placed in media that do not reach the target audience—whether new media or traditional media—will be much like the proverbial tree that falls in the forest with no one around: Does it make a sound? Students will read about the major media options available to advertisers today, the media-planning process, computer modeling in media planning, and the challenges that complicate the media-planning process.

Chapter 15: Media Evaluation: Print and Broadcast Media. Using the brilliant and creative Absolut vodka print campaign as the chapter's opening vignette, this chapter focuses on evaluating media as important means for advertisers to reach audiences. The chapter details the advantages and disadvantages of newspapers, magazines, radio, and television as media classes and describes the buying and audience measurement techniques for each.

Chapter 16: Media Evaluation: Traditional and Emerging Support Media. This chapter makes students aware of the vast number of support media options available to advertisers: event sponsorship, signage, outdoor billboards, transit, aerial, point of purchase, directory, specialty, CD-ROM, interactive television, commercial online services, and the Internet and World Wide Web. If students do not already appreciate the challenge of integrating marketing communications before they get to this chapter, they certainly will afterwards!

Chapter 17: Advertising on the Internet. *Advertising* is the first introductory advertising book to devote an entire chapter to advertising on the Internet. Today's employers expect college advertising students to know about the Internet and the creative and selling opportunities it presents to advertisers as part of their IMC strategy. This chapter presents a complete overview of advertising on the Internet and provides numerous Net activities to give students hands-on experience visiting and analyzing advertisers' Web sites. The chapter describes who's using the Internet today and the ways they are using it, identifies the advertising and marketing opportunities presented by the Internet, discusses fundamental requirements for establishing sites on the WWW, and lays out the challenges inherent in measuring the cost effectiveness of the Internet versus other advertising media. This chapter doesn't assume that all students are already Internet gurus, but it won't insult those who are.

Chapter 18: Sales Promotion. Sales promotion is a multibillion-dollar business in the United States and is emerging as a global force as well. This chapter explains the rationale for different types of sales promotions. It differentiates between consumer and trade sales promotions and highlights the risks and coordination issues associated with sales promotions. All of the following are discussed: coupons, price-off deals, premiums, contests, sweepstakes, sampling, trial offers, product placements, refunds, rebates, frequency programs, point-of-purchase displays, incentives, allowances, trade shows, and cooperative advertising.

Chapter 19: Direct Marketing. This chapter opens with an example of direct marketing from the mayor of Beverly Hills promoting the virtues of her fair city and then moves quickly on to L. L. Bean and the well-known L. L. Bean mail-order catalog. Students quickly learn about Bean's emphasis on building an extensive mailing list, which serves as a great segue to database marketing. Students will learn why direct marketing continues to grow in popularity, what media is used by direct marketers to deliver their messages, and how direct marketing creates special challenges for achieving integrated marketing communications.

Chapter 20: Public Relations and Corporate Advertising. This chapter begins with the story of Intel's Pentium chip public relations disaster. It illustrates the point that while some public relations crises are beyond the control of the organization, some are of the company's own doing. This dynamic and engaging chapter explains the role of public relations as part of an organization's overall IMC strategy and details the objectives and tools of public relations in a way that attracts and holds student interest. The chapter differentiates between proactive and reactive public relations, and it discusses corporate advertising as a means for building the reputation of an organization in the eyes of key constituents.

Inside Every Chapter

Inside every chapter of *Advertising* you will find features that make this new book eminently teachable and academically solid, while at the same time fun to read. As we said earlier, this text was written and the examples were chosen to facilitate an effective meeting place for student and teacher.

Who said learning has to be pure drudgery? It doesn't and shouldn't.

Dynamic Graphics and Over 400 Ads and Exhibits.

Ask any student and almost any instructor what an advertising book must include, and you will get as a top response—lots of ads. As you will see by quickly paging through *Advertising*, this is a book full of ads. Over 300 ads are used to illustrate important points made in the chapters. Each ad is referenced in the text narrative, tying in the visual with the concept being discussed.

As you can see, the book's clean, classic, graphic layout invites you to read it, dares you to put it down without reading just one more caption or peeking at just the next chapter.

Opening Vignettes. Every chapter in *Advertising* includes a classic or current real-world advertising story to draw students into the chapter and to stimulate classroom discussions. Each vignette illustrates important concepts that will be discussed in the chapter. For example, in Chapter 1, "Advertising as a Process," students read about Phil Knight, founder of Nike, and his initial intense dislike of the advertising process. Today, Nike spends about $400 million a year on advertising and almost that much on endorsements. In Chapter 2, "The Structure of the Advertising Industry," students read how Creative Artists Agency (CAA) stole the Coca-Cola account from one of the world's largest ad agencies, McCann-Erickson Worldwide. In Chapter 6, "Market Segmentation, Positioning, and Product Differentiation," students see how 7-Eleven saved the Slurpee (a true piece of Americana) with its "Brain Freeze" campaign aimed at males ages 12 to 18. And, in Chapter 9, "Advertising Planning: An International Perspective," students are treated to a short scene from the movie *Pulp Fiction,* and an important lesson: If you want to advertise "there," you must pay attention to "there's" culture.

In-Chapter Boxes. Every chapter in *Advertising* contains boxed material that highlights interesting, unusual, or just plain entertaining information as it relates to the chapter. The boxes are not diversions unrelated to the text; rather, they provide information that can be fully integrated into classroom lectures. The boxes are for teaching, learning, and reinforcing chapter content. Questions in the supplementary test bank are provided for instructors who wish to test on the material provided in the in-chapter boxes. We think so highly of our boxed discussions that we anticipated the desire to have questions targeted at their content. All box test questions are designated as such in the test bank.

Five types of boxes are included in the text: New Media, Global Issues, Ethical Issues, Contemporary Issues, and Regulatory Issues. Let's take a look at each:

New Media. A New Media box appears in every chapter. There is no greater challenge in the ad industry today than coping with the number and diversity of new media options available. This is especially true with respect to the Internet, and much of the coverage in the New Media boxes focuses on issues related to advertising and the Internet. Following is a sampling of the issues discussed in the New Media boxes:

- *The Virtual Sale: DEC Alpha Stations Silences Skeptics Online,* Chapter 1
- *The Wild West of Advertising: Online Services and the World Wide Web,* Chapter 4
- *Cyberspace for Rent: Brand Builders Take to the Internet,* Chapter 5
- *Testing the Waters: Marketers Wade First before Surfing the Net,* Chapter 7
- *Writing Cybercopy: Don't Abandon All the Old Rules,* Chapter 11
- *Radio Goes Off Air, Online,* Chapter 13
- *Should It Be WWW or www?,* Chapter 14
- *Digizines: Don't Look for One While You Wait for the Dentist,* Chapter 15
- *Building Marketing Databases in Cyberspace,* Chapter 19
- *Turning Green in the Cybermall,* Chapter 20

Global Issues. The Global Issues boxes provide an insightful real-world look at the numerous challenges advertisers face internationally. Many issues are discussed in these timely boxes, including the development of more standardized advertising across cultures with satellite-based television programming, how U.S.-based media companies like MTV and Disney/ABC are pursuing the vast potential in global media, obstacles to advertising in emerging markets, and cross-cultural global research. Below is a sampling of the Global Issues boxes you'll find in *Advertising:*

- *It's a Small World after AOL: Europe Goes Online,* Chapter 3
- *Advertising Russian Style: Many Obstacles Have Marketers Seeing Red,* Chapter 5
- *I Want My MTV: Information Age Heralds The First Global Consumers,* Chapter 6
- *One for All: Cross-Cultural Research Allows Global Ad Planning,* Chapter 7
- *America's Newest Contribution to World Culture: Infomercials Go Global,* Chapter 10
- *Forget Cyberspace—We're Talking Outer Space Here,* Chapter 11

- *Reaching the Latin American Consumer: Advertisers Plug In to Cable,* Chapter 14
- *Gaining a Global Foothold: Music and News Television Worldwide,* Chapter 15

Ethical Issues. The Ethical Issues boxes scrutinize advertising practices from an ethical standpoint. There is no shortage of material, as you can see from the titles below:

- *A Long-Distance Joust: MCI and AT&T Battle over Market Share,* Chapter 1
- *Beyond Psychics and Spray-On Hair: Infomercials Gain New Respectability,* Chapter 3
- *Be Careful When Claiming Pollution Solutions: It's Not That Easy Being Green,* Chapter 8
- *Déjà Vu All Over Again?,* Chapter 13
- *The Four Rs: Readin', 'Ritin', 'Rithmetic, and (Ad) Revenue,* Chapter 16
- *With Friends Like These, Who Needs Enemies?,* Chapter 20

Contemporary Issues. The content of the Contemporary Issues boxes runs the gamut from the practical to the cutting edge, much as contemporary advertising does. Each title below is guaranteed food for the discussion fodder:

- *"Hi!" 20-Somethings: Neon Launch Targeted Squarely at Generation X,* Chapter 1
- *Think Big: Agencies Vie for Volkswagen of America Account,* Chapter 2
- *Inside Intel: Component Part Branding Pulls Channel Demand,* Chapter 3
- *Saturday Morning Merchandising: Animated Peddlers Dominate Children's Programming,* Chapter 4
- *Sweetening Sour Gripes: Savvy Companies Learn from Customer Complaints,* Chapter 7
- *Down and Out on Madison Avenue: Commissions Give Way to Fees and Incentives,* Chapter 8
- *Okay, Here's the Advertising Message Strategy: None,* Chapter 10
- *It Doesn't Always Have to Be Expensive,* Chapter 13
- *The Rush to Talk Radio,* Chapter 15
- *Chevy Media Event Targets Women,* Chapter 16
- *Winning Business at Trade Shows,* Chapter 18
- *To Be or Not to Be An Event Sponsor—That Is the Question,* Chapter 20

Regulatory Issues. Last, but not least, are the Regulatory Issues boxes, which provide examples of the impact of current advertising regulations around the world, as the following titles illustrate:

- *Sino Snake Oil: Advertising Ethics Now Enforced in Mainland China,* Chapter 4
- *Don't Mention It: Postrevolutionary Regs Rule Iran,* Chapter 9
- *The Fed's Crackdown on Fraudulent Telemarketers,* Chapter 19

Web Sightings. In keeping with the new media focus of this new book, you will find Web Sightings in each chapter. You can spot these Web Sightings by looking for the Web-sighting banner found above selected ads in each chapter. Students are asked to go to the Web site address provided to explore the advertiser's home page, bringing the ad in the book online and into real time. Questions are provided to prompt students to explore, explain, describe, compare, contrast, summarize, rethink, or analyze the content or features of the advertiser's home page. You can think of these Web Sightings as in-chapter experiential exercises and real-time cases. Suggested answers to the questions can be found in the Instructor's Manual. You can assign these Web Sightings as individual or group activities. They are also excellent discussion starters. A note: Most Web sites are listed with the prefix *http://*. While this is the technical address, most Web browsers don't require the user to type out this prefix, so it has been dropped from the sites in this book.

Concise Chapter Summaries. Each chapter ends with a summary that distills the main points of the chapter. Chapter summaries are organized around the learning objectives so that students can use them as a quick check on their achievement of learning goals.

Key Terms with Page Citations. Each chapter ends with an alphabetical listing of the key terms found in the chapter along with page citations for easy reference. Key terms also appear in boldface in the text. Students can prepare for exams by scanning these lists to be sure they can define or explain each term.

Questions for Review and Critical Thinking. These end-of-chapter questions, written by the authorship team, are designed to challenge students' thinking and to go beyond the "read, memorize, and regurgitate" learning process. The Questions for Review and Critical Thinking sections require students to think analytically and to interpret data and information provided for them in the text. Detailed responses to these questions are provided in the Instructor's Manual.

Below is a sampling of the types of critical-thinking questions found in *Advertising:*

- If a firm developed a new line of athletic shoes, priced them competitively, and distributed them in appropriate retail shops, would there be any need for advertising? Is advertising really needed for a good product that is priced right?
- The 1950s were marked by great suspicion about advertisers and their potential persuasive powers. Do you see any lingering effects of this era of paranoia in attitudes about advertising today?
- Some contend that self-regulation is the best way to ensure fair and truthful advertising practices. Why would it be in the best interest of the advertising community to aggressively pursue self-regulation?
- Explain the difference between individualism and collectivism as core values. Pick up a recent issue of your favorite magazine and see if it contains any advertisements that appeal to the values of individualism or collectivism.
- Explain the two basic strategies for developing corporate home pages, exemplified in this chapter by Saturn and Reebok.
- Visit some of the corporate home pages described in this chapter, or think about corporate home pages you have visited previously. Of those you have encountered, which would you single out as being most effective in giving the visitor a reason to come back? What conclusions would you draw regarding the best ways to motivate repeat visits to a Web site?
- Everyone has their own opinion on what makes advertisements effective or ineffective. How does this fundamental aspect of human nature complicate a copywriter's life when it comes to winning approval for his or her ad copy?

Experiential Exercises. At the end of each chapter, Experiential Exercises require students to apply the material they have just read by researching topics, writing short papers, or preparing brief presentations. They require students to get out of the classroom to seek information not provided in the text. A number of these exercises are especially designed for teamwork, and many are classroom tested. Additional Experiential Exercises can be found in the Instructor's Manual. Suggested answers for all of the exercises are provided in the Instructor's Manual.

Internet Exercises. This unique set of Internet Exercises is designed to get students on the Internet to see the quality of advertising that is there, to analyze the effectiveness of what they find, and to apply the Internet to fundamental advertising concepts presented in the text. Because the focus of these exercises is hands-on in nature, students will spend time accessing home pages using the Web site addresses provided and evaluating what they find. Application questions are provided for each exercise for students to answer after their Web site excursions. The application questions require students to apply the concepts taught in each chapter, making these surfing-the-net exercises worthwhile and focused, not just browsing time. Additional Internet Exercises can be found in the Instructor's Manual—for real diehard cyberhounds! Suggested answers to all of the Internet exercises can be found in the Instructor's Manual. Additionally, *Advertising*'s appendix provides the Web address of nearly every major advertiser that appears in the text.

Learning Objectives and a Built-In Integrated Learning System

The text and test bank are organized around the learning objectives that appear at the beginning of each chapter, to provide you and students with an easy-to-use, integrated learning system. A numbered icon like the one shown here ❶ identifies each chapter objective and appears next to its related material throughout the chapter. This integrated learning system can provide you with a structure for creating lesson plans, as well as tests. A correlation table at the beginning of every chapter in the test bank enables you to create tests that fully cover every learning objective or that emphasize the objectives you feel are most important.

The integrated system also gives structure to students as they prepare for tests. The icons identify all the material in the text that fulfill each objective. Students can easily check their grasp of each objective by reading the text sections and reviewing the corresponding summary sections. They can return to appropriate text sections for further review if they have difficulty with end-of-chapter questions.

End-of-Part IMC Campaign: Delta Air Lines

No introductory text would be complete without giving special attention to integrated marketing communications. At the end of each of the four parts of *Advertising* is an ongoing case study of Delta Air Lines and its "Cincinnati Instead" IMC campaign. The color-coded sections at the end of each text part will help students better understand IMC by examining the topic in two ways. First, each section discusses methods for creating effective integrated marketing communications. Second, each section applies the basic principles of IMC to the promotional programs of Delta Air Lines. As students will discover, Delta uses a wide range of communications tools to support its goal of gaining and sustaining market share in a fiercely competitive global market. Of course, these campaign sections are fully and colorfully illustrated.

A Full Array of Teaching/Learning Supplementary Materials

Instructor's Manual

The author-written Instructor's Manual that accompanies *Advertising* provides comprehensive lecture outlines for each of the text's 20 chapters. These outlines average 10 to 12 pages per chapter and offer a complete and structured approach for presenting class lectures. The outlines also include marginal notations suggesting where the supplementary videos, PowerPoint slides, and color transparencies can be used to demonstrate points made in the text. A full set of 83 PowerPoint acetate transparency masters are included in the manual. In addition, the manual includes suggested answers for all exercises found in the text: Web Sightings, Questions for Review and Critical Thinking, Experiential Exercises, and Internet Exercises. Finally, the manual contains additional Experiential and Internet Exercises, with suggested answers, for instructors seeking variety.

PowerPoint Slides

All 83 images prepared as transparency masters in the Instructor's Manual are also available on PowerPoint software, 4.0 and 7.0 versions. All you need is Windows to run the PowerPoint viewer, and an LCD panel for classroom display. The PowerPoint images can also be downloaded from our Web site at: www .swcollege.com/oguinn.html.

Comprehensive Test Bank

This comprehensive test bank is organized around the text's learning objectives. At the beginning of each test bank chapter is a correlation table that classifies each question according to type, complexity, and learning objective covered.

Using this table, you can create exams with the appropriate mix of question types and level of difficulty for your class. You can choose to prepare tests that cover all learning objectives or emphasize those you feel are most important.

For each text chapter the test bank provides true/false, multiple choice, scenario application, and essay questions. There are a total of 1,200 questions. All questions have been carefully reviewed for clarity and accuracy. Questions are identified by topic and show the rationales and text pages where the rationales appear.

Testing Software

All items from the printed test bank are available on disk through Westest, an automated testing program that allows instructors to create exams by selecting provided questions, modifying existing questions, or adding questions. Westest is available in Windows and MS-DOS versions and is provided free of charge to instructors at educational institutions that adopt *Advertising* by O'Guinn, Allen, and Semenik. Instructors can also have tests created and printed by calling International Thomson Publishing Academic Resource Center at 1-800-423-0563 (8:30 A.M.–6:00 P.M. EST).

Color Transparency Package and Slides

Also available to instructors is a high-quality selection of full-color overhead transparencies (also available as 35-mm slides). These transparencies include 25 ads and exhibits taken from the text as well as 75 additional ads not used in the text, including winners of 1996 Clios. Suggestions for incorporating these ads into lectures are included in the lecture outlines in the Instructor's Manual.

Award-Winning Video Package

The following three comprehensive and exciting video programs, which represent the best package going, are available to supplement *Advertising*. These three programs are designed to bring to life, in a fresh, cutting-edge, and energetic way, the advertising principles presented in the text.

BusinessLink Video Series. Two videos were produced exclusively for *Advertising* by LEARNet, a team of experienced advertising and marketing professors and video producers who specialize in creating instructional media. These two videos have been custom scripted and produced to specifically illustrate topics in the text. Critical-thinking issues segment the video presentations, allowing you to easily stop the tapes to discuss pertinent issues. A video instructor's guide provides descriptions of the video segments and other information to help you integrate the videos into your classroom lectures. Descriptions of the two LEARNet videos follow:

Advertising Agency Relationships: W.B. Doner and Red Roof Inn. Red Roof Inns has been using the advertising slogan "Sleep Cheap." The W. B. Doner Advertising Agency was hired to develop a new integrated marketing communications strategy that emphasized value instead of low price. The successful new campaign used humorous messages featuring celebrity Martin Mull. [*13.10*]

Client-Based Advertising: Andersen Consulting. In 1989, Andersen Consulting (AC) had two advertising challenges: to define their image in the marketplace, and to establish a distinctive position. AC conducted marketing research and then initiated a very innovative corporate image advertising campaign that has achieved impressive results. [*14:02*]

Clio Awards 1996 Show Reel. This show reel (40-plus minutes long) contains the best of television advertising in 1996. No other advertising text on the market today includes the Clio awards as part of its supplementary package. We pursued the Clio ads not just because of their entertainment value but to expose students to the creative work of the best and brightest advertising minds. Today and for the past 38 years, Clio has heralded great accomplishments in advertising. The purpose of the Clios is to honor and inspire advertising excellence worldwide. You will find incorporating the Clio ads into your classroom lectures not only entertaining and inspiring, but an effective way to illustrate concepts presented in the text chapters.

The Advertising Education Foundation, Inc. (AEF). Two videos produced by The Advertising Education Foundation, Inc., are also available as supplements to *Advertising*. The first is the 27-minute video entitled "Good-Bye Guesswork: How Research Guides Today's Advertisers." This documentary probes the dynamics of advertising research, strategic thinking, and concept testing from the viewpoint of three major advertisers and their ad agencies in three 9-minute segments: Campbell Soup Company with FCB/ Leber Katz Partners, Maidenform with Ogilvy & Mather, and AT&T with McCann-Erickson Worldwide.

The second AEF-produced video is a 30-minute video entitled "Behind the Scenes: The Advertising Process at Work." This video, presented in three 10-minute segments, follows the advertising process from inception to completion, with all the tension and drama included, for three campaigns: Acuvue (Johnson & Johnson with Lintas Worldwide), Jell-O Gelatin (General Foods Corporation and Young & Rubicam), and Coke (Coca-Cola Company and McCann-Erickson Worldwide).

This entire award-winning video package was designed to show students how advertising works in the real world from the perspective of both the ad agency and the client and to demonstrate for students some of the most current and creative examples of advertising worldwide. It's a dynamic, attention-getting, and engaging package you'll enjoy using in your classes.

IMC: An Integrated Marketing Communications Exercise

This comprehensive supplementary package puts students in the role of client services manager at a major, full-service integrated marketing communications agency. The client, the Republic of Uruguay, wants the agency to create and manage a total marketing program for a new resort in Uruguay called Punta del Este. This approximately 100-page, semester-long project workbook includes step-by-step directions for students to follow. Cost tables are supplied, as are how-to worksheets on creative and media planning assignments. In addition to the traditional IMC mix, this exercise also takes students into the world of interactive media, because any successful presentation in the real world today will have to include a proposal integrating the Internet and other interactive media.

To begin the exercise, students are briefed on all aspects of the new resort: facts and details about Punta del Este, competition, research data, and the lore surrounding the resort. After the briefing, students are guided through the development of a four-part campaign recommendation for their client. They will create (1) a generalized communications statement complete with objectives and a strategy for segmentation, targeting, and product positioning; (2) a copy platform with their recommendations for TV and magazine ads; (3) a media plan, including interactive media; and (4) a promotion plan for travel industry intermediaries and travel consumers.

The correlating Instructor's Manual contains numerous suggestions and guidelines for the smooth implementation of this exercise into your course. It also offers suggestions for condensing the material, if you prefer a shorter exercise or one that focuses exclusively on advertising without the IMC topics.

This outstanding supplement was written by Bernard C. Jakacki of Ramapo College. In addition to writing this exercise, Professor Jakacki has tested it for four years with many college students and with advertising agency trainees. The response from users has been spectacular in terms of both its comprehensive content and the fun they have promoting Punta del Este. This tested and proven package is truly real-world in both orientation and design. [ISBN 0-538-87794-4]

Ad Campaign Workbook

Developed by Shay Sayre, of California State University, Fullerton, this workbook presents compete yet concise instructions for developing an advertising campaign for one of two accounts. Using a series of specially designed worksheets, students are guided through the process of building a campaign step by step. Students organize an agency, profile a target market, conduct primary and secondary research, analyze the competition, develop an industry overview, evaluate the product/service, and prepare media plans, creative strategies, and promotions. Then, drawing on their worksheets, they construct and end-of-term written proposal and/or presentation. A sample campaign is included. [ISBN 0-538-87894-0]

Thomas C. O'Guinn
Chris T. Allen
Richard J. Semenik

Acknowledgments

The most pleasant task in writing a textbook is the expression of gratitude to people and institutions that have helped the authors. We appreciate the support and encouragement we received from many individuals, including:

- The people at Delta Air Lines who gave us tremendous in the help and support in creating the IMC sections. In top management, Paul Matsen, Tim Mapes, and Brad Gerdeman embraced the concept and gave us permission to use a wide range of Delta materials to support our effort. But more than just supporting the idea, they played an active role in fleshing out how the Delta experience could bring to life the basic concepts of IMC being covered in the special sections. How much of a commitment did they make? They gave us their home telephone numbers! We owe a special debt of thanks to Sue King in Delta's advertising department. Not only did Sue make sure everything was provided to us in a timely fashion, she scrutinized every word of every section and made some important suggestions. And, in the eleventh hour, it was Sue who made a critical decision that preserved the quality of the effort. We also want to thank Mimi Bean at BBDO South for the important role she played in helping us with the advertising materials for the Delta discussions.
- David Moore, vice president/executive producer at Leo Burnett, who gave us invaluable insights on the broadcast production process and helped us secure key materials for the text.
- Bernard C. Jakacki, Ramapo College, for providing a truly excellent IMC supplement. The timing of his work was serendipitous, and we're glad to have it as part of the *Advertising* package.
- Shay Sayre, California State University, Fullerton, for creating an ad campaign workbook of exceptional quality.
- Nick Bean, Bean Enterprises, for taking on the challenge of preparing the box discussions for the early chapters. Nick set the tone for the lively and informative boxes throughout the text. We are also indebted to him for creating the Power-Point transparencies, which serve as a truly useful lecture aid.

- Jon B. Freiden and Scott Takacs, Florida State University, for their fine efforts in preparing the Experiential Exercises for the text and the supplementary Internet Exercises in the Instructor's Manual.
- Peter Sheldon, University of Illinois, Urbana-Champaign, for his outstanding diligence and unfailing sense of humor in preparing an exceptionally good test bank without missing a single deadline! Our thanks to Peter, as well, for all of his assistance and professional input reading, reviewing, and revising chapters—and tracking down endless pieces of artwork. We couldn't have completed this project without him.
- Peter Newman, University of Illinois, Urbana-Champaign, for his tireless efforts in tracking down ads for every chapter in the book and tying up a million loose ends every step of the project.
- Rajiv Shah and Kyle Zolner, University of Illinois, Urbana-Champaign, who deserve all the credit for their exemplary and cutting-edge work on the Internet chapter, as well as for writing the text Internet Exercises.
- Gina Malopsy, Treehouse Consultants, Inc., for coordinating this massive project and providing important quality control.
- Jeff Bivona, Treehouse Consultants, Inc., who was dragged into the project at the eleventh hour to finalize permissions for many of the text exhibits. His patience and professionalism under tight deadline pressure were refreshing.
- Matt Smith of Arnold, Finnegan & Martin for providing us with the Watermark ad and sketches in Chapter 12.
- To James M. Smyth, Peter Zapf, and the entire staff of the Clio Awards, a special acknowledgement is owed for providing us with the best advertising awards reel in the industry (www.clioawards.com).
- Linda Scott, University of Illinois, just for being so damn smart.

We would also like to thank the many people at South-Western Publishing who made this project take shape and helped guide its development from start to finish: Valerie Ashton, John Szilagyi, Cinci Stowell, Craig LaGesse Ramsdell, Jennifer Mayhall, Meghan Kenney, Steve Ray, Steve Scoble, and Sue Disselkamp. We express gratitude, also, to our publisher's professional and committed sales force for the critically important customer feedback that we received all along the way.

We would also like to thank Dreis Van Landuyt, acquisitions editor, for his hard work, dedication, suggestions, and support throughout the project. Our special thanks go to Mary Pommert, who served as our developmental editor. Her patience, encouragement, organizing skills, and thoughtful interventions were vital in our completion of this project.

A special thanks goes to Judy O'Neill, our production manager at South-Western, and Lachina Publishing Services, Inc., who skillfully and professionally guided the production of this book under the tightest of production deadlines.

We are particularly indebted to our reviewers, who read and reviewed manuscript in all stages of development. Their comments and suggestions were instrumental in preparing final-draft manuscript. Our thanks go to:

Jon Freiden
Florida State University

Corliss L. Green
Georgia State University

Karen James
Louisiana State University–Shreveport

James Kellaris
University of Cincinnati

Patricia Kennedy
University of Nebraska–Lincoln

Robert Kent
University of Delaware

Sue King
Delta Air Lines

Tina M. Lowrey
Rider University

Nancy Mitchell
University of Nebraska–Lincoln

David Moore
Leo Burnett

Darrel Muehling
Washington State University

Jan Slater
Syracuse University

Patricia Stout
University of Texas–Austin

Lynn Walters
Texas A & M

Brian Wansink
*The Wharton School of the University of
Pennsylvania*

Marc Weinberger
University of Massachusetts–Amherst

Gary B. Wilcox
University of Texas–Austin

Kurt Wildermuth
University of Missouri–Columbia

Chriss Wright-Isak
Young & Rubicam

Molly Ziske
Michigan State University

We are also indebted to the following individuals who also shaped the content of
Advertising with their thoughtful comments and responses to our inquiries:

Christopher S. Alexander
King's College

Renae Allen
Grand Island College

Robert P. Allerheiliger
Colorado State University

Bob Alter
Framingham State College

Moses Altsech
Penn State University

Steven J. Anderson
Austin Peay State University

Verl Anderson
Eastern Oregon State College

David L. Antes
University of Massachusetts–Dartmouth

Robert Anthony
Western Montana College

Edward Applegate
Middle Tennessee State University

Joan Atkins
Morehead State University

Tullan Avard
Muskingum Area Technical College

Jim Avery
University of Alaska–JPC

Laurie Babin
University of Southern Mississippi

Greg Bach
Bismarck State College

Marsha Bagley
Iowa Wesleyan College

Deborah Baird
Utah Valley State College

Gregory Baleja
Alma College

Al Barnhart
MMCC

Michael Barone
Florida International University

Anne Heineman Batory
Wilkes University

Fred Beard
University of Oklahoma

Jack Bell
Metropolitan State College of Denver

Richard F. Beltramini
Wayne State University

Stephanie Bibb
Chicago State University

Rachel Bickerstaff
Holmes Community College

Carla Bickert
Bismarck State College

Cliff Bieberly
Elliott School of Communications

Frank William Biglow
University of Wisconsin–Oshkosh

Roy E. Blackwood
Bemidji State University

Gregory Blase
Kent State University

David A. Bodkin
Cumberland University

Courtney C. Bosworth
University of Georgia

Karen Bowman
Morgan State University

Robert S. Boyd
University of Nevada–Las Vegas

Janet Brav
Fashion Institute of Technology

Greg M. Broekemier
University of Nebraska–Kearney

Robert Brown
Salem State College

Brian Buckler
Avila College

Janice Bukovac
Michigan State University

Laura Bulas
Central Community College

John Bunnell
Broome Community College

Margaret L. Burk
Muskingum College

Louis F. Butterfield
Harding University

Chris Cakebread
Boston University

James W. Camerius
Northern Michigan University

T. Camp
Glendale Community College

M. E. Campbell
University of Montana

Rene Castilla
North Lake College

Rajesh Chandrashekaran
Trenton State College

Frederick A. Chapman
Grand Valley State University

Glenn Chappell
Meredith College

Newell Chiesl
Indiana State University

David W. Claire
Johnson & Wales University

J. William Click
Winthrop University

Gene Conyers
North Georgia College

Cristanna Cook
Husson College

Ernest F. Cooke
Loyola College (Maryland)

Ron Cooley
South Suburban College

Doug Cords
California State University–Fresno

Steve Corker
Gonzaga University

John J. Cronin
Western Connecticut State University

Larry Crowson
Florida Institute of Technology

Richard Cummins
Williams Baptist College

Barb Cunningham
Olivet College Conservatory

Datha Damron-Martinez
Western New Mexico University

Judy F. Davis
Eastern Michigan University

Irmagard Davis
Kapi'olani Community College

Robert Davis
University of Central Florida

Robert A. DeMarais
Arkansas Technical University

Bruce Dickinson
Southeast Technical Institute

Gordon DiPaolo
College of Staten Island

Glenna Dod
Wesleyan College

Laura Dollar
Sam Houston State University

Kathleen V. Donnelly
Point Park College

Bonnie Ann Dowd
Palomar College

Richard M. Dubiel
University of Wisconsin–Stevens Point

Linda Duckworth
Northeast Mississippi Community College

Rick Dudkowski
Genesee Community College

Sid Dudley
Eastern Illinois University

Jacqueline K. Eastman
Valdosta State University

Gayle V. Economos
Gouchor College

Martin Edu
Grambling State University

James Eiseman
Loyola University–New Orleans

Edmund Elfers
Wayne State College

Roberta Elins
State University of New York

Katherine Ellis-Donner
Daemen College

Ronald Engeldinger
Bassist College

Stuart Esrock
University of Louisville

Linda Evans
Hofstra University

Ron Faber
University of Minnesota

Karen Fager
Umpqua Community College

Mercer Fellouris
Bridgewater State College

David Ferrell
Central College

Nancy P. Floyd
Eastern Mennonite University

B. Foskit
Drake University

Patrick D. Fountain
Methodist College

Michael Fowler
Brookdale Community College

George R. Franke
University of Alabama

Alan Fried
University of South Carolina

Karen Fritz
Pellissippi State Technical Community College

Nancy Frontczak
Metropolitan State College of Denver

William Fudge
University of South Florida

Amy Gambale
Fashion Institute of Technology

Gary W. Garrett
University of Detroit–Mercy

Gerald A. Garrity
Anna Maria College

Leonard Gaston
Central State University

John Gauthier
Gateway Technical College

Salma Ghanem
University of Texas–Pan American

Ron Gilbert
Lee College

Jim Gilliand
Idaho State University

Richard Gist
Towson State University

Marc H. Goldberg
Portland State University

Larry Goldstein
Iona College

Ronald M. Gordon
Florida Metropolitan University

Robert F. Grant
Carthage College

Nancy Grassilli
Tunxis Community Technical College

Mark Green
Simpson College

Michael J. Greene
University of Nebraska

Laura Gresens
Louisiana State University

Tom Groth
University of West Florida

Chuck Gulas
Wright State University

Robert Gustafson
Ball State University

Larry Haase
Central Missouri State

Robert A. Habermas
Liberty University

Samuel Haft
Nassau Community College

William B. Hall
Moorhead State University

James Hamilton
SUNY Geneseo

Anne Hammond
Oklahoma Baptist University

John Hanc
New York Institute of Technology

Lea Anna Harrah
Marion Technical College

Greg Harrell
Johnson County Community College

Robert C. Harris
University of Northern Colorado

Bernie Harris
University of Wisconsin–Platteville

S. L. Harrison
University of Miami

John Hart
Fullerton College

Susanne Hartl
Nyack College

Thomas R. Hartley
Oklahoma State University

Dale Hatfield
Clackamas Community College

Jerry M. Hayes
Defiance College

Joo-Gin Heaney
Franklin and Marshall College

Jeffrey R. Hefel
Saint Mary's University

Richard Heiens
University of Texas at Tyler

Kristel J. Heinz
Aquinas College

Joe Helgert
Grand Valley State University

Lucy L. Henke
University of New Hampshire

Teri Henley
Loyola University–New Orleans

Volker Henning
Southern Adventist University

Lise Heroux
SUNY Plattsburgh

Bill Herrington
North Central Texas College

Cliff Hesse
Kingsborough Community College

Joe Bob Hester
Southwest Texas State University

Kae K. Hineline
McLennan Community College

Randall W. Hines
East Tennessee State University

Mike Hitchins
Florida State University

Larry Hoffman
Long Beach City College

John Holmes
Skidmore College

Brooks Honeycutt
Frostburg State University

Douglas Housknecht
University of Akron

Marie Huba
Adirondack Community College

Jerry Hudson
Texas Tech University

Jean A. Husby
Chippewa Valley Technical College

Robert J. Illidge
University of Central Oklahoma

Kay F. Israel
Rhode Island College

Marti Tomas Izral
Loyola University–Chicago

Joseph Izzo
Wesley College

Randy Jacobs
University of Hartford

P. Jacoby
Purdue University

Janice S. Jenny
Herkimer County Community College

Myra Johnson
Isothermal Community College

Keith F. Johnson
Texas Tech University

Thomas L. Johnson
Bethel College

Tom Jordan
San Jose State University

Richard Kagel
Brigham Young University

Gerald S. Kapela
Sullivan County Community College

Kevin Keenan
University of Maryland

Richard King
Washtenaw College

Dan Kirchner
California State University

Bart Kittle
Youngstown State University

C. M. Kochunny
University of South Alabama

D. A. Kornemann
MATC

Bob Kosmidek
Champlain College

Carl J. Kranendonk
Florida International University

Peggy J. Kreshel
University of Georgia

Jim Kress
Central Oregon Community College

Darwin L. Krumrey
Kirkwood Community College

John R. Kuzma
Mankato State University

Elena Kyle
Fitchburg State College

Geoffrey Lantos
Stonehill College

Robert W. Larson
Pittsburg State University

Edmund O. Lawler
DePaul University

Keith Lawson
West Liberty State College

Philip Lee
Dixie College

Monle Lee
Indiana University–South Bend

Varnell Lee
Spring Hill College

Tim Leutwiler
University of Wisconsin–Eau Claire

David Light
University of San Diego

Mary Lou Lockerby
College of DuPage

Gordon Long
Georgia College and State University

Roxanne Lucchesi
South Dakota State University

Ann Lucht
MATC

Sondra Luke
Meridian Community College

Peter M. Lynagh
University of Baltimore

Mary Ann Machanic
University of Massachusetts–Boston

Lynda M. Maddox
George Washington University

Larry Maes
Detroit College of Business

Jill K. Maher
Kent State University

Michael Mandel
Housatonic Community/Technical College

Frank M. Marion
Christian Brothers University

Richard Marsh
Greenville Technical College

Wendy Martin
Judson College

Elizabeth Marzoni
Arapahoe Community College

James M. Maskulka
Lehigh University

Barbara C. Massar
Orange County Community College

Dennis Mathern
University of Findlay

Jack Mauch
Idaho State University

Gary H. Mayer
Stephen F. Austin State University

Michael McBride
Southwest Texas State University

Patrick H. McCaskey
Millersville University

Robert L. McChesney
McKendree College

Ellen McDonough
Emerson College

Nancy McGormley
Maryville University

Sam McNeely
Murray State University

Debra Merskin
University of Oregon

Tim Meyer
University of Wisconsin

Pamela L. Mickelson
Morningside College

David W. Miller
Dana College

Chip E. Miller
Pacific Lutheran University

Darryl Miller
Washburn University

Avantika Modi
University of Maryland

Dennis Morgan
Mt. St. Mary's College

Jay Mower
University of Houston

Babaz Mueller
San Diego State University

Lynn F. Muller
Minot State University

Jeanne Munger
University of Southern Maine

Reginald Murphy
University of Tennessee at Knoxville

Blaise Newman
Detroit College of Business

Laura Nicholson
Northern Oklahoma College

Mel A. Novak
Indiana Institute of Technology

Gillian Oakenfull
University of Houston

Ray Oakes
Franklin Pierce College

Rosa L. Okpara
Albany State University

Gary Olsen
University of Dubuque

Anita M. Olson
North Hennepin Community College

P. B. Orman
University of Southern Colorado

Anne Owen
Florida International University

Lewis D. Owens
Oakland University

Kartik Pashupati
University of West Florida

Charles Pearce
Kansas State University

Mike Pearson
Loyola University–New Orleans

James Peltier
University of Wisconsin–Whitewater

Jennifer L. Peters
Louisiana State University

Karla Peterson
University of North Dakota–Williston

R. J. Pfingstler
Edinboro University of Pennsylvania

Julie M. Pharr
Tennessee Technical University

Melodie Phillips
Middle Tennessee State University

Bill B. Pierce
Morehead State University

J. Kent Pinney
University of Nevada–Las Vegas

Raymond E. Polchow
MATC

Patrick Quinlan
Adrian College

Richard A. Rauch
Long Island University, C.W. Post Campus

Cassandra Reese
Ohio University

Sarah M. Regan
University of Tennessee–Chattanooga

Jane Reid
Youngstown State University

Pierre J. Rener
University of Missouri–Kansas City

Glen Riecken
East Tennessee State University

Joe Ries
San Francisco State University

Judy Rinehimer
Consumnes River College

Penelope B. Roberts
Fashion Institute of Technology

Jerry Rogers
Pittsburg State University

Stuart Rogers
University of Denver

John Ronchetto
University of San Diego

Gregory M. Rose
University of Mississippi

Richard L. Roth
University of Kentucky

Morleen Getz Rouse
University of Cincinnati

Barbara C. Rugnell
Southern Illinois University–Edwardsville

Marilyn Sarow
Winthrop University

Paul Sauer
Canisius College

Shay Sayre
California State University–Fullerton

Duane Schecter
Muskegon Community College

Edward C. Scheiner
Marshall University

Ron Schie
West Virginia University

Peter A. Schneider
Seton Hall University

Edwin M. Schultheis
Five Towns College

Lisa M. Sciulli
Indiana University of Pennsylvania

T. Randall Scott
Liberty University

E.A. Sekeres
Youngstown State University

Jeff Seyfert
Southern Nazarene University

Richard D. Shaw
Rockhurst College

William Shelburn
University of South Carolina–Aiken

Rasak O. Shidi
Knoxville College

Jon A. Shidler
Southern Illinois University–Carbondale

Alan P. Shields
Suffolk Community College

Bruce Siegmund
Grambling State University

Teresa L. Simmons
Western Illinois University

Mandeep Singh
Western Illinois University

Lewis F. Small
York College of Pennsylvania

Allen E. Smith
Florida Atlantic University

James R. Smith
SUNY College at New Paltz

LaTanya Smith
Edinboro University of Pennsylvania

Lois Smith
University of Wisconsin–Whitewater

Tom Smith
Texas Wesleyan University

Mary F. Smith
Georgia Southern University

Peter W. Smith
University of Wisconsin–Green Bay

Robin L. Snipes
Columbus State University

Al South
Treasure Valley Community College

Randy Sparks
University of Dayton

Richard S. Squire
Northwest State Community College

Tom Stafford
Cameron University

Gary Stanton
Erie Community College–City Campus

James A. Stephens
Emporia State University

Karen Stewart
Richard Stockton College of New Jersey

Terry Stone
College of Notre Dame

Carolyn Stringer
Western Kentucky University

Jack D. Summerfield
New York Institute of Technology

Scott Takacs
Florida State University

Faruk Tanyel
University of South Carolina–Spartanburg

Jan Taylor
Miami University

David K. Terwische
Eastern Washington University

Marye Tharp
University of Texas at Austin

Judith M. Thorpe
University of Wisconsin–Oshkosh

L. K. Thumuluri
Miami University

Kathy Toler
A-B Technical Community College

Ron Tremmel
Rend Lake College

Vincent P. Troccoli
Pierce College

Leslie Turner
University of Nebraska at Omaha

Don Umphrey
Southern Methodist University

Ron Utecht
Texas Lutheran University

Rajiv Vaidyanathan
University of Minnesota

Helen Varner
Hawaii Pacific University

Sandy Veltri
Trinidad State Jr. College

Karen K. Vignare
Alfred State College of Technology

William E. Vincent
Santa Barbara Community College

Ottilia N. Voegtli
University of Missouri–St. Louis

Randy Wade
Rogue Community College

Michael W. Wakefield
Black Hills State University

Amanda G. Watlington
Terra Community College

Roger L. Watson
Ohio University

Fredric A. Weiss
San Antonio College

Rosemary Werner
Teikyo Post University

Jerry Wheaton
NACTC

Bill White
California State University–Los Angeles

Charles W. White
Hardin–Simmons University

J. Chris White
Texas A & M University

Laura Widmer
Northwest Missouri State University

David A. Wiley
Anne Arundel Community College

Alan R. Wiman
Rider University

Jennifer B. Winningham
Arkansas State University

Robert F. Witherspoon
Triton College

C. Wittmayer
Dakota State University

Charles Wood
University of Missouri

Gregory J. Worosz
Schoolcraft College

Timothy W. Wright
Lakeland Community College

William Yates
St. Joseph's College

Wayne A. Yerxa
Mount Vernon Nazarene College

William J. Ziegler
Bethune–Cookman College

Advertising

Part 1 | The Process: Advertising in Business and Society

This first part, "The Process: Advertising in Business and Society," sets the tone for our study of advertising. The chapters in this part of the book emphasize that advertising is much more than a wonderfully creative interpretation of important corporate and marketing strategies. While it very much serves that purpose, advertising is a fundamental business and societal process that has evolved over time with technology and tradition. To appreciate the true nature of advertising, we must first understand advertising as the complex, dynamic business and social process it is. Part 1 examines the first of the four Ps of advertising. It describes the *process* of developing and using advertising as a marketing tool. In this first part of the text, the roots of the advertising process are revealed. Advertising is defined as both a business *and* a communications process, and the structure of the industry through which modern day advertising is carried out is described. The evolution of advertising is traced from fairly modest beginnings through periods of growth and maturation. The complex and controversial social, ethical, and regulatory aspects of advertising conclude this opening part of the text. Part 1 gives us a first look at advertising and reveals some of what advertising is and can be. From a broad societal process that helps consumers learn about products and services to a fast-paced and highly competitive business tool, advertising is revealed as a complex, dynamic, and sophisticated process.

Chapter 1, "Advertising as a Process," defines advertising and positions it within a firm's overall marketing scheme. This chapter also analyzes advertising as a basic communications tool and as a marketing communications *process*. We introduce the concept of integrated marketing communications (IMC), which provides a new perspective on the way in which a full range of communications options is exercised to compete effectively, develop customer loyalty, and generate profits.

Chapter 2, "The Structure of the Advertising Industry," shows that effective advertising requires the participation of a variety of organizations, not just that of the advertiser. Advertising agencies, research firms, special production facilitators, and media companies are just some of the organizations that form the structure of the industry. Each plays a different role, and billions of dollars are spent every year for the services of various participants. But the structure of the industry is in flux. New media and advertisers' interest in integrated marketing communications are forcing change in the industry. This chapter looks at the basic structure of the industry and at how that structure is changing.

Chapter 3, "The Evolution of Advertising," sets the process of advertising into a contemporary context. Advertising has evolved and proliferated because of fundamental influences related to free enterprise, economic development, and tradition. Advertising as a business process and a reflection of social values has experienced many evolutionary periods as technology, business management practices, and social values have changed.

Chapter 4, "Social, Ethical, and Regulatory Aspects of Advertising," examines the broad societal aspects of the advertising process. From a social standpoint, we must understand that advertising has positive effects on the standard of living, addresses needs, supports the mass media, and is a contemporary art form. Critics argue, though, that advertising wastes resources, promotes materialism, is offensive, and perpetuates stereotypes. The ethical issues in advertising focus on truth in advertising, advertising to children, and the advertising of controversial products.

Chapter 1

Advertising

as a Process

After reading and thinking about this chapter, you will be able to do the following:

1 Have an informed discussion about what constitutes advertising and what does not.

2 Discuss a basic model of advertising communication.

3 Describe a variety of different audiences for advertising.

4 Explain the key roles of advertising as a business process.

5 Recognize the aggregate effects of advertising in a national economy.

In 1974, there wasn't a bank that would lend his company money. He and his wife were feeding their family on a $25-a-week budget. He was a CPA but had given up his full-time job to teach accounting classes at a local university at night so he could devote all day to his fledgling and struggling company. And the company was, indeed, struggling. The name of the company, Dimension Six, meant nothing to anyone and seemed to excite people even less. So strapped was the firm for cash that in the early 1970s, it had to pass up sponsoring a young tennis star who demanded $1,500 to wear its shoes in major tournaments—the young tennis star turned out to be Jimmy Connors.

The company was stuck. In a market dominated by Converse and Adidas, it needed recognition. It needed visibility. What it needed was a new brand name and some good advertising. But the founder didn't have any good ideas for a brand name and thought advertising was both phony and adversarial. Still, he had to do something to save the company.

For starters, he paid a student at Portland State University $35 to come up with a logo. From the dozens of proposals she submitted, he picked the one he disliked the least—it looked like a "fat, lazy check mark." When Phil Knight, founder of Nike, was finally convinced that his company and its product needed advertising desperately, he walked into an advertising agency, stuck out his hand, and said, "Hi, I'm Phil Knight, and I don't believe in advertising."

All this happened more than 20 years ago. The $10 billion Nike empire that employs fifteen thousand people now spends about $500 million a year on worldwide advertising and almost that much every year on endorsements by the likes of Bo Jackson, Michael Jordan, Andre Agassi, and Sigourney Weaver. Advertising has helped make the Nike brand name as well known around the world as Coke and Levi's.[1] Nike's advertising campaigns are among the most memorable in advertising history: "Bo Knows," "Just Do It," "It's Gotta Be the Shoes," "Rock 'n' Roll Tennis," and "Michael Jordan and Bugs Bunny." By the way, it seems Phil Knight, the founder and CEO of Nike, has now changed his mind about advertising.

Just as Phil Knight misunderstood, or at least underestimated, advertising, many people have misperceptions about the process of advertising and what it's supposed to do, what it can do, and what it can't do. The general public's attitude toward advertising is ambivalent—most people like individual ads, while they may hate advertising in general. Many think advertising deceives others, but rarely them. Most think it's a glamorous profession, but one in which people are either morally bankrupt con artists or pathological liars. At worst, advertising is seen as hype, unfair capitalistic manipulation, banal commercial noise, mind control, modern voodoo, or outright deception. Some of these descriptions of advertising reflect suspicions that have long surrounded the industry, and some of these descriptions are, on occasion, regrettably precise.

At best, the average person sees advertising as amusing, informative, helpful, and occasionally hip. It can help consumers see possibilities and meanings in the things they buy and the services they use. It can connect goods and services to the culture and liberate meanings that lie below the surface. It can turn mere products into meaningful brands and important possessions. For example, the advertising of Doyle, Dane, Bernbach for Volkswagen (see Exhibit 1.1) helped turn an unlikely automobile into a mobile social statement. Decades of advertising by Coca-Cola (an example is shown in Exhibit 1.2) have helped turn this brand of soft drink into a nearly universally recognized cultural icon. There are many less-dramatic and less well known examples of the way advertising helps locate meaning for common products. Such an ad, for the Gillette Sensor razor, is shown in Exhibit 1.3.

1.   Statistics about Nike and quotes taken from Frank Deford, "Running Man," *Vanity Fair*, August 1993, 52–72.

Lemon.

This Volkswagen missed the boat.
The chrome strip on the glove compartment is blemished and must be replaced. Chances are you wouldn't have noticed it; Inspector Kurt Kroner did.
There are 3,389 men at our Wolfsburg factory with only one job: to inspect Volkswagens at each stage of production. (3000 Volkswagens are produced daily; there are more inspectors

than cars.)
Every shock absorber is tested (spot checking won't do), every windshield is scanned. VWs have been rejected for surface scratches barely visible to the eye.
Final inspection is really something! VW inspectors run each car off the line onto the Funktionsprüfstand (car test stand), tote up 189 check points, gun ahead to the automatic

brake stand, and say "no" to one VW out of fifty.
This preoccupation with detail means the VW lasts longer and requires less maintenance, by and large, than other cars. (It also means a used VW depreciates less than any other car.)
We pluck the lemons; you get the plums.

EXHIBIT 1.1

Advertising helps shape a product's image in the minds of consumers. Explain how Volkswagen used this ad to get consumers to rethink the image of cars as "lemons" with the image of thrifty, dependable VWs. What image is today's VW campaign trying to promote through TV and print ads? How do the elements of the VW Web site **www.vw.com/** *contribute to this image? Compare the VW image with Harley-Davidson's image at* **www.harley davidson.com**.

EXHIBIT 1.2 *Decades of creative and memorable advertising have made Coca-Cola one of the most recognizable brand names around the world.* **www.cocacola.com/**

EXHIBIT 1.3 *Advertising can help turn common, everyday products into important, meaningful brands. This ad for the Gillette Sensor razor is an example of advertising that elevates a common product to a more meaningful possession.*

The truth about advertising lies somewhere between the extremes. Sometimes advertising is hard-hitting and powerful; other times, it is boring and ineffective. Advertising can be enormously creative and entertaining, and it can be simply annoying. One thing is for sure: Advertising is anything but unimportant. Advertising plays a pivotal role in world commerce. It is also part of our language. It reflects the way we think about things and the way we see ourselves. It is both a complex communication process and a business process. Advertising is an important topic for you to study.

What Is Advertising?

❶ Advertising means different things to different people. It's a business, an art, an institution, and a cultural phenomenon. To the CEO of a multinational corporation, such as Phil Knight, advertising is an essential marketing tool that helps create brand awareness and loyalty and stimulates demand. To the art director in an advertising agency, advertising is the creative expression of a concept. To a media planner, advertising is the way a firm uses the mass media to communicate to current and potential customers. To scholars and museum curators, it is an important cultural artifact and historical record. Advertising means something different to all these people. In fact, sometimes determining just what is and what is not advertising is a difficult task. Keeping that in mind, we offer this definition:

Advertising *is a paid, mass-mediated attempt to persuade.*

As direct and simple as this definition seems, it is loaded with distinctions. Advertising is *paid* communication by a company or organization that wants its information disseminated. In advertising language, the company or organization that pays for advertising is called the **client** or **sponsor.**

First, if communication is not paid for, it's not advertising. For example, a form of promotion, called publicity, is not advertising because it is not paid for. Let's say Bruce Willis appears on the *Late Show with David Letterman* to promote his newest *Die Hard* movie. Is this advertising? No, because the producer or film studio did not pay the *Late Show with David Letterman* for airtime. In this example, the show gets an interesting and popular guest, the guest star gets exposure, and the film gets plugged. Everyone is happy, but no advertising took place. But when the film studio produces and runs ads for the newest *Die Hard* movie on television and in newspapers across the country, this communication is paid for by the studio, and it most definitely is advertising.

For the same reason, public service announcements (PSAs) are not advertising, either. When you hear a message on the radio that implores you to "Just Say No" to drugs, this sounds very much like an ad, but it is a PSA. While many PSAs sound like ads, they are excluded from the definition of advertising because they are unpaid communication. Consider the two messages in Exhibits 1.4 and 1.5.

These two messages have similar copy and deliver similar advice. Exhibit 1.4 has persuasive intent, is paid-for communication, and appears in the mass media. It is an advertisement. Exhibit 1.5 also has persuasive intent and appears in mass media outlets, but it is not advertising because it is not paid-for communication.

Second, advertising is *mass mediated.* This means it is delivered through a communication medium designed to reach more than one person, typically a large number—or mass—of people. Advertising is widely disseminated through familiar means—television, radio, newspapers, and magazines—and other media like direct mail, billboards, online services, and videocassettes. Even the simple posters placed around college campuses are designed to be seen by more than one person, making posters a medium for advertising. The mass-mediated nature of advertising creates a communication environment where the message is not delivered in a face-to-face manner. This distinguishes advertising from personal selling as a form of communication.

Third, all advertising includes an *attempt to persuade.* To put it bluntly, ads are communication designed to get someone to do something. Even an advertisement with a stated objective of being purely informational still has persuasion at its core. The ad informs the consumer for a purpose, and that purpose is to get the consumer to like the brand and to eventually buy the brand. In the absence of this persuasive intent, a communication might be news, but it would not be advertising.

At this point, we can say that for a communication to be classified as advertising, three essential criteria must be met:

1. The communication must be paid for.
2. The communication must be delivered to an audience via mass media.
3. The communication must be attempting persuasion.

The messages in Exhibits 1.4 and 1.5 communicate nearly identical information to the audience, but one is an advertisement and one is not. The message in Exhibit 1.4, sponsored by Trojan, is an advertisement because it is a paid-for communication. The message in Exhibit 1.5, sponsored by the Health Education Authority, has a persuasive intent similar to the Trojan ad, but it is not advertising—Exhibit 1.5 is a PSA. Why isn't the Health Education Authority message an ad?
www.linkmag.com/trojan/

"I didn't use one because I didn't have one with me."

GET REAL

If you don't have a parachute, don't jump, genius.

Helps reduce the risk

HOW FAR WILL YOU GO BEFORE YOU MENTION CONDOMS?

THIS FAR?

THIS FAR?

THIS FAR?

THIS FAR?

Today, no one can ignore the need to mention condoms. Have sex with someone without using one and not only could you risk an unwanted pregnancy, but you also risk contracting one of the many sexually transmitted diseases.

Like Herpes, Chlamydia, Gonorrhoea, and of course HIV, the virus which leads to AIDS.

So the question isn't if, but when you mention condoms. You could mention them at any moment leading up to sexual intercourse. In reality, it's not quite so easy.

Mention them too early and you might feel you look pushy or available. Leave it too late and you risk getting so carried away you might not mention them at all.

When is the easiest moment to say you want to use one? How about while you're still wearing your knickers? In this instance it would be picture three.

By now you've gone far enough to make it obvious that you both want to have sex. But not so far that you're in danger of getting emotionally and sexually carried away.

It's a perfect opportunity. So take it. Say you want to use a condom.

Say he hasn't got one? Well have one of your own at the ready just in case. It really doesn't matter whose you use.

And then you can go just as far as you like.

FOR MORE INFORMATION OR ADVICE ABOUT AIDS OR HIV, PHONE THE FREE NATIONAL AL PINE ON 0800 567 123. IT'S OPEN 24 HOURS A DAY AND IS COMPLETELY CONFIDENTIAL.

It is important to note here that advertising can be persuasive information not only about a product or service, but also about an idea, a person, or an entire organization. When Colgate and Honda use advertising, this is product advertising and meets all three criteria. Likewise, when Dean Witter, Delta Air Lines, Terminex, or your dentist run advertisements, it is service advertising and meets all three criteria.

But what about political advertising? Political ads "sell" candidates rather than commercial goods or services. Political advertisements are special because they are the only completely unregulated form of advertising; they are viewed as "political speech" and thus enjoy complete First Amendment protection. Still, political advertising meets our definitional test because it is paid-for communication, is mass mediated, and has a

The following is a paid political announcement

ANNCR: The following is a paid political announcement.

"Change must be guided by principle."

PRESIDENT BUSH: Everyone wants change.

America must want change.

But change must be guided by principle.

And there are three basic principles that must lead our quest for change.

First, we must control wasteful government spending.

That's absolutely essential for the kind of change the American people want.

And second, we must strengthen the American family.

The decline of the American family is hurting the soul of America.

And we've got to change that.

Third, we're a nation of laws.

We must increase respect for the law.

We must pass strong legislation to help the fight against crime and to back up our police officers and law enforcement officers

out on the street. These are the kind of changes that America needs

President Bush

and I am convinced I can bring about that change.

The preceding has been a paid political announcement

ANNCR: The proceeding has been a paid political announcement.

EXHIBIT 1.6

While this political message for George Bush during the 1992 presidential campaign is promoting a person and ideas, it meets the definitional test for advertising in general—it is paid-for communication, is placed in mass media, and has a persuasive intent. Check out **www .democrats.org** *and* **www.rnc.org**.

persuasive intent. Political advertising can be for a candidate, as shown in Exhibit 1.6, or for a political organization, such as the National Rifle Association (NRA).

Although the Bush Campaign ad does not ask anyone to buy anything, it is (1) paid for, (2) placed in a mass medium, and (3) an attempt to persuade members of the electorate to view George Bush and his agenda favorably. It represents another way advertising can persuade beyond the purchase of products and services. Many political candidates, environmental groups, human rights organizations, and political groups buy advertising and distribute it through mass media to persuade people to accept their way of thinking.

Advertising, Advertisements, and Advertising Campaigns

Now that we have a working definition of advertising, we turn our attention to other important dimensions of defining advertising. An **advertisement** refers to a specific message that an organization has placed to persuade an audience. An **advertising campaign** is a series of coordinated advertisements and other promotional efforts that communicate a single theme or idea. Successful advertising campaigns can be developed around a single advertisement placed in multiple media. Or, an advertising campaign may be made up of several different advertisements all with a similar look, feel, and message. Advertising campaigns can run for a few weeks or for many years. The advertising campaign is, in many ways, the most challenging aspect of advertising execution. It requires a keen sense of the complex environments within which an advertiser must communicate to different audiences.

The vast majority of ads you see each day are part of broader campaigns. Furthermore, most individual ads would make little sense without the knowledge the audience members have about ads for this particular product or for the category in general. Ads are interpreted by consumers through their experiences with the product and with previous ads about the product. When you see a new Coca-Cola ad, you make sense of the ad through your history with Coca-Cola and its previous advertising. Even ads for a new brand or a new product are situated within audiences' broad knowledge of products, brands, and advertising. After years of viewing ads and buying brands, audiences bring a rich history and knowledge base to every communications encounter. Just how these encounters between consumers and communications work is our next topic.

Advertising as a Communications Process

❷ Communication is fundamental to life itself. Advertising is communication. To understand advertising at all, you must understand something about communication in general, and mass communication in particular. At the outset, you must understand the most basic aspects of how advertising works as a means of communication. To accomplish this, let's consider a contemporary model of mass communication. We will apply this basic model of communication as a first step in understanding advertising communication.

A Model of Mass-Mediated Communication

As we said earlier, advertising is mass-mediated communication. It is communication that occurs not face-to-face, but through a medium (such as radio, magazines, television, or a computer). A contemporary model of mass-mediated communication is presented in Exhibit 1.7.

This model shows mass communication as a process of interacting individuals and institutions. It has two major components, each representing quasi-independent processes: (1) production and (2) reception.

Moving from left to right in the model, we first see the process of communication production. This is where the content of any mass communication is produced. An advertisement, like other forms of mass communication, is the product of institutions (such as networks, corporations, advertising agencies, and governments) interacting to produce content (what physically appears on a page or on an audiotape or videotape or computer screen). The creation of the advertisement is a complex interaction of the advertiser; the advertiser's expectations regarding the target audience; the advertiser's assumptions about how the audience will interpret the ad; and the conventions, rules, and regulations of the medium itself.

Moving to the right, we see the communication reception process. Within the reception process, individual members of the audience interpret an ad according to a set of factors governed largely by their salient social networks (their family, friends, and peers), their previous experience, and their motivations. This is where the meaning of the ad is determined. The advertiser has significant input into the creation of *content,* but what the audience member makes of the ad (his or her interpretation) is the *meaning* the audience member gives it. It is critical to remember that content and meaning are not synonymous. For example, you and one of your friends can read the same book but interpret it very differently. The same is true of ads.

The audience also acts with *intent.* Individuals exercise choice in their selection of advertising, or at least of the media that carry advertising. They also bring with them their own rules of membership in the audience, that is, their own rules on how they will approach a message and interpret it. A condom ad, for example, will most likely have different meanings depending on one's personal views toward sex. You and your grandmother may see things differently. You create your own, separate meanings based on the social and cultural context and your own unique background and experiences.

We say that the processes of production and reception are partially independent because the producers of the message cannot control or even closely monitor the actual reception and interpretation of the content. Audience members are exposed to advertising outside of the direct observation of the advertiser and are capable of interpreting advertising any way they want. Likewise, audience members have little control over or

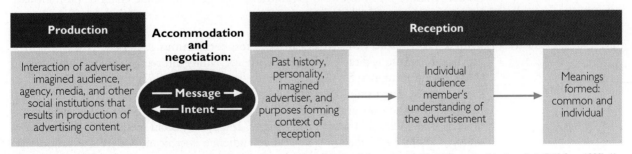

Source: Adapted from a model that appears in James A. Anderson and Timothy P. Meyer, *Mediated Communication: A Social Perspective* (Newbury Park, Calif.: Sage, 1988), 41.

EXHIBIT 1.7

A model of mass-mediated communication.

WEB SIGHTING

EXHIBIT 1.8

This ad is a good example of how the meaning of an ad can vary for different people. How would you interpret the meaning of this ad? Think of someone very different from you. What meaning might that person give this ad? At the Coke Web site **www.cocacola.com/**, *what message do you think Coke is trying to convey? What meaning might other people see in this same presentation? For comparison, summarize the meaning you get from the Pepsi site at* **www.pepsi.com**.

input into the actual production of the message. Both producers and receivers are thus "imagined," in the sense that the two don't have significant direct contact with one another but have a general sense of what the other is like.

The model in Exhibit 1.7 underscores the critical point that no ad contains a single meaning for all audience members. An ad for a pair of women's shoes means something different for women versus men. A popular ad for Diet Coke (shown in Exhibit 1.8) may be interpreted differently by men and women. For example, does the ad suggest that men drink Diet Coke so they can be the object of intense daily admiration by a group of female office workers? Or does the ad suggest that Diet Coke is a part of a modern woman's lifestyle, granting her "permission" to freely admire attractive men in the same way women have been eyed by male construction workers (or executives) for years? The audience decides. Keep in mind that although individual audience members' interpretations will differ to some extent, they may be close enough to the advertiser's intent to make the ad effective. When members of an audience are similar in their background, social standing, and goals, they generally yield similar enough meaning from an ad.

The Audiences for Advertising

3 In the language of advertising, an **audience** is a group of individuals who receive and interpret messages sent from advertisers through mass media. The level of interpretation might be minimal (recognition), or it might be extensive (thoughtful, elaborate processing of an ad). In advertising, audiences are often targeted. A **target audience** is a particular group of consumers singled out for an advertisement or advertising campaign. Target audiences are *potential* audiences because advertisers can never be sure that the message will actually get through to them as intended. While advertisers can identify dozens of different target audiences, five broad audience categories are commonly described: household consumers, members of business organizations, members of a trade channel, professionals, and government officials and employees.

Audience Categories.   **Household consumers** are the most conspicuous audience in that most mass media advertising is directed at them. Unilever, Miller Brewing, Saturn, The Gap, and Nationwide Insurance have products and services designed for the consumer market, and so their advertising targets household consumers. The most recent information indicates that there are about 96.5 million households in the United States and approximately 270 million household consumers.[2] Total yearly retail spending by these households is about $4.43 trillion.[3] This huge audience is typically where the action is in advertising. Under the very broad heading of "consumer advertising," you will soon

2.   "1995 Survey of Buying Power," *Sales and Marketing Management* (1995): B2.
3.   Ibid., B3.

learn that very fine audience distinctions are made by advertisers. Target audience definitions such as men 25 to 45, living in metropolitan areas, with incomes greater than $50,000 per year, are common.

Members of business organizations are the focus of advertising for firms that produce business and industrial goods and services, such as office equipment, production machinery, supplies, and software. While products and services targeted to this audience often require personal selling, advertising is used to create an awareness and a favorable attitude among potential buyers. Not-for-profit businesses like universities, some research laboratories, philanthropic groups, and cultural organizations represent an important and separate business audience for advertising.

Members of a trade channel include retailers, wholesalers, and distributors; they are an audience for producers of both household and business goods and services. Unless a producer can obtain adequate retail and wholesale distribution through a trade channel, the firm's products will not reach customers. Therefore, it is important to direct advertising at the trade level of the market. Various forms of advertising and promotion are instrumental in cultivating demand among members of a trade channel. Generally, the major promotional tool used to communicate with this group is personal selling. This is because this target audience represents a relatively small, easily identifiable group that can be reached with personal selling. When advertising is also directed at this audience, it can serve an extremely useful purpose, as we will see later in the section on advertising as a business process. (See Exhibits 1.9 and 1.10 for two examples of advertising directed at members of a trade channel.)

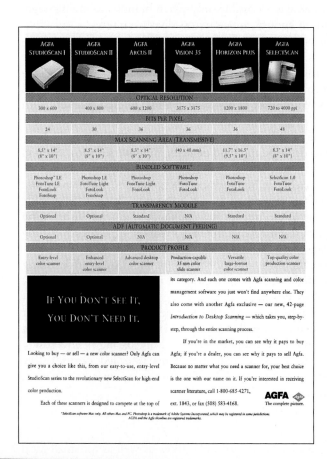

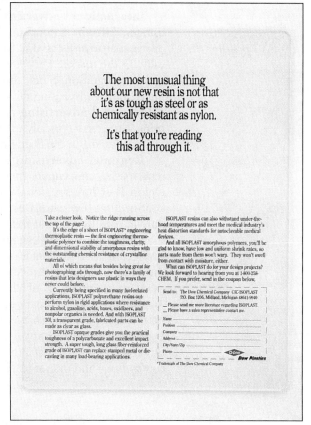

EXHIBITS 1.9 AND 1.10

These two ads, one for Agfa scanners and the other for Dow Chemical resins, are examples of advertising aimed at members of a trade channel. Business and industrial firms often use advertising to develop awareness of their goods and services within a trade channel of retailers and wholesalers.
www.agfahome.com/ *and* **www.dow.com/**

Professionals form a special target audience and are defined as doctors, lawyers, accountants, teachers, or any other professionals who have received special training or certification. This audience warrants separate classification because its members have specialized needs and interests. Advertising directed at professionals thus highlights products and services often uniquely designed to serve their narrowly defined needs. In addition, the language and images used in advertising to this target audience rely on the esoteric terminology and unique circumstances that members of the professions readily recognize. Advertising to professionals is predominantly carried out through trade publications. The ad for Prevacid in Exhibit 1.11 is an example of advertising directed to doctors.

Government officials and employees constitute an audience in themselves due to the large dollar volume of buying that federal, state, and local governments represent. Government organizations such as schools and road maintenance operations buy huge amounts of various products. Producers of items like furniture, construction materials, vehicles, fertilizers, computers, and business services all target this group with their advertising. Advertising to this audience group is dominated by direct mail advertising.

Audience Geography. Audiences can also be thought of in geographic terms. Because of cultural differences, very few ads can be effective for all consumers worldwide. However, **global advertising** is used for brands like Pepsi, IBM, Levi's, Sony, and Pirelli Tires. Exhibits 1.12 and 1.13, for example, show similar German and Italian executions of a Rolex ad. Firms that market brands like these will attempt to develop and place advertisements with a common theme and presentation in all markets around the world where the firm's brands are sold. Global placement is possible only when brands and the messages about those brands have a common enough appeal across diverse cultures.

International advertising occurs when firms prepare and place different advertising in different national markets. Each international market will often require unique or original advertising due to product adaptations or message appeals tailored specifically for the market. Very few firms have products with truly cross-cultural appeal and global recognition. Since this is true, most firms must pursue foreign markets with international advertising rather than global advertising.

National advertising reaches all geographic areas of one nation. National advertising is the term typically used to describe the kind of advertising we see most often in the mass media in the domestic U.S. market.

Regional advertising is carried out by producers, wholesalers, distributors, and retailers that concentrate their efforts in a relatively large, but not national, geographic region. Best Buy, a regional consumer electronics and appliance chain, has distribution confined to a few states. Because of the nature of the firm's market, it places advertising only in regions where it has stores.

Local advertising is essentially the same as regional advertising. **Local advertising** is directed at an audience in a single trading area, either a city or state. Exhibit 1.14 shows an example of this type of advertising.

Retail shopkeepers of all types rely on local media to reach their customers. Under special circumstances, national advertisers will share advertising expenses in a market with local dealers to achieve specific advertising objectives. This sharing of advertising expenses between national advertisers and local merchants is called **cooperative advertising** (or **co-op advertising**). Exhibit 1.15 illustrates a co-op advertisement run by Sony and one of its retailers.

Advertising as a Business Process

❹ For multinational organizations like IBM, as well as for small local retailers, advertising is a basic business tool that helps them communicate with current and potential customers. We will discuss advertising as a business process in two ways. First, we will consider the role advertising plays in the overall marketing program in firms. Second, we will take a broader look at the impact of advertising across economic systems.

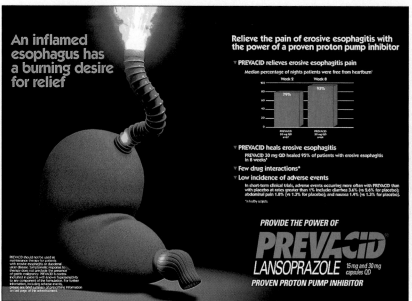

Professional audiences for advertising, like doctors, lawyers, and engineers, have special needs and interests. This ad for Prevacid was run in a trade publication and offers medical doctors the kind of specialized information they desire about pharmaceutical products.

When a brand has a common appeal across cultures, a firm can create global advertising that uses similar ads in different geographic markets. Rolex has created very similar ads for the German market (Exhibit 1.12) and for the Italian market (Exhibit 1.13), even though the cultures are quite different. Be aware, however, that most firms must customize their advertising from culture to culture.

WHEN A CLOTHING STORE HAS A SALE ON SELECTED MERCHANDISE, WHY IS IT ALWAYS MERCHANDISE YOU'D NEVER SELECT?

At Daffy's you'll find 40-70% off all our clothes, every day. 5th Ave. & 18th St., Madison Ave. & 44th St.

DAFFY'S®

CLOTHES THAT WILL MAKE YOU, NOT BREAK YOU.™

EXHIBIT 1.14

Daffy's is a clothing retailer with just one shop in New York City; it services a local geographic market. Retailers that serve a small geographic area use local advertising to reach their customers.

The Role of Advertising in Marketing

To truly appreciate advertising as a business process, we have to understand the role advertising plays in a firm's marketing effort. Every organization must make marketing decisions. These decisions involve developing, pricing, promoting, and distributing products and services for some target audience. The role of advertising in marketing relates to four important aspects of the marketing process in organizations: the marketing mix; market segmentation, product differentiation, and positioning; revenue and profit generation; and customer satisfaction.

Advertising's Role in the Marketing Mix. A formal definition of marketing suggests the importance of advertising (or promotion) as one of the primary marketing tools available to any organization:

Marketing is the process of planning and executing the conception, pricing, promotion, and distribution of ideas, goods, and services to create exchanges that satisfy individual and organizational objectives.[4]

Marketing assumes a wide range of responsibilities related to the conception, pricing, promotion, and distribution of ideas, goods, or services. These four responsibilities of marketing are referred to as the **marketing mix.** The word *mix* is used to describe these responsibilities because decision makers decide on the proper emphasis on the product, its price, its promotion (including advertising), and its distribution. This blend of emphases, or mix, results in the overall marketing program for a brand. Advertising is important, but it is only one of the promotional tools relied on in the marketing mix. Effective advertising planning and execution often depend on activities in the other areas of the marketing mix as well. For example, allowing customers to sample a product can often be a potent tactic for winning them over. The New Media box on page

---

4.   This American Marketing Association definition appeared in *Marketing News,* March 1, 1985, 1.

National advertisers will often share advertising expenses with local retail merchants if the retailer features the advertiser's brand in local advertising. This sharing of expenses is called co-op advertising. Good Vibes is featuring Sony products in this co-op ad. **www.sony.co.jp/**

17 illustrates a creative sampling program that produced impressive results using the Internet.

Effective advertising communicates to a target audience the value of a product or service that a firm has to offer. Value consists of more than simply the product or service, though. Consumers look for value beyond the product or service itself and demand such things as convenient location, credit terms, warranties and guarantees, and delivery. Because of consumers' search for value, marketers must determine which marketing mix ingredients to emphasize and how to blend the elements in just the right way to attract and serve customers. These mix ingredients should play a significant role in determining the nature of the advertising effort.

Exhibit 1.16 lists the most common factors considered when addressing each component of the marketing mix. You can see that product, price, promotion, and distribution really refer to a wide range of strategies that can be used to attract customers. The important point is that a firm's advertising effort must complement the overall marketing strategy being used by a firm.

Advertising's Role in Market Segmentation, Product Differentiation, and Positioning.

For advertising to be effective, it must work to support the organization's general marketing strategies. Some of the most basic strategies for cultivating customers are market segmentation, product differentiation, and positioning. Advertising plays an important role in helping a firm execute these marketing strategies.

Market segmentation is the breaking down of a large, heterogeneous market into submarkets or segments that are more homogeneous. Underlying the strategy of market segmentation are the facts that consumers differ in their wants and that the wants of one person can differ under various circumstances. For example, the market for automobiles can be divided into submarkets for different types of automobiles based on the needs and desires of various groups of buyers. Identifying those groups, or segments, of the population who want and will buy large or small, luxury or economy, sport, sedan, or minivan models is an important part of basic marketing strategy. Advertising's role in the market segmentation process is to develop messages that appeal to the wants and desires of different segments and then to transmit those messages via appropriate media. As discussed in the Contemporary Issues box on page 18, Chrysler applied a market segmentation strategy in targeting its "Hi!" campaign to young adults.

Product differentiation is the process of creating a perceived difference, in the mind of the consumer, between an organization's product or service and the competition's. Notice that this definition emphasizes that product differentiation is based on consumer perception. The perceived differences can be tangible differences, or they may be based on intangible, image, or style factors. The critical issue is that consumers *perceive* a difference between brands. If consumers do not perceive a difference, then whether "real" differences exist or not does not matter: In the mind of the consumer, there are no differences. Product differentiation is one of the most critical marketing

Product	Promotion
Functional features	Amount and type of advertising
Aesthetic design	Number and qualifications of salespeople
Accompanying services	Extent and type of personal selling program
Instructions for use	Sales promotion—coupons, contests, sweepstakes
Warranty	Trade shows
Product differentiation	Public relations activities
Product positioning	Direct mail or telemarketing
	Event sponsorships
	Internet communications

Price	Distribution
Level:	Number of retail outlets
Top of the line	Location of retail outlets
Competitive, average prices	Types of retail outlets
Low-price policy	Catalog sales
Terms offered:	Other nonstore retail methods
Cash only	Number and type of wholesalers
Credit:	Inventories—extent and location
Extended	Services provided by distribution:
Restricted	Credit
Interest charges	Delivery
Lease/rental	Installation
	Training

strategies. If a firm's product or service is not perceived as distinctive and attractive by consumers, then consumers will have no reason to choose the brand over one from the competition or to pay higher prices for the "better" brand. The same can be said for political candidates who offer their positions to the public during political campaigns.

Advertising can help create a difference, in the mind of the consumer, between an organization's brand and its competitors' brands. The advertisement may feature performance features, or it may create the difference with imagery. The essential task for advertising is to develop a message that is distinctive and unmistakably linked to the organization's brand. The ads in Exhibits 1.17 and 1.18 are distinctive and pursue product differentiation.

Positioning is the process of designing a product or service so that it can occupy a distinct and valued place in the target consumer's mind, and then communicating this distinctiveness through advertising. Notice that positioning, like product differentiation, is dependent on a perceived image. The importance of positioning can be understood by recognizing that consumers will create a perceptual space in their minds for all the brands they might consider. A perceptual space is how one brand is seen on any number of dimensions—such as quality, taste, price, or social display value—in relation to those same dimensions in other brands.

The positioning decision is really comprised of two different decisions. A firm must decide on the **external position** for a brand—that is, the competitive niche the brand will pursue. Additionally, an **internal position** must be achieved with regard to the other similar brands a firm markets. For example, Procter & Gamble has to be careful not to cannibalize, or steal share from, one of its own brands. With regard to the external-positioning decision, a firm must achieve a distinctive competitive position based on design features, pricing, distribution, or promotion or advertising strategy. Some brands are positioned at the very top of their product category, like BMW's 750iL, priced around $75,000 (see Exhibit 1.19). Other brands seek a position at the low end of all market offerings, like the Chevrolet Geo shown in Exhibit 1.20.

Effective internal positioning is accomplished by either developing vastly different products within a product line (Ben & Jerry's® ice cream, for example, offers plenty of distinctive flavors, as shown in Exhibit 1.21) or creating advertising messages that appeal to different consumer needs and desires. Procter & Gamble has successfully internally positioned very similar brands using a combination of product design and effective advertising. Procter & Gamble's soap products line includes eight or more laundry detergent brands (see Exhibit 1.22). While some of these brands assume different positions in the line due to substantive differences (a liquid versus a powder soap, for example), others with minor differences achieve distinctive positioning through advertising. One brand is advertised as being

NEW MEDIA

THE VIRTUAL SALE: DEC ALPHA STATIONS SILENCES SKEPTICS ONLINE

Digital Equipment Corporation's new line of Alpha workstations faced a major credibility problem at their 1993 launch. Quite simply, nobody believed that the systems could possibly be as fast or as powerful as claimed. While seeing is believing, how could DEC possibly hope to demonstrate its new system to every doubting potential business buyer? Virtually, of course. To separate fact from fiction and substantiate the awesome power of its new offerings, DEC allowed potential customers to use its Internet gateway, directly access an Alpha client-server, load their own software, and let it fly. The result: More than 1,400 accesses were recorded each day, making believers out of skeptics and generating a substantial number of qualified buyers. Ira Machefsky, DEC's West Coast product manager in the Internet Business Group, says that the gateway access alone accounted for $15 million of Alpha systems sales over a 12-month period. Who'd have believed it?

Source: "Betting on the 'Net," *Sales and Marketing Management* (June 1995): 47.

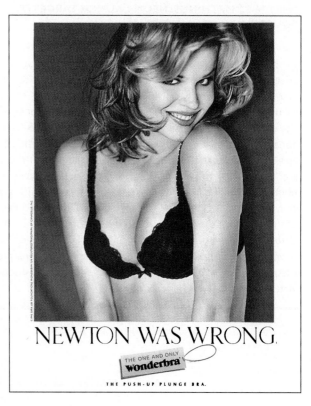

EXHIBITS 1.17 AND 1.18

An important role for advertising is to help a firm differentiate its brand from the competition with distinctive presentations. The Honda del Sol ad in Exhibit 1.17 draws attention to the car's removable roof as a basis for differentiation. The Wonderbra ad in Exhibit 1.18 also highlights this brand's superior design as a basis for differentiation. **www.honda .com/**

Advertising helps brands pursue a position in the market. Here, BMW is positioning the 750iL at the top end of the market, and this ad helps achieve that goal. **www .bmwusa.com/**

effective on kids' dirty clothes, while another brand is portrayed as effective for preventing colors from running (see Exhibit 1.23). In this way, advertising helps to create a distinctive position, both internally and externally, and minimizes cannibalization among similar brands.

CONTEMPORARY ISSUES

"HI!" 20-SOMETHINGS: NEON LAUNCH TARGETED SQUARELY AT GENERATION X

How do you target products at Generation X? Subtly, very subtly. Research has shown that the X'ers are wary and skeptical of traditional advertising. How then do you launch a new car to the 24-to-30-year-old crowd, which comprises half of the two-million-unit small-car market, without succumbing to portrayals of the target audience lifestyle? Feature the car, not the group, and imbue the vehicle with its own separate personality. Witness the Dodge and Plymouth Neon, a zippy, inexpensive, and "huggable" car that personally greets viewers of the BBDO ads with a cheerful "Hi!" and a smiling, inviting visage. Later, savvy changes to the ubiquitous "Hi!" billboards created fresh meaning with graffiti-like additions to form phrases like "it's a **Hit**." The Dodge and Plymouth versions of the car share the Neon name and differ only in the Dodge or Plymouth emblem on the hood. This common branding approach saved precious development dollars and allowed Chrysler to concentrate promotional resources around a central campaign theme that positioned Neon as a virtual brand.

Sources: "Neon Lights Up Fast Lane in Noeltime X-Country Road Trip," *Brandweek*, September 20, 1993, 1; and "Gen X Makes Neon Product of the Year," *Advertising Age*, December 26, 1994, 17.

The methods and strategic options available to an organization with respect to market segmentation, product differentiation, and positioning will be fully discussed in Chapter 6. For now, recognize that advertising plays an important role in assisting an organization to put these essential market strategies into operation.

Advertising's Role in Revenue and Profit Generation. The fundamental purpose of marketing can be stated quite simply: to generate revenue. No other part of an organization has this primary purpose. In the words of highly regarded management consultant and scholar Peter Drucker, "Marketing and innovation produce results: all the rest are 'costs.' "[5] The results Drucker is referring to are revenues. The marketing process in organizations is designed to generate sales and therefore revenues for the firm.

5.   Peter F. Drucker, *People and Performance: The Best of Peter Drucker on Management* (New York: HarperCollins, 1977), 90.

EXHIBIT 1.20

Just as BMW pursued positioning with the ad in Exhibit 1.19, Chevrolet is using advertising to position the Geo Metro—this time at the low-price, value position in the market. **www .chevrolet.com/geo/ a300.htm**

It doesn't cost a lot,
and it has two air bags.

The newest Geo. Metro, *from* $8,595.*

◆ Metro is the lowest-priced car around that comes with two air bags! ◆

◆ And every new Metro comes with big safety ideas like

a steel safety cage and crush zones. ◆

◆ If you want anti-lock brakes, you can get those, too. ◆

◆ The side-impact protection meets Uncle Sam's safety laws for 1997. ◆

◆ For all the running around you do,

every new Metro comes with daytime running lamps. ◆

◆ Get to know the newest Geo. Metro. At your Chevrolet/Geo dealer's. ◆

◆ Want to know more? Give us a call. 1-800-Get-2-Kno. ◆

GET TO KNOW

Geo
metro

WEB SIGHTING

INTRODUCING
Smooth **BEN & JERRY'S**
NO CHUNKS! NEW flavors of ice cream unfettered by chunks.

Vanilla Bean | White Russian | Double Chocolate Fudge Swirl

Vanilla Caramel Fudge | Aztec Harvests Coffee | Deep Dark Chocolate

Vanilla | Mocha Fudge

EXHIBIT 1.21

Firms with multiple brands in a single product category have to internally position these brands to differentiate them from each other in the minds of consumers. Ben & Jerry's® achieves its product positioning by emphasizing the distinctly different flavors of each of its ice creams. How does the Ben & Jerry's® Web site **www.benjerry .com/** *help position its products? What does the site do to differentiate the company from other companies? For comparison, visit the site of G & D's Ice Cream and Café at* **www.gdhq.com /ice_cream.html**, *the British version of the Ben & Jerry's® approach.*

It is in this sales part of the revenue-generating process where advertising plays a role. As we have seen, advertising communicates descriptive and persuasive information to audiences based on the values created in the marketing mix. This communication, which can highlight brand features, price, or availability through distribution, attracts customers. When a brand has the *right* features, the *right* price, the *right* distribution, and the *right* communication, sales will likely occur, and the firm generates revenue. In this way, advertising makes a direct contribution to the marketing goal of revenue generation. Notice that advertising *contributes* to the process of creating sales and revenue. Some organizations will mistakenly see advertising as a panacea—the salvation for marketing mix strategy. Advertising alone cannot be held solely responsible for sales. Sales occur when a brand has a well-conceived overall marketing mix—including good advertising.

The effect of advertising on profits is a bit more involved. This effect comes about when advertising can help give a firm greater flexibility in the price it charges for a product or service. Advertising can help create pricing flexibility by (1) contributing to economies of scale, and (2) creating brand loyalty. When a firm creates large-scale demand for its product, the quantity of product produced is increased. As production reaches higher and higher levels, fixed costs (such as rent and equipment costs) are spread over a greater number of units produced. The result of this large-scale production is that the cost to produce each item is reduced. Lowering the cost of each item produced because of high-volume production is known as **economies of scale.**

EXHIBIT 1.22

When a firm has multiple brands within a single product category—like Procter & Gamble's soap products line—then ads must be created to successfully position these brands against one another without causing cannibalization. **www.pg.com**

EXHIBIT 1.23

Procter & Gamble successfully achieves both a competitive external position and a distinctive internal product line position for Cheer laundry detergent by advertising the brand as the leader in preventing colors from running. **www.pg.com**

When Procter & Gamble manufactures hundreds of thousands of tubes of Crest toothpaste and ships them in large quantities to warehouses, the fixed costs of production and shipping per unit are greatly reduced. With lower fixed costs per unit, a firm can realize greater profits on each item sold. Advertising contributes to demand stimulation by communicating to the market about the features and availability of a product or service. By contributing to demand stimulation, advertising contributes to the process of creating economies of scale, which ultimately translates into higher profits per unit.

Brand loyalty occurs when a consumer repeatedly buys the same brand. This loyalty can result from pure habit, brand images and brand names that are prominent in the consumer's memory, barely conscious associations with a brand's image, or some fairly deep meanings consumers have attached to the brands they buy. When consumers, through whatever set of influences and meanings, are brand loyal, they are generally less sensitive to price increases for the brand. In economic terms, this is known as **inelasticity of demand.** When consumers are less price sensitive, firms have the flexibility to raise prices and increase profit margins. Advertising contributes directly to brand loyalty, and thus to inelasticity of demand, by persuading and reminding consumers of the satisfactions and values related to the brand.

Advertising's Role in Customer Satisfaction. How does advertising play a role in creating customer satisfaction? Once again, advertising can communicate how a brand addresses certain needs and desires, and it therefore plays an important role in attracting customers to products and services they will find useful and satisfying. But advertising can go further. It can help link a brand's image and meaning to a consumer's social environment and to the larger culture, and it can thus deliver a sense of personal connection for the consumer. Without advertising as a way to reveal the availability of these products and services and draw out these connections of broader meaning, a firm's ability to deliver customer satisfaction would be compromised. Other promotional tools, like personal selling, sales promotions, public relations, and event sponsorship, simply do not have the reach and creative power of advertising to communicate all the meanings of a product or service.

Types of Advertising   Advertisers develop and place advertisements for many reasons. Some of the most basic types of advertising are based on functional goals, that is, what it is the advertiser is trying to accomplish. The functional goals for advertising include primary and selective ad stimulation, direct and delayed response advertising, and corporate advertising.

One function for advertising is primary demand stimulation. In **primary demand stimulation,** the advertiser is seeking to create demand for a product category in general. In its pure form, the purpose of this type of advertising is to educate potential buyers about the fundamental values of the type of product, rather than emphasizing a specific brand within the product category. Both the National Fluid Milk Processor Promotion Board and the Florida Department of Citrus have used primary demand stimulation advertising for their products, as shown in Exhibits 1.24 and 1.25.

Primary demand stimulation is challenging and costly. Consumers in the market need to be convinced that a product category itself is valuable. Although primary demand stimulation is typically undertaken by trade organizations, occasionally a manufacturer will attempt to stimulate primary demand through category advertising. When the VCR was first introduced in the United States, RCA, Panasonic, and Quasar ran primary demand stimulation advertising to explain to household consumers the value and convenience of taping television programs—something almost no one had ever done before at home. One of the early ads in this category is shown in Exhibit 1.26. More recently, Thermoscan has been running advertisements in an attempt to stimulate primary demand for a thermometer that measures a baby's temperature in the ear rather than in the traditional location (see Exhibit 1.27).

While some corporations have tried primary demand stimulation, the true power of advertising is when it functions to stimulate demand for a particular company's brand. This is known as **selective demand stimulation.** The purpose of selective demand stimulation advertising is to point out a brand's unique benefits compared to the competition. For example, look at the Fuji ad in Exhibit 1.28—it touts this brand's superiority.

EXHIBITS 1.24 AND 1.25

These ads promoting milk (Exhibit 1.24) and orange juice (Exhibit 1.25) are both attempting to stimulate primary demand. Primary demand is demand for a product category—like milk or orange juice—rather than demand for a particular brand within a product category.

Likewise, now that the VCR is past the stage of primary demand stimulation—households accept the value of this product—each brand is selectively appealing to different consumer needs. Current advertising for VCRs emphasizes brand features like hi-fi sound, remote control, and voice recognition programming, as Exhibit 1.29 illustrates. This is selective demand stimulation.

Another important type of advertising involves functional goals related to the immediacy of consumer response. **Direct response advertising** is a type of advertising that asks the receiver of the message to act immediately. When an ad suggests that you "call this toll-free number" or "mail your $19.95 before midnight tonight," it is an example of direct response advertising. The General Motors insert card shown in Exhibit 1.30 is a good example. Here, recent college graduates can obtain a $400 rebate certificate by calling the 1-800 number or by returning the response card. That's direct response.

While exceptions exist, direct response advertising is most often used for products that consumers are familiar with, do not require inspection at the point of purchase, and are relatively low cost. The proliferation of toll-free numbers and the widespread use of credit cards have been a boon to direct response advertisers.

Delayed response advertising relies on imagery and message themes that emphasize the benefits and satisfying characteristics of a brand. Rather than trying to stimulate an immediate action from an audience, delayed response advertising attempts to develop recognition and approval of a brand over time. In general, delayed response advertising attempts to create brand awareness, reinforce the benefits of using a brand, and develop a general liking for the brand. When a consumer enters the purchase process, the information from delayed response advertising comes into play. Most advertisements we see on television and in magazines are of the delayed response type. Exhibit 1.31, an ad for hypoallergenic detergent, provides an example of this common form of advertising.

Corporate advertising is not designed to promote a specific brand, but rather functions to establish a favorable attitude toward the company as a whole. Prominent users of corporate advertising are Phillips Petroleum, Xerox, and IBM. These firms have long-established corporate campaigns aimed at generating favorable public opinion toward the corporation and its products. This type of advertising can also have an

EXHIBIT 1.26

In the early days of the VCR, manufacturers stimulated primary demand for the product category with advertising that touted the basic value of the machines and the taping process itself.

EXHIBIT 1.27

Advertising for ear thermometers is a recent attempt at primary demand stimulation, as this ad by Thermoscan demonstrates quite well.

Funny, nobody complains that Douglas Walker's vacation pictures are boring.

It could be the type of vacations Douglas takes. But more likely, it's the type of film he takes on vacation. In this case it's Fuji film. Capture crisp images with saturated colors on Fujicolor Super G Plus. It delivers enhanced image quality, natural looking skin tones and has improved film storage characteristics. If you want a superior color transparency film, try Fujichrome Sensia. This ultra-fine grain film has the ability to capture vivid, true-to-life color and smooth realistic gradation. Nothing captures the subtleties of natural color quite like the human eye or Fujicolor Reala. And only Reala combines a fourth layer of emulsion with an ultra-fine grain. So, whether you decide to trek the Appalachian trail or take shots along a deserted beach, plan on taking a more colorful vacation with Fuji film.

© 1995 FUJI PHOTO FILM U.S.A. INC.

Fujifilm. A new way of seeing things.

EXHIBIT 1.28

Selective demand stimulation advertising highlights a brand's superiority in providing satisfaction. In this ad, Fuji film is advertised as providing superior color reproduction compared to other films. www.fujifilm.co.jp/

THIS IS THE HEART OF TOSHIBA'S REVOLUTIONARY VCR CHASSIS.

INTRODUCING V3. ONLY FROM TOSHIBA.

TOSHIBA

EXHIBIT 1.29 *With primary demand well established for the VCR product category, marketers now use selective demand stimulation to tout the distinctive features of their individual brands, as Toshiba is doing in this ad that features the V3 head cylinder.* www.toshiba.com/

EXHIBIT 1.30

Direct response advertising asks consumers to take some immediate action. While direct response advertising is most often used with low-price products, even high-price products like automobiles can use this type of advertising effectively. www.gm.com

effect on the shareholders of a firm. When shareholders see good corporate advertising, it instills confidence and, ultimately, long-term commitment to the firm and its stock.

Another form of corporate advertising is carried out by members of a trade channel. Often, corporate advertising within a trade channel is referred to as *institutional advertising*. Retailers like Nordstrom, County Seat, and Wal-Mart advertise to persuade consumers to shop at their stores. While these retailers may occasionally feature a particular manufacturer's brand in the advertising (County Seat often features Levi's, in fact), the main purpose of the advertising is to get the audience to shop at their store.

Competitive pressures in the early 1990s have produced an important hybrid advertising category, wherein retailers aggressively promote their own brands. Retailers have developed private label brands in an attempt to increase profit margins and gain greater control over their product mix. **Private label brands** are brands developed and marketed by members of a trade channel. The Limited, The Gap, Sears, and Wal-Mart are retailers that have successfully developed the Forenzia, Gap, Kenmore, and Sam's Choice brands. Exhibit 1.32 shows an ad for one of these private label brands, Kenmore.

The Economic Effects of Advertising

⑤ Our discussion of advertising as a business process has focused strictly on the use of advertising by individual business organizations. There are aspects of advertising, however, that relate to broad effects across the entire economic system of a country, and beyond.

EXHIBIT 1.31

Delayed response advertising attempts to reinforce the benefits of using a brand and create a general liking for the brand. This ad for "all" detergent is an example of delayed response advertising.

EXHIBIT 1.32 *Retailers use advertising to promote their own private label brands. Here, Sears is advertising its line of Kenmore cooking appliances.* **www.sears.com**

Advertising's Effect on Gross Domestic Product. As demand is stimulated, consumer spending rises and increases the gross revenues of firms in an economic system. When this occurs, the gross domestic product of the country will rise. **Gross domestic product (GDP)** is a measure of the total value of goods and services produced within an economic system. Advertising is related to GDP in that it can contribute to levels of overall consumer demand and play a key role in introducing new products, like VCRs, microcomputers, the Internet, or alternative energy sources. As demand for these products grows, the resultant consumer spending fuels retail sales, housing starts, and corporate investment in finished goods and capital equipment. Consequently, GDP is affected.[6]

Advertising's Effect on Business Cycles. Advertising can have a stabilizing effect on downturns in business activities. There is evidence that many firms increase advertising during times of recession in an effort to spend their way out of a business downturn. Similarly, there is research to suggest that firms that maintain advertising during a recession perform better afterward, relative to firms that cut advertising spending.[7]

Advertising's Effect on Competition. Advertising is alleged to stimulate competition and therefore motivate firms to strive for better products, better production methods, and other competitive advantages that ultimately benefit the economy as a whole. Additionally, when advertising serves as a way to enter new markets, competition across the economic system is fostered. For example, Exhibit 1.33 shows an ad in which plastics manufacturers present themselves as a competitor to manufacturers of other packaging materials.

Advertising is not universally hailed as a stimulant to competition. Critics point out that the amount of advertising dollars needed to compete effectively in many industries is often prohibitive. As such, advertising can act as a barrier to entry into an industry—that is, a firm may have the capability to compete in an industry in every regard except that the advertising expenditures needed to compete are so great that the firm cannot afford to get into the business. In this way, advertising can actually serve to decrease the overall amount of competition in an economy.[8]

Advertising's Effect on Prices. One of the widely debated effects of advertising has to do with its effect on the prices consumers pay for products and services. Since advertising is a relatively costly process, then products and services would surely cost much less if firms did no advertising. Right? This is an incorrect conclusion for several reasons. First, across all industries, advertising costs incurred by firms range from about 2 percent of sales in the automobile and retail industries to about 15 percent of sales in the personal care products business. Exhibit 1.34 shows the ratio of advertising to sales for various firms in selected industries. Notice

A Little Plastic Packaging Can Help Prevent Bruising.

PLASTIC MAKES IT POSSIBLE™

EXHIBIT 1.33

Advertising affects the competitive environment in an economy. This ad by a plastics manufacturers council is fostering competition with manufacturers of other packaging materials.

6.   There are several historical treatments on how advertising affects aggregate demand. See, for example, Neil H. Borden, *The Economic Effects of Advertising* (Chicago, Ill.: Richard D. Irwin, 1942), 187–189; and John Kenneth Galbraith, *The New Industrial State* (Boston, Mass.: Houghton Mifflin Company, 1967), 203–207.

7.   See, for example, Marion L. Elmquist, "100 Leaders Parry Recession with Heavy Spending," *Advertising Age,* September 8, 1983, 1; and Rebecca Quarles, "Marketing Research Turns Recession into a Business Opportunity," *Marketing News,* January 7, 1991, 27.

8.   This argument was well articulated many years ago by Colston E. Warn, "Advertising: A Critic's View," *Journal of Marketing,* Vol. 26, no. 4 (October 1962), 12.

that there is no consistent and predictable relationship between advertising spending and sales. Circuit City Stores, Wal-Mart, and Intel all spent around $350 million in advertising in 1995, but these firms generated vastly different sales totals, ranging from more than $93 billion for Wal-Mart to just $7 billion for Circuit City Stores. Different products and different market conditions demand that firms spend more or less money on advertising. These same conditions make it difficult to identify a predictable relationship between advertising and sales.

It is true that the costs for advertising are built into the costs for products, which are ultimately passed on to consumers. But this effect on price must be judged against how much time and effort a consumer would have to spend in searching for a product or service without the benefit of advertising.

Second, the effect of economies of scale, discussed earlier, has a direct impact on prices. Recall that economies of scale serve to lower the cost of production by spreading fixed costs over a large number of items. This lower cost can be passed on to consumers in terms of lower prices, as firms search for competitive advantage with lower prices. The Ethical Issues box on page 27 describes a recent price war involving MCI and AT&T. These companies certainly are heavy advertisers, but their cutthroat competition seems to be benefiting consumers.

EXHIBIT 1.34

Advertising spending as a proportion of sales in selected industries, 1995 (dollars in millions).

Industry	Advertiser	U.S. Ad Spending	U.S. Sales	Advertising Spending as % of Sales
Apparel	Levi Strauss	$ 250.6	$ 4,171.7	5.99
	Nike	298.1	3,972.8	7.50
Automobiles	General Motors	2,046.9	132,594.4	1.54
	Ford	1,149.2	95,253.0	1.20
	Chrysler	1,222.4	47,289.0	2.58
	Mitsubishi Motors	168.0	13,300.0	1.26
	Volkswagen	135.2	3,596.4	3.75
Computers	IBM	419.8	26,789.0	1.56
	Intel	339.8	7,922.0	4.27
Food	Nestle SA	487.3	9,906.9	4.91
	Kellogg	739.7	4,080.3	18.11
	Campbell Soup	253.4	4,561.1	5.54
	H. J. Heinz	246.9	5,235.8	4.69
Personal care	Procter & Gamble	2,777.1	17,133.0	16.2
	Unilever NV	858.3	9,215.8	9.31
	Gillette	215.1	2,064.8	10.41
	Estee Lauder	134.9	1,800.0	7.4
Retail	Sears	1,225.7	31,558.0	3.88
	J.C. Penney	602.1	21,419.0	2.81
	Kmart	482.4	33,105.0	1.45
	Circuit City Stores	343.0	7,029.1	4.87
	Wal-Mart	338.7	93,627.0	0.36

Source: "100 Leading National Advertisers," *Advertising Age*, September 30, 1996, 51. Reprinted with permission from the September 30, 1996, issue of *Advertising Age*. Copyright © Crain Communications Inc. 1996.

Advertising's Effect on Value. *Value* is the password for successful marketing in the nineties. **Value** refers to a perception by consumers that a product or service provides satisfaction beyond the cost incurred to acquire the product or service. The value perspective of the modern consumer is based on wanting every purchase to be a good deal. Value is added to the consumption experience by advertising. For example, many advertising professionals and academic researchers believe that the experience of eating at McDonald's or drinking a Coke is significantly enhanced by the expectations the advertising has created and reinforced within the consumer.

Advertising also affects a consumer's perception of value by contributing to the symbolic value and the social meaning of a brand. **Symbolic value** refers to what a product or service means to consumers in a nonliteral way. For example, automobiles have been said to symbolize self-concept for some consumers. Exhibits 1.35 and 1.36 show examples of ads seeking to create symbolic value for two well-known brands.

Social meaning refers to what a product or service means in a societal context. For example, social class is marked by any number of products used and displayed to signify class membership, such as cars, beverages, and clothes. Exhibit 1.37 shows an ad for a service with clear social-class connections. Often, the product's connection to a social class addresses a need within consumers to move up in class.

ETHICAL ISSUES

A LONG-DISTANCE JOUST: MCI AND AT&T BATTLE OVER MARKET SHARE

AT&T introduced its "true" this and "true" that calling programs and ridiculed MCI's Friends & Family Plan, playing upon social fears of calling circles. MCI countered with "Shame on You, AT&T" ads and eventually introduced a *new* Friends & Family Plan. The salvos and potshots have continued ad infinitum. Finally, after years of battle in the fiercest advertising war of recent memory, a clear victor has emerged: the ad agencies! With an estimated $600 million spent on U.S. long-distance marketing in 1994 and even greater spending in 1995, consumers have reached new heights of anxiety and stress as they wonder aloud if their rates are lowest. "It's clearly a war of confusion," said Jeffrey Kagan, president of Atlanta-based Kagan Telecom Associates, "and advertising is the weapon."

Many feel that the battle of telecommunications giants will merely undermine and erode brand loyalty. This is already in evidence as a new breed of "rate surfers" has thrown loyalty out the window, continually switched services, and snatched up the offered incentives. Meanwhile, the third-largest U.S. long-distance provider, Sprint, has waited in the wings for an eventual fallout from the increasingly disloyal feelings toward AT&T and MCI. "We're doing quite well by going after consumers who don't want all the confusion, the calling circles, and the games," said Wally Meyer, vice president of marketing and sales for Sprint.

Sources: "Barrage of New Offers Sparks Phone Price War," *Advertising Age,* January 16, 1995, 36; "How AT&T Finally Found Its True Calling," *Advertising Age,* January 30, 1995, 3; and "MCI: A Smaller Family and Fewer Friends," *Business Week,* February 6, 1995, 147.

Researchers from various disciplines have long argued that objects are never just objects. They take on meaning from culture, society, and communities, and from consumers. It is important to remember that these meanings often become just as much a part of the product as some physical feature.[9] Since advertising is an essential way in which the image of a brand is developed, it contributes directly to consumers' perception of the value of the brand. The more value consumers see in a brand, the more they are willing to pay to acquire the brand. If the image of a Gucci watch, Lexus coupe, or Four Seasons hotel is valued by consumers, then consumers will pay a premium to acquire that value. Waterford crystal and a Gucci watch, shown in Exhibits 1.38 and 1.39, are examples of products that consumers will pay a premium to own.

9.   Ernest Dichter, *Handbook of Consumer Motivations* (New York: McGraw-Hill, 1964), 6.

EXHIBITS 1.35 AND 1.36

Advertising can contribute to the symbolic value that brands have for consumers. The ad for Levi's jeans in Exhibit 1.35 and the ad for Ray Ban sunglasses in Exhibit 1.36 both contribute to the symbolic value of these brands. **www.levi.com/menu** *and* **www.bushnell.com/bausch.html**

Advertising and Integrated Marketing Communications

It is important to recognize that advertising is only one of many promotional tools available. It is not always the main choice of companies because in many situations, another tool, like sales promotion or direct marketing, is better suited to the task at hand.

The concept of mixing various promotional tools has recently received widespread attention in the advertising industry and is referred to as integrated marketing communications.[10] **Integrated marketing communications (IMC)** is the process of using promotional tools in a unified way so that a synergistic communications effect is created. Although the basic ideas of IMC are not new,[11] the concept of coordinating and integrating promotional efforts to achieve a synergistic effect—that is, to ensure that the promotional effort is greater than the sum of its parts—has gained much greater sophistication and industry commitment in recent years.[12] Because of the growing emphasis on IMC in the advertising industry, special sections of this book are

10.   Don E. Schultz, Stanley Tannenbaum, and Robert Lauterborn, *Integrated Marketing Communications* (Lincolnwood, Ill: NTC Books, 1993).

11.   As an example of a basic and traditional treatment of promotion that suggested coordination and integration of the promotional mix variables, see Roy T. Shaw, Richard J. Semenik, and Robert H. Williams, *Marketing: An Integrated-Analytical Approach,* 4th ed. (Cincinnati, Ohio: South-Western Publishing, 1981), 237–238.

12.   Tom Duncan, "Integrated Marketing? It's Synergy," *Advertising Age,* March 8, 1993, 1.

EXHIBIT 1.37

Ads can communicate social meaning to consumers—a product or service carries meaning in a societal context beyond its use or purpose. This ad for United Airlines puts the company's service into such a context. **www.ual.com/**

EXHIBITS 1.38 AND 1.39 *Waterford crystal and a Gucci watch are two advertised products that consumers will pay premium prices to own. Both products have intrinsic value in that they epitomize the highest levels of quality craftsmanship. Such craftsmanship, in itself, may be enough to command premium prices in the marketplace.*

devoted to integrated marketing communications. These special sections conclude each of the four major parts of the book, parallel the emphasis of the text, and feature Delta Air Lines:

- *Delta Air Lines:* The Process of Integrated Marketing Communications
- *Delta Air Lines:* Planning Integrated Marketing Communications
- *Delta Air Lines:* Preparing the Integrated Marketing Communications Message
- *Delta Air Lines:* Placing and Coordinating Advertising and Supportive Communications

These special IMC sections are easy to find because each section begins with the red and blue logo of Delta Air Lines. These sections focus on the real-world IMC challenges faced by Delta Air Lines in planning, developing, executing, and coordinating its integrated marketing communications. Delta Air Lines and its advertising agency, BBDO South in Atlanta, have generously provided their advertising and other communication materials for use in this text. You will follow the development of an IMC campaign for Delta Air Lines from the initiation of the process, through planning and creative development, to the coordination of media and supportive communications. These sections serve as a real-world demonstration of all aspects of an integrated marketing communications effort.

SUMMARY

❶ Have an informed discussion about what constitutes advertising and what does not.

Since advertising has become so pervasive, it would be reasonable to expect that you might have your own working definition for this critical term. Advertising can be recognized by its three essential elements: Its intent is to persuade, someone sponsors it, and it is mass mediated. An advertisement is a specific message that an advertiser has placed to persuade or inform an audience.

❷ Discuss a basic model of advertising communication.

Advertising cannot be effective unless some form of communication takes place between the advertiser and the audience. But advertising is about mass communication. There are many models that might be used to help explain how advertising works or doesn't work as a communication platform. The model introduced in this chapter features basic considerations like the message-production process versus the message-reception process, and it says that consumers create their own meanings when interpreting advertisements.

❸ Describe a variety of different audiences for advertising.

While it is possible to provide a simple and clear definition of what advertising is, it is also true that advertising takes many forms and serves different purposes from one application to the next. One way to appreciate the complexity of advertising is to classify it by audience type, by geographic focus, and by function. For example, advertising might be directed at households versus government officials; it can be global or local in its focus; and it may be used to support a specific brand or to enhance the general image of a corporation.

❹ Explain the key roles of advertising as a business process.

Many different types of organizations use advertising to achieve their business objectives. For major multinational corporations, like Procter & Gamble, and for smaller, more localized businesses, like the San Diego Zoo, advertising is part of a critical business process referred to as marketing. Advertising is one element of the marketing mix; the other key elements are the firm's products, their prices, and the distribution network. Advertising must work in conjunction with these other mix elements if the organization's marketing objectives are to be achieved.

❺ Recognize the aggregate effects of advertising in a national economy.

In North America alone, billions and billions of dollars are spent on advertising every year. Viewed in the aggregate, all this advertising has several broad effects on the economy. Advertising can stimulate primary demand in many product categories, and it thus contributes to growth in gross domestic product and affects business cycles. It is also clear that the way organizations compete in the marketplace, the prices consumers pay for products, and the value consumers derive from brands are all influenced by aggregate investments in advertising.

KEY TERMS

advertising (6)
client, or sponsor (6)
advertisement (8)
advertising campaign (8)
audience (10)
target audience (10)
household consumers (10)
members of business organizations (11)
members of a trade channel (11)
professionals (12)
government officials and employees (12)
global advertising (12)
international advertising (12)

national advertising (12)
regional advertising (12)
local advertising (12)
cooperative advertising (12)
marketing (14)
marketing mix (14)
market segmentation (15)
product differentiation (15)
positioning (16)
external position (16)
internal position (16)
economies of scale (19)
brand loyalty (20)

inelasticity of demand (20)
primary demand stimulation (21)
selective demand stimulation (21)
direct response advertising (22)
delayed response advertising (22)
corporate advertising (22)
private label brands (24)
gross domestic product (GDP) (25)
value (27)
symbolic value (27)
social meaning (27)
integrated marketing communications (IMC) (28)

QUESTIONS FOR REVIEW AND CRITICAL THINKING

1. What does it mean when we say that advertising is intended to persuade? How do different ads persuade in different ways?

2. Explain the differences among regional advertising, local advertising, and cooperative advertising. What would you look for in an ad to identify it as a cooperative ad?

3. How do the goals of direct response versus delayed response advertising differ? How would you explain marketers' growing interest in direct response advertising?

4. When can a firm use global advertising? How does global advertising differ from international advertising?

5. Give an example of an advertising campaign that you know has been running for more than one year. Why do some advertising campaigns last for years, whereas others come and go in a matter of months?

6. If a firm developed a new line of athletic shoes, priced them competitively, and distributed them in appropriate retail shops, would there be any need for advertising? Is advertising really needed for a good product that is priced right?

7. Many companies now spend millions of dollars to sponsor and have their names associated with events like stock-car races or rock concerts. Do these event sponsorships fit the definition for advertising given in this chapter?

8. How does the process of market segmentation lead an organization to spend its advertising dollars more efficiently and more effectively?

9. What does it mean to say that a brand has symbolic value? Is there any good reason to believe that consumers will actually pay higher prices for brands with symbolic value?

EXPERIENTIAL EXERCISE

Find ads that fit the definition of primary demand, selective demand, direct response, and corporate advertising. What is the intended purpose of each type of advertising? Do the ads you selected achieve their objective? Explain why or why not.

USING THE INTERNET

Pick a consumer product. Then go to Yahoo! (www.yahoo .com) and search for the product. Visit five sites that carry information about this product. To search on Yahoo!, place a keyword in the empty box, then hit SEARCH. You may need to use different keywords to achieve the desired results. For each of the five sites, answer the following questions:

1. Is the site promoting the product category or promoting a specific brand? What value does the site offer consumers?

2. How helpful is the site for making a purchase decision in this product category?

3. Do you think this Web site is a reliable source of information? Why or why not?

4. How effective is this site in communicating its message? If it has a persuasive message, how effective is it?

jane's brain bulletin board

COMMUNICATIONS

jane's brain is officially 1 month old! How 'bout a party? Or better yet, why not fill us in on what you like, what you don't like, & what you'd like to see--do it in YOU TELL US. We love hearing from you & giving you what you want (like the new HOMEWORK topic), so don't be shy! If you asked Mariella a makeup question, look for your answer in BEAUTY BYTES, & Binki sez "HEY WRITERS!!" see Our Magazine sub/WRITERS CRAMP, NOW!

Guidelines & Info

Read Notes posted since you last visited:

09/23 06:00 PM Eastern

Choose a Topic

GIRL TALK

Your last visited Topic

Optionally, see Notes only:

To Member ID

or

From Member ID

Begin Reading Notes

Customize This Board

Write a Public Note

 jane's got great colors, great products & 1 great price: everything jane is $2.99!

jane. Everything Great About Being A Girl.
Copied from the PRODIGY(R) service 10/19/94 09:18

M J P A-Z X Z A P T E   FREE

Chapter 2

The Structure

of the

Advertising

Industry

After reading and thinking about this chapter, you will be able to do the following:

1 Discuss six important trends transforming the advertising industry.

2 Describe the size and scale of the advertising industry.

3 Explain who the participants in the advertising industry are and the role each plays in the formulation and execution of advertising campaigns.

4 Detail the diverse services that advertising agencies supply in the planning, preparation, and placement of advertising and explain how agencies are compensated for their services.

In the fall of 1992, what was basically a Hollywood talent agency, Creative Artists Agency (CAA), won the Coca-Cola advertising business from one of the world's largest advertising agencies, McCann-Erickson Worldwide. Executives at Coca-Cola believed that in the consumer market—where channel surfing and ad zapping were undermining traditional advertising presentations—new and unusual ads were the only solution. CAA made a pitch for Coca-Cola's advertising business that included 50 ideas in many different creative styles, including the now-famous computer-generated polar bears. CAA won the $300 million account and unveiled the new ads in 1993. The campaign has been praised as "innovative, playful, and breathtaking" and criticized as "entertainment gymnastics."[1] Despite the critics, ads like the polar bear ad illustrated in Exhibit 2.1 proved to be very popular with consumers. The "Always Coca-Cola" tag line is included on everything from elaborate television ads to banners in basketball arenas, making Coca-Cola one of the most visible brand names in the world.

Despite innovative efforts by advertising agencies like CAA, the truth is that the fundamental features of the process of advertising have changed very little over the past 75 years. Certainly, the process has evolved with social and cultural trends and advances in technology. But the essence of the process—persuasive communication designed to stimulate demand and delivered to targeted audiences—has remained constant.

What has changed over the past 75 years is the structure of the advertising industry. As one analyst put it, "Just like manufacturing, the advertising industry is undergoing seismic change" in the 1990s.[2] How has the industry changed, and how is it continuing to change? Well, media options, advertising agency structure, client demands, compensation schemes, and creative techniques are just a few of the aspects of the industry undergoing significant and fundamental change.

The central issues in the story of how CAA won the Coca-Cola account highlight several aspects of change that have taken place in the structure of the advertising industry. First, advertisers like Coca-Cola believe that to maintain brand leadership in highly competitive markets characterized by impatient consumers, new and different creative executions are essential. Second, the traditional factory-like advertising agencies are being replaced with a new, more adaptable and responsive type of agency. Many ad agencies formed by megamergers in the 1980s are dismantling their vertically integrated, multilayered management structures and reengineering themselves into more nimble multiservice organizations that use dynamic management structures to prioritize creative thinking. Third, the old commission method of paying for advertising (based on media spending) is giving way to fee-based systems. Now, only about 14 percent of advertisers still pay agencies the once-standard 15 percent commission.[3]

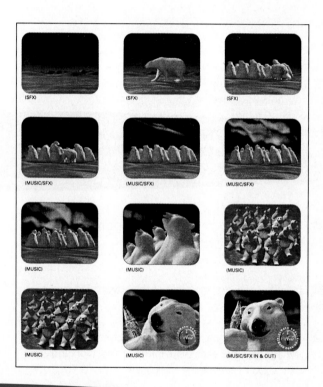

EXHIBIT 2.1

Creative Artists Agency won the much sought after $300 million Coca-Cola account based on its creative prowess. One of CAA's first campaigns for Coca-Cola featured these polar bears and was immensely popular with television audiences. **www.cocacola.com/**

1.   Patricia Sellers, "Do You Need Your Ad Agency?" *Fortune,* November 15, 1993, 148.
2.   Ibid., 156.
3.   "Say Adieu to 15%, but Lower Rates Alive, Kickin'," *Advertising Age,* May 15, 1995, 1.

❶ While Coca-Cola's newest advertising effort illustrates some important aspects of change in the advertising industry, it does not tell of all the changes in structure taking place. The structure of the industry today is being altered by six important trends:

1. With the proliferation of cable television and direct marketing, and with the development of interactive television, media have become fragmented.
2. The tremendous proliferation of ads in an array of media, ranging from TV ads to billboards to the Internet, has resulted in so much clutter that the probability of any one advertisement breaking through and making a real difference continues to diminish.
3. New retail channels, including catalogs, home shopping, and price clubs, are growing in influence.
4. A fragmentation of marketing budgets has occurred, with a greater proportion of these budgets going to trade and consumer sales promotions.
5. Improved information systems are allowing retailers and distributors to exercise more control over many kinds of marketing decisions.[4]
6. More and more advertisers are focusing their efforts on integrated marketing communications (IMC) programs. Advertisers now look to sales promotions, event sponsorships, new media options, and public relations as means to support and enhance the primary advertising effort.

For years to come, these fundamental changes will affect the way advertisers think about communicating, the way advertising agencies serve their clients, and the way advertising is transmitted to audiences. Large advertisers like Procter & Gamble and Sprint are already demanding new and innovative programs to enhance the impact of their advertising. While the goal of informative and persuasive communication remains intact, the changing structure used by the advertising industry to accomplish that goal is the topic of this chapter.

The Scope of the Advertising Industry

❷ To fully understand the structure of the advertising industry, we first must appreciate the scope of advertising. By any measure, advertising is an enormous, global business. Annual expenditures on advertising in the United States total about $160 billion, with nearly $400 billion being spent worldwide.[5] Advertising expenditures worldwide have been growing about 5 to 6 percent a year during the 1990s, with the United States, Great Britain, Asia, and Latin America leading the way.[6]

Another indicator of the scope of advertising is the investment made by individual firms. Exhibit 2.2 shows the top twenty U.S. advertisers' spending for 1994 and 1995. The hundreds of millions of dollars—and in the case of the four largest spenders, even billions of dollars—is truly a huge amount of money to spend annually on advertising. But we have to realize that the $2.0 billion for advertising spent by General Motors was just 1.5 percent of sales. Similarly, Sears spent $1.2 billion for advertising, but this amount represented about 4 percent of sales. So, while the absolute dollars are large, the relative spending is much more reasonable. Overall, the 100 leading advertisers in the United States spent $47.3 billion on advertising in 1995, which was a healthy 9.3 percent increase over 1994.

4.   Adapted from a summary of a conference presentation by John Deighton, "The Future of the Marketing Communications Industry: Implications of Integration and Interactivity," *Marketing Communications Strategies Today and Tomorrow: Integration, Allocation, and Interactive Technologies,* conference summary prepared by Corinne Faure and Lisa Klein, report number 94–109 (Cambridge, Mass.: Marketing Science Institute, July 1994), 40–43.
5.   "Advertising's Top 100," *Advertising Age,* September 30, 1996, 54.
6.   "Hubris and Humble Pie," *The Economist,* August 27, 1994, 55.

EXHIBIT 2.2

Top twenty leading national advertisers.

Company	1995 U.S. Ad Dollars (in millions)	1994 U.S. Ad Dollars (in millions)	% Change
Procter & Gamble Co.	$2,777.1	$2,696.5	3.0
Philip Morris Cos.	2,576.9	2,386.7	8.0
General Motors Corp.	2,046.9	1,909.4	7.2
Time Warner	1,307.1	1,077.8	21.3
Walt Disney	1,296.0	978.5	32.4
Sears, Roebuck & Co.	1,222.4	1,064.3	15.2
Chrysler Corp.	1,222.4	971.4	25.8
PepsiCo	1,197.0	1,097.8	9.0
Johnson & Johnson	1,173.3	945.2	24.1
Ford Motor Co.	1,149.2	1,186.0	–3.1
AT&T Corp.	1,063.5	1,103.8	–3.7
Warner-Lambert Co.	978.9	852.7	14.8
Grand Metropolitan	950.5	782.0	21.6
McDonald's Corp.	880.0	763.7	9.0
Unilever NV	858.3	801.0	6.4
Kellogg Co.	739.7	732.9	0.9
Toyota Motor Corp.	733.4	765.9	–4.2
Sony Corp.	674.3	546.4	23.4
Viacom	647.0	473.2	36.7
American Home Products	634.4	573.3	10.7

Source: "100 Leading National Advertisers," *Advertising Age*, September 30, 1996, S-4. Reprinted with permission from the September 30, 1996, issue of *Advertising Age*. Copyright © Crain Communications Inc.

The Structure of the Advertising Industry

❸ Knowledge of the structure of the advertising industry gives us a perspective on *who* does *what* in *what order* during the advertising process. The advertising industry is actually a collection of separate participants, all of whom have specialized expertise and perform necessary tasks in planning, preparing, and placing of advertising. Exhibit 2.3 represents the structure of the advertising industry by showing who the different participants are in the process.

Exhibit 2.3 demonstrates simply that *advertisers* can employ the services of *advertising agencies* that may contract for specialized services with various *external facilitators* in the process, which results in advertising being transmitted with the help of various *media organizations* to one or more *target audiences*. Note the dashed line on the left side of Exhibit 2.3. This line indicates that advertisers do not always employ the services of advertising agencies. Nor do advertisers or agencies always seek out the services of external facilitators. Some advertisers deal directly with media organizations for placement of their advertisements, sometimes receiving technical assistance in the preparation of advertisements. This happens either when the advertiser has an advertising department that prepares all the materials for the advertising process, or when the media organizations (especially radio, television, and newspapers) provide technical assistance to advertisers in exchange for significant purchases of media time and space. The new interactive

EXHIBIT 2.3

The structure of the advertising industry.

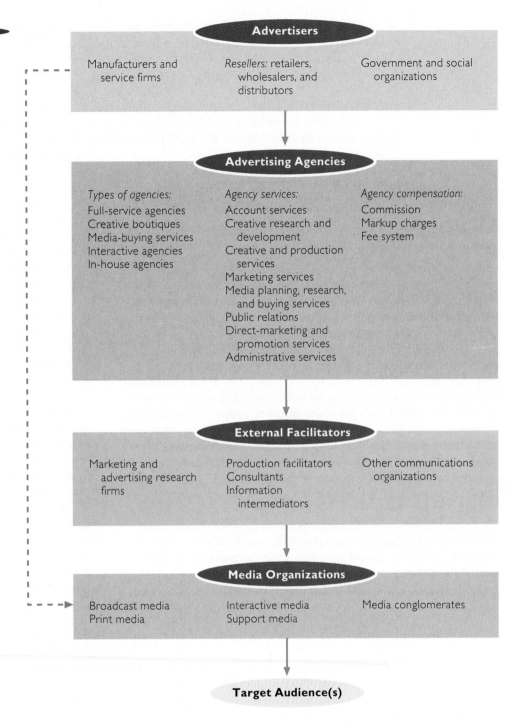

media formats also provide advertisers the opportunity to work directly with entertainment programming firms, like Walt Disney and Sony, to provide integrated programming that features brand placements in the programming.

Each level in the structure of the advertising industry is complex. We will now discuss each level, with particular emphasis on the nature and activities of advertising agencies. Advertising agencies provide the essential creative firepower to the advertising process and represent a critical link in the structure. As the New Media box on page 38 exemplifies, it is also true that advertising agencies are being transformed by technological changes, like the rush of many major newspapers to establish an online presence.

Advertisers

A wide range of organizations seek to benefit from the effects of advertising. The advertisers listed in Exhibit 2.2 each use advertising somewhat differently, given the type of product or service they sell or the position in the channel of distribution they occupy.

Manufacturers and Service Firms.

Large national manufacturers of consumer products and services are the most prominent users of advertising, often spending hundreds of millions of dollars annually. Procter & Gamble, General Foods, MCI, and Merrill Lynch all have national or global markets for their products and services. The use of advertising by these firms is essential to creating awareness and preference for their brands. But advertising is not just useful to national or multinational firms; regional and local producers of household goods and services also rely heavily on advertising. For example, regional dairy companies sell milk, cheese, and other dairy products in regions usually comprised of a few states. Several breweries and wineries also serve only regional markets. Local producers of products are relatively rare, but local service organizations are common. Medical facilities, hair salons, restaurants, and art organizations are examples of local service providers that use advertising to create awareness and stimulate demand.

Firms that produce business goods and services also use advertising on a global, national, regional, and local basis. IBM and Xerox are examples of global companies that produce business goods and services. At the national and regional level, firms that supply agricultural and mining equipment and repair services are common advertisers, as are consulting and research firms. At the local level, firms that supply janitorial, linen, and bookkeeping services use advertising.

NEW MEDIA

GOOD NEWS FOR TREES: MAJOR NEWSPAPERS GO ONLINE AND INTERACTIVE

America's newspapers are rushing headlong to take part in the interactive craze. Because most subscribers read only portions of their daily paper (such as the sports page), newspaper publishers envision great potential for interactivity and selectivity in their forum. Electronic delivery embodies the natural extension of a newspaper's mission.

"Online editions are not only a great way to attract more advertisers, but they also preserve the newspaper's role in pulling the community together," says Randy Bennet, director of new media at the Newspaper Association of America. The first forms of advertising on the new services include classified ads and the sponsorship of special events, but the newspapers anticipate that the medium will eventually attract advertisers not normally interested in newspapers. Knight-Ridder's Mercury News Center has been on America Online for two years and has already established a site on the Internet's World Wide Web. Although access to the Internet has been free in the past, Knight-Ridder now charges a fee for users to visit the Mercury News Center. Bob Ingle, Knight-Ridder's vice president of new media, feels that the charges won't deter the established user base. "We could really take a bath with this one, but we think subscribers should pay a little, and advertisers should pay a lot." Time will tell.

Sources: "Top Newspapers Link for Online Network," *Advertising Age*, April 24, 1995, 14; and "Online Soon to Snare 100-Plus Newspapers," *Advertising Age*, April 24, 1995, S-6.

Resellers.

The term *reseller* is simply a general description for all organizations in the channel of distribution that buy products to resell to customers. As Exhibit 2.3 shows, resellers can be retailers, wholesalers, or distributors. These resellers deal with both household consumers and business buyers at all geographic levels.

Retailers that sell in national or global markets are the most visible reseller advertisers. Sears, The Limited, and McDonald's are examples of national and global retail companies that use various forms of advertising to communicate with customers. Regional retail chains, typically grocery chains like Albertson's or department stores like Dillard's, serve multistate markets and use media advertising appropriate for their customers. At the local level, small retail shops of all sorts rely on newspaper, radio, television, and billboard advertising to reach a relatively small geographic area.

Wholesalers and distributors, like American Lock & Supply (which supplies contractors with door locks and hardware), are a completely different breed of reseller.

Technically, these two groups deal with business customers only, since their position in the distribution channel dictates that they sell products either to producers (who buy goods to produce other goods) or to retailers (who resell goods to household consumers). Occasionally, an organization will call itself a wholesaler and sell to the public. Such an organization is actually operating as a retail outlet.

Wholesalers and distributors have little need for the mass media. Also, these firms tend to rely more heavily on personal selling and trade shows as promotional tools. Trade publications, catalogs, and direct mail are also common advertising vehicles for the wholesaler and distributor.

Government and Social Organizations. It may seem odd to include the government as an advertiser, but government bodies invest millions of dollars in advertising annually. In fact, in 1995 the U.S. government spent more than $408 million on advertising. The federal government's spending on advertising is concentrated in two areas: armed forces recruiting and social issues. In 1995, the U.S. government launched a new television ad campaign with a budget of $55 million for U.S. Army recruiting. The government purchased time on MTV and during NCAA basketball games.[7] In addition, a large number of government publications are aimed at businesses to alert them to government programs or regulations.

State and local government agencies, especially health care and welfare organizations, attempt to shape behaviors (reduce child abuse, for example) or communicate with citizens who can use their services, like potential Social Security and Medicare recipients. State governments also invest millions of dollars in promoting state lotteries and tourism.

Advertising by social organizations at the national, state, and local level is common. The American Cancer Society and United Way advertise their programs, seek donations, and attempt to shape behavior (deter drug use or encourage breast self-examination procedures, for example). National organizations like these use both the mass media and direct mail.

Every state has its own unique statewide organizations, such as Citizens against Hunger, a state arts council, or a historical society. Social organizations in local communities represent a variety of special interests, from computer clubs to neighborhood child care organizations. The advertising used by social organizations has the same fundamental purposes as the advertising carried out by major multinational corporations: to stimulate demand and disseminate information.

Few of the advertisers just discussed have the expertise or resources to strategically plan and then prepare effective advertising. This is where advertising agencies play such an important role in the structure of the advertising industry.

Advertising Agencies

Many advertisers, particularly those with national or global markets, choose to enlist the services of an advertising agency in planning, preparing, and placing advertisements. The reason so many firms rely on advertising agencies is that such agencies house a collection of professionals with very specialized expertise. A formal definition of an advertising agency is as follows:

*An **advertising agency** is an organization of professionals who provide creative and business services to clients related to planning, preparing, and placing advertisements.*

Advertising agencies can be global businesses. During the 1980s several megamergers occurred, creating worldwide organizations to serve clients' advertising and marketing communications needs. Exhibit 2.4 shows the 1995 worldwide gross income of the ten largest advertising agencies in the world. Note that the list is dominated by agencies with headquarters in New York City. The top 500 U.S.-based agencies had worldwide income of more than $17 billion in 1995.[8]

7.   Kevin Goldman, "Army Launches New TV Ad Campaign," *Wall Street Journal,* March 7, 1995, B10.
8.   "Agency Report," *Advertising Age,* April 15, 1996, S-1.

World's top ten advertising agencies in 1995.

Rank	Agency	Worldwide Gross Income (in millions of U.S. dollars)	% Change 1994–1995
1	WPP Group, London	$3,129.7	12.7
2	Omnicom Group, New York	2,576.7	16.7
3	Interpublic Group of Cos., New York	2,337.2	9.9
4	Dentsu Inc., Tokyo	1,998.6	21.8
5	Cordiant, London	1,337.8	11.5
6	Young & Rubicam, New York	1,197.5	14.4
7	Hakuhodo Inc., Tokyo	958.6	23.8
8	Havas Advertising, Levallios-Perret, France	909.4	11.8
9	Grey Advertising, New York	896.5	10.9
10	Leo Burnett, Chicago	803.9	18.7

Source: "Agency Report," *Advertising Age*, April 15, 1996, S-2. Reprinted with permission from the April 15, 1996, issue of *Advertising Age*. Copyright © Crain Communications Inc.

The types of agency professionals who can help advertisers in the planning, preparation, and placement of advertising and other promotional activities include the following:

Account supervisors
Art directors
Creative directors
Copywriters
Radio and television producers
Researchers
Artists
Technical staff—printing, film editing, and so forth
Marketing specialists
Media buyers
Public relations specialists
Sales promotion and event planners
Direct-marketing specialists

As this list suggests, an advertising agency provides an advertiser with a host of services, from campaign planning through creative concepts to measuring advertising effectiveness. Several different types of agencies are available to the advertiser. An appreciation of the differences between types of agencies is important.

Full-Service Agencies. A **full-service agency** typically includes an array of advertising professionals to meet all the promotional needs of clients. Often, such an agency will also offer a global reach to the client, as discussed in the Global Issues box on page 41. Leo Burnett, Young & Rubicam, and McCann-Erickson Worldwide are examples of full-service agencies with global capabilities.

A full-service agency will attempt to have available not only the creative and technical personnel associated with advertising preparation, but also marketing and research personnel to help in the planning process. Additionally, various administrative services personnel are provided, which include everyone from high-level management (such as account supervisors) to clerical services. Account supervisors typically act as the liaison between the agency and the client. Administrative services can take care of such costly details as scheduling and billing procedures.

Creative Boutiques. A **creative boutique** emphasizes copywriting and artistic services to its clients. An advertiser can employ this alternative for the strict purpose of infusing greater creativity into the message theme or individual advertisement. Other aspects of advertising planning and placement are handled internally by the advertiser or contracted out to other external facilitators. Some large global agencies like McCann-Erickson World-wide are setting up "creative-only" project shops that mimic the services provided by creative boutiques.[9]

GLOBAL ISSUES

BBDO WORLDWIDE: FULL-SERVICE GLOBAL AGENCY EXCELS IN BRAND MANAGEMENT

A truly global force in both size and focus, BBDO has separate centers with prime responsibility for at least one principle multinational client, plus other contrasting accounts of varied sizes. Within the advertising industry, BBDO is known for brand building, positioning, and image enhancement. This global ad agency also enjoys a reputation for building strong relationships with its clients. After representing Apple Computer in every key market except Japan for the past nine years (the longest agency relationship with any major computer manufacturer), Apple has sought to strengthen the relationship and expand BBDO's international assignments. Not everything about this relationship has been perfect for BBDO, however. In this era of increasing personal computer competition and uncertain futures, the effective commission rate for Apple's business (with an estimated $150 million plus in annual billings) is said to be well under 10 percent already, far below the historical 15 percent industry norm.

Sources: "Apple Brings in Advisor to Revise BBDO Pact," *Advertising Age,* January 23, 1995, 2; and "Apple Gets Bruised by Shrinking Share," *Advertising Age,* April 24, 1995, 44.

Media-Buying Services. While not technically an agency, a **media-buying service** is an independent organization that specializes in buying media time and space, particularly on radio and television, as a service to advertising agencies and advertisers. The task of buying media space has become more complex because of the proliferation of media options. An agency or advertiser will do the strategy planning for media placement and then turn to a media-buying service to do the actual buying of time and space. One additional advantage of using a media-buying service is that since it buys media in large quantities, it often acquires media time at a much lower cost than an agency or advertiser could.

Interactive Agencies. The era of new media has created a new form of agency—the interactive agency. **Interactive agencies** help advertisers prepare communications for new media like the Internet, interactive kiosks, CD-ROMs, and interactive television. Sometimes referred to as *cyberagencies,* these new ad agencies have specialized talent and expertise that many traditional full-service agencies do not have. Organizations like Modem Media in Norwalk, Connecticut, Organic Online in San Francisco, and Network Publishing in Salt Lake City have created new media communications for some big-name companies: AT&T, Adolph Coors, Delta Air Lines, Saturn, and Kraft Foods.

Interactive agencies have technical personnel to help advertisers develop new media communications. They also keep other specialized talent to maintain computer file servers that not only manage the interactions with clients' communication, but also build databases for clients' future use—with both new and traditional media. At this point, many of the interactive agencies are dealing with clients' established full-service agency. The creative history embodied in the general agency is valuable in preparing new media communications.

This is not to say that traditional full-service agencies are sitting idly by. Ogilvy & Mather, Grey Advertising, and Leo Burnett—some of the oldest agencies in the business —have developed special groups within their agencies to handle clients' new media needs. Chrysler, Toshiba, IBM, and American Express are relying on their full-service agencies for their new media materials. It will be interesting to see if the new cyberagencies move to provide broader services or remain specialized.

9.   Melanie Wells, "McCann Eyes Boutique," *Advertising Age,* June 27, 1994, 4.

In-House Agencies. An **in-house agency** is often referred to as the advertising department of a firm. This option has the advantage of greater coordination and control in all phases of the advertising process. The advertiser's own personnel have greater control over and knowledge of marketing activities, such as product development and distribution tactics. Another advantage is that the firm can essentially keep all the profits from commissions an external agency would have earned.

While these advantages are formidable and attractive, there are severe limitations to an in-house agency. First, there may be a lack of objectivity, thereby constraining the execution of all phases of the advertising process. Second, it is highly unlikely that an in-house agency could ever match the breadth and depth of expertise available in an external agency.

Advertising agencies represent an important link in the structure of the industry. At this point, we will consider the broad range of services agencies can provide to advertisers.

Agency Services

4 The types of services provided by an agency vary with the types of agencies just discussed. In a full-service agency, a wide range of creative, marketing, media, and administrative services are often provided to serve a client's complete advertising needs. A typical organizational structure for a full-service agency is shown in Exhibit 2.5. Exhibit 2.6 is an ad from Leo Burnett, the largest U.S. full-service agency. While not every full-service agency offers every service, the types of services that can be found in full-service agencies are discussed in the following sections.

EXHIBIT 2.5

Organizational structure of a full-service advertising agency.

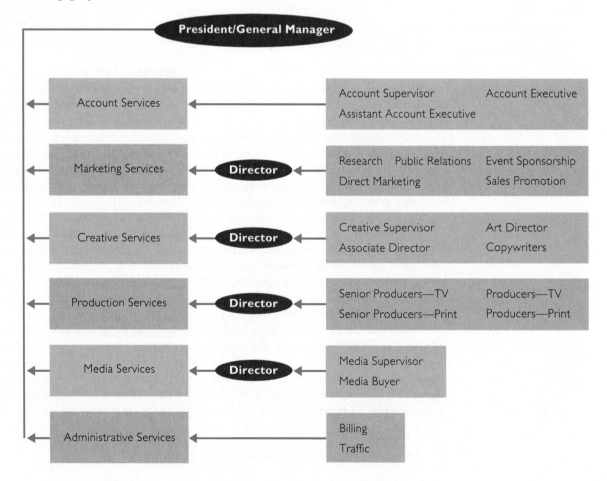

SCRATCH QUALITY. IT'S EASY AS...

PILLSBURY REFRIGERATED PIE CRUST.

SIMPLY UNFOLD,

FILL,

AND BAKE.

EXHIBIT 2.6

This ad created by full-service agency Leo Burnett demonstrates the staying power of a successful ad theme. Because Burnett has a full range of marketing support services to maintain and update Pillsbury's Doughboy, it can provide its creative and production people with information they need to adapt this well-known theme to changing consumer tastes. At Pillsbury's Web site **www.pillsbury.com/**, *this commitment to progressive continuity is evident in its pages on the company's history and its products. To see how another icon in the food industry is updating its image, visit the Birds Eye site at* **www.birdseye.com**

Account Services. Account services managers, who have titles like account executive, account supervisor, or account manager, work with the client to determine how the client's product or service can benefit most from advertising. Account services entail identifying the benefits a product or service provides, its potential target audiences, and the best competitive positioning, and then developing a complete advertising plan. In some cases, account services in an agency can provide basic marketing and consumer behavior research. Some agencies have analysts doing research on basic consumer behavior and consumer values, product concept testing, and campaign evaluation.

Account services managers also work with the client in translating cultural and consumer values into advertising messages through the creative services in the agency. And finally, they work with media services to develop an effective media strategy for the best placement of advertisements to reach targeted audiences. One of the primary tasks in account services is to keep the various agency teams—creative, production, media—on schedule and within budget. In many agencies, account services are referred to as account management activities.

Marketing Services. Marketing services in an agency commonly include four areas: research, sales promotion and event sponsorship, direct marketing, and public relations. Research conducted by an agency for a client usually consists of the agency locating studies (conducted by commercial research organizations) that have bearing on a client's market or advertising objectives. The research group will help the client interpret the research and communicate these interpretations to the creative and media people. Another type of research may actually be conducted by the agency. As mentioned in the account services discussion, some agencies can assemble consumers from the target audience to evaluate different versions of proposed advertising and determine if messages are being communicated effectively. BBDO has several proprietary research methods it employs for clients.

The sales promotion and event sponsorship marketing services that an agency may provide include the development of contests, sweepstakes, premiums, or special offers and in-store merchandising materials for a client. Many firms are adding event-marketing specialists in this area. These are marketing experts who help clients identify whether and how to sponsor events, like major golf tournaments, auto races, or local community events, like parades and marathons.

Some agencies have developed in-house direct-marketing departments to serve clients' needs for direct mail and telemarketing efforts. This department plans and integrates direct-marketing activities with a firm's primary advertising effort. Direct mail pieces or phone campaigns can target audience members for special advertising messages or sales promotion efforts.

In this era of integrated marketing communications, agencies are finding that more clients demand assistance with integrating all forms of communication with the advertising effort. Some full-service agencies are adding public relations to their list of marketing services available. These firms are attempting to achieve as much control as possible over a client's marketing communications to ensure truly integrated marketing communications. We touched on IMC in Chapter 1, and we will continue to examine the issue throughout the text, with special emphasis in Part 4.

Creative and Production Services. Creative services personnel come up with the concepts that express to a target audience the value and benefits offered by their clients' brands. In simple terms, the creative group develops the advertising message. The creative group in an agency will typically include a creative director, art director, illustrators, and copywriters.

Production services includes producers (and sometimes directors) who take the creative ideas and turn them into radio, television, and print advertisements. Producers are the ones who scout locations, hire directors, find the right actors and actresses, contract with production and postproduction houses, and generally manage and oversee the production of the finished advertisement. Creative and production services personnel in an agency bring to life the value clients have to offer the market and express that value by producing polished advertising messages.

Media-Planning and -Buying Services. Media-planning and -buying services handle the placement task in the advertising effort. The central challenge is to determine how a client's message can most effectively and efficiently reach the target audience. Media planners and buyers examine an enormous number of options to put together an effective media plan within the client's budget. But media planning and buying is much more than simply buying ad space. A wide range of media strategies can be implemented to enhance the impact of the message. Agencies are helping clients sort through the blizzard of new media options like CD-ROM, videocassettes, interactive media, and the Internet. Some agencies like Chiat/Day and Fallon McElligott have already set up their own sites on the Internet in response to client demands that the Internet media option be made available to them.[10] The three positions typically found in the media area are media planner, media buyer, and media researcher.

Administrative Services. Like other businesses, advertising agencies have to manage their business affairs. Agencies have personnel departments, accounting and billing departments, and sales staffs that go out and sell the agency to clients. Most important to clients is the traffic department, which has the responsibility of monitoring projects to be sure that deadlines are met. Traffic managers make sure the creative group and media services are coordinated so that deadlines for getting ads into media are met. The job requires tremendous organizational skills and is critical to delivering the other services to clients.

Agency Compensation, Promotion, and Redesign

The way agencies get paid is somewhat different from the way other professional organizations are compensated. While accountants, doctors, lawyers, and consultants often work on a fee basis, advertising agencies often base compensation on a commission or markup system. We will examine the three most prevalent agency compensation methods: commission, markup charges, and the fee system.

Commission. One method of agency compensation is the **commission system,** which is based on the amount of money the advertiser spends on media. Under this method, 15 percent of the total amount billed by the media organization is retained by the advertising agency as compensation for all costs in creating advertising for the client. The only variation is that the rate typically changes to 16⅔ percent for outdoor media. Exhibit 2.7 provides a simple example of how an agency is compensated for an advertising campaign that cost $1 million for media time.

10. Kevin Goldman, "Ad Agencies Slowly Set Up Shop at New Addresses on the Internet," *Wall Street Journal,* December 29, 1994, B5.

EXHIBIT 2.7

*Commission-based agency
compensation system.*

Over the past ten years, the wisdom of the commission system has been questioned by both advertisers and agencies themselves. As the chairman of Leo Burnett, Rick Fizdale, has said, "It's incenting us to do the wrong thing, to recommend network TV and national magazines and radio when other forms of communication like direct marketing or public relations might do the job better."[11] As Exhibit 2.8 shows, about 59 percent of all advertisers compensate their advertising agencies using a commission system. Only about 14 percent of advertisers responding to a recent survey still use the traditional 15 percent commission, however. More advertisers use other percentage levels of commission—often negotiated levels—as the basis for agency compensation.[12]

Markup Charges. Another method of agency compensation is to add a percentage **markup charge** to a variety of services the agency purchases from outside suppliers. In many cases, an agency will turn to outside contractors for art, illustration, photography, printing, research, and production. The agency then, in agreement with the client, adds a markup charge to these services. The reason markup charges became prevalent in the industry is that many service providers do not give the agency a commission, as do the media. There is thus no way, other than adding a markup percentage, for the agency to receive compensation for managing the work of outside contractors. A typical markup on outside services is from 17.65 percent to 20 percent.

Fee System. A **fee system** is much like that used by consultants or attorneys, whereby the advertiser and the agency agree on an hourly rate for different services provided. The hourly rate can be based on average salaries within departments or on some agreed-upon hourly rate across all services. Recently, Leo Burnett and one of its long-standing clients, Olds-mobile, agreed to a fee system in which "compensation will be based on the agency's work and its thinking."[13]

EXHIBIT 2.8

*Agency compensation
programs: 1992 versus
1995.*

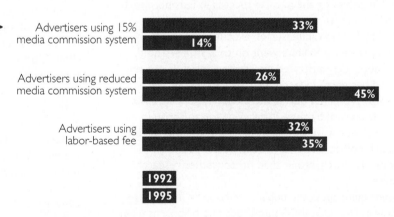

Source: Iris Cohen Selinger, "Big Profits, Risks, with Incentive Fees," *Advertising Age,* May 15, 1995, 3. Reprinted with permission from the May 15, 1995, issue of *Advertising Age.* Copyright © Crain Communications Inc.

11. Sellers, "Do You Need Your Ad Agency?" 151–52.
12. "Say Adieu to 15%, but Lower Rates Alive, Kickin'."
13. Raymond Serafin, "GM Tests Fee-Based Compensation System," *Advertising Age,* February 19, 1996, 3.

Another version of the fee system is a fixed fee set for a project between the client and the agency. It is imperative that the agency and the advertiser agree on precisely what services will be provided, by what departments in the agency, over what specified period of time. In addition, the parties must agree on which supplies, materials, travel costs, and other expenses will be compensated beyond the fixed fee. Fixed-fee systems have the potential for causing serious rifts in the client-agency relationship.

Agency Self-Promotion. To receive any form of compensation, an agency must win and keep clients. As the Contemporary Issues box below demonstrates, winning clients can be an expensive and risky undertaking. Exhibits 2.9 and 2.10 furnish other examples of how agencies promote themselves, practicing what they preach.

Agency Redesign. As highlighted at the opening of the chapter, advertising agencies are reconsidering their role and structure in the contemporary advertising environment. Major advertisers are now questioning the traditional role of mass media as the primary delivery mechanism for advertising. All of this has led many agencies to redesign themselves to better meet the needs of advertisers.

Much redesign is being done to serve all of an advertiser's marketing communications needs, and it is turning agencies into integrated marketing communications organizations. While few agencies are willing to change their designation from "advertising agency" to "IMC agency," more agencies are adding public relations, sales promotion, direct-marketing, and event-marketing departments. As more corporate dollars are being spent on these other forms of promotion, agencies are trying to keep that spending rather than letting it go to specialists in these areas.

Another issue in agency redesign is preparing to serve clients' needs in applying interactive media to the process of communicating with customers. What can agencies do to retain an important role in this emerging media communication process? One firm that is keeping its agency involved by relying on both traditional advertising and the new interactive information superhighway is Sassaby Cosmetics. Sassaby's strategy for the introduction of a line of teen cosmetics called "jane" included a

CONTEMPORARY ISSUES

THINK BIG: AGENCIES VIE FOR VOLKSWAGEN OF AMERICA ACCOUNT

Donny Deutsch, CEO of Deutsch advertising in New York, wanted the VW account in a big way. Make that 360,000 big ways—the colossal dollar amount spent preparing for the final pitch, ranging from dealer interviews and other market research to renting the film *Patton,* for inspiration, and shelling out $20,000 for a new black Jetta. The agency spent 95 days and used the talents of 50 of its 175 employees to compete for the prestigious honor of winning the auto account. Weeks of work culminated in a three-hour final presentation from Deutsch's top executives.

"I think we blew them away!" commented Donny Deutsch afterward. "Something special happened in that room."

The following day, the announcement came: Arnold, Fortuna, Lawner & Cabot, of Boston—a firm best known for producing run-of-the-mill retail advertising—won the account. It would later be known that Deutsch did not even run a close second, but fell third behind Richards Group, Dallas. Volkswagen, having suffered a 20-year identity crisis in the United States while achieving spectacular success in Europe, clearly perceived a need to "strengthen the brand and heighten consumer awareness," as stated by Steve Wilhite, senior executive in charge of Volkswagen sales and marketing. Wilhite went on to say that Arnold, Fortuna, Lawner & Cabot "demonstrated exceptional insights into the Volkswagen brand and business." In fact, the "Drivers Wanted" one-with-the-road campaign presented during the pitch has gone straight to production, which is unusual because firms vying for an account typically err on the overly creative side. It would seem then, in retrospect, that the Deutsch dollars would have been better spent on Volkswagen of America research, rather than on consumer research and creative fireworks.

Still, you can never quite guess the public's reaction to a campaign until it hits the airwaves. The "Drivers Wanted" ads and billboards from AFL&C have Volkswagen dealerships across the United States turning away would-be applicants seeking the advertised "driving" position.

Sources: "Behind the Scenes with an Ad Agency," *USA Today,* March 28, 1995, 1; "Untying the Knot at VW," *Advertising Age,* December 12, 1994, 37; and "VW Picks Arnold, Fortuna, Lawner," *Wall Street Journal,* March 28, 1995, B7.

Self-promotion is an important advertising goal for any agency. By showcasing its creative prowess in this ad, J. Walter Thompson seeks both new clients and leverage in setting its compensation system. What does this ad say to you about JWT? The Internet offers agencies a unique medium. How does JWT promote itself in its Web site **www.jwtworld.com/**? *Would the site influence you to employ this company? Why or why not? For a view of how BBDO Worldwide uses the Web to promote itself, check out their Tech Setter hotline site at* **www.techsetter.com/**

Advertising agencies need to sell their "product" just like any other organization. Arian, Lowe & Travis uses an advertisement (what else?) to promote itself to potential clients.

AFTER SEEING OUR WORK THE BURNETT CREATIVE REVIEW BOARD DUBBED IT "PROVOCATIVE, OUTRAGEOUS, AND NASTY." WE MUST BE DOING SOMETHING RIGHT.

SEE FOR YOURSELF. CALL DARYL TRAVIS FOR
A COPY OF OUR AGENCY'S LATEST REEL.

ARIAN, LOWE & TRAVIS
833 WEST CHICAGO AVENUE CHICAGO ILLINOIS 60622 (312) 243-3500

$3 million magazine advertising campaign supported by a 24-hour chat service on Prodigy online information services. The Sassaby Cosmetics online, interactive media ad is shown in Exhibit 2.11. The ad has been dubbed "jane's brain" and will give teenage girls a forum to talk to each other and to Sassaby about a range of topics including but not limited to cosmetics and fashion.[14]

Precisely how agencies will reinvent themselves to better address client needs and adapt to new media options remains to be seen. Many agencies have already made significant organizational commitments. Ogilvy & Mather Direct has 40 full-time staff in its Interactive Marketing Group working on interactive advertising disks with Forbes, kiosk-based systems with Kraft, and interactive television with AT&T. Saatchi & Saatchi has created Interactive Plus within its agency, and the group is doing extensive research on the future of interactive television and CD-ROM applications. Other agencies are setting up interactive task forces to determine how they will adapt to the new media options.[15] These actions signal changes to the structure of advertising agencies as well as to the evolving structure of the industry.

External Facilitators

While advertising agencies offer clients many services and are adding more, advertisers often need to rely on specialized external facilitators in planning, preparing, and placing advertisements. **External facilitators** are organizations or individuals that provide specialized services to advertisers and agencies. The most important of these external facilitators are discussed in the following sections.

Marketing and Advertising Research Firms.

Many firms rely on outside assistance during the planning phase of advertising. Research firms like Burke International can perform original research for advertisers using focus groups, surveys, or experiments to assist in understanding the potential market or consumer perceptions of a product or services. Other research firms like SRI International routinely collect data (from grocery store scanners, for example) and have these data available for a fee.

Advertisers and their agencies also seek measures of advertising effectiveness. After an advertisement has been running for some reasonable amount of time, firms like Starch INRA Hooper will run recognition tests on print advertisements. Other firms like Burke offer day-after recall tests of broadcast advertisements. There are also firms that specialize in message testing to determine if consumers find advertising messages appealing and understandable. The exact nature and full range of research that can be conducted is covered in Chapter 7.

Consultants.

A variety of consultants specialize in areas related to the advertising process. Advertisers can seek out marketing consultants for assistance in the planning stage. Creative and communications consultants provide insight on issues related to message strategy and message themes. Media experts can help an advertiser determine the proper media mix and efficient media placement. The newest type of consultant is a database consultant, who works with both advertisers and advertising agencies. Organizations like Shepard Associates help firms identify and then manage databases that allow for the development of integrated marketing communications programs. Diverse databases from research sources discussed earlier can be merged or cross-referenced in developing effective communications programs.

Production Facilitators.

External production facilitators offer essential services both during and after the production process. Production is the area where advertisers and their agencies rely most heavily on external facilitators. All forms of media advertising require special

---

14.   Pat Sloan, "A Sassy Approach to Cosmetics," *Advertising Age,* May 23, 1994, 17.
15.   Melanie Wells, Jeff Jansen, Gary Levine, and others, "Desperately Seeking the Interactive Superhighway," *Advertising Age,* special section on interactive media and marketing, August 22, 1994, 14–15.

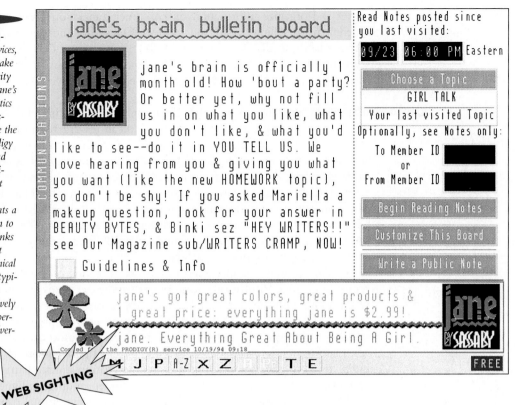

expertise that even the largest full-service agency, much less an advertiser, may not retain on staff. In broadcast production, directors, production managers, songwriters, camera operators, audio and lighting technicians, and performers are all essential to preparing a professional, high-quality radio or television ad. Production houses can provide the physical facilities, including sets, stages, equipment, and crews, needed for broadcast production. Similarly, in preparing print advertising, graphic artists, photographers, models, directors, and producers may be hired from outside the advertising agency or firm to provide the specialized skills and facilities needed in preparing advertisements.

Once an advertisement has gone through the production process, further expertise is needed before the ad is placed in a medium. Postproduction processes in broadcast advertising include film developing and transferring, editing, special effects, sound mixing, and color matching. In print advertising, film developing and photo enhancement are typically carried out by external organizations.

The specific activities performed by external facilitators and the techniques employed by the personnel in these firms will be covered in greater detail at various points in the text. For now, it is sufficient to recognize the role these firms play in the advertising industry.

Information Intermediators. This form of external facilitator has emerged as a result of new technology and the desire on the part of advertisers to more precisely target audiences. An **information intermediator** collects customer purchase transaction histories, aggregates them across many firms that have sold merchandise to these customers, and then sells the customer names and addresses back to the firms that originally sold to these customers.[16] Firms like American Express, AT&T, and regional telephone companies are uniquely situated in the information management process to accumulate and organize such data, and they will likely emerge as information intermediators. These firms will

16. Deighton, *Marketing Communications Strategies Today and Tomorrow,* 40.

gather and organize information on consumer transaction histories across a variety of different firms selling goods and services. Once this information is organized by an intermediator, it allows an advertiser to merge information about important target segments—what they buy, when they buy, and how they buy. With this information, both message themes and media placement can be more effectively and efficiently developed.

Other Communications Organizations. A complete discussion of the structure of the advertising industry must recognize that other types of communications organizations, beyond advertising agencies, play an important role in fulfilling the communications needs of advertisers. In an era when the concept of integrated marketing communications is receiving more and more attention, it is necessary to consider other organizations that provide advertisers with alternative opportunities to communicate with their target audiences. These other communications organizations act much like other external facilitators and provide advertisers with services that an advertising agency may not offer. The three communications organizations most often relied on are public relations firms, direct-marketing firms, and sales promotion specialists.

Public relations was identified in Chapter 1 as one of the components of a firm's promotional mix. **Public relations firms** handle the needs of organizations regarding relationships with the local community, competitors, industry associations, and government organizations. The tools of public relations include press releases, feature stories, lobbying, spokespeople, and company newsletters. Some public relations firms can conduct research to develop and test the impact of public relations efforts. The goal of public relations efforts is to communicate information about a firm, its products, and its employees so as to achieve public awareness, understanding, and goodwill.

Direct-marketing firms handle another of the promotional mix variables listed in Chapter 1. **Direct-marketing firms** maintain large databases of mailing lists as one of their services. Several of these firms can also design direct-marketing campaigns either through the mail or by telemarketing. Finally, **sales promotion specialists** design and then operate contests, sweepstakes, special displays, or couponing campaigns for advertisers. Since sales promotion is a specialized form of communication, there are experts in this area that plan and then execute such promotions.

Media Organizations

The next level in the industry structure shown in Exhibit 2.3 on page 37 comprises the media available to advertisers. The media available for placing advertising, such as broadcast and print media, are well known to most of us simply because we're exposed to them daily. Exhibit 2.12, however, organizes this information into five specific categories.

Advertisers and their agencies turn to organizations that own and manage these media categories. Major television networks like NBC or FOX, as well as national magazines like *U.S. News & World Report* or *People,* provide advertisers with time and space—at considerable expense—for their messages. Other media options are more useful for reaching narrowly defined target audiences. Specialty programming on cable television, tightly focused direct mail pieces, and a well-designed outdoor campaign may be better ways to reach a specific audience. Note the inclusion in this list of "Media Conglomerates." This category is included because organizations like Time Warner and Viacom own and operate companies in broadcast, print, and interactive media. These media organizations may soon control, coordinate, and integrate a variety of separate media options to the benefit (and no doubt expense) of advertisers.

The obvious importance of the various media is that each provides access to an audience. Each of the media options listed in Exhibit 2.12 has its own unique advantages for transmitting information and reaching a particular audience. Strategic use of media options is critical to an effective and efficient advertising process. The strategic opportunities and challenges of each medium are discussed in great detail in Part 4 of this text.

EXHIBIT 2.12

Media organizations available to advertisers.

Broadcast

Television
Major network
Independent station
Cable

Radio
Network
Local

Interactive Media

Online Computer Services

Home-Shopping Broadcasts

**Interactive Broadcast
Entertainment Programming**

Kiosks

CD-ROM

Internet

Media Conglomerates

Multiple Media Combinations
Time Warner
Viacom
TCI
Turner Broadcasting
Comcast
AT&T

Print

Magazines
By geographic coverage
By content

Direct Mail
Brochures
Catalogs
Videos

Newspapers
National
Statewide
Local

Specialty
Handbills
Programs

Support Media

Outdoor
Billboards
Transit
Posters

Directories
Yellow pages
Electronic directories

Premiums
Keychains
Calendars
Logo clothing
Pens

Point-of-Purchase Displays

**Film and Program Product
Placement**

Event Sponsorship

SUMMARY

1 Discuss six important trends transforming the advertising industry.

The 1990s have proved to be a period of dramatic change for the advertising industry. Many factors have served to propel this change. Cable television has increased its reach, and the growing popularity of direct-marketing programs and home shopping have diluted the impact of advertising delivered via mass media. Marketers have altered their budget allocations, with more funding going to sales promotion and event sponsorship, and less money allocated for conventional advertising. These changes have contributed to the emphasis on integrated marketing communications.

2 Describe the size and scale of the advertising industry.

Advertising is an immense, globalized business. Counting the many forms of advertising, annual global expenditures on advertising have surpassed $400 billion. In the United States, companies like Procter & Gamble, Philip Morris, and General Motors allocate billions of dollars to advertising their various brands every year. The advertising agencies that help companies like these develop advertising campaigns employ tens of thousands of people worldwide.

3 Explain who the participants in the advertising industry are and the role each plays in the formulation and execution of advertising campaigns.

Many different types of organizations make up the advertising industry. To truly appreciate what advertising is all about, one must have a good handle on *who* does *what* and in *what order* in the creation and delivery of an advertising campaign. The process begins with an organization that has a message it wishes to communicate to a target audience. Advertising agencies typically are hired to launch a campaign, but other external facilitators are often brought in to perform specialized functions, like identifying a sporting event for the advertiser to sponsor, or helping the advertiser set up a Web page on the Internet. Since most campaigns use some type of mass media, advertisers and their agencies must also work with companies that have advertising time or space to sell.

4 Detail the diverse services that advertising agencies supply in the planning, preparation, and placement of advertising and explain how agencies are compensated for their services.

Advertising agencies come in many varieties and offer diverse services to clients with respect to planning, preparing, and placing advertising. These services include market research and marketing planning, the actual creation and production of ad materials, the buying of media time or space for placement of the ads, and traffic management—keeping production on schedule. Some advertising agencies appeal to clients by offering a full array of services under one roof; others—like creative boutiques—develop a particular expertise and win clients with their specialized skills. The three most prevalent ways to compensate an agency for services rendered are the commission, markup, and fee systems.

KEY TERMS

advertising agency (39)
full-service agency (40)
creative boutique (41)
media-buying service (41)
interactive agencies (41)
in-house agency (42)
commission system (44)

markup charge (45)
fee system (45)
external facilitators (48)
information intermediary (49)
public relations firms (50)
direct-marketing firms (50)
sales promotion specialists (50)

QUESTIONS FOR REVIEW AND CRITICAL THINKING

1. Explain why in 1992 Coca-Cola was willing to take the risk of moving its advertising business from one of the world's largest and best-known advertising agencies to a Hollywood talent agency—CAA.

2. As cable-TV channels continue to proliferate and the TV-viewing audience becomes ever more fragmented, how would you expect the advertising industry to be affected?

3.   The U.S. Army spends millions of dollars each year trying to recruit young men and women into the armed services. Given the definition of advertising offered in Chapter 1, would it be correct to conclude that the U.S. Army is spending millions on advertising?

4.   Huge advertisers like Procter & Gamble spend billions of dollars on advertising every year, yet they still rely on advertising agencies to prepare most of their advertising. Why doesn't a big company like this just do all its own advertising in-house?

5.   As marketers become more enamored with the idea of integrated marketing communications, why would it make sense for an advertising agency to develop a reputation as a full-service provider?

6.   Explain the viewpoint that a commission-based compensation system may actually give ad agencies an incentive to do the wrong things for their clients.

7.   What is it that makes ad production the area where advertisers and their agencies are most likely to call on external facilitators for expertise and assistance?

8.   Give an example of how the skills of a public relations firm might be employed to reinforce the message that a sponsor is trying to communicate through conventional ads.

EXPERIENTIAL EXERCISE

During a two-day period, observe and list all of the media you come in contact with that carry advertising messages. Which media are most suitable for local advertisers? Which medium do you think is most effective in reaching you?

Which do you think is least effective? If you were planning to open a pizza restaurant, which media choices do you think would be best for advertising? Explain your reasoning.

USING THE INTERNET

Visit the following five sites:

Bozell Worldwide: www.poppe.com

Proxima: www.proxima.com

DD&B Needham Interactive Communications: www.ddbniac.com

J. Walter Thompson: www.jwtworld.com

Trilium Interactive: www.trilium.com

For each of the sites, answer these questions:

1.   Is this a full-service advertising agency or a boutique that specializes in Internet advertising services?

2.   What specific services does the firm offer? What is its client base?

3.   Based on the Web site, what is the creative style of each firm?

4.   If you were a company selling mountain bikes, which firm would you choose? Justify your choice based on your answers to the preceding questions.

Chapter 3

The Evolution

of Advertising

After reading and thinking about this chapter, you will be able to do the following:

1 Explain why advertising is a natural feature of capitalistic economic systems.

2 Appreciate manufacturers' dependence on advertising and branding in achieving balanced relationships with retailers.

3 Discuss ten important eras in the evolution of advertising in the United States, and relate important changes in advertising practice to more fundamental changes in society and culture.

4 Identify forces that may make the next decade a period of dramatic change for the advertising industry.

The 1935 Lux advertisement shown in Exhibit 3.1 is undoubtedly curious to contemporary audiences. It is, however, typical of its time. In the 1930s, in the middle of the Great Depression, anxiety about losing one's spouse—and thus one's economic well-being—to divorce was not unfounded. This ad was surely not read the same way it would be today. Ads are part of their times. We see the 1930s in this ad the same way that students of the future viewing ads of the 1990s will no doubt see our times.

This chapter is about the evolution of advertising. Over the decades, advertisers have tried many different strategies and approaches, and you can learn a lot from their successes and failures. Besides being interesting, this history is very practical.

Fundamental Influences

In many discussions of the evolution of advertising, the process is often portrayed as having its origins in ancient times, with even primitive peoples practicing some form of advertising. Frankly, this is unlikely. Whatever those ancients were doing, they weren't advertising. Remember, advertising exists only as mass-mediated communication. As far as we know, there was no Mesopotamia Messenger or Rome: Live at Five. So, while cavemen and cavewomen certainly were communicating with one another with persuasive intent, and even in a commercial context, they were not using advertising. Before offering a brief social history of American advertising, we will first discuss some of the major factors that gave rise to it. Advertising, as we have defined it, came into being as a result of at least four major developments:

1. The rise of capitalism
2. The Industrial Revolution
3. Manufacturers' pursuit of power in the channel of distribution
4. The rise of modern mass media

The Rise of Capitalism

For advertising to become prominent in a society, the society must rely on aspects of capitalism in its economic system. The tenets of capitalism warrant that organizations compete for resources, called capital, in a free market environment. Part of the competition for resources involves stimulating demand for the organization's goods or services. When an individual organization successfully stimulates demand, it attracts capital to the organization in the form of money (or other goods, in a barter system) as payment. One of the tools used to stimulate demand is advertising.

The Industrial Revolution

A capitalistic economic system is a necessary condition for advertising to function. But capitalism alone is not enough. Historically, the industrialization of societies has been the foundation for advertising's emergence as a business and communication process.

The **Industrial Revolution** began about 1750 in England. The revolution spread to the United States and progressed slowly until the early 1800s, when the War of 1812 boosted domestic production. The emergence of the principle of interchangeable parts and the perfection of the sewing machine, both in 1850, coupled with the Civil War a decade later, laid the foundation for widespread industrialization. The Industrial Revolution took American society away from household self-sufficiency as a method of fulfilling material needs to marketplace dependency as a way of life. And the Industrial Revolution was a basic force behind the rapid increase in a mass-produced supply of goods that required stimulation of demand, something that advertising can be very good at. By providing a need for advertising, the Industrial Revolution was a basic influence in its emergence.

As part of the broad Industrial Revolution, there were other equally revolutionary developments. First, there was a revolution in transportation. This was most dramatically

EXHIBIT 3.1

While this ad for Lux laundry powder may seem curious to us today, it reflected the anxiety of the 1930s, during the Great Depression. Just as today's advertising reflects the values of contemporary society, this ad emphasized some very real concerns of the time—economic well-being and the status of women.

symbolized by the east-west connection of the United States in 1869 by the railroad. This connection represented the beginnings of the distribution network needed to move the mass quantities of goods for which advertising would help stimulate demand. In the 1840s, the **principle of limited liability**—which allows an investor to risk only his or her shares of a corporation, rather than personal wealth, in business ventures—gained acceptance and resulted in the accumulation of large amounts of capital to finance the Industrial Revolution. Finally, rapid population growth and urbanization began taking place in the 1800s. From 1830 to 1860, the population of the United States increased nearly threefold, from 12.8 million to 31.4 million. During the same period, the number of cities with more than 20,000 inhabitants grew to 43. Historically, there is a strong relationship between per capita outlays for advertising and an increase in the size of cities.[1] Overall, the growth and concentration of population provided the marketplaces essential to the widespread use of advertising.

This brief discussion of the Industrial Revolution and other related developments in the United States is not meant to be a complete documentation of the effects these influences had on the evolution of advertising. Rather, it is included to highlight the kinds of economic and social changes that provided a framework for the use of advertising by organizations. As the potential grew for goods to be produced, delivered, and introduced to large numbers of people residing in concentrated areas, the stage was set for advertising to emerge and flourish.

Manufacturers' Pursuit of Power in the Channel of Distribution

❷ Another fundamental influence on the emergence and growth of advertising relates to manufacturers' pursuit of power in the channel of distribution. If a manufacturer can stimulate sizeable demand for a brand, then that manufacturer can develop power in the distribution channel and essentially force wholesalers and retailers to sell that particular brand. Demand stimulation among consumers causes them to insist on the item at the retail or wholesale level; retailers and wholesalers have virtually no choice but to comply with consumers' desires and carry the desired item. Thus, the manufacturer has power in the channel of distribution and not only can force other participants in the channel to stock the brand, but also is in a position to command a higher price for the item. The marketing of Intel's Pentium chip is an excellent example of how one manufacturer, Intel, has developed considerable power in the computer distribution channel, establishing its product, the Pentium chip, as a premium brand. This is discussed in the Contemporary Issues box on page 58.

A factor that turned out to be critical to manufacturers' pursuit of power was the strategy of **branding** products. Manufacturers had to develop brand names so that consumers could focus their attention on a clearly identified item. Manufacturers began branding their products in the late 1800s, with Levi's (1873), Maxwell House

1.   Julian Simon, *Issues in the Economics of Advertising* (Urbana, Ill.: University of Illinois Press, 1970), 41–51.

Coffee (1873), Budweiser (1876), Ivory (1879), and Coca-Cola (1876) being among the first branded products to show up on shopkeepers' shelves. Once a product had a brand mark and name that consumers could identify, the process of demand stimulation could take place. Of course, the essential tool in stimulating demand for a brand is advertising. Even today, when Procter & Gamble and Philip Morris spend many billions of dollars each year to stimulate demand for such popular brands as Crest, Charmin, Kraft cheese, and Miller Lite, wholesalers and retailers carry these brands because advertising has stimulated demand and brought consumers into the retail store looking for and asking for the brands.

Manufacturers' pursuit of power in the distribution channel is associated with advanced versions of free enterprise, capitalistic economic systems. Generally, the economic system also needs to be advanced enough to feature a national market and sufficient communication and distribution infrastructure as tools through which power in the channel is pursued. It is just this sort of pursuit of power by manufacturers that is argued to have had a tremendous influence on the widespread use of advertising in the United States.[2]

CONTEMPORARY ISSUES

INSIDE INTEL: COMPONENT PART BRANDING PULLS CHANNEL DEMAND

Microprocessors such as Intel's Pentium chip serve as the brains of a computer and are the greatest single-cost component part in 90 percent of today's PCs. As a component part, the chips have no substantive value alone (except as costume jewelry) and are subject to derived demand from the overall PC market. By targeting consumers directly, however, Intel has sought to differentiate its component product, circumvent derived demand, and employ a pull strategy through the channels of distribution in which customers specifically ask for personal computers with the Intel Pentium chip inside. By promoting microprocessors directly to the public, Intel has also established itself as a premium brand and can charge more for its products than rivals like Advanced Micro Devices and Cyrix.

Sources: "A Conflict of Ambition," *Forbes,* October 10, 1994, 45; and "The Education of Andrew Grove," *Business Week,* January 16, 1995, 60.

NEW MEDIA

MASS COMMUNICATION ONLINE: ADVERTISERS FUND FREE E-MAIL SERVICES

Electronic mail, once relegated solely to interoffice memos, has finally come of age. Two new online service providers, Freemark communications and Juno Online Services, will launch the industry's first free E-mail services to anyone with a modem. Advertisers ultimately pay for (and gain from) the new service: Each piece of mail is delivered with an advertiser's stamp and a sponsor banner that can be accessed for more information. While only 9 million U.S. households currently subscribe to existing pay-as-you-go online services, over 22 million own personal computers with modems, representing a huge potential market for the new class of no-cost service providers. As the medium gains momentum, E-mail may yet reach the critical mass of mass communication and grow to global use and acceptance. Advertisers are banking on the possibility; the first on board with the Freemark service include Nabisco's Planters Peanuts and Upjohn's Rogaine.

Could free E-mail eventually supplant the tried-and-true letter with postage? The prospect of mailing hundreds of virtual holiday greeting cards at the stroke of a single key holds great promise, to be sure. "Happy Holidays—but first, a word from our sponsor."

Source: "E-mail Offered for Free," *Advertising Age,* November 6, 1995, 1.

The Rise of Mass Communication

Advertising is also tied to the rise of mass communication. With the invention of the telegraph in 1844, a communication revolution was set in motion. The telegraph not only allowed the young nation to benefit from the inherent efficiencies of rapid communication, but also did a great deal to engender a sense of national, or at least regional, community. People began to know and care about things going on thousands of miles away. Probably even more important in terms of advertising was the rise of the mass circulation magazines. The upper classes were

2.　Vincent P. Norris, "Advertising History—According to the Textbooks," *Journal of Advertising* 9, no. 3 (1980): 3–12.

not the only ones privy to magazines; during this period, many new magazines designed for larger and less socially privileged audiences made magazines both a viable mass advertising medium and a democratizing influence on American society.[3]

Likewise, the ads that were now reaching a more diverse audience were also promoting a type of **democracy of goods**—that is, products previously unavailable to the masses were now available across the social spectrum. The ads themselves took on social-class identities and helped link products with class, circumstance, and aspiration. Without the proliferation of print vehicles, advertising would never have flourished.

It is critical to realize that for the most part, mass media in the United States is advertising supported. Television networks, radio stations, newspapers, and magazines produce shows, articles, films, and programs not for the ultimate goal of entertaining or informing, but to make a healthy profit from the sale of advertising. As indicated in the New Media box opposite, the same motives appear to be at work for those who provide E-mail services.

Advertising in Practice

So far, our discussion of the evolution of advertising has identified the fundamental social and economic influences that fostered its rise. Now we'll turn our focus to the evolution of advertising in practice. Several periods in this evolution can be identified to give us various perspectives on the process of advertising.

The Preindustrialization Era (pre-1800)

While advertising did not flourish before industrialization and the creation of concentrated urban markets, it still existed in a variety of simplistic forms. Societies that relied on a marketplace for the distribution of goods reveal evidence of the use of advertising.

An important development occurred in the seventeenth century with the appearance of the printed **handbill.** Printed on engraved wood or copper, these handbills were used to announce the availability of grocery products, household goods, druggists' wares, and various other commodities and services. The artistic quality of the lettering and illustrations of the handbills have made them worthy of preservation in British museums as representatives of period artwork.

Also in the seventeenth century, printed advertisements appeared in newsbooks (the precursor to the newspaper).[4] The messages were informational in nature and appeared on the last pages of the tabloid. In America, the first newspaper advertisement is said to have appeared in 1704 in the *Boston News Letter.* Two notices were printed under the heading "Advertising" and offered rewards for the return of merchandise stolen from an apparel shop and a wharf.[5]

Advertising grew in popularity during the eighteenth century both in Britain and the American colonies. The *Pennsylvania Gazette* printed advertisements and was the first newspaper to separate ads with lines of white space.[6] As far as we know, it was also the first newspaper to use illustrations in advertisements. But advertising made little progress for the next 70 years. While the early 1800s saw the advent of the penny newspaper, which resulted in widespread distribution of the news medium, advertisements in penny newspapers were dominated by simple announcements by skilled laborers. As one historian notes, "Advertising was closer to the classified notices in newspapers than to product promotions in our media today."[7] Advertising was about to change dramatically, however.

3.   Christopher P. Wilson, "The Rhetoric of Consumption: Mass-Market Magazines and the Demise of the Gentle Reader, 1880–1920," in *The Culture of Consumption: Critical Essays in American History,* 1880-1980, ed. Richard Wightman Fox and T. J. Jackson Lears (New York: Pantheon, 1983), 39-65.

4.   Frank Presbrey, *The History and Development of Advertising* (Garden City, N.Y.: Doubleday, Doran & Company, 1929), 7.

5.   Ibid., 11.

6.   Ibid., 40.

7.   James P. Wood, *The Story of Advertising* (New York: The Ronald Press, 1958), 45–46.

The Era of Industrialization (1800 to 1875)

In practice, users of advertising in the mid- to late-1800s were trying to cultivate markets for growing production in the context of a dramatically increasing population. A middle class, spawned by the economic windfall of regular wages from factory jobs, was beginning to emerge. This newly developing populace with economic means was concentrated geographically in cities more than ever before.

By 1850, circulation of the **dailies,** as newspapers were called, was estimated at 1 million copies per day. The first advertising agent—thought to be Voleny Palmer, who opened shop in Philadelphia—basically worked for the newspapers by soliciting orders for advertising and collecting payment from advertisers.[8] This new opportunity to reach consumers was embraced readily by merchants, and at least one newspaper doubled its advertising volume from 1849 to 1850.[9]

With the expansion of newspaper circulation fostered by the railroads, a new era of opportunity emerged for the advertising process. Advertising was not universally hailed as an honorable practice, however. Without any formal regulation of advertising, the process was considered an embarrassment by many segments of society, including some parts of the business community. At one point, firms even risked their credit ratings if they used advertising—banks considered the practice a sign of financial weakness. This image wasn't helped much by advertising for patent medicines, which were the first products heavily advertised on a national scale. These advertisements promised a cure for everything from rheumatism and arthritis to "consumption" and respiratory affliction, as Exhibit 3.2 shows.

EXHIBIT 3.2

The expansion of newspaper circulation fostered more widespread use of advertising. Unfortunately, some of this new advertising did not contribute positively to the image of the practice. Ads like this one for a patent medicine carried outrageous claims, such as "Keep the blood pure."

The P. T. Barnum Era (1875 to 1918)

Shortly after the Civil War in the United States, modern advertising began. This is advertising we would begin to recognize as advertising. While advertising existed during the era of industrialization, it wasn't until America was well on its way to being an urban, widely industrialized nation that advertising became a vital and integral part of the social landscape. During the years from about 1875 to 1918, advertising ushered in what is known as **consumer culture,** or a way of life centered around consumption. Advertising became a full-fledged industry in this period. It was the time of advertising legends: Albert Lasker, head of Lord and Thomas in Chicago, possibly the most influential agency of its day; Francis W. Ayer, founder of N. W. Ayer; John E. Powers, the most important copywriter of the period; Charles Austin Bates, another brilliant advertising copywriter; Earnest Elmo Calkins, champion of advertising design; Claude Hopkins, influential in promoting ads as "dramatic salesmanship"; and John E. Kennedy, creator of "reason why" advertising.[10] These were the founders, the visionaries, and the artists who played principal roles in the establishment of the advertising business.

---

8.   Daniel Pope, *The Making of Modern Advertising and Its Creators* (New York: William Morrow and Company, 1984), 14.
9.   Cited in Stephen Fox, *The Mirror Makers: A History of American Advertising and Its Creators* (New York: William Morrow and Company, 1984), 14.
10.   Ibid.

By 1900, total sales of patent medicines had reached $75 million—providing an early demonstration of the power of advertising.[11] This demonstration sent advertising in a new direction and set the stage for its modern form. It was during this period that the first advertising agencies were founded and the practice of branding products became the norm. Advertising at this time was motivated by the need to sell the vastly increased supply of goods brought on by mass production and by the demands of an increasingly urban population seeking social identity through branded products. In earlier times when shoppers went to the general store and bought soap sliced from a large locally produced cake, advertising had little or no place. Now advertising, which created a difference between identical soaps, suddenly held a very prominent place.

The advertising of this period was, until 1906, completely unregulated. In that year, Congress passed the **Pure Food and Drug Act,** which required manufacturers to list the active ingredients of their products on their labels. Still, its effect on advertising was minimal; advertisers could continue to say just about anything—and usually did. Many advertisements took on the style of a sales pitch for snake oil. The tone and spirit of advertising owed more to P. T. Barnum—"There's a sucker born every minute"—than to any other influence. The ads were bold, carnivalesque, garish, and often full of dense copy that hurled fairly incredible claims at prototype "modern" consumers. Ads from this era are shown in Exhibits 3.3 and 3.4.

Several things are notable about these ads: lots of copy (words); the prominence of the product itself and the corresponding lack of surrounding social space, or context in which the product was to be used; small size; little color; few photographs; and plenty of hyperbole. Over this period there was some evolution, but this style was fairly consistent up until World War I.

You should also consider the social context of these ads. It was a period of rapid urbanization, massive immigration, labor unrest, and significant concerns about the abuses of capitalism. It was the age of the first wave of the feminist movement (suffrage), the progressive movement, motion pictures, and mass culture. The world changed rapidly in this period, and it was no doubt disruptive and unsettling to many—but advertising was there to offer solutions to the stresses of modern life.

EXHIBIT 3.3

During the late 1800s and early 1900s, advertising began to make claims aimed at the "modern" consumer. Here, the 1900 Washer Company promises relief from all the drudgery of wash day.

EXHIBIT 3.4 *Ads from the P. T. Barnum era were often densely packed with fantastic promises. This 1902 Saturday Evening Post advertisement featured many reasons why potential customers should get into the duck-raising business.*

11. Presbrey, *The History and Development of Advertising,* 16.

The 1920s
(1918 to 1929)

In many ways, the Roaring '20s really began a couple of years early. After World War I, advertising found respectability, fame, and glamour. The prewar reform movement was completely dissipated by the distractions of the war and advertising's role in the war effort.

The 1920s were prosperous times. Most Americans enjoyed a previously unequaled standard of living. It was an age of hedonism, and the pleasure principle was appreciated, openly and often. The Victorian Age was over, and a great social experiment in the joys of consumption began. Victorian sexual repression and modesty gave way to a more open sexuality and a love affair with modernity. Advertising played right into this. Ads of the era exhorted consumers to have a good time and enjoy life. Consumption was not only respectable, but expected. The average citizen had become a "consumer" instead.

During this post–World War I economic boom, advertising instructed consumers how to be thoroughly modern and how to avoid the pitfalls of this new age. It was during this era that consumers learned of halitosis from Listerine advertising, and about body odor from Lifebuoy advertising (see Exhibit 3.5, a Lifebuoy ad from 1926). Amazingly, there just happened to be a product with a cure for just about every social anxiety and personal failing.

Other ads from the 1920s emphasized themes of modernity, the division between public work space (the male domain of the office) and the private, "feminine," space of the home. Science and technology were in many ways the new religions of the day. Ads stressed the latest scientific offerings for child rearing and "domestic science," as Exhibits 3.6 and 3.7 demonstrate.

The style of the 1920s ads was much more visual and far less wordy than those of the preceding decades. They showed slices of life, or lessons in what historian Roland

EXHIBIT 3.5

Many ads from the 1920s promised to relieve just about any social anxiety imaginable. Here, Lifebuoy offered a solution for people concerned that body odor could be standing in the way of career advancement.

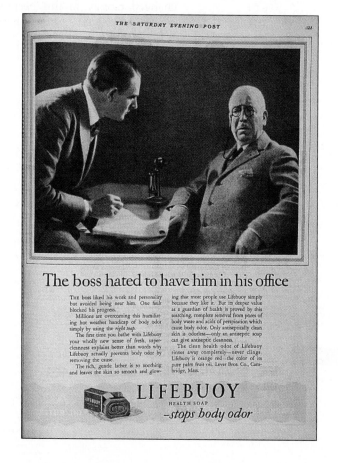

The cultural theme of modernity in the 1920s emphasized science and technology. These ads for Van Camp's Pork and Beans (Exhibit 3.6) and Pet Milk (Exhibit 3.7) tout the "domestic science" these brands brought to the home.

Marchand called **social tableau.**[12] These lessons were about how to fit in with the smart crowd, how to be urbane and modern by using the newest modern conveniences. Advertising during the 1920s chronicled the state of technology and current styles for clothing, furniture, and social functions. Advertising specified social relationships between people and products by depicting the social settings and circumstances into which the products would fit. Some of the best illustrators, artists, and writers in the world worked on advertisements during this period, and some of the ads are now being collected and sold as art. The 1922 Standard plumbing fixtures ad, shown in Exhibit 3.8, is an example of an ad now prized as a work of art.

The Struggle (1929 to 1941)

Just as sure as advertising was heroic in the 1920s, it was villainous in the 1930s. It was part of big business, and big business, big greed, and big lust had gotten America into the great economic depression beginning in 1929—or so the story goes. The public now saw advertising as something bad, something that had seduced them into the excesses for which they were being punished.

Advertisers responded by adopting a tough, no-nonsense advertising style. The stylish and highly aesthetic ads of the 1920s gave way to harsher and more cluttered ads. As one historian said, "The new hard-boiled advertising mystique brought a proliferation of 'ugly,' attention-grabbing, picture-dominated copy in the style of the tabloid newspaper."[13] Clients wanted their money's worth, and agencies responded by cramming

12. See Roland Marchand, *Advertising the American Dream: Making Way for Modernity, 1920–1940* (Berkeley: University of California Press, 1985).
13. Ibid., 303–304.

"Standard"
PLUMBING FIXTURES

Standard Sanitary Mfg. Co., Pittsburgh
Write for Catalogue

EXHIBIT 3.8

*In an effort to make their advertising depict the technology and style of
the era, advertisers in the 1920s enlisted the services of some
of the best illustrators and artists of the time. So fine were the illustrations
that many of them, like this Standard plumbing fixtures ad from 1922,
are now prized as works of art.*

every bit of copy and image they could into their ads. This type of advertising persisted, quite likely making the relationship between the public and this institution even worse. The themes in advertisements traded on the anxieties of the day: Losing one's job meant being a bad provider, spouse, or parent, unable to give the family what it needed. The cartoon-strip style also became very popular during this period. Exhibit 3.9 offers a typical 1930s-style ad.

Another notable event during these years was the emergence of radio as a significant advertising medium. During the 1930s, the number of radio stations rose to 814, and the number of radio sets in use more than quadrupled to 51 million. Radio was in its heyday as a news and entertainment medium, and it would remain so until the 1950s when television emerged as a new and powerful medium. An important aspect of radio was its ability to create a new sense of community in which people thousands of miles apart listened to and became involved with their favorite radio soap opera, so termed in reference to the soap sponsors of these shows.

The J. Walter Thompson advertising agency was the dominant agency of the period. Stanley and Helen Resor and James Webb Young brought this agency to a leadership position through intelligent management, vision, and great advertising. Helen Resor was the first prominent woman advertising executive and was instrumental in J. Walter Thompson's success. Still, the most famous ad person of the era was a very interesting man named Bruce Barton. He was not only the leader of BBDO, but also a best-selling author, most notably of a 1924 book called *The Man Nobody Knows.*[14] The book was about Jesus and portrayed him as the archetypal ad man. This blending of Christian and capitalist principles was enormously attractive to a people struggling to reconcile the traditional religious dogma, which preached against excess, and the new religion of consumption, which preached just the opposite.

Advertising, like the rest of the country, suffered dark days during this period. Agencies cut salaries and forced staff to work four-day weeks without being paid for the mandatory extra day off. Clients demanded frequent review of work, and agencies were compelled to provide more and more free services to keep accounts. Advertising would emerge from this depression, just as the economy itself did, during World War II. However, it would never again reach its predepression status. It became the subject of a well-organized and angry consumerism movement. Congress passed real reform in this period.

War, Paranoia, and Economic Growth (1941 to 1960)

Many people mark the end of the depression with the start of America's involvement in World War II, in late 1941. During the war, advertising often made direct reference to the war effort, as the ad in Exhibit 3.10 shows, linking the product with patriotism and helping to rehabilitate the tarnished image of advertising.

14. Bruce Barton, *The Man Nobody Knows* (New York: Bobbs-Merrill, 1924).

EXHIBIT 3.9

Another notable feature of 1930s advertising was the increasing use of the cartoon-strip style. The cartoon strip, like this one for Dr. West's toothpaste, could tell a fairly complex story of devastating social failure and then offer a wondrous solution with the advertiser's brand. This ad also shows how agencies were responding to advertisers' demands for copy-heavy ads.

EXHIBIT 3.10 *Advertisers often used America's involvement in World War II as a way to link their products with patriotism. This link provided advertising with a much-needed image boost after the dark period of the late 1930s.* **www.cocacola.com/**

Following World War II, the economy continued to improve, and the consumption spree was on again. This time, however, public sentiment toward advertising was fundamentally different from what it had been in the 1920s, because of several sociopolitical forces. During World War II and again during the 1950s, when there was great concern about the rise of communism, the issue of "mind control" became an American paranoia, and many people suspected that advertising was a tool of mind control. The country was filled with suspicion related to McCarthyism, nuclear threats, and aliens from outer space. Otherwise normal people were building bomb shelters in their backyards and wondering whether their neighbors were communists.

In this environment of fear, stories began circulating in the 1950s that advertising agencies were doing motivation research and using the psychological sell, which served only to fuel an underlying suspicion of advertising. It was also during this period that Americans began to fear they were being seduced by **subliminal advertising** (subconscious advertising) to buy all sorts of things they didn't really want or need. There had to be a reason that homes and garages were filling up with so much stuff; it must be all that powerful advertising—or so the story went. In fact, a best-selling 1957 book, *The Hidden Persuaders,* offered the answer: slick advertising worked on the subconscious.[15]

15.   Vance Packard, *The Hidden Persuaders* (New York: D. McKay Co., 1957).

This era also saw growth in the U.S. economy and in household incomes. The suburbs emerged, and along with them there was an explosion of consumption. Technological change was relentless, and it fascinated the nation. The television, the telephone, and the automatic washer and dryer became common to the American lifestyle. Advertisements of this era were characterized by scenes of modern life, social promises, and a reliance on science and technology.

Two of the most significant advertising personalities of the period were Rosser Reeves of the Ted Bates agency, who is best remembered for his ultra-hard-sell style, and consultant Ernest Dichter, best remembered for his motivational research, which focused on the subconscious and symbolic elements of consumer desire.

Exhibits 3.11 through 3.13 are representative of the advertising from this contradictory and jumbled period in American advertising.

Peace, Love, and the Creative Revolution (1960 to 1972)

You say you want a revolution,
well, you know,
we all want to change the world.
—John Lennon and Paul McCartney, "Revolution"[16]

Advertising in the United States during the 1960s was slow to respond to the massive social revolution going on all around it. While the nation was struggling with civil rights, the Vietnam War, and the sexual revolution, advertising was often still portraying women and minorities in subservient roles. Based on the ads of the day, one would conclude that only white people bought and used products, and that women had few aspirations beyond service in the kitchen and the bedroom.

The only thing really revolutionary about 1960s advertising was the **creative revolution.** This revolution was characterized by the "creatives" (art directors and copywriters) having a bigger say in the management of their agencies. The emphasis in advertising turned "from ancillary services to the creative product; from science and research to art, inspiration, and intuition."[17] The look of advertising during this period was clean, minimalist, and sparse, with simple copy and a sense of self-effacing humor. The creative revolution, and the look it produced, is most often associated with three famous advertising agencies: Leo Burnett in Chicago; Ogilvy & Mather in New York; and Doyle, Dane, Bernbach in New York. They were led in this revolution by Leo Burnett, David Ogilvy, and Bill Bernbach. The Kellogg's Special K® cereal, Sears, and Avis ads pictured in Exhibits 3.14, 3.15, and 3.16 are 1960s ads prepared by these three famous agencies.

Of course, it would be wrong to characterize the entire period as a creative revolution. Many of the ads in the 1960s still reflected traditional values and relied on relatively uncreative executions. Typical of many of the more traditional ads during the era are the Pepsi and Goodyear ads in Exhibits 3.17 and 3.18.

A final point that needs to be made about the era from 1960 to 1972 is that this was a period when advertising became generally aware of its own role in consumer culture —that is, advertising itself was an icon of a culture fascinated with consumption. While advertising played a role in encouraging consumption, it had become a symbol of consumption itself.

The 1970s (1973 to 1980)

Mr. Blutarski, fat, drunk, and stupid
is no way to go through life.
—Dean Vernon Wormer, Faber College

Dean Wormer's admonition to John Belushi's character in the 1977 hit movie *Animal House* captured essential aspects of the 1970s, a time of excess and self-induced numbness.

---

16. John Lennon and Paul McCartney, "Revolution," Northern Songs, 1968.
17. Fox, *The Mirror Makers,* 218.

EXHIBITS 3.11, 3.12, AND 3.13

Advertising during the 1950s offered consumers contradictory messages. On one hand, technological change and economic progress created the widespread enthusiasm reflected in the IBM and Chrysler ads in Exhibits 3.11 (lower left) and 3.12 (top). On the other hand, consumer suspicions about slick advertising that worked on the subconscious led some advertisers to use hard-sell messages, like the one in the Serta ad shown in Exhibit 3.13 (lower right). www.ibm.com/ *and* www.chryslercorp.com/

We're watching your weight.

A good breakfast is an essential part of any weight control program. Scale down and get back into things, with the Kellogg's® Special K® Breakfast. Only 240 calories, 99% fat-free. Delicious.

© 1968 by Kellogg Company

Avis is only No.2 in rent a cars. So why go with us?

We try harder.

(When you're not the biggest, you have to.)

We just can't afford dirty ash-trays. Or half-empty gas tanks. Or worn wipers. Or unwashed cars. Or low tires. Or anything less than seat-adjusters that adjust. Heaters that heat. Defrost-ers that defrost.

Obviously, the thing we try hardest for is just to be nice. To start you out right with a new car, like a lively, super-torque Ford, and a pleasant smile. To know, say, where you get a good pastrami sandwich in Duluth. Why?

Because we can't afford to take you for granted. Go with us next time.

The line at our counter is shorter.

WEB SIGHTING

EXHIBIT 3.16   *This Avis ad, developed by Doyle, Dane, Bernbach in New York, was typical of the 1960s creative revolution in advertising. The clean, simple, almost humble claims of the ad contrast sharply with the inflated product claims made in earlier eras. Why do you think Avis's approach worked? Today, at the Avis home page* **www.avis .com/**, *the company offers quick links to services and information, as well as other fun information and links. Describe the approach that competitor Hertz takes in its Asian office's home page at* **www.singapore.com/ companies/hertz/**

Yesterday's nylon was never like this!

Sears has the greatest floor show in town

EXHIBITS 3.14 AND 3.15

The new era of advertising in the 1960s was characterized by the creative revolution, during which the creative side of the advertising process rose to new prominence. The ads in Exhibits 3.14 (top) and 3.15 (bottom) reflect the advertising of the day—clean, minimalist, and sparse, with simple copy. These ads were developed by two advertising agencies closely associated with the creative revolution of the sixties: Leo Burnett in Chicago and Ogilvy & Mather in New York. **www.kelloggs.com/**

EXHIBITS 3.17 AND 3.18

Not all the advertising in the 1960s was characterized by the spirit of the creative revolution. The ads in Exhibits 3.17 and 3.18 rely on more traditional styles and values. **www.pepsi.com/** *and* **www.goodyear.com/**

This was the age of polyester, disco, and driving 55. The reelection of Richard Nixon in 1972 marks the real start of the 1970s. America had just suffered through its first lost war, four student protesters had been shot and killed by the National Guard at Kent State University in the spring of 1970, mideast nations appeared to be dictating the energy policy of the United States, and we were, as President Jimmy Carter said late in this period, in a national malaise. In this environment, advertising again retreated into the tried-and-true but hackneyed styles of decades before. The creative revolution of the 1960s gave way to a bad economy and a return to the hard sell. This period also marked the beginning of the second wave of the American feminist movement. In the 1970s, advertisers actually started to present women in "new" roles and to include people of color, as the 1978 Polaroid OneStep ad in Exhibit 3.19 shows.

Often, advertisements focused on the product itself, rather than on creative technique, as illustrated in the product-focused Alpo and Spirit ads in Exhibit 3.20 and Exhibit 3.21. During this period, management took control and dominated agency activities. Alas, the MBA age was upon us.

The process of advertising encountered a new round of challenges on several fronts. First, there was growing concern over what effect $200 million a year in advertising had on children. A group of women in Boston formed **Action for Children's Television (ACT),** which lobbied the government to limit the amount and content of advertising directed at children. Established regulatory bodies, in particular the **Federal Trade Commission (FTC)** and the industry's **National Advertising Review Board,** demanded higher standards of honesty and disclosure from the advertising industry. Several firms were subject to legislative mandates and fines because their advertising was judged to be misleading. Most notable among these firms were Warner-Lambert (for advertising that Listerine mouthwash could cure and prevent colds), Campbell's (for putting marbles in the bottom of a soup bowl to bolster its look), and Anacin (for advertising that its aspirin could help relieve tension). While advertising during this period featured more African-Americans and women, the effort to adequately represent and serve these consumers was minimal; advertising agency hiring and promotion practices with respect to minorities were formally challenged in the courts.

EXHIBIT 3.19

While a bad economy and a national malaise caused a retreat to the tried-and-true styles of decades before, a bright spot of 1970s advertising was the portrayal of people of color. This Polaroid ad is from 1978. **www.polaroid .com/**

EXHIBITS 3.20 AND 3.21 *One of the significant differences between advertising prepared in the 1960s and in the 1970s is that ads began focusing on the product itself, rather than on creative techniques. The Alpo ad in Exhibit 3.20 and the Spirit ad in Exhibit 3.21 represent this product-focused feature of 1970s advertising, which reflects the fact that management had taken control of agency activities during this era.* **www.chryslercorp.com/**

The most positive aspect of this period was not the result of efforts on the part of advertisers or their agencies, but rather the contribution of technology to the process of advertising. The 1970s signaled a period of growth in communications technology. Consumers began to surround themselves with devices related to communication. The development of the VCR, cable television, and the laser disc player all occurred during the 1970s. Cable TV claimed 20 million subscribers by the end of the 1970s. Similarly, cable programming grew in quality, with viewing options like ESPN, CNN, TBS, and Nickelodeon. As cable subscribers and their viewing options grew, advertisers learned how to reach more specific audiences through the diversity of programming on cable systems.

The process of advertising was being restricted by both consumer and formal regulatory challenges, yet technological advances posed unprecedented opportunities. It was the beginning of the merger mania that swept the industry throughout the end of the decade and into the next, a movement that saw most of the major agencies merge with one another and with non-U.S. agencies as well. This period in the evolution of advertising presented enormous challenges.

The Republican Era (1980 to 1993)

The political, social, business, and advertising landscape changed again around 1980 with the election of Ronald Reagan. The country made a sharp right, and conservative politics was the order of the day. There was, of course, some backlash and many countercurrents, but the conservatives were in the mainstream.

Many ads from the Republican era are social-class and values conscious. They openly promote consumption, but in an understated and conservative way. The Royal Viking Line ad in Exhibit 3.22 is a good example of understated, class-conscious advertising. The quintessential 1980s ad may be the 1984 television ad for President Ronald Reagan's reelection campaign called "Morning in America." The storyboard for this ad is shown in Exhibit 3.23. This ad is soft in texture, but it gives an impression of firm reaffirmation of family and country. Other advertisers quickly followed with ads that looked similar to "Morning in America."

EXHIBIT 3.22

Advertising from the Republican era openly promoted consumption, but in an understated way. This ad for the Royal Viking Line exemplifies this subtle emphasis on consumption.

EXHIBIT 3.23 *An ad that embodied the tone and style of 1980s advertising was Ronald Reagan's 1984 reelection campaign ad "Morning in America." The ad is soft in texture but firm in its affirmation of the conservative values of family and country.*

At the same time, several new, high-technology trends were emerging in the industry, which led to more-creative, bold, and provocative advertising. Television advertising of this period was influenced by the rapid-cut editing style of MTV, and some advertising near the end of the period played to at least someone's idea of Generation X, as the 1993 Pepsi ad in Exhibit 3.24 illustrates.

This was also the age of the **infomercial,** a long advertisement that looks like a talk show or a half-hour product demonstration. If you watch late-night cable television, you've probably seen some guy lighting his car on fire as part of a demonstration for car wax. These very long ads initially aired in late-night television time slots, when audiences were small in number and airtime was relatively inexpensive. Infomercials have since spread to other off-peak time slots, including those with somewhat larger audiences, and they have gained respect along the way, as the Ethical Issues box on page 73 discusses. The Psychic Friends Network, Soloflex, and Cher's hair care line are all examples of products and services recently promoted on infomercials.

The Present Era   ❹ In May of 1994, Edwin L. Artzt, then chairman and CEO of Procter & Gamble, the $40-billion-a-year marketer of consumer packaged goods, dropped a bomb on the advertising industry. During an address to participants at the American Association of Advertising Agencies (4As) annual conference, he warned that agencies must confront a "new media" future that won't be driven by traditional advertising. While at that time P&G was spending about $1 billion a year on television advertising, Artzt told the 4As audience, "From where we stand today, we can't be sure that ad-supported TV programming will have a future in the world being created—a world of video-on-demand, pay-per-view, and subscription TV. These are designed to carry no advertising at all."[18] Then, just when the industry had almost

18.   This quote and information from this section can be found in Steve Yahn, "Advertising's Grave New World," *Advertising Age,* May 16, 1994, 53.

EXHIBIT 3.24

While the success of the Republican era in using advertising to create political images led to many imitations, the Pepsi ad here marked a counter-current of rebellion that appealed to the younger markets. Is there evidence that this cultivated, youth-oriented image for Pepsi still drives the company's advertising? When you visit the Pepsi home page at **www.pepsi.com/**, *see if you can draw direct comparisons to the past campaign illustrated in this exhibit. Also compare this campaign to competitor Coca-Cola's at* **www.cocacola.com/**

recovered from Artzt's blast, William T. Esrey, chairman and CEO of Sprint, fired another volley almost exactly a year later at the same annual conference. Esrey's point was somewhat different but equally challenging to the industry. He said that clients are "going to hold ad agencies more closely accountable for results than ever before. That's not just because we're going to be more demanding in getting value for our advertising dollars. It's also because we know the technology is there to measure advertising impact more precisely than you have done in the past."[19] Esrey's point: Interactive media will allow direct measurement of ad exposure and impact, quickly revealing those that perform well, and those that do not. The emergence of interactive media options is a central issue in this present era.

The Interactive Media Revolution. As you might imagine, the perspectives offered by the heads of Procter & Gamble and Sprint sent shock waves through the advertising industry. The technological changes that will occur during the last few years of the twentieth century and the early years of the twenty-first century may create the era of greatest upheaval for advertising. Or, they may not.

At the crux of the turmoil is the new technology generally referred to as **interactive media.** With interactive media, consumers are able to call up games, entertainment, shopping opportunities, and educational programs on a subscription or pay-per-view basis. The belief is that consumers want the wide range of choices, the convenience, and the control such programming provides. To reach consumers through this new technology, big firms like Procter & Gamble will most likely form joint ventures with major entertainment companies and participate in all phases of **integrated programming.** Using this approach, advertisers control the content of new media—like CD-ROMs, interactive television, and online information services—to better control the destiny of their advertising.[20] The system would work something like this: A firm like P&G finances media expenses; entertainment companies like Sony provide production funding; cable TV operators like Time Warner and TCI provide the airtime; and all parties promote the programming together and create a media event. In such a system, interactive technology can be used to actually engage consumers in commercials. For example, if a viewer wants to know what nail polish will match the lipstick she just saw in a commercial, she can interact with the programming and get an immediate answer. Thus, target audiences do not have to be broadly defined by age or geographic groups—individual households can be targeted through direct interaction with the audience member.

Reinventing the Advertising Process. The glaring omission in this new world of programming is traditional advertising as we know it today. This is a world where half-hour prime-time programming with 10 to 12 minutes of commercial interruption does not exist. How can advertising as a process survive in such a world? One answer lies in reinventing the process to fit the new ways of reaching audience members.

19.   Kevin Godman, "Sprint Chief Lectures Agencies on Future," *Wall Street Journal,* April 28, 1995, B6.
20.   Scott Donaton and Pat Sloan, "Control New Media," *Advertising Age,* March 13, 1995, 1.

But we shouldn't jump to the conclusion that the very nature of advertising as a process will change. Advertising will still be a paid, mass-mediated attempt to persuade. As a business process, advertising will still be one of the primary marketing mix tools that contribute to revenues and profits by stimulating demand and nurturing brand loyalty. It is also safe to argue that consumers will still be highly involved in some product decisions and not so involved in others, so that some messages will be particularly relevant and others will be completely irrelevant to forming and maintaining attitudes about brands.

ETHICAL ISSUES

BEYOND PSYCHICS AND SPRAY-ON HAIR: INFOMERCIALS GAIN NEW RESPECTABILITY

Remember the infomercial, the quasi–talk show/news program that hawked wares of dubious origin and quality? The infomercial format we now know became available in 1984 when the FCC (Federal Communications Commission) rescinded regulations limiting advertising to 16 minutes per hour, and many of the early purveyors have gone bankrupt or have been prosecuted for false product claims. The hucksters and scam artists have had their day in the sun, and mainstream manufacturers have now discovered that the format has tremendous potential and room for growth. Traditional 30-second advertisements simply do not have the ability to deeply engross and involve an audience. As such, the short ads are principally oriented toward indirect action, a positive disposition toward the product, and long-term brand and logo recognition. The greatest strength of the infomercial, on the other hand, is the ability to motivate action and direct response to immediately close the sale. The infomercial is a powerful selling tool; it is not placed for future positive effect. The 30-minute format has also proven to be a powerful educational tool for retailers. An Apple Computer infomercial promoting the Performa line drove computer sales on the retail and the direct level and resulted in more than 100,000 phone inquiries. The increased visibility of blue-chip marketers such as Apple has caught the attention of Madison Avenue and has lent respectability to the format. Other firms of note experimenting with the 30-minute format include Volkswagen, Texaco, Sega of America, Magnavox, and Fidelity Investments.

Sources: "Infomercials Are Attracting More Converts," *Advertising Age*, March 13, 1995, 21; "The Wild West of Advertising," *Forbes*, January 16, 1995, 50; and "Apple Performa Infomercial Bags 100,000 Calls," *Advertising Age*, January 30, 1995, 6.

If advertising retains its character as both a business and a communication process, then how must the process be reinvented? The most dramatic change will be in the way advertising is prepared and delivered to the target audience. The likely scenario for the integrated, interactive advertisement of the future goes something like this: Prospective car buyers, from the comfort of their home, consider a variety of cars on their television screen. They change the model, position, color, and options on the vehicle with a click of a mouse. Then, having constructed one or more appealing versions of the desired vehicle, another click of the mouse sets an appointment for a test drive with a nearby dealer. The dealer brings the requested car to prospective buyers. If a buyer is ready to take action, the dealer representative can go online with a laptop computer to check inventory and leasing programs and then signal the dealership to prepare the necessary paperwork.[21]

Of course, like all predictions, this one is probably wrong, but not completely wrong. Advertising is changing dramatically and rapidly. Several firms are already experimenting with early, hybrid versions of interactive advertising and promotion:

- Shopper Vision, a Georgia home-grocery-shopping service, and Shoppers Express, a Maryland grocery-ordering and delivery service, are merging to form ShopperVisionExpress and will develop interactive applications for television and online services.
- Intel has announced agreements with Prodigy, America Online, and others for test delivery of multimedia online services via cable.
- CUC International provides catalog-shopping services on CompuServe, and America Online is adding video to its text-based service.
- U.S. West is working with Nordstrom and J.C. Penney to develop interactive home-shopping services in the firm's new Interactive Video Services division.

21. Jonathan Berry and Kathy Rebello, "What Is an Ad in the Interactive Future?" *Business Week,* May 2, 1994, 103.

- Turner Broadcasting System has introduced Turner Interactive—a line of interactive CD-ROMs.
- Procter & Gamble has agreed to participate in the Time Warner full-service network test in Orlando, Florida. This test is a prototype of cable interactive systems of the future.

The present era is certainly full of change and challenge for advertising, advertisers, and advertising agencies. But there is enormous opportunity as well, both in the United States and in foreign markets, as the Global Issues box on this page discusses. One research study estimates that by the year 2003, the total dollar volume of interactive TV transactions will be $7.2 billion and that advertisers will have a clear role in bringing about consumer use of the technology.[22] Consumers will still need descriptive and persuasive information; how that information is developed and delivered will be the fascination of advertisers and their agencies for the coming years.

The Value of an Evolutionary Perspective

To understand advertising in an evolutionary perspective is to appreciate the reasons for advertising's use in a modern industrialized society. Advertising was spawned by a market-driven system and grew through self-interest in capitalistic, free enterprise market economies. Efficient methods of production made advertising essential as a demand stimulation tool. Urbanization, transportation expansion, and communications advancements all facilitated the use and growth of advertising. The result is that advertising has become firmly entrenched as a business function, with deeply rooted economic and cultural foundations. This evolutionary perspective allows us to understand the more basic aspects of the role and impact of advertising.

Corporate leaders like Artzt from Procter & Gamble and Esrey from Sprint have issued a challenge to traditional advertising methods and media. New technologies and the interactive media options they present are an important issue. But this should not be interpreted as the death of advertising, as some have argued.[23] In fact, paraphrasing Mark Twain, the death of advertising has been greatly exaggerated. Just when people were starting to describe advertising's sorrowful death at the hands of new media, we witnessed a surge in demand for traditional mass media space that set off a bidding war and the prospect of rationing time slots during the

GLOBAL ISSUES

IT'S A SMALL WORLD AFTER AOL: EUROPE GOES ONLINE

As personal computer and modem sales skyrocket in Europe, market researchers forecast that the number of homes online in Europe may surpass 15 million by the year 2000. Several online services, such as CompuServe, have already entered the fray, and new services from a partnership between America Online (the largest online service in the United States) and the German entertainment giant Bertelsmann AG are getting under way. Initially, Bertelsmann plans to offer information on its vast publishing and music empire. European online networks are also planned by Microsoft and a European consortium named Europe Online SA. When it comes to content, however, the American companies may lag behind. Europe Online plans to begin hundreds of local services in French, English, and German and is now testing automatic translation software that would allow members of different nationalities to converse. When it comes to advertising, the new European services have proceeded with caution. Steve Case, president and CEO of America Online, has said of the AOL-Bertelsmann venture that "we need a critical mass of consumers first" and that the European service will not be available initially to marketers. Europe Online has also declined online advertising for the present. With a history of closely shadowing American computer trends by a year or two, however, European online ads are likely to follow. As U.S. advertisers now learn to cultivate online sales at home, they may well enjoy the advantage in online Europe when that market becomes available.

Sources: "Online's Next Battlefront: Europe," *Advertising Age*, March 6 1995, 18; "Bertelsmann, American Online Set Service," *Wall Street Journal*, March 1, 1995, B6; and "Europe Enters the Cyberspace Race," *Business Week*, February 13, 1995, 91.

---

22. Scott Donaton, "Bates USA Survey Is Bullish on Interactive," *Advertising Age*, July 11, 1994, 26.
23. Roland Rust and Richard W. Oliver, "The Death of Advertising," *Journal of Advertising* 23, no. 4 (December 1994): 71–77.

1995–96 prime-time network television season![24] A record $10 billion in advance media time was purchased, and advertisers were scrambling for airtime. In addition, advertising agencies experienced an 11.1 percent rise in gross income in 1995—one of the largest increases in industry history, bringing total revenues in the industry to nearly $130 billion worldwide.[25] The death of advertising at the hands of interactive media does, indeed, seem to have been greatly exaggerated.

The 1990s have also brought changes to the concept of power in the distribution channel, which was discussed earlier as a fundamental influence on advertising. Power retailers—like Wal-Mart, The Gap, Toys "R" Us, and Home Depot—are struggling to wrestle power away from manufacturers. The retailers' power in the channel is being exercised in two ways. First, mass merchandise discounters like Wal-Mart and Home Depot are using **value pricing**—pricing that emphasizes quality and low price—to attract customers. Manufacturers must comply with the power of these retailers in the channel, and they are having a more difficult time getting consumers to demand their products when the retailer suddenly has a power base. Second, the emergence and popularity of retailers' **private label brands**—brands that carry the retailer name—have also affected manufacturers' use of advertising. Private label brands have emerged as formidable competition for national brands. The appeal of the private labels is their lower price. Because of this, manufacturers have had to rely more on direct mail campaigns and sales promotions like coupons and premiums to attract attention back to the national brands.

SUMMARY

1 Explain why advertising is a natural feature of any capitalistic economic system.

Although some might contend that the practice of advertising began thousands of years ago, it is more meaningful to connect advertising as we know it today with the emergence of capitalistic economic systems. In such systems, business organizations must compete for survival in a free market setting. In this setting, it is natural that a firm would embrace a tool that assists it in persuading potential customers to choose its products over those offered by others. Of course, advertising is such a tool. The explosion in production capacity that marked the Industrial Revolution gave demand stimulation tools added importance.

2 Appreciate manufacturers' dependence on advertising and branding in achieving balanced relationships with retailers.

Advertising and branding play a key role in the ongoing power struggle between manufacturers and their retailers. U.S. manufacturers began branding their products in the late 1800s. Advertising could thus be used to build awareness of and desire for the various offerings of a particular manufacturer. Retailers have power in the marketplace deriving from the fact that they are closer to the customer.

When manufacturers can use advertising to build customer loyalty to their brands, they take part of that power back. Of course, in a capitalistic system, power and profitability go hand in hand.

3 Discuss ten important eras in the evolution of advertising in the United States, and relate important changes in advertising practice to more fundamental changes in society and culture.

Social and economic trends, along with technological developments, are major determinants of the way advertising is practiced in any society. Before the Industrial Revolution, advertising's presence in the United States was barely noticeable. With an explosion in economic growth around the turn of the century, modern advertising was born: the P. T. Barnum era and the 1920s established advertising as a major force in the U.S. economic system. With the Great Depression and World War II, cynicism and paranoia began to grow regarding advertising. This concern led to refinements in practice and more careful regulation of advertising in the 1960s and 1970s. Consumption was once again in vogue during the Republican era of the 1980s. The new communication technologies that have emerged in the present era may effect significant changes in future practice.

24.   Joe Mandese, "Sizzling TV Ad Sales May Spark Rationing," *Advertising Age,* May 15, 1995, 1.
25.   R. Craig Endicott, "Shops Soar on Growth of 9.2 % to $17 Billion," *Advertising Age,* April 15, 1996, S-2.

4 Identify forces that may make the next decade a period of dramatic change for the advertising industry.

Integrated and *interactive* have become the advertising buzzwords of the nineties. These words represent notable developments that may reshape advertising practice. Integrated marketing communications may grow in importance as advertisers work with more-varied media options to reach markets that are becoming even more fragmented. A variety of advertisers are now experimenting with interactive media to learn how to make effective use of this new tool. Advertising in the next decade will continue to be a vibrant and challenging profession.

KEY TERMS

Industrial Revolution (56)
principle of limited ability (57)
branding (57)
democracy of goods (59)
handbill (59)
dailies (60)
consumer culture (60)
Pure Food and Drug Act (61)
social tableau (63)
subliminal advertising (65)

creative revolution (66)
Action for Children's Television (ACT) (69)
Federal Trade Commission (FTC) (69)
National Advertising Review Board (69)
infomercial (71)
interactive media (72)
integrated programming (72)
value pricing (75)
private label brands (75)

QUESTIONS FOR REVIEW AND CRITICAL THINKING

1.   As formerly communist countries make the conversion to free market economies, advertising typically becomes more visible and important. Why would this be the case?

2.   Explain why there is a strong relationship between increasing urbanization and per capita spending.

3.   Why are manufacturers like Nabisco and First Brands losing power in their channels of distribution? To whom, exactly, are they losing this power?

4.   Describe the various factors that produced an explosion of advertising activity in the P. T. Barnum era.

5.   The 1950s were marked by great suspicion about advertisers and their potential persuasive powers. Do you see any lingering effects of this era of paranoia in attitudes about advertising today?

6.   There were many important developments in the seventies that set the stage for advertising in the Reagan era. Which of these developments are likely to have the most enduring effects on advertising practice in the future?

7.   Ed Artzt, then chairman and CEO of Procter & Gamble, made a speech in May of 1994 that rattled the cages of many advertising professionals. What did Artzt have to say that got people in the ad business so excited?

8.   Review the technological developments that have had the greatest impact on the advertising business. What new technologies are emerging that promise more profound changes for advertisers in the next decade?

EXPERIENTIAL EXERCISE

As discussed in the chapter, one of the more popular forms of advertising today is the infomercial. Watch two infomercials. Describe the products advertised and what action the advertiser wants you to take. Do you think the infomercials are persuasive and believable? Why or why not? Call one of the two 800 numbers you saw advertised and ask a few pertinent questions about the product or request additional information. Describe the nature of your conversation and the outcome. Note: You *do not* have to buy anything to complete this exercise.

USING THE INTERNET

The Internet is an emerging communication medium that offers businesses fresh opportunities for satisfying customer needs. The following businesses each take advantage of the unique characteristics of the Internet to offer added value in competitive environments:

Southwest: www.iflyswa.com

FedEx: www.fedex.com

General Electric: www.ge.com

Holiday Inn: www.holiday-inn.com

Ticketmaster: www.ticketmaster.com

For each site, answer these questions:

1.   What new service does the site offer to consumers?

2.   What is the value added by the Web site, as compared to traditional media?

3.   How does the site strengthen the company's image? Increase profitability? Facilitate sales?

4.   How does the site build stronger relationships between buyers and sellers?

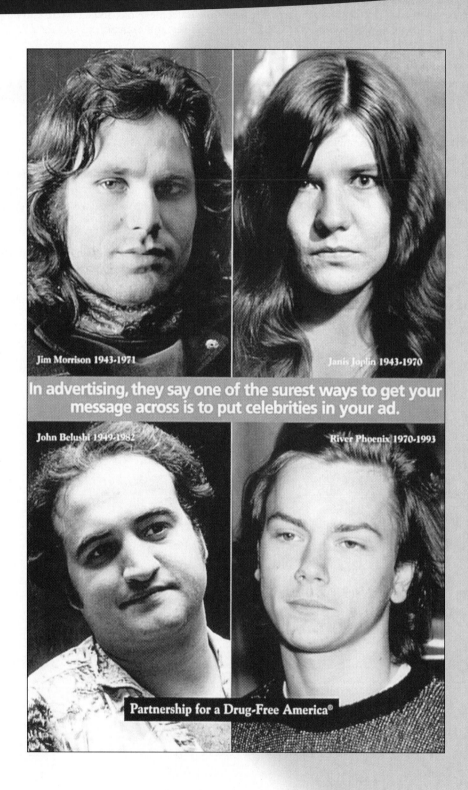

Jim Morrison 1943-1971 Janis Joplin 1943-1970

In advertising, they say one of the surest ways to get your message across is to put celebrities in your ad.

John Belushi 1949-1982 River Phoenix 1970-1993

Partnership for a Drug-Free America®

Chapter 4

Social, Ethical, and Regulatory Aspects of Advertising

After reading and thinking about this chapter, you will be able to do the following:

1 Assess the benefits and drawbacks of advertising in a capitalistic society and debate a variety of issues concerning advertising's effects on societal well-being.

2 Explain how ethical considerations affect the development of advertising campaigns.

3 Discuss the role of government agencies in the regulation of advertising.

4 Explain the meaning and importance of self-regulation for an advertising practitioner.

The social, ethical, and regulatory aspects of advertising are as dynamic and controversial as any of the strategic or creative elements of the process. What is socially responsible or irresponsible, ethically debatable, politically correct, or legal? The answers are constantly changing. As a society changes, so too do its perspectives. Like anything else with social roots and implications, advertising will be affected by these changes.

The social, ethical, and regulatory aspects of advertising provide some of its most memorable and defining moments. Consider these episodes in the history of advertising:

- In the late 1800s, patent medicine advertising dominated the media. Elixirs and medical devices promised cures for everything from paralysis to spinal irritation and malaria.
- Warner-Lambert began running advertising in 1921 that claimed Listerine mouthwash could prevent colds and sore throats. In 1975, the advertising was judged to be deceptive, and the firm was required to spend $10 million on "corrective advertising" to undo the misimpressions created by the claims.
- In 1990, an ad for Volvo automobiles showed a monster truck with oversized tires rolling over the roofs of a row of cars, crushing all of them except a Volvo. Volvo, which had developed a reputation for building safe and durable cars, had rigged the demonstration; the Volvo's roof had been reinforced, while the other cars' roof supports had been weakened.[1]
- In 1994, General Nutrition agreed to stop making unsubstantiated claims for more than 40 products, including Sleepers Diet, which the company claimed would help users lose weight while they slept. The company also agreed to pay a $2.4 million civil penalty.[2]

Advertising history includes all sorts of social, ethical, and legal lapses on the part of advertisers. However, advertising has also had its triumphs, financial as well as moral. Whether justified or not, criticisms of advertising can be naive and simplistic, often failing to consider the complex social and legal environment in which contemporary advertising operates.

The Social Aspects of Advertising

The social aspects of advertising are often volatile. For the person who feels advertising is intrusive and manipulative, it is usually the social aspects that provide the most fuel for heated debate.

We can consider the social aspects of advertising in several broad areas. On the positive side, we will consider advertising's effect on consumers' standard of living, its support of the mass media, and the role it plays in providing exposure to issues. Advertisers like Anheuser-Busch devote millions of dollars to promoting responsible drinking with advertisements like the one shown in Exhibit 4.1. Government organizations use advertising for many purposes, including the education of consumers about social programs, as illustrated in Exhibit 4.2.

On the negative side, we will examine a variety of social criticisms of advertising, ranging from the charge that advertising wastes resources and promotes materialism to the argument that advertising perpetuates stereotypes.

Our approach will be to offer pros and cons on several issues that critics and advertisers commonly argue about. Be forewarned—these are matters of opinion, with no clear right and wrong answers. You will have to draw your own conclusions.

Advertising Educates Consumers

Does advertising provide valuable information to consumers, or does it seek only to confuse or entice them? Here's what the experts on both sides have to say.

---

1.   Steven W. Colford and Raymond Serafin, "Scali Pays for Volvo Ad: FTC," *Advertising Age,* August 26, 1991, 4.
2.   Jeanne Saddler, "General Nutrition to Pay FTC Penalty of $2.4 Million over False Advertising," *Wall Street Journal,* April 29, 1994, B10.

EXHIBIT 4.1

This ad represents time and money spent by Anheuser-Busch to project a positive social message, yet the ad doesn't attempt to sell its products. Why is this choice important in a social responsibility ad? See if Budweiser continues its social responsibility theme on its home page at **www.budweiser.com/**. *Describe the difference in tone and style at the Miller Brewing Company's home page at* **www.careermosaic .com/cm/miller/**

EXHIBIT 4.2 *Many types of organizations use advertising to get their message out. In this case the message is very serious.*

Pro: Advertising Informs. Supporters of advertising argue that advertising educates consumers, equipping them with the information they need to make informed purchase decisions. By regularly assessing information and advertising claims, consumers become more educated regarding the features, benefits, functions, and values of products. Further, consumers can become more aware of their own tendencies toward being persuaded and relying on certain types of product information. The argument has been offered that advertising is "clearly an immensely powerful instrument for the elimination of ignorance."[3] According to this argument, better-educated consumers enhance their lifestyles and economic power through astute marketplace decision making.

A related argument is that advertising *reduces search time*—that is, the amount of time an individual must spend to search for desired products and services is reduced because of advertising. The large amount of readily available information allows consumers to easily assess the potential value of a particular product or service in the marketplace, without spending time and effort to evaluate the product in a retail setting. The information contained in an advertisement "reduces drastically the cost of search."[4]

Con: Advertising Is Superficial. Critics argue that advertising does not provide good product information. The basic criticism of advertising here is that it frequently carries little, if any, actual product information. What it does carry is said to be hollow ad-speak.

---

3.   George J. Stigler, "The Economics of Information," *The Journal of Political Economy* (June 1961), 213–20.
4.   Ibid., 220.

Critics claim that ads should contain information on functional features and performance results. Advertisers argue in response that, in many instances, consumers are interested in more than a physical, tangible material good with performance features and purely functional value. The functional features of a product may be secondary in importance to consumers in both the information search and the choice process. Advertising's critics often dismiss or ignore the totality of product benefits, including the hedonic (pleasure-seeking) aspects. The relevant information for the buyer is information that relates to the criteria being used to judge the satisfaction potential of the product, and that satisfaction is quite often nonutilitarian.

Advertising Improves the Standard of Living

Whether advertising raises or lowers the general standard of living is hotly debated. Opinions vary widely on this issue and go right to the heart of whether advertising is a good use or a waste of energy and resources.

Pro: Advertising Lowers the Cost of Products. First, supporters argue that due to the economies of scale produced by advertising, consumers actually realize less-expensive products. As broad-based demand stimulation results in lower production and administrative costs, lower prices are passed on to consumers. Second, a greater variety of choice in products and services stems from the increased probability of success firms realize from being able to introduce new products with the assistance of advertising. Third, the pressures of competition and the desire to have advertisable products stimulate firms to produce improved products. Fourth, the speed and reach of the advertising process aids in the diffusion of innovations. This means that new discoveries can be communicated to a large percentage of the marketplace very quickly. Innovations succeed when advertising communicates their benefits to the customer.

All four of these factors can contribute positively to the standard of living and quality of life in a society. Advertising may be instrumental in bringing about these effects because it serves an important role in demand stimulation and keeping customers informed.

Con: Advertising Wastes Resources. One of the traditional criticisms of advertising is that it represents an inefficient, wasteful process that channels monetary and human resources in a society to the "shuffling of existing total demand," rather than to the expansion of total demand.[5] Advertising thus brings about economic stagnation and a lower standard of living. Critics say that a society is no better off with advertising because it does not stimulate demand—it only shifts demand from one brand to another. Similarly, critics argue that brand differences are trivial and the proliferation of brands does not offer a greater variety of choice, but rather a meaningless waste of resources.

Advertising Affects Happiness and General Well-Being

Critics and supporters of advertising differ significantly in their views about how advertising affects consumers' happiness and general well-being. As you will see, this is a complex issue with multiple pros and cons.

Con: Advertising Creates Needs. A common cry among critics is that advertising creates needs and makes people buy things they don't really need or even want. The argument is that consumers are relatively easy to seduce into wanting the next shiny bauble offered by marketers. For example, the advertisement in Exhibit 4.3 features a line of spectacular blankets and bedding that will make your bedroom a showplace. But does anyone really need a $15,000 bedspread?

5.   Richard Caves, *American Industry: Structure, Conduct, Performance* (Englewood Cliffs, N.J.: Prentice-Hall, 1964), 102.

EXHIBIT 4.3

Extravagance is a concern of many of advertising's critics. Does this ad seek to create needs beyond what is reasonably required for sleep and comfort?

Pro: Advertising Addresses a Variety of Needs. A good place to start in discussing whether advertising can create needs is to consider the nature of needs. Abraham Maslow, a pioneer in the study of human motivation, conceived that human behavior progresses through the following hierarchy of need states:

- *Physiological needs.* Biological needs that require the satisfaction of hunger, thirst, and basic bodily functions.
- *Safety needs.* The need to provide shelter and protection for the body and to maintain a comfortable existence.
- *Love and belonging needs.* The need for affiliation and affection. A person will strive for both the giving and receiving of love.
- *Esteem needs.* The need for recognition, status, and prestige. In addition to the respect of others, there is a need and desire for self-respect.
- *Self-actualization needs.* This is the highest of all the need states and is achieved by only a small percentage of people, according to Maslow. The individual strives for maximum fulfillment of individual capabilities.

It must be clearly understood that Maslow was describing basic human needs and motivations, not consumer needs and motivations. But, in the context of an affluent society, individuals will turn to goods and services to satisfy needs. Many products are said to directly address the requirements of one or more of these need states. Food and health care products, for example, like those in Exhibits 4.4 and 4.5, relate to physiological needs. Home security systems and smoke detectors help address safety needs. Many personal care products, such as the skin care system shown in Exhibit 4.6, promote feelings of self-esteem, confidence, glamour, and romance.

In the pursuit of esteem, many consumers buy products they perceive to have status and prestige: expensive jewelry, clothing, automobiles, and homes are examples. Though it may be difficult to buy self-actualization, ownership of some products can help promote feelings of pride and accomplishment. Supporters maintain that advertising may be directed at many different forms of need fulfillment, but it is of little use in creating new needs.

Con: Advertising Promotes Materialism. It is also claimed that individuals' wants and aspirations may be distorted by advertising. The long-standing argument is that in societies characterized by heavy advertising, there is a tendency for conformity and status-seeking behavior, both of which are considered materialistic and superficial.[6] Material goods are placed ahead of spiritual and intellectual pursuits. Advertising, which portrays products as symbols of status, success, and happiness, contributes to the materialism and superficiality in a society. It creates wants and aspirations that are artificial and self-centered. This results in an overemphasis on the production of private goods, to the detriment of public goods (such as highways, parks, schools, and infrastructure).[7]

6.   Vance Packard, *The Status Seekers* (New York: David McKay Company, 1959).
7.   See, for example, George Katona, *The Mass Consumption Society* (New York: McGraw-Hill, 1964), 54–61; and John Kenneth Galbraith, *The Affluent Society* (Boston: Houghton Mifflin, 1958).

We know exactly how you feel about fruit

How would you feel if we topped that?

If you love fruit, and you love crunch, you'll love new BREYERS® Mix'N Crunch.™
You'll love the cool, creamy texture and the crunchy goodness of POST® cereals you mix right
in. It's just what you'd expect from BREYERS. Yogurt pure and delicious. So full of fruit
and flavor, so full of crunch. Enjoy it to your heart's content.

New BREYERS® Mix'N Crunch Yogurt. The Full-of-Fruit & Crunch Yogurt.™

BREYERS® is a registered trademark owned and licensed by Unilever N.V.

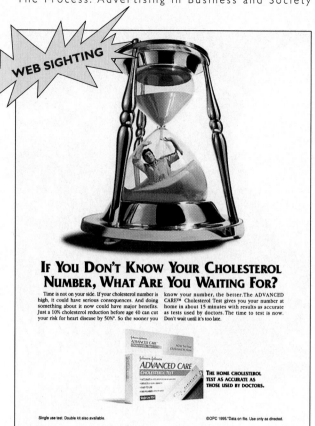

IF YOU DON'T KNOW YOUR CHOLESTEROL
NUMBER, WHAT ARE YOU WAITING FOR?

Time is not on your side. If your cholesterol number is
high, it could have serious consequences. And doing
something about it now could have major benefits.
Just a 10% cholesterol reduction before age 40 can cut
your risk for heart disease by 50%*. So the sooner you

know your number, the better. The ADVANCED
CARE™ Cholesterol Test gives you your number at
home in about 15 minutes with results as accurate
as tests used by doctors. The time to test is now.
Don't wait until it's too late.

THE HOME CHOLESTEROL
TEST AS ACCURATE AS
THOSE USED BY DOCTORS.

Single use test. Double kit also available.   ©OPC 1995. *Data on file. Use only as directed.

EXHIBIT 4.4

*Consumers always want products that taste good. Many advertisements
appeal to this basic desire.*

EXHIBIT 4.5 *Many Johnson & Johnson products attempt to satisfy
physiological needs. Does this ad provide motivation, need satisfaction, or
both? At the J&J home page* **www.jnj.com/**, *how is this emphasis
on basic need satisfaction carried through? How does the company credo
support its products? Compare this approach with that of competitor
Bristol-Myers-Squibb at* **www.bms.com/**

Pro: Advertising Reflects Society's Priorities. Although advertising is undeniably in the business of promoting the good life, defenders of advertising argue it did not create the American
emphasis on materialism. For example, in the United States, major holidays like Christmas (gifts), Thanksgiving (food), and Easter (candy and clothing) have become festivals
of consumption. This is the American way. Stephen Fox concludes his treatise on the
history of American advertising as follows:

> One may build a compelling case that American culture is—beyond redemption—money-mad,
> hedonistic, superficial, rushing heedlessly down a railroad track called Progress. Tocqueville and
> other observers of the young republic described America in these terms in the early 1800s, decades
> before the development of national advertising. To blame advertising now for these most basic ten-
> dencies in American history is to miss the point. . . . The people who have created modern adver-
> tising are not hidden persuaders pushing our buttons in the service of some malevolent purpose.
> They are just producing an especially visible manifestation, good and bad, of the American Way of
> life.[8]

While we clearly live in the age of consumption, goods and possessions have been used
by all cultures to mark special events, play significant roles in rituals, and serve as vessels
of special meaning long before there was modern advertising.

8.   Stephen Fox, *The Mirror Makers: A History of American Advertising and Its Creators* (New York: William Morrow,
1984), 330.

"All you need is Guinot." In what sense might a person need Guinot?
www.lotions.com/guinot.html

Con: Advertising Perpetuates Stereotypes.

Advertisers often portray their target customer in advertisements, with the hope that individuals will relate to the ad and attend to its message. Critics charge that this practice yields a very negative effect—it perpetuates stereotypes. The portrayal of women, the elderly, and ethnic minorities is of particular concern. It is argued that women are still predominantly cast as homemakers or sex objects in advertising, despite the fact that women now hold top management positions and deftly head households. The elderly are often shown as helpless or ill, even though many active seniors enjoy a rich lifestyle. Critics contend that advertisers' propensity to feature African-American or Latin athletes in ads is simply a more contemporary form of stereotyping.

Pro: Advertisers Are Showing Much More Sensitivity.

Much of this sort of stereotyping is becoming part of the past. Advertisements from prior generations do show a stereotyping problem. The ad in Exhibit 4.7 illustrates the gender stereotype that a good woman is one who can keep her man happy with her cooking abilities. Today, FedEx's advertising features an African-American woman prevailing over a group of white male executives in an important business deal. Advertisers are realizing that a diverse world requires diversity in the social reality that ads represent and help construct. Still, many remain dissatisfied with the pace of change.

Con: Advertising Is Often Offensive.

A pervasive and long-standing criticism of advertising is that it is often offensive and the appeals are typically in poor taste. Of course, taste is just that, a personal and inherently subjective evaluation. What is offensive to one person is satiric to another. What should we call an ad prepared for the International Advertising Festival in Cannes, designed to show the durability of Kadu surfer shorts? The ad showed Kadu shorts emerging from the stomach of a gutted shark.[9] (By the way, the agency that conceived this ad is now defunct.) Another ad was prepared to plug a Hong Kong television station. The newspaper ad showed a photo of Adolf Hitler, and the copy implied that if he had been wise enough to advertise on the Hong Kong station, he would have won World War II and dominated the world.[10]

But not all advertising deemed offensive has to be as extreme as these examples. Many times, advertisers get caught in a firestorm of controversy because certain, and sometimes relatively small, segments of the population are offended. The AIDS prevention campaign run by the Centers for Disease Control (CDC) has been criticized for

9.   "Objection, Your Honor," *Advertising Age,* December 19, 1994, 19.
10.   Pamposh Dhar, "Hitler-Theme Ad Sparks Furor," *Advertising Age,* November 21, 1994, 28.

Most people today would view this ad as being in poor taste. Maybe things have changed when it comes to stereotypes in advertising.

being too explicit. A spokesperson for the Family Research Council said about the ads, "They're very offensive—I thought I was watching *NYPD Blue.*" A highly popular ad seen as controversial by some was the "People Taking Diet Coke Break." In this television spot, a group of female office workers is shown eyeing a construction worker as he takes off his T-shirt and enjoys a Diet Coke (see Exhibit 1.8 in Chapter 1). Coca-Cola has been criticized for using reverse sexism in this ad.[11] While Coca-Cola and the CDC may have ventured into delicate areas, consider these advertisers, who were caught completely by surprise in finding that their ads were deemed offensive:

- In a public service spot developed by Aetna Life & Casualty insurance for measles vaccine, a wicked witch with green skin and a wart resulted in a challenge to the firm's ad from a witches' rights group.

- A Nynex spot was criticized by animal-rights activists because it showed a rabbit colored with blue dye.

- A commercial for Black Flag bug spray had to be altered after a war veterans' group objected to the playing of taps over dead bugs.

It should be emphasized that most consumers did not find these ads particularly offensive.[12] Perhaps it is the spirit of political correctness that causes such scrutiny, or maybe it is that consumers are so overwhelmed with ads that they have simply lost their tolerance. Or, maybe some people are just plain silly. Whatever the explanation, advertisers today are more challenged than ever before to avoid being offensive with their ads.

Pro: Advertising Is a Source of Fulfillment and Liberation.   On the other end of the spectrum, there are those who argue that the consumption that advertising glorifies is actually quite good for members of society. Most sincerely appreciate modern conveniences that liberate us from the more foul facets of the natural, such as body odor, close contact with dirty diapers, and washing clothes by hand. Furthermore, this view holds that consumption is more likely to set one free than the slavish worship of an unpleasant, uncomfortable, and likely odoriferous, but natural, condition. Some observers remind us that when the Berlin Wall came down, those in the East did not immediately run to libraries and churches—they ran to department stores and shops. Before the modern consumer age, the consumption of many goods was restricted by social class. Modern advertising has helped bring us a democracy of goods. These observers argue that there is a liberating quality to advertising and consumption that should be appreciated and encouraged.

Con: Advertisers Deceive via Subliminal Stimulation.   There is much controversy, and almost a complete lack of understanding, regarding the issue of subliminal (below the threshold of consciousness) communication and advertising. Since there is much confusion surrounding

---

11.   Kevin Goldman, "From Witches to Anorexics, Critical Eyes Scrutinize Ads for Political Correctness," *Wall Street Journal,* May 19, 1994, B1, B10.
12.   Ibid.

the issue of subliminal advertising, perhaps this is the most appropriate point to provide some clarification: No one ever sold anything by putting images of breasts in ice cubes or the word *sex* in the background of an ad. Furthermore, no one at an advertising agency, except the very bored or the very eager to retire, has time to sit around dreaming up such things. We realize it makes for a great story, but hiding pictures in other pictures doesn't work to get anyone to buy anything. Although it is true that there is some evidence for some types of unconscious ad processing, these are effects related to repetition and ease of recall from memory, not the Svengali-type hocus-pocus that has become advertising mythology. If the rumors are true that advertisers are actually using subliminal messages in their ads (and they aren't), the conclusion should be that they're wasting their money.[13]

Pro: Advertising Is Art. Finally, there are those who argue that one of the best aspects of advertising is its artistic nature. The pop art movement of the late 1950s and 1960s, particularly in London and New York, was characterized by a fascination with commercial culture. Some of this art critiqued consumer culture and simultaneously celebrated it. Above all, Andy Warhol, himself a commercial illustrator, demonstrated that art was for the people and that the most accessible art was advertising. Art was not something restricted to museum walls; it was on Campbell's soup cans, Lifesaver rolls, and Brillo Pads. Advertising is anti-elitist, democratic art. As Warhol said about America, democracy, and Coke,

> *What's great about this country is that America started the tradition where the richest consumers buy essentially the same things as the poorest. You can be watching TV and see Coca-Cola, and you can know that the President drinks Coke, Liz Taylor drinks Coke, and just think, you can drink Coke, too. A Coke is a Coke and no amount of money can get you a better Coke than the one the bum on the corner is drinking. All the Cokes are the same and all the Cokes are good. Liz Taylor knows it, the President knows it, the bum knows it, and you know it.*[14]

Advertising Has a Powerful Effect on the Mass Media

One final issue that advertisers and their critics debate is the matter of advertising's influence on the mass media. Here again, we find a very wide range of viewpoints.

Pro: Advertising Fosters a Diverse and Affordable Mass Media. Advertising fans argue that advertising is the best thing that ever happened to an informed democracy. Magazines, newspapers, and television and radio stations are supported by advertising expenditures. In 1995, advertising expenditures in the United States reached nearly $160 billion, with worldwide advertising expenditures estimated to be around $400 billion.[15] Much of this spending went to support television, radio, magazines, and newspapers. With this sort of monetary support of the media, citizens have access to a variety of information and entertainment sources at low cost. Network television and radio broadcasts would not be free commodities, and newspapers would likely cost two to four times more, in the absence of advertising support. Further, the demands of various segments of the population for specialized television and radio programming or special interest magazines could not be economically served without the support of advertisers.

Others argue that advertising provides invaluable exposure to issues. When noncommercial users of advertising rely on the advertising process, members of society receive information on important social and political issues. Political candidates and

13.   Timothy E. Moore, "Subliminal Advertising: What You See Is What You Get," *Journal of Marketing* 46, no. 2 (spring 1982): 38–47.

14.   Andy Warhol, *The Philosophy of Andy Warhol: From A to B and Back Again* (New York: Harcourt Brace Jovanovich, 1975), 101.

15.   *Advertising Age,* September 30, 1996, 54.

Andy Warhol
Three Coke Bottles. 1962
Synthetic polymer paint and silkscreen ink on canvas, 20 × 16 in.

Jim Morrison 1943-1971   Janis Joplin 1943-1970

In advertising, they say one of the surest ways to get your message across is to put celebrities in your ad.

John Belushi 1949-1982   River Phoenix 1970-1993

Partnership for a Drug-Free America®

Here, the Partnership for a Drug-Free America makes provocative use of celebrities to send a powerful message.

proponents of political causes (for example, tax reform or environmental regulation) use advertising to inform voters. Similarly, various philanthropic organizations, such as the United Way and Special Olympics, use advertising to inform people of organization activities and to generate donations. At the local level, community fund-raisers for various artistic or community service organizations can benefit from advertising's ability to provide information efficiently to large numbers of people.

A dramatic example of the noncommercial use of advertising is the Centers for Disease Control's advertising campaign promoting AIDS awareness and prevention. These unusually explicit ads on television and radio urged young, sexually active adults to use latex condoms as a means of AIDS prevention. The ads were aired in both English and Spanish.[16] An ad from the Partnership for a Drug-Free America, shown in Exhibit 4.8, also carries a similar, compelling message.

Con: Advertising Affects Programming.
Critics argue that advertisers who place ads in media have an unhealthy effect on shaping the content of information contained in the media. For example, if a magazine that reviews and evaluates stereo equipment tests the equipment of one of its large advertisers, the contention is that the publication will hesitate to criticize the advertiser's equipment.

Another charge leveled at advertisers is that they purchase airtime only on programs that draw large audiences. Critics argue that these mass market programs lower the quality of television because cultural and educational programs, which draw smaller and more selective markets, are dropped in favor of mass market programs. Additionally, television programmers have a difficult time attracting advertisers to shows that may be valuable, yet controversial. Programs that deal with abortion, sexual abuse, or AIDS may have trouble drawing advertisers who fear the consequences of being associated with controversial issues.

The Ethical Aspects of Advertising

❷ Many of the ethical aspects of advertising border on and interact with both the social and legal considerations of the advertising process. **Ethics** are moral standards and principles against which behavior is judged. Honesty, integrity, fairness, and sensitivity are all included in a broad definition of ethical behavior. Much of what is judged as ethical or unethical comes down to personal judgment. We will discuss the ethical aspects of advertising in three areas: truth in advertising, advertising to children, and advertising controversial products.

16. Helene Cooper, "CDC Advocates Use of Condoms in Blunt AIDS-Prevention Spots, *Wall Street Journal,* January 5, 1994, B1, B7.

Truth in Advertising

While truth in advertising is a key legal issue, it has ethical dimensions as well. The most fundamental ethical issue has to do with **deception**—making false or misleading statements in an advertisement. The difficulty regarding this issue, of course, is in determining just what is deceptive. A manufacturer who claims a laundry product can remove grass stains is exposed to legal sanctions if the product cannot perform the task. Another manufacturer who claims to have "The Best Laundry Detergent in the World," however, is perfectly within its rights to employ superlatives. Just what constitutes "The Best" is a purely subjective determination; it cannot be proved or disproved. The use of absolute superlatives like "Number One" or "Best in the World" is sometimes called **puffery** and is considered completely legal. The courts have long held that superlatives are understood by consumers as simply the standard language of advertising and are interpreted by consumers as such.

It is likewise impossible to legislate against emotional appeals such as those made about the beauty or prestige-enhancing qualities of a product, because these claims are unquantifiable. Since these types of appeals are legal, the ethics of such appeals fall into a gray area. Beauty and prestige, it is argued, are in the eye of the beholder, and such appeals are neither illegal nor unethical. Although there are some narrowly defined legal parameters for truth in advertising (as we will discuss shortly), the ethical issues are not as clear-cut.

Advertising to Children

The desire to restrict advertising to children is based on three concerns. First, it is believed that advertising promotes superficiality and values founded in material goods and consumption—as we discussed earlier in the broader context of society as a whole. Second, children are considered inexperienced consumers and easy prey for the sophisticated persuasions of advertisers. Third, advertising influences children's demands for everything from toys to snack foods. These demands create an environment of child-parent conflict. Parents find themselves having to say no over and over again to children whose desires are piqued by effective advertising. As suggested in the Contemporary Issues box on page 91, Saturday morning remains a prime time for reaching youthful consumers.

There is also concern that many programs aimed at children constitute program-length commercials. Many critics argue that programs featuring commercial products, especially products aimed at children, are simply long advertisements. In 1990, critics pointed out that 70 programs were based on commercial products like He-Man, Smurfs, and the Muppets.[17] More recent examples include elaborate, hour-long television productions like "Treasure Island: The Adventure Begins." Critics claim that a program such as this, which features a young boy's vacation at the Las Vegas resort Treasure Island, blurs the boundary between programming and advertising. The program was produced by the Mirage Resorts (owners of Treasure Island), and the one-hour time slot was purchased from a major network, as advertising time, for an estimated $1.7 million.[18] While the program looks like an adventure show, critics argue it merely promotes the theme park and casino to kids, without ever revealing its sponsor. There have been several attempts by special interest groups to strictly regulate this type of programming aimed at children, but, to date, the Federal Communications Commission permits such programming to continue.

Advertising Controversial Products

Some people question the wisdom of allowing the advertising of controversial goods and services, such as tobacco, alcoholic beverages, gambling and lotteries, and firearms. Most frequently criticized are the advertising of cigarettes and alcoholic beverages. Critics charge these firms with tar-

---

17.   Patrick J. Sheridan, "FCC Sets Children's Ad Limits," *1990 Information Access Company* 119, no. 20 (1990): 33.
18.   Laura Bird, "NBC Special Is One Long Prime-Time Ad," *Wall Street Journal*, January 21, 1994, B1, B4.

geting children with their advertising and with making dangerous and addictive products appealing.[19] While advertising in all of these product areas is already restricted, there are serious efforts to impose even stricter constraints, such as banning pictures and image advertising in outdoor cigarette advertising or banning the advertising of these products altogether.

Critics have also called into question the targeting of ethnic and minority groups with products and advertising, such as with malt liquor ads. Similarly, the tobacco and alcohol industries have been the target of boycotts over their sponsorship of professional sporting events. These industries answer the critics with the counterclaim that the advertising is aimed at smokers and drinkers of legal age.[20] The firms argue that they have no intention of illegally selling products to minors.

Gambling and state-run lotteries represent another controversial product area with respect to advertising. What is the purpose of this advertising? Is it meant to inform gamblers and lottery players of the choices available? This would be selective demand stimulation. Or is such advertising designed to stimulate demand for engaging in wagering behavior? This would be primary demand stimulation. What of compulsive gamblers? What is the state's obligation to protect "vulnerable" citizens by restricting the placement or content of lottery advertising? When these vulnerable audiences are discussed, questions as to what is the basis for this vulnerability can become complex and emotionally charged. Those on one side of the issue argue that special audiences are among the "information poor," while those on the other side find such claims demeaning, patronizing, and paternalistic.

It is also critical to recognize that the courts have given limited First Amendment protection to advertising. As long as these products and services are legal and what is said about them is true, commercial free speech advocates argue that there should be no further restrictions. One of the dangers civil libertarians point to is the so-called slippery slope, or the scenario that once government is given one opportunity to restrict the advertising of one legal product, this action will begin the slow but inevitable slide down a slippery slope to unwanted and broadly applied government censorship. The issues involved are a long way from being resolved and play themselves out virtually every day in the news.

While we can group the ethical issues of advertising into some reasonable categories, it is not as easy to make definitive statements about the status of ethics in advertising. Ethics will always be a matter of personal values and personal interpretation.

CONTEMPORARY ISSUES

SATURDAY MORNING MERCHANDISING: ANIMATED PEDDLERS DOMINATE CHILDREN'S PROGRAMMING

Animated children's programming, once the home of Bugs Bunny and friends, has evolved into clever infomercial-like segments that serve to promote the retail merchandising of cartoon characters and toys. As a result, many children are becoming increasingly brand conscious at an early age. In addition, child-development experts feel that children's play mimics that of their screen heroes and action figures, and it thus may not be developmentally appropriate. The current influx of programming oriented around merchandising efforts began in the late 1980s with the Teenage Mutant Ninja Turtle craze. While turtlemania has dissipated, other characters have come to the fore, including the ubiquitous Power Rangers and newly animated versions of superheroes like Batman and Spiderman. That the advertising is encapsulated within seemingly standard programming has angered many parent groups, but the response of U.S. government has fallen short of further regulation. Interestingly, in several European countries—including Sweden, Denmark, and Norway—the Power Rangers and other similar programs have been summarily banned.

19.   Kathleen Deveny, "Joe Camel Ads Reach Children Research Finds," *Wall Street Journal,* December 11, 1991, B1, B6.
20.   Kevin Goldman, "Coors Ads Try Not to Attract Teen-Agers," *Wall Street Journal,* November 10, 1992, B10.

The Regulatory Aspects of Advertising

❸ The term *regulation* immediately brings to mind government scrutiny and control of the advertising process. There are, indeed, various government bodies that regulate advertising. But consumers themselves and several different industry organizations exert as much regulatory power over advertising as government bodies. Three primary groups—consumers, industry organizations, and government bodies—regulate advertising in the truest sense: They shape and restrict the process. The government relies on legal restrictions, while consumers and industry groups use less-formal controls.

First we will consider the areas of regulation most ardently pursued, whether it be by the government, consumers, or industry groups. Then we will examine the specific nature of the regulation exerted by these groups.

Areas of Advertising Regulation

There are three basic areas of advertising regulation: the content of advertisements, competitive issues, and advertising to children. Each of these areas is subject to regulation. At the outset, it is necessary to understand the factors related to each of these areas.

The Content of Advertisements.

Probably the majority of complaints against advertisers and their advertising efforts has to do with the content of advertising. In general, critics and those who desire greater regulation of the advertising process feel that advertising does not provide enough information for consumers to make informed decisions. There are two main content issues related to regulation: deception and unfairness, and poor taste.

Deception and Unfairness.

Agreement is widespread that deception in advertising is unacceptable. The problem, of course, is that it is as difficult to determine what is deceptive from a regulatory standpoint as from an ethical standpoint. The Federal Trade Commission (FTC) and a variety of court decisions have produced the following conclusions with regard to the nature of deception in advertising:

1. It is necessary only to establish the tendency or capacity to deceive, not the actual deception itself.
2. Misrepresentation of fact is considered deceptive.
3. A totally false statement cannot be qualified or modified.
4. A statement may be deceptive even though it is not literally construed to be misrepresentation.
5. In making product performance claims, substantial test data are needed to support the claims.
6. Products must be reasonably related to the size of the containers in which they are presented for sale.
7. There must be a reasonable basis for making product claims.
8. Ambiguous statements susceptible to both misleading and yet truthful interpretations will be construed against the advertiser.
9. Failure to disclose material facts where the effect is to deceive a substantial segment of the public is equal to deception.[21]

Many of these interpretations of what constitutes deceptive advertising and packaging have resulted in formal government programs designed to regulate such practices. But as we also discussed earlier, there can be complications in regulating puffery. Conventional wisdom has argued that consumers don't actually believe extreme claims and realize that advertisers are just trying to attract attention. There are those, however,

---

21. Drawn from an interpretation of FTC rulings and court decisions in William E. Francois, *Mass Media and Regulation* (Columbus, Ohio: Grid Publishing, 1975), 247–48.

who disagree with this view of puffery and feel that it actually represents "soft-core" deception, because some consumers believe the claims.[22]

While the FTC and the courts have been reasonably specific about what constitutes deception, the definition of unfairness has been left relatively vague until recently. In 1994, Congress ended a long-running dispute in the courts and in the advertising industry by approving legislation that defines **unfair advertising** as "acts or practices that cause or are likely to cause substantial injury to consumers, which is not reasonably avoidable by consumers themselves and not outweighed by the countervailing benefits to consumers or competition."[23] This definition will allow the FTC to proceed with the regulation of advertising it deems as unfair.

Poor Taste. We earlier discussed poor taste in advertising as a social issue. Advertising that is considered offensive or in poor taste is also subject to regulation. If deception in advertising is an elusive issue, then poor taste is a nearly impossible issue. Individual perceptions of what is tasteful and proper vary so widely that standardized criteria for advertising have never been defined. Some percentage of the population finds the mass media advertising of feminine hygiene products and contraceptive aids offensive. Others take a more liberalized view of these products and do not find such ads inappropriate. The use of sex in advertising is another prime area of controversy regarding taste. Sexually explicit or suggestive ads regularly create a furor within certain segments of the population. Conversely, marketers around the world, particularly in France and Brazil, commonly use nudity as an artistic expression in advertisements.

Media and industry associations act as watchdogs over advertisements and can apply pressure to advertisers whose ads are deemed in poor taste. Further, the Federal Communications Commission (FCC) has a long list of words that are specified as obscene.

Competitive Issues. Because the large dollar amounts spent on advertising can lead to unfair competition, there are several advertising practices relating to competition that can result in regulation: cooperative advertising, comparison advertising, and using monopoly power.

Vertical cooperative advertising is an advertising technique whereby a manufacturer and dealer (either a wholesaler or retailer) share the expense of advertising. This technique is commonly used in regional or local markets where a manufacturer wants a brand to benefit from a special promotion run by local dealers. There is nothing illegal, per se, about the technique, and it is used regularly. The competitive threat inherent in the process, however, is that dealers (especially since the advent of department store chains) can be given bogus cooperative advertising allowances. These allowances require no effort or expenditure on the part of the dealer and thus represent hidden price concessions. As such, they are a form of unfair competition and are deemed illegal. If an advertising allowance is granted to a dealer, that dealer must demonstrate that the funds are applied specifically to advertising.

The potential exists for firms to engage in unfair competition if they use comparison ads inappropriately. **Comparison advertisements** are those in which an advertiser makes a comparison between the firm's brand and competitors' brands. The comparison may or may not explicitly identify the competition. Again, comparison ads are completely legal and are used frequently by all sorts of organizations. However, if the advertisement is carried out in such a way that the comparison is not a fair one, then there is an unjust competitive effect. The American Association of Advertising Agencies (4As) has issued a set of guidelines, shown in Exhibit 4.9, regarding the use of comparison ads. Further, the Federal Trade Commission may require a firm using comparison to substantiate the claims made in the advertisement.

22.   Ivan Preston, *The Great American Blow Up* (Madison, Wis.: University of Wisconsin Press, 1975), 4.
23.   Christy Fisher, "How Congress Broke Unfair Ad Impasse," *Advertising Age*, August 22, 1994, 34.

EXHIBIT 4.9

*American Association of
Advertising Agencies'
guidelines for comparison
advertising.*

The Board of Directors of the American Association of Advertising Agencies recognizes that when used truthfully and fairly, comparative advertising provides the consumer with needed and useful information. However, extreme caution should be exercised. The use of comparative advertising, by its very nature, can distort facts and, by implication, convey to the consumer information that misrepresents the truth. Therefore, the Board believes that comparative advertising should follow certain guidelines:

1. The intent and connotation of the ad should be to inform and never to discredit or unfairly attack competitors.
2. When a competitive product is named, it should be one that exists in the marketplace as significant competition.
3. The competition should be fairly and properly identified, but never in a manner or tone of voice that degrades the competitive product or service.
4. The advertising should compare related or similar properties or ingredients of the product, dimension to dimension, feature to feature.
5. The identification should be for honest comparison purposes and not simply to upgrade by association.
6. If a competitive test is conducted, it should be done by an objective testing source, preferably an independent one, so that there will be no doubt as to the veracity of the test.
7. In all cases, the test should be supportive of all claims made in the advertising based on the test.
8. The advertising should never use partial results or stress insignificant differences to cause the consumer to draw an improper conclusion.
9. The property being compared should be significant in terms of value or usefulness of the product to the consumer.
10. Comparatives delivered through the use of testimonials should not imply that the testimonial is more than one individual's thought unless that individual represents a sample of the majority viewpoint.

Source: American Association of Advertising Agencies.

Finally, some firms are so powerful in their use of advertising that **monopoly power** by virtue of the advertising can become a problem. This issue normally arises in the context of mergers and acquisitions. As an example, the U.S. Supreme Court blocked the acquisition of Clorox by Procter & Gamble because the advertising power of the two firms combined would (in the opinion of the Court) make it nearly impossible for another firm to compete.

Advertising Aimed at Children. Critics argue that continuously bombarding children with persuasive stimuli can alter their motivation and behavior. While government organizations like the Federal Trade Commission (FTC) have been active in trying to regulate advertising directed at children, industry and consumer groups have been more successful in securing restrictions. The consumer group known as Action for Children's Television (discussed in Chapter 3) was actively involved in getting Congress to approve the Children's Television Act (1990). This act limits the amount of commercial airtime during children's programs to 10½ minutes on weekdays and 12 minutes on weekends. The Council of Better Business Bureaus established a Children's Advertising Review Unit and has issued a set of guidelines for advertising directed at children. These guidelines emphasize that advertisers be sensitive to the level of knowledge and sophistication of children as decision makers. The guidelines also urge advertisers to make a constructive contribution to the social development of children by emphasizing positive social standards in advertising, like friendship, kindness, honesty, and generosity. Similarly, the major television networks have set their own guidelines for advertising aimed at children. The guidelines restrict the use of celebrities, prohibit exhortive language (such as "Go ask dad"), and restrict the use of animation to one-third of the total time of the commercial.

Regulatory Agents

At the outset of this chapter, it was pointed out that consumers and industry and government bodies all participate in the regulation of advertising. We will now discuss each of these agents of regulatory influence in advertising and the kind of influence they exert.

Government Regulation. Governments have a powerful tool available for regulating advertising: the threat of legal action. As suggested in the Regulatory Issues box on page 96, advertising regulation can vary dramatically from country to country. In the United States, several different government agencies have been given the power and responsibility to regulate the advertising process. Exhibit 4.10 identifies the six agencies that have legal powers over advertising and their areas of regulatory responsibility.

There are several other agencies with minor powers in the regulation of advertising, such as the Civil Aeronautics Board (advertising by air carriers), the Patent Office (trademark infringement), and the Library of Congress (copyright protection). The agencies listed in Exhibit 4.10 are the most directly involved in advertising regulation. Most active among these agencies is the Federal Trade Commission. It is this agency that has the most power and is most directly involved in controlling the advertising process. The FTC has been granted legal power through legislative mandates and also has developed programs for regulating advertising.

EXHIBIT 4.10

Primary government agencies regulating advertising.

Government Agency	Areas of Advertising Regulation
Federal Trade Commission (FTC)	Most widely empowered agency in government. Controls unfair methods of competition, regulates deceptive advertising, and has various programs for controlling the advertising process.
Federal Communications Commission (FCC)	Prohibits obscenity, fraud, and lotteries on radio and television. Ultimate power lies in the ability to deny or revoke broadcast licenses.
Food and Drug Administration (FDA)	Regulates the advertising of food, drug, cosmetic, and medical products. Can require special labeling for hazardous products like household cleaners. Prohibits false labeling and packaging.
Securities and Exchange Commission (SEC)	Regulates the advertising of securities and the disclosure of information in annual reports.
U.S. Postal Service	Responsible for regulating direct mail advertising and prohibits lotteries, fraud, and misrepresentation. It can also regulate and impose fines for materials deemed to be obscene.
Bureau of Alcohol, Tobacco, and Firearms	Most direct influence has been on regulation of advertising for alcoholic beverages. This agency was responsible for putting warning labels on alcoholic beverage advertising and banning active athletes as celebrities in beer ads. It has the power to determine what constitutes misleading advertising in these product areas.

The FTC's Legislative Mandates. The Federal Trade Commission was created by the FTC Act in 1914. The original purpose of the agency was to prohibit unfair methods of competition. In 1916, the FTC concluded that false advertising was one way in which a firm could take unfair advantage of another, and advertising was introduced as a primary concern of the agency.

It was not until 1938 that the effects of deceptive advertising on consumers became an issue for the FTC. Until the passage of the Wheeler-Lea Amendment (1938), the commission was concerned only with the effect of advertising on competition. The amendment broadened the FTC's powers to include regulation of advertising that was misleading to the public (regardless of the effect on competition). Through this amendment, the agency could apply a cease and desist order, which required a firm to stop its deceptive practices. It also granted the agency specific jurisdiction over drug, cosmetic, and food advertising.

Several other acts provide the FTC with legal powers over advertising. The Robinson-Patman Act (1936) prohibits firms from providing phantom cooperative-advertising allowances as a way to court important dealers. Regulatory power over labeling and advertising disclosure was provided to the commission by the Wool Products Labeling Act (1939), the Fur Products Labeling Act (1951), and the Textile Fiber Products Act (1958). Consumer protection legislation, which seeks to increase the ability of consumers to make more-informed product comparisons, includes the Fair Packaging and Labeling Act (1966), the Truth in Lending Act (1969), and the Fair Credit Reporting Act (1970). The FTC Improvement Act (1975) expanded the authority of the commission by giving it the power to issue trade regulation rules.

Recent legislation is related to the FTC's role in monitoring and regulating advertising. The Nutrition Labeling and Education Act (1990) requires uniformity in the nutrition labeling of food products and establishes strict rules for health claims and the nutritional attributes of food products. Finally, as mentioned, the Children's Television Act (1990) limits the minutes of advertising allowable during television programs for children.

The legislation just described provides the FTC with various methods of recourse when advertising practices are judged to be deceptive or misleading. The spirit of all these acts relates to the maintenance of an equitable competitive environment and the protection of consumers from misleading information. It is interesting to note, however, that direct involvement of the FTC in advertising practices more often comes about from its regulatory programs and remedies than from the application of legal mandates.

REGULATORY ISSUES

SINO SNAKE OIL: ADVERTISING ETHICS NOW ENFORCED IN MAINLAND CHINA

The Chinese economic boom of recent years has been accompanied by a rapid growth of advertising in that country. In the last decade alone, ad spending has multiplied nearly 100 times over, with literally thousands of advertising agencies sprouting up in just the past few years. With the state-owned media companies under increasing pressure to remain profitable, however, the government stations have been loath to police advertising content and turn away vital ad dollars. Numerous misleading, inflated, or false product claims have ensued, with toothpaste that cures cancer, soap that wipes ten years off a woman's face, and a single-pill cure for hepatitis, among others. To curb abuse of the ill-defined regulations, Chinese officials passed their first comprehensive advertising law late in 1994. The enforcement has been both swift and sure; following a screening of nearly 1,500 television commercials in January 1995, the Chinese State Administration for Industry and Commerce found that 90 of the ads were in violation of the new law and blocked them from airing. The Chinese advertising community has taken notice. "Before they were just regulations," says Dennis Wong, managing director of Leo Burnett's Chinese operations. "Now they're laws."

Source: "Chinese Officials Attempt to Ban False Ad Claims," *Wall Street Journal*, February 28, 1995, B1.

The FTC's Regulatory Programs and Remedies. The application of legislation has evolved as the FTC exercises its powers and expands its role as a regulatory agency. This evolution of the FTC has spawned several regulatory programs and remedies to help enforce legislative mandates in specific situations.

The **advertising substantiation program** of the FTC was initiated in 1971 with the intention of ensuring that advertisers make available to consumers supporting evidence for claims made. The program was strengthened in 1972 when the commission forwarded the notion of "reasonable basis" for the substantiation of advertising. This extension suggests not only that advertisers should substantiate their claims, but also that the substantiation should provide a reasonable basis for believing the claims are true.[24] The implication is that if a claim has not been reasonably substantiated before being made in an advertisement, then it is considered unlawful whether or not the FTC can in fact prove it is false.

Affirmative disclosure is another remedy available to the FTC. An advertisement that fails to disclose important material facts about a product can be deemed deceptive, and the FTC may require **affirmative disclosure** in future advertising, whereby the important material absent from prior ads must be included in subsequent advertisements. The absence of important material information may cause consumers to make false assumptions about products in comparison to the competition. Such was the case with Geritol; the FTC ordered the makers of the product to disclose that "iron poor blood" was not the universal cause of tiredness.

The consent order and the cease and desist order are the most basic remedies used by the FTC in dealing with deceptive or unfair advertising. In a **consent order,** an advertiser accused of running deceptive or unfair advertising agrees to stop running the advertisements in question, without admitting guilt. For advertisers who do not comply voluntarily, the FTC can issue a **cease and desist order,** which requires that the advertising in question be stopped within 30 days so a hearing can be held to determine whether the advertising is deceptive or unfair.

The most severe remedy for advertising determined to be misleading is **corrective advertising.**[25] In cases where evidence suggests that consumers have developed false beliefs about a brand based on misleading or deceptive advertising, the firm may be required to run corrective ads in an attempt to dispel those false beliefs. The commission has specified not only the message content for corrective ads, but also the budgetary allocation, the duration of transmission, and the placement of the advertising. Corrective advertising attempts to rectify false beliefs created by deceptive advertising.

The final area of FTC regulation and remedy has to do with **celebrity endorsements.** The FTC has specific rules for advertisements that use an expert or celebrity as a spokesperson to endorse the use of a product. In the case of experts (those whose experience or training allows a superior judgment of products), the endorser's actual qualifications must justify his or her status as an expert. In the case of celebrities (such as Michael Jordan as a spokesperson for McDonald's), FTC guidelines indicate that the celebrity must be an actual user of the product, or the ad is considered deceptive.

These regulatory programs and remedies provide the FTC a great deal of control over the advertising process. Numerous ads have been interpreted as questionable under the guidelines of the programs, and advertisements have been altered. It is likely also that advertisers and their agencies, who are keenly aware of the ramifications of violating

24. For a discussion of the FTC advertising substantiation program and its extension to require reasonable basis, see Debra L. Scammon and Richard J. Semenik, "The FTC's 'Reasonable Basis' for Substantiation of Advertising: Expanded Standards and Implications," *Journal of Advertising* 12, no. 1 (1983): 4–11.

25. A history of the corrective-advertising concept and several of its applications is provided by Debra L. Scammon and Richard J. Semenik, "Corrective Advertising: Evolution of the Legal Theory and Application of the Remedy," *Journal of Advertising* 11, no. 1 (1982): 10–20.

FTC precepts, have developed ads with these constraints in mind. However, as indicated by the New Media box on this page, advertising regulation is clearly dynamic: with each new medium that emerges, new regulatory challenges emerge as well.

Industry Self-Regulation.   ❹ Advertisers have come a long way in terms of their self-control and restraint. Some of this improvement is due to tougher government regulation, and some to industry self-regulation. Self-regulation is the industry's attempt to police itself. Supportors say it is a shining example of how unnecessary government intervention is, while critics point to it as a joke, an elaborate shell game. According to the critics, meaningful self-regulation occurs only when the threat of government action is imminent. How you see this controversy is largely dependent on your own personal experience and level of cynicism.

Several industry and trade associations and public service organizations have voluntarily established guidelines for advertising within their industries. The reasoning is that self-regulation is good for the advertising community as a whole and promotes the credibility, and therefore the effectiveness, of advertising itself. Exhibit 4.11 lists the various business organizations that have taken on the task of regulating and monitoring advertising, and the year when each established a code by which to judge the acceptability of advertising.

The purpose of self-regulation by these organizations is to evaluate the content and quality of advertisements specific to their industries. The effectiveness of such organizations depends on the cooperation of members and the policing mechanisms used. Each organization exerts an influence on the nature of advertising in its industry. Some are particularly noteworthy in their activities and warrant further discussion.

NEW MEDIA

THE WILD WEST OF ADVERTISING: ONLINE SERVICES AND THE WORLD WIDE WEB

"On the Net there are no real rules," says Deborah Young, a spokeswoman for CompuServe. While the American online companies (America Online, Prodigy, and CompuServe) claim to monitor and regulate their offerings, all bets are off once the services provide access to the freewheeling Internet. Goldschlager, one of the fastest-growing liqueur brands in the United States, has developed a virtual billboard that users can download as a screen saver, and Jim Beam Brands now maintains a virtual bar on the Internet, where users can copy drink recipes and even scrawl graffiti on the virtual bathroom walls. The question for regulators: Is cyberspace like television or like magazines? Neither, really. As brands move online and compete for exposure, they must provide *real* content to the user, and this is where the media differ widely. Watching television is a rather passive experience, and advertising is easily avoided through flipping channels. Print media, while more engrossing, may also be dismissed easily. The consumer's reactions to both television and magazines are *reactive,* while navigating the world of online Internet choices is decidedly *proactive.* Lynn Upshaw, managing director of Ketchum Interactive Group, San Francisco, says that "you can't just throw an ad in front of someone. A commercial presence on the Internet should offer about 80 to 90 percent value, and 10 to 20 percent ad." Users must then be enticed to visit a particular web site, and the ethical questions posed by this arrangement may well invite future government regulation. Indeed, many in the advertising world feel it is simply a question of time.

Sources: "Cheers! It's Happy Hour in Cyberspace," *Wall Street Journal,* March 15, 1995, B1; and "New Rules Apply As Brands Move Online," *Advertising Age,* May 8, 1995, 41.

The National Advertising Review Board.
One important self-regulation organization is the Council of Better Business Bureaus' National Advertising Review Board (NARB). The NARB is the operations arm of the National Advertising Division (NAD) of the Council of Better Business Bureaus. Complaints received from consumers, competitors, or local branches of the Better Business Bureau are forwarded to the NAD. After a full review of the complaint, the issue may be forwarded to the NARB and evaluated by a panel. The complete procedure for dealing with complaints is detailed in Exhibit 4.12.

The NAD maintains a permanent professional staff that works to resolve complaints with the advertiser and its agency before the issue gets to the NARB. If no resolution

EXHIBIT 4.11

*Selected business organiza-
tions and industry associations
with advertising self-regulation
programs.*

Organization	Code Established
Advertising Associations	
American Advertising Federation	1965
American Association of Advertising Agencies	1924
Association of National Advertisers	1972
Business/Professional Advertising Association	1975
Special Industry Groups	
Council of Better Business Bureaus	1912
Household furniture	1978
Automobiles and trucks	1978
Carpet and rugs	1978
Home improvement	1975
Charitable solicitations	1974
Children's Advertising Review Unit	1974
National Advertising Division/National Advertising	
Review Board	1971
Media Associations	
American Business Press	1910
Direct Mail Marketing Association	1960
Direct Selling Association	1970
National Association of Broadcasters	
Radio	1937
Television	1952
Outdoor Advertising Association of America	1950
Selected Trade Associations	
American Wine Association	1949
Wine Institute	1949
Distilled Spirits Association	1934
United States Brewers Association	1955
Pharmaceutical Manufacturers Association	1958
Proprietary Association	1934
Bank Marketing Association	1976
Motion Picture Association of America	1930
National Swimming Pool Institute	1970
Toy Manufacturers Association	1962

is achieved, the complaint is appealed to the NARB, which appoints a panel made up of three advertiser representatives, one agency representative, and one public representative. This panel then holds hearings regarding the advertising in question. The advertiser is allowed to present the firm's case. If no agreement can be reached by the panel either to dismiss the case or to convince the advertiser to change the advertising, then the NARB initiates two actions. First, the NARB publicly identifies the advertiser,

EXHIBIT 4.12

Flow diagram of the NAD and NARB regulatory process.

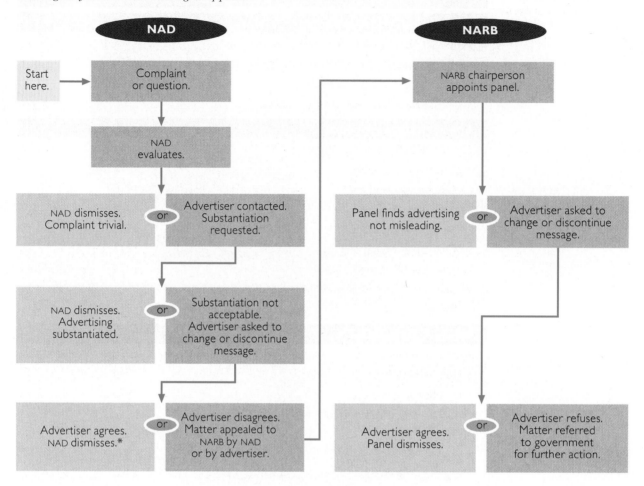

*If the complaint originated outside the system, the outside complainant can appeal at this point to the NARB chairperson for a panel adjudication. Granting of such an appeal is at the chairperson's discretion.

the complaint against the advertiser, and the panel's findings. Second, the case is forwarded to an appropriate government regulatory agency (usually the Federal Trade Commission).

The NAD and the NARB are not empowered to impose penalties on advertisers, but the threat of going before the board acts as a deterrent to deceptive and questionable advertising practices. Further, the regulatory process of the NAD and the NARB is probably less costly and time consuming for all parties involved than if every complaint were handled by a government agency.

State and Local Better Business Bureaus. Aside from the national Better Business Bureau (BBB), there are more than 140 separate local bureaus. Each local organization is supported by membership dues paid by area businesses. The three divisions of a local BBB—merchandise, financial, and solicitations—investigate the advertising and selling practices of firms in their areas. A local BBB has the power to forward a complaint to the NAD for evaluation.

Beyond its regulatory activities, the Better Business Bureau tries to avert problems associated with advertising by counseling new businesses and providing information to advertisers and agencies regarding legislation, potential problem areas, and industry standards.

Advertising Agencies and Associations. It makes sense that advertising agencies and their industry associations would engage in self-regulation. An individual agency is legally responsible for the advertising it produces and is subject to reprisal for deceptive or misleading claims. The agency is in a difficult position in that it must monitor not only the activities of its own people, but also the information provided to the agency by clients. Should a client direct an agency to use a product appeal that turns out to be untruthful, the agency is still responsible.

The American Association of Advertising Agencies has no legal or binding power over its agency members, but it can apply pressure when its board feels industry standards are not being upheld. The 4As also publishes guidelines for its members regarding various aspects of advertising messages. One of the most widely recognized industry standards is the 4As' Creative Code. The code outlines the responsibilities and social impact advertising can have and promotes high ethical standards of honesty and decency.

Media Organizations. Individual media organizations evaluate the advertising they receive for broadcast and publication. The National Association of Broadcasters (NAB) has a policing arm known as the Code Authority, which implements and interprets the separate radio and television codes. These codes deal with truth, fairness, and good taste in broadcast advertising.

Newspapers have historically been rigorous in their screening of advertising. Many newspapers have internal departments to screen and censor ads believed to be in violation of the newspaper's advertising standards. While the magazine industry does not have a formal code, many individual publications have very high standards. We are all familiar with the Good Housekeeping Seal of Approval. The Good Housekeeping Institute claims to spend more than $1 million a year testing products to ensure that advertising appeals are in fact truthful.

Direct mail may have a poor image among many consumers, but its industry association, the Direct Marketing Association (DMA), is active in promoting ethical behavior and standards among its members. It has published guidelines for ethical business practices. In 1971, the association established the Direct Mail Preference service, which enables consumers to have their names removed from most direct mail lists.

A review of all aspects of industry self-regulation suggests not only that there are a variety of programs and organizations designed to monitor advertising, but also that many of these programs are effective. Those whose livelihoods depend on advertising are just as interested as consumers and legislators in maintaining high standards. If advertising deteriorates into an unethical and untrustworthy business activity, the economic vitality of many organizations will be compromised. Self-regulation can help prevent such a circumstance and, as such, is in the best self-interest of all the organizations discussed here.

Consumers as Regulatory Agents. Consumers themselves are motivated to act as regulatory agents based on a variety of interests, including product safety, reasonable choice, and the right to information. Advertising tends to be a focus of consumer regulatory activities because of its conspicuousness. Consumerism and consumer organizations have provided the primary vehicles for consumer regulatory efforts.

Consumerism. Consumerism, the actions of individual consumers to exert power over the marketplace activities of organizations, is by no means a recent phenomenon. The earliest consumerism efforts can be traced to seventeenth-century England. In the United States, there have been recurring consumer movements throughout the twentieth century.

In general, these movements have focused on the same issue: Consumers want a greater voice in the whole process of product development, distribution, and information dissemination. Most consumer movements try to create pressures on firms by withholding patronage through boycotts. Some boycotts have been effective. Firms as powerful as Procter & Gamble, Kimberly-Clark, and General Mills all have responded to threats of boycotts by pulling advertising from programs consumers found offensive.[26]

Consumer Organizations. The other major consumer effort to bring about regulation is through consumer organizations. The following are the most prominent consumer organizations and the activities they engage in:

- *Consumer Federation of America (CFA).* This organization was founded in 1968 and now includes over 200 national, state, and local consumer groups and labor unions as affiliate members. The goals of the CFA are to encourage the creation of consumer organizations, provide services to consumer groups, and act as a clearinghouse for information exchange between consumer groups.
- *Consumers Union.* This nonprofit consumer organization is best known for its publication of *Consumer Reports.* Established in 1936, Consumers Union has as its stated purpose "to provide consumers with information and advice on goods, services, health, and personal finance; and to initiate and cooperate with individual and group efforts to maintain and enhance the quality of life for consumers."[27] This organization supports itself through the sale of publications and accepts no funding, including advertising revenues, from any commercial organization.
- *Action for Children's Television (ACT).* ACT has been active in conjunction with the national Parent-Teacher Association in trying to initiate boycotts against the products of advertisers who sponsor programs that are violent in nature. On its own, ACT has lobbied government bodies to enact legislation restricting the use of premiums in advertising to children and the use of popular cartoon characters in promoting products.

These three consumer organizations are the most active and potent of the consumer groups, but there are literally hundreds of such groups organized by geographic location or product category. Consumers have proved that with an organized effort, corporations can and will change their practices. In one of the most publicized events in recent times, consumers applied pressure to Coca-Cola and, in part, were responsible for forcing the firm to remarket the original formula of Coca-Cola (as Coca-Cola Classic). If consumers are able to exert such a powerful and nearly immediate influence on a firm like Coca-Cola, one wonders what other changes they could effect in the market.

---

26.   Alix M. Freedman, "Never Have So Few Scared So Many Television Sponsors," *Wall Street Journal,* March 20, 1989, B4.
27.   This statement of purpose can be found on the inside cover of any issue of *Consumer Reports.*

SUMMARY

❶ Assess the benefits and drawbacks of advertising in a capitalistic society and debate a variety of issues concerning advertising's effects on societal well-being.

Advertisers have always been followed by proponents and critics. Proponents of advertising argue that it offers benefits for individual consumers and society at large. At the societal level, proponents claim, advertising helps promote a higher standard of living by allowing marketers to reap the rewards for product improvements and innovation. Advertising also "pays for" mass media in many countries, and provides consumers with a constant flow of information not only about products and services, but also about political and social issues.

Over the years critics have leveled many charges at advertising and advertising practitioners. Advertising expenditures in the multibillions are condemned as wasteful, offensive, and a source of frustration for many in society who see the lavish lifestyle portrayed in advertising, knowing they will never be able to afford such a lifestyle. Critics also contend that advertisements rarely furnish useful information but instead perpetuate superficial stereotypes of many cultural subgroups. For many years, some critics have been concerned that advertisers are controlling us against our will with subliminal advertising messages.

❷ Explain how ethical considerations affect the development of advertising campaigns.

Ethical considerations are a concern when creating advertising, especially when that advertising will be targeted to children or will involve controversial products like firearms, gambling, alcohol, or cigarettes. While ethical standards are a matter for personal reflection, it certainly is the case

that unethical people can create unethical advertising. It is also true that there are many safeguards against such behavior, including the corporate and personal integrity of advertisers.

❸ Discuss the role of government agencies in the regulation of advertising.

Governments typically are involved in the regulation of advertising. It is important to recognize that advertising regulations can vary dramatically from one country to the next. In the United States, the Federal Trade Commission (FTC) has been especially active in trying to deter deception and unfairness in advertising. The FTC was established in 1914, and since then a variety of legislation has been passed to expand the powers of the FTC. The FTC has also developed regulatory remedies that have expanded its involvement in advertising regulation, like the advertising substantiation program.

❹ Explain the meaning and importance of self-regulation for an advertising practitioner.

Some of the most important controls on advertising are voluntary; that is, they are a matter of self-regulation by advertising and marketing professionals. For example, the American Association of Advertising Agencies has issued guidelines for promoting fairness and accuracy when using comparative advertisements. Many other organizations, such as the Better Business Bureau, the National Association of Broadcasters, and Action for Children's Television, participate in the process to help ensure fairness and assess consumer complaints about advertising.

KEY TERMS

ethics (89)
deception (90)
puffery (90)
unfair advertising (93)
vertical cooperative advertising (93)
comparison advertisements (93)
monopoly power (94)

advertising substantiation program (97)
affirmative disclosure (97)
consent order (97)
cease and desist order (97)
corrective advertising (97)
celebrity endorsements (97)
consumerism (101)

QUESTIONS FOR REVIEW AND CRITICAL THINKING

1.   Advertising has been a focal point of criticism for many decades. In your opinion, what are some of the key factors that make advertising controversial?

2.   You have probably been exposed to hundreds of thousands of advertisements in your lifetime. In what ways does exposure to advertising make you a better consumer?

3.   Use Maslow's well-known hierarchy of needs to address critics' concerns that too much of advertising is directed at creating demand for products that are irrelevant to people's true needs.

4.   What does it mean to suggest that an advertisement projects a stereotype? How might this problem of stereotyping be related to the process of market segmentation?

5.   One type of advertising that attracts the attention of regulators, critics, and consumer advocates is advertising directed at children. Why is it the focal point of so much attention?

6.   What is comparison advertising, and why does this form of advertising need a special set of guidelines to prevent unfair competition?

7.   Explain why a marketer might be tempted to misuse cooperative advertising allowances to favor some kinds of retailers over others. What piece of legislation empowered the FTC to stop these bogus allowances?

8.   Some contend that self-regulation is the best way to ensure fair and truthful advertising practices. Why would it be in the best interests of the advertising community to aggressively pursue self-regulation?

EXPERIENTIAL EXERCISE

In this chapter you read about the social aspects of advertising. Imagine you are speaking with an individual who is totally unfamiliar with life in the United States. To inform your companion about life here, find five magazine ads that reflect societal characteristics of Americans. Describe for your companion how each ad reflects American society and values.

USING THE INTERNET

Visit the following four sites and consider the social and ethical issues each raises about advertising.

Global Casino: www.gamblenet.com

Stoli: www.stoli.com

Playboy: www.playboy.com

Loopy: www.loopy.com

1.   What issues would consumer advocate groups raise for this site? What personally concerns you about this site? Justify your arguments with information from the site.

2.   Many children surf the net. Does that affect your previous evaluation of the site?

3.   What steps have these companies taken to regulate themselves?

4.   What regulations would you suggest for Internet advertising in light of these issues?

Now, visit the FTC site at www.ftc.gov and read the latest FTC news.

5.   Are there any pending regulations affecting advertising on the Internet?

▲ Delta Air Lines

The Process of Integrated Marketing Communications

In Chapter 1, we introduced the concept of integrated marketing communications (IMC). The discussion there highlighted the relationship between IMC and the advertising process. Now we want to focus on integrated marketing communications itself. The rise in prominence of IMC makes it essential that this evolving perspective on communications be understood as a context for the advertising process. Sophisticated marketers like Upjohn, Pepsi, and Mercedes are more frequently using promotional tools like direct marketing, event sponsorship, the Internet, and CD-ROMs in conjunction with advertising.[1]

The sections at the end of each part of this text will help you better understand integrated marketing communications by examining the topic in two ways. First, each section will discuss IMC relative to each part of the text. These discussions will lay out the principles of IMC as a method for creating effective communications. Second, we will apply these basic principles of IMC to the promotional programs of Delta Air Lines. Delta uses a wide range of communications tools to support its goal of gaining and sustaining market share in the fiercely competitive global airline services market. Together, these two kinds of discussions—the general principles of IMC and its application in a real-world setting—result in a complete view of this new and important perspective on communications. This first section, "The Process of Integrated Marketing Communications," offers a definition and industry perspective on IMC.

Its Nature and Scope

The American Association of Advertising Agencies (4As) defines **integrated marketing communications** this way:

a concept of marketing communications planning that recognizes the added value of a comprehensive plan that evaluates the strategic role of a variety of communications disciplines—for example, general advertising, direct response, sales promotion, and public relations—and combines these disciplines to provide clarity, consistency and maximum communications impact.[2]

Schultz, Tannenbaum, and Lauterborn, the most vigorous proponents of IMC, offer this observation:

What is integrated marketing communications? It's a new way of looking at the whole, where once we only saw parts such as advertising, public relations, sales promotion, purchasing, employee communications, and so forth. It's realigning communications to look at it the way the customer sees it—as a flow of information from indistinguishable sources.[3]

Notice that these descriptions highlight that IMC programs use many different promotional tools, from advertising through employee communications (like newsletters), to create unified and memorable communications.

Factors Contributing to Its Rising Prominence

But why is it that IMC has become so popular over the past few years? Several significant and pervasive changes in the communications environment have contributed to the rising prominence of IMC:

- *Fragmentation of media.* Media options available to marketers have proliferated at an astounding rate. Broadcast media now offer "narrowcasting" so specific that advertisers can reach consumers at precise locations, like airports and supermarket checkout counters. The print media have proliferated dramatically as well. At one point, there were 197 different sports magazines on the market in the United States! The proliferation and fragmentation of media have resulted in less reliance on mass media and more emphasis on other promotional options, like direct mail and event sponsorship.

- *Consumer empowerment.* Consumers today are more powerful than their predecessors. Fostering this greater power are more single person households, smaller families, higher education levels, and more experienced consumers. Empowered consumers are more skeptical of commercial messages and are demanding information tailored to their precise information desires.
- *Database technology.* The ability of firms to generate, collate, and manage databases has created diverse communications opportunities beyond mass media. These databases can be used to create customer and noncustomer profiles. With this information, highly targeted direct response and telemarketing programs can be implemented.
- *Channel power.* In some product and market categories, there has been a shift in power away from big manufacturers and toward big retailers. The new "power retailers," like Wal-Mart, The Gap, Toys 'R' Us, and Home Depot, are able to demand promotional fees and allowances from manufacturers, which diverts funds away from advertising and into events or special promotions.
- *Accountability.* In an attempt to achieve greater accountability for promotional spending, firms have reallocated promotional dollars from advertising to more short-term and more easily measurable methods like direct response and sales promotion.

All of these factors have contributed to an increase in the diversity and complexity of the communications tools used by firms to inform and persuade target audiences. Advertising, of course, still plays a lead role in the communications programs of most firms, whether they are IMC oriented or not. But the opportunity to use other promotional tools makes coordinating and integrating communications more challenging than in the past. Both clients and advertising agencies, however, see the payoff as great:

Integrated marketing communications is emerging as one of the most valuable "magic bullets" a firm can use to gain competitive advantage.

—James C. Reilly, IBM

Integrated marketing communications identifies the dynamics of today's marketplace and teaches us how easy it is to prosper under the new rules [of communication].

—Richard Fizdale, Leo Burnett[4]

Its Participants and Tools

The process of IMC as it is typically implemented by an organization and its advertising and specialty agencies is shown in Exhibit IMC 1.1. Notice that the firm itself brings to the IMC process a marketing plan, goals and objectives, and any databases that will identify customers and prospective customers. These databases are developed from customer contacts or are purchased from specialty research firms. The firm's advertising agency will help in researching the market, suggesting creative strategies, and producing integrated marketing communications materials. In addition, agencies can aid in strategically placing materials in outlets that range from traditional mass media to event sponsorship and even unique efforts like product placements in films or television programs.

The IMC process as it is depicted in Exhibit IMC 1.1 shows the participants and the tools of IMC. At the end of Part 2 of the text, the "Planning Integrated Marketing Communications" section will look at the strategic planning that goes into the development of an IMC program. For now, let's turn our attention to how the integrated marketing communications process is organized at Delta Air Lines.

The Process of Integrated Marketing Communications at Delta Air Lines

Headquartered in Atlanta, Georgia, Delta Air Lines has grown to become one of the premier airlines in the world. With 4,900 flights per day to over 300 cities in 41 countries, Delta alone serves more passengers than any other airline.[5]

And the airline has done it in fine style. In 1995, Delta won the Best Airline in Overall Satisfaction award from J. D. Powers and Associates; the Best Airline award from *Robb Report,* as voted by readers of *Robb Report* magazine; the Top U.S. Carrier award from *Business Traveler International;* and the Best U.S. Domestic Airline award from *USA Today (International Edition)*. More recently, Delta has won Best Economy Class and Best Cellars (for their wine selection) from *Business Traveler International.*

As much as any organization in the world, Delta Air Lines has enormous communications opportunities and challenges. The airline industry is complex and intensely competitive. There are multiple segments to be served, a broad range of competent competitors, and several different types of messages that need to be communicated to Delta's many different customer groups. These factors combine to make the

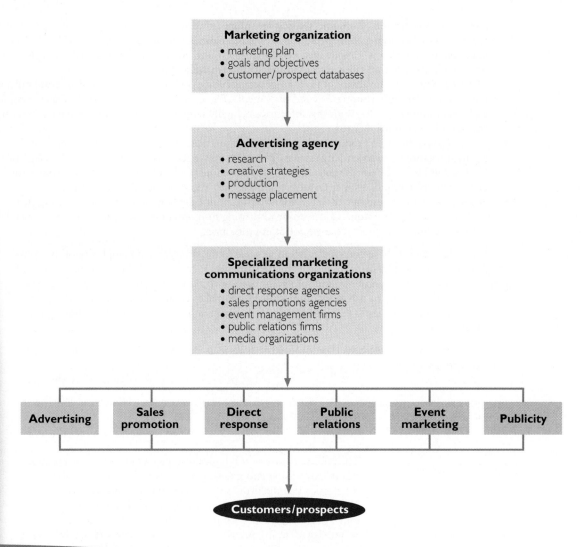

EXHIBIT IMC 1.1

The integrated marketing communications process.

integrated marketing communications effort a massive undertaking. In this section, we will consider how Delta and its support agencies go about the process of integrating the communications Delta uses to attract and retain customers in the many segments it serves.

Building a Structure to Support Integrated Marketing Communications at Delta Air Lines

To appreciate Delta's communications process, one has to first appreciate the extraordinary relationship between Delta and its general agency, BBDO South. Delta and BBDO celebrated their 50th anniversary as business partners in 1995. During this time, BBDO has helped Delta with its advertising and communications needs as the airline grew from a regional carrier to an international industry leader.

An important part of effectively managing Delta's communications process is the organizational structure both agency and client have developed. Exhibit IMC 1.2 shows how BBDO South has put in place an account management organizational structure to serve Delta.

Notice that the structure includes a global accounts director, a director of strategic planning, two management supervisors, account executives, and assistant AEs. Also notice that along the bottom of the chart are listed the many areas of responsibility and programs handled by the account group. BBDO South prepares advertising for Delta in national mass media—newspapers, magazines, and broadcast. BBDO also takes responsibility for other areas including trade advertising, advertising in several international markets, northeast shuttle service advertising, military programs, youth marketing, minority programs, the in-flight

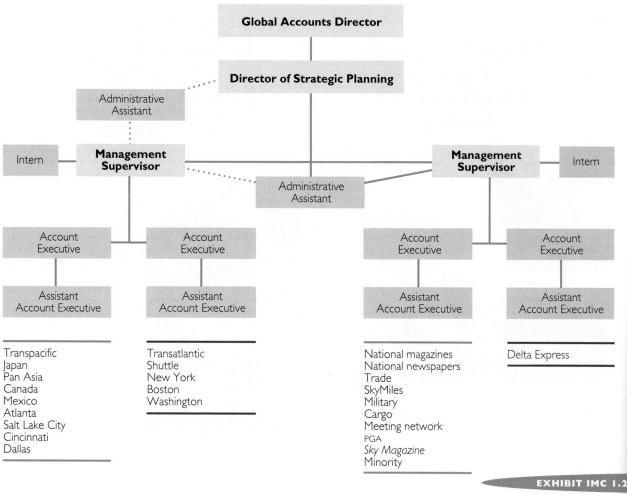

Global Accounts Director

Director of Strategic Planning

Administrative Assistant

Intern

Management Supervisor

Administrative Assistant

Management Supervisor

Intern

Account Executive

Account Executive

Account Executive

Account Executive

Assistant Account Executive

Assistant Account Executive

Assistant Account Executive

Assistant Account Executive

Transpacific
Japan
Pan Asia
Canada
Mexico
Atlanta
Salt Lake City
Cincinnati
Dallas

Transatlantic
Shuttle
New York
Boston
Washington

National magazines
National newspapers
Trade
SkyMiles
Military
Cargo
Meeting network
PGA
Sky Magazine
Minority

Delta Express

EXHIBIT IMC 1.2

BBDO South account management for Delta Air Lines.

Sky Magazine, and regional ads for four of Delta's main hubs—Atlanta, Salt Lake City, Cincinnati, and Dallas/Fort Worth. It is this account team that works directly with the Delta Air Lines marketing division and advertising group to determine how communications programs can be implemented to best serve Delta's marketing goals and objectives.

With direction from Delta management regarding the goals, objectives and creative platform for advertising, BBDO South has produced award-winning advertising for Delta in many areas. Exhibit IMC 1.3 shows examples of ads related to programs listed in Exhibit IMC 1.2. Shown here are two ads prepared for particular market applications. For the New York market, ease of international travel was promoted with the "More Cities to Europe" ad. The "SkyMiles Never Expire" ad was targeted to the Dallas/Fort Worth market. These ads, along with four others, were scheduled in national publications like *USA Today* and run as copy splits, in which certain ads, as indicated above, ran only in designated markets.

Of course, Delta has its own organizational structure to handle the communications decision-making process. A distillation of the vast organizational complex of Delta's marketing, advertising, and promotions activities, which includes 85 people in-house, from secretaries to the vice president of consumer marketing, is represented in Exhibit IMC 1.4. Notice in this structure that the communications process is managed through the Marketing Division. But other Delta divisions, like Operations and the Corporate Communications Division, have direct input through Marketing. The Marketing Division sets the communications goals and objectives in terms of communications strategy and targeting particular customer and prospect audiences. Delta is able to draw on several databases. The firm itself has developed two large databases: the world's largest database of children under 12 years old in the Fantastic Flyer database, and 18 million travelers in the SkyMiles frequent flyer database. In addition, Delta can rely on corporate partners, like American Express, to generate other databases for specifically targeted communications.

*These ads are part of Delta's
multifaceted IMC program.*

What is important to recognize about this organizational structure is the many agencies used by Delta to prepare communications across all forms of consumer-marketing programs. The general agency, BBDO South, takes primary responsibility for advertising and creative services. For interactive communications and Web site development, Modem Media is used. Delta's Web site (www.delta-air.com) provides breaking news, information on flight schedules, real-time flight information, seating charts, aircraft statistics, maps, booking ability, and other relevant information for travelers. For Delta's highly successful SkyMiles frequent flyer program, Rapp Collins Worldwide, which specializes in frequency programs, is the main support agency. Most of Delta's target- and direct-marketing communications, which includes programs like Family Fares, are handled by the Lacek Group Worldwide and the Rapp Collins Worldwide agency. For partnership programs, Delta and its support agencies help coordinate activities with partnership firms. For example, Delta's Target/Direct/Partnership Marketing department, along with American Express and its support agency, launched the SkyMiles Card program in early 1996. Materials from the SkyMiles and American Express programs are shown in Exhibit IMC 1.5.

Promotional Marketing, shown on the lower right side of Exhibit IMC 1.4, works directly with local affiliates to respond to local market needs, including event sponsorships. Delta provides a wide range of sponsorship support (nearly 300 official sponsor programs a year), from being an official sponsor of the centennial Olympic Games in Atlanta in 1996 to ongoing sponsorship of the Delta Center arena in Salt Lake City to small events like community fund-raisers. Also represented on the right side of Exhibit IMC 1.4 is International Marketing, which maintains offices in London. Delta's main international advertising agency in London coordinates communications throughout Europe. Finally, notice that Delta's Corporate Communications Division manages public relations in conjunction with the Ketchum Advertising agency. The coordination of these communications is less direct in that the link is through the Marketing Division rather than managed by the Marketing Division.

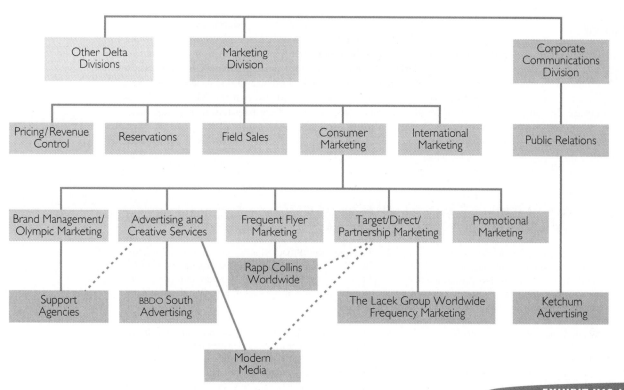

EXHIBIT IMC 1.4

Delta Air Lines structure for marketing communications.

EXHIBIT IMC 1.5

SkyMiles and American Express SkyMiles mailers.

Coordinating Communications of Delta Air Lines

With respect to coordinating the communications process, Exhibit IMC 1.4 shows that the Marketing Division is responsible for implementing corporate goals and objectives through the Consumer Marketing level of the organization. Consumer Marketing then determines what forms of communication prepared by which agencies will be used to pursue the goals and objectives. The activities of these agencies is coordinated through the Marketing Division to ensure that all communications to all segments is consistent and coordinated. In the next IMC section, "Planning Integrated Marketing Communications," we will look at how Delta planned a specific communications program to take advantage of a marketing opportunity discovered by corporate strategists.

IMC EXERCISES

1. Analysts argue that firms are relying on more and more communications tools in addition to advertising. Do you notice that you are targeted with communications in addition to advertising? What materials have you encountered? What firms have targeted you with these materials?

2. For the next few weeks, check your local newspaper for special events in town—festivals, concerts, fund-raisers. What organizations are listed as sponsors? How many of these firms are national firms, and how many are local organizations?

3. Examine the BBDO South organizational structure used to manage the communications needs of Delta. How does the BBDO South structure compare to the general structure of agencies discussed in this section of the text?

4. Delta Air Lines has broadened its communications mix like many other firms. Where have you seen Delta Air Lines communications? Identify both national mass media and more narrowly transmitted communications, such as direct marketing and event sponsorship. Do you think you are in one of Delta's target audiences? If yes, what communications have been specifically directed to you?

ENDNOTES

1. For discussions of how these and other marketers are using multiple communications options in an integrated way see Robert Frank, "Pepsi Bets a Blue Can Will Spur Sales Abroad," *Wall Street Journal,* April 2, 1996; Jeffery D. Zbar, "Upjohn Database Rallies Rogaine, *Advertising Age,* January 23, 1995; and Raymond Serafin, "Mercedes E-Class Embarks," *Advertising Age,* November 6, 1995.

2. This definition by the American Association of Advertising Agencies appeared in Don E. Schultz, "Integrated Marketing Communications: Maybe Definition Is in the Point of View," *Marketing News,* January 18, 1993, 17.

3. Don E. Schultz, Stanley I. Tannenbaum, and Robert F. Lauterborn, *Integrated Marketing Communications* (Lincolnwood, Ill.: NTC Business Books, 1993), xvii.

4. These quotes are taken from Schultz, Tannenbaum, and Lauterborn, pages ix, xi, xii (Fizdale).

5. Based on cities served by Delta, Delta Connecton carriers, and Worldwide Partners.

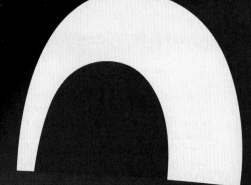

Part 2 | The Planning: Analyzing the Advertising Environment

Successful advertising campaigns generally rely on a clear understanding of how and why consumers make their purchase decisions. Successful campaigns are also usually rooted in sound marketing strategies and careful research about one's market. This understanding, strategy, and research are brought together in a formal advertising plan. Part 2, "The Planning: Analyzing the Advertising Environment," discusses several important bases for the development of an advertising plan and concludes with a look at ad planning for international markets. Part 2 reveals the care and detail needed to effectively plan an advertising campaign. This planning stage provides advertisers with the information and insights needed to take on the creative challenges of the next stage of advertising, the preparation.

CHAPTER 5

Advertising and Consumer Behavior

Chapter 5, "Advertising and Consumer Behavior," begins with an assessment of the way consumers make product and brand choices. These decisions depend on consumers' involvement and prior experiences with the product in question. This chapter also addresses consumer behavior and advertising from both psychological and sociological points of view. It concludes with a discussion of how external factors, such as culture and reference groups, affect the way individuals make decisions.

CHAPTER 6

Market Segmentation, Positioning, and Product Differentiation

Chapter 6, "Market Segmentation, Positioning, and Product Differentiation," details how these three fundamental planning efforts are developed by an organization. With this combination of audience and competitive information, products and services are developed that include features both valued by customers and different from those of the competition.

CHAPTER 7

Advertising Research

Chapter 7, "Advertising Research," discusses the types of research conducted by advertisers and the role information plays in planning an advertising effort. Advertisers do research before messages are prepared, during the preparation process, and after messages are running in the market. Without effective research, advertising planning is greatly compromised.

CHAPTER 8

The Advertising Plan

Chapter 8, "The Advertising Plan," explains how formal advertising plans are developed. The inputs to the advertising plan are laid out in detail, and the process of setting advertising objectives—both communications and sales objectives—is described. The methods for setting an advertising budget are presented, including the widely adopted objective-and-task approach.

CHAPTER 9

Advertising Planning: An International Perspective

Chapter 9, "Advertising Planning: An International Perspective," introduces issues related to planning advertising targeted to international audiences. Global forces are creating markets that are more affluent, more accessible, and more predictable. In the midst of these trends toward international trade, marketers are redefining the nature and scope of the markets for their goods and services while adjusting to the creative, media, and regulatory challenges of competing across national boundaries.

Cool like them   or   Cool like us

YOU ARE WHAT YOU WATCH

Chapter 5

Advertising
and Consumer
Behavior

After reading and thinking about this chapter, you will be able to do the following:

1 Describe the four basic stages of consumer decision making.

2 Explain how consumers adapt their decision-making processes as a function of involvement and experience.

3 Discuss how advertising may influence consumer behavior through its effects on various psychological states.

4 Discuss the interaction of culture and advertising.

5 Discuss the role of sociological factors in consumer behavior and advertising response.

Through the 1980s, Japanese automobiles surged into the North American market. During this decade, the Japanese share of the U.S. market increased from 20 to 28 percent, while the combined market share of the U.S. big three (Chrysler, Ford, and General Motors) fell to 65 percent.[1] Japanese automotive success had been based historically on building quality cars priced for the mass market. The Honda Civic and Toyota Corolla typified the Japanese approach. These economical and reliable vehicles were (and are) extremely popular with younger, less-affluent consumers. By the end of the 1980s, nearly half of all new cars purchased by persons under the age of 45 were from Japanese companies like Honda, Toyota, and Nissan.[2]

Two things happen to a younger, less-affluent market: All of its members get older, and some move into higher income brackets. Would the more fortunate of these consumers continue to buy Civics and Corollas? Some might, but many were, in fact, choosing to move to larger, more prestigious vehicles. Japanese managers noticed this change in consumer preferences and began to design more-sophisticated and expensive autos for those consumers looking to trade up to higher quality and prestige. This change in the Japanese market strategy was dramatically illustrated in 1989 when both Toyota and Nissan introduced new luxury divisions—Lexus and Infiniti. These cars were priced in the $35,000 to $50,000 range (in 1989-90) and were targeted to compete with European nameplates like Mercedes Benz and BMW.

Of course, new advertising campaigns emerged with the introduction of the two new Japanese luxury divisions. The two campaigns were, however, very different. The Lexus campaign by Team One, El Segundo, California, used a high-tech demonstration style, as the storyboard in Exhibit 5.1 shows.

In contrast, Nissan's Infiniti division chose advertising by Hill-Holiday, which had a style referred to as Zen-like. Rather than showing the car or touting its performance, Infiniti commercials featured natural scenes with trees, rocks, and assorted flora and fauna. Judging from the ad, this car was to be like no other and would deliver not only performance and prestige, but a plateau of peace and serenity as well.

The Infiniti ads were unconventional. There was no obligatory performance-driving footage, no rapid-cut montage, no look at the "rich interior," and no hunk or hunkess. What was this? Was this a car ad? It didn't look like a car ad. In fact, it violated all the conventions and audience expectations of this genre, or type of ad. This generated controversy and a good deal of criticism.

Nissan introduced the Infiniti on November 8, 1989. By the end of that year, only 1,723 cars had been sold—well below Nissan's goals for the car.[3] By contrast, in its first three months on the market, the Lexus exceeded Toyota's sales goal of 16,000 vehicles.[4] Lexus dealers couldn't have been happier, while Nissan dealers grew impatient with the Zen-like ads and demanded a change. The merits of the Infiniti campaign were debated in the business press, and even late-night talk-show hosts got in on the action. Jay

EXHIBIT 5.1

Traditional automobile advertising makes the car the star of the show. In this ad, Lexus uses the traditional approach. With its controversial campaign in the late 1980s, Infiniti broke with tradition to create a short-lived, Zen-like style. **www.lexususa.com/**

1.   David Woodruff, "A New Era for Auto Quality," *Business Week,* October 22, 1990, 84–96.
2.   Ibid.
3.   Bradley A. Stertz, "Nissan's Infiniti Gets Off to Slow Start; Zen-Like Advertising Comes under Fire," *Wall Street Journal,* January 8, 1990, B4.
4.   Ibid.

Leno summed things up this way: "That new Japanese car, Infiniti, isn't selling well. I guess the advertising isn't working, although I understand that the sale of rocks and trees is up 300 percent."[5]

The circumstances surrounding the Nissan Infiniti campaign raise some critical questions in our attempt to appreciate and understand advertising. How do consumers make buying decisions for an automobile, and how much impact should we expect a few television commercials to have on such a decision? Is advertising more important as a sales generator in categories like soft drinks or fast-food restaurants, than for big-ticket items like cars and home entertainment systems? If advertising cannot be expected to have much impact on the sales of an automobile, why do car companies like Ford, Honda, and Chrysler continue to spend literally billions of dollars on advertising campaigns every year? These are central questions about the relationship of advertising and consumer behavior.

The primary goal for advertising is to persuade consumers to behave in certain ways. Not surprisingly, an understanding of consumer behavior is crucial to advertising professionals. Before advertisers initiate campaigns for any product or service, they need a thorough understanding of the way consumers make their buying decisions. This understanding greatly increases the advertiser's chance of effecting the desired behavior.

Consumer behavior is defined as those activities directly involved in obtaining, consuming, and disposing of products and services, including the decision processes that precede and follow these actions.[6] Like all human behavior, the behavior of consumers is complicated. However, advertisers must make it their job to understand consumers if they are to have sustained success in creating effective advertising. Sometimes this understanding comes in the form of comprehensive research efforts; other times in the form of years of experience and implicit theories; other times in the form of blind, dumb luck (rarely attributed as such). However this understanding comes about, it is a key factor for advertising success.

This chapter provides a summary of the concepts and frameworks we believe are most helpful in trying to understand consumer behavior. We will describe consumer behavior and attempt to explain it, in its incredible diversity, from two different perspectives. The first portrays consumers as systematic decision makers who seek to maximize the benefits they derive from their purchases. The second views consumers as active interpreters (meaning makers) of advertising, whose membership in various cultures, subcultures, societies, and communities significantly affects their interpretation and response to advertising. These two perspectives are merely different ways of looking at the exact same people and the exact same behaviors. Though different in essential assumptions, both of these perspectives are valid, and both are necessary to the task of actually getting the work of advertising done.

The point is that no one perspective can adequately explain consumer behavior. Consumers are both psychological and social at the same time. Suppose a sociologist and a psychologist both saw someone buying a car. The psychologist might explain this behavior in terms of attitudes, decision criteria, and the like, while the sociologist would probably explain it in terms of the buyer's social environment and circumstances (that is, income, housing conditions, social class, and so on). Both explanations may be valid, but they are also incomplete. The bottom line is that all consumer behavior is complex and multifaceted. Why you or any other consumer buys Levi's rather than Lee, or Pepsi rather than Coke, or Duracell rather than Eveready, is a function of psychological, economic, sociological, anthropological, historical, and other forces. No single explanation is sufficient. With this in mind, we offer two basic perspectives on consumer behavior.

5.   Cleveland Horton, "Infiniti Ads Trigger Auto Debate," *Advertising Age,* January 22, 1990, 49.
6.   James F. Engel, Roger D. Blackwell, and Paul W. Miniard, *Consumer Behavior* (Fort Worth, Tex.: Dryden Press, 1995), 4.

Perspective One: The Consumer as Decision Maker

❶ One way to view consumer behavior is as a logical, sequential process culminating with the individual reaping a set of benefits from a product or service that satisfies that person's perceived needs. In this basic view, we can think of individuals as purposeful decision makers who take matters one step at a time. All consumption episodes might then be conceived as a sequence of four basic stages:

1. Need recognition
2. Information search and alternative evaluation
3. Purchase
4. Postpurchase use and evaluation

The Consumer Decision-Making Process

A brief discussion of what typically happens at each stage will give us a foundation for understanding consumers, and it can also illuminate opportunities for developing powerful advertising.

Need Recognition. The consumption process begins when people perceive a need. A **need state** arises when one's desired state of affairs differs from one's actual state of affairs. Need states are accompanied by a mental discomfort or anxiety that motivates action; the severity of this discomfort can be widely variable depending on the genesis of the need. For example, the need state that arises when one runs out of toothpaste would involve very mild discomfort for most people, whereas the need state that accompanies the breakdown of one's automobile on a dark and deserted highway in Minnesota in mid-February can approach true desperation.

One way advertising works is to point to and thereby activate needs that will motivate consumers to buy a product or service. For instance, nearly every fall, advertisers from product categories as diverse as autos, snowblowers, and footwear roll out predictions for another severe winter and encourage consumers to prepare themselves before it's too late. Such an appeal is very productive when the previous winter was especially severe and the advertiser does a good job of capturing the sights and sounds of last year's terrible storms.

Following an especially severe winter in the Northeast, Jeep dealers in New York State warned, "Last year's winter produced 17 winter storms. . . . This year, the *Old Farmer's Almanac* is predicting another winter with above-average snowfall." As a result of this campaign, Jeep dealers in the New York region sold every vehicle they could get their hands on.[7] Consumers in New York obviously responded to the advertiser's effort to activate a need state.

Many factors can influence the need states of consumers. For example, as suggested by Maslow's well-known hierarchy of needs, a consumer's level of affluence can have a dramatic impact on the types of needs he or she might perceive as relevant. The less fortunate are concerned with fundamental needs, such as food and shelter; more-affluent consumers may fret over which new piece of Williams Sonoma kitchen gadgetry or other accoutrement to place in their uptown condo. The former's needs are predominantly for physiological survival and basic comfort, while the latter's may have more to do with seeking to validate personal accomplishments and derive status and recognition through consumption. While income clearly matters in this regard, it would be a mistake to believe that the poor have no aesthetic concerns, or that the rich are always oblivious to the need for basic essentials. The central point is that a variety of needs can be fulfilled through consumption, and it is reasonable to suggest that consumers are looking to satisfy needs when they buy products or services.

7.   Fara Warner, "Relishing and Embellishing Forecasts for Frigid Winter," *Wall Street Journal,* December 1, 1994, B1.

Products and services should provide benefits that fulfill consumers' needs; hence, one of the advertiser's primary jobs is to make the connection between the two for the consumer. Benefits come in many forms. Some are more functional—that is, they derive from the more objective performance characteristics of a product or service. Convenience, reliability, nutrition, durability, and economy are descriptors that refer to **functional benefits.**

Consumers may also choose products that provide **emotional benefits;** these are not typically found in some tangible feature or objective characteristic of a product. Emotional benefits are more subjective and may be perceived differently from one consumer to the next. Products and services help consumers feel pride, avoid guilt, relieve fear, and experience intense pleasure. These are powerful consumption motives that advertisers often try to activate. Can you find the emotional benefits promised in Exhibit 5.2?

EXHIBIT 5.2

All parents want to be good to their child. This ad promises both functional benefits and emotional rewards for diligent parents.
www.jnj.com/

Any advertiser must develop a keen appreciation for the kinds of benefits that consumers might derive from its product and brand. Even in the same product category, the benefits promised may be quite disparate. As shown in Exhibit 5.3, the makers of the Geo Metro portray their vehicle as the epitome of functional transportation. The Dodge Neon offers inexpensive transportation along with hipness and cuteness, per Exhibit 5.4. The makers of the Acura Integra GS-R sports coupe appeal to the emotional rewards of ownership with ads like that in Exhibit 5.5.

The ads for these three cars demonstrate the diversity of needs perceived by consumers, along with benefits offered by advertisers. If consumers do not know about or forget the benefits that a particular brand is supposed to provide, the maker's advertising effort is likely at fault.

Information Search and Alternative Evaluation.

Given that a consumer has recognized a need, it is often not obvious what would be the best way to satisfy that need. For example, if you have a fear of being trapped in a blizzard in upstate New York, a condo on Miami Beach may be a much better solution than a Jeep or new snow tires. Need recognition simply sets in motion a process that may involve an extensive information search and careful evaluation of alternatives prior to purchase. Of course, during this search and evaluation, there are numerous opportunities for the advertiser to influence the final decision.

Once a need has been recognized, information for the decision is acquired through an internal or external search. The consumer's first option for information is to draw on personal experience and prior knowledge. This **internal search** for information may be all that is required. When a consumer has considerable prior experience with the products in question, attitudes about the alternatives may be well established and determine choice, as is suggested in the ad for Campbell's soup shown in Exhibit 5.6.

An internal search can also tap into information that has accumulated in one's memory as a result of repeated advertising exposures. Affecting people's beliefs about a brand before their actual use of it, or merely establishing the existence of the brand in the consumer's consciousness, is a critical function of advertising. As noted in Chapter 1, the purpose of delayed response advertising is to generate recognition of and a favorable predisposition toward a brand so that when consumers enter into the search mode,

EXHIBIT 5.3

Functional benefits rule in this ad. Of course, the "tiny, little price tag" of the Geo Metro is a good place to start when promoting functionality. www.chevrolet.com/geo/a300.htm

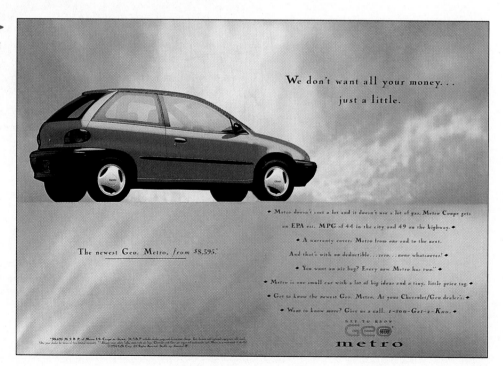

EXHIBIT 5.4

While the Dodge Neon and Geo Metro both target youthful, first-time car buyers, the Neon's promise has a different twist. Is the Neon promising just functional benefits? **www.4adodge.com/neon/**

EXHIBIT 5.5

This ad makes no concession to functional benefits. Driving is about emotional rewards. But which emotional rewards? **www.acura.com**

EXHIBIT 5.6

For a cultural icon like Campbell's soup, an advertiser can assume that consumers have some prior knowledge. Here the advertiser seeks to enhance that knowledge to lead people to use more canned soup. **www.campbellsoups.com**

that brand will be one they immediately consider as a possible solution to their needs. If the consumer has not used a brand previously and has no recollection that it even exists, then that brand probably will not be the brand of choice.

It is certainly plausible that an internal search will not turn up enough information to yield a decision. The consumer then proceeds with an external search. An **external search** involves visiting retail stores to examine the alternatives, seeking input from friends and relatives about their experiences with the products in question, or perusing professional product evaluations furnished in various publications like *Consumer Reports* or *Car and Driver*. In addition, when consumers are in an active information-gathering mode, they also may be receptive to detailed, informative advertisements delivered through any of the print media.

During an internal or external search, consumers are not merely gathering information for its own sake. They have some need that is propelling the process, and their goal is to make a decision that yields benefits. The consumer searches and is simultaneously forming attitudes about the possible alternatives. This is the alternative-evaluation component of the decision process, and it is another key phase for the advertiser to target.

Alternative evaluation will be structured by the consumer's consideration set and evaluative criteria. The **consideration set** is the subset of brands from a particular product category that becomes the focal point of the consumer's evaluation. Most product categories contain too many brands for all to be considered, so the consumer finds some way to focus the search and evaluation. For example, for autos, consumers may consider just cars priced less than $10,000, or only cars that have antilock brakes, or just foreign-made cars, or just cars sold at dealerships within a five-mile radius of their work or home. A critical function of advertising is to make consumers aware of the brand and keep them aware, so that the brand has a chance to be part of the consideration set. Virtually all ads try to do this.

As the search-and-evaluation process proceeds, consumers will form evaluations based on the characteristics or attributes that brands in their consideration set have in common. These product attributes or performance characteristics are referred to as **evaluative criteria.** Evaluative criteria will differ from one product category to the next and can include many factors, such as price, texture, warranty terms, color, scent, or fat content. As Exhibit 5.7 suggests, one traditional evaluative criteria for judging airlines has been on-time arrivals.

It is critical for advertisers to have as complete an understanding as possible of the evaluative criteria that consumers are using to make their buying decisions. They must also know how consumers rate their brand in comparison with others from the consideration set. Understanding consumers' evaluative criteria furnishes a powerful starting point for any advertising campaign and will be examined in more depth later in the chapter.

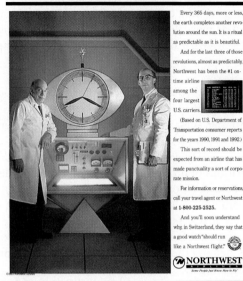

Every 365 days, more or less, the earth completes another revolution around the sun. It is a ritual as predictable as it is beautiful.

And for the last three of those revolutions, almost as predictably, Northwest has been the #1 on-time airline among the four largest U.S. carriers.

(Based on U.S. Department of Transportation consumer reports for the years 1990, 1991 and 1992.)

This sort of record should be expected from an airline that has made punctuality a sort of corporate mission.

For information or reservations, call your travel agent or Northwest at 1-800-225-2525.

And you'll soon understand why, in Switzerland, they say that a good watch "should run like a Northwest flight."

NORTHWEST AIRLINES
Some People Just Know How to Fly

EXHIBIT 5.7

Advertisers must know the relevant evaluative criteria for their products. For an airline, on-time arrival is certainly an important matter. **www .nwa.com/**

Back to Infiniti. When we left the Infiniti example, the car was not selling well, and automotive experts, Infiniti dealers, and late-night talk-show hosts were questioning the merits of an ad campaign that didn't even show the car. Understanding how consumers make their decisions can help us appreciate the nature, and perhaps virtues, of this unusual campaign.

Nissan executives created this vehicle because they believed that the market for luxury cars was growing. However, given that consumers were recognizing needs that could be fulfilled only by a vehicle costing $40,000 or more, one would expect considerable internal and external search. Here is where Infiniti's Zen-like advertising was effective. The curious campaign did accomplish important goals. It made people aware of the new vehicle, moved the car into many buyers' consideration set, and prompted many consumers to visit Infiniti showrooms as part of their external search. In the first six weeks after the car's introduction, about 35,000 persons visited 50 Infiniti dealers around the United States, and another 60,000 people called these dealers for information about the new car.[8]

That's the good news. The bad news is that very few Infinitis were sold. While traditional luxury car dealers commonly sell vehicles to 25 percent of their shoppers, Infiniti dealers could convince only 5 percent of their visitors to buy.[9] Perhaps the Infiniti campaign was simply too effective in arousing people's curiosity about the car. Perhaps it could be criticized for bringing into showrooms people who had no real sense of what an Infiniti automobile was like and who could not afford its $40,000 sticker price. The high volume of showroom traffic may have been a problem for dealers as they tried to identify the real luxury car purchasers from the merely curious. Perhaps the advertising conveyed a certain pretense or even silliness that on the one hand made people curious, but on the other hand became the butt of jokes, leaving the car itself to be painted by the same broad brush of public skepticism with which the ad campaign was painted. Maybe the ads promised a revolutionary vehicle, and prospective buyers saw only a Japanese version of a Buick or Chrysler.

8.   Horton, "Infiniti Ads Trigger Auto Debate."
9.   Stertz, "Nissan's Infiniti Gets Off to Slow Start."

In retrospect, it's impossible to say whether Nissan's Zen-like ad campaign was an unequivocal success or failure. Like many campaigns, it did some things well and others not so well. The point here is to illustrate the importance of understanding consumer decision-making processes if we are to have any hope of planning consistently successful advertising programs. Concepts like need recognition, internal and external searches, consideration sets, and evaluative criteria are part of the advertising lexicon because they have such enormous impact on the development of successful advertising.

Purchase. At this third stage, purchase occurs. The consumer has made a decision, and a sale is made. Great, right? Well, to a point. As nice as it is to make a sale, things are far from over at the point of sale. In fact, it would be a big mistake to view purchase as the culmination of the decision-making process. No matter what the product category, the consumer is likely to buy from it again in the future. So, what happens after the sale is very important to advertisers.

Postpurchase Use and Evaluation. The goal for marketers and advertisers must not be simply to generate a sale; it must be to create satisfied and perhaps ultimately loyal customers. The data to support this position are quite astounding. Research shows that about 65 percent of the average company's business comes from its present, satisfied customers, and that 91 percent of dissatisfied customers will never buy again from the company that disappointed them.[10] Thus, consumers' evaluations of products in use become a major determinant of which brands will be in the consideration set the next time around.

Customer satisfaction derives from a favorable postpurchase experience. It may develop after a single use, but more likely it will require sustained use. Advertising can play an important role in inducing customer satisfaction by creating appropriate expectations for a brand's performance, or by helping the consumer who has already bought the advertised brand to feel good about doing so.

Advertising plays an important role in alleviating the cognitive dissonance that can occur after a purchase. **Cognitive dissonance** is the anxiety or regret that lingers after a difficult decision. Often, rejected alternatives can have attractive features that lead people to second-guess their own decisions. If the goal is to generate satisfied customers, this dissonance must be resolved in a way that leads consumers to conclude that they did make the right decision after all. Purchasing high-cost items or choosing from categories that include many desirable and comparable brands can yield high levels of cognitive dissonance.

When dissonance is expected, it makes good sense for the advertiser to reassure buyers with detailed information about its brands. Postpurchase reinforcement programs might involve direct mail or other types of personalized contacts with the customer. This postpurchase period represents a great opportunity for the advertiser to have the undivided attention of the consumer and to provide information and advice about product use that will increase customer satisfaction.[11] It can also help marketers in getting consumers to think about their new purchase in the way advertisers want them to. For an example, see the ad for Isuzu shown in Exhibit 5.8.

Four Modes of Consumer Decision Making

As you may be thinking about now, consumers aren't always deliberate and systematic; sometimes they are hasty, impulsive, or even irrational. The search time that people put into their purchases can vary dramatically for different types of products. Would you give the purchase of a toothbrush the same amount of effort as the purchase of a new stereo system? Probably not, unless you've been chastised by your dentist recently. Why

10.   Terry G. Vavra, *Aftermarketing: How to Keep Customers for Life through Relationship Marketing* (Homewood, Ill.: Business One Irwin, 1992), 13.
11.   Ibid.

is that T-shirt you bought at the Nirvana concert more important to you than the brand of orange juice you had for breakfast this morning? Does buying a Valentine's gift from Victoria's Secret create different feelings than buying a newspaper for your father? (We're guessing here.) When you view a TV ad for car batteries, do you carefully memorize the information being presented so that it will be there to draw on the next time you're evaluating the brands in your consideration set? (For the sake of society and any innocent bystanders, we hope not.)

Some purchase decisions are just more engaging than others. In the following sections we will elaborate on the view of consumer as decision maker by explaining four decision-making modes that help advertisers appreciate the richness and complexity of consumer behavior. These four modes are determined by a consumer's involvement and prior experiences with the product or service in question.

Sources of Involvement. To accommodate the complexity of consumption decisions, those who study consumer behavior typically talk about the involvement level of any particular decision. **Involvement** is the degree of perceived relevance and personal importance accompanying the choice of a certain product or service within a particular context.[12] Many factors contribute to an individual's level of involvement with any given decision. People can develop interests and avocations in many different areas, like cooking, photography, pet ownership, or exercise and fitness. Such ongoing personal interests can enhance involvement levels in a variety of product categories. Also, any time a great deal of risk is associated with a purchase—perhaps as a result of the high price of the item, or because the consumer will have to live with the decision for a long period of time—one should also expect elevated involvement.

Consumers can also derive important symbolic meaning from products and brands. Ownership or use of some products can help people reinforce some aspect of their self-image or make a statement to other persons who are important to them. If a purchase carries great symbolic and real consequences—like choosing the right gift for someone on Valentine's Day—it will be highly involving.

---

12. Engel, Blackwell, and Miniard, *Consumer Behavior,* 161.

Some purchases can also tap into deep emotional concerns or motives. For example, many marketers, from Wal-Mart to Marathon Oil, have solicited consumers with an appeal to their patriotism. The ad for Casio watches (a Japanese product) in Exhibit 5.9 demonstrates that a product doesn't have to be American to wrap itself in the stars and stripes. For some individuals, this can be a powerful appeal that strikes an emotional chord. Here, the appeal to emotion influences the consumer's involvement with the decision.

You'll feel so proud it'll bring a tear to your eye.

(Don't worry, it's water resistant.)

The new Landmark watch is more than a mere timepiece — it's a patriotic exercise in state-of-the-art electronics. This rugged watch proudly serves, with features like water resistance and a 7-year battery life. And, in a glowing display of national pride, the illuminated LCD shines with images of Americana. Indeed, at such a reasonable price, the Landmark even pays a dutiful respect to our national deficit.

CASIO®

Casio, Inc., 570 Mt. Pleasant Avenue, Dover, NJ 07801

EXHIBIT 5.9

The emotional appeal in this Casio ad is just one of many involvement devices. The play on water resistance also increases involvement as the reader perceives the double meaning. Describe how these devices work. How does Casio use involvement devices at its Web site **www.casio-usa.com/** *to encourage visitors to further explore its products on the site? Describe the involvement devices used by competitor Timex at its home page* **www.timex.com/**.

Involvement levels vary not only among product categories for any given individual, but also among individuals for any given product category. For example, some pet owners will feed their pets only the expensive canned products that look and smell like people food. Iams, whose ad is featured in Exhibit 5.10, understands this and made a special premium dog food for consumers who understand the nature of the dog–owner relationship. Many other pet owners, however, are perfectly happy with fifty-pound economy sizes.

Now we will use the ideas of involvement and prior experience to help conceive four different types of consumer decision making. These four modes are shown in Exhibit 5.11. Any specific consumption decision is based on a high or low level of prior experience with the product or service in question, and a high or low level of involvement. This yields the four modes of decision making: (1) extended problem solving; (2) limited problem solving; (3) habit or variety seeking; and (4) brand loyalty. Each is described in the following sections.

Extended Problem Solving. When consumers are inexperienced in a particular consumption setting yet find the setting highly involving, they are likely to engage in **extended problem solving.** In this mode, consumers go through a deliberate decision-making process that begins with explicit need recognition, proceeds with careful internal and external search, continues through alternative evaluation and purchase, and ends with a lengthy postpurchase evaluation.

Examples of extended problem solving come with decisions like choosing a home or a diamond ring, as shown in Exhibit 5.12. These products are expensive, are publicly evaluated, and can carry a considerable amount of risk in terms of making an uneducated decision. Selecting one's first new automobile or choosing a college are two other consumption settings that may require extended problem solving. Extended problem solving is the exception, not the rule.

Limited Problem Solving. In this decision-making mode, experience and involvement are both low. **Limited problem solving** is a more common mode of decision making. In this mode, a consumer will be less systematic in his or her decision making. The consumer has a new problem to solve, but it is not a problem that is interesting or engaging, so the information search is limited to simply trying the first brand encountered. For example, let's say a young couple have just brought home a new baby, and suddenly

EXHIBIT 5.10

When people think of their pets as human beings, they take their selection of pet food very seriously. Iams offers serious pet food for the serious dog owner. www .iamsco.com/

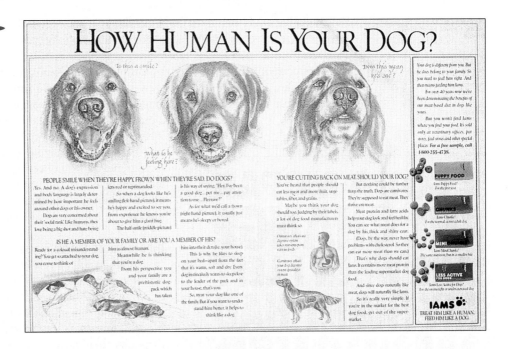

EXHIBIT 5.11

Four modes of consumer decision making.

	High Involvement	Low Involvement
Low Experience	Extended problem solving	Limited problem solving
High Experience	Brand loyalty	Habit or variety seeking

EXHIBIT 5.12

High involvement and low experience typically yield extended problem solving. Buying an engagement ring is a perfect example of this scenario. This ad offers lots of advice for the extended problem solver.

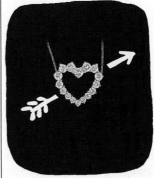

they perceive a very real need for disposable diapers. At the hospital they received complimentary trial packs of several products, including Pampers disposables. They try the Pampers, find them an acceptable solution to their messy new problem, and take the discount coupon that came with the sample to their local grocery, where they buy several packages. In the limited problem-solving mode, we often see consumers simply seeking adequate solutions to mundane problems. It is also a mode in which just trying a brand or two may be the most efficient way of collecting information about one's options. Of course, smart marketers realize that trial offers can be a preferred means of collecting information, and they facilitate trial offers for consumers through free samples, inexpensive "trial sizes," or discount coupons, as seen in the Mopar ad in Exhibit 5.13.

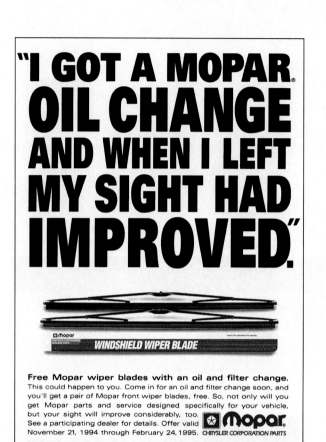

EXHIBIT 5.13

Trial offers are a common tactic with less-involving products.
www.chryslercars.com/

Habit or Variety Seeking. Habit or variety seeking occur in settings where a decision is uninvolving and a consumer repurchases from the category over and over again. In terms of sheer numbers, habitual purchases are probably the most common decision-making mode. Consumers find a brand of laundry detergent that suits their needs, they run out of the product, and they buy it again. The cycle repeats itself dozens of times per year in an almost mindless fashion. Getting in the habit of buying just one brand can be a way to simplify life and minimize the time invested in "nuisance" purchases. When a consumer perceives little difference among the various competitive brands, it is easier to buy the same brand repeatedly. A lot of consumption decisions are boring but necessary. Habits help us minimize the inconvenience.

In some product categories where a buying habit would be expected, an interesting phenomenon called variety seeking may be observed instead. Remember, **habit** refers to buying a single brand repeatedly as a solution to a simple consumption problem. This can be very tedious, and some consumers fight the boredom through variety seeking. **Variety seeking** refers to the tendency of consumers to switch their selection among various brands in a given category in a seemingly random pattern. This is not to say that a consumer will buy just any brand; he or she probably has two to five brands that all provide similar levels of satisfaction to a particular consumption problem. However, from one purchase occasion to the next, the individual will switch brands from within this set, just for the sake of variety.

Variety seeking is most likely to occur in frequently purchased categories where sensory experience, such as taste or smell, accompanies product use. Satiation will occur after repeated use and may leave the consumer looking for a fresh sensory experience. Product categories like soft drinks and alcoholic beverages, snack foods, breakfast cereals, and fast food are prone to variety seeking, as you can see in the Wendy's ad in Exhibit 5.14.

Brand Loyalty. The final decision-making mode is typified by high involvement and rich prior experience. In this mode, **brand loyalty** becomes a major consideration in the purchase decision. Consumers demonstrate brand loyalty when they repeatedly purchase a single brand as their choice to fulfill a specific need. In one sense, brand-loyal purchasers may look like they have developed a simple buying habit; however, it is important to distinguish brand loyalty from simple habit. Brand loyalty is based on highly favorable attitudes toward the brand and a conscious commitment to find this brand each time the consumer purchases from this category. Conversely, habits are merely consumption simplifiers that are not based on deeply held convictions. Habits can be disrupted through skillful advertising and promotions. Spending advertising dollars to convince truly brand-loyal consumers to try an alternative can be a great waste of resources.

"Why run for the border?"

"Just walk into a Wendy's for our Taco Salad. We take our rich, meaty chili and combine it with fresh lettuce, tomatoes, shredded cheese and tortilla chips. I think it's the best taco salad either side of the border."

Wendy's   Salads made fresh all day, every day.

EXHIBIT 5.14

Dave Thomas of Wendy's combines the reliability of an easily recognizable celebrity with an appeal to variety-seeking behavior. How does this pairing encourage consumers to seek variety? How does Wendy's Web site **www.wendys.com/** *encourage consumers to seek variety? How does rival McDonald's offer variety at its site* **www.mcdonalds.com/a_ welcome***?*

Brands like Sony, Gerber, Levi's, Harley-Davidson, FedEx, and the Grateful Dead have inspired loyal consumers. Brand loyalty is something that any marketer aspires to have, but in a world filled with more-savvy consumers and endless product proliferation, it is becoming harder and harder to attain. Brand loyalty may emerge because the consumer perceives that one brand simply outperforms all others in providing some critical functional benefit. For example, the harried business executive may have grown loyal to FedEx's overnight delivery service as a result of repeated satisfactory experiences with FedEx—and as a result of FedEx advertising that has repeatedly posed the question, Why fool around with anyone else?

Perhaps even more important, brand loyalty can be due to the emotional benefits that accompany certain brands. One of the strongest indicators for brand loyalty has to be the tendency on the part of some loyal consumers to tattoo their bodies with the insignia of their favorite brand. While statistics are not kept on this sort of thing, it would be reasonable to speculate that the worldwide leader in brand-name tattoos is Harley-Davidson. What accounts for Harley's fervent following? Is Harley's brand loyalty simply a function of performing better than its many competitors? Or does a Harley rider derive some deep emotional benefit from taking that big bike out on the open road and leaving civilization far behind? To understand loyalty for a brand like Harley, one must turn to the emotional benefits, like feelings of pride, kinship, and nostalgia that attend "the ride."

Owning a Harley—perhaps complete with tattoo—makes a person feel different and special. Harley ads are designed to reaffirm the deep emotional appeal of this product.

Strong emotional benefits might be expected from consumption decisions that we classify as highly involving, and they are major determinants of brand loyalty. Indeed, with so many brands in the marketplace, it is becoming harder and harder to create loyalty for one's brand through functional benefits alone. To break free of this brand-parity problem and provide consumers with enduring reasons to become or stay loyal, advertisers are investing more and more effort in communicating the emotional benefits that might be derived from brands in categories as diverse as film (trust your important memories to Kodak) and tires (your family is safer on Michelins).

In addition, as suggested by the New Media box on page 132, more and more companies are exploring ways to use interactive media to create a dialogue with customers. The hope is that this dialogue may help foster brand loyalty.

Key Psychological Processes

❸ To complete our consideration of the consumer as a thoughtful decision maker, one key issue remains. We need to examine the explicit psychological consequences of advertising. What is it that advertising leaves in the minds of consumers that ultimately may influence their behavior? For those of you who have previously taken psychology courses, many of the topics in this section will sound familiar.

As we noted earlier in the chapter, a good deal of advertising is designed to ensure recognition and create favorable predispositions toward a brand so that as consumers search for solutions to their problems, the brand will be thought of immediately. The goal of any delayed response ad is to effect some psychological state that will subsequently influence a purchase.

Two ideas borrowed from social psychology are usually the center of attention when discussing the psychological aspects of advertising. First is attitude. **Attitude** is defined as an overall evaluation of any object, person, or issue that varies along a continuum, like favorable to unfavorable or positive to negative. Attitudes are learned, and if they are based on substantial experience with the object or issue in question, they can be held with great conviction. Attitudes make our lives easier because they simplify decision making; that is, when faced with a choice among several alternatives, there is no need to process new information or analyze the merits of the alternatives. One merely selects the alternative thought to be the most favorable. We all possess attitudes on thousands of topics, ranging from a religious sect to underage drinking. Marketers and advertisers, however, are most interested in one particular class of attitudes—brand attitudes.

Brand attitudes are summary evaluations that reflect preferences for various products and brands. The next time you are waiting in a checkout line at the grocery, take a good look at the items in your cart: Those items are a direct reflection of your brand attitudes.

But what is the basis for these summary evaluations? Where do brand attitudes come from? Here we need a second idea from social psychology. To understand *why* people hold certain attitudes, we need to assess their specific beliefs. **Beliefs** represent the knowledge and feelings a person has accumulated about an object or issue. They can be logical and factual in nature, or biased and self-serving. A person might believe that Cadillacs are large, garlic consumption promotes weight loss, and pet owners are lonely people. For that person, all these beliefs are valid and can serve as a basis for attitudes toward Cadillacs, garlic, and pets.

If we know a person's beliefs, it is usually possible to infer attitude. Consider the two consumers' beliefs about Cadillacs summarized in Exhibit 5.15. From their beliefs, we might suspect that one of these con-

NEW MEDIA

CYBERSPACE FOR RENT: BRAND BUILDERS TAKE TO THE INTERNET

The premise of interactive media seems ideally suited for brand development. After all, *interactive* by definition ensures a two-way communication between buyer and seller; communication builds relationships, and relationships translate into brand loyalty. Right? Well, the rules of online selling are far from clear, but the medium may prove to be the most powerful tool ever in creating long-term relationships with brand-conscious consumers.

The challenge in moving established brands online revolves around the need to integrate marketing acumen with technical ability. Traditional software developers may contribute entertainment and interactivity, but the content must also be focused around marketing objectives and the brand-identity expertise of creative agencies. The multiple creative dimensions to cyberbranding have marketers scrambling to enlist new talent. In one recent move, MCI hired the former number-two executive from Prodigy to manage the branding of its online products and services.

While established household brands may attract Internet users familiar with an established image, start-up brands have surprised many by stimulating trial of their interactive offerings. Whether this initial curiosity will persist is unclear, but Internet consumers are typically more outgoing and inquisitive because they retain a semblance of anonymity. One thing is clear, however: Content is king. The ultimate strength of cyberbrands will live or die by "What can you do for me?"

Sources: "The Keys to Building Cyberbrands," *Advertising Age*, May 29, 1995, 18; and "New Rules Apply As Brands Move Online," *Advertising Age*, May 5, 1995, 41.

EXHIBIT 5.15

An example of two consumers' beliefs about Caddies.

Consumer 1	Consumer 2
Cadillacs are clumsy to drive	Cadillacs are sturdy and safe
Cadillacs are expensive	Cadillacs are a good investment
Cadillacs are gas guzzlers	Cadillacs are simple to maintain
Cadillacs are large	Cadillacs are good for long trips
Cadillacs are for senior citizens	Cadillacs are a symbol of one's success

sumers is a Cadillac owner, while the other will need a dramatic change in beliefs to ever make Cadillac part of his or her consideration set. It follows that the brand attitudes of the two individuals are at opposite ends of the favorableness continuum.

People have many beliefs about various features and attributes of products and brands. It is noteworthy that some beliefs are more important than others in determining a person's final evaluation of a brand. Typically, a small number of beliefs—on the order of five to nine—underlie brand attitudes.[13] These beliefs are the critical determinants of an attitude and are referred to as **salient beliefs.**

Clearly, we would expect the number of salient beliefs to vary between product categories. The loyal Harley owner who proudly displays a tattoo will have many more salient beliefs about his bike than he has about his brand of shaving cream. Also, salient beliefs can be modified, replaced, or extinguished. Exhibit 5.16 is a two-page ad from a recent Sears campaign designed to modify the salient beliefs of its target audience.

Since belief shaping and reinforcement can be one of the principal goals of advertising, it should come as no surprise that advertisers make belief assessment a focal point in their attempts to understand consumer behavior.

Multi-Attribute Attitude Models (MAAMs).
Multi-attribute attitude models (MAAMs) provide a framework and set of procedures for collecting information from consumers to assess their salient beliefs and attitudes about competitive brands. Chapter 7 will furnish more detail on the topic of data collection procedures, so our purpose here is to highlight the basic components of a MAAMs analysis and illustrate how such an analysis can benefit the advertiser.

Any MAAMs analysis will feature four fundamental components:

- *Evaluative criteria* are the attributes or performance characteristics that consumers use in comparing competitive brands. In pursuing a MAAMs analysis, an advertiser must identify all evaluative criteria relevant to its product category.
- *Importance weights* reflect the priority that a particular evaluative criterion receives in the consumer's decision-making process. Importance weights can vary dramatically from one consumer to the next; for instance, some people will merely want good taste from their bowl of cereal, while others will be more concerned about fat and fiber content.
- The *consideration set* is that group of brands that represents the real focal point for the consumer's decision. For example, the potential buyer of a luxury sedan might be focusing on Acuras, BMWs, and Saabs. These and comparable brands would be featured in a MAAMs analysis. Cadillac could have a model, like its Seville, that aspired to be part of this consideration set, leading General Motors to conduct a MAAMs analysis featuring the Seville and its foreign competitors. Conversely, it

---

13.   Icek Ajzen and Martin Fishbein, *Understanding Attitudes and Predicting Social Behavior* (Englewood Cliffs, N.J.: Prentice-Hall, 1980), 63.

EXHIBIT 5.16

Belief change is a common goal in advertising. With its "Softer side" campaign, Sears attempted to change beliefs about its stores as a source for women's fashions. **www.sears.com**

would be silly for GM to include the Geo Metro in a MAAMs analysis with this set of imports.

- *Beliefs* represent the knowledge and feelings that a consumer has about various brands. In a MAAMs analysis, beliefs about each brand's performance on all relevant evaluative criteria are assessed. Beliefs can be matters of fact—Raisin Nut Bran has five grams of fat per serving—or highly subjective—the Acura Integra sports coupe is the sleekest, sexiest car on the road. It is common for beliefs to vary widely among consumers.

In conducting a MAAMs analysis, we must specify the relevant evaluative criteria for our category, as well as our direct competitors. We then go to consumers and let them tell us what's important and how our brand performs or fares against the competition on the various evaluative criteria. The information generated from this research will give us a better appreciation for the salient beliefs that underlie brand attitudes, and it may suggest important opportunities for changing our marketing or advertising to yield more favorable brand attitudes.

Three basic attitude-change strategies can be developed from the MAAMs framework. First, a MAAMs analysis may reveal that consumers do not have an accurate perception of the relative performance of our brand on an important evaluative criterion. For example, consumers may perceive that Crest is far and away the best brand of toothpaste for fighting cavities, when in fact all brands with a fluoride additive perform equally well on cavity prevention. Correcting this misperception could become our focal point if we compete with Crest.

Second, a MAAMs analysis could uncover that our brand is perceived as the best performer on an evaluative criterion that most consumers do not view as very important.

The task for advertising in this instance would be to convince consumers that what our brand does offer (say, more baking soda than any other toothpaste) is more important than they had thought previously.

Third, the MAAMs framework may lead to the conclusion that the only way to improve attitudes toward our brand would be through the introduction of a new attribute to be featured in our advertising. Tartar Control Crest was one of the ways Procter & Gamble responded to its many competitors when they copied Crest's original cavity-prevention claim.

When marketers use the MAAMs approach, good things can result in terms of more-favorable brand attitudes and improved market share. When marketers carefully isolate key evaluative criteria, bring products to the marketplace that perform well on the focal criteria, and develop ads that effectively shape salient beliefs about the brand, the results can be dramatic. If you don't believe it, turn to Chapter 7 and read how Goodyear used this approach to shape salient beliefs about its Aquatred tires.

Information Processing and Perceptual Defense. At this point you may have the impression that creating effective advertising is really a straightforward exercise. We carefully analyze consumers' beliefs and attitudes, construct ads to address any problems that might be identified, and choose various media to get the word out to our target customers. Yes, it would be very easy if consumers would just pay close attention and believe everything we tell them, and if our competition would kindly stop all of its advertising so that ours would be the only message that consumers had to worry about. Of course, these things aren't going to happen.

Why would we expect to encounter resistance from consumers as we attempt to influence their beliefs and attitudes about our brand? One way to think about this problem is to portray the consumer as an information processor who must advance through a series of stages before our message can have its intended effect. If we are skillful in selecting appropriate media to reach our target, then the consumer must (1) pay attention to the message, (2) comprehend it correctly, (3) accept the message exactly as we intended, and (4) retain the message until it is needed for a purchase decision. Unfortunately, problems can and do occur at any or all of these four stages, completely negating the effect of our advertising campaign.

There are two major obstacles that we must overcome if our message is to have its intended effect. The first—the **cognitive consistency** impetus—stems from the individual consumer. Remember, a person develops and holds beliefs and attitudes for a reason: These cognitions help him or her make efficient decisions that yield pleasing outcomes. When a consumer is satisfied with these outcomes, there is really no reason to alter the belief system that generated them. New information that challenges existing beliefs can be ignored or disparaged to prevent modification of the present cognitive system. The consumer's desire to maintain cognitive consistency can be a major roadblock for an advertiser that wants to change beliefs and attitudes.

The second obstacle—**advertising clutter**—derives from the context in which ads are processed. Even if a person wanted to, it would be impossible to process and integrate every advertising message that he or she is exposed to each day. Pick up today's newspaper and start reviewing every ad you come across. Will you have time today to read them all? The clutter problem is further magnified by competitive brands making very similar performance claims. Now, was it Advil, Anacin, Aleve, Avia, Motrin, Nuprin, or Tylenol Gelcaps that promised you 12 hours of relief from your headache? (Can you even select the brand from this list that isn't a headache remedy?) The simple fact is that each of us is exposed to hundreds of ads each day, and no one has the time or inclination to sort through them all.

Consumers thus employ perceptual defenses to simplify and control their own ad processing. It is important here to see that the consumer is in control, and the advertiser must find some way to engage the consumer if an ad is to have any impact. Of course, the best way to engage consumers is to offer them information about a product or service that will address an active need state. Simply stated, it is difficult to get people to process a message about your headache remedy when they don't have a headache. **Selective attention** is certainly the advertiser's greatest challenge and produces tremendous waste of advertising dollars. Most ads are simply ignored by consumers. They turn the page, change the station, mute the sound, head for the refrigerator, or just daydream or doze off—rather than process the ad.

Advertisers employ a variety of tactics to break through the clutter. Popular music, celebrity spokespersons, sexy models, rapid scene changes, and anything that is novel are devices for combating selective attention.

LIVE THEATRE. CASINO GAMBLING.

Imagine a place where the two of you can enjoy all this, and more...The Museum of

JAZZ CLUBS. AND 300 RESTAURANTS THAT

African American History, the Motown Museum and shopping to rival Fifth Avenue.

DON'T SERVE A TOY WITH DINNER.

The place is Detroit and there's a lot to discover in a weekend...including yourselves.

For a free Visitors Guide, call 1-800-DETROIT, *ext. 1116.*

DETROIT
EXPECT A LOT

EXHIBIT 5.17

Cities too can engage in persuasive communications. Does this ad present an image of Detroit that is compatible with your prior beliefs? www .detroit.com

The battle for consumers' attention poses a major dilemma for advertisers. Without attention, there is no chance that an advertiser's message will have its desired impact; however, the provocative, attention-attracting devices used to engage consumers often become the focal point of consumers' ad processing. They remember seeing an ad featuring 27 Elvis Presley impersonators, but they can't recall what brand was being advertised or what claims were being made about the brand. If advertisers must entertain consumers to win their attention, they must be careful that the brand and message don't get lost in the shuffle.

Let's assume that an ad gets attention and the consumer comprehends its claims correctly. Will acceptance follow and create the enduring change in brand attitude that is desired, or will there be further resistance? If the message is asking the consumer to alter beliefs about the brand, expect more resistance. When the consumer is involved, attentive, and comprehends a claim that challenges current beliefs, the cognitive consistency impetus kicks in, and cognitive responses can be expected. **Cognitive responses** are the thoughts that occur to individuals at that exact moment in time when their beliefs and attitudes are being challenged by some form of persuasive communication. When these thoughts are negative in any way, the advertiser's goals are not served.[14] Messages designed to reinforce existing beliefs, or shape beliefs for a new brand that the consumer was unaware of previously, are more likely to win uncritical acceptance. Look at the ad in Exhibit 5.17. Is the ad's message designed to reinforce or change existing beliefs about the city of Detroit?

Shaping Attitudes via a Peripheral Route. For low-involvement products, like batteries or tortilla chips, cognitive responses to advertising claims are not expected.[15] In such situations, attitude formation will often follow a more peripheral route, and peripheral cues become the focal point for judging the ad's impact. **Peripheral cues** refer to features of the ad other than the actual arguments about the brand's performance. They include an attractive spokesperson, novel imagery, humorous incidents, or a catchy jingle. Any feature of the ad that prompts a pleasant emotional response could be thought of as a peripheral cue.

14.   For an expanded discussion of these issues, see Richard E. Petty, John T. Cacioppo, Alan J. Strathman, and Joseph R. Priester, "To Think or Not to Think: Exploring Two Routes to Persuasion," in *Persuasion: Psychological Insights and Perspectives,* ed. Sharon Shavitt and Timothy C. Brock (Boston: Allyn and Bacon, 1994), 113–47.
15.   Ibid.

In the peripheral route the consumer can still learn from an advertisement, but the learning is passive and typically must be achieved by frequent association of the peripheral cue (for example, the Eveready Energizer bunny) with the brand in question. It has even been suggested that classical conditioning principles might be employed by advertisers to facilitate and accelerate this associative learning process.[16] As consumers learn to associate pleasant feelings and attractive images with a brand, their attitude toward the brand should become more positive.

What do Paula Abdul, Jerry Seinfeld, the Pillsbury Doughboy, Joe Montana, the Keebler elves, and the song "Instant Karma!" by John Lennon have in common? They and many others like them have been used as peripheral cues in advertising campaigns. When all brands in a category offer similar benefits, the most fruitful avenue for advertising strategy is likely to be the peripheral route, where the advertiser merely tries to maintain positive or pleasant associations with the brand by constantly presenting it with appealing peripheral cues. This strategy can yield enhanced interest in the brand, but it is expensive because any gains made along the peripheral route are short-lived. Expensive TV airtime, lots of repetition, and a never-ending search for the freshest, most popular peripheral cues demand huge advertising budgets. When you think of the peripheral route, think of the advertising campaigns for high-profile, mature brands like Coke, Pepsi, Miller Lite, McDonald's, and Doritos.

Perspective Two: The Consumer as Social Being

The view of the consumer as decision maker is a popular and useful one. It taps into valuable knowledge of consumer psychology, or how consumers think about goods and services. It is not, however, without its limitations. It tells only part of the story. In its effort to isolate psychological mechanisms, this approach often takes consumer behavior out of its natural social context, making consumers appear utilitarian and overly rational. This section presents a second perspective on consumer behavior, a perspective concerned with social and cultural processes. It draws on basic ideas from anthropology, sociology, and communications, and it should be considered another part of the larger story of how advertising works.

But remember, this is just another perspective. We are still talking about the very same consumers we discussed in the preceding section; we are just viewing their behavior from a different vantage point. When it comes to the complexities of consumer behavior, we really can't have too many perspectives.

Let's now consider some of the elements of this second major perspective.

Advertising in a Cultural Context

❹ **Culture** is what a people do, or "the total life ways of a people, the social legacy the individual acquires from his group."[17] It is the way we eat, groom ourselves, celebrate, and mark our space and position. It is the way things are done. If you have traveled beyond your own country, you will have no doubt noticed that people in other cultures do things differently. If you were to point this out to one of the locals, say to a Parisian, and say something like, "Boy, you guys sure do things funny over here in France," you would no doubt be struck (perhaps literally) with the local's belief that it is not they, but you, who behave oddly. This is a manifestation of culture and points out that members of a culture find the ways they do things to be perfectly natural. Culture is thus said to be invisible to those who are immersed in it. Everyone around us behaves in a similar fashion, so we do not think about the existence of some large and powerful force acting on us all. But it's there; this constant background force is culture. Make no mistake, culture is real, and it affects

16.   For additional discussion of this issue, see Frances K. McSweeney and Calvin Bierley, "Recent Developments in Classical Conditioning," *Journal of Consumer Research* 11 (September 1984): 619–31.
17.   Gordon Marshall, ed., *The Concise Oxford Dictionary of Sociology* (New York: Oxford University Press, 1994), 104–105.

every aspect of human behavior, including consumer behavior and response to advertising. Culture surrounds the creation, transmission, reception, and interpretation of ads. Advertisements are cultural products. As suggested in the Global Issues box on this page, even general acceptance of advertising can vary dramatically between cultures.

Values. **Values** are the defining expressions of culture. They express in words and deeds what is important to a culture. For example, some cultures value individual freedom, while others value duty to the society at large. Some value propriety and restrained behavior, while others value open expression. Values are cultural bedrock. Values are enduring. They cannot be changed quickly or easily. They are thus very different from attitudes, which advertisers believe can be changed through a single advertising campaign, or even a single ad. Think of cultural values as the very strong and rigid foundation on which the much more mutable attitudes rest. Exhibit 5.18 illustrates this relationship. Values are the foundation of this structure. Attitudes are, in turn, influenced by values, as well as by many other sources. Advertising has to be consistent with, but cannot easily or quickly change, values.

It is thus senseless for an advertiser to speak of using advertising to change values in any substantive way. It can't happen. If advertising influences values at all, it does so in the same way a persistent drip of water wears down a granite slab—very slowly and through cumulative impact, over years and years—and even that is debatable.

Typically, advertisers try to either associate their product with a cultural value or criticize a competitor for being out of step with one. For example, in America, to say that a product "merely hides or masks odors" would be damning criticism indeed, because it suggests that anyone who would use such a product doesn't really value cleanliness and thus isn't like the rest of us.

GLOBAL ISSUES

ADVERTISING, RUSSIAN STYLE: MANY OBSTACLES HAVE MARKETERS SEEING RED

While advertising in traditional Eastern Bloc countries such as Poland is thriving under new market reforms, ad acceptance in the former heart of communism has been slow in coming. The reasons are varied. While consumer products advertising is relatively new in Russia, many consumers equate advertising in general with cold war state-sponsored propaganda. In fact, Russian consumers and their ex-Soviet neighbors are the most skeptical worldwide. In a global survey of some 40,000 individuals dispersed among 40 different countries, Roper Starch Worldwide found that only 9 percent of former Soviet Union residents believe that advertising actually contains useful information, compared with a global average of 38 percent.

Other reasons for lethargic Russian ad diffusion include political graft and instability. John Riley, the general manager of Russian operations for H. J. Heinz, states that "in the north, you're dealing with the cold; in the south, there's the war in the Caucasus; and everywhere in the country you're dealing with organized crime." Television advertising ceased altogether in Russia from May to August of 1995, as the ORT-Reklama (the media control board for the nation's largest network) sought to curb media wholesalers from price-gouging the state-owned channel. Shortly thereafter, ORT-Reklama's new executive director was slain, and his murder is believed to be ad-ban related. Next on the agenda for Russian regulators: higher advertising rates for foreign marketers than for Russian concerns.

Sources: "Consumer-Goods Firms Set Sights on Burgeoning Russian Market," *Wall Street Journal,* March 17, 1995, B5B; "Russian Ads Returning," *Advertising Age,* July 31, 1995, 2; and "Ex-Soviet States Lead World in Ad Cynicism," *Advertising Age,* June 5, 1995, 3.

indeed, because it suggests that anyone who would use such a product doesn't really value cleanliness and thus isn't like the rest of us.

Advertisements must be consistent with the values of a people. If they are not, they will likely be rejected. Many argue that the best (most effective) ads are those that best express and affirm core cultural values. For example, one core American value is individualism, or the predisposition to value the individual over the group. This value has been part of American culture for as long as there has been an America. It is at the center of American social identity. Advertisements that celebrate or affirm this value are more likely to succeed than ones that denigrate or ignore it. Exhibit 5.19 shows an ad that leans heavily on this value. As a practical matter, American advertisers can rarely go wrong by celebrating this core cultural value of individualism.

EXHIBIT 5.18
*Cultural values, attitudes, and consumer behavior.
Some believe advertising can directly affect consumer
behavior and, over time, cultural values as well.*

Rituals. Rituals are "often-repeated formalized behaviors involving symbols."[18] Cultures participate in rituals. Cultures affirm, express, and maintain their values through rituals. Rituals are core elements of culture. They are a way in which individuals are made part of the culture, and a method by which the culture constantly renews and perpetuates itself. For example, ritual-laden holidays like Thanksgiving, Christmas, and the Fourth of July help perpetuate aspects of American culture through their repeated reenactment. Because they include consumption (for example, feasts and gift giving), they help intertwine national culture and consumption practices (see Exhibit 5.20). For example, Jell-O may have attained the prominence of a national food because of its regular usage as part of the Thanksgiving dinner ritual.[19]

But rituals don't have to be the biggest events of the year. There are also everyday rituals, such as the way we eat, clean ourselves, and groom. Think about all the habitual,

EXHIBIT 5.19

Everybody deserves a chance to express their individuality. Right?

EXHIBIT 5.20 *Pumpkin pie is a food that many in America include as part of the Thanksgiving dinner ritual. Notice in this ad that Mrs. Smith's pies are offered as a perfect fit for such holiday rituals.*

18.   Ibid., 452.
19.   Melanie Wallendorf and Eric J. Arnould, "We Gather Together: Consumption Rituals of Thanksgiving Day," *Journal of Consumer Research* 18, no. 1 (June 1991): 13–31.

routine things you do from the time you get up in the morning until you crawl into bed at night. These things are done in a certain way; they are not random. Members of a common culture tend to do them one way, and members of other cultures do them other ways. Again, if you've ever visited another country, you have no doubt noticed significant differences. An American dining in Paris might be surprised to have a dessert to begin the meal and a salad to end it.

Daily rituals seem inconsequential because they are habitual and routine. If, however, someone tried to get you to significantly alter the way you do these things, he or she would quickly learn just how important and resistant to change these rituals are.

If a product or service cannot be incorporated into an already-existing ritual, it is very difficult and expensive for advertisers to effect a change. If, on the other hand, an advertiser can successfully incorporate the consumption of its good or service into an existing ritual, then success is much more likely.

How Ads Transmit Cultural Meaning. The link between culture and advertising is key. Anthropologist Grant McCracken has offered the model in Exhibit 5.21 to explain how advertising (along with other cultural agents) functions in the transmission of meaning. To understand advertising as a mechanism of meaning transfer is to understand a great deal about advertising. In fact, one could legitimately say that advertisers are really in the meaning-transfer business.

Think about McCracken's model as you examine the ad for Johnston and Murphy in Exhibit 5.22. The product—in this case, shoes—exists "out there" in the culturally constituted world, but it needs advertising to link it to certain social representations, certain slices of life. The advertiser places the advertised product and the slice of social life in an ad to get the two to rub off on each other, to intermingle, to become part of the same social reality. In other words, the product is given social meaning by being placed within an ad that represents some social reality. This slice of life, of course, is the type of social setting in which potential customers might find, or desire to find, themselves. According to McCracken's model, meaning has moved from the world to the product (shoes) by virtue of its sharing space within the social frame of the advertisement. When a consumer purchases or otherwise incorporates that good or service into his or her own life, the meaning is transferred to the individual consumer. Meaning is thus moved from the world to the product (via advertising) to the individual. When the individual uses the product, that person conveys to others the meaning he or she and the advertisement have now given it. Their use incorporates various rituals that facilitate the movement of meaning from good to consumer.

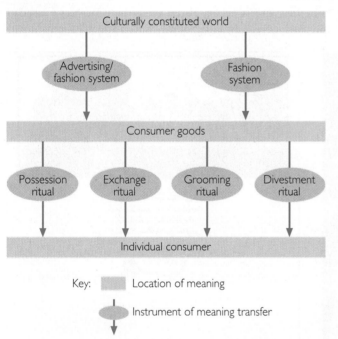

EXHIBIT 5.21

The movement of meaning.

Key: [ ] Location of meaning

[ ] Instrument of meaning transfer

Source: Grant McCracken, *Culture and Consumption* (Bloomington: Indiana University Press, 1988), 72. Reprinted with permission of Indiana University Press.

Advertising in a Societal Context

5 While culture is essentially what a people do, **society** is "a group of people who share a common culture, occupy a particular territorial area, and feel themselves to constitute a unified and a distinct entity."[20] Examples are American society, Southern society, and Eastern society. Within a society, many

20. Marshall, 498.

social forces and social institutions operate. Consumer behavior and advertising are dependent on the actions of these social institutions, agents, and forces. Social factors like class, reference groups, gender, race, family, and community all have a significant impact on consumer behavior and the way consumers respond to advertising.

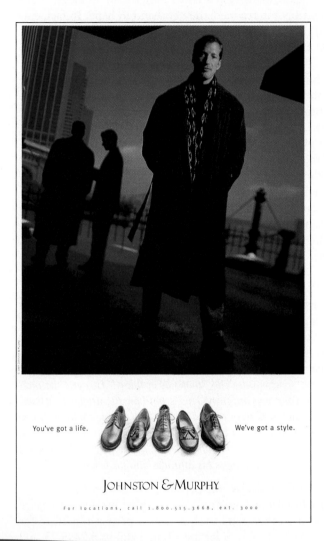

You've got a life.   We've got a style.

JOHNSTON &MURPHY.

For locations, call 1.800.515.3668, ext. 3000

EXHIBIT 5.22

A Johnston & Murphy shoe is not just any shoe. One goal of this adver-tisement is to create a special meaning for this brand of men's shoes.

Social Class. **Social class** refers to a person's relative standing in a social hierarchy resulting from systematic inequalities in the social system. (These systematic inequalities are also known as social stratification.) Social class is a type of social stratification. Wealth, power, prestige, and status are not distributed equally within our society. People are rich or poor, powerful or powerless, possess low status or high status, and so on. Race and gender are likewise unequally distributed within classes of power, income, and status. Thus, a cross section, or slice, of American society would reveal many different levels (or strata) of the population in these different dimensions.

Social class has historically been a fairly slippery concept. For example, some individuals possess higher social class than their income indicates and vice versa. Successful plumbers often have higher incomes than college professors, but their occupation is (perhaps) less prestigious. Education also has something to do with social class, but a person with a little college experience and a lot of inherited wealth will probably rank higher than an insurance agent with an MBA. Thus income, education, and occupation are three important variables for indicating social class, but are still individually, or even collectively, inadequate at capturing its full meaning. Clearly, complex combinations of social rewards and social opportunities comprise social class.[21] Others have argued that the emergence of the New Class, a class of technologically skilled and highly educated individuals with great access to information and information technology, will change the way we define social class: Knowledge of, and access to, information may begin to challenge property as a determinant of social class.[22]

Here, we use the term *social class* in a very inclusive sense. To us, social class includes not only economic criteria (such as income and property), but prestige, status, mobility, and a felt sense of similarity or communal belonging. Members of a social class tend to live in a similar way, have similar views and philosophies, and, most critically, tend to consume in similar ways.

Markers of social class include what one wears, where one lives, and how one talks. In a consumer society, consumption marks or indicates social class in a myriad of ways. In fact, some believe that social class is the single biggest predictor of consumer behavior and consumer response to advertising. Despite the contributions to advertising practice by psychologists, in real-world advertising agencies, social class (and correlates) dwarfs anything else in terms of its use in actual advertising planning.

21.   James R. Kluegel and Eliot R. Smith, *Beliefs About Inequality: Americans' View of What Is and What Ought to Be* (New York: Aldine de Gruyter, 1986).
22.   Alvin W. Gouldner, "The Future of Intellectuals and the Rise of the New Class," in *Social Stratification in Sociological Perspective: Class, Race and Gender,* ed. David B. Grusky (San Francisco: Westview Press, 1994), 711–29.

One reason for this is the power of social class in determining consumption tastes and preferences, including media habits, and thus exposure to various advertising media vehicles, for example *RV Life* versus *Wine Spectator*. We think of tennis more than bowling as belonging to the upper classes, chess more than checkers, and Brie more than Velveeta. Ordering wine instead of beer has social significance, as does wearing Tommy Hilfiger rather than Lee jeans, or driving a Volvo rather than a Chevy. Social class and consumption are undeniably intertwined; they go hand in hand. In fact, cultural theorist Pierre Bourdieu argues that social class is such a powerful socializing factor that it "structures the whole experience of subjects," particularly when it comes to consumption tastes.[23]

Consider some examples. Think about the purchases of equivalently priced cars, say a Saab and a Cadillac. The Saab is owned by a young architect, the Cadillac by the owner of small construction company. Now, these two consumers don't frequent the same restaurants, drink in the same bars, or eat the same kinds of foods. They don't belong to the same social class, and it is evident in their consumption.

Consider the contents of the living rooms of those in various social classes, as shown in Exhibit 5.23. The differences are not due to money only, or the lack of it. Clearly, there is another dynamic at work here. Social-class-related consumption preferences are reflective of class-related value differences and of different ways of seeing the world and the role of things in it.

Class also becomes apparent when a person moves from one class into another. Consider the following example:

Movin' on Up

Bob and Jill move into a more-expensive neighborhood. Both had grown up in lower-middle-class surroundings and had, after graduate school, moved into high-paying jobs. They have now moved into a fairly upscale neighborhood, comprised mostly of "older money." On one of the first warm Sundays, Bob goes out to his driveway and begins to do something he has done all his life, change the oil in his car. One of Bob's neighbors comes over and chats, and ever so subtly suggests to Bob that people in this neighborhood have "someone else" do "that sort of thing." Bob gets the message: It's not cool to change your oil in your own driveway. This is not how the neighbors behave. It doesn't matter if you like to do it or not, it is simply not done. To Bob, paying someone else to do this simple job seems wasteful and uppity. He's a bit offended, and a little embarrassed. But, over time, he decides that it's better to go along with the other people in the neighborhood. Over time, Bob begins to see the error of his ways and changes his attitudes and his behavior.

This is an example of the effect of social class on consumer behavior. Bob will no longer be a good target for Fram, Puralator, AutoZone, or any other product or service used to change oil at home. On the other hand, Bob is now a perfect candidate for quick oil change businesses, like Jiffy Lube. Consider the ads in Exhibits 5.24, 5.25, and 5.26 in terms of social-class considerations. Which social classes do you believe are being targeted by these ads?

Family. The consumer behavior of families is also of great interest to advertisers. Advertisers want to not only discern the needs of different kinds of families, but also discover how decisions are made within families. The first is possible; the latter is much more difficult. For a while, consumer researchers tried to determine who in the traditional nuclear family (that is, mom, dad, and the kids) made various purchasing decisions. This was largely an exercise in futility. Due to errors in reporting and conflicting perceptions between husbands and wives, it became clear that the family purchasing process is anything but clear. While some types of purchases are handled by one family member, many decisions are actually diffuse nondecisions, arrived at through what consumer

23.   Pierre Bourdieu, "Distinction: A Social Critique of the Judgement of Taste," in *Social Stratification in Sociological Perspective: Class, Race and Gender*, ed. David B. Grusky (San Francisco: Westview Press, 1994), 711–29.

EXHIBIT 5.23

Living room clusters and social status.

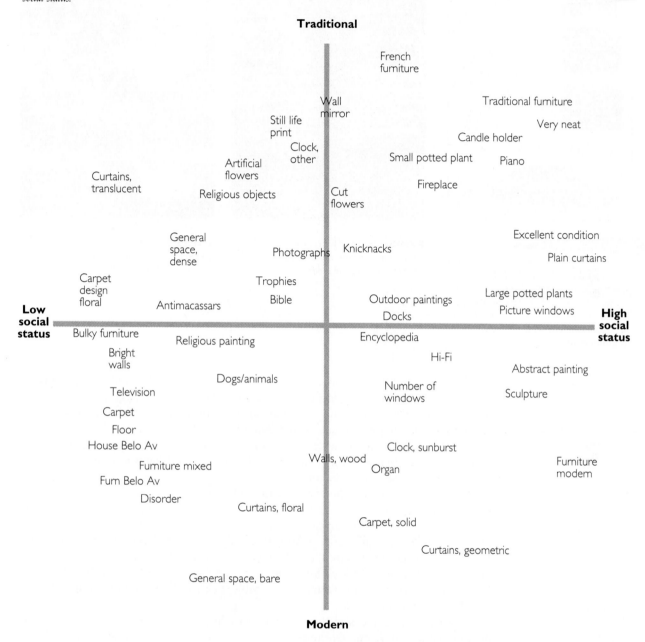

researcher C. W. Park aptly calls a "muddling through" process.[24] These "decisions" just get made, and no one is really sure who made them, or even when. For an advertiser to influence such a diffuse and vague process is indeed a challenge. The consumer behavior of the family is a complex and often subtle type of social negotiation. One person handles this, one takes care of that. Sometimes, specific purchases fall along gender

24.   C. Whan Park, "Joint Decisions in Home Purchasing: A Muddling-Through Process," *Journal of Consumer Research* 9 (September 1982): 151–62.

EXHIBIT 5.24

Automobiles offer tremendous symbolic meaning that may reflect their owner's social status. To protect its status potential, Jaguar refuses to be associated with an unrefined phrase like used car. Instead, we see used Jaguars presented as Select Edition Pre-Owned Jaguars. www .jaguarcars.com/

EXHIBIT 5.25 *Wolverine boots are obviously for no-nonsense, working people. They are merely durable and comfortable.*

EXHIBIT 5.26 *Leisure-time pursuits vary by social class.* planetreebok.com/ *and* www.jcpenney.com/

lines, but sometimes they don't.[25] Still, some advertisers capitalize on the flexibility of this social system by suggesting in their ads who should take charge of a given consumption task, and then arming that person with the appearance of expertise so that whoever wants the job can take it and defend his or her purchases. (While they may not be the buyer in many instances, children can play important roles as initiators, influencers, and users in many categories, like cereals, clothing, vacation destinations, fast-food restaurants, and even computers.)

We also know that families have a lasting influence on the consumer preferences of family members. One of the best predictors of the brands adults use is the ones their parents used. This is true for cars, toothpaste, household cleansers, and many more products. Say you go off to college. You eventually have to do laundry, so you go to the store, and you buy Tide. Why Tide? Well, you're not sure, but you saw it around your house when you lived with your parents, and things seemed to have worked out okay for them, so you buy it for yourself. The habit sticks, and you keep buying it. This is called an *intergenerational effect*.

Advertisers often focus on the major or gross differences in types of families, because different families have different needs, buy different things, and are reached by different media. Family roles often change when both parents (or a single parent) are employed outside the home. For instance, a teenage son or daughter may be given the role of initiator and buyer, while the parent or parents serve merely as influences. Furthermore, we should remember that Ward, June, Wally, and the Beaver are not (if they ever were) the norm. There are a lot of single parents and second and third marriages. *Family* is a very open concept. In addition to the "traditional" nuclear family and the single-parent household, there is the extended family (nuclear family plus grandparents, cousins, and others) and the so-called alternative family (single and never-married mothers and gay and lesbian households with and without children, for example).

25.   For an excellent article on this topic, see Craig J. Thompson, William B. Locander, and Howard R. Pollio, "The Lived Meaning of Free Choice: An Existential–Phenomenological Description of Everyday Consumer Experiences of Contemporary Married Women," *Journal of Consumer Research* 17 (December 1990): 346–61.

Beyond the basic configuration, advertisers are often interested in knowing things like the age of the youngest child, the size of the family, and the family income. The age of the youngest child living at home tells an advertiser where the family is in terms of their needs and obligations (that is, toys, investment instruments for college savings, clothing, and vacations). When the youngest child leaves home, the consumption patterns of a family radically change.

Reference Groups.   Obviously, other people can have a dramatic impact on our consumption priorities, as the Fox ad in Exhibit 5.27 shows. The term **reference group** refers to any configuration of other persons that a particular individual uses as a point of reference in making his or her own consumption decisions.

Reference groups can be small and intimate (you and the persons sharing your neighborhood) or large and distant (you and all other persons taking an advertising course). Reference groups can also vary in their degree of formal structure. They can exist as part of some larger organization—like any business or employer—with formal rules for who must be part of the group and what is expected of the group in terms of each day's performance. Or they may be informal in their composition and agenda, like a group of casual friends who all live in the same apartment complex.

Another way of categorizing reference groups involves the distinction between membership and aspirational groups.[26] **Membership groups** are those that we interact with in person on some regular basis; we have personal contact with the group and its other members. **Aspirational groups** are made up of people we admire or use as role models, but it is likely we will never interact with the members of this group in any meaningful way. However, because we aspire to be like the members of this group, they can set standards for our own behavior. Professional athletes, movie stars, rock 'n' roll bands, and successful business executives become role models whether they like it or not. Of course, advertisers are keenly aware of the potential influence of aspirational groups, and they commonly employ celebrities, from Shaq to Cher, as endorsers for their products. (See Exhibit 5.28.) After all, who wouldn't want to be, to paraphrase another ad, like Michael Jordan?

Reference groups affect our consumption in a variety of ways. At the simplest level, they can furnish information that helps us evaluate products and brands, and if we will actually consume a particular product (for example, tonight's dinner), with the group, the group's preferences may become hard to distinguish from one's own. Additionally, reference groups play an important role in legitimizing the symbolic value of some forms of consumption—that is, individuals choose some brands because they perceive that using these products will enhance their image with a reference group, signal to others the particular reference group they belong to, or serve as a gift to another member of the group to let that person know how special he or she is. And where do products and brands get their symbolic meaning that makes them valuable as props for communicating with others? How did Cadillac become a symbol of status and Nike become a symbol of devotion to

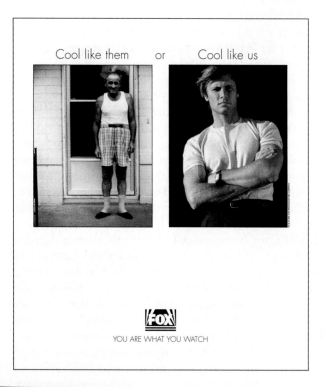

EXHIBIT 5.27

Fox wants to be perceived as the modern, hip alternative to those stodgy old television networks. So if you watch Fox, you'll be just like the guy on the right. Cool. **www.foxnetwork.com/**

26.   For additional explanation of this distinction, see Michael R. Solomon, *Consumer Behavior* (Boston: Allyn and Bacon, 1994), 368–70.

performance? Such symbolism is shaped and reaffirmed by years of consistent advertising, as long as the status conferred is consistent with the other coexisting social forces. Even great advertising will not succeed against the tide.

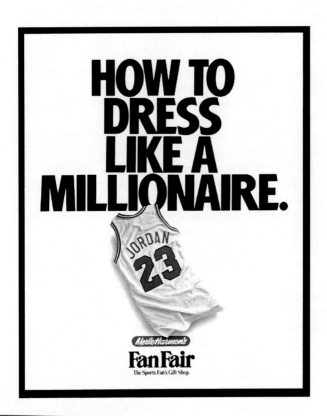

EXHIBIT 5.28

Michael Jordan has proved to be one of the best celebrity endorsers of all time. From Wheaties to basketball gear to Hanes underwear, he has sold it all. Did you ever want to be like Mike?

Race and Ethnicity. Race and ethnicity provide other ways to think about important social groups. Answering the question of how race figures into consumer behavior is difficult. Our discomfort stems from having, on the one hand, the desire to say, "Race doesn't matter, we're all the same," and on the other hand not wanting (or not being able) to deny the significance of race in terms of reaching ethnic subcultures and influencing a wide variety of behaviors, including consumer behavior. Obviously, a person's pigmentation, in and of itself, has almost nothing to do with preferences for one type of product over another. But because race has mattered in culture, it does matter in consumer behavior. To the extent that race is part of culture, it matters. Race clearly affects cultural and social phenomena. But how do we (and should we) deal with that reality?

There probably isn't an area in consumer behavior where research is more inadequate. We simply know next to nothing about the role of race in consumer behavior. This is probably because everyone is terrified to discuss it, and because most of the findings we do have are suspect. What is attributed to race is often due to another factor that is itself associated with race. For example, consumer behavior textbooks commonly say something to the effect that African-Americans and Hispanics are more brand loyal than their Anglo counterparts. Data on the frequency of brand switching is offered, and lo and behold, it does appear that white people switch brands more often. But why? Some ethnic minorities live in areas where there are fewer retail choices. When we statistically remove the effect of income disparities between whites and people of color, we see that the brand-switching effect often disappears. This suggests that brand loyalty is not a function of race, but of disposable income and shopping options.

Still, race is something that does inform one's social identity to varying degrees. One is not blind to one's own ethnicity. African-Americans, Latinos and Latinas, and other ethnic groups have culturally related consumption preferences. It is not enough, however, for advertisers to say one group is different from another group. If they really want a good, long-term relationship with their customers, they must acquire, through good consumer research, a deeper understanding of who their customers are and how this identity is informed by culture, felt ethnicity, and race. In short, advertisers must ask why groups of consumers are different, and not settle for an easy answer. It wasn't until the mid to late 1980s that most American corporations made a concerted effort to court the African-American consumer.[27] Efforts to serve the Hispanic consumer have been intermittent and inconsistent. Ads directed toward these audiences are shown in Exhibits 5.29, 5.30, and 5.31.

27.   Jannette L. Dates, "Advertising," in *Split Image: African Americans in the Mass Media,* ed. Jannette L. Dates and William Barlow (Washington, D.C.: Howard University Press, 1990), 421–54.

EXHIBIT 5.29

Diversity is a fact of life in modern America. General Mills and many other companies reflect this fact in their advertising.

EXHIBIT 5.30 *This ad ran in the publication* Hispanic Business. *However, the basic message of the ad is relevant for any businessperson traveling to Latin America.* **www.ual.com/**

EXHIBIT 5.31 *This Sprint ad recognizes the importance of reference groups, particularly the ethnicity of membership groups, in attracting consumers in new markets. Select a specific reference group. What would you include in an ad to appeal to this group? How does the Sprint Web site* **www.sprint.com/** *appeal to different reference groups? Does the site appeal to your reference group? For comparison, visit MCI's Web site* **www.mci.com/**. *How does MCI handle reference-group issues?*

Gender. Gender is the social expression of sexual biology, sexual choice, or both. Obviously, gender matters in consumption. But are men and women really that different in any meaningful way in their consumption behavior, beyond the obvious? Again, to the extent that gender informs a "culture of gender," the answer is yes. As long as men and women are the products of differential socialization, then they will continue to be different in some ways. There is, however, no definitive list of gender differences in consumption, because the expression of gender, just like anything else social, depends on the situation and the social circumstances. In the 1920s, advertisers openly referred to women as less logical, more emotional, the cultural stewards of beauty.[28] (Some argue that the same soft, irrational, emotional feminine persona is still invoked in 1990s advertising.) Advertising helps construct a social reality, with gender a predominant feature. Not

28. Roland Marchand, *Advertising: The American Dream* (Berkeley, Calif.: University of California Press, 1984).

only is it a matter of conscience and social responsibility to be aware of this construction, but it is good business as well. Advertisers must keep in mind, though, that it's hard to do business with people you patronize, insult, or ignore.

Obviously, gender's impact on consumer behavior is not limited to heterosexual men and women. Gay men and lesbian women are large and significant markets. Of late, these markets have been much more publicly courted. Again, these are markets that desire to be acknowledged and served, but not stereotyped and patronized. Exhibits 5.32 and 5.33 are ads targeted at lesbian and gay audiences.

In the late 1970s, advertisers discovered working women. In the 1980s, marketers discovered African-American consumers, about the same time they discovered Latino and Latina consumers. Later they discovered Asian-Americans, and just lately they discovered gays and lesbians. Of course, these people weren't missing. They were there all along. These "discoveries" of forgotten and marginalized social groups create some interesting problems for advertisers. Members of these groups, quite reasonably, want to be served just like any other consumers. To reach these markets, one should remember what Julian Bond said that black Americans want from advertisers:

To believe that we are buying the best of the top of the line ticket item . . . that the company that sells to us hires us and has us on its board . . . that our pictures will be in some of the ads without the use of patronizing, specious jargon.

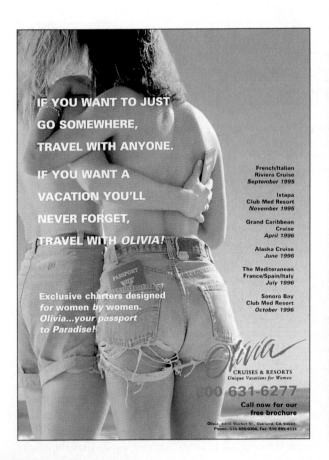

EXHIBIT 5.32

Same-sex partners may have distinctive preferences when choosing vacation packages. Olivia Cruises & Resorts makes an explicit appeal to lesbian couples with its exclusive packages designed for women by women. **www.oliviatravel.com/**

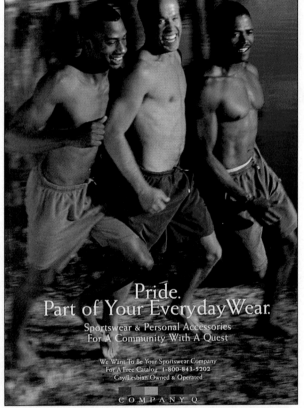

EXHIBIT 5.33 *Gay men and lesbian women are becoming a significant force in the marketplace. This ad makes a direct appeal to these gender segments.*

Attention without stereotyping from a medium and a genre that is known for stereo-typing might be a lot to expect, but it's not that much.

Community. **Community** is a powerful and traditional sociological variable. It is considered by some to be the fundamental concept in sociology. It is defined as a "wide-ranging relationship of solidarity over a rather undefined area of life and interests."[29] Advertisers are becoming increasingly aware of its power. It is important in at least two major ways. First, it is where consumption is grounded, where consumption literally lives. To speak about consumption outside of community is unnecessarily limiting. Products have social meanings, community is the quintessential social domain, so consumption is inseparable from the notion of where we live. Communities may be the fundamental reference group, and they exhibit a great deal of power. A community may be your neighborhood, or it may be persons like you with whom you feel a kinship, such as members of social clubs, other consumers who collect the same things you do, or persons who have the same interests you do. In a consumer society, goods and services figure prominently into the symbolic fabric of communities. Communities may also transcend geography to include those who may never know one another but who connect through a common text (such as an ad) or a product.

Second, the extent to which brands can derive power is determined in part by something called brand community. **Brand communities** are groups of consumers who feel a commonality and a shared purpose grounded or attached to a consumer good or service.[30] When owners of Doc Martens or Saabs, Mountain Dews or Saturns, experience a sense of connectedness by virtue of their common ownership or usage, a brand community exists. When two perfect strangers stand in a parking lot and act like old friends simply because they both own Saturns, a type of community is revealed. Indeed, Saturn's Spring Hill Homecoming, described in the Contemporary Issues box on page 150, is considered a great marketing success story in the area of cultivating brand community. Exhibit 5.34 reinforces the communal appeal of Saturn.

Advertising as Social Text

Remember, the meaning of an ad does not exist inviolate and immutable within its borders. In fact, it doesn't exist there at all. Meaning is constructed in the minds of consumers, not delivered by advertisements. What an ad means is determined through a subtle, but nonetheless powerful, process of meaning construction by consumers. What something means depends on who the consumer is, the strategy or motivation with which he or she receives the ad, and the ad itself. Consider texts in general: For some African-Americans, reading *Huckleberry Finn* is a very different experience than it is for white suburban middle-class kids. In fact, if the experience is so entirely different, then so is the text for these two groups. In other words, there is no single text. Since what a text means is really up to the reader, then we must acknowledge that who the reader is, in terms of major psychological and sociological factors, matters as well.[31]

Textual meaning is created through the interaction of sociological, cultural, and individual factors. So it is for ads. Ads are no less texts than *Huckleberry Finn*. Consumers determine what ads mean, and since they are socially situated within significant groups, their interpretations will be affected by those group memberships.[32] Ads are created by organizations (social entities) through social processes, all affected by social actions.

29.   Gordon Marshall, ed., *The Concise Oxford Dictionary of Sociology* (New York: Oxford University Press, 1994), 72–73.
30.   Thomas C. O'Guinn and Albert Muniz Jr., *Brand Communities* (Urbana, Ill.: University of Illinois Press, 1994).
31.   Stanley Fish, *Is There a Text in This Class?* (Cambridge, Mass.: Harvard University Press, 1980).
32.   Linda M. Scott, "The Bridge from Text to Mind: Adapting Reader Response Theory for Consumer Research," *Journal of Consumer Research* 21 (December 1994): 461–86; and David Glenn Mick and Claus Buhl, "A Meaning-Based Model of Advertising Experiences," *Journal of Consumer Research* 19 (December 1992): 312–38.

GM's Saturn division has been a leader in promoting a sense of community among its owners. In this ad, that sense of community is cultivated through photographs from the Spring Hill Homecoming. Savvy Saturn marketers used the homecoming as a feature in advertising campaigns to show that the bond between Saturn owners and their cars is something special. www.saturncars.com/index.html

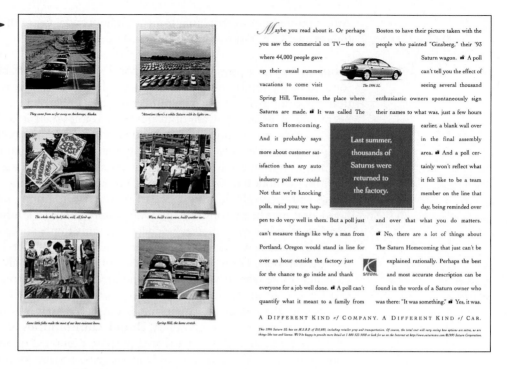

They are then interpreted according to social conventions and have their meanings determined through social interpretive processes.

CONTEMPORARY ISSUES

COMING TOGETHER ... OVER SATURN

It sounded like a goofy idea: Invite every Saturn owner to a "homecoming" at the Spring Hill, Tennessee, plant where their cars were "born." After all, who in their right mind would plan their vacation around a remote manufacturing facility? About 44,000 Saturn owners, that's who. And another 135,000 at Saturn retailers across the United States for tie-in events. Add in the national publicity provided from the news media and ensuing Saturn ads depicting the event, and the idea isn't so goofy anymore.

Retention marketing is the most cost-effective means of generating future sales. In fact, it costs up to ten times more to generate new customers than to retain existing ones. The genius of the Spring Hill Homecoming (and subsequent ads) is that Saturn's primary marketing strategy revolves around strong customer relations and service. The four-day event at the Tennessee plant rewarded customers for their purchase behavior and provided reassurance for new car shoppers seeking the trust and relationships that allay service-related fears and the general mystery of new car buying. Saturn's innovative approach is also integral to the overall marketing strategy of its parent company, General Motors; the overwhelming majority of Saturn sales come from previous import owners, and not at the expense of other GM divisions. Actually, Saturn's retention programs just may be the greatest tangible benefit to arise from GM's earth-shaking $5 billion initial investment in the Saturn project.

Think about how different individuals might interpret the ads shown in Exhibits 5.35 and 5.36. Of course, the different meanings will not be random. While there will be variations, the meanings will have a certain commonality about them, because members of the same culture tend to bring similar cultural baggage to the interpretive event (reading the ad) and thus render similar interpretations. When advertisers include social and cultural factors in their analysis of consumer behavior, they dramatically enhance their chances of anticipating the meaning consumers will draw from advertisements.

Sources: "Savvy Companies Hold Customers," *Sales & Marketing Management* (December 1994): 15; and "The Superstars behind 100 Success Stories," *Advertising Age*, June 6, 1995, S-12.

SUMMARY

❶ Describe the four basic stages of consumer decision making.

Advertisers need a keen understanding of their consumers as a basis for developing effective advertising. This understanding begins with a view of consumers as systematic decision makers who follow a predictable process in making their choices among products and brands. The process begins when consumers perceive a need, and it proceeds with a search for information that will help in making an informed choice. The search-and-evaluation stage is followed by purchase. Postpurchase use and evaluation then become critical as the stage in which customer satisfaction is ultimately determined.

❷ Explain how consumers adapt their decision-making processes as a function of involvement and experience.

Some purchases are more important to people than others, and this fact adds complexity to any analysis of consumer behavior. To accommodate this complexity, advertisers

often think about the level of involvement that attends any given purchase. Involvement and prior experience with a product or service category can lead to four diverse modes of consumer decision making. These modes are extended problem solving, limited problem solving, habit or variety seeking, and brand loyalty.

❸ Discuss how advertising may influence consumer behavior through its effects on various psychological states.

Advertisements are developed to influence the way people think about products and brands. More specifically, advertising is designed to affect consumers' beliefs and brand attitudes. Multi-attribute attitude models are a tool used by advertisers to help them ascertain the beliefs and attitudes of target consumers. However, consumers have perceptual defenses that allow them to ignore or distort most of the commercial messages they are exposed to. When consumers are not motivated to thoughtfully process an advertiser's message, it may be in that advertiser's best interest to feature one or more peripheral cues as part of the message.

❹ Discuss the interaction of culture and advertising.

Advertisements are cultural products, and culture provides the context in which an ad will be interpreted. Advertisers who overlook the influence of culture are bound to struggle in their attempt to communicate with the target audience. Two key concepts in managing the impact of culture are values and rituals. Values are enduring beliefs that provide a foundation for more-transitory psychological states, like brand attitudes. Rituals are patterns of behavior shared by individuals from a common culture. Violating cultural values and rituals is a sure way to squander advertising dollars.

❺ Discuss the role of sociological factors in consumer behavior and advertising response.

Consumer behavior is an activity that each of us undertakes before a broad audience of other consumers. Advertising helps the transfer of meaning. Reference groups of various types have a dramatic influence on the consumption behavior of their individual members. Reference groups can be either groups we merely aspire to be part of, or groups, like our families, that count us as members.

KEY TERMS

consumer behavior (119)
need state (120)
functional benefits (121)
emotional benefits (121)
internal search (122)
external search (124)
consideration set (124)
evaluative criteria (125)
customer satisfaction (126)
cognitive dissonance (126)
involvement (127)
extended problem solving (128)
limited problem solving (128)
habit (130)
variety seeking (130)
brand loyalty (130)
attitude (132)
brand attitudes (132)
beliefs (132)

salient beliefs (133)
multi-attribute attitude models (MAAMs) (133)
cognitive consistency (135)
advertising clutter (135)
selective attention (136)
cognitive responses (136)
peripheral cues (136)
culture (137)
values (138)
rituals (139)
society (140)
social class (141)
reference group (145)
membership groups (145)
aspirational groups (145)
gender (148)
community (149)
brand communities (149)

QUESTIONS FOR REVIEW AND CRITICAL THINKING

1. When consumers have a well-defined consideration set and a list of evaluative criteria for assessing the brands in that set, they in effect possess a matrix of information about that category. Drawing on your experiences as a consumer, set up and fill in such a matrix for the category *fast-food restaurants*.

2. Is cognitive dissonance a good thing or a bad thing from an advertiser's point of view? Explain how and why advertisers should try to take advantage of the cognitive dissonance their consumers may be experiencing.

3. Most people quickly relate to the notion that some purchasing decisions are more involving than others. What kinds of products or services do you consider highly involving? What makes these products more involving from your point of view?

4. Explain the difference between brand-loyal and habitual purchasing. When a brand-loyal customer arrives at a store and finds her favorite brand is out of stock, what would you expect to happen next?

5. Describe three attitude-change strategies that could be suggested by the results of a study of consumer behavior using multi-attribute attitude models. Provide examples of different advertising campaigns that have employed each of these strategies.

6. Watch an hour of prime-time television and for each commercial you see, make a note of the tactic the advertiser employed to capture and hold the audience's attention. How can the use of attention-attracting tactics backfire on an advertiser?

7.   What does it mean to say that culture is "invisible"? Explain how this invisible force serves to restrict and control the activities of advertisers.

8.   Give three examples of highly visible cultural rituals practiced annually in the United States. For each ritual you identify, assess the importance of buying and consuming for effective practice of the ritual.

9.   Are you a believer in the intergenerational effect? Make a list of the brands in your cupboards, refrigerator, and medicine cabinet. Which of these brands would you also expect to find in your parents' cupboards, refrigerator, and medicine cabinet?

10.   "In today's modern, highly educated society, there is simply no reason to separate men and women into different target segments. Gender just should not be an issue in the development of marketing and advertising strategies." Comment.

EXPERIENTIAL EXERCISE

In this chapter, you learned about MAAMs. Divide into teams. Go to the toothpaste, toothbrush, cereal, or shampoo section of a grocery store. How many different brands are displayed? Develop a list of attributes for the product category your team chose. Are there any attributes associated with new products? What are they, and what brands have them? Which attributes are especially important to team members when buying a brand in this product category? Which attributes do team members find irrelevant? Discuss with the class the beliefs and attitudes various team members have toward the brands.

USING THE INTERNET

Consumers often follow a predictable decision-making process when purchasing products. Web sites can be configured to influence a specific stage or several stages of the decision-making process. Visit the following sites:

Edmund's Automobile Buyer's Guides:
www.edmund.com

Isuzu: www.isuzu.com

1.   Which stage or stages of the consumer decision-making process does each site address?

2.   How do the sites differ in addressing the process of buying a car?

3.   How do the sites differ in addressing functional and emotional benefits?

Now, compare the Amazon.com Books and Reebok sites:

Amazon.com Books: www.amazon.com

Reebok: www.reebok.com

4.   Which stage or stages of the consumer decision-making process does each site address?

5.   How do the sites differ in developing brand loyalty?

6.   How do the sites differ in producing customer satisfaction?

Chapter 6

Market
Segmentation,
Positioning,
and Product
Differentiation

After reading and thinking about this chapter, you will be able to do the following:

1 Explain the process known as STP marketing.

2 Describe different bases that marketers use to identify target segments.

3 Discuss the criteria used for choosing a target segment.

4 Identify the essential elements of an effective positioning strategy.

5 Compare and contrast market segmentation and product differentiation strategies.

Segmenting, Targeting, Positioning, and . . . the Slurpee

Consider the problem faced by 7-Eleven stores a few years ago with their beverage product, the Slurpee. While 7-Eleven's executives considered their 30-year-old slush drink "a true piece of Americana," the marketplace had become bored with the Slurpee. Sales were stagnant, and consumer surveys showed that most 7-Eleven customers knew about the product but had little interest in purchasing it.[1]

How could an organization like 7-Eleven revive the Slurpee? One way involves going back to the drawing board and reinventing the market segmentation strategy. The first step is to identify possible target segments for the Slurpee. Next, select one segment of the market as a target and create a new marketing program with this target segment in mind. The 7-Eleven marketing managers chose males age 12 to 18 as the target for their renewed marketing efforts and set out to reposition the product to make it more attractive to this segment. New flavors were created with assistance from the Coca-Cola Company, and cups, lids, and straws were redesigned to make them something that "kids would want to be seen with while they were rollerblading down the street."

Next, 7-Eleven's advertising agency was brought in to create the campaign that would introduce the new Slurpee to the target segment. Working with its agency, 7-Eleven conceived a novel benefit for the new Slurpee and called it the brain freeze. If one slurps one's Slurpee rapidly—especially on a hot summer day after inline skating—one's temples start to throb. To reach the target segment with this great news about the Slurpee, the ad agency selected media like MTV and the 1993 summer movie *Super Mario Bros.*

The Slurpee was saved! From May to December of 1993, Slurpee sales rose 9 percent, and in the first quarter of 1994, sales were up again 14 percent. Nancy Smith, the 7-Eleven executive who managed the revival effort, was praised in *Advertising Age* as one of 1994's top 100 marketing managers.[2] At the heart of Smith's success was careful development of a complete, new marketing strategy for her brand, which culminated in the "Brain Freeze" ad campaign. Exhibit 6.1 shows one television ad from the "Brain Freeze" campaign.

Careful market analysis and target-segment identification are crucial for marketing success. While the process can get rather complicated, market segmentation is based on the simple premise that you cannot be all things to all people. What rings true and holds appeal for teenage males rarely is of interest to their sisters, parents, or grandparents. Every organization must compete for the attention and business of some customer groups while de-emphasizing or ignoring others. In this chapter we will examine in detail the way organizations decide who to target and who to ignore in laying the foundation for their marketing programs and advertising campaigns.

(MUSIC/SFX-DOG BARKING)   (MUSIC/SFX-MAN SIPS)   (SFX-SCREAMS)

(SFX-SCREAMS)   (SFX-SCREAMS)   MAN: Huh.

Brain freeze. ANNCR: So good, it hurts.   Slurpee, the coolest thing on Earth.   (MUSIC/SFX OUT)

ANNCR: Get your 32-ounce Slurpee   (SFX-CARTOONS ON CUPS SCREAM) and a Sega Eternal Champions Cup with a free tatoo underneath. (SFX OUT)   Buy 4 and get $5 rebate off the Sega game cartridge. CARTOONS ON CUPS: Huh, brain freeze!

EXHIBIT 6.1

This Slurpee "Brain Freeze" ad targeted adolescent males with a rather unusual product claim: "so good, it hurts."

1.   Jeff Smyth, "Slurpee," *Advertising Age,* July 4, 1994, S-2.
2.   Ibid.

STP Marketing and the Evolution of Marketing Strategies

❶ The Slurpee example nicely illustrates a process that marketers use time and again to produce marketing strategies. The 7-Eleven executives started with the diverse market of all who shop at their stores, and they broke the market down by age segments. They then selected teenage males as their **target segment.** The target segment is the subgroup (of the larger market) chosen as the focal point for the marketing program and advertising campaign.

While markets are segmented, products are positioned. To pursue the target segment, a firm organizes its marketing and advertising efforts around a coherent positioning strategy. **Positioning** is the act of designing and representing one's product or service so that it will occupy a distinct and valued place in the consumer's mind. **Positioning strategy** involves the selection of key themes or concepts that the organization will feature for communicating this distinctiveness to the target segment. In the Slurpee case, 7-Eleven executives designed packaging and created flavors that would make their product fit the inline-skating lifestyle of the teenage male. They reinforced this distinctive fit with the brain freeze benefit, which made perfect sense for a target segment of adolescent sensation seekers. Finally, through skillful advertising, they communicated their distinctive benefits to the target segment.

Notice the specific sequence, illustrated in Exhibit 6.2, that was played out in the Slurpee example: the marketing strategy evolved as a result of segmenting, targeting, and positioning. This sequence of activities is often referred to as STP marketing, and it represents a sound basis for generating effective advertising.[3] While there are no formulas or models that guarantee success, the STP approach is strongly recommended for markets characterized by diversity in consumers' needs and preferences. In markets with any significant degree of diversity, it is impossible to design one product that would appeal to everyone, or one advertising campaign that would communicate with everyone. Organizations that lose sight of this simple premise often run into trouble.

For example, back in the mid-1980s Nike developed its first (and last) generic casual shoe. Nike recognized that many consumers were wearing their athletic footwear to

EXHIBIT 6.2

Laying the foundation for effective advertising campaigns through STP marketing.

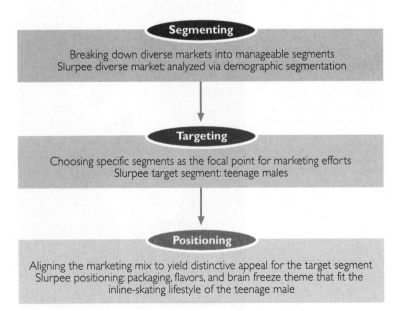

3.   For a more extensive discussion of STP marketing, see Philip Kotler, *Marketing Management* (Englewood Cliffs, N.J.: Prentice-Hall, 1994), Chapters 11 and 12.

watch TV or go grocery shopping, so they reasoned that just about everyone would want a casual shoe from Nike. Not so. In the words of Phil Knight, founder and CEO of Nike:

We got our brains beat out. We came out with a functional shoe we thought the world needed, but it was funny looking and the buying public didn't want it. . . . People got confused and Nike began to lose its magic. Retailers were unenthusiastic, athletes were looking at the alternatives, and sales slowed. So not only was the casual shoe effort a failure, but it was diluting our trademark and hurting us in running.[4]

When organizations create products that attempt to appeal to everybody, the typical outcome is that the product doesn't suit anyone.

Nike reversed its tailspin in the mid-1980s through meticulous application of STP marketing. Rather than making one generic shoe for a broad but poorly defined market, they began creating many different athletic shoes for a variety of specific target segments. There were shoes for basketball players, joggers, walkers, cross-trainers, and tennis players. Within each of these segments were subsegments; the tennis player segment was divided into the brash, more-youthful, and rebellious players versus the older, more affluent, "country-club" players. Each of the targeted subsegments had a line of shoes positioned specifically for them. In the tennis subsegments, these lines were known as the Challenge Court and Supreme Court Collections, respectively.[5] This strategy has remained effective for Nike over the years. As Exhibit 6.3 shows, the company continues to fit the mindset, as well as the feet, of the consumer.

Notice also from the Nike example that the STP framework does not preclude the targeting of multiple segments. In fact, it encourages it. By targeting multiple segments, an organization like Nike can end up serving a wide variety of consumers. But keep in mind that appealing to diverse consumers with products designed for the preferences of different segments is very different from trying to reach many consumers with one product. As the Nike casual shoe illustrates, a single product developed for no one in particular usually appeals to no one in particular.

EXHIBIT 6.3

Nike understands that when it comes time to "Just Do It," one segment of players wants shoes that let them do it like young phenom Andre Agassi. Another segment is better able to relate to former-bad-boy-turned-elder-statesman John McEnroe. **www.nike.com**

4.   Geraldine E. Willigan, "High-Performance Marketing: An Interview with Nike's Phil Knight," *Harvard Business Review* (July/August 1992): 91–101.
5.   Ibid.

Beyond STP Marketing

If an organization uses STP marketing as its framework for strategy development, at some point it will find the right strategy, develop the right advertising, make a lot of money, and live happily ever after. Right? As you might expect, it's not quite that simple. Even when STP marketing yields profitable outcomes, one must presume that success will not last indefinitely. Indeed, an important feature of marketing and advertising—a feature that can make these professions both terribly interesting and terribly frustrating—is their dynamic nature. To paraphrase a popular saying, Shifts happen—consumer preferences shift. Competitors improve their marketing strategies, or technology changes and makes a popular product obsolete. Successful marketing strategies need to be modified or may even need to be reinvented as shifts occur in the organization's competitive environment.

To maintain the vitality and profitability of its products or services, an organization has two options. The first entails reassessment of the segmentation strategy. This may come through a more-detailed examination of the current target segment to develop new and better ways of meeting its needs, or it may be necessary to change the target and reposition the offering to a new segment, as was the case with Slurpee.

The second option is to pursue a product differentiation strategy. As defined in Chapter 1, product differentiation focuses the firm's efforts around emphasizing or even creating differences for its brands to distinguish them from the offerings of established competitors. Advertising plays a critical role as part of the product differentiation strategy because often the consumer will have to be convinced that the intended difference is in fact meaningful. Product differentiation strategies try to make a brand appear different from competing brands, but it is consumers' perceptions of the difference that will determine the success of the strategy.

For example, when Church & Dwight Company introduced its Arm & Hammer Dental Care baking soda toothpaste, major toothpaste marketers like Procter & Gamble and Colgate-Palmolive were not impressed. The product had a distinctive difference from traditional brands like Crest and Colgate, but would consumers find this difference meaningful? The answer turned out to be yes—the slightly salty taste and gritty texture of the Arm & Hammer brand proved popular with consumers, and in no time sales of baking soda toothpastes approached $300 million annually.[6] Both Procter & Gamble and Colgate-Palmolive were forced to create baking soda toothpastes as a result of Arm & Hammer's success.

The basic message is that marketing strategies and the advertising that supports them are never really final. Successes realized through proper application of STP marketing can be short-lived in highly competitive markets where any successful innovation is almost sure to be copied by competitors. Thus, the value creation process for marketers and advertisers is continuous; STP marketing must be pursued over and over again and often complemented with product differentiation strategies.

The remainder of this chapter is devoted to a more detailed assessment of how organizations develop market segmentation, positioning, and product differentiation strategies. The critical role of advertising campaigns in executing these strategies is also highlighted.

Identifying Target Segments

❷ The first step in STP marketing involves breaking down large, diverse markets into more-manageable submarkets or segments. As mentioned earlier, this activity is known as market segmentation. It can be accomplished in many ways, but keep in mind that advertisers need to identify a segment with common characteristics that will lead the members of that segment to respond distinctively to a marketing program. For example, if teenage males and females respond in the same way to Slurpee's "Brain Freeze" ad campaign, then

---

6.   Kathleen Deveny, "Anatomy of a Fad: How Clear Products Were Hot and Then Suddenly Were Not," *Wall Street Journal,* March 15, 1994, B1.

males and females should not be considered separate segments. Additionally, for a segment to be really useful, advertisers must be able to reach that segment with information about the product. Typically this means that advertisers must be able to identify some media the segment uses that will allow them to get an advertising message to the segment. For example, teenage males can be reached efficiently through media like MTV and selected rap, contemporary rock 'n' roll, or alternative radio stations.

In this section we will review several ways that consumer markets are commonly segmented. Markets can be segmented on the basis of usage patterns and commitment levels, demographic and geographic information, psychographics and lifestyles, or benefits sought. Many times, segmentation schemes evolve in such a way that multiple variables are used to identify and describe the target segment. Such an outcome is desirable because more knowledge about the target will usually translate into better marketing and advertising programs.

Usage Patterns and Commitment Levels

One of the most common ways to segment markets is by consumers' usage patterns or commitment levels. With respect to usage patterns, it is important to recognize that for most products and services, some users will purchase much more frequently than others. It is common to find that **heavy users** in a category account for the majority of a product's sales and thus become the preferred or primary target segment. For example, Campbell Soup Company has discovered what it refers to as its extra-enthusiastic core users: folks who buy nearly 320 cans of soup per year.[7] That's enough soup to serve Campbell's at least six days a week every week. To maintain this level of devotion to the product, standard marketing thought holds that it is in Campbell's best interest to know these heavy users in great detail and make them a focal point of the company's marketing strategy.

While being the standard wisdom, the heavy-user focus has some potential downsides. For one, devoted users may need no encouragement at all to keep consuming. In addition, a heavy-user focus takes attention and resources away from those who do need encouragement to purchase the marketer's brand. Perhaps most importantly, various heavy users may be significantly different in terms of their motivations to consume, their approach to the product, or their image of the product.

Another segmentation option combines prior usage patterns with commitment levels to identify four fundamental segment types—brand-loyal customers, switchers (or variety seekers), nonusers, and emergent consumers.[8] Each segment represents a unique opportunity for the advertiser. **Nonusers** offer the lowest level of opportunity relative to the other three groups. **Brand-loyal users** are a tremendous asset if they are the advertiser's customers, but they are difficult to convert if they are loyal to a competitor.

Switchers, or **variety seekers,** often buy what is on sale or choose brands that offer discount coupons or other price incentives. Whether they are pursued through price incentives, high-profile advertising campaigns, or both, switchers turn out to be an expensive segment to try to win. Much can be spent in getting their business merely to have it disappear just as quickly as it was won.

Emergent consumers, however, offer the organization an important business opportunity. In most product categories, there is a gradual but constant influx of first-time buyers. The reasons for this influx vary by product category and include purchase triggers like college graduation, marriage, birth of a child, divorce, job promotions, and retirement. Generation X attracts the attention of marketers and advertisers because it is a large group of emergent adult consumers.[9] Immigration can also be a source of numerous new customers for many product categories.

7.   Rebecca Piirto, *Beyond Mind Games: The Marketing Power of Psychographics* (Ithaca, N.Y.: American Demographics Books, 1991), 230.
8.   Further discussion of this four-way scheme is provided by David W. Stewart, "Advertising in Slow-Growth Economies," *American Demographics* (September 1994): 40–46.
9.   Renee H. Frengut, "What's All the Fuss about Xers?" *Marketing News,* July 18, 1994, 4.

Emergent consumers are motivated by many different factors, but they share one important characteristic: Their brand preferences are still under development. Targeting emergents with messages that fit their age or social circumstances may produce modest effects in the short run, but it eventually may yield a brand loyalty that pays handsome rewards for the discerning organization. For example, credit card marketers actively recruit college students who have limited financial resources but excellent potential as long-term customers. Exhibit 6.4 shows an American Express ad run in a college catalog and designed to tap this potential.

Demographic Segmentation

Demographic segmentation is widely used in selecting target segments and includes basic descriptors like age, gender, race, marital status, income, education, and occupation. Demographic information has special value in market segmentation because if an advertiser knows the demographic characteristics of the target segment, choosing media to efficiently reach that segment is much easier. Also, as indicated by the Global Issues box on page 162, demographic characteristics can be used in identifying target segments around the world.

Demographic information has two specific applications. First, demographics are commonly used to describe or profile segments that have been identified with some other variable. If an organization had first segmented its market in terms of product usage rates, the next step would be to describe or profile its heavy users in terms of demographic characteristics like age or income. In fact, one of the most common approaches for identifying target segments is to combine information about usage patterns with demographics.

EXHIBIT 6.4

Emergent consumers represent an important source of long-term opportunity for many organizations. Have you ever thought of yourself as an emergent consumer? **www.americanexpress.com/**

Recently, Mobil Oil Corporation used such an approach in segmenting the market for gasoline buyers and identified five basic segments: Road Warriors, True Blues, Generation F3, Homebodies, and Price Shoppers.[10] Extensive research on more than 2,000 motorists revealed considerable insight about these five segments. At the one extreme, Road Warriors spend at least $1,200 per year at gas stations; they buy premium gasoline and snacks and beverages and sometimes opt for a car wash. Road Warriors are generally more-affluent, middle-aged males who drive 25,000 to 50,000 miles per year. (Note how Mobil combined information about usage patterns with demographics to provide a detailed picture of the segment.) In contrast, Price Shoppers spend no more than $700 annually at gas stations, are generally less affluent, rarely buy premium, and show no loyalty to particular brands or stations. In terms of relative segment sizes, there are about 25 percent more Price Shoppers on the highways than Road Warriors.

If you were the marketing vice president at Mobil Oil Corporation, which of these two segments would you target? Think about it for a few pages—we'll get back to you.

GLOBAL ISSUES

I WANT MY MTV: INFORMATION AGE HERALDS THE FIRST GLOBAL CONSUMERS

What do Big Macs, *Beverly Hills 90210,* Coca-Cola, Net surfing, and Levi's have in common? They are all a part of today's teen scene around the globe. Over the past few years, an explosion of information available worldwide through satellite-based television programming and the World Wide Web has helped to bridge the gaps of language and culture and form the first global teen lifestyles. "It's not just Levi's and Nikes," claims Elissa Moses, senior vice president and director of strategic planning for the advertising agency DMB&B. "Movies, TV, and music come from America. It's a cultural force as well as a consumer goods force."

While standardized global campaigns with their inherent economies of scale have been a distant dream in the past for advertisers, the emerging teen lifestyle may provide enough shared meaning to launch truly integrated, global ad efforts. At the forefront of this global trend is the MTV network, now broadcast over several geographic regions worldwide. As both the source and medium of global teen trends, MTV stands to benefit greatly. In the United States alone, an MTV home-shopping program called *The Goods* managed to sell $1 million in wristwatches in a four-hour period and more than $1.5 million in Rolling Stones merchandise. Can a global home-shopping network and online catalogs for teens be far behind?

Sources: "Home Shopping Network Targets Young Audience," *Marketing News,* July 17, 1995, 13; and "Teens Seen as the First Truly Global Consumers," *Marketing News,* March 27, 1995, 9.

Second, demographic categories are frequently used as the starting point in market segmentation. This was the case in the Slurpee example, where teenage males turned out to be the segment of interest. Additionally, film makers like Konica USA, Kodak, and Fuji have attempted to tap diverse demographic segments with products like high-speed "baby film" for new parents, complete photo-hobby kits for preteens, and hassle-free cardboard cameras for older persons who want last-minute photos of the grandchildren.[11]

One demographic group that will receive increasing attention from advertisers in the years to come is the "woopies," or well-off older people. In the United States, consumers over 50 have more discretionary income than all other age segments combined. By the year 2025, the number of persons over 50 will grow by 80 percent to become a third of the U.S. population. This growth in the woopie segment will be even more dramatic in other countries, like Japan and the nations of Western Europe.[12] Still, like any other age segment, older consumers are a diverse group, and the temptation to stereotype must be resisted. Some marketers advocate partitioning older consumers into groups aged 50–64, 65–74, 75–84, and 85 or older as a means for reflecting important differences in needs. Still, more-thorough knowledge of this population is clearly needed.

10.   Allanna Sullivan, "Mobil Bets Drivers Pick Cappuccino over Low Prices," *Wall Street Journal,* January 30, 1995, B1.
11.   Joan E. Rigdon, "Photography Companies Focus on Niches," *Wall Street Journal,* March 12, 1993, B1.
12.   "The Rich Autumn of a Consumer's Life," *The Economist,* September 5, 1992, 67–68.

Geographic Segmentation

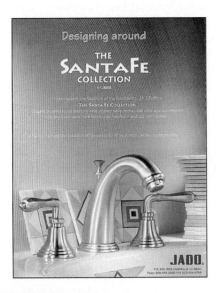

Each region of the United States has distinctive preferences that subsume many product categories. For a hint of the Southwest in your bathroom, choose the Santa Fe collection from JADO.

Geographic segmentation needs little explanation other than to emphasize how useful geography is in segmenting markets. Geographic segmentation may be conducted within a country by region (for example, Pacific Northwest versus New England), by state or province, by city, or even by neighborhood. Climate and topographical features yield dramatic differences in consumption by region for products like snow tires and surfboards, but geography can also correlate with other differences that are not so obvious. Eating and food preparation habits, entertainment preferences, recreational activities, and other aspects of lifestyle have been shown to vary along geographic lines. Exhibit 6.5 features an ad from Jado fixtures with a distinctly southwestern flavor. Exhibits 6.6 and 6.7 show U.S. consumption patterns for Twinkies and for Obsession versus Old Spice. As you can see, where one lives does seem to affect preferences.

In recent years skillful marketers have merged information on where people live with the U.S. Census Bureau's demographic data to produce a form of market segmentation known as **geodemographic segmentation.** Geodemographic segmentation identifies neighborhoods (that is, zip codes) around the country that share common demographic characteristics. One such system, known as PRIZM (potential rating index by zip marketing), identifies 62 market segments that encompass all the zip codes in the United States.[13] Each of these segments indicates similar lifestyle characteristics and can be found throughout the country.

For example, the American Dreams segment is found in many metropolitan neighborhoods and is comprised of upwardly mobile ethnic minorities, many of whom were foreign-born. This segment's product preferences are different from those of persons belonging to the Rural Industria segment, who are young families with one or both parents working at low-wage jobs in small-town America. Systems like PRIZM are very popular because of the depth of segment description they provide, along with their ability to precisely identify where the segment can be found.

Source: Michael Weiss, *Latitudes and Attitudes* (Boston: Little, Brown, 1994), 17. Reprinted with permission of Simmons Market Research Bureau, Inc.

People who eat Hostess Twinkies.

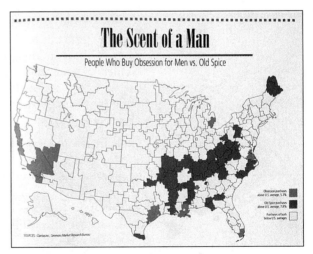

Source: Michael Weiss, *Latitudes and Attitudes* (Boston: Little, Brown, 1994), 45. Reprinted with permission of Simmons Market Research Bureau, Inc.

EXHIBIT 6.7 *People who buy Obsession for Men versus Old Spice.*

13.   Christina Del Valle, "They Know Where You Live—And How You Buy," *Business Week,* February 7, 1994, 89.

Psychographics and Lifestyle Segmentation

Psychographics is a term that advertisers created in the mid-1960s to refer to a form of research that emphasizes the understanding of consumers' activities, interests, and opinions (AIOs).[14] Many advertising agencies were using demographic variables for segmentation purposes, but they wanted insights into consumers' motivations, which demographic variables did not provide. Psychographics were created as a tool to supplement the use of demographic data. Because a focus on consumers' activities, interests, and opinions often produces insights into differences in the lifestyles of various segments, this approach usually results in a **lifestyle segmentation.** Knowing details about the lifestyle of a target segment can be valuable for creating advertising messages that ring true to the consumer.

Lifestyle, or psychographic segmentation, can be customized with a focus on the issues germane to a single product category, or it may be pursued so that the resulting segments have general applicability to many different product or service categories. An example of the former is research conducted for Pillsbury to segment the eating habits of American households.[15] This "What's Cookin'" study involved consumer interviews with more than 3,000 people and identified five segments of the population, based on their shared eating styles:

- *Chase & Grabbits,* at 26 percent of the population, are heavy users of all forms of fast food. These are people who can make a meal out of microwave popcorn; as long as the popcorn keeps hunger at bay and is convenient, this segment is happy with its meal.
- *Functional Feeders,* at 18 percent of the population, are a bit older than the Chase & Grabbits but no less convenience oriented. Since they are more likely to have families, their preferences for convenient foods involve frozen products that are quickly prepared at home. They constantly seek faster ways to prepare the traditional foods they grew up with.
- *Down-Home Stokers,* at 21 percent of the population, involve blue-collar households with modest incomes. They are very loyal to their regional diets, such as meat and potatoes in the Midwest versus clam chowder in New England. Fried chicken, biscuits and gravy, and bacon and eggs make this segment the champion of cholesterol.
- *Careful Cooks,* at 20 percent of the population, are more prevalent on the West Coast. They have replaced most of the red meat in their diet with pastas, fish, skinless chicken, and mounds of fresh fruit and vegetables. They believe they are knowledgeable about nutritional issues and are willing to experiment with foods that offer healthful options.
- *Happy Cookers* are the remaining 15 percent of the population but are a shrinking segment. These cooks are family oriented and take substantial satisfaction from preparing a complete homemade meal for the family. Young mothers in this segment are aware of nutritional issues but will bend the rules with homemade meat dishes, casseroles, pies, cakes, and cookies.

Even these abbreviated descriptions of Pillsbury's five psychographic segments should make it clear that very different marketing and advertising programs are called for to appeal to each group. Exhibits 6.8 and 6.9 show ads from Pillsbury. Which segments are these ads targeting?

As noted, lifestyle segmentation studies can also be pursued with no particular product category as a focus, and the resulting segments could prove useful for many different marketers. The most notable example of this approach is the VALS™ (for values and lifestyles) system developed by SRI International and marketed by SRI Consulting of Menlo Park, California.[16] The VALS framework was first introduced in 1978 with nine potential segments, but in recent years it has been revised as VALS™ 2 with eight market segments.

14. Piirto, *Beyond Mind Games,* 21–23.
15. Ibid., 222–23.
16. Ibid.; see Chapters 3, 5, and 8 for an extensive discussion of the VALS™ system.

EXHIBIT 6.8

Which lifestyle segment is Pillsbury targeting with this ad? It looks like a toss-up between Chase & Grabbits and Functional Feeders. info .pillsbury.com/

EXHIBIT 6.9   *The convenience-oriented Functional Feeders seem the natural target for this novel ad. That Pillsbury Doughboy sure gets around!* info.pillsbury.com/

As shown in Exhibit 6.10, these segments are organized in terms of resources (which includes more than age, income, and education) and personal orientation. For instance, the Experiencer is relatively affluent and action oriented. This is an enthusiastic and risk-taking group that has yet to establish predictable behavioral patterns. Its members look to sports, recreation, exercise, and social activities as outlets for their abundant energy. SRI Consulting sells detailed information and marketing recommendations about the eight segments to a variety of marketing organizations. Recently, SRI has also developed a separate VALS™ system for the Japanese market.

Benefit Segmentation   Another segmentation approach developed by advertising researchers and used extensively over the past 30 years is **benefit segmentation.** In benefit segmentation, target segments are delineated by the various benefit packages that different consumers want from the same product category. For instance, different people want different benefits from their automobiles. Some consumers just want economical and reliable transportation; others want speed and excitement; and still others want luxury, comfort, and prestige. One product could not possibly serve such diverse benefit segments. Exhibits 6.11, 6.12, and 6.13 show three car ads that appeal to three different benefit segments.

This notion of attempting to understand consumers' priorities and assess how different brands might perform based on criteria deemed important by various segments should have a familiar ring. If not, turn back to Chapter 5 and revisit our discussion of multi-attribute attitude models (MAAMs). The importance weights collected from individual consumers in MAAMs research provide the raw material needed for identifying benefit segments.

*The eight VALS™ 2
Segments.*

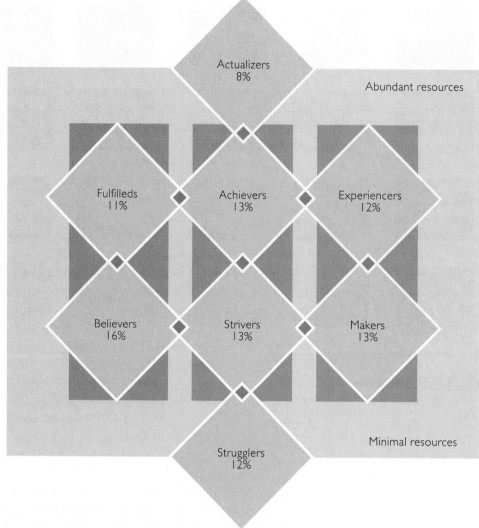

Source: SRI Consulting. VALS™/Simmons, 1996.

Segmenting Business-to-Business Markets

Thus far, our discussion of segmentation options has focused on ways to segment **consumer markets.** Consumer markets are the markets for products and services purchased by individuals or households to satisfy their specific needs. Consumer marketing is often compared and contrasted with business-to-business marketing. **Business markets** are the institutional buyers who purchase items to be used in other products and services or to be resold to other businesses or households. While advertising is much more prevalent in consumer markets, products and services like fax machines, cellular phones, and overnight delivery are commonly promoted to business customers. Hence, segmentation strategies are also valuable for business-to-business marketers.

Business markets can be segmented using several of the options already discussed.[17] For example, business customers differ in their usage rates and geographic locations, so these variables may be productive bases for segmenting business markets. Additionally, one of the most common approaches uses the Standard Industrial Classification (SIC) codes prepared by the U.S. Census Bureau. SIC information is helpful for identifying categories of businesses and then pinpointing the precise locations of these organizations.

17. Kotler, 278.

EXHIBIT 6.11

Benefit segmentation really comes to life in the automobile market. For example, the Mitsubishi Spyder presents a distinctive set of benefits for one group of car buyers. www.mitsucars.com/

EXHIBIT 6.12

Here we see Infiniti abandon its ill-fated Zen-like advertising style and adopt the conventional approach in automotive advertising: Make the car the star of the show, and describe features and benefits. www.infiniti-motors.com/

WEB SIGHTING

EXHIBIT 6.13

For years, Volvo has employed a benefit segmentation strategy by emphasizing safety features in its ads. How does this segment differ from the benefits targeted in the Infiniti and Mitsubishi ads? At the Volvo home page www.volvo.se/, *you might be surprised to learn that cars are just one of their product lines. For comparison, visit Infiniti at* www.infinitimotors.com/ *and Mitsubishi at* www.mitsucars.com/

Some of the more sophisticated segmentation methods used by firms that market to individual consumers do not translate well to business markets.[18] For instance, rarely would there be a place for psychographic or lifestyle segmentation in the business-to-business setting. In business markets, advertisers fall back on simpler strategies that are easier to work with from the perspective of the sales force. Segmentation by a potential customer's stage in the purchase process is one such strategy. It turns out that first-time prospects, novices, and sophisticates want very different packages of benefits from their vendors, and thus they should be targeted separately in advertising and sales programs.

Prioritizing Target Segments

3 Whether it is done through usage patterns or demographic characteristics or geographic location or benefit packages or any combination of options, segmenting markets typically yields a mix of segments that vary in their attractiveness to the advertiser. In pursuing STP marketing, the advertiser must get beyond this potentially confusing mixture of segments to a selected subset that will become the target for its marketing and advertising programs. Recall the example of Mobil Oil Corporation and the segments of gasoline buyers it identified via usage patterns and demographic descriptors. What criteria should Mobil use to help decide between Road Warriors and Price Shoppers as possible targets?

Perhaps the most fundamental criteria in segment selection revolve around what the members of the segment want versus the organization's ability to provide it. Every organization has distinctive strengths and weaknesses that must be acknowledged when choosing its target segment. The organization may be particularly strong in some aspect of manufacturing, like Gillette, which has particular expertise in mass production of intricate plastic and metal products, such as the highly successful Sensor razor. Or perhaps its strength lies in well-trained and loyal service personnel, like those at FedEx, who can effectively implement new service programs initiated for customers, such as next-day delivery "absolutely, positively by 10:30 A.M." To serve a target segment, an organization may have to commit substantial resources to acquire or develop the capabilities to provide what that segment wants. If the price tag for these new capabilities is too high, the organization must find another segment.

Another major consideration in segment selection entails the size and growth potential of the segment. Segment size is a function of the number of persons, households, or institutions in the segment, plus their willingness to spend in the product category. When assessing size, advertisers must keep in mind that the number of persons in a segment of heavy users may be relatively small, but the extraordinary usage rates of these consumers can more than make up for their small numbers. In addition, it is not enough to simply assess a segment's size as of today. Segments are dynamic, and it is common to find marketers most interested in devoting resources to segments projected for dramatic growth. As we have already seen, the purchasing power and growth projections for persons at least 50 years old have made this a segment that many companies are targeting.

So does bigger always mean better when choosing target segments? The answer is a function of the third major criterion for segment selection. In choosing a target segment, an advertiser must also look at the **competitive field**—companies that compete for the segment's business—and then decide whether it has a particular expertise, or perhaps just a bigger budget, that would allow it to serve the segment more effectively.

When an advertiser factors in the competitive field, it often turns out that smaller is better when selecting target segments. Almost by definition, large segments are usually established segments that many companies have identified and targeted previously. Trying to enter the competitive field in a mature segment isn't easy because established competitors can be expected to respond aggressively with advertising campaigns or price promotions in an effort to repel any newcomer.

18.   Thomas S. Robertson and Howard Barich, "A Successful Approach to Segmenting Industrial Markets," *Planning Forum* (November/ December 1992): 5–11.

Alternatively, large segments may simply be poorly defined segments; that is, a large segment may need to be broken down into smaller categories before a company can understand consumers' needs well enough to serve them effectively. Again, the segment of older consumers—age 50 or older—is huge, but in most instances it would simply be too big to be valuable as a target. Too much diversity exists in the needs and preferences of this age group, so further segmentation based on other demographic variables, or perhaps via psychographics, is called for before an appropriate target can be located.

The smaller-is-better principle has become so popular in choosing target segments that it is now referred to as niche marketing. A **market niche** is a relatively small group of consumers who have a unique set of needs and who typically are willing to pay a premium price to the firm that specializes in meeting those needs.[19] The small size of a market niche often means it would not be profitable for more than one organization to serve it. Thus, when a firm identifies and develops products for market niches, the threat of competitors developing imitative products to attack the niche is reduced. As the New Media box on page 170 illustrates, growing competition among online services has spawned a search for market niches.

Niche marketing will continue to grow in popularity as the mass media splinters into a more and more complex and narrowly defined array of specialized vehicles. Specialized programming—like the Health & Fitness Channel, the Cooking Channel, or Arnold Palmer's 24-hour golf channel—attracts small and very distinctive groups of consumers, providing advertisers with an efficient way to communicate with market niches.[20] Exhibit 6.14 is an example of an ad directed toward a very small niche, those who prefer imported Russian tubes for their high-end tube stereo amplifiers.

So now let's return to the question faced by Mobil Oil Corporation. Who should it target—Road Warriors or Price Shoppers? Hopefully you will see this as a straightforward decision. Road Warriors are a more attractive segment in terms of both segment size and growth potential. Although there are more Price Shoppers in terms of sheer numbers, Road Warriors spend more at the gas station, making them the larger segment from the standpoint of revenue generation. Road Warriors are much more prone to buy those little extras, like a sandwich and a car wash, that could be extremely profitable sources of new business. Mobil also came to the conclusion that too many of its competitors were already targeting Price Shoppers. Mobil thus selected Road Warriors as its target segment and developed a positioning strategy it referred to as "Friendly Serve." Gas prices went up at Mobil stations, but Mobil also committed new resources to improving all aspects of the gas-purchasing experience.[21] Cleaner restrooms and better lighting alone yielded sales gains between 2 percent and 5 percent. Next, more attendants were hired to run between the pump and the snack bar to get Road Warriors in and out quickly—complete with their sandwich

EXHIBIT 6.14

Niche marketers are usually able to charge a premium price for their distinctive products. If you decide to go with Svetlana the next time you are buying amplifier tubes, expect to pay a little extra. **www.svetlana.com/**

19. Kotler, 267.
20. Patricia Sellers, "The Best Way to Reach Your Buyers," *Fortune,* Autumn/Winter 1993, 14–17.
21. Sullivan.

and beverage. Early results indicated that helpful attendants boosted station sales by another 15 to 20 percent. The Mobil case is a good example of how the application of STP marketing can rejuvenate sales, even in a mundane product category like gasoline.

Formulating the Positioning Strategy

4 Now that we have discussed the ways markets are segmented and the criteria used for selecting specific target segments, we turn our attention to positioning strategy. If a firm has been careful in segmenting the market and selecting its targets, then a positioning strategy—like Mobil's "Friendly Serve"—should occur naturally. In addition, as an aspect of positioning strategy, we will begin to entertain ideas about how a firm can best communicate to the target segment what it has to offer. This is where advertising plays its vital role. A positioning strategy will include particular ideas or themes that must be communicated effectively if the marketing program is to be successful.

Essentials for Effective Positioning Strategies

Any sound positioning strategy includes several essential elements. Effective positioning strategies are based on meaningful commitments of organizational resources to produce substantive value for the target segment. They also are consistent internally and over time, and they feature simple and distinctive themes. Each of these essential elements is described and illustrated in this section.

Let's begin with the issue of substance. For a positioning strategy to be effective and remain effective over time, the organization must be committed to creating substantive value for the customer. Take the example of Mobil Oil Corporation and its target segment, the Road Warriors. Road Warriors are willing to pay a little more for gas if it comes with extras like prompt service or fresh coffee. So Mobil must create an ad campaign that depicts its employees as the brightest, friendliest, most helpful people you'd ever want to meet. The company asks its ad agency to come up with a catchy jingle that will remind people about the great services they can expect at a Mobil station. It spends millions of dollars running these ads over and over and wins the enduring loyalty of the Road Warriors. Right? Well, maybe, and maybe not. Certainly, a new ad campaign will have to be created to make Road Warriors aware of what the company has to offer, but it all falls apart if they drive in with great expectations and the company's people do not live up to them.

NEW MEDIA

ONLINE SERVICES SEEK NEW NICHES AS COMPETITION INTENSIFIES

As basic service fees for America Online, CompuServe, and Prodigy fall to relative parity, many consumers have come to see these services as homogenous and interchangeable. In fact, as subscribers have begun to switch services looking for the best deal, online purveyors are discovering that they must distinguish their brand image and array of offerings from their competitors'. This has led the three companies to revamp the look and feel of their online interfaces, initiate new brand-awareness campaigns, and focus new service developments around targeting specific niche markets.

America Online, considered by many as the hippest of the three, has turned to the Los Angeles firm of Chiat/Day to further develop and exploit its image. America Online also plans to introduce an Internet-only service to attract new users. CompuServe, traditionally associated with the computer savvy, is slated to launch Wow!, a new service for novice users. And finally, Prodigy is developing future online additions, including Prodigy for Kids and Prodigy for Seniors.

This change in approach for the three branded services is timely; a new venture from Microsoft has further intensified the competition. The new Microsoft Network (MSN) offers even lower monthly rates and includes a novel distribution strategy to wrest valuable market share. Traditional marketing practices for online services have centered around the direct-mail promotion of access software and the bundling of online services with sales from PC manufacturers. MSN is accessed simply by clicking an icon on the Windows 95 operating system, now standard issue on over 80 percent of new PCs sold worldwide.

Sources: "CompuServe to Revamp Service, Cut Prices Prior to Microsoft's New Service," *Wall Street Journal*, August 2, 1995, B3; and "On-Line Services Try to Define Their Identities," *Wall Street Journal*, July 12, 1995, B1.

Effective positioning begins with substance. In the case of Mobil's "Friendly Serve" strategy, this means things like keeping restrooms attractive and clean, adding better lighting to all areas of the station, and upgrading the quality of the snacks and beverages available in each station's convenience store. It also means hiring more attendants, outfitting them in blue pants, blue shirts, ties, and black Reeboks, and then training and motivating them to anticipate and fulfill the needs of the harried Road Warrior.[22] Effecting meaningful change in service levels at its 8,000 stations nationwide will be an expensive and time-consuming process for Mobil, but without some substantive change, there can be no hope of retaining the Road Warrior's lucrative business.

A positioning strategy also must be consistent internally and consistent over time. Regarding internal consistency, everything must work in combination to reinforce a distinct perception in the consumer's eyes about what a brand stands for. If we have chosen to position our airline as the one that will be known for on-time reliability, then we certainly would invest in things like extensive preventive maintenance and state-of-the-art baggage-handling facilities. There would be no need for exclusive airport lounges as part of this strategy, nor would any special emphasis need to be placed on in-flight food and beverage services. If our target segment wants reliable transportation, then this and only this should be the obsession in running our airline.

A strategy also needs consistency over time. As we saw in Chapter 5, consumers have perceptual defenses that allow them to screen or ignore most of the ad messages they are exposed to. Breaking through the clutter and establishing what a brand stands for is a tremendous challenge for any advertiser, but it is a challenge made easier by consistent positioning. If year in and year out an advertiser communicates the same basic themes to the target segment, then the message may get through and shape the way consumers perceive the brand. An example of a consistent approach is the long-running "Good Neighbor" ads of State Farm Insurance. While the specific copy changes, the thematic core of the campaign does not change. Exhibit 6.15 shows a contemporary ad from this long-running campaign.

Of course, things don't always work out. An interesting but unsuccessful campaign by Leo Burnett for Oldsmobile consistently promised consumers that "this is not your father's Oldsmobile." In fact, this campaign, designed to fight Olds' geriatric image, resulted in the average age of owners actually increasing. This prompted industry critics to suggest wryly, "No, it's your grandfather's Oldsmobile!"

Finally, there is the matter of simplicity and distinctiveness. Simplicity and distinctiveness are essential to the advertising task. No matter how much substance has been built into a product, it will fail in the marketplace if the consumer doesn't perceive what the product can do. Keep in mind, in a world of harried consumers who can be expected to interrupt, ignore, or completely forget most of the ads they are exposed to, complicated, imitative messages simply have no chance of getting through. The basic premise of a positioning strategy must be simple and distinctive if it is to be communicated effectively to the target segment.

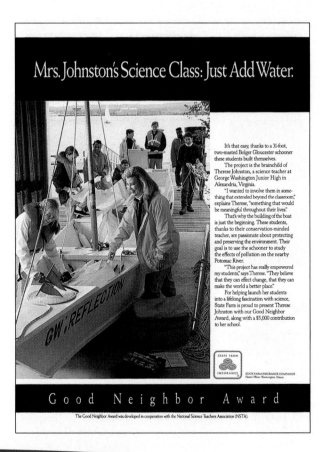

EXHIBIT 6.15

Consistency is a definite virtue in choosing and executing a positioning strategy. State Farm's "Good Neighbor" theme has been a hallmark of its advertising for many years. **www.statefarm.com/**

22. Ibid.

The value of simplicity and distinctiveness in positioning strategy is perfectly illustrated by the success of GM's Pontiac division in the mid-1980s. Remember, this was a period when Japanese automakers were taking market share from their U.S. counterparts, and no American car company was being hit harder than General Motors. Pontiac, however, grew its market share in this period with a positioning strategy that involved a return to Pontiac's heritage from the 1960s as a performance car.[23] Pontiac's positioning strategy, which was communicated with a relentless barrage of advertisements like that shown in Exhibit 6.16, was "We Build Excitement."

This was certainly a distinctive claim relative to GM's other stodgy divisions of that era, and its beauty was its simplicity. Pontiac's Grand AM featured distinctive styling and mechanics that furnished the substance to support the advertising claim, and it became a best-seller for Pontiac. Indeed, in this Pontiac positioning strategy we see substance, consistency, and simplicity and distinctiveness—all the essential elements for an effective positioning strategy.

Another elegant and successful positioning strategy was Apple's tag line for the Macintosh—"A Computer for the Rest of Us"—illustrated in Exhibit 6.17. This computer was positioned as easy to use, hip, and a bit countercultural, and it was targeted to a segment that saw themselves as the antithesis of the techno-nerd (in their view) who used IBM-platform machines. Macintosh was a computer with an alternative attitude for a group of consumers with similar attitudes.

EXHIBIT 6.16

"We Build Excitement" is a perfect example of a single-benefit positioning theme. Pontiac has used this theme, with recent adaptations ("We Are Driving Excitement"), for more than ten years. www.pontiac.com /index.html

EXHIBIT 6.17 *Apple's "A Computer for the Rest of Us" campaign provides a nice example of a competitive positioning theme. This ad for the Macintosh ran during the Summer Olympics in 1984.* www .apple.com/

23.   Paul Ingrassia, "Pontiac Revives 'Sporty' Image, Setting a Marketing Example for Other GM Units," *Wall Street Journal,* August 15, 1986, 13.

Fundamental Positioning Themes

Positioning themes that are simple and distinctive help an organization make internal decisions that yield substantive value for customers, and they assist in the development of focused advertising campaigns to break through the clutter of competitors' advertising. Thus, choosing a viable positioning theme is one of the most important decisions faced by marketers and advertisers. In many ways, the *raison d'être* for STP marketing is to generate viable positioning themes.

Positioning themes take many forms, and like any other aspect of marketing and advertising, they can benefit from creative breakthroughs. Yet while novelty and creativity are valued in developing positioning themes, there are basic principles that should be considered when selecting a theme. Whenever possible, it is helpful if the organization can settle on a single premise—like "We Build Excitement" or "Friendly Serve"—to reflect its positioning strategy.[24] In addition, three fundamental options should always be considered in selecting a positioning theme. These options are benefit positioning, user positioning, and competitive positioning.[25]

"We Build Excitement" and "Friendly Serve" are examples of **benefit positioning.** Notice in these premises that a distinctive customer benefit is featured. This single-benefit focus is the first option that should be considered when formulating a positioning strategy. Consumers purchase products to derive functional or emotional benefits, so an emphasis on the primary benefit they can expect to receive from a brand is fundamental. While it might seem that more-compelling positioning themes would result from promising consumers a wide array of benefits, keep in mind that multiple-benefit strategies are hard to implement. Not only will they send mixed signals within an organization about what it stands for, but they will also place a great burden on advertising. Even for complex and expensive products like automobiles, single-benefit positioning themes, such as "We Build Excitement," are often the best way to break through competitive clutter to register a message with the consumer.

Another fundamental option is **user positioning.** Instead of featuring a benefit or attribute of the product, this option takes a specific profile of the target user as the focal point of the positioning strategy. For example, Rykä is positioned as the aquatic aerobic shoe just for women. This is apparent in the ad in Exhibit 6.18.

United is positioned as the airline of the harried business traveler, and as we saw earlier, Slurpee is positioned as the beverage of choice for thrill-seeking teenage males. User-oriented positioning themes are common when demographic and psychographic variables have been combined to reveal a target segment's distinctive lifestyle. The task then becomes the positioning of products or services to fit that particular lifestyle. Exhibits 6.19 and 6.20 show ads for the Norwegian and Carnival cruise lines; the former clearly sets itself apart as a young person's romantic experience (that is, no kids), while the latter reaches out to families with children.

EXHIBIT 6.18

The Aqueous 9H2O from Rykä is made for the female aqua fitness enthusiast. This is a nice example of user positioning. **www.ryka .com/**

24.   A more elaborate case for the importance of a single, consistent positioning premise is provided in Al Ries and Jack Trout, *Positioning: The Battle for Your Mind* (New York: Warner Books, 1982).

25.   Other basic options are discussed in David A. Aaker and J. Gary Shansby, "Positioning Your Product," *Business Horizons,* May/June 1982, 56–62.

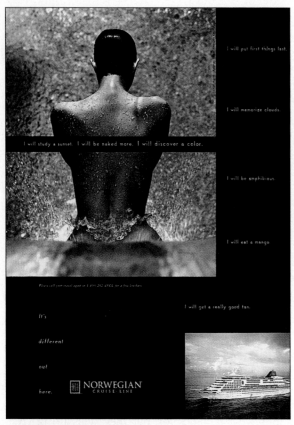

I will put first things last.

I will memorize clouds.

I will study a sunset. I will be naked more. I will discover a color.

I will be amphibious.

I will eat a mango

I will get a really good tan.

It's

different

out

here.

NORWEGIAN
CRUISE LINE

EXHIBIT 6.19

This ad does not come right out and say it, but the message is clear: Norwegian Cruise Line is about fun and not about kids. **www.ncl.com**

There's Something For Everyone On A "Fun Ship" Cruise.

There's no one too young, too old or too middle-aged to enjoy a Carnival cruise vacation. That's because each ship is designed with one concept in mind — to let you have "Your Kind of Fun," no matter what your age or interests.

The beauty of a Carnival cruise is that you can do almost anything you want. You can enjoy tropical days of poolside games or just relax in the sunshine. You can kick up your heels in a glittering

discotheque or kick back with a classic novel. And a "Fun Ship" cruise is the perfect family vacation. Children enjoy a wide variety of supervised daily activities for tots, tweens and teens that our Camp Carnival program offers.

No matter what your age, you'll have the vacation of a lifetime on a Carnival cruise. So call your Travel Agent today for special savings on Carnival, a leader in quality cruise vacations.

the "Fun Ships"

Carnival.
THE MOST POPULAR CRUISE LINE IN THE WORLD!
Registered in Liberia, Panama and The Bahamas

FESTIVALE • TROPICALE • HOLIDAY • JUBILEE • CELEBRATION • FANTASY • ECSTASY • SENSATION • FASCINATION • IMAGINATION

EXHIBIT 6.20   *Contrast the tone of this ad with that in Exhibit 6.19. See any differences?* **www.thetravelguide.com/carnival/**

The third option for a positioning theme is **competitive positioning.** This option is sometimes useful in well-established product categories with a crowded competitive field. Here, the goal is to use an explicit reference to an existing competitor to help define precisely what the brand can do. Many times this approach is used by smaller brands to carve out a position relative to the market share leader in their category. For instance, in the analgesics category, many competitors have used market leader Tylenol as an explicit point of reference in their positioning strategies. Excedrin, for one, has attempted to position itself as the best option to treat a simple headache, granting that Tylenol might be the better choice to treat the various symptoms of a cold or the flu.

Distinctiveness is essential for effective positioning strategy, and distinctiveness is always judged relative to the competition. In benefit and user positioning, a firm seeks to distinguish itself from the competition implicitly. In competitive positioning, a firm explicitly uses key competitors to delineate what its brand represents. Exhibit 6.21 shows an ad for Volvo that refers directly to a key competitor, BMW.

Repositioning

STP marketing is far from a precise science, so marketers do not always get it right the first time.[26] Furthermore, markets are dynamic. Things change. Even when marketers do get it right, competitors can react, or consumers' preferences may shift for any number of reasons, and what once was a viable positioning strategy must be altered if the brand is to survive. One of the best ways to revive an ailing

26.   Michael Gershman, *Getting It Right the Second Time* (Reading, Mass.: Addison-Wesley, 1990).

brand or to fix the lackluster performance of a new market entry is to redeploy the STP process to arrive at a revised positioning strategy. This type of effort is commonly referred to as **repositioning.**

While repositioning efforts are a fact of life for marketers and advertisers, they present a tremendous challenge. When brands that have been around for some time are forced to reposition, perceptions of the brand that have evolved over the years must be changed through advertising. This problem is common for brands that become popular with one generation but fade from the scene as that generation ages and emergent consumers come to view the brand as passé.

This was Hush Puppies' problem as the decade of the nineties began. Hush Puppies footwear became popular in the United States during the Kennedy administration, so by 1993 it had a severe positioning problem. At that point the makers of Hush Puppies finally realized that their brand was dying, and they decided to revive it by repositioning their shoes to "nifty, natural, contemporary, younger people." A $5 million campaign was launched in 1993, with print ads in magazines like *GQ, Details,* and *Glamour* featuring Hush Puppies on the feet of glamorous, youthful models.[27] During this same period, Nike and Reebok were spending approximately $200 million to communicate their positioning strategies to the same youthful segment that the makers of Hush Puppies had targeted. When brands are not revitalized on a regular basis and strong competitors emerge to fill the void, the repositioning challenge can be formidable.

A successful repositioning was that of Mountain Dew, which was taken from relative obscurity to the official brand of Generation X. Exhibit 6.22 shows the storyboard for one television ad from Mountain Dew's popular "Thrill" campaign.

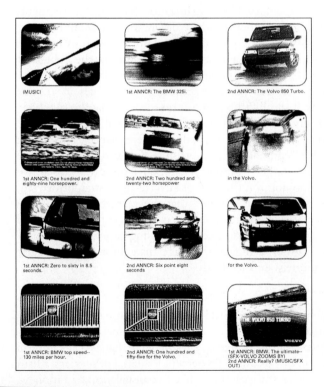

EXHIBIT 6.21

Here, Volvo seeks to expand on its safety-first positioning by going head-to-head with BMW on horsepower, acceleration time, and top speed. This could be risky business for Volvo and may leave consumers confused. Does Volvo stand for safety and security, or speed and power? Can Volvo have it both ways? **www.volvo.se/**

EXHIBIT 6.22 *Mel Torme accepts the "Do the Dew" challenge. Not bad, but has he ever experienced brain freeze?* **www.dewbeep.com/**

27.   Oscar Suris, "Ads Aim to Sell Hush Puppies to New Yuppies," *Wall Street Journal,* July 28, 1993, B1.

Product Differentiation

5 STP marketing can lay the foundation for successful advertising campaigns, but such successes are by no means permanent. Any money-making product or program can eventually be copied or improved on by a competitor, forcing a firm to go back to the drawing board to renew its brand. One path to renewal, as just discussed, is to reapply the STP framework to refine the segmentation strategy and then reposition the brand. But as the Hush Puppies' case illustrates, if a firm waits too long to pursue revitalization, the process is much more difficult.

There are limits on how frequently the STP framework can be applied and still be expected to produce valuable outcomes. In mature markets with established brands, the STP framework may be applied over and over again to the point where all relevant market segments are well known and hotly contested by several competitors. In this case, a firm needs another path for maintaining the vitality of its brands. This alternative path for creating marketing and advertising strategies is commonly referred to as product differentiation.

Product differentiation is an approach to brand building that takes the offerings of established competitors as its focal point and emphasizes the creation of differences to distinguish a firm's brand from competitors' brands. In product differentiation, the focus is on making a product unique to avoid head-to-head competition. By contrast, in market segmentation, the focus is on the identification of groups of consumers that may be served in some specific way.[28] Although product differentiation and market segmentation are sometimes presented as opposing or incompatible alternatives, it is more productive to view them as supplementary. If an organization has targeted segments that no other competitors are targeting, then product differentiation should not be necessary. In the more common situation in which several organizations are competing for the business of the same target segment (for example, the minivan or the light-beer segment), product differentiation is a valuable supplement to STP marketing.

As emphasized repeatedly, consumers purchase products or services to receive functional and emotional benefits. It should thus come as no surprise that the two basic paths to product differentiation entail either functional or emotional appeals. Before detailing these options, note that when pursuing product differentiation, advertising carries a heavy burden. In market segmentation, advertising's job is to communicate how a product fits the needs of the target segment. If a product possesses substantive value that the target segment is looking for, the role of advertising is straightforward. But in product differentiation, it cannot be assumed that the market will value the newly created point of difference. It is likely that consumers will have to be persuaded that the new feature is something they really do need. Persuading larger, general audiences to see things differently is always a bigger challenge than informing a smaller target segment that a product uniquely suits its needs.

Functional Differentiation

In functional differentiation, the goal is to build a feature or performance characteristic into a brand to set it apart from the competition. For products, this could involve features like color, size, scent, handy packaging, a special additive, or a special deletion (for example, 25 percent less fat). For services, a firm could pursue functional differentiation through things like free installation or a money-back guarantee if the pizza doesn't arrive in 30 minutes or less. Remember, the goal with any form of product differentiation is to build something—and perhaps anything

---

28.   For a more elaborate comparison of product differentiation and market segmentation, see Steven P. Schnaars, *Marketing Strategy: A Customer-Driven Approach* (New York: Free Press, 1991).

—into the offering that will set it apart from the competition. Exhibit 6.23 shows a Toshiba ad that underscores the functional attributes of the machine.

Functional differentiation comes in many forms. For less-involving product categories characterized by high levels of variety seeking, the point of difference may be little more than a novelty that makes consumers curious enough to try the brand. For example, Barbara's Bakery of Petaluma, California, makes potato chips called True Blues from real blue potatoes.[29] The chips turn out a deep purple color. A purple potato chip is obviously different, but only the consumer can decide whether it's a difference worth buying.

In a product category like minivans, we should expect functional differentiation to take a more substantive character. Such was the case in 1995 when Honda introduced its first entry into the crowded minivan segment. The Honda Odyssey contained several differentiating features—it had four carlike doors with power windows, and a fold-down rear seat that Honda ad's claimed could be folded away in just 3.5 seconds. The introduction of these new features sent established competitors like Chrysler and Ford back to the drawing board to come up with better door and seat configurations for their vehicles.

Although the prime goal of differentiation is always to make a brand different, simply having something different is by no means a guarantee of success. Take all those clear products that were introduced back in the early 1990s. On the heels of the success of a clear beverage product—Clearly Canadian—many marketers decided that they, too, would differentiate their brands by creating a clear version. Makers of Ivory Clear dishwashing soap, Crystal Pepsi, Miller-Clear transparent beer, and Mennen Lady Speed Stick Crystal all hoped that the clear feature would distinguish their brands and increase their market share. It didn't work out that way. Marketers were creating clear versions of their brands because they saw other marketers doing it, not because it was something that the consumer valued.[30] It became obvious that the clear craze was nothing more than a faddish differentiation tactic when Amoco started promoting its Crystal Clear Ultimate gasoline. While all these clear products are nice examples of functional differentiation, they also illustrate how seeking pure differentiation can lead a firm to lose sight of its customers. The designer water described in the Ethical Issues box on page 178 also suggests the faddish character of some product differentiation strategies.

WEB SIGHTING

GET PENTIUM.

Pentium™ Power:
The super-quick Pentium™ processor is designed specifically for notebooks and is engineered to perform 91% faster than 75MHz Intel DX4™ processors.

GET CD-ROM.

CD-ROM to Go:
The power of multimedia is all packed up and ready to go. The Satellite Pro™ 400CDT comes with an integrated, modular Quad-Speed CD-ROM drive that you can swap with the floppy drive in seconds. Or plug in the floppy drive externally and use both.

GET GOING.

Classic Car

In Touch with Tomorrow
TOSHIBA
Toshiba. The World's Best Selling Portable Computers.

Satellite Pro
The New Satellite Pro™ with Modular CD-ROM.

Lithium Ion Battery:
Toshiba's long-life Lithium Ion battery provides many hours of power while you travel.

Enhanced Port Replicator:
The new optional Enhanced Port Replicator provides two Type III PC Card slots, and allows one-step connection to your desktop environment.

Built-in Power Supply:
A built-in power supply means you don't have to carry a bulky external AC adapter. This slim power cord is all you need.

FEATURES:
400CDT:
• 10.4" dia. color active matrix display
• Integrated modular Quad-Speed CD-ROM
• Modular 3.5" FDD included

400CS²:
• 10.4" dia. color dual-scan display
• Integrated modular 3.5" FDD
• Optional modular Quad-Speed CD-ROM

BOTH MODELS:
• 75MHz Pentium™ processor (2.9v)
• Supports 24-bit true color (16.7 million colors)
• 810 Million Bytes (=772MB) HDD
• 8MB EDO RAM expandable to 40MB
• VL local-bus video
• Two stacked PC Card slots (two Type II or one Type III)
• Plug and Play connectivity
• Sound Blaster™ Pro compatible, 30AV and MIDI sound support
• AccuPoint™ integrated pointing device
• Toll-free Technical Support—7 days a week, 24 hours a day

Call 1-800-457-7777
for more information or a dealer near you.

intel inside
pentium™

All specifications and availability are subject to change. T 400CS comes with the modular FDD only. A Quad-Speed CD-ROM is available as an optional upgrade. ²The 400CS is sold at selected retailers as the 400CS with additional pre-installed software. © 1995 Toshiba America Information Systems, Inc. All products indicated by trademark symbols are trademarked and/or registered by their respective companies. The Intel Inside logo is a trademark of Intel Corporation.

EXHIBIT 6.23

This Toshiba ad is a good example of functional differentiation. Notice how both copy and pictures highlight specific product features related to how the laptop functions. What other differentiation strategy might have been used here? At the Toshiba home page **www.toshiba.com/,** *compare how features are presented on the site to the presentation in the sample ad in Exhibit 6.23. At competitor Dell Computer's Website at* **www.dell.com/,** *check out how this company presents its features. Which site—Toshiba's or Dell's—do you feel is most effective? Why?*

29.   Wendy Bounds, "Mood Is Indigo for Many Food Marketers," *Wall Street Journal,* September 2, 1993, B1.
30.   Kathleen Deveny, "Anatomy of a Fad: How Clear Products Were Hot and Then Suddenly Were Not," *Wall Street Journal,* March 15, 1994, B1.

Emotional Differentiation

In many mature product categories, there are few ways to functionally differentiate a brand. In these instances, the organization may turn to emotion in an effort to distinguish its offerings. The approach often used in advertising campaigns is to create distinctive images or personalities for brands and then invite consumers into brand communities. These brand images or personalities can be of value to individuals as they use the brands to make statements about themselves to other people. For example, feelings of status, pride, and prestige might be derived from the imagery associated with brands like BMW, Rolex, and Ralph Lauren. Brand imagery can also be valued in gift-giving contexts. A woman who gives a man Obsession by Calvin Klein is certainly expressing something different than the woman who gives Old Spice. Advertisers help brands have meaning and symbolic value to distinguish them beyond their functional forms.

Sometimes, the line between functional and emotional differentiation is blurred, as in the ad shown in Exhibit 6.24, which stresses a functional benefit (firmer thighs) with an arresting image. In the Saab advertising shown in Exhibit 6.25, brand image is an invitation to reject brand image or adopt an anti-image image. This form of differentiation can be difficult for a competitor to emulate.

Another way to effect emotional differentiation involves linking one's brand with social causes that provoke intense feelings. Avon Products' CEO, James E. Preston, believes that tie-ins with high-profile social issues can cut through the clutter of rival marketing messages.[31] His company supports breast cancer research in the United States and child nourishment programs in China. Likewise, Sears helps raise money for the homeless, Star-Kist has promoted dolphin-safe fishing practices, and Coors Brewing has funded public literacy programs—all as ways of striking distinctive emotional chords with their customers. Exhibit 6.26 demonstrates this type of emotional appeal in an ad for Virginia Power.

ETHICAL ISSUES

DESIGNER WATER? HAUTE COUTURE CLOTHIERS TAP THIRSTY THOUSANDS

The latest fashion craze from the design houses of New York and Los Angeles may evaporate very quickly: designer-label drinking water. For now, however, status-minded consumers are lapping up the pricey new offerings in surprising numbers.

The clothing designers have linked the new products to a desired lifestyle. The full range of products are then meant to evoke a central group of values, such as purity, simplicity, and refreshment. In this manner, the design houses employ a $1.50-a-glass price strategy to cash in on their brand equity and exclusive cachet. While haute couture clothier Maxfield's actually claims a degree of functional differentiation with its 100 percent glacier water, other houses such as Donna Karan New York (DKNY) are content simply to paste their distinctive logos on common bottled water, available (under a different name) at drugstores and supermarkets for a mere 99 cents a quart. DKNY may have the better approach: Maxfield's glacier water is said to "taste like an oil slick."

Other new bottled-water products venture beyond image alone into outright puffery, promising specific health benefits. Mo'Beta, from Odwalla, claims that its added antioxidants and beta-carotene will refresh overworked cells and guard against a host of medical problems, including aging. Other offerings promise to restore healthy hair and skin or to help control blood-sugar levels. *Caveat emptor.*

While some may see these latest fads as the ultimate triumph of marketing over substance, history has shown that these so-called marketing gimmicks come and go quite rapidly. Anyone remember the pet rock?

Sources: "Products New, but Puffery Same as Always," *Marketing News*, November 7, 1994, 14; and "The Latest Fashion Makes a Big Splash with the In Crowd," *Wall Street Journal*, October 18, 1994, A1.

---

31.   Geoffrey Smith and Ron Stodghill, "Are Good Causes Good Marketing?" *Business Week,* March 21, 1994, 64–65.

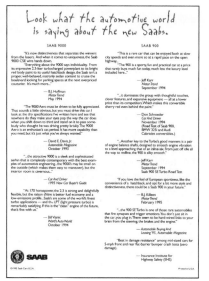

EXHIBIT 6.24

Do firmer thighs represent a functional or an emotional benefit? Is this ad really about a benefit promise, or is it image building for Donna Karan hosiery? Remember, it could be both. **www.donnakaran.com/**

EXHIBIT 6.25 *Saab advertising often emphasizes quality and performance, but there is symbolism here as well. Think of Saab imagery as anti-image imagery.*   **www.saabusa.com/**

EXHIBIT 6.26

Cause-related advertising can effect emotional differentiation for a company. Localized efforts like this one by Virginia Power can be very compelling. **www.vapower.com/**

SUMMARY

1 Explain the process known as STP marketing.

The phrase *STP marketing* refers to the process of segmenting, targeting, and positioning. Marketers pursue this set of activities in formulating marketing strategies for their brands. STP marketing also provides a strong foundation for the development of advertising campaigns. While no single approach can guarantee success in marketing and advertising, STP marketing should always be considered when consumers in a category have heterogeneous wants and needs.

2 Describe different bases that marketers use to identify target segments.

In market segmentation, the goal is to break down a heterogeneous market into more manageable subgroups or segments. Many different bases can be used for this purpose. Markets can be segmented on the basis of usage patterns and commitment levels, demographics, geography, psychographics, lifestyles, benefits sought, SIC codes, or stage in the decision process. Different bases are typically applied for segmenting consumer versus business-to-business markets.

3 Discuss the criteria used for choosing a target segment.

In pursuing STP marketing, an organization must get beyond the stage of segment identification and settle on one or more segments as a target for its marketing and advertising efforts. Several criteria are useful in establishing the organization's target segment. First, the organization must decide whether it has the proper skills to serve the segment in question. The size of the segment and its growth potential must also be taken into consideration.

Another key criterion involves the intensity of the competition the firm is likely to face in the segment. Often, small segments, known as market niches, can be quite attractive because they will not be hotly contested by numerous competitors.

4 Identify the essential elements of an effective positioning strategy.

The *P* in STP marketing refers to the positioning strategy that must be developed as a guide for all marketing and advertising activities that will be undertaken in pursuit of the target segment. As exemplified by Pontiac's "We Build Excitement" campaign, effective positioning strategies are rooted in the substantive benefits offered by the brand. They are also consistent internally and over time, and they feature simple and distinctive themes. Benefit positioning, user positioning, and competitive positioning are options that should be considered when formulating a positioning strategy.

5 Compare and contrast market segmentation and product differentiation strategies.

Formulating a market segmentation strategy begins with an analysis of the market. Conversely, formulating a product differentiation strategy begins with an analysis of the competitive brands currently in the marketplace. In product differentiation, the focal point is identifying some unique feature or aspect for the brand that the firm can promote as a point of difference vis-à-vis the brands of established competitors. The two primary options for creating this perception of uniqueness with consumers are functional or emotional differentiation.

KEY TERMS

target segment (157)
positioning (157)
positioning strategy (157)
heavy users (160)
nonusers (160)
brand-loyal users (160)
switchers, or variety seekers (160)
emergent consumers (160)
demographic segmentation (161)
geodemographic segmentation (163)
psychographics (164)

lifestyle segmentation (164)
benefit segmentation (165)
consumer markets (166)
business markets (166)
competitive field (168)
market niche (169)
benefit positioning (173)
user positioning (173)
competitive positioning (174)
repositioning (175)

QUESTIONS FOR REVIEW AND CRITICAL THINKING

1. Explain the logic that led Nike to create its casual shoe. What was the flaw in Nike's logic? Explain how Nike was able to recover from this casual-shoe debacle.

2. While STP marketing often produces successful outcomes, there is no guarantee that these successes will last. What factors can erode the successes produced by STP marketing, forcing a firm to reformulate its marketing strategy?

3. Explain the appeal of emergent consumers as a target segment. Identify a current ad campaign targeting an emergent-consumer segment.

4. It is often said that psychographics were invented to overcome the weaknesses of demographic information for describing target segments. What unique information can psychographics provide that would be of special value to advertisers?

5. What criteria did Mobil Oil Corporation weigh most heavily in its selection of Road Warriors as a target seg-

ment? What do you think will be the biggest source of frustration for Mobil in trying to make this strategy work?

6. Explain why smaller is better when selecting segments to target in marketing strategies.

7. What essential elements of a positioning strategy can help overcome the consumer's natural tendency to ignore, distort, or forget most of the advertisements she or he is exposed to?

8. Identify examples of current advertising campaigns featuring benefit positioning, user positioning, and competitive positioning.

9. Why does the persuasion required with a product differentiation strategy present more of a challenge than the persuasion required with a market segmentation strategy?

10. Who would you rather compete against—a firm that uses functional differentiation to impress the consumer, or a firm that uses emotional differentiation to impress the consumer? Explain your position.

EXPERIENTIAL EXERCISE

General Motors is attempting to reposition the image of Oldsmobile in the minds of consumers. Ask three adults to discuss with you their current impression of, beliefs about, and attitude toward Oldsmobile. Would they purchase an Oldsmobile today? Why or why not? Briefly describe what

each adult said and indicate the extent to which you think the brand needs to be repositioned. Develop two rough ads for Oldsmobile using competitive, benefit, or user positioning.

USING THE INTERNET

The soft drink market has become increasingly competitive, with several companies seeking to capture market share and sustain consistent growth. What was once referred to as the cola wars has now expanded to the Internet and includes more companies than Coca-Cola and Pepsi. Visit each of these sites supported by soft drink companies:

Pepsi: www.pepsi.com

Snapple: www.snapple.com

Jolt: www.joltcola.com

Gatorade: www.gatorade.com

1. Describe each brand's target segment in terms of demographics, psychographics, and lifestyles.

2. Compare the four sites and describe their positioning strategies. How does each site create a specific position?

3. How does the positioning reflected in each Web site match with the target segment?

4. How effective is each site at differentiating its brand from its competitor's?

Chapter 7

Advertising

Research

After reading and thinking about this chapter, you will be able to do the following:

1 Explain the purposes served by and methods used in developmental advertising research.

2 Discuss the various procedures used for pretesting advertising messages prior to a complete launch of an advertising campaign.

3 Discuss the various methods used to track the effectiveness of ad executions during and after the launch of a full-blown advertising campaign.

4 Identify the many sources of secondary data that can aid the ad-planning effort.

The Goodyear Aquatred tire was one of the most successful new tire introductions of all time. Goodyear's ability to compete successfully against foreign competitors, particularly Michelin and Yokohama, has been greatly enhanced by the Aquatred. It also contributed significantly to Goodyear's recent record profits. Managers at Goodyear attribute much of the success of the introduction of the Aquatred to the initial advertising campaign. This campaign featured "The Bucket," which showed how many buckets of water an Aquatred tire can disperse every mile.

Strategists at Goodyear believe "The Bucket" advertising was so successful because the ad went through extensive and rigorous testing before and during the product's release. While the product was being developed, marketing strategists at Goodyear determined that a unique tread design with outstanding performance features would provide clear brand differentiation in the market. Then, before the tire was ready for market introduction, Goodyear and its advertising agency, J. Walter Thompson Detroit, started researching several alternative television messages. First, the agency tested two different basic message formats. One was a testimonial by a user (called "Richard on Aquatreds"), the other was an ad that featured the tire's traction on wet, snowy roads (called "Skiing"). Based on this preliminary research, Goodyear and its agency concluded that a product performance ad that also demonstrated brand differentiation would be the best format for the introductory Aquatred campaign.

The agency moved forward based on the research and developed "The Bucket" as an ad that specifically featured both the performance and demonstration dimensions. "Skiing" and "The Bucket" were aired during the four-week introductory period for Aquatred. Exhibit 7.1 shows the **storyboard** (the frame-by-frame sequence agencies use to depict the scenes from a television ad) for "The Bucket."

(MUSIC) MAN: This is a Goodyear Aquatred

and this is a gallon of water.

At highway speeds in a rain storm

Goodyear Aquatred pumps a gallon of water every second

thanks to its computer designed deep groove Aqua Channel.

It channels water away as you drive

to keep more of the tire in contact with the road

for outstanding wet weather traction.

It's only from Goodyear

and it comes with a 60,000 miles tread life warranty.

The All Season Aquatred, try a set.

We like to say the best tires in the world have Goodyear written all over them. (MUSIC OUT)

EXHIBIT 7.1

Goodyear and its ad agency determined that a demonstration ad would be most effective in launching the new Aquatred tire. **www.goodyear .com/**

Once the product was introduced, Goodyear tracked the effectiveness of "The Bucket" and "Skiing" using a persuasion rating system. These results were compared to the sales of the Aquatred in various market areas. The firm discovered that both ads were having a significant and positive impact on sales, that "The Bucket" campaign was the most powerful, and that both ads became less effective after a four-week period. Goodyear also realized that the ads were contributing to a level of consumer demand beyond the firm's production capacity, so the advertising was actually scaled back to balance demand with supply.

Goodyear and its advertising agency used several different types of research to plan the introductory advertising campaign for the new Aquatred tire. First, marketing research performed by Goodyear determined what product features and performance characteristics would provide a basis for clear brand differentiation in the market. Next, advertising research determined that a product demonstration ad, rather than a testimonial, would be more effective. Finally, when the two demonstration ads began running during the tire's introduction, persuasion and sales measures were tracked to assess the ads' relative effectiveness.[1]

1.   Information on Goodyear's development of Aquatred advertising is adapted from Ronald P. Conlin, "Goodyear Advertising Research: Past, Present, and Future," *Journal of Advertising Research,* Research Currents (May/June 1994): RC-7–RC-10.

The Role of Research

The experience of Goodyear highlights the role of research. Managerial experience in a product category and a history of marketing to a particular market segment are extremely valuable but generally insufficient to fully meet the challenges of advertising planning.

By drawing on research, an advertiser can better understand what will be useful in an advertisement. This is not to say that research information makes decisions for advertisers. It's more that research increases the probability of making a good decision or, conversely, reduces the probability of making a bad one. Still, no matter how comprehensive the research may be, decision making still relies on decision makers' interpretations, and ultimately on their judgment.

Several issues must be addressed regarding marketing and advertising research. First, what is the difference between marketing and advertising research? **Marketing research** is defined as the systematic gathering, recording, and interpretation of information related to all marketing mix variables. **Advertising research** is a specialized form of marketing research that focuses on the planning, preparation, and placement of advertising. More simply stated, advertising research is any research conducted by an advertising agency. While some agencies have all but gotten out of the research business, others are scrambling to take on any research jobs that will bring in a little extra revenue (those that bill on a fee basis) or allow them to hang on to an important client. The distinction between advertising research and marketing research is, as a practical matter, not terribly significant.

Research comes into the advertising process at several points. It is often used to assist a marketer in determining which segment of the market to target. Research also plays a role in helping the creatives understand the audience members to whom their ads will speak, and which buttons to push. It is also used to make go/no-go decisions, to determine when to pull an ad that is worn out, and to evaluate the performance of an ad agency.

As you can see, advertising research is used to judge advertising, but who judges advertising research, and how? First of all, not enough people, in our opinion, question and judge research. Research is not magic or truth, and it should never be confused with such. Issues of reliability, validity, trustworthiness, and meaningfulness should be seriously considered when research is used to make important decisions. **Reliability** means that the method generates generally consistent findings over time. **Validity** means that the information generated is relevant to the research questions being investigated. In other words, the research measured what it sought to measure. **Trustworthiness** is a term usually applied to qualitative data, and it means exactly what it implies: Can one, knowing how the data were collected, trust them, and to what extent? Most difficult of all is the notion of **meaningfulness.** Just what does a piece of research really mean? It is important for advertising professionals to take a moment and consider the limitations inherent in their data and in their interpretations. Too few take the time.

Developmental Advertising Research

❶ Developmental advertising research is used to generate advertising opportunities and messages. It helps the creatives and account team figure out things like the target audience's street language and profile. It provides critical information used by creatives in actually producing ads. It is conducted early in the process so there is still an opportunity to influence the way the ads come out. Developmental advertising research is broadly defined and serves many purposes. Because of this, it is considered by many to be the most valuable kind of advertising research. Several of the purposes served by developmental research are reviewed in the following sections.

Idea Generation

Sometimes an ad agency is called on to invent new, yet meaningful, ways of presenting an advertised good or service to a target audience. The outcome might take the form of a repositioning strategy for the advertiser. For example, after many years of representing its parks as the ultimate family destination, Disney and its ad agencies have now positioned its theme parks as adult vacation alternatives for couples whose children have grown and gone off on their own.

Where does an advertiser get the ideas for new and meaningful ways to portray a brand? Direct contact with the customer can be an excellent place to start. Qualitative research involving observation of customers, brainstorming sessions with customers, and extended interviews with customers can be great devices for fostering fresh thinking about a brand. (Disney probably got its idea for repositioning by simply observing how many older couples were visiting its parks without children in tow!) As discussed in the Contemporary Issues box on page 189, customer complaint patterns can be another key information source in idea generation. Direct contact with and aggressive listening to the customer can fuel the creative process at the heart of any great advertising campaign.

Environmental Analysis

Environmental analysis generates information on the uncontrollable variables in the broad business environment. **Environmental analysis** tries to assess the potential influence of social and cultural trends, economics, and politics on the consumer and the social environment into which the advertising will be injected. Such analysis provides useful information for advertising planning in terms of both the opportunities to communicate effectively with audiences and the barriers to implementation. Exhibit 7.2 shows the type of information gathered during environmental analysis. All of these data help situate (put in context) the advertising message.

Audience Definition

Market segmentation is one of the first and most important marketing decisions a firm must make. As discussed in the last chapter, the goal of market segmentation research is to identify consumer groups that represent the best match between the firm's market offering and the consumer's needs and desires.

Furthermore, new market opportunities can also be discovered. As an example, the national hardware trade association discovered in 1993 that 49.6 percent of the purchases of tools needed for simple emergency repairs—plungers, ladders, fire extinguishers, pipe decloggers—were made by women.[2] Once a target segment or segments have been identified, advertising planning can proceed with a determination of the message information that will be most meaningful to the consumers in the segment. In addition, information about the best potential segments allows for the efficient media placement of advertisements. The finding on women's purchases of hardware items has led Builders Square, the home improvement retailer, to run ads targeting the women's market in *Home, House Beautiful,* and *Better Homes & Gardens,* as the ad in Exhibit 7.3 shows.[3]

Audience Profiling

Perhaps the most important service provided by developmental advertising research is the profiling of target audiences for the creatives. Creatives need to know as much as they can about the people to whom their ads will speak. This research is done in many ways. One of the most popular is through lifestyle research. Lifestyle research, also known as AIO research, uses survey data from consumers who have answered questions regarding a wide array of activities, interests, and opinions (thus AIO). From the answers to close to a thousand questions, advertisers are able to

---

2.   Jeffery D. Zbar, "Hardware Builds Awareness among Women," *Advertising Age,* July 11, 1994, 18.
3.   Ibid.

EXHIBIT 7.2

Environmental analysis.

Environment	Information Gathered
Demographic	Demographics are population characteristics. Among the important dimensions of the demographic environment are population density, age distribution, geographic population distribution, household size and composition, and population ethnicity. The demographic environment is of critical importance to advertisers because population characteristics affect demand for various goods and services. Further, accurate information on the demographic environment allows marketers to make inferences regarding behavior, thus providing a basis for predicting future consumption patterns.
Social and cultural	One of the most important and yet most difficult external environmental factors to gauge is the social and cultural environment. The social and cultural environment is related to the broad-based values evident in a society. In recent history, changes in such social and cultural values have spawned multibillion-dollar industries in the United States. The value placed on health and fitness has given rise to the health food industry and the spa and fitness center industry, as well as a huge boost to the outdoor recreation industry. Social and cultural trends may evolve slowly but have an enormous effect on goods and services (and advertising) prevalent in a society. Among the significant social and cultural trends over the past 30 years that have shaped demand in the United States are the changing family structure, the importance of time and convenience, the emphasis on health and fitness, the changing gender roles, a concern for the natural environment, and attitudes toward wealth and status seeking.
Economic	Several economic factors affect the ability of firms to successfully market and advertise goods and services. Fundamental features of the economy, like gross domestic product, interest rates, and inflation, influence the ability (and desire) of both household and business consumers to spend. Some industries are more sensitive to economic conditions than others. Traditionally, the automobile industry (and other durable goods industries), tourism, and housing suffer the most if economic conditions sour. Conversely, basic consumer packaged goods, pharmaceuticals, and some business goods categories suffer little from a general slowdown in the economy. Of the enormous number of economic statistics available, some of the more popular for firms to monitor are household income and spending patterns, the consumer price index, and consumer confidence.
Political/regulatory	The effects of the political and regulatory environment come from both government and nongovernment sources. Numerous restrictions have been imposed on marketing and advertising practices by both federal and state governments. The federal agencies that have the most direct and obvious effect on marketing and advertising practices are the Federal Trade Commission (FTC), the Food and Drug Administration (FDA), and the Federal Communications Commission (FCC). Recall that consumers, industry associations, and the media all have informal regulatory powers over a firm's marketing and advertising practices. Consumers can boycott products or form special interest groups. Industry trade associations and media organizations have codes of behavior they generally follow.
Technological	Technological change doesn't just affect the products or services a firm can market. Technology affects the values and behavior of a society. With regard to advertising specifically, if the information superhighway makes it feasible to communicate with individual consumers in an interactive media format, the nature of advertising will change dramatically. Similarly, if technology promotes telecommuting, then consumption of and demand for automobiles, gasoline, fast food, clothing, and a variety of other work-related products will be changed. A long-term and visionary perspective on technology and its impact is essential.
Competitive	The activities of competitors have an obvious effect on both marketing and advertising planning. Firms must monitor competitors to respond to competitive maneuvers. What is less obvious, though, is the threat from indirect competition. This is the threat of competition from new alternatives. For example, there is the threat to the airline industry from teleconferencing. The primary decision with regard to the competitive environment for advertising planning is the extent to which a direct response to competition will be undertaken or whether more basic, noncompetition-based strategies will be pursued.

get a pretty good profile of those consumers they are most interested in talking to. Since the data also contain other product usage questions, advertisers are able to account for a consumption lifestyle as well. These profiles present the creative staff with a finer and finer grained picture of the target audience, their needs, wants, and motivations. Of course, the answers to these questions are only as valuable as the questions are valid. Some believe that depth interviews provide a better method.

Builders Square targets a new segment for hardware: women.

Methods and Procedures Used in Developmental Research

One of the key methods for developmental research purposes is the **focus group.** A focus group is a brainstorming session with target customers to come up with new insights about the brand—"Six people sitting around a table eating pizza and discussing your product category with market researchers watching through a one-way mirror is the essence of focus groups."[4] This method brings together from 6 to 12 consumers with a professional moderator to guide the discussion. These consumers are first asked some general questions, and then, as the session progresses, the questioning becomes more focused and moves to detailed issues about the brand in question. Clients tend to like focus groups because they can understand them and observe the data being collected.

While focus groups provide an opportunity for in-depth discussion with consumers, they are not without limitations. Even multiple focus groups represent a very small sample of the target audience, and advertisers must remember that generalization is not the goal. The real goal is to get or test a new idea and gain depth of information. Greater depth of information allows for a greater understanding of the context of actual usage and its subtleties.

It also takes great skill to lead a focus group effectively. Without a well-trained and experienced moderator, some individuals will completely dominate, or at least annoy, the others. Focus group members feel empowered and privileged; they have been made experts by their selection, and they will sometimes give the moderator all sorts of strange answers that may be more a function of trying to impress other group members than anything having to do with the product in question.

Projective techniques are designed to allow consumers to project thoughts and feelings (conscious or unconscious) in an indirect and unobtrusive way onto a theoretically neutral stimulus. (Seeing faces in clouds, or breasts in ice cubes, is an example of projection.) Projective techniques share a history with Freudian psychology and depend on notions of unconscious or even repressed thoughts. Projective techniques often consist of offering consumers fragments of pictures or words and asking them to complete the fragment. The most common projective techniques are association tests, sentence or picture completion, dialogue balloons, and story construction. While there is

---

4.   Jeffery A. Trachtenberg, "Listening the Old-Fashioned Way," *Forbes,* October 5, 1987, 202, 204.

little doubt that people can, and do, project, the trustworthiness and validity of these techniques are often suspect.

Association tests ask consumers to express their feelings or thoughts after hearing a brand name or seeing a logo. In **sentence and picture completion,** a researcher presents consumers with part of a picture or a sentence with words deleted and then asks that the stimulus be completed. The picture or sentence relates to one or several brands of products in the category of interest. For example, a sentence completion task might be

Most American-made cars are _____ .

The basic idea is to elicit honest thoughts and feelings. Of course, consumers usually have some idea of what the researcher is looking for. Still, one can get some reasonably good data from this method.

CONTEMPORARY ISSUES

SWEETENING SOUR GRIPES: SAVVY COMPANIES LEARN FROM CUSTOMER COMPLAINTS

First, the bad news: No matter how hard you try, you simply cannot please everyone. Now, the good news: Those you don't please are a valuable source of information and may offer many ideas for improving your marketing efforts. While tracking individual complaints may enhance overall performance and customer service, tracking *complaint trends* may point to overall inefficiencies that need attention. To better identify these complaint trends, many firms have developed proprietary software and other tracking systems to identify complaint relationships. Toyota Motor Sales USA uses a measurement system it calls the "blue-card process" to follow changing grievance patterns over time. When unusual complaints are received, each is recorded on a blue card and reviewed weekly by a team of customer service supervisors. From that point, the team may launch a statistical analysis of recurring concerns against its complaint database, discover meaningful patterns and relationships, and recommend specific remedies.

Following complaints closely allows a company to respond quickly and provides a cost-effective means of preventing similar problems from arising. John Goodman, president of TARP, an Arlington, Virginia, customer service consulting firm, explains that "you get complaints quickly after the incident took place. So as a source of quality information, they are timely and less expensive than doing systematic surveys." What marketers must ultimately realize is that customers rarely demand unswerving perfection. The main factor in retaining an unsatisfied customer's loyalty is the process of validating personal concerns and providing a remedy. People generally want to be listened to with respect, and the original problem itself often pales in comparison. The opportunity to satisfy an unhappy customer through resolving a complaint then provides a unique opportunity to build relationships and long-term brand loyalty. Consequently, those with excellent listening and communication skills are in high demand, and the average annual salary for customer service personnel responsible for answering 800 numbers is nearly $30,000. No complaints there.

Sources: "You Can Get Satisfaction," *Sales & Marketing Management* (July 1995): 106; and "Cashing In on Complaints," *Sales & Marketing Management* (May 1995): 86.

Dialogue balloons offer consumers the chance to fill in the dialogue of cartoonlike stories, much like those in the comics in the Sunday paper. The story usually has to do with a product use situation. **Story construction** asks consumers to tell a story about people depicted in a scene or picture. Respondents might be asked to tell a story about the personality of the people in the scene, what they are doing, what they were doing just before this scene, what type of car they drive, and what type of house they live in.

Again, the idea is to use a less direct method to less obtrusively bring to the surface some often-unconscious mapping of the brand and its associations.

Many times advertisers need feedback about new ideas before they spend a lot of money to turn the idea into a new marketing or advertising initiative A **concept test** seeks feedback designed to screen the quality of a new idea, using consumers as the final judge and jury. Concept testing may be used to screen new ideas for specific advertisements or to assess new product concepts. How the product fits current needs and how much consumers are willing to pay for the new product are questions a concept test attempts to answer. For example, would consumers trust a yogurt product coming from the makers of Jell-O? Exhibit 7.4 makes one think so. Concept tests of many kinds are commonly included as part of the agenda of focus groups to get quick feedback on new product or advertising ideas. Concept testing may also be pursued via survey research when more generalizable feedback is desired.

Everything
yogurt
should be.

Plus fun.

Finally, a lowfat yogurt with the fun of Jell-O® Brand, and the nutrition of, well, yogurt. Jell-O™ Yogurt. Kids love the fruity flavors. And moms love that kids love it.

JELL-O
YOGURT

EXHIBIT 7.4

Yogurt seems a natural fit with the other products for which Jell-O is best known.

The Experiences of the Consumer

Consumers live real lives, and their behavior as consumers is intertwined throughout their lives. More and more, researchers are attempting to capture more of the experiences of consumers.[5] Advertising researchers can situate their messages far better if they understand the lives of their target audience. Various types of qualitative research attempt to do this. This general type of research uses prolonged engagement and in-depth study of individuals or small groups of consumers, typically in their own social environment. This work is usually accomplished through field work, going where the consumer lives and consumes. The advertising industry has long appreciated the value of qualitative data and is currently moving to even more strongly embrace extended types of field work.

Fundamental Issues in Message Evaluation

At the heart of any successful advertising campaign is a message that engages a consumer and gives him or her a reason to believe in the brand. It should thus come as no surprise that much of the research conducted by ad agencies and their clients deals with message testing. Message-testing research comes in two basic types: one occurs before an ad is placed (a pretest); the other occurs after an ad is placed (a posttest). There is no one right way to test a message, and as a result one can find conflicting advice about how to execute this research function. This diversity of opinion stems from multiple and sometimes competing testing criteria or outright confusion about what an ad must do to be considered effective.

Motives and Expectations

Message testing can be a function of logic and adaptive decision making, or it may be driven by custom and history. In the best case, reliable, valid, trustworthy, and meaningful tests are appropriately applied. In the worst case, tests in which few still believe continue to thrive because they represent "the way we have always done things." More typically, however, industry practice falls somewhere in between. The pressure of history and the felt need for normative data (which allows comparisons with the past) partially obscure questions of appropriateness and validity. This makes for an environment in which the best test is not always done, and the right questions are not always asked.

5.   Craig J. Thompson, William B. Locander, and Howard Pollio, "Putting Consumer Experience Back into Consumer Research: The Philosophy and Method of Existential Phenomenology," *Journal of Consumer Research* 16, number 1 (1989): 133–47.

This brings us to motives and expectations. Just what is it that advertising people want out of their message tests? The answer, of course, depends on who you ask. Generally speaking, the account team wants some assurance that the commercial or ad does essentially what it's supposed to do. Many times, the team simply wants whatever the client wants. The client typically wants to see some numbers, generally meaning normative test scores; in other words, the client wants to see how well a particular ad scored against the average commercial of its type. The creatives who produced the ad often believe there is no such thing as the average commercial, and they are quite sure that if there are average commercials, theirs are not among them. Besides benefiting the sales of the advertised good or service, the creatives wouldn't mind another striking ad on their reel or in their book. Message-testing tools also generate a type of report card, and some people, particularly those who like to think of themselves as artists, resent getting report cards from people in suits. (Who wouldn't?) Creatives also argue that these numbers are often misleading and misapplied. Sometimes they're right.

Whenever people begin looking at the numbers, there is a danger that trivial differences can be made monumental. Other times, the required measure is simply inappropriate. Still other times, creatives, wishing to keep their jobs, simply give the client what he or she wants, as suggested in Exhibit 7.5.

If simple recall is what the client wants, then increasing the frequency of brand mentions might be the answer. It may not make for a better commercial, but it may make for a better score and, presumably, a happy client in the short run.

Despite the politics involved, message-testing research is a good idea most of the time. Properly conducted, such research can yield important data that management can then use to determine the suitability of an ad. It's far better to shelve an expensive commercial than run (or continue to run) something that will produce little good and may even do harm.

Dimensions for Message Assessment

There are many standards against which ads are judged. Of course, picking the right criteria is not always an easy task, but it is the essence of effective message evaluation. An ad like that in Exhibit 7.6 could be judged along many dimensions and with several criteria. However, we will discuss four basic dimensions on which a message could be evaluated: whether or not the ad imparts knowledge about the brand, shapes attitudes and preferences, attaches feeling and emotion, or legitimizes the brand as one that is right for its target audience.

Impart Knowledge. It is commonly assumed that advertising generates thoughts, some of which are at some point retrieved to then influence purchase. Some ads are judged effective if

Bob, a creative at a large agency, has learned from experience how to deal with lower-than-average day-after-recall (DAR) scores. As he explains it, there are two basic strategies: (1) Do things that you know will pump up the DAR. For example, if you want high DARs, never simply super (superimpose) the brand name or tag at the end of the ad. Always voice it over as well, whether it fits or not. You can also work in a couple of additional mentions in dialogue; they may stand out like a sore thumb and make consumers think, "Man, is that a stupid commercial," because people don't talk that way. But it will raise your DARs. (2) Tell them (the account executive or brand manager and other suits) that this is not the kind of product situation that demands high DARs. In fact, high DARs would actually hurt them in the long run due to quick wearout and annoyance. Tell them, "You're too sophisticated for that ham-handed kind of treatment. It would never work with our customers." You can use the second strategy only occasionally, but it usually works. It's amazing.

they leave this cognitive residue, or knowledge about the brand. This knowledge may take many different forms. It could be a jingle, a tag line, the recognition of a product symbol, or merely brand-name recognition. Generally, tests of recall and recognition are featured when knowledge generation is the advertiser's primary concern.

EXHIBIT 7.6

This Sun-Maid raisins ad could be judged with several criteria. **www**
.sunmaid.com/

Shape Attitudes. Attitudes can tell us a lot about where a brand stands in the consumer's eyes. Attitudes can be influenced both by what people know and by what people feel about a brand. In this sense, attitude or preference is a summary evaluation that ties together the influence of many different factors. Advertisers thus may view attitude shaping or attitude change as a key dimension for assessing advertising effectiveness. Message-testing research is frequently structured around the types of attitude measures discussed extensively in Chapter 5.

Attach Feelings and Emotions. Advertisers have always had a special interest in feelings and emotions. Ever since the atmospheric ads of the 1920s, there has been the belief that feelings may be more important than thoughts as a reaction to certain ads. While this philosophy waxes and wanes, there has been a renewed interest in developing better measures of the feelings and emotions generated by advertising.[6] This has included better paper-and-pencil measures as well as dial-turning devices with which those watching an ad turn a dial in either a positive or negative direction to indicate their emotional response to the ad. Participants' responses are tracked by computer and can be aggregated and superimposed over the ad during playback to allow account executives and brand managers to see the pattern of affective reactions generated by the ad.

Legitimize the Brand. A **resonance test** is one in which the goal is to determine to what extent the message resonates or rings true with target audience members.[7] This method fits well with consumer-experience research. The question becomes, Does this ad match consumers' own experiences? Does it produce an affinity reaction? Do consumers who view it say, "Yeah, that's right; I feel just like that"? Do consumers read the ad and make it their own?[8] In the view of some, this is the direction in which message evaluation research needs to move. The assessment dimension here reflects the effectiveness of advertising for legitimizing a brand with its target audience.

Pretest Message Research

2 Because so much time, effort, and expense are involved in the development of advertising messages, most organizations pretest their message to gauge consumer reaction *before* advertisements are placed. A variety of tools may be used in pretesting.

---

6.   Stuart J. Agres, Julie A. Edell, and Tony M. Dubitsky, eds., *Emotion in Advertising* (Westport, Conn.: Quorum Books, 1990). See especially Chapters 7 and 8.

7.   David Glenn Mick and Claus Buhl, "A Meaning-Based Model of Advertising Experiences," *Journal of Consumer Research* 19 (December 1992), 317–38.

8.   Linda Scott, "The Bridge from Text to Mind: Adapting Reader Response Theory for Consumer Research," *Journal of Consumer Research* 21 (December 1994), 461–86.

Communications Tests   A **communications test** simply seeks to see if a message is communicating something close to what is desired. Communications tests are usually done in a group setting, with data coming from a combination of pencil-and-paper questionnaires and group discussion. They are done with one major thought in mind: to prevent a major disaster, to prevent communicating something the creators of the ad are too close to see but that is entirely obvious to those consumers first seeing the ad. This could be an unintended double entendre or an unseen sexual allusion. It could be an unexpected interpretation of the visual imagery in an ad as that ad is moved from country to country around the world. Remember, if the consumer sees unintended things, it doesn't matter if they're intended or not—to the consumer, they're there. However, advertisers should balance this against the fact that communications test members feel privileged and special, and thus they may try too hard to see things. This is another instance where well-trained and experienced researchers must be counted on to draw a proper conclusion from the testing.

Magazine Dummies   **Dummy advertising vehicles** are mock-ups of magazines that contain editorial content and advertisements, as a real magazine would. Inserted in the dummy vehicle is one or more test advertisements. Once again, consumers representing the target audience are asked to read through the magazine as they normally would. The test is usually administered in consumers' homes and therefore has some sense of realism. Once the reading is completed, the consumers are asked questions about the content of both the magazine and the advertisements. Questions relating to recall of the test ads and feelings toward the ad and the featured product are typically asked. This method is most valuable for comparing different message options.

Theater Tests   Advertisements are also tested in small theaters, usually set up in or near shopping malls. Members of the theater audience have an electronic device through which they can express how much they like or dislike the advertisements shown. Simulated shopping trips can also be a part of this type of research. The problem with the **theater test** is that it is difficult to determine whether the respondent is really expressing feelings toward the ad or the product being advertised. Furthermore, the environment could hardly be more unrealistic. Given the artificial and demanding conditions of the test, experienced researchers are again needed to interpret the results. Interestingly, theater tests disguised as TV-show previews do appear to be winning advocates for ad testing around the world. See the Global Issues box on page 194 for a discussion of this development.

Thought Listings   It is commonly assumed that advertising generates thoughts, or cognitions, during and following exposure. Message research that tries to identify specific thoughts that may be generated by an ad is referred to as **thought listing,** or cognitive response analysis.

Here the researcher is interested in the thoughts that a finished or near-finished ad generated in the mind of the consumer. Typically, cognitive responses are collected by having individuals watch the commercial in groups and, as soon as it is over, asking them to write down all the thoughts that were in their minds while watching the commercial. The hope is that this will capture what the potential audience members made of the ad and how they responded, or talked back, to it.

These verbatim responses can then be analyzed in a number of ways. Usually, simple percentages or box scores of word counts are used. The ratio of favorable to unfavorable thoughts may be the primary interest of the researcher. Alternatively, the number of times the person made a self-relevant connection—that is, "That would be good for me" or "That looks like something I'd like"—could be tallied and compared for different ad executions.

Attitude Change Studies

The typical **attitude change study** uses a before-and-after ad exposure design. People from the target market are recruited, and their pre-exposure attitudes toward the advertised brand as well as competitors' brands are taken. Then they are exposed to the test ad, along with some dummy ads. Following this exposure, their attitudes are measured again. The goal, of course, is to gauge the potential of specific ad versions for changing brand attitudes.

Attitude change studies are often conducted in a theater test setting. These tests often use a constant-sum measurement scale. A subject is asked to divide a sum (for example, 100 points) among several (usually three) brands. For example, they would be asked to divide 100 points among three brands of deodorants in relation to how likely they are to purchase each. They do this before and after ad exposure. A change score is then computed. Sometimes this change score is adjusted by the potential change, so as not to unfairly penalize established brands.

GLOBAL ISSUES

ONE FOR ALL: CROSS-CULTURAL RESEARCH ALLOWS GLOBAL AD PLANNING

With the advent and growth of satellite broadcasting, global television programming may soon be possible. Even now, Ted Turner's Cable News Network nearly spans the globe. The problem for advertisers, however, is that the ads that play well in Britain may alienate consumers in Japan. What marketers need is a way to measure advertising's effectiveness across cultures if they hope to create standardized ad campaigns for worldwide distribution.

At least two different research firms now claim that their respective testing techniques can predict the effectiveness of advertising across traditional cultural boundaries. Research Systems Corporation (RSC) of Evansville, Indiana, attempts to quantify changes in behavior through simulated shopping exercises. Subjects are asked to choose from an array of products in a store setting. They then sit through a television preview with actual TV programming interspersed with commercials, in an attempt to replicate the viewing environment of their home. The trial subjects, not knowing any specifics about the ads being tested, then repeat the shopping exercise, and RSC records any shifts in purchase behavior. Another firm, Research International (RI) in New York, also takes a behavioral approach to cross-cultural ad research but is more interested in how consumers learn the advertising message and relate it to their lives. Both firms claim that by directly measuring intended purchase behavior and personal affect, the cultural bias that invalidates traditional research methods is circumvented. When consumers from some Far Eastern countries are directly interviewed, for example, the desire to please the interviewer may skew responses to the positive. Other cultures may tend to be cynical or wary of the interviewing process; direct attitudinal assessments simply aren't valid across cultures. While media buyers have traditionally seen the world as a series of pan-regional marketing units (Europe, Asia, Latin America), the global placement of standardized advertising is sure to benefit from the new research methods. Perhaps in the near future, advertisers will be able to think *and* act globally.

Sources: "Few Marketers Acting Globally in Buying Media," *Advertising Age International*, July 17, 1995, I–13; "Researchers Probe Ad Effectiveness Globally," *Marketing News*, August 29, 1994, 6; and "Pan-Regional Media Studies Surging," *Advertising Age International*, July 17, 1995, I–16.

The reliability of these procedures is fairly high. Yet, how meaningful are change scores? This is change premised on a single ad exposure (sometimes two) in an unnatural viewing environment. Many advertisers believe that commercials don't register their impact until after three or four exposures.

Still, a significant swing in before and after scores with a single exposure suggests that something is going on, and that some of this effect can be expected when the ad reaches real consumers in the comfort of their homes.

To test attitude change in regard to print ads, test ads can be dropped off at the participants' homes in the form of magazines. The test ads have been tipped in, or inserted. Subjects are told that the researcher will call the next day for an interview. They are told that as part of their compensation for participating, they are being entered in a drawing. At that point, they are asked to indicate their preferences on a wide range of potential prizes. The next day when the interviewer "finishes," he or she tells the subjects that their original preference forms were inadvertently misplaced, and they will have to fill out another. What they are really completing is the postexposure attitude measure.

There aren't many attitude change studies in radio. This may be because most people view radio as a medium best used for building awareness and recall, and not for the higher-order goal of attitude change.

Physiological Measures

There are several message pretests that use physiological measurement devices. **Physiological measures** detect how consumers react to messages, based on physical responses. **Eye-tracking systems** have been developed to monitor eye movements across print ads. With one such system, respondents wear a goggle-like device that records (on a computer system) pupil dilations, eye movements, and length of view by sectors within a print advertisement. Another physiological measure is a **psychogalvanometer,** which measures galvanic skin response (GSR). GSR is a measure of minute changes in perspiration, which suggest arousal related to some stimulus—in this case, an advertisement.

Voice response analysis is another high-tech research procedure. The idea here is that inflections in the voice when discussing an ad indicate excitement and other physiological states. In a typical application, a subject is asked to respond to a series of ads. These responses are tape recorded and then computer analyzed. Deviations from a flat response are claimed to be meaningful. Other, less frequently used physiological measures record brain wave activity, heart rate, blood pressure, and muscle contraction.

All physiological measures suffer from the same drawbacks. While we may be able to detect a physiological response to an advertisement, there is no way to determine if the response is to the ad or the product, or which part of the advertisement was responsible for the response. In some sense, even the positive-negative dimension is obscured. Without being able to correlate specific effects with other dimensions of an ad, physiological measures are of minimal benefit.

Since the earliest days of advertising, there has been a fascination with physiological measurement. Advertising's fascination with science is well documented, with early attempts at physiology being far more successful as a sales tool than as a way to actually gauge ad effectiveness. There is something provocative about scientists (sometimes even in white lab coats) wiring people up; it seems so scientific and legitimate, as reflected in Exhibit 7.7. Unfortunately—or fortunately, depending on your perspective—these measures tell us little beyond the simple degree of arousal attributable to an ad. For most advertisers, this minimal benefit doesn't justify the expense and effort involved with physiological measurement.

EXHIBIT 7.7

The legitimatizing effect of science on advertising testing.

Commercial Pretest Services

Pretest message research can often be conducted by an advertiser in conjunction with its advertising agency. There are, however, several commercial pretesting services that provide full-service pretesting for both television and print advertisements. Some of these service providers are described in Exhibit 7.8.

Television Pretesting Services

Research Systems Corporation: ARS Persuasion System. This is the system Goodyear used to pretest its Aquatred advertisements. The ARS System employs 800 to 1,200 respondents in several market areas. These respondents view television ads embedded in television programs. Before and after viewing, respondents are asked to choose sets of products they would pick if they were chosen as a winner of a door prize. The persuasion measure is the number of respondents who choose the test product after exposure versus those who chose the product before exposure. Three days after exposure, a subsample is telephoned to measure recall and understanding of the test ad.

Gallup & Robinson InTeleTest. This test uses in-home viewing of a videotaped program with six test commercials and six normal commercials embedded. Testing is done in ten different cities, with 150 male and female respondents. Respondents are told they are viewing a proposed new television program. The day after viewing the program, a researcher conducts a telephone interview and takes recall measures related to the advertising in the program. Later, respondents view a tape that contains only the test ads, and they then provide an evaluation of recognition, likability, and general reaction to each ad.

Video Storyboard Tests (VST). The VST is specifically designed to test rough versions of television ads. The ads are prepared from storyboards and music soundtracks by VST. VST. One-on-one interviews are conducted after individual respondents are shown the storyboard ads on a television monitor. Respondents are asked questions relating to persuasion, liking, believability, and other features of the ad. VST can provide benchmark measures for other products in the category as a basis for rating the test ad.

Print Pretesting Services

Perception Research Services (PRS). PRS evaluates all types of print advertising using an eye-tracking camera that follows the respondent's eye movement around a print advertisement. Respondents that fit a target audience profile are allowed to view a print ad as long as they desire. The camera records the length of time for which and the sequence in which some ad elements are viewed, other elements are overlooked, and copy is read. A postsession interview identifies recall, likability of the ad, main idea perceptions, purchase interest, and product image.

ASI: Print Plus. ASI offers print ad pretesting through national magazines or its own dummy magazine vehicle, called *Reflections*. Testing is done in five markets in the United States. Test participants are told they are taking part in a public opinion survey and are given a magazine to read in their home. A telephone interview is conducted the following day to determine recall and other dimensions of the test ad. Participants are asked to review four ads, after which a feature evaluation and product interest list is administered.

Video Storyboard Tests (VST). VST tests all forms of rough and fully finished print ads in its dummy vehicle magazine, called *Looking At Us*. Respondents are told they are examining a pilot issue of a new magazine. Individual interviews are conducted in shopping malls, where respondents rate ads on persuasion, product uniqueness, believability, competitive strength, likes and dislikes, and reactions to headlines.

Source: Adapted from descriptions in Jack Haskins and Alice Kendrick, *Successful Advertising Research Methods* (Chicago: NTC Business Books, 1993), 318–28.

Experimentation in the Marketplace— Pilot Testing

Before committing to the expense of a major campaign, advertisers often take their message-testing programs into the field. Pursuing message evaluation with experimentation in the marketplace is known as **pilot testing.** This extended testing can be of the do-it-yourself variety, or it can be accomplished via a commercial service provider. Several well-known service providers are featured in Exhibit 7.9.

The fundamental options for pilot testing fall into one of three classes. **Split-cable transmission** allows testing of two different versions of an advertisement through direct transmission to two separate samples of similar households within a single, well-defined market area. This method provides exposure in a natural setting for heightened realism. Factors such as frequency of transmission and timing of transmission can be carefully controlled. The advertisements are then compared on measures of exposure, recall, and persuasion.

Split-run distribution uses the same technique as split-cable transmission except the print medium is used. Two different versions of the same advertisement are placed in every other copy of a magazine. This method of pilot testing has the advantage of using direct response as a test measure. Ads can be designed with a reply card that can serve as a basis of evaluation. Coupons and toll-free numbers can also be used. The realism of this method is a great advantage in the testing process. Expense is, of course, a major drawback.

EXHIBIT 7.9

Commercial services for pilot testing advertising messages.

Television Pilot Testing

Gallup & Robinson: In-View. This service provides on-air testing of both rough and finished advertisements. One market area in the East, Midwest, and West is selected, and randomly selected samples of 100 to 150 subjects are targeted for the test. The test ad is aired on an independent network station with a former prime-time program now in syndication. Subjects are called *before* the program is aired and invited to watch for the purpose of evaluating the program itself. Researchers obtain day-after recall measures and ask questions regarding idea communication and persuasion for the test ad.

ASI: Recall Plus and Persuasion Plus. Unlike the Gallup & Robinson test, ASI uses cable transmission to test ads on a recruited audience. A standard random sample is 200 respondents drawn from a minimum of two test cities. In Recall Plus, respondents are called the day of the test and invited to preview a new television program. The program includes four noncompeting test advertisements and one filler nontest ad. Day-after recall and effectiveness measures are then taken. The Persuasion Plus test uses the same methods as Recall Plus, with the addition of brand-choice measures. More extensive screening of participants is done in the recruiting stage with respect to brand usage and preference. Then, within two hours after viewing the test program, Persuasion Plus respondents are interviewed and, in the context of prize drawing, asked to choose the brands they would most like to have. A "Tru-Share" persuasion score is calculated on the pretest and posttest brand preferences.

Print Pilot Testing

Gallup & Robinson: Rapid Ad Measurement (RAM). Regular readers of *Time* and *People* magazines are recruited in five metropolitan areas to participate in studies. Gallup & Robinson then offers advertisers the chance to buy advertising space in test issues of these magazines, which are delivered to 150 participants' homes in each test area. A telephone interview is conducted the day after delivery, and, after magazine reading has been verified, respondents are asked if they recall ads for a list of brands and companies. Detailed measures are obtained for recall, idea communication, and persuasion of the text ad.

Source: Adapted from descriptions in Jack Haskins and Alice Kendrick, *Successful Advertising Research Methods* (Chicago: NTC Business Books, 1993), 334–37.

Finally, a **split-list experiment** tests the effectiveness of various aspects of direct mail advertising pieces. Multiple versions of a direct mail piece are prepared and sent to various segments of a mailing list. The version that pulls (produces sales) the best is deemed superior. The advantage of all the pilot-testing methods is the natural and real setting within which the test takes place. A major disadvantage is that competitive or other environmental influences in the market cannot be controlled and may affect the performance of one advertisement without ever being detected by the researcher. Such effects provide an inaccurate comparison between test ads. As suggested by the New Media box on page 199, pilot testing of advertising messages may one day soon become yet another use for the Internet.

Posttest Message Tracking

3 **Posttest message tracking** assesses the performance of advertisements during or after the launch of an advertising campaign. Common measures of an ad's performance are recall, recognition, awareness and attitude, and purchase behavior.

Recall Testing

By far the most common method of advertising research is the recall test. The basic idea is that if the ad is to work, it has to be remembered. Following on this premise is the further assumption that the ads best remembered are the ones most likely to work. Thus the objective of these tests is to see just how much, if anything, the viewer of an ad remembers of the message. Recall is used in the testing of print, television, and radio advertising.

In television, the basic procedure is to recruit a group of individuals from the target market who will be watching a certain channel during a certain time on a test date. They are asked to participate ahead of time, and simply told to watch the show. A day after exposure, the testing company calls the individuals on the phone and determines, of those who actually saw the ad, how much they can recall. The procedure generally starts with questions such as, Do you remember seeing an ad for laundry detergent? If so, do you remember the brand? If the respondent remembers, she or he is asked to replay the commercial; if not, further aids or prompts are given. The interview is generally tape recorded and transcribed. The verbatim interview is coded into various categories representing levels of recall, typically reported as a percentage. Recall testing for radio ads follows procedures similar to those for television.

In a typical print recall test, a consumer is recruited from the target market, generally at a shopping mall. He or she is given a magazine to take home. Many times the magazine is an advance issue of a real publication; other times it is a fictitious magazine created only for testing purposes. The ads are tipped in, or inserted into the vehicle. Some companies alter the mix of remaining ads, others do not. Some rotate the ads (put them in different spots in the magazine) so as not to get effects due to either editorial context or order. The participants are told that they should look at the magazine and that they will be telephoned the following day and asked some questions. During the telephone interview, aided recall is assessed. This involves a product-category cue, such as, Do you remember seeing any ads for personal computers? The percentage who respond affirmatively and provide some evidence of actually remembering the ad are scored as exhibiting aided recall. Other tests go into more detail by actually bringing the ad back to the respondent and asking about various components of the ad, such as the headline and body copy. Recall tests are more demanding for participants than recognition tests, which are described next.

Some research indicates there is little relation between recall scores and sales effectiveness.[9] But doesn't it make sense that the best ads are the ads best remembered? This seemingly simple question has perplexed academics and practitioners for a long time.

9.   Rajeev Batra, John G. Meyers, and David A. Aaker, *Advertising Management,* 5th ed. (Upper Saddle River, N.J.: Prentice-Hall, 1996), 469.

Recognition Testing

Recognition tests ask magazine readers and television viewers whether they remember having seen particular advertisements and whether they can name the company sponsoring the ad. For print advertising, the actual advertisement is shown to respondents, and for television advertising, a script with accompanying photos is shown. For instance, a recognition test might ask, Do you remember seeing the ad in Exhibit 7.10? This is a much easier task than recall in that respondents are cued by the very stimulus they are supposed to remember, and they aren't asked to do anything more than say yes or no. (By the way, the authors hope you answered yes to the question about Exhibit 7.10. You saw this ad previously in Chapter 5—surely you remember Exhibit 5.6!)

Companies that do this kind of research follow some general procedures. Subscribers to a relevant magazine are contacted and asked if an interview can be set up in their home. The readers must have at least glanced at the issue to qualify. Then, each target ad is shown, and the readers are asked if they remember seeing the ad (if they *noted* it), if they read or saw enough of the ad to notice the brand name (if they *associated* it), and if they claim to have read at least 50 percent of the copy (if they *read most* of it). This testing is usually conducted just a few days after the current issue becomes available.

There is a longer history of recognition scores than of any other testing method. There are normative data on many types of ads. The biggest problem with this test is that of a yea-saying bias. In other words, many people say they recognize an ad that in truth they haven't seen. After a few days, do you really think you could correctly remember which of the three ads in Exhibits 7.11, 7.12, and 7.13 you really saw, if you saw the ads under natural viewing conditions?

Recognition tests suffer from

NEW MEDIA

TESTING THE WATERS: MARKETERS WADE FIRST BEFORE SURFING THE NET

Imagine a virtual automobile dealership out in the far reaches of cyberspace. You have the freedom to bypass high-pressure salespeople. Prices, options, colors, and video footage are all readily at hand. You navigate around your prospective purchase in a realistic 3-D world and give the virtual tires a kick with the click of your mouse. Welcome to the present. In the here and now, marketers are probing new and creative ways to promote their wares online, and several automakers, including Chrysler and General Motors, are testing the interactive waters. Even Rolls-Royce, the automotive paragon of old-world craftsmanship, is contemplating a new media online forum for well-heeled customers to interact with the people responsible for sculpting their $300,000 luxury vehicles.

In yet another corner of cyberspace, Pillsbury's Jolly Green Giant invites you to download nutritious recipes and cooking tips, complete with color photos of the prepared meals. Any takers? About 60,000 Prodigy subscribers have visited the Green Giant promotion, a one-month Pillsbury pilot test to assess the viability of interactive marketing. Online pilot testing seems ideally suited to technology marketers, as the medium and message are even more congruent with their wares. To demonstrate the processing power and unbelievable speed of Digital Equipment's Alpha chip and related workstations, Internet surfers can actually log onto an Alpha client server, load their own software from a remote Internet connection, and take the Alpha out for a virtual test drive. The result: more than 1,400 accesses are being recorded each day, making believers out of skeptics and generating a substantial number of qualified buyers.

While interactive online advertising and promotion may well be the next wave in reaching prospective audiences, most are approaching the new medium with caution. Some GM marketing executives see the online efforts as risky and want to avoid becoming roadkill on the information autobahn. The same tenuous view of cyberspace is predominant at Green Giant. "We know that the online services reach a limited number of consumers at this time, but our feeling is that online advertising is a nice component of a larger advertising and promotion program," a Pillsbury spokeswoman said. For now, at least, the Green Giant approach may be just the recipe for success.

Sources: "Pillsbury Takes a Giant Step Online," *Advertising Age*, June 5, 1995, 19; "Auto Makers Are Test-Driving Marketing Campaigns On-Line," *Wall Street Journal*, April 7, 1995, B2; and "Betting on the 'Net," *Sales & Marketing Management* (June 1995): 47.

---

two other problems. First, because direct interviewing is involved, the test is expensive. Second, because respondents are given visual aids, the risk of overestimation threatens the meaningfulness of the collected data.

EXHIBIT 7.10

Recognition testing uses the ad itself to test whether the consumer remembers the ad and associates it with the brand and message. Would you immediately associate this ad with its brand? What makes the ad memorable to you? At the Campbell Soup Company home page **www.campbellsoups .com/**, *see how the company uses the familiar red and white label to enhance recognition. In contrast, competitor Lipton at* **www.lipton.com/**, *although in the soup business, is more recognized by its tea icons.*

Awareness and Attitude Tracking

Tracking studies measure the change in an audience's brand awareness and attitude before and after an advertising campaign. This common type of advertising research is almost always conducted as a survey. Members of the target market are surveyed on a fairly regular basis to detect any changes. Any change in awareness or attitude is usually attributed (rightly or wrongly) to the advertising effort. The problem with these types of tests is the inability to isolate the effect of advertising on awareness and attitude amid a myriad of other influences—media reports, observation, friends, competitive advertising, and so forth.

Behavior-Based Evaluation

Advertisements in both print and broadcast media that offer the audience the opportunity to place an inquiry or respond directly through a reply card or toll-free phone number are called **inquiry/direct response measures.** An example is displayed in Exhibit 7.14. These measures are quite straight-forward in the sense that advertisements that generate a high number of inquiries or direct responses, compared to historical benchmarks, are deemed effective. An additional measure compares the number of inquiries or responses to the number of sales generated. These measures are not suitable for all types of advertising. Ads designed to have long-term image-building or brand-identity effects should not be judged using such short-term response measures.

With the advent of universal product codes (UPCs) on product packages and the proliferation of cable television, research firms are now able to engage in single-source research to document the behavior of individuals in a respondent pool by tracking their behavior from the television set to the checkout counter. **Single-source tracking measures** provide information from individual households about brand purchases, coupon use, and television advertising exposure by combining grocery store scanner data and devices attached to the households' televisions (called *peoplemeters*) which monitor viewing behavior.[10] These sophisticated measures are used to gauge the impact of advertising and promotions on consumers' actual purchases. The main

---

10. The peoplemeter is a rather cumbersome device employed by A. C. Nielsen. It requires members of the test household to push buttons each time they turn on the television, or leave and re-enter the room. Rival research firm Arbitron is about to introduce a new monitoring device that will require greatly reduced subject interaction. A discussion of the differences is found in Elizabeth Jensen, "Nielsen Rival to Unveil New 'Peoplemeter,'" *Wall Street Journal,* December 4, 1992, B4.

The use of an 800 number or other behavior-based activity is an attractive feature of inquiry/direct response measures for evaluating advertising effectiveness. What are the key advantages to this kind of research? The E★Trade home page www.etrade.com/html/index.html demonstrates a key advantage of the Internet for advertising: its interactivity. Customers can respond easily and quickly, making a response more likely. Also, the interactivity goes both ways—the company can respond to the customer. How does this two-way interactivity benefit the company? See how competitor Charles Schwab www.schwab.com/ takes advantage of Internet interactivity.

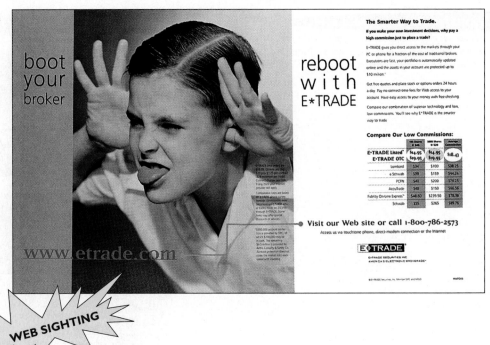

WEB SIGHTING

problem with these measures is that it is impossible to determine what aspects of advertising had positive effects on consumers. In the absence of such specific information, message planning and media placement strategy are given minimal assistance.

Commercial Services

Exhibit 7.15 lists the most widely recognized commercial posttest message services. Overall, posttesting is appealing because of the strong desire to track the continuing effectiveness of advertising in a real-world setting. However, the problems of expense, delay of feedback, and inability to separate sources of effect are compromises that need to be understood and evaluated when using this form of message testing.

A Final Thought on Message Testing

None of these methods are perfect. There are enormous challenges to reliability, validity, trustworthiness, and meaningfulness with all of them. Advertisers sometimes think that consumers watch new television commercials the way they watch new, eagerly awaited feature films, or that they listen to radio spots like they listen to a symphony, or read magazine ads like a Steinbeck novel. Work by Lull and other naturalistic researchers and ethnographers demonstrates what we as Americans know: We watch TV while we work, talk, eat, and study; we use it as a night-light, background noise, and baby-sitter.[11] Likewise, we typically thumb through magazines very, very quickly. While these traditional methods of message testing have their strengths, more naturalistic methods are clearly recommended.

Secondary Data

❹ Apart from the primary data collection methods just discussed, there is a wealth of available secondary data. Information obtained from existing sources is referred to as **secondary data.** Secondary data have the distinct advantages of being far less costly to obtain than primary data and more immediately available.

11. James Lull, "How Families Select Television Programs: A Mass Observational Study," *Journal of Broadcasting* 26, no. 4 (1982): 801–11.

Gallup & Robinson: Magazine Impact Research Service (MIRS). This service from Gallup & Robinson tests advertisements that appear in selected issues of major consumer magazines, including *Time, Playboy, Sports Illustrated, Business Week, Bon Appetit, People,* and others. Male and female respondents who have read at least two of the last four issues of one or more of the test magazines (but not the current issues used for the testing) are recruited in ten metropolitan areas. Test magazines are delivered to participants, who are interviewed by phone the next day. Fifteen brand and product categories are examined, with questions relating to recall, idea communication, and persuasion.

ASI: Print Plus. This service is similar to ASI's pretesting service, discussed earlier. Male and female samples are drawn in five test markets for posttesting general consumer magazines. Participants are told they are in a public opinion survey of magazines. A distinct feature of the ASI test is that brand attitude is measured before exposure to the test ad, in the context of a prize drawing for a dollar amount of a product (and brand) chosen by the participant. After delivery of the test magazines and verification of reading, recall and feature communication are tested. Re-exposure to four test ads is carried out to measure interest in the product. A postexposure brand preference is taken in the prize-drawing context for each category of advertisement tested. Pretest and posttest preference measures provide a persuasion index.

Starch INRA Hooper: Message Report Service. Starch provides the most extensive posttesting service available. Testing is available for 700 issues of all forms of magazines, including professional and trade publications. More than 75,000 subjects are interviewed each year by Starch. Starch draws samples from 20 to 30 urban locations for each test. Interviewers turn the pages of a publication and ask subjects about each ad under study. Along with demographic data on subjects, Starch produces the following evaluations for each ad:

- *Noted readers*—the percentage who remember having previously seen the ad in the issue being studied.
- *Associated readers*—the percentage who remember seeing the ad and are able to associate it with a brand or advertiser.
- *Read-most readers*—the percentage who read at least half of the material in the ad.

Starch INRA Hooper: Impression Study. This Starch service is designed to posttest ads that appear in print, television, and outdoor media. The measures are more qualitative and designed to identify the communication effects of advertising. Personal interviews are conducted in which subjects are shown an ad and then asked to describe in their own words their reactions with respect to the ad's meaning, the outstanding features of the ad, and the impressions formed from both the visual and written aspects of the ad.

Information Resources (IRI): Panel Data. While IRI's national sample of homes that maintain a diary on their purchases and media habits is not strictly designed to give detailed posttest message information, the panel data can provide some insights. The data from the households can be used to correlate promotional efforts with sales, which gives an indirect measure of message effectiveness. Of course, lack of control makes such a measure tenuous at best.

Secondary Data Sources

Secondary data are abundant and should be considered before an advertiser initiates primary research. Four typical places to find secondary data are internal company sources, government sources, commercial sources, and professional publications.

Internal Company Sources. Some of the most valuable data are available within a firm itself and are, therefore, referred to as internal company sources of secondary data. Commonly available information within a company includes strategic marketing plans, old research reports, customer service records, warranty registration cards, letters from customers, customer complaints, and various sales figures (by region, by customer type, by product line). All provide a wealth of information relating to the proficiency of the company's marketing practices and, more generally, changing consumer tastes and preferences.

Government Sources. Various government organizations generate data on factors of interest to advertising planners; information on population and housing trends, transportation, consumer spending, and recreational activities in the United States is available through government documents. Exhibit 7.16 gives a listing and brief description of some relevant government sources of secondary data. Many of these secondary sources are now easily accessed via the World Wide Web.

The array of consumer data available from government sources is a particularly useful starting place in advertising planning for businesses of all sizes, as the data in Exhibit 7.17 show. Such publications are reasonably current, and many are available at public libraries. This means that even a small-business owner can access large amounts of information for advertising-planning purposes at little cost.

EXHIBIT 7.16

Government sources of secondary data pertinent to advertising.

Government Data Source	Type of Information
Census of population	This counts the population of the nation. Information can be obtained for the nation as a whole or by state, city, county, or region. Different volumes identify the citizenry by age, gender, income, race, marital status, and other demographic features. Published every ten years in years ending with 0.
Census of housing	Housing units are described based on size, number of inhabitants, type of fuel used, number and type of major appliances, and condition and value of structures. Major urban areas are broken down by city block. Published every ten years in years ending with 0.
Census of retail trade	Provides detailed information on retail activity, including number of retail outlets, total sales and employment. Also published in years ending in 2 and 7. Statistics are available for relatively small geographic areas, such as counties and cities.
Census of service industries	Identifies service providers by category and geographic area and indicates sales, employment, and number of units. Taken in years ending in 2 and 7.
Census of transportation	Identifies usage of three major transportation modes: passenger car, truck, and bus. Some 24,000 households were surveyed in 1977, and information includes number of trips, number of persons taking trips, duration, means of travel, and destination. Taken in years ending in 2 and 7.
Survey of current business	This survey is published monthly by the Bureau of Economic Analysis of the Department of Commerce. It provides information on general business indicators, real estate activity, commodity prices, personal consumption expenditures, and income and employment by industry. There are 2,600 different series in the survey, most of which contain data on the past four years.

Commercial Sources. Since information has become such a critical resource in marketing and advertising decision making, commercial data services have emerged to provide data of various types. Firms specializing in this sort of information tend to concentrate their data-gathering efforts on household consumers. Exhibit 7.18 lists some of the more prominent commercial sources of marketing and advertising information.

Information from these sources is reasonably comprehensive and is normally gathered using sound methods. The cost of information from these sources is greater than information from government sources. Despite the greater expense, information from commercial sources still generally costs less than primary data generation.

Professional Publications. Another secondary data source is professional publications. Professional publications are periodicals in which marketing and advertising professionals report significant information related to industry trends or new research findings. Exhibit 7.19 provides a listing of publications that frequently contain secondary data for advertising planning.

In marketing and advertising, there are several academic, trade, and general business publications carrying research studies and industry statistics that can contain valuable secondary data. It may be that precisely the information a firm needs has been reported in a recent publication. Failure to explore such publications before initiating primary data collection is a major oversight.

Sporting Goods—Sales and Purchases 239

No. 406. Sporting Goods Sales, by Product Category: 1980 to 1990

[**In millions of dollars, except percent.** Based on a sample survey of consumer purchases of 80,000 households, except recreational transport, which was provided by industry associations. Excludes Alaska and Hawaii]

SELECTED PRODUCT CATEGORY	1980	1981	1982	1983	1984	1985	1986	1987	1988	1989	1990, proj.
Sales, all products	**16,691**	**18,725**	**18,684**	**23,111**	**26,401**	**27,446**	**30,614**	**33,942**	**42,093**	**44,371**	**45,996**
Annual percent change [1]	-1.4	12.2	5.8	23.7	14.2	4.0	11.5	10.9	24.0	5.4	3.7
Percent of retail sales	1.7	1.8	1.7	2.0	2.1	2.0	2.1	2.2	2.6	2.6	(NA)
Athletic and sport clothing [2]	**3,127**	**3,201**	**3,014**	**3,226**	**3,432**	**3,376**	**3,931**	**4,645**	**10,736**	**11,557**	**12,286**
Athletic and sport footwear [3]	**1,731**	**1,785**	**1,900**	**2,189**	**2,381**	**2,610**	**3,199**	**3,524**	**3,772**	**5,246**	**5,583**
Walking shoes	(NA)	(NA)	(NA)	(NA)	(NA)	263	368	512	752	1,237	1,422
Gym shoes, sneakers	465	616	659	639	669	656	642	693	783	1,125	1,193
Jogging and running shoes	397	372	421	557	591	572	476	475	460	515	526
Tennis shoes	359	284	287	340	371	470	448	367	353	508	543
Aerobic shoes	(NA)	(NA)	10	29	54	178	333	401	327	425	404
Basketball shoes	86	80	81	119	159	185	187	169	226	293	319
Golf shoes	68	78	99	115	110	109	120	130	128	129	138
Athletic and sport equipment [3]	**6,487**	**6,762**	**7,114**	**7,925**	**8,317**	**8,922**	**9,477**	**9,900**	**10,705**	**11,249**	**11,752**
Firearms and hunting	1,351	1,454	1,567	1,666	1,620	1,699	1,675	1,804	1,894	2,033	2,093
Exercise equipment	(NA)	(NA)	723	960	1,055	1,216	1,206	1,191	1,452	1,728	1,836
Golf	386	413	493	633	630	730	828	946	1,111	1,168	1,261
Camping	646	663	735	790	699	724	833	858	945	990	1,029
Bicycles (10-12-15-18+ speed)	(NA)	(NA)	656	761	765	975	1,089	930	819	843	(NA)
Fishing tackle	539	689	586	606	616	681	773	830	766	738	760
Snow skiing	379	307	332	386	502	593	622	661	710	589	613
Tennis	237	254	277	293	315	273	260	238	264	315	337
Archery	149	169	168	179	212	212	214	224	235	244	254
Baseball and softball	158	157	154	173	153	176	180	173	174	193	198
Water skis	123	123	106	133	146	125	132	148	160	96	96
Bowling accessories	107	107	103	106	108	106	114	129	129	132	136
Recreational transport	**5,345**	**6,977**	**6,656**	**9,771**	**12,271**	**12,539**	**14,007**	**15,873**	**16,880**	**16,319**	**16,375**
Pleasure boats	2,718	3,656	3,684	4,612	6,209	6,753	7,372	8,906	9,637	9,269	9,270
Recreational vehicles	1,178	1,820	1,701	3,368	4,082	3,515	3,940	4,507	4,839	4,481	4,392
Bicycles and supplies	1,233	1,299	1,148	1,638	1,840	2,109	2,518	2,272	2,131	2,259	2,372
Snowmobiles	216	202	123	153	140	162	177	188	273	310	341

NA Not available. [1] Change from prior year shown; for 1980, change from 1979. Minus sign (-) indicates decrease. For explanation of average annual percent change, see Guide to Tabular Presentation. [2] Category expanded in 1988; not comparable with earlier years. [3] Includes other products not shown separately.

Source: National Sporting Goods Association, Mt. Prospect, IL, *The Sporting Goods Market in 1989*, and prior issues. (Copyright.)

No. 407. Consumer Purchases of Sporting Goods, by Consumer Characteristics: 1989

[**In percent.** Based on sample survey of consumer purchases of 80,000 households. Excludes Alaska and Hawaii]

CHARACTERISTIC	Total households	FOOTWEAR				EQUIPMENT					
		Aerobic shoes	Gym shoes/ sneakers	Jogging/ running shoes	Walking shoes	Bicycles [1]	Camping equipment	Exercise equipment	Rifles	Shotguns-	Golf-equipment
Total	**100.0**	**100.0**	**100.0**	**100.0**	**100.0**	**100.0**	**100.0**	**100.0**	**100.0**	**100.0**	**100.0**
Age of user:											
Under 14 years old	20.3	4.7	34.6	8.3	2.8	22.4	9.0	1.0	1.0	3.3	1.0
14 to 17 years old	5.4	5.4	13.8	10.5	1.9	6.3	5.0	3.0	2.5	7.1	3.0
18 to 24 years old	10.7	11.5	9.7	10.0	3.3	10.7	8.0	6.0	11.6	11.6	4.0
25 to 34 years old	17.7	30.9	16.9	28.5	12.9	21.8	29.0	24.0	34.5	22.3	30.0
35 to 44 years old	14.7	22.5	10.3	24.0	19.7	16.1	21.0	25.0	21.3	23.4	18.0
45 to 64 years old	18.7	17.6	10.7	15.2	35.7	7.2	12.0	30.0	20.3	20.1	31.0
65 years old and over	12.5	7.4	4.0	3.5	23.7	1.3	3.0	8.0	5.8	10.5	8.0
Multiple ages	-	-	-	-	-	14.2	12.0	3.0	3.0	1.7	6.0
Sex of user:											
Male	48.8	15.7	53.0	64.9	33.0	56.9	64.0	47.0	91.8	93.9	78.0
Female	51.2	84.3	47.0	35.1	67.0	30.8	21.0	46.0	7.1	5.1	15.0
Both sexes	-	-	-	-	-	12.3	15.0	6.0	1.1	1.0	7.0
Education of household head:											
Less than high school	12.7	6.8	7.6	4.7	10.7	5.0	6.0	13.0	11.2	5.0	13.0
High school	30.5	25.5	32.2	22.0	28.2	19.8	25.0	30.0	33.3	26.3	30.0
Some college	27.2	29.9	27.5	27.3	27.5	30.4	29.0	27.0	33.9	38.1	27.0
College graduate	29.6	37.8	32.7	46.0	33.6	44.8	40.0	30.0	21.6	30.6	30.0
Annual household income:											
Under $15,000	24.9	14.1	13.6	9.8	20.4	12.3	11.0	8.0	11.0	12.3	25.0
$15,000 to $24,999	18.2	15.2	16.1	12.4	16.7	14.0	15.0	15.0	25.2	12.6	18.0
$25,000 to $34,999	16.1	16.4	17.3	16.3	15.8	16.8	16.0	12.0	19.3	18.6	16.0
$35,000 to $49,999	18.8	20.0	22.9	20.8	18.0	23.9	24.0	23.0	32.0	22.4	19.0
$50,000 and over	22.0	34.3	30.1	40.7	29.1	33.0	34.0	42.0	12.5	34.1	22.0

- Represents or rounds to zero. [1] 10-12-15-18+ speed.

Source: National Sporting Goods Association, Mt. Prospect, IL, *The Sporting Goods Market in 1989*, and prior issues. (Copyright.)

EXHIBIT 7.17

A sample of secondary data available from the government, in this case the Statistical Abstract of the United States.

238 Parks, Recreation, and Travel

No. 405. Participation in Sports Activities, by Selected Characteristics: 1989

[**In thousands, except rank.** For persons 7 years of age or older. Except as indicated, a participant plays a sport more than once in the year. Based on a sampling of 10,000 households]

ACTIVITY	ALL PERSONS		SEX		AGE								HOUSEHOLD INCOME (dol.)				
	Number	Rank	Male	Female	7-11 yrs.	12-17 yrs.	18-24 yrs.	25-34 yrs.	35-44 yrs.	45-54 yrs.	55-64 yrs.	65 yrs. and over	Under 15,000	15,000-24,999	25,000-34,999	35,000-49,999	Over 50,000
Total	**222,551**	**(X)**	**108,000**	**114,551**	**17,886**	**20,127**	**26,556**	**44,042**	**36,536**	**24,883**	**21,546**	**30,975**	**53,397**	**39,253**	**34,476**	**41,507**	**53,917**
Number participated in:																	
Aerobic exercising [1]	25,108	9	4,173	20,935	1,047	2,181	4,950	8,228	4,644	2,089	955	1,014	4,150	3,912	3,798	5,343	7,905
Backpacking/wilderness camping	11,357	21	7,269	4,088	866	1,699	2,076	3,774	1,917	760	220	45	2,480	2,078	2,059	2,351	2,390
Baseball	15,406	17	12,132	3,273	5,014	4,365	2,131	2,084	1,256	395	59	100	3,056	2,267	2,459	3,009	4,614
Basketball	26,182	8	19,091	7,091	4,986	7,680	5,125	5,067	2,403	733	167	23	4,964	4,656	3,736	5,839	6,988
Bicycle riding [1]	56,941	3	28,354	28,587	11,909	9,986	6,545	11,810	7,878	3,670	2,640	2,503	11,532	9,327	9,340	11,437	15,305
Bowling	40,810	6	21,252	19,556	4,244	5,147	7,650	10,617	5,972	3,139	1,933	2,108	7,780	6,814	6,964	8,519	10,732
Calisthenics [1]	15,141	18	6,816	8,325	1,866	2,368	2,613	3,906	2,070	934	669	714	2,637	2,324	2,367	3,113	4,700
Camping (vacation/overnight)	46,514	4	24,577	21,936	6,174	5,725	4,830	12,756	8,151	4,293	2,779	1,806	9,319	7,597	8,567	10,108	10,922
Exercise walking [1]	66,558	2	23,680	42,879	2,308	3,177	6,164	14,258	12,640	9,920	8,213	9,877	14,664	12,206	9,922	12,554	17,213
Exercising with equipment [1]	31,476	7	16,477	14,998	489	2,948	6,846	8,552	5,708	3,155	2,091	1,687	4,392	5,120	4,788	6,975	10,200
Fishing—fresh water	41,005	5	27,902	13,104	4,908	4,477	4,919	10,454	6,972	4,136	2,751	2,388	9,310	7,394	7,823	7,869	8,609
Fishing—salt water	11,326	22	8,311	3,015	1,012	988	1,162	2,725	1,952	1,617	923	947	1,900	1,620	1,698	2,834	3,274
Football	14,728	19	12,779	1,949	2,606	4,573	4,330	2,242	679	232	13	53	3,198	2,709	2,259	2,681	3,881
Golf	23,156	13	17,411	5,745	1,001	1,693	3,237	6,234	4,095	2,779	1,948	2,171	2,376	3,221	3,230	5,030	9,298
Hiking	23,516	12	12,606	10,910	2,366	2,467	2,774	6,400	4,420	2,571	1,492	1,026	4,968	3,982	3,585	4,845	6,136
Hunting with firearms	17,715	16	16,129	1,586	538	2,009	2,797	4,938	3,655	2,213	1,006	560	3,385	3,389	3,573	3,673	3,695
Racquetball	8,244	25	6,151	2,093	225	965	2,568	2,641	1,260	449	80	56	1,193	1,152	1,305	1,864	2,730
Running/jogging [1]	24,803	11	14,485	10,318	2,731	4,325	5,199	6,156	3,551	1,690	628	524	4,845	4,395	3,466	4,609	7,488
Skiing—alpine/downhill	11,034	24	6,886	4,148	725	1,475	2,562	3,569	1,670	782	217	32	909	1,137	1,302	2,804	4,882
Skiing—cross country	4,906	26	2,359	2,547	389	523	673	1,403	984	592	245	97	641	684	786	1,132	1,663
Soccer	11,168	23	7,450	3,718	4,708	3,518	1,214	1,106	452	123	28	18	2,204	1,156	1,581	2,213	4,015
Softball	22,092	14	13,437	8,655	3,531	4,121	4,437	6,424	2,548	767	170	93	3,862	4,060	3,411	4,975	5,784
Swimming [1]	70,489	1	33,213	37,277	11,216	11,644	10,060	14,372	10,977	5,237	3,620	3,363	12,057	11,317	11,410	15,308	20,397
Target shooting	12,607	20	10,039	2,569	1,145	1,605	2,018	3,887	2,152	1,208	292	300	2,873	2,278	2,339	2,739	2,379
Tennis	18,844	15	10,420	8,424	1,299	3,319	4,039	5,315	2,551	1,401	643	277	2,650	2,716	2,272	4,032	7,173
Volleyball	25,071	10	12,972	12,098	2,185	5,614	5,353	7,160	3,162	1,125	381	91	5,022	4,253	4,314	5,178	6,304

X Not applicable. [1] Participant engaged in activity at least six times in the year.

Source: National Sporting Goods Association, Mt. Prospect, IL, *Sports Participation in 1989: Series I*. (Copyright.)

EXHIBIT 7.18

Examples of commercial sources of secondary data.

Commercial Information Source	Type of Information
Dun and Bradstreet Market Identifiers	DMI is a listing of 4.3 million businesses that is updated monthly. Information includes number of employees, relevant SIC codes that relate to the businesses' activities, location, and chief executive. Marketing and advertising managers can use the information to identify markets, build mailing lists, and specify media to reach an organization. (www.dnb.com)
Nielsen Retail Index	Nielsen auditors collect product inventory turnover data from 1,600 grocery stores, 750 drugstores, and 150 mass merchandise outlets. Information is also gathered on retail prices, in-store displays, and local advertising. Data from the index are available by store type and geographic location. (www.nielsenmedia.com)
SAMI/Burke	The SAMI/Burke report is similar to the Nielsen index except that sales volume figures are based on warehouse withdrawals rather than retail sales. SAMI/Burke data track only food operators but do include all forms of grocery operations, including mom-and-pop stores. Samscan is a SAMI/Burke service that uses supermarket scanner data.
National Purchase Diary Panel	With more than 13,000 families participating, NPD is the largest diary panel in the United States. Families record on preprinted sheets their monthly purchases in 50 product categories. Information recorded includes brand, amount purchased, price paid, use of coupons, store, specific version of the product (flavor, scent, etc.), and intended use.
Roper Starch Advertisement Readership	The Roper Starch service tracks readership of more than 70,000 advertisements appearing in 1,000 consumer and farm publications, newspapers, and business periodicals. More than 100,000 personal interviews are conducted each year to determine the readership of the ads. Starch uses a recognition approach, which rates each ad on the extent of readership it was able to stimulate. Data on headlines, copy, and other component parts of an ad are also recorded.
Nielsen Television Index	This is one of the most familiar commercial services since the Nielsen ratings receive so much popular press. The index provides estimates of the size and characteristics of the audience for television programs. Data are gathered through an electronic device attached to participating households' television sets. The device records the times the TV is on and what channel is tuned in. Reports on viewership are published biweekly.
Consumer Mail Panel	This panel is operated by a firm called Market Facts. There are 45,000 active participants at any point in time. Samples are drawn in lots of 1,000. The overall panel is said to be representative of different geographic regions in the United States and Canada, then broken down by household income, urbanization, and age of the respondent. Data are provided on demographic and socioeconomic characteristics as well as type of dwelling and durable goods ownership.
Information Resources	One of the leading organizations in single-source research, where all phases of a consumer's media exposure and, ultimately, purchase behavior are tracked. This firm is also recognized for its research on the impact of grocery store promotional programs (PromotioScan) and coupon redemption.

Limitations of Secondary Data

As convenient and cost-effective as secondary data can be, they are not perfect. There are several potential problems with secondary data, and these problems may make the information poorly suited for decision making:

- The information can be out-of-date.
- The data may be expressed in categories different from the information desired. For example, the variable of interest to a firm may be the total number of women between the ages of 18 and 25 in a certain geographic area. Published secondary data may provide statistics on women less than 18 and from 19 to 29 years of age.
- The unit of measurement may be different from the unit needed for analysis. Secondary data sources may report income figures for individuals, families, households, or spending units. If the unit of measure is not the same as the one desired by the decision maker, then the data are useless.
- The source of the data may not be totally objective. For example, industry trade associations may generate and report data that make the industry look good.
- The data may be completely irrelevant.

Secondary data offer a low-cost and speedy method for gaining information, but they should be scrutinized for currency, the qualifications of the data collection organization, any special interests associated with the data generation effort, and, most importantly, relevance and meaning.

EXHIBIT 7.19

Examples of professional publications often containing secondary data for advertising planning.

Trade Publications	General Business Publications
Adweek	Forbes
Advertising Age (www.adage.com)	Fortune
New Media	Business Week
Chain Store Age	Wall Street Journal (www.wsj.com)
Progressive Grocer	Barron's
Stores	Investors Daily
Sales and Marketing	Inc.
Management	
INFOWORLD (www.infoworld.com)	
Promo	

SUMMARY

1 Explain the purposes served by and methods used in developmental advertising research.

Advertising research can serve many purposes in the development of a campaign. There is no better way to generate fresh ideas for a campaign than careful listening to the customer. Environmental analysis is also valuable in the planning process to help determine opportunities for effective communication. Audience definition and profiling are fundamental to effective campaign planning and rely on advertising research. In the developmental phase, advertisers use diverse tools for gathering information. Survey research, focus groups, projective techniques, and concept testing are

some of the most common tools used for developmental purposes.

2 Discuss the various procedures used for pretesting advertising messages prior to a complete launch of an advertising campaign.

Another major type of advertising research is that devoted to message testing prior to the launch of a campaign. Communications tests, dummy advertising vehicles, and theater tests are basic tools used for message pretesting. The thought-listing technique and attitude change studies are important approaches for pretesting the persuasiveness of a message. Commercial testing services may be used prior to launch of a full-blown campaign for both pretesting and pilot testing. Pilot testing is a form of marketplace experimentation that provides data about how messages may perform when they reach the consumer. Since there is no one right way to test a message, it is important for an advertiser to be aware of the various options and the virtues and limitations of each.

3 Discuss the various methods used to track the effectiveness of ad executions during and after the launch of a full-blown advertising campaign.

Advertisers commonly track the performance of their messages during and after the launch of an ad campaign. Recall and recognition testing are two traditional tools that allow an advertiser to assess whether a message has broken through the competitive clutter to register with the target audience. Brand awareness and attitude surveys are also

commonly employed in tracking a campaign's impact. Behavior-based evaluation has a strong following and is made possible by direct response measures and single-source research. There are a number of commercial suppliers of posttest evaluation services.

4 Identify the many sources of secondary data that can aid the ad-planning effort.

Before investing in new or primary research, an advertiser is well advised to examine the information available through secondary sources. Secondary data are inexpensive and immediately accessible. The ongoing evolution of the Internet and World Wide Web will put more and more secondary data at the researcher's fingertips. Sources of secondary data include a firm's internal records, the government, commercial suppliers, and professional publications. Knowing the limitations of secondary data is a necessary prerequisite for informed use of this important tool.

KEY TERMS

storyboard (184)
marketing research (185)
advertising research (185)
reliability (185)
validity (185)
trustworthiness (185)
meaningfulness (185)
environmental analysis (186)
focus group (188)
projective techniques (188)
association tests (189)
sentence and picture completion (189)
dialogue balloons (189)
story construction (189)
concept test (189)
resonance test (192)

communications test (193)
dummy advertising vehicles (193)
theater test (193)
thought listing (193)
attitude change study (194)
physiological measures (195)
eye-tracking systems (195)
psychogalvanometer (195)
pilot testing (197)
split-cable transmission (197)
split-run distribution (197)
split-list experiment (198)
posttest message tracking (198)
inquiry/direct response measures (201)
single-source tracking measures (200)
secondary data (202)

QUESTIONS FOR REVIEW AND CRITICAL THINKING

1. What does it mean to profile the target audience? What is the value of audience profiling? Identify three different types of information commonly used in developing audience profiles.

2. Focus groups turn out to be one of the advertising researcher's most versatile tools. Explain how focus groups are valuable in conducting concept tests, resonance tests, and communications tests. Describe the basic features of focus group research that could lead to inappropriate gen-

eralizations about the preferences of the target audience.

3. Identify issues that could become sources of conflict between brand managers and advertising creatives in the message-pretesting process. What could be wrong with people in an ad agency taking the position that what the client wants, the client gets?

4. Explain the key distinction between pretesting and pilot testing. What is it about direct mail advertising that

makes it so amenable to pilot testing? Do you think the ease of pilot testing has anything to do with the growing popularity of direct mail as an advertising option?

5.   Attitude change research is another versatile tool for message testing. Identify the key differences that distinguish an attitude change study being conducted for pretesting purposes from an attitude change study being conducted for posttesting purposes.

6.   How would you explain the finding that ads that achieve high recall scores don't always turn out to be ads that do a good job in generating sales? Are there some features of ads that make them memorable but could also turn off consumers and dissuade them from buying the brand? Give an example from your experience.

7.   What is the meaning of the phrase *single-source research?* What is the connection between the UPCs one finds on nearly every product in the grocery store and this thing called single-source research?

8.   Discuss in detail the limitations of secondary data. Given these limitations, how do you justify the statement in this chapter that the failure to explore secondary data sources before initiating primary data collection represents a serious oversight?

EXPERIENTIAL EXERCISE

In this chapter you learned about advertising research methods that help managers avoid costly mistakes. Find an example of a print ad or describe a broadcast ad you feel is truly awful. Explain your objections. Now imagine that you have the opportunity to conduct advertising research before the ad actually runs. What type or types of research would you recommend that management conduct? Explain your recommendations and how the research might have changed the ad you selected.

USING THE INTERNET

Visit *The X-Files* site (www.thex-files.com) and continue to the fan forum.

1.   How could the makers of *The X-Files* use the information exchanged in the fan forum to better understand their viewers?

2.   What other established research method or methods is this discussion forum similar to?

Visit the Nielsen site (www.nielsenmedia.com) and continue to the executive summary of Nielsen's survey with CommerceNet. Identify and compare the different research methods used to study and describe Internet usage.

3.   Which methods were most appropriate? What are the shortcomings of each method?

4.   How does the use of multiple methods increase your confidence in the final results?

Visit the Interse site (www.interse.com/ourproducts/) and continue to the standard analysis report. Read a few different standard analysis reports.

5.   If you were interested in the characteristics of visitors to a specific site, which reports would be most important, and why?

Visit the Hot Wired site (www.hotwired.com) and find the user registration form.

6.   As a potential registrant, are you comfortable with giving out this information?

7.   Pick out a few questions you think are important, and suggest their value to Hot Wired. As a marketer, what additional information would you request?

Chapter 8

The

Advertising

Plan

After reading and thinking about this chapter, you will be able to do the following:

1 Describe the basic components of an advertising plan.

2 Compare and contrast two fundamental approaches for setting advertising objectives.

3 Explain various methods for setting advertising budgets.

4 Discuss the role of the advertising agency in formulating an advertising plan.

I have no idea. I just got caught up.

—Response of a New Zealand man when asked why he waited in line for hours to be the first person in the world to own Windows 95.

The fact that all over the world, people stood in line to buy a computer operating system may help explain why *Promo* magazine named Microsoft its Marketer of the Year. The launch of Windows 95 by Microsoft may have been the largest new-product launch in history. Microsoft spent around $200 to $300 million to introduce its new operating system for personal computers. The launch became news well beyond the techno-press and was truly front-page news. The campaign was an integrated effort, with every form of promotion imaginable being brought to bear, from joint advertising efforts with several major retailers, such as CompUSA and Best Buy, to actually painting the Windows 95 flag in farmers' fields in England so that airplane passengers could look down and marvel at the scope of Microsoft's efforts.[1]

The launch of Windows 95 on August 24, 1995, actually followed the sun from Wellington, New Zealand—near the international date line—across the entire planet. Exhibit 8.1 details the launch highlights.

Still, the really big show was in Redmond, Washington, Microsoft's corporate headquarters, where a full-scale carnival with 120 or so computer-related companies comprised the midway. Bill Gates and Jay Leno were the headliners. Of course, the entire spectacle could be accessed on-line as well.

Still, something was missing. What would a launch be without a launch tune? To solve this problem, Microsoft paid Mick Jagger and Keith Richards a reported "few million" for the right to use the Rolling Stones 1981 classic "Start Me Up" for the launch ads. (See Exhibit 8.2.) The first few notes of the song make up one of the most immediately recognizable guitar hooks in rock and roll. The song is high energy and fits the rapid-cut montage of the introductory TV ads perfectly. The song was thought to be particularly appropriate since the new product's key icon is a start button. According to Brad Chase at Microsoft, "We wanted to take one thematic element of the product, which was the start button, and carry it through the ads in the music and in visuals."[2]

EXHIBIT 8.1

August 24, 1995: launch day for Windows 95.

Australia: A four-story-high Windows box sailed into Sydney harbor on a barge accompanied by live musicians.

Hong Kong: Local celebrities appeared at numerous malls to support the launch.

Philippines: The first package of Windows 95 went to President Fidel Ramos in a staged ceremony.

Russia: More than 2,000 journalists and customers attended a launch party in Moscow.

Poland: Microsoft took journalists down in a submarine to show them what it is like "to live in a world without Windows."

Spain: Some 800 people attended the launch and participated in a live Q & A with Bill Gates. Interview was taped for TV news broadcast.

Britain: Microsoft bought out the entire pressrun of the August 24 edition of the *London Times* and distributed 1.5 million copies compliments of Windows 95.

Toronto: On August 14 a giant letter *O* appeared on the CN Tower in Toronto, Canada's tallest building, and each day another letter appeared until August 24, when there was a 300-foot-high Windows 95 banner.

Source: *Promo,* 9, no. 1, December 1995, 69–70.

1.   Dottie Enrico, "Microsoft Turns to Hard Rock Pitch," *USA Today,* August 18, 1995, 1B–2B. The idea of advertising for airline passengers was advanced in the early 1970s by Connie Johnson.
2.   Ibid., B-1.

EXHIBIT 8.2

Mick and Keith.

Furthermore, it was a brilliant choice in that almost every sports venue in the United States plays a few bars of "Start Me Up" several times a game to inspire the crowd. If consumers begin to think of Windows 95 when they hear the song, then this represents a lot of free advertising. The launch of Windows 95 was truly great integrated marketing communications.

The storyboard for the launch ad by Wieden and Kennedy of Portland, Oregon, is shown in Exhibit 8.3. If you haven't seen this ad by now, something's very, very wrong.

While the story of the Windows 95 launch is interesting, what happened immediately before the Windows 95 campaign was perhaps even more significant. Bill Gates, Microsoft's founder and chairman, wanted to transform his firm from a business software company to a consumer technology company. At the heart of the transformation is a new on-line service developed by the firm called MSN™, the *Microsoft Network*. The homepage for MSN is shown in Exhibit 8.4. The on-line service allows consumers to access news, weather, science, business, and sports information. Not too surprisingly, the service capability is included in the Windows 95 software. Some industry analysts believe that MSN, an on-line Internet access service and browser, is the real significance for Microsoft and holds the real profit potential.[3]

To pave the way for the Windows 95 launch, Gates and Microsoft needed an advertising plan. In reality, the firm had relatively little experience with the consumer market. Certainly, many consumers were familiar with Microsoft from exposure to its software programs in the workplace and at home. The Microsoft Network was, however, designed to cultivate the millions of consumers—worldwide—that had little experience with computers and no significant brand loyalty to Microsoft programs. Gates had set a new marketing direction for the firm—to cultivate the consumer market for a new product. An advertising plan would have to be put into place to raise awareness among consumers and help implement this marketing strategy. Rather than merely seeking brand-related attitude change, consumers needed to really start thinking about computer technology in a different way; they needed to start thinking about

3.   Peter Lewis, "Technology: On the Net, the Real Significance of Windows 95 Is Reaching the Web with a Single Click of the Mouse," *New York Times,* July 31, 1995, D6, late New York edition.

EXHIBIT 8.3

This ad uses the Rolling Stones well-known song as part of a continuing theme that plays on both the song and the start button of Microsoft's Windows 95 computer operating system. Can you think of other ways in which this campaign uses an integrated marketing communications program? At the Microsoft Web site **www.microsoft.com/**, *other involvement devices are used as well, including access to lots of Windows 95-related products and lots of giveaways linked to increasingly higher levels of involvement in using and promoting Microsoft software. This advertising approach is best understood in the context in which it was created: as a competitive response to the success of Netscape Communications, Microsoft's arch rival in the battle for the heart and soul of the Internet. Check out Netscape's home page at* **home.netscape.com/**

how it connected in their own lives in a much more personal and even intimate way. Microsoft had to do something much more than just introduce some new software. It needed to change the way people thought about computers and link that new mental imagery to Microsoft.

To get things rolling, Microsoft relied on a $100 million pre–Windows 95 launch advertising plan with the stated purpose of making Microsoft a household name. The plan specified that the campaign would give a singular and distinctive look and feel to the Microsoft global brand. To accomplish these goals, a television, print, and outdoor ad campaign was initiated in late 1994. Microsoft allocated $25 million for the U.S. market and another $75 million for Germany, France, the United Kingdom, and Canada. The campaign included 30- and 60-second television commercials, an eight-page insert in consumer magazines, and newspaper ad spreads all featuring the tag line "Where do you want to go today?"

The television ads showed 52 different people of all ages and ethnic backgrounds, including a violinist, schoolchildren, and a European trolley driver. The visuals and the copy in the ad—including phrases like "It makes you powerful. Take it. Gather up your ideas"—were designed to communicate a sense of democracy in a borderless world of initiative, ideas, and individuality. While the Microsoft name appears for a scant two seconds at the end of the TV spot, over time a strong, unique image and brand recognition were expected.[4] Exhibit 8.5 shows one of the print ads from this campaign. This prelaunch campaign was part of an integrated marketing communications (IMC) effort.

Bill Gates and Microsoft relied on a well-executed advertising plan to build brand awareness among a new target audience—household consumers. As you will see in this chapter, Gates and Microsoft followed the process of building an advertising effort based on several key features of the advertising plan. An advertising plan is the culmination of the planning effort needed to create effective advertising.

---

4.   Information about the Microsoft campaign was taken from Bradley Johnson, "Microsoft's New World," *Advertising Age,* November 14, 1994, 1, 8; Don Clark, "Microsoft Launches Its On-Line Network," *Wall Street Journal,* November 15, 1994, B6; and Bob Garfield, "Wieden Waves Nike-Like Wand to Weave Microsoft Magic," *Advertising Age,* November 14, 1994, 3.

This Web site shows how Microsoft is attempting to move into a new area of business as an online Internet service provider (ISP). How does the Microsoft Network fit into the overall integrated marketing communications program for Microsoft products? The MSN home page provides perhaps the ultimate in individualization of products and services on demand: the ability to customize the look of the page to suit your personal preferences. Contrast this approach with the Web site of America Online at www.aol.com/, with its emphasis on interconnectivity, and featuring, among other things, links to the top twenty-five ISP sites.

WEB SIGHTING

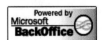

Windows 95 integrated prelaunch campaign.

The Advertising Plan and Its Marketing Context

① An ad plan must be an integrated extension of a firm's marketing plan. The marketing plan articulates the company's entire marketing effort, from product to distribution. The advertising plan, including all integrated marketing communications, is a subset of the larger marketing plan. The IMC component must be built into the plan in a seamless and synergistic way. Everything has to work together, whether the plan is for Microsoft or for a business with far fewer resources. Advertising agencies have a tendency to forget this from time to time, and marketers frequently don't remember to keep the agency fully informed of their plans, either. Such lapses can be disastrous.

An **advertising plan** specifies the thinking and tasks needed to conceive and implement an effective advertising effort. Exhibit 8.6 shows the components of an advertising plan. It should be noted that there is a great deal of variation in advertising plans from advertiser to advertiser. Our discussion of the advertising plan will focus on the seven major sections shown in Exhibit 8.6: the introduction, situation analysis, objectives, budgeting, strategy, execution, and evaluation. Each of these advertising plan components is discussed on the following pages.

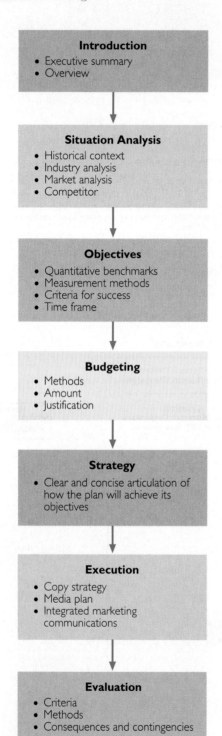

Introduction
- Executive summary
- Overview

Situation Analysis
- Historical context
- Industry analysis
- Market analysis
- Competitor

Objectives
- Quantitative benchmarks
- Measurement methods
- Criteria for success
- Time frame

Budgeting
- Methods
- Amount
- Justification

Strategy
- Clear and concise articulation of how the plan will achieve its objectives

Execution
- Copy strategy
- Media plan
- Integrated marketing communications

Evaluation
- Criteria
- Methods
- Consequences and contingencies

EXHIBIT 8.6

The advertising plan.

Introduction

The introduction of an advertising plan consists of an executive summary and an overview. An executive summary, typically two paragraphs to two pages in length, is offered to state the most important aspects of the plan. This is the take-away; that is, it is what the reader should remember from the plan. It is the essence of the plan.

As with many documents, an overview is also customary. An overview ranges in length from a paragraph to a few pages. It sets out what is to be covered, and it structures the context. All plans are different, and some require more of a setup than others. Don't underestimate the benefit of a good introduction. It's where you can make or lose a lot of points with the client.

Situation Analysis

When someone asks you to explain a decision you've made, you may say something like: "Well, here's the situation . . ." In what follows, you probably try to distill the situation down to the most important points and how they are connected in order to explain why you made the decision. An ad plan **situation analysis** is no different. It is where the agency lays out the most important factors that define the situation, and then explains the importance of each factor.

There is an infinite list of potential factors (for example, demographic, social and cultural, economic, political/regulatory) that define a situation analysis. Some books offer long but incomplete lists. We prefer to play it straight with you: there is no complete list of situational factors. The idea is not to be exhaustive or encyclopedic when writing a plan, but to be smart in choosing the few important factors that really describe the situation, and then explain how the factors relate to the advertising task at hand. Market segmentation, product positioning, and consumer behavior research provide the organization with insights that can be used for a situation analysis, but ultimately you have to decide which of the many factors are really the most critical to address in your advertising. This is the essence of management.

Let's say you represent American Express. How would you define the firm's current advertising situation? What are the most critical factors? What image has recent advertising, like that in Exhibit 8.7, established for the card? Would you consider the changing view of prestige cards to be critical? What about the problem of hanging onto an exclusive image while trying to increase your customer base by having your cards accepted at discount stores, such as Kmart? Does the proliferation of gold and platinum cards by other banks rate as critical? Do the very low interest rates offered by bank cards seem critical to the situation? What about changing social attitudes regarding the responsible use of credit cards? What about the current high level of consumer debt?

Think about how credit card marketing is influenced by the economic conditions of the day and the cultural beliefs about the proper way to display status. In the early eighties, it was acceptable for advertisers to tout the self-indulgent side of plastic (for example, MasterCard's slogan "MasterCard, I'm bored"). Today, charge and credit card ads often point out just how prudent it is to use your card for the right reasons. Now, instead of just suggesting you use your plastic to hop off to the islands when you feel the first stirrings of a bout with boredom, charge and credit card companies are far more likely to detail a few of the functional benefits of their cards, as shown in Exhibit 8.8. The Ethical Issues box on page 221 also addresses the role of public opinion, current thinking, and ad planning.

Simple demographic trends may be the single most important situational factor in advertising plans. Whether it's boomers or X'ers, where the numbers are is often where

EXHIBIT 8.7

What is the image this ad establishes for the American Express card? How is this image a response to the company's situation analysis? Link your answer to a discussion of market segmentation and product positioning. Who is reached by this ad and how does reaching this segment fit into the overall strategy for American Express? At the home page for American Express at **www.americanexpress.com/** *you can get information on credit and financial services, as well as information about company strategy. For services designed around your needs as a student, check out* **www.americanexpress.com/student/**

WEB SIGHTING

the sales are. As the population distribution varies with time, new markets are created and destroyed. The baby-boom generation of post–World War II dictates consumer offerings and demand simply because of its size. As the boomers age, companies that offer the things needed by tens of millions of aging boomers will have to devise new appeals. Think of the consumers of this generation needing long-term health care, geriatric products, and things to amuse themselves in retirement. Will they have the disposable income necessary to have the bountiful lifestyle many of them have had during their working years? After all, they aren't the greatest savers. And what of the X'ers? Are the needs of the current 20-somethings fundamentally different from those of boomers? (See Exhibit 8.9.)

Historical Context. No situation is entirely new, but all situations are unique. Just how a firm arrived at the current situation is very important. Before trying to design Microsoft's Windows 95 campaign, an agency should certainly know a lot about the history of all the principal players, the industry, the brand, the corporate culture, critical moments in the company's past, its big mistakes and big successes. All new decisions are situated in a firm's history, and an agency should be diligent in studying that history. For example, would an agency pitch new business to Green Giant without knowing something of the brand's history and the rationale behind the Green Giant? The history of the Green Giant dates back decades, as the ad in Exhibit 8.10 shows. The fact is that no matter what advertising decisions are made in the present, the past has a significant impact.

Apart from history's intrinsic value, sometimes the real business goal is to convince the client that the agency knows the client's business, its major concerns, and its corporate culture. A brief history of the company and brand are included to demonstrate the thoroughness of the agency's research, the depth of its knowledge, and the scope of its concern.

Industry Analysis. An **industry analysis** is just that; it focuses on developments and trends within an industry and on any other factors that may make a difference in how an advertiser proceeds with an advertising plan. An industry analysis should enumerate and discuss the most important aspects of a given industry, or the supply side of the supply-demand

EXHIBIT 8.9

Chasing X.

Soon to be publisher of his own GenX magazine, buster journalist Nathaniel Wice attended the first GenX marketing conference, which promised to teach participants how to create "profitable and targeted marketing programs for the twentysomething generation." Most fascinatingly, he comes to the conclusion that as far as these nostalgic marketing experts are concerned, GenX does not represent a real population or social movement but a reflection of their own boomer identity in flux.

As Ann Glover, Strategy Manager for Mountain Dew at Pepsico, makes points in her speech, they come up on a slide screen one by one for the hundred-plus attendees of the first-ever marketing conference devoted to the newly discovered demographic bulge of 46 million Americans born between 1963 and 1974. The screen beside her spells out UNDER-RATED BRAND MEETS UNDER-RATED GENERATION. . . .

Glover is straining to connect her product with a very desirable market. Over the last year, the first significant generation gap since the sixties has been declared, not atop student barricades, but in a flood of soft news features about "Generation X," "twentysomethings," and "baby busters." And in the media trade press young adults have emerged as the "hot" target audience.

Companies as diverse as Taco Bell, Ford Motor, and Bugle Boy Jeans have come to this Generation X conference to get a fix on kids today. ("A $125 Billion Market" shouts the conference brochure. It's sponsored by the Institute for International Research, a market research group specializing in conferences.) Presenters share their experiences marketing to this elusive generation, and at the same time promote their own products or services. Everyone in attendance hopes a little Generation X excitement will rub off on them.

The Mountain Dew presentation, called "Getting Busters to 'Do Diet Dew,'" is one of the heavy-handed ones. Glover argues that Mountain Dew and Gen X—as it is referred to at the conference—have a lot in common. Not only do they stand for similar values—"X'ers prioritize physical self-improvement" and Mountain Dew advertising features "lots of physical activity"—they are each badly misunderstood. Gen X is unfairly labeled dumb, hopeless, and angry, while Mountain Dew is mistakenly regarded as a small regional brand with a minuscule advertising budget. Let the facts show, though, click, chunk goes the projector, that Mountain Dew is the sixth most popular soft drink brand in the country, and that its ad budgets are comparable to those of Sprite and Gatorade. . . .

Another focus-group researcher to speak at the conference, Marian Salzman, strives to help the middle-aged marketers understand. Still in her early thirties, Salzman is the founder of her own marketing firm, BKG Youth. She is the sensible older sister, trying to explain her younger sibling to her parents. It is one of the more careful presentations, interpreting Gen X's reputation for apathy and cynicism—especially as regards advertisers—as fidelity to traditional values like honesty and quality. Her recommendations for crafting ad campaigns turn the contradictions of Gen X hype—and they are innumerable—into guidelines for advertisers. Craving simplicity, Gen X supposedly responds well to outdoors imagery: with commitments such as home ownership out of reach, they "feather their nests with electronic luxuries recast as 'essentials.'"

Gen X, another speaker explains, "demands to be entertained." Wieden & Kennedy, responsible for some of Nike's best ad campaigns, is ridiculed by conference speakers for an overzealous Subaru ad which they executed. In this spot, a young man who looks like a cross between Corey Feldman and Christian Slater compares the Subaru to punk rock. Hopelessly unhip. Much more popular is a Converse ad that the sneaker company showcases at the conference: A street punk unleashes a Dennis Leary-like diatribe against the tyranny of beautiful people pictured in ads. The spot, called "Ugly," ends with the tagline, "I don't want to live in a beer commercial." It is currently running on MTV. . . .

Source: Nathaniel Wice, "Generalization X," in *The GenX Reader,* ed. Douglas Rushkoff (New York: Ballantine Books, 1994), 279–286.

equation. For example, if you were designing advertising for Blockbuster Video, you might be concerned that movie rentals have been significantly lower industrywide. Are consumers watching fewer movies? No. In this particular industry, film distributors are discovering that they can make more money by selling films directly to the public at deeply discounted prices. Also, satellite distribution of the movies is cutting directly into the sales by video rental chains. There is also the problem of changing home technologies. What if the new DV disk completely does in the inferior videocassette?

Certainly these issues have an impact on the long-term future of companies like Blockbuster, but even in the short term they have a meaning. If you're Blockbuster, you want someone to come up with some advertising that slows or reduces this trend. You want your agency to figure out what is unique about going to a video store. Maybe it means more integrated marketing efforts, such as tie-ins with fast-food restaurants and toy stores, appearances by celebrities, or a chance to win tickets to a sporting event. One thing is clear—you can't ignore the trends in an industry.

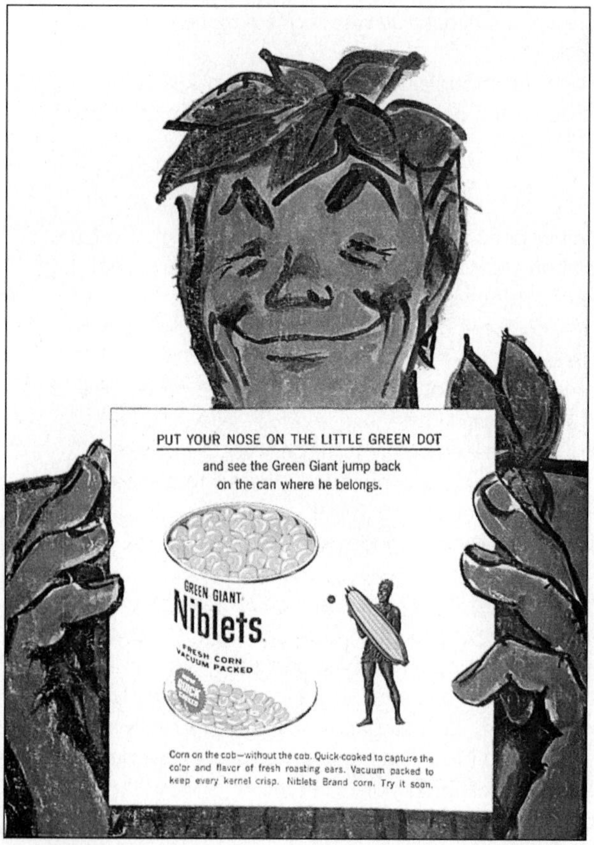

Market Analysis. A **market analysis** is the flip side of industry analysis; it is the demand side of the equation. In a market analysis, an advertiser examines the factors that drive and determine the market for the firm's product or service. First, the advertiser needs to decide just exactly what the market is for the product. Most often, the market for a given good or service is simply defined as current users. The idea here is that consumers figure out for themselves if they want the product or not and thus define the market for themselves, and for the advertiser. This approach has some wisdom to it. It's simple, easy to defend, and very conservative. Few executives get fired for choosing this target market. However, it completely ignores those consumers who might otherwise be persuaded to use the product.

A market analysis commonly begins by stating just who the current users are and why they are current users. Consumers' motivations for using one product or service but not another may very well provide the advertiser with the means toward a significant expansion of the entire market. If the entire pie grows, the firm's slice usually does as well. The advertiser's job in a market analysis is to find out the most important market factors and why they are so important.

Competitor Analysis. Once the industry and market are studied and analyzed, attention is turned to **competitor analysis.** Here an advertiser determines just exactly who the competitors are, discussing their strengths, weaknesses, tendencies, and any threats they pose.

For example, suppose you are advertising Fuji 35-mm film. Who are your competitors? Is Kodak a competitor, with more than an 80 percent share of the market? Are AGFA and Konica worth worrying about? Would stealing share from these fairly minor players amount to much? What has Kodak done in the past when Fuji has made a move? What are Kodak's advantages? For one, it may have successfully equated memories with photographs and with trusting the archiving of these memories to Kodak film. Does Kodak have any weaknesses? Is it as technologically advanced as Fuji? Japanese

EXHIBIT 8.10

Knowing a brand's history can guide the development of future campaigns.

technologies are often thought to be superior to American. Could Kodak be characterized as stodgy and old-fashioned? What of recent product innovations? What about financial resources? Can Kodak swat Fuji like a fly? Or does Fuji have deep pockets, too? What would happen if Fuji tripled its advertising and directly compared its product to Kodak's? All of these questions would be addressed for each competitor in a competitor analysis.

Objectives

Advertising objectives lay the framework for the subsequent tasks in an advertising plan and take many different forms. Objectives identify the goals of the advertiser in concrete terms. The advertiser, more often than not, has more than one objective for an ad campaign. An advertiser's objectives may be (1) to increase consumer awareness of its product, (2) to change consumers' beliefs or attitudes about its product, (3) to influence the purchase intent of its customers, (4) to stimulate trial use of its product, (5) to convert one-time product users into repeat purchasers, (6) to switch consumers from a competing brand to its brand, or (7) to increase sales. (Each of these objectives is discussed briefly in the following paragraphs.) The advertiser may have more than one objective at the same time. For example, a swimwear company may state its advertising objectives as follows: to maintain the company's brand image as the market leader in adult female swimwear and to increase revenue in this product line by 15 percent.

Creating or maintaining brand awareness is a popular advertising objective. Brand awareness is an indicator of consumer knowledge about the existence of the brand and how easily that knowledge can be retrieved from memory. For example, an advertiser might ask a consumer to name five brands of coffee. **Top-of-the-mind awareness** is represented by the brand listed first. Ease of retrieval from memory is important because for many consumer goods or services, ease of retrieval is predictive of market share.

Beliefs are knowing with some degree of certainty that certain things are true. For example, you may believe that FedEx is the most reliable next-day delivery service or that Saturn has a no-pressure sales environment. You may believe that gingivitis is the scourge of the Western world, and no one is safe from it. These are all important beliefs for marketers. In the case of Crest or any other toothpaste that promises to prevent gingivitis, the idea that this disease is prevalent is important when setting advertising objectives.

Creating or changing attitudes is another popular advertising objective. Attitudes about products are typically measured by tracking studies and survey research. Attitudes

ETHICAL ISSUES

BE CAREFUL WHEN CLAIMING POLLUTION SOLUTIONS: IT'S NOT THAT EASY BEING GREEN

Just when are soiled disposable diapers safe for the environment? Well, it depends. At present, every state that restricts green claims in advertising has a different definition of what constitutes environmental friendliness. This spells trouble for ecosensitive national advertisers seeking to ride the green bandwagon, extol their earth-safe virtues, and garner greater greenbacks. While no federal regulations exist at present, an *Advertising Age* survey of 240 adults from New York, Denver, and San Francisco found that 77 percent of respondents agree that the government should actively regulate advertisers' environmental claims. The survey also found that respondents would favor federal regulations over state regulations, citing a greater degree of uniformity and believability. As the movement to save the planet from pollution gathers momentum, perhaps we'll see the FTC step into the fray and issue new regulations. Still, the safest way for an advertiser to capitalize on environmental marketing efforts is to compare its product or process with an existing one. The advertiser then has the ability to make verifiable product claims against known industry benchmarks, such as the degree of photodegradability or the ratio of recycled material content. The overall effect of environmental advertising is difficult to quantify in the minds of consumers, however. While 70 percent of survey respondents agreed that environmental claims influence their purchase decisions, it has yet to be shown conclusively that green ads lead from the red to the black.

Source: "Saving Endangered 'Green' Ad Claims," *Advertising Age*, May 22, 1995, 19

can also be measured in forced-exposure copy research, but remember that the predictive ability of attitudes toward actual buying behavior is nowhere near a one-to-one relationship.

Purchase intent is another popular criterion in objective setting. Purchase intent is determined by asking consumers whether or not they intend to buy a product or service in the near future. The appeal of influencing purchase intent is that intent is closer to actual behavior, and thus closer to the desired sale, than are attitudes. While this makes sense, it does presuppose that consumers can express their intentions with a reasonably high degree of reliability. Sometimes they can, sometimes they cannot. Purchase intent, however, is generally reliable as an indicator of relative intention to buy, and it is, therefore, certainly worth attempting to influence.

Trial use is an indicator of actual behavior and is commonly used as an advertising objective. In the case of new products, stimulating trial use is critically important. In the marketing realm, the angels truly sing when the initial purchase rate of a new product or service is high.

The **repeat purchase,** or conversion, objective is aimed at the percentage of consumers who try a new product and then purchase it a second time. A second purchase is reason for great rejoicing. The odds of long-term product success go way up when this percentage is high.

Brand switching is the last of the advertising objectives mentioned here. In some brand categories, switching is commonplace, even the norm. In others it is rare. When setting a brand-switching advertising objective, the advertiser must neither expect too much, nor rejoice too much, over a temporary gain. Convincing consumers to switch brands can be a long and arduous task.

Communications versus Sales Objectives.

Some analysts argue that as a single variable in a firm's overall marketing mix, it is not reasonable to set sales expectations for advertising when other variables in the mix might undermine the advertising effort or be responsible for sales in the first place.

In fact, some advertising analysts argue that communications objectives are the *only* legitimate objectives for advertising. This perspective has its underpinnings in the proposition that advertising is but one variable in the marketing mix and cannot be held solely responsible for sales. Rather, advertising should be held responsible for creating awareness of a brand, communicating information about product features or availability, or developing a favorable attitude that can lead to consumer preference for a brand. All of these outcomes are long term in nature and based on communications impact. Central to a strict communications perspective is the belief that since it is impossible to judge sales impact directly from advertising, then sales objectives should not be part of advertising objectives.

There are some major benefits to maintaining a strict communications perspective in setting advertising objectives. First, by viewing advertising as primarily a communications effort, marketers can consider a broader range of advertising strategies. Second, they can gain a greater appreciation for the complexity of the overall communications process. Designing an integrated marketing communications program with sales as the sole objective neglects aspects of message design, media choice, public relations, or sales force deployment that can be effectively integrated across all phases of a firm's communications efforts. Using advertising messages to reinforce the efforts of the sales force is an example of coordinating the communications process and the IMC effort.

The desire of organizations to tie the advertising effort to sales is certainly understandable. After all, the average person assumes a fairly direct relationship between advertising and sales. With more and more emphasis on accountability in spending, firms are scrutinizing budgets and the performance of all aspects of the marketing program, including advertising. Despite all the compelling arguments to maintain a heavy emphasis on communications, firms still have a keen eye trained on sales.

While there is a natural tension between those who advocate sales objectives and those who push communications objectives, nothing precludes a marketer from using both categories of objectives when developing an advertising plan. Indeed, combining sales objectives like market share and household penetration with communication objectives like awareness and brand imagery can be an excellent means of motivating and evaluating an advertising campaign.[5]

Characteristics of Workable Advertising Objectives.

Objectives that enable a firm to make intelligent decisions about resource allocation must be stated in an advertising plan in terms specific to the organization. Articulating such well-stated objectives is easier when advertising planners do the following:

1. *Establish a quantitative benchmark.* Objectives for advertising are measurable only in the context of quantifiable variables. Advertising planners should begin with quantified measures of the current status of market share, awareness, attitude, or other factors that advertising is expected to impact. The measurement of effectiveness in quantitative terms requires a knowledge of the level of variables of interest *before* an advertising effort, and then afterward. For example, a statement of objectives in quantified terms might be "Increase the market share of heavy users of the product category using our brand from 22 to 25 percent." In this case, a quantifiable and measurable market share objective is specified.

2. *Specify measurement methods and criteria for success.* It is important that the factors being measured are directly related to the objectives being pursued. It is of little use to try to increase the awareness of a brand with advertising and then judge the effects based on changes in sales. If changes in sales are expected, then measure sales. If increased awareness is the goal, then change in consumer awareness is the only legitimate measure of success. This may seem obvious, but in a classic study of advertising objectives, it was found that claims of success for advertising were unrelated to the original statements of objective in 69 percent of the cases studied.[6] In this research, firms cited increases in sales as proof of success of advertising when original objectives related to factors such as awareness, conviction to a brand, or product use information. Yet another recent complication for measurement stems from vehicles like the World Wide Web. As indicated in the New Media box on page 224, the interactive media present a substantial challenge with respect to establishing success criteria.

3. *Specify a time frame.* Objectives for advertising should include a statement of the period of time allowed for the desired results to occur. In some cases, like with direct response advertising, the time frame may be immediate or a 24-hour period. For communications-based objectives, the measurement of results may not be undertaken until the end of an entire 13-week campaign. The point is that the time period for accomplishment of an objective and the related measurement period must be stated in advance in the ad plan.

These criteria for setting objectives help ensure that the planning process is organized and well directed. By relying on quantitative benchmarks, an advertiser has guidelines for making future decisions. Linking measurement criteria to objectives provides a basis for the equitable evaluation of the success or failure of advertising. Finally, the specification of a time frame for judging results keeps the planning process moving forward. As in all things, however, moderation is a good thing. A single-minded obsession with watching the numbers can be dangerous in that it minimizes or entirely misses the importance of qualitative and intuitive factors.

---

5.   John Philip Jones, "Advertising's Crisis of Confidence," *Marketing Management* 2, no. 1 (1993): 15–24.
6.   Stewart Henderson Britt, "Are So-Called Successful Advertising Campaigns Really Successful?" *Journal of Advertising Research* 9 (1969): 5.

Budgeting

❸ One of the most agonizing tasks is budgeting the funds for an advertising effort. Firms often spend millions of dollars on advertising. Normally, the responsibility for the advertising budget lies with the firm itself. Within a firm, budget recommendations come up through the ranks, from a brand manager to a product manager and ultimately to the executive in charge of marketing. The sequence then reverses itself for the allocation and spending of funds. In a small firm, such as an independent retailer, the sequence just described may include only one individual who plays all the roles.

In some cases, a firm will rely on its advertising agency to make recommendations regarding the size of the advertising budget. When this is done, it is typically the account executive in charge of the brand who will analyze the firm's objectives and its creative and media needs and then make a recommendation to the company. The account supervisor's budget planning will likely include working closely with brand and product group managers to determine an appropriate spending level.

To be as judicious and accountable as possible for spending money on advertising, advertisers rely on various methods for setting an advertising budget. To appreciate the benefits (and failings) of each of these methods, we will consider each of them separately.

Percentage of Sales.

A **percentage-of-sales approach** to advertising budgeting calculates the advertising budget based on a percentage of the prior year's sales or the projected year's sales. This technique is easy to understand and operationalize. The budget decision makers merely specify that a particular percentage of either last year's sales or the current year's estimated sales be allocated to the advertising process. It is common to spend between 2 and 12 percent of sales on advertising.

While ease is certainly an advantage in decision making, the percentage-of-sales approach is fraught with problems. First, when a firm's sales are decreasing, the advertising budget will automatically decline. Periods of decreasing sales may be precisely the time when a firm needs to increase spending on advertising; if a percentage-of-sales budgeting method is being used, this won't happen. Second, this budgeting method can easily result in overspending on advertising. Once funds have been earmarked, the tendency is to find ways to spend the budgeted amount. Third, the most serious drawback from a strategic standpoint is that the percentage-of-sales approach does not relate advertising dollars to advertising objectives. Basing spending on past or future sales is devoid of analytical evaluation and implicitly presumes a direct cause-and-effect relationship between advertising and sales.

NEW MEDIA

CAUGHT IN THE WEB: MEDIA RESEARCH SPINS NEW INTERNET MEASURES

While some firms rush headlong into interactive ventures, many question the new medium's effectiveness. After all, no industrywide standards exist to measure Internet reach or frequency, and individual claims vary widely. "The info that's out there right now is totally unverified and unaudited," says Alec Gerster, executive vice president and director of media at Grey Advertising, New York. He goes on to say that the current predicament is "like having ABC, NBC, CBS, and Fox supply their own ratings." Clearly, then, some standard is needed to assess the quantity and quality of online advertising.

The battle for online measurement rights has been engaged, but uncertainty still exists as to what constitutes relevant measurement criteria. One new tracking company, Internet Profiles of Palo Alto, California, promises to provide Web site owners with a detailed analysis, complete with the total number of users, time spent per page, user demographics, and even user spending habits. While the criteria debate ensues, some leading Web publishers like Netscape Communications and InfoSeek are introducing advertising rate structures based on cost per thousand impressions (CPMs), a measure often used for traditional media, such as television and magazines. The problem with using CPMs, however, is that they only quantify passive exposure to advertising, while Web browsers must actively search out messages on the Internet.

The ultimate benefit of Internet advertising—interactivity—allows advertisers to build relationships with their customers that go well beyond mere exposure to a brand or product. With the proper measurement tools, then, evaluating the degree of interactivity may provide a rating of actual customer involvement.

Sources: "New Media Digging Up Old Tools," *Advertising Age*, July 10, 1995, 16; "Now Marketers Can Track Internet Usage," *Wall Street Journal*, April 5, 1995, B9; and "MPA Joins Web Measurement Fray," *Advertising Age*, July 17, 1995, 13.

A variation on the percentage-of-sales approach that firms may use is the unit-of-sales approach. **Unit-of-sales approach** to budgeting simply allocates a specified dollar amount of advertising for each unit of a brand sold (or expected to be sold). This is merely a translation of the percentage-of-sales method into dollars per units sold. The unit-of-sales approach has the same advantages and disadvantages as the percentage-of-sales approach.

Share of Market/Share of Voice.

With this method, employed by many firms, a firm monitors the amount spent by various significant competitors on advertising and allocates an amount equal to the amount of money spent by competitors or an amount proportional to (or slightly greater than) the firm's market share relative to the competition.[7] Exhibit 8.11 shows the relationship between share of market and share of voice for two fierce competitors: Coke and Pepsi.

With this method, an advertiser will achieve a **share of voice,** or an advertising presence in the market, equal to or greater than the competitors' share of advertising voice. This method is often used for advertising budget allocations in new-product introductions. Conventional wisdom suggests that some multiple, often 2.5 to 4 times the desired first-year market share, should be spent in terms of share-of-voice advertising expenditures. For example, if an advertiser wants a 2 percent first-year share, it would need to spend up to 8 percent of the total dollar amount spent in the industry (for an 8 percent share of voice). The logic is that a new product will need a significant share of voice to gain notice among a group of existing, well-established brands.[8]

Although this technique is sound in the sense that it shows a heightened awareness of competitors' activities, there is some question as to whether it can or should be used. First, it may be difficult to gain access to precise information on competitors' spending. Second, there is no reason to believe that competitors are spending their money wisely or in a way even remotely related to what the decision-making firm wants to accomplish. Third, a likely outcome of budgeting advertising in this fashion is that the firm employing this technique will make little headway on the competition and simply maintain the status quo. There are situations where the status quo certainly does not

EXHIBIT 8.11

Share of market versus share of voice, 1992 cola market.

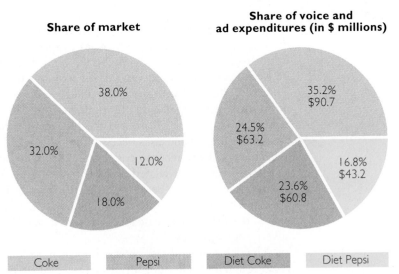

Source: Taken from *Market Share Reporter* (Detroit: Gale Research, 1994). 100. Share of voice/ad expenditures computed from January to December 1992 in LNA/Media Watch Multi-Media Service (New York: 1992), 186, 209, 392. Copyright © 1994, Gale Research, Inc. All rights reserved. Reproduced by permission.

7.   The classic treatment of this method was first offered by James O. Peckham, "Can We Relate Advertising Dollars to Market-Share Objectives?," in *How Much to Spend for Advertising,* ed. Malcolm A. McGiven (New York: Association of National Advertisers, 1969), 24.
8.   James C. Shroer, "Ad Spending: Growing Market Share," *Harvard Business Review* (January–February 1990): 44.

relate to strategic objectives. For example, to achieve significant share of voice for its new toothpaste with baking soda and peroxide, Colgate-Palmolive spent $40 million in the first six months on advertising.[9] This sort of massive spending on a product launch can give a brand visibility in a crowded market but would be far out of line relative to competitors' spending.

Finally, the flaw in logic in this method is the presumption that every advertising effort is of the same quality and will have the same effect from a creative execution standpoint. Nothing could be further from the truth. Multimillion-dollar advertising campaigns have been miserable failures, and limited-budget campaigns have been huge successes.

Response Models. Using response models to aid the budgeting process is a fairly widespread practice among larger firms.[10] The belief is that greater objectivity can be maintained with such models. While this may or may not be the case, response models do provide useful information on what a given company's advertising response function looks like. An **advertising response function** is a mathematical relationship that associates dollars spent on advertising and sales generated. To the extent that past advertising predicts future sales, this method is valuable. Using marginal analysis, an advertiser would continue its spending on advertising as long as its marginal spending was exceeded by marginal sales. Marginal analysis answers the advertiser's question, "How much more will sales increase if we spend an additional dollar on advertising?" As the rate of return on advertising expenditures declines, the wisdom of additional spending is analyzed.

Theoretically, this method leads to a point where an optimal advertising expenditure results in an optimal sales level and, in turn, an optimal profit. The relationship between sales, profit, and advertising spending is shown in the marginal analysis graph in Exhibit 8.12. Data on sales levels, prior advertising expenditures, and consumer awareness are typical of the numerical input to such quantitative models.

Unfortunately, the advertising-to-sales relationship assumes simple causality, and we know that assumption isn't true. Many other factors, in addition to advertising, affect sales directly. Still, some feel that the use of response models is a better budgeting method than guessing or applying the percentage-of-sales or other budgeting methods discussed so far.

Objective and Task. The methods for establishing an advertising budget just discussed all suffer from the same fundamental deficiency: a lack of specification of how expenditures are related to advertising goals. The only method of budget setting that focuses on the relationship between spending and advertising objectives is the **objective-and-task approach.** This method begins with the stated objectives for an advertising effort. Goals related to production costs, target audience reach, message effects, behavioral effects, media placement, duration of the effort, and the like are specified. The budget is formulated by identifying the specific tasks necessary to achieve different aspects of the objectives.

There is a lot to recommend this procedure for budgeting. A firm identifies any and all tasks it believes are related to achieving its objectives. Should the total dollar figure for the necessary tasks be beyond the firm's financial capability, then a reconciliation must take place. But even if a reconciliation and a subsequent reduction of the budget results, the firm has at least identified what *should* have been budgeted to pursue its advertising objectives.

The objective-and-task approach is the most logical and defensible method for calculating and then allocating an advertising budget. It is the only budgeting method that specifically relates advertising spending to the advertising objectives being pursued. It is widely used among major advertisers. For these reasons, we will consider the specific procedures for implementing the objective-and-task budgeting method.

9.   Pat Sloan, "Colgate Packs $40M behind New Toothpaste," *Advertising Age,* December 12, 1994, 36.
10.   James E. Lynch and Graham J. Hooley, "Increasing Sophistication in Advertising Budget Setting," *Journal of Advertising Research* (February–March, 1990): 72.

EXHIBIT 8.12

Graph on sales, profit, and advertising curves used in marginal analysis.

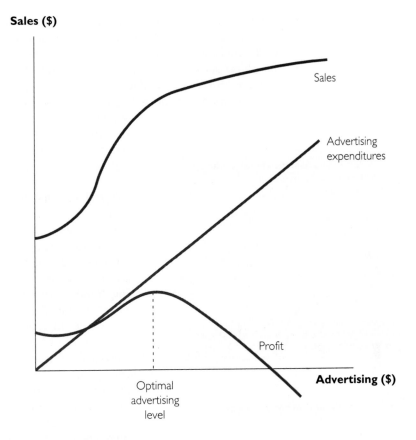

Source: David A. Aaker, Rajeev Batra, and John G. Meyers, *Advertising Management*, 4th ed. (Englewood Cliffs, N.J.: Prentice-Hall, 1992), 469. Reprinted by permission of Prentice-Hall, Inc., Upper Saddle River, N.J.

Implementing the Objective-and-Task Budgeting Method. Proper implementation of the objective-and-task approach requires a data-based, systematic procedure. Since the approach ties spending levels to specific advertising goals, the process is dependent on proper execution of the objective-setting process described earlier. Once a firm and its agency are satisfied with the specificity and direction of stated objectives, a series of well-defined steps can be taken to implement the objective-and-task method. These steps are shown in Exhibit 8.13 and summarized in the following sections.

Determine Costs Based on Build-Up Analysis. Having identified specific objectives, an advertiser can now begin determining what tasks are necessary for the accomplishment of those objectives. In using a **build-up analysis**—building up the expenditure levels for tasks —the following factors must be considered in terms of costs:

- *Reach:* Identification must be made of the geographic and demographic exposure the advertising is to achieve.
- *Frequency:* Determination must be made of the number of exposures required to accomplish desired objectives.
- *Time frame:* There must be an estimate of when communications will occur and over what period of time.
- *Production costs:* The decision maker can rely on creative personnel and producers to provide an estimate of costs associated with the planned execution of advertisements.
- *Media expenditures:* Given the preceding factors, the advertiser can now define the appropriate media, media mix, and frequency of insertions that will directly address objectives. Further, differences in geographic allocation, with special attention to regional or local media strategies, are considered at this point.

- *Ancillary costs:* There will be a variety of related costs not directly accounted for in the preceding factors. Prominent among these are costs associated with advertising to the trade, specialized research unique to the campaign, and other costs.
- *Integrating other promotional costs:* In this era of integrated marketing communications, an advertising budget must be considered in the context of spending on other promotional efforts. Some of these promotional expenditures will be directly supportive of mass media advertising. Others will have distinct objectives, but as we have seen from an IMC standpoint, the theme and any spending issues need to be coordinated with advertising.

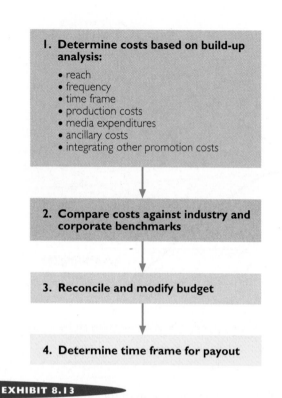

1. **Determine costs based on build-up analysis:**
   - reach
   - frequency
   - time frame
   - production costs
   - media expenditures
   - ancillary costs
   - integrating other promotion costs

2. **Compare costs against industry and corporate benchmarks**

3. **Reconcile and modify budget**

4. **Determine time frame for payout**

EXHIBIT 8.13

Steps in implementing the objective-and-task approach.

Compare Costs against Industry and Corporate Benchmarks. After compiling all the costs through a build-up analysis, an advertiser will want to make a quick reality check. This is accomplished by checking the percentage of sales the estimated set of costs represents relative to industry standards for percentage of sales allocated to advertising. If most competitors are spending 4 to 6 percent of gross sales on advertising, how does the current budget compare to this percentage? Another technique recommended is to identify the share of industry advertising that the firm's budget represents. Another relevant reference point is to compare the current budget with prior budgets. If the total dollar amount is extraordinarily high or low compared to previous years, this variance should be justified based on the objectives being pursued. The use of percentage of sales on both an industry and internal corporate basis provides a reference point only. The percentage-of-sales figures are not used for decision making per se, but rather as a baseline comparison to judge if the budgeted amount is so unusual as to need reevaluation.

Reconcile and Modify the Budget. It is always a fear that the proposed budget will not meet with approval. It may not be viewed as consistent with corporate policy related to advertising expense, or it may be considered beyond the financial capabilities of the organization. Modifications to a proposed budget are common. Having to make radical cuts in proposed spending is disruptive and potentially devastating. The objective-and-task approach is designed to identify what a firm will need to spend in order to achieve a desired advertising impact. To have the budget level compromised after such planning can result in a totally impotent advertising effort because necessary tasks cannot be funded.

Every precaution should be taken against having to radically modify a budget. Planners should be totally aware of corporate policy and financial circumstance *during* the objective-setting and subsequent task-planning phases. This will help reduce the extent of budget modification, should any be required.

Determine Time Frame for Payout. It is important that budget decision makers recognize when the budget will be available for funding the tasks associated with the proposed effort. Travel expenses, production expenses, and media time and space are tied to specific calendar dates. For example, media time and space are often acquired and paid for far in advance of the completion of finished advertisements. Knowing when and how much money is needed will usually increase the odds of the plan being carried out smoothly.

If these procedures are followed for the objective-and-task approach, an advertiser will have a defendable and agreeable advertising budget with which to pursue advertising objectives. One point to be made, however, is that the budget should not be viewed as the final word in funding an advertising effort. The dynamic nature of the market and rapid developments in media require flexibility in budget execution. This can mean changes in expenditure levels, but it can also mean changes in payout allocation.

Like any other business activity, an advertiser must take on an advertising effort with clearly specified intentions for what is to be accomplished. Intentions and expectations for advertising are embodied in the process of setting objectives. Armed with information from marketing planning and an assessment of the type of advertising needed to support marketing plans, advertising objectives can be set. These objectives should be in place before steps are taken to determine a budget for the advertising effort, and before the creative work begins. Again, this is not always the order of things, even though it should be. These objectives will also affect the plans for media placement.

Strategy

Strategy represents the mechanism by which something is to be done. It is an expression of the means to an end. All of the other factors are supposed to result in a strategy. Strategy is what you do, given the situation and objectives. There are an infinite number of possible advertising strategies. For example, if you are trying to get more top-of-the-mind awareness for your brand of chewing gum, a simple strategy would be to employ a high-frequency, name-repetition campaign. More sophisticated goals call for more sophisticated strategies. You are limited only by your resources: financial, organizational, and creative. Ultimately, strategy formulation is a creative endeavor. It is best learned through the study of what others have done in similar situations. Experience counts.

Execution

The actual "doing" is the execution of an ad plan. It is the making and placing of ads across all media. To quote a famous bit of advertising copy from a tire manufacturer, this is where "the rubber meets the road." There are two elements to the execution of an advertising plan: determining the copy strategy and devising a media plan.

Copy Strategy. A copy strategy consists of copy objectives and methods, or tactics. The objectives state what the advertiser intends to accomplish, while the methods describe how the objectives will be achieved. Chapters 10 and 11 detail the copy strategy and copywriting processes.

Media Plan. The media plan specifies exactly where ads will be placed and what strategy is behind their placement. In a truly integrated marketing communications environment, this is much more complicated than it might appear. Back when there were just three broadcast television networks, there were already more than a million different combinations of placements that could be made. With the explosion of media and promotion options today, the permutations are almost infinite. It is at this point, devising a media plan, where all the money is spent, and so much could be saved. This is where the profitability of many agencies is really determined. Media placement strategy can make a huge difference in profits or losses and is considered in great depth in Part 4 of this text.

Integrated Marketing Communications. The IMC effort should be spelled out in the media plan. It should be seamless with the rest of the plan. Sometimes IMC is the dominant aspect of the marketing effort, as is the case with Rhino Records. One could argue that Rhino is the all-time undisputed champion of creative sales promotion, an integral part of IMC. Rhino Records began as a used-album record store in west Los Angeles. Records were displayed in fruit crates on sawhorses. Rhino management would do just about anything to gain loyal customers. For example, they offered customers a nickel if they would take home a copy of a Danny Bonaduce album and promise to actually listen to it.[11] They pressed records in the shapes of animals. Perhaps their greatest feat was recording and selling a kazoo-orchestra recording of Led Zeppelin's "Whole Lotta Love." It sold 15,000 copies. A well-known street person in Los Angeles, Wild Man Fischer, was asked to record "Go to Rhino Records." At first the recording was given out as a promotional bonus to customers, but then it found its way to the BBC and actually made the pop charts in the UK.[12] Rhino issued offerings like *The World's Worst Records,* which actually came with a barf bag,[13] and a collection of seventies tunes called *Have a Nice Day.* Soon Rhino was a record label as well as a record store. In 1978 it produced an influential album of then-unsigned LA bands, called *Saturday Night Pogo,* and *Cover Me,* a collection of bands covering Bruce Springsteen. Today you can find Rhino on the World Wide Web and in ads in popular magazines.

Everything Rhino does has a synergy and integration to it. The lesson from Rhino should not be lost: Don't make IMC a static, me-too formula. When practiced creatively, IMC is at its best. (See Exhibit 8.14.)

EXHIBIT 8.14

Rhino Records practices integrated gonzo.

And now to the business at hand: how to create interest in yet another compilation of party music, *Frat Rock 3: Grandson of Frat Rock,* aimed at either college students, former college students or high-school grads with Dobie Gillis's outlook on what college must be like.

"We could give away condoms," someone suggests.

"Yeah, 'Wooly Bully' Trojans, great idea."

"How about a toll-free number with test answers?"

"I'd like to stick with more *retail*-oriented promotions," the leader warns in a tone that sounds almost authoritative.

"How about an in-store toga party?"

"Show up in a toga, get $1 off!"

"That's almost worth the humiliation."

Source: Stephen Fried, "Loony Tunes: Rhino Records' Utterly Gonzo Sensibility Is Turning Out to Be Good Business," *GQ,* April 1992, 76.

Evaluation

Last but not least in an ad plan is the evaluation component. This is where an advertiser determines how the agency will be graded: what criteria will be applied and how long the agency will have to achieve the agreed-upon objectives. It's critically important for the advertiser and agency to understand the evaluation criteria up front. Of course, the advertiser has the power to change its agency anytime it wishes, regardless of whether or not the criteria are being met. In short, advertising agencies are at the mercy of their clients, fair or unfair.

The Role of the Advertising Agency in Advertising Planning

Now that we have covered key aspects of the advertising planning process, one other issue should be considered. Because many advertisers rely heavily on the expertise of an advertising agency, understanding the role an agency plays in the advertising planning process is important. What contribution to the planning effort can and should an advertiser expect from its agency? As described in the Contemporary Issues box on page 231, the issue of contribution is directly tied to the compensation that many agencies now expect from their clients.

11. Stephen Fried, "Loony Tunes: Rhino Records' Utterly Gonzo Sensibility Is Turning Out to Be Good Business," *GQ,* April 1992, 76.
12. "B-Rated Rock and Roll," *Newsweek,* October 7, 1985, 90.
13. Fried, "Loony Tunes."

The discussion of advertising planning to this point has emphasized that the advertiser is responsible for the marketing planning inputs as a type of self-assessment that identifies the firm's basis for offering value to customers. This assessment should also clearly identify, in the external environment, the opportunities and challenges that can be addressed with advertising. A firm should bring to the planning effort a well-articulated statement of a brand's competitive position and the marketing mix strategies designed to gain and sustain competitive advantage.

The advertising agency's role, as a partner in the advertising effort, is to translate the current market and marketing status of a firm and its advertising objectives into advertising strategy and, ultimately, finished advertisements. An agency can serve its clients best by taking charge of the preparation and placement stages. Here, message strategies and tactics for the advertising effort and for the efficient and effective placement of ads in media need to be hammered out. At this point, the firm (as a good client) should turn to its agency for the expertise and talent needed for planning and executing at the stage where creative execution brings marketing strategies to life. There are two basic models for the relationship between agencies and their clients: adversarial or partnering. The former is too common; the latter is certainly preferred.

CONTEMPORARY ISSUES

DOWN AND OUT ON MADISON AVENUE: COMMISSIONS GIVE WAY TO FEES AND INCENTIVES

The 1990s are all about lean and mean. As major corporations downsize, they learn that tighter cost controls can ensure survival. Agencies have gotten the message: when advertisers are struggling themselves to maintain profit margins in the neighborhood of 10 to 12 percent, traditional 15 percent media commissions seem wholly unreasonable. As a result, advertisers and agencies are moving more toward fee- and incentive-based programs, in which agencies receive compensation in direct relation to their creative input and their impact on sales or other concrete marketing objectives. Tom Eppes, president of Price/McNabb Advertising in Charlotte, North Carolina, favors this value-added approach to agency compensation: "We eliminated commissions as a choice for agency compensation. Now we offer only one compensation program: hourly fees."

The move to fee-based compensation also helps to ensure the long-term relationship between advertiser and agency. Many firms that had seen lean years during the last recession, such as Apple Computer, have received generous concessions from their agencies of record as the firms have struggled near the breakeven point.

Keith Reinhard, chair and CEO at DDB Needham Worldwide, New York, agrees that the traditional 15 percent commission for media buys is outdated and not responsive to clients' needs: "We should find ways to be compensated for our core competency in brand-building communications instead of how much media we can buy. We need a results-based program agreed to by the client and agency so everybody knows what they should be expecting and there's no arguing over how many ads you run." At long last, it seems that agencies may be compensated according to what they can do for the client.

Sources: "Driving Home a Point," *Sales & Marketing Management*, August 1995, 104; and "Big Profits, Risks, with Incentive Fees," *Advertising Age*, May 15, 1995, 3.

SUMMARY

❶ Describe the basic components of an advertising plan.

An advertising plan is motivated by the marketing planning process and provides the direction that ensures proper implementation of an advertising campaign. An advertising plan incorporates decisions about the segments to be tar- geted, communications and/or sales objectives with respect to these segments, and salient message appeals. The plan should also specify the dollars budgeted for the campaign, the media that will be employed to deliver the messages, and the measures that will be relied on to assess the campaign's effectiveness.

② Compare and contrast two fundamental approaches for setting advertising objectives.

Setting appropriate objectives is a crucial step in developing any advertising plan. These objectives are typically stated in terms of communications or sales goals. Both types of goals have their proponents, and the appropriate type of objectives to emphasize will vary with the situation. Communications objectives feature goals like building brand awareness or reinforcing consumers' beliefs about a brand's key benefits. Sales objectives are just that: they hold advertising directly responsible for increasing sales of a brand.

③ Explain various methods for setting advertising budgets.

Perhaps the most challenging aspect of any advertising campaign is arriving at a proper budget allocation. Companies and their advertising agencies work with several different methods to arrive at an advertising budget. A percentage-of-sales approach is a simple but naive way to deal with this issue. In the share-of-voice approach, the activities of key competitors are factored into the budget-setting process. A variety of quantitative models may also be used for budget determination. The objective-and-task approach is difficult to implement, but with practice it is likely to yield the best value for a firm's advertising dollars.

④ Discuss the role of the advertising agency in formulating an advertising plan.

An advertising plan will be a powerful tool when firms partner with their advertising agencies in its development. The firm can lead this process by doing its homework with respect to marketing strategy development and objective setting. The agency can then play a key role in managing the preparation and placement phases of ad campaign execution.

KEY TERMS

advertising plan (216)
situation analysis (216)
industry analysis (218)
market analysis (220)
competitor analysis (220)
top-of-the-mind awareness (221)
purchase intent (222)

repeat purchase (222)
percentage-of-sales approach (224)
unit-of-sales approach (225)
share of voice (225)
advertising response function (226)
objective-and-task approach (226)
build-up analysis (227)

QUESTIONS FOR REVIEW AND CRITICAL THINKING

1. Explain the connection between marketing strategies and advertising plans. What is the role of target segments in making this connection?

2. Describe five key elements in a situation analysis and provide an example of how each of these elements may ultimately influence the final form of an advertising campaign.

3. How would it ever be possible to justify anything other than sales growth as a proper objective for an advertising campaign? Is it possible that advertising could be effective yet not yield growth in sales?

4. What types of objectives would you expect to find in an ad plan that featured direct response advertising?

5. Write an example of a workable advertising objective that would be appropriate for a product like Crest Tartar Control toothpaste.

6. In what situations would share of voice be an important consideration in setting an advertising budget? What are the drawbacks of trying to incorporate share of voice in budgeting decisions?

7. What is it about the objective-and-task method that makes it the preferred approach for the sophisticated advertiser? Describe how build-up analysis is used in implementing the objective-and-task method.

8. Briefly discuss the appropriate role to be played by advertising agencies and their clients in the formulation of marketing and advertising plans.

EXPERIENTIAL EXERCISE

In this chapter you read about the role of industry analysis in marketing and advertising planning. Divide into teams and select one product category, such as soft drinks, fast foods, vitamin supplements, health foods, or athletic footwear. Identify the external variables that tend to impact that industry. Assign the variables to group members. Describe how each variable should be monitored by industry advertisers. Find one newspaper or magazine article that examines a variable you have targeted, and discuss the significance of the article for your industry.

USING THE INTERNET

A successful advertising plan should include an integrated marketing communications strategy. The following companies have extensive advertising budgets allocated across multiple media vehicles. Explore the following sites and determine the creative style and type of information available at each site:

Budweiser: www.budweiser.com

Guess: www.guess.com

Jeep: www.jeepunpaved.com

NBA: www.nba.com

For each site, answer the following questions:

1.   From your experience with past and current promotions for the company or organization, how does the site fit with all of these communications? Are there similarities? Differences? Does the site reinforce the promotions? Does it offer additional information?

2.   In what ways are the differences you have noticed between the site and other media due to the different characteristics of the Internet itself?

3.   Create a personal standard for advertising quality by listing several criteria that apply to different media. Compare the quality of the Web site with that of promotions in other media. In your judgment, did the company or organization allocate too much, too little, or just the right amount of resources on its Web site?

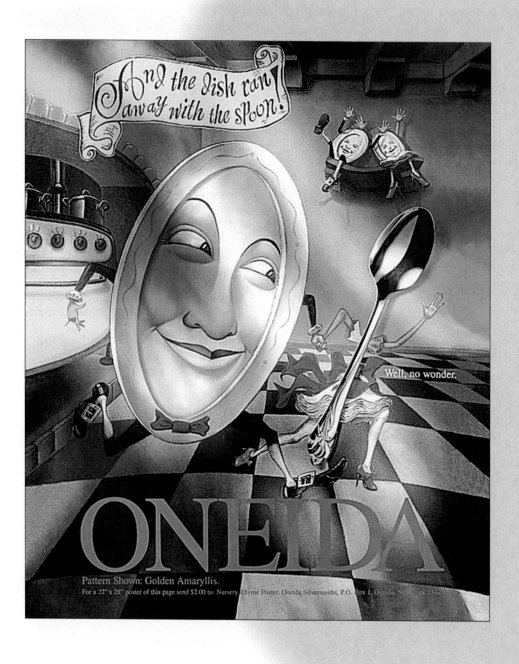

Chapter 9

Advertising Planning: An International Perspective

After reading and thinking about this chapter, you will be able to do the following:

1 Explain the types of audience research that are useful for understanding cultural barriers that can interfere with effective communication.

2 Identify three distinctive challenges that complicate the execution of advertising in international settings.

3 Describe the three basic types of advertising agencies that can assist in the placement of advertising around the world.

4 Discuss the advantages and disadvantages of globalized versus localized advertising campaigns.

In the movie *Pulp Fiction,* two famous consumers discuss the finer points of cross-cultural consumption:

JULES: What'd they call it?
VINCENT: They call it a Royale with Cheese.
JULES: (repeating) Royale with Cheese.
VINCENT: Yeah, that's right.
JULES: What'd they call a Big Mac?
VINCENT: Well, Big Mac's a Big Mac, but they call it Le Big Mac.
JULES: Le Big Mac. What do they call a Whopper?
VINCENT: I dunno, I didn't go to a Burger King. But you know what they put on French Fries in Holland instead of ketchup?
JULES: What?
VINCENT: Mayonnaise.[1]

As Vincent explained to Jules, "There, it's a little different." "There" has its own culture. If you want to advertise "there," you must pay attention to "there's" culture.

International advertising is advertising that reaches across national and cultural boundaries. Unfortunately, a great deal of international advertising in the past was nothing more than translations of domestic advertising. Oftentimes, these translations were at best ineffective, at worst offensive. The day has passed, however—if there ever was such a day—when advertisers based in industrialized nations could simply "do a foreign translation" of their ads. Today, international advertisers must pay greater attention to local cultures. While this chapter is written by Americans, we have tried hard to write about advertising from an international perspective. We argue that the real issue is not nations, but national cultures.

As we said in Chapter 5, culture is a set of values, rituals, and behaviors that define a way of life. Culture is typically invisible to those who are immersed within it. Communicating *across* cultures is not easy. It is, in fact, one of the most difficult of all communication tasks, largely because there is no such thing as culture-free communication. Advertising is a cultural product; it means nothing outside of culture. Culture surrounds advertising, informs it, gives it meaning. To transport an ad across cultural borders, one must respect, and hopefully understand, the power of culture.

This chapter augments and extends the advertising planning framework offered in Chapter 8. We add some necessary international planning tools along with a discussion of the special challenges found in advertising around the world.

Ads ask consumers to do something. Ads depend on effective communication, and effective communication depends on shared meaning. The degree of shared meaning is significantly affected by cultural membership. When an advertiser in culture X wants to communicate with consumers in culture Y, it is culture Y that will surround the created message, form its cultural context, and significantly affect how it will be interpreted.

Some few, rare products and brands may belong to a global consumer culture more than to any one national culture. Such brands travel well, as do their ads, because there is already common cultural ground on which to build effective advertising. The Apple computer and McDonald's ads in Exhibits 9.1 and 9.2 provide examples of brands with this kind of appeal. Apple may be thought of as a truly global product because it is part of a product category forged at a time when technology created its own culture, fairly independent of national boundaries. McDonald's, although clearly an American product, has become a part of the global landscape, thus facilitating a global image. Such brands, however, are few and far between, and as global as they may be, they are still affected by the local culture as to their use and, ultimately, their meaning.

1.   Quentin Tarantino, *Pulp Fiction: A Quentin Tarantino Screenplay* (New York: Miramax Books and Hyperion, 1994), 14–15.

International advertising requires that an advertising message and appeal for a brand be adapted to the cultural context where the ad is being run. Some brands, however, like Apple and McDonald's, belong to a more global consumer culture. These global brands travel well, and their advertising requires far less local-culture adaptation, except for language considerations. www.apple.com/ *and* www.mcdonalds.com/

The Pepsi Challenge in Brazil: Confronting a Global Brand

Consider this cross-cultural advertising challenge: Your major competitor has 88 percent of the market; you have 7 percent. The market has a history of loyalty to your competitor; you're considered an upstart. Although you have made recent market gains, your competitor claims that the gains are merely a result of its inability to keep up with demand. Welcome to the battle between Pepsi and Coke, the dominant market leader, in the $6 billion Brazilian soft drink market.

The stakes in the Brazilian cola market are indeed high. Brazil is not only a huge market—it ranks as the world's fourth largest in soft drink consumption—but also a young market. More than 30 percent of Brazil's population is between 10 and 24 years old—the prime cola-drinking age. These youthful consumers, if captured now, may be brand loyal for a lifetime.

Pepsi has an enormous challenge. Coca-Cola has carefully nurtured massive market share over decades. So much so that when a person in Brazil asks for *uma coca,* it doesn't mean "a cola" to most Brazilians, it means "a Coke." What's more, Coke is in no way complacent. It regularly launches $40 to $50 million advertising campaigns in Brazil to defend market share. What can Pepsi do, and why does Pepsi think that challenging Coke in the Brazilian market is even feasible?

Brazil is in the midst of a massive economic revolution that is changing the lives and lifestyles of most Brazilians. The Brazilian government's economic reform program—called the "plan *real*" after the new monetary unit, the *real,* on which it is based—has brought inflation down from more than 1,000 percent a year into single digits. The removal of this "inflation tax" has given Brazilians a new standard of living. To the extent that Pepsi's advertising appeal can be wrapped up in this social change, Pepsi may have an opportunity to create common cultural ground between a brand known for youth and irreverence and a culture in the midst of dramatic change.

In 1995, Pepsi started a massive $500 million marketing and advertising offensive to gain the loyalty of the 145 million prime cola drinkers. The campaign takes an integrated marketing communications approach—advertising, sales promotions, support media, and public relations. The program is anchored by 20 television commercials produced by the Brazilian ad agency Almap BBDO in São Paulo. This $100 million TV campaign employs ads featuring young people touting the recent changes in Brazil. Each television ad ends with the same shot—a Brazilian teen holding up a can of Pepsi and speaking the tag line of the ad, "Now we have a choice."[2] Another part of the campaign is the print ad in Exhibit 9.3, which connects Brazil's cultural change with Pepsi.

Pepsi's challenge is formidable. Coca-Cola is one of the most highly respected marketing and advertising organizations in the world, with more than 70 percent of its $16 billion in annual sales coming from markets outside the United States.[3] Some argue that Coke is one of the few brands that is part of a global consumer culture. In the view

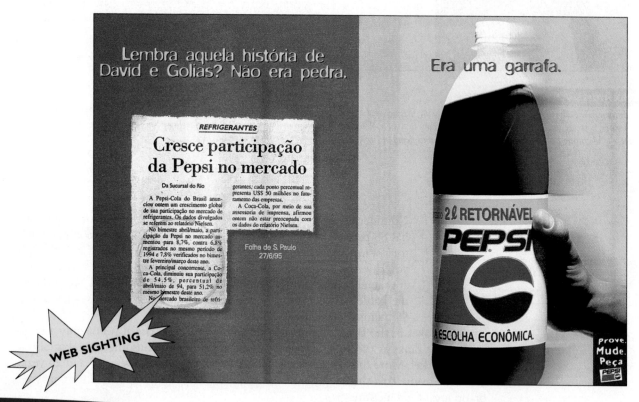

EXHIBIT 9.3

As an example of international advertising, how does this Pepsi ad take advantage of the particular cultural and economic conditions in Brazil? Does the use of an integrated marketing communications approach have special considerations when implemented in international markets? How do Pepsi and Coca-Cola expand upon integrated marketing communications at their Web sites **www.pepsi.com/** *and* **www.cocacola.com/?**

2.   Claudia Penteado, "Pepsi's Brazil Blitz," *Advertising Age,* January 16, 1995, 12.
3.   "In Japan, Coke Is Still It," *International Herald Tribune,* July 18, 1995, 15.

of Coca-Cola strategists, there is enough homogeneity across cultures that the look and feel of both the product and the advertising for Coke can be highly standardized, with a few minor adaptations. For example, as adaptations, Coca-Cola uses Coke Lite as a brand name instead of Diet Coke in countries where the word *diet* is legally restricted for commercial use, due to medical connotations. Coke also uses a slightly sweeter formula for the syrup in Middle Eastern markets to accommodate local tastes.

What is important, though, is that Coca-Cola has a global perspective whereby the entire world is viewed as a market, and the product and advertising planning proceeds from that premise. Coca-Cola may be the ultimate global brand, with more loyalty around the world than any other. Just ask the folks at Pepsi.

Overcoming Cultural Barriers

Global trade initiatives like the General Agreement on Tariffs and Trade (GATT) and the European Union (EU) are designed to facilitate trade and economic development on a worldwide basis. These initiatives signal the emergence of international markets that are larger, more accessible, and perhaps more homogeneous. In the midst of this trend toward more and more international trade, marketers are redefining the nature and scope of the markets for their goods and services, which, in turn, redefines the nature and scope of advertising and the advertising planning effort. This means that firms must be more sensitive to the social and economic differences of individual international markets.

For giant firms like Colgate-Palmolive and Procter & Gamble, an international perspective is essential. These two consumer goods firms now realize 64 percent and 55 percent of their respective sales outside North America.[4] They also expect that nearly 60 percent of their revenue growth will come from outside the United States by the year 2000. With more access to established international markets and multiple emerging markets, firms of all types are cultivating markets outside their domestic one.

Today, most marketers consider their markets to extend beyond national boundaries and across cultural boundaries. Hence, advertisers must come to terms with how they are going to effectively overcome cultural barriers in trying to communicate around the world.

Barriers to Successful International Advertising

Adopting an international perspective is often difficult for marketers. The reason is that experiences gained over a career and a lifetime create a cultural "comfort zone"—that is, one's own cultural values, experiences, and knowledge serve as a subconscious guide for decision making and behavior. International advertisers are particularly beset with this problem. Managers must overcome two related biases to be successful in international markets. **Ethnocentrism** is the tendency to view and value things from the perspective of one's own culture. A **self-reference criterion (SRC)** is the unconscious reference to one's own cultural values, experiences, and knowledge as a basis for decisions. These biases are primary obstacles to success when conducting marketing and advertising planning that demands a cross-cultural perspective.

A decision maker's SRC and ethnocentrism can inhibit the ability to sense important cultural distinctions between markets. This in turn can blind advertisers to their own culture's "fingerprints" on the ads they've created. Sometimes these are offensive or, at a minimum, markers of "outsider" influence. Outsiders aren't always welcome; other times, they just appear ignorant.

For example, AT&T's "Reach Out and Touch Someone" advertising campaign was viewed as much too sentimental for most European audiences. Similarly, AT&T's "Call USA" campaign, aimed at Americans doing business in Europe, was negatively perceived

4.   Zachary Schiller, "Ed Artzt's Elbow Grease Has P&G Shining," *Business Week,* October 10, 1994.

by many Europeans. The ad featured a harried American businessman whose language skills were so poor that he could barely ask for assistance in a busy French hotel to find a telephone. European businesspeople are typically fluent in two or three languages and have enough language competence to ask for a telephone. This ad, with its portrayal of Americans as culturally inept and helpless, created a negative association for AT&T among European businesspeople. Granted, the target market was Americans assigned to foreign markets, but the perspective of the ad was still decidedly ethnocentric and offensive to Europeans.

The most effective way to counteract the negative influences that ethnocentrism and SRC can have on international decision making is to constantly be sensitive to potential differences between cultures. To avoid errors in advertising planning, it is necessary to conduct cross-cultural analysis in an attempt to isolate key differences. There is no substitute for careful audience research as the primary means for overcoming cultural barriers.

Cross-Cultural Audience Research

Analyzing audiences in international markets can be a humbling task. If firms have worldwide product distribution networks—as do Revlon, Unilever, and Philip Morris—then international audience analysis will require dozens of separate analyses. There really is no way to avoid the task of specific audience analysis. This typically involves research in each different country, generally from a local research supplier. There are, however, good secondary resources that may provide broad-based information to advertisers about international markets. The U.S. Department of Commerce has an International Trade Administration (ITA) division that helps companies based in the United States develop foreign market opportunities for their products and services. The ITA publishes specialized reports that cover most of the major markets in the world and provide economic and regulatory information. The United Nations Statistical Yearbook is another source of general economic and population data. The yearbook, published annually, provides information for more than 200 countries. This type of source provides some helpful information for the international advertiser. Unfortunately, it's rarely enough.

An international audience analysis will also involve evaluation of economic conditions; demographic characteristics; values; custom and ritual; and product use and preferences.

Economic Conditions.

One way to think about the economic conditions of a potential international audience is to break the world's markets into three broad classes of economic development: less-developed countries, newly industrialized countries, and highly industrialized countries. These categories provide a basic understanding of the economic capability of the average consumer in a market and thus help place consumption in the context of economic realities.

Less-developed countries represent nearly 75 percent of the world's population. Some of these countries are plagued by drought and civil war, and their economies lack almost all the resources necessary for development: capital, infrastructure, political stability, and trained workers. Many of the products sold in these less-developed economies are typically not consumer products, but rather business products used for building infrastructure (such as heavy construction equipment) or agricultural equipment.

Newly industrialized countries have economies defined by change; they are places where traditional ways of life that have endured for centuries are changing and modern consumer cultures have emerged in a few short years. This creates a very particular set of problems for the outside advertiser trying to hit a moving target, or a culture in rapid flux. Tremendous economic growth in countries such as South Korea, Singapore, Hong Kong, and Taiwan has created a new middle class of consumers with radically different expectations than their counterparts of a mere decade ago.

Achieving compound economic growth rates of 8 to 9 percent over the past three decades, many Asian nations have followed Japan in performing a feat never before seen: combining fast growth in the early stages of economic takeoff with an increase, rather than a decline, in income equality. Asian consumers are relatively heavy users of media-based information. The latest global trends in fashion, music, and travel have shorter and shorter lag times in reaching this region of the world. Also, many U.S. firms already have a strong presence in these markets with both their products and their advertising. The Tropicana brand shown in Exhibit 9.4 is well known throughout Southeast Asia.

The **highly industrialized countries** of the world are the countries with both a high GNP (as shown in Exhibit 9.5) and a high standard of living. These countries have also invested heavily over many years in infrastructure—roads, hospitals, airports, power-generating plants, and educational institutions. Within this broad grouping, an audience assessment will focus on more-detailed analyses of the market, including the nature and extent of competition, marketing trade channels, lifestyle trends, and market potential. Firms pursuing opportunities in highly industrialized countries proceed with market analysis in much the same way it would be conducted in the United States. While the advertising in these countries will often vary based on unique cultural and lifestyle factors, consumers in these markets are accustomed to seeing a full range of creative appeals for goods and services.

EXHIBIT 9.4

This ad for Tropicana exemplifies the rapid changes occurring in many Southeast Asian countries. Traditional values are giving way to a focus on consumption and consumer culture.

Demographic Characteristics. Information on the demographic characteristics of nations is generally available. Both the U.S. Department of Commerce and the United Nations publish annual studies of population for hundreds of countries. Advertisers must be sensitive to the demographic similarities and differences in international markets. The demographics of a population, including size of population, age distribution, income distribution, education levels, occupations, literacy rates, and household size, can dramatically affect the type of advertising prepared for a market. Large-scale demographic trends are important to advertisers. For example, those thinking of entering international markets should keep in mind that roughly 20 percent of the world's population, generally residing in the highly industrialized countries, controls 75 percent of the world's wealth and accounts for 75 percent of all consumption.[5]

Country	GNP ($ in billions)
United States	$5,695
Japan	3,370
Germany	1,586
France	1,191
Italy	1,128
United Kingdom	1,106
Canada	570
Spain	522
Brazil	395
Netherlands	287
Australia	282
Switzerland	243
Mexico	234
Sweden	231
Belgium/Luxembourg	213

Source: *The World Competitiveness Report 1993* (IMD and the World Economic Forum).

EXHIBIT 9.5

World economies ranked by GNP in U.S. dollars, 1991.

While much has been written about the graying of the U.S. population, other parts of the world do not follow this pattern. In the Middle East, Africa, and Latin America, roughly 40 percent of the population is currently under the age of 20.[6] Increases and decreases in the proportion of the population in specific age groups are closely related to the demand for particular products and services. As populations continue to increase in developing countries, new market opportunities emerge for products and services for young families and children. Similarly, as advanced-age groups continue to increase in countries with stable population rates, the demand for consumer products and services such as health aids, health care, travel services, and retirement planning will also increase.

One of the most interesting demographic evolutions is taking place in Asian countries. By the year 2010, an additional 400 million people will be born in the Pacific Rim region. While the current demographic profile shows a relatively young population, by the year 2000, 30 percent of the population will be in their 30s and 40s and will have migrated from rural to urban areas. In just 30 years, South Korea's population has flip-flopped to 73 percent urban from 72 percent rural.[7] Advertising messages must accommodate the new experiences of the now urban and middle-age audiences. In addition, advertising strategies must place ads in media that efficiently reach these audiences.

Values. Cultural values are enduring beliefs about what is important to the members of a culture. They are the defining bedrock of a culture. They are an outgrowth of the culture's history and its collective experience. One of America's core values is individualism, or the sanctity of the individual. America's history is replete with examples of valuing the individual over the group. Many other cultures, however, value the group, or the collective. If the values of the group conflict with the values of the individual, the individual is expected to set aside his or her own desires. One such culture is Japan, where organizational loyalty and social interdependence are values that promote a group mentality.

5.   Clive Cook, "Catching Up," in *The World in 1994,* a special issue of *The Economist,* Winter 1993, 15–16.
6.   Adapted from Richard Sookdeo, "The New Global Consumer," *Fortune,* Autumn/Winter 1993, 68–79.
7.   Ford S. Worthy, "A New Mass Market Emerges," *Fortune,* Fall 1991.

Japanese consumers are much more sensitive to appeals that feature stability, longevity, and reliability, and they find appeals using competitive comparisons to be confrontational and inappropriate.[8]

This continuum from individualism to collectivism is one of the more stable and dependably observed cultural differences among the peoples of the world. Exhibits 9.6 and 9.7 show two ads that reflect this issue. The scotch ad in Exhibit 9.6 shows an appeal to individualism; it ran in the United States. The IBM ad shown in Exhibit 9.7 reflects a collectivist approach; it ran in Korea. Scotch certainly has a social component in actual use, and computers are not typically considered group products by Americans. But IBM, advertising in a collectivist culture, adapted its message accordingly.[9]

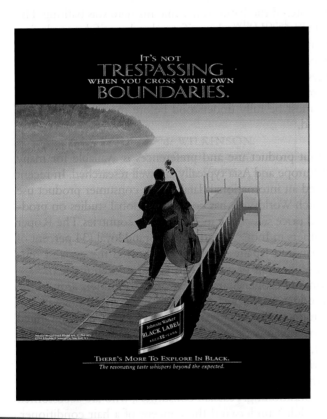

EXHIBIT 9.6

Individualism is a core value in U.S. culture and is reflected by the message theme of the Johnnie Walker ad. In contrast, the IBM ad in Exhibit 9.7, which ran in Korea, appeals to the collectivist nature of that culture's values.

EXHIBIT 9.7 *How does the IBM ad shown here underscore the collectivist values important to Korean consumers? Even if you don't read Korean, what is it about the ad that communicates these values right away? How do IBM and Apple offer country-specific choices at their Web sites* **www.ibm.com** *and* **www.apple.com***? Which is more effective? Why?*

8.   Johny Johanson, "The Sense of Nonsense: Japanese TV Advertising," *Journal of Advertising* (March 1994): 17–26.
9.   S. Han and S. Shavitt, "Persuasion and Culture: Advertising Appeals in Individualistic and Collectivistic Societies," *Journal of Experimental Social Psychology* 30 (1994): 326–350.

market, the firm ran into a fairly severe language problem. The word *mist* spelled and pronounced precisely the same way in German means "manure." The word *stick* translates roughly as "wand." Sunbeam was attempting to introduce a "manure wand" for use in German food preparation.[13]

What is less obvious, however, is the role of **picturing** in cross-cultural communication. There is a widely held belief that pictures are less culturally bound than are words, and that pictures can speak to many cultures at once. International advertisers are increasingly using ads that feature few words and rely on pictures to communicate. This is, as you might expect, a bit more complicated than it sounds.

First, picturing *is* culturally bound. Different cultures use different conventions or rules to create representations (or pictures) of things. People living in Western cultures assume that everyone knows what a certain picture means. This is not true and is another example of ethnocentrism. Photographic two-dimensional representations are not even recognizable as pictures to those who have not learned to interpret such representations. Symbolic representations that seem so absolute, common, and harmless in one culture can have varied, unusual, and even threatening meaning in another. A picture may be worth a thousand words, but those words may not mean something appropriate —or they may be entirely unintelligible—to those in another culture. Think about the ads in Exhibits 9.10 through 9.13. Which of these ads seem culture bound? Which would seem to easily cross cultural borders? Why?

CONTEMPORARY ISSUES

PIRELLI TIRES: OLYMPIC GOLD MEDALIST ANCHORS GLOBAL AD CAMPAIGN

It's rare to find a standardized global advertisement. After all, successful global advertising must be free of self-reference criteria to transcend the barriers of language and culture. How then do multinational corporations develop messages that play to a worldwide audience? The phenomenon of international sporting events and the adulation of sport heroes worldwide forge a link between cultures through shared meaning and experience. Therein lies the opportunity for a global campaign from Pirelli tires. Olympic track and field star Carl Lewis is recognized around the globe as an uncompromising competitor, and he serves to energize Pirelli's global theme as the physical embodiment of both power and control. The firm's slogan also succeeds on several levels. "Power Is Nothing without Control" translates well in many languages and illustrates the functional purpose (control) of Pirelli's line of high-performance tires. Appeals such as this prove effective in a global campaign when they stir the heart and surmount cross-cultural barriers.

All of these ads depend on knowing the way to correctly interpret the ad, but some require more cultural knowledge than others. For example, if the audience doesn't know the story of the dish who ran away with the spoon, then the Oneida ad in Exhibit 9.12 is probably not as engaging as it otherwise might be. Do you have to know who Tiny Tim was to understand the ad for Kenwood? What does giving a rose mean in other cultures?

A few human expressions, such as a smile, are widely accepted to mean a positive feeling. Such expressions and their representations, even though culturally connected, have widespread commonality. But cultureless picture meanings do not exist. A much larger contributor to cross-cultural commonalities is those representations that are a part of a far-flung culture of commerce and have thus taken on similar meanings in many different nations. With sports playing an ever-larger role in international commerce, the sports hero is often used to symbolize common meaning across cultural boundaries. The Contemporary Issues box on this page reflects this approach with an Olympic hero who has gained a global following.

13.   David Ricks, *Big Business Blunders: Mistakes in Multi-National Marketing* (Homewood, Ill.: Dow Jones–Irwin, 1983), 66.

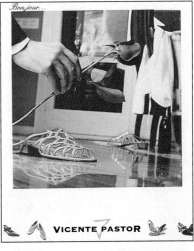

EXHIBITS 9.10 TO 9.13

Which of these ads seem bound to their national cultures, based on the pictures used in the ads? Which feature pictures that are less culturally bound? www.kenwoodcorp.com/ *and* www .oneida.com/ *and* www.piper.heidsieck.com/

The Media Challenge

Of all the challenges faced by advertisers in international markets, the media challenge may be the greatest. Exhibit 9.14 shows many of the best options for reaching consumers around the world.

Media Availability and Coverage.

Some international markets simply have too few media options. In addition, even if diverse media are available in a particular international market, there may be severe restrictions on the type of advertising that can be done or the way in which advertising is organized in a certain medium.

Many countries have dozens of subcultures and language dialects within their borders, each with its own newspapers and radio stations. This complicates the problem of deciding which combination of newspapers or radio stations will achieve the desired coverage of the market. The presence of a particular medium in a country does not necessarily make it useful for advertisers if there are restrictions on accepting advertising. The most prominent example is the BBC networks in the United Kingdom, where advertising is still not accepted. While the UK does have commercial networks in both radio and television, the BBC stations are still widely popular. Or consider the situation with regard to television advertising in Germany and the Netherlands. On the German government-owned stations, television advertising is banned on Sundays and holidays and restricted to four five-minute blocks on other days. In the Netherlands, television advertising cannot constitute more than 5 percent of total programming time, and most time slots must be purchased nearly a year in advance. Similar circumstances exist in many markets around the world.

Newspapers are actually the most localized media worldwide, and they require the greatest amount of local market knowledge to be correctly used as an advertising option. In Mexico, for example, advertising space is sold in the form of news columns, without any notice or indication that the "story" is a paid advertisement. This situation influences both the placement and layout of ads. Turkey has more than 350 daily national newspapers, but the Netherlands has only three. Further, many newspapers (particularly regional papers) are positioned in the market based on a particular political philosophy. Advertisers must be aware of this, making certain that their product's position with the target audience is not in conflict with the politics of the medium.

The best news for advertisers from the standpoint of media availability and coverage is the emergence of several global television networks made possible by satellite technology. MTV estimates its worldwide audience to be more than 250 million viewers and expects its coverage to reach 600 million by the year 2000. CNN, the worldwide news network, can be seen in 100 countries; it offers newly acquired access to the vast Indian market.[14]

Another recent development affecting Europe and Asia is direct broadcast by satellite (DBS). DBS transmissions are received by households through a small, low-cost receiving dish. STAR TV, which stands for Satellite Televisions Asian Region, currently sends BBC and U.S. programming to 17 million Asian households and hotels. Ultimately, STAR TV could reach 3 billion people, making it the most widely viewed medium in the world.[15] An ad for one of STAR TV's competitors in the Asian market is shown in Exhibit 9.15.

Additionally, as suggested by the New Media box on page 250, global expansion of the Internet may one day offer advertisers economical access to huge new markets.

Media Costs and Pricing.

Confounding the media challenge is the issue of media costs and pricing. As discussed earlier, some markets have literally hundreds of media options (recall the 350 Turkish newspapers). Whenever a different medium is chosen, separate payment and placement must be made. Additionally, in many markets, media prices are subject to

14.   Todd Pruzan, "Global Media: Distribution Slows but Rates Climb," *Advertising Age International,* January 16, 1995, I-19; and "India Will Allow CNN Broadcasts," July 1–2, 1995, 9.
15.   Thomas McCarroll, "New Star over Asia," *Time,* August 9, 1993, 53.

EXHIBIT 9.14

Advertising Age International's global media lineup.

Media and Location	Total Worldwide Distribution		
	1995	1994	Change
DAILIES			
The Financial Times, London	294,217	292,248	+0.7%
International Herald Tribune,			
Neuilly-sur-Seine, France*	n/a	188,711	n/a
Nihon Keizai Shimbun, Tokyo	2,870,268	n/a	n/a
USA Today International, New York[†]	2,098,157	2,106,705	−0.4%
The Wall Street Journal, New York	3,563,811	2,937,059	+21.3%
The Yomiuri Shimbun, Tokyo	10,230,000	10,230,000	0%
WEEKLIES			
Business Week, New York[†]	993,000	987,000	+0.6%
ComputerWorld, Boston[‡]	1.7 million	n/a	n/a
The Economist, London	598,501	568,683	+5.2%
The Guardian Weekly, London	106,577	104,688	+1.8%
L'Express, Paris[§]	n/a	547,837	n/a
Le Point, Paris[§]	n/a	305,388	n/a
Madame Figaro, Paris	990,000	n/a	n/a
Time, New York	5,604,281	5,705,830	−1.8%
MONTHLIES			
Cosmopolitan, New York[‖]	4,700,597	5,755,795	−18.3%
Elle, Levallois Perret, France	4,819,899	4,788,843	+0.9%
Esquire, New York[‖]	683,143	1,207,478	−43.4%
Good Housekeeping, New York[‖]	6,052,577	5,715,865	+5.9%
MacWorld, Boston	860,000	n/a	n/a
Marie Claire, Issy-les–Moulineaux, France[‖]	2,795,633	n/a	n/a
National Geographic, Washington	8,812,000	9,138,000	−3.6%
Network World, Boston[#]	620,000	n/a	n/a
PC World, Boston	2.8 million	n/a	n/a
Reader's Digest, Pleasantville, New York	27,322,000	26,954,000	+1.4%
Redbook, New York[‖]	3,760,824	3,826,869	−1.7%
Scientific American, New York	733,716	755,138	−2.8%
The WorldPaper, Boston	776,000	262,000	+196.2%
OTHER PRINT			
Fortune, New York	878,822	917,921	−4.3%
TV			
CNN International, Atlanta[†]	133.4 million	118 million	+13.1%
Cartoon Network International,			
Atlanta[†]	58.9 million	34.4 million	+71.2%
CMT: Country Music Television,			
New York	41.3 million	34.8 million	+18.7%
The Discovery Channel, Bethesda, Md.	90 million	85 million	+5.9%
Dow Jones' ABN and EBN networks,			
New York	23 million	n/a	n/a
ESPN, New York	166.45 million	137.7 million	+20.9%
MTV: Music Television, New York[†]	163.8 million	134.1 million	+22.1%
NBC, New York**	231.5 million	212.5 million	+8.9%
TNT International, Atlanta[†]	100.6 million	84.5 million	+19.1%
USA Networks and the Sci-Fi			
Channel, New York[††]	108.9 million	82.9 million	+31.4%

Data unavailable from BBC Worldwide TV, GEMS TV, *Harper's Bazaar,* Middle East Broadcasting Centre, *Runner's World.* *Latest circulation figures available are 1994. [†]Europe and Middle East/Africa figures are combined. 1995 *USA Today International* worldwide circulation is an estimate. [‡]Bi-monthly distribution in selected markets. [§]North America figures include Latin America. Latest circulation figures available are 1994. [‖]U.S. ad rates given. Rates vary by country. [#]Weekly distribution in selected markets. **Includes CNBC. Europe includes Middle East. [††]Total gross buy across both networks.

Source: *Advertising Age International,* February 12, 1996, I-10. Reprinted with permission from the February 12, 1996, issue of *Advertising Age International.* Copyright © Crain Communications Inc. 1996.

negotiation—no matter what the official rate cards say. The time needed to negotiate these rates is a tremendous cost in and of itself.

Global coverage is an expensive proposition. For example, a four-color ad in *Readers Digest* costs nearly half a million dollars.[16] Should the advertiser desire to achieve full impact in *Readers Digest,* then the ad should be prepared in all twenty of the different languages for the international editions—again, generating substantial expense.

Aside from the absolute cost of media for global coverage, a recent study shows that media costs in nine international markets are rising at a rate of 10 to 15 percent annually —a rate of increase even greater than in the United States.[17] In some markets, advertising time and space are in such short supply that, regardless of the published rate, a bidding system is used to escalate the prices. As you will see in Chapter 14, media costs represent the majority of costs in an advertising budget. With the seemingly chaotic buying practices in some international markets, media costs are indeed a great challenge.

NEW MEDIA

AFRICA ONLINE: IS THE WORLD WIDE WEB A THIRD-WORLD WHITE ELEPHANT?

The race is on: AT&T has signed on a dozen of the 30 or so nations it needs to launch Africa One, a $2 billion underwater fiber-optic cable network that surrounds the African continent and connects constituent nations to one another and to the World Wide Web. Meanwhile, the 15-year-old Pan African News Agency (PANA) has taken a wireless approach and plans to expand a skeleton satellite network that currently allows bureaus in 13 African nations to send and receive articles instantly. Someday soon, we may freely converse online with our African cousins and welcome them to the cyberfold. Or maybe not. In many regions of sub-Saharan Africa, some 90 percent of individuals have never placed a phone call, let alone connected to the Net via a modem. Even in Africa's most developed nation, South Africa, the stated priorities do not include networks and interactivity. President Nelson Mandela frequently lists the hierarchy of needs for his country, such as basic medical care, schooling, fresh water, and electricity, without mention of either computers or telephones.

Still, many feel that the African voice may be lost in the current information revolution, and that divisions between information societies and the Third World may deepen further. The larger question looming for the next century may prove to be, What will separate the information haves from the have-nots? Babcar Fall, the 43-year-old Senegalese journalist and communications expert given charge of the PANA effort, believes that "without information, there can be no development. It is our hope that this is the beginning of the end of our isolation." Ironically, one possibility for Internet development lies with the explosive growth in advertising on the African continent, as nations relax and remove archaic statutes that formerly banned the practice. Given the infrastructure (courtesy of AT&T, PANA, or others), customized Internet advertising may yet prove to be a motivating force behind Africa online.

Sources: "Advertising's Heart of Darkness," *Advertising Age,* May 15, 1995, 1–10; "Builders of Info-Highway Hope to Reshape Priorities in Africa," *Wall Street Journal,* June 9, 1995, B5B; and "Linked to Internet, Could Africa's Voice Be Heard?" *New York Times,* October 1, 1994, 2.

The Regulatory Challenge

The regulatory restrictions on international advertising are many and varied, reflecting cultural values within markets. The range and specificity of regulation can be aggravatingly complex. Tobacco and liquor advertising are restricted (typically banned from television) in many countries, although several lift their ban on liquor after 9 or 10 P.M. With respect to advertising to children, Austria, Canada, Germany, and the United States have specific regulations. Other products and topics monitored or restricted throughout the world are drugs (Austria, Switzerland, Germany, Greece, and the Netherlands), gambling (United Kingdom, Italy, and Portugal), and religion (Germany, United Kingdom, and the Netherlands).

This regulatory complexity is now spreading to emerging media options. For instance, the European Union is proposing restrictions for the placement of advertising on teleshopping, pay-per-view, and movie-on-demand channels.[18] Generally, advertisers must be sensitive to the fact that advertising regulations can, depending on the international market, impose limitations on the following:

16. Pruzan, I-19
17. Tim Harper, "UK Eyes New Channel to Ease Demand, Prices," *Advertising Age,* May 16, 1988, 68.
18. Bruce Crumley, "EU Proposal May Limit TV Spots," *Advertising Age,* January 9, 1995, 12.

- The types of products that can be advertised
- The types of appeals that can be used
- The times during which ads for certain products can appear on television
- Advertising to children
- The use of foreign languages (and talent) in advertisements
- The use of national symbols, such as flags and government seals, in advertisements
- The taxes levied against advertising expenditures

In short, just about every aspect of advertising can be regulated, and every country has its own peculiarities with respect to ad regulation. More examples of the regulatory differences among nations are featured in Exhibit 9.16 and in the Regulatory Issues box on page 255.

EXHIBIT 9.15

Direct broadcast by satellite allows households to receive television transmissions via a small, low-cost receiving dish. This is an ad for Skyport TV promoting such a dish in the Asian market.

Advertising Agencies around the World

❸ An experienced and astute agency can help an advertiser deal with the creative, media, and regulatory challenges just discussed. In Brazil, using a local agency is essential to get the creative style and tone just right. In Australia, Australian nationals must be involved in certain parts of the production process. And in China, trying to work through the government and media bureaucracy is nearly impossible without the assistance of a local agency.

Advertisers in the United States have three basic alternatives in choosing an agency to help them prepare and place advertising in other countries; they can use a global agency, an international affiliate, or a local agency.

The Global Agency

The consolidation and mergers taking place in the advertising industry are creating more and more **global agencies,** or worldwide agencies. Agencies with a global presence have experienced tremendous revenue growth in the past few years. In 1995 these agencies had one of their best years ever, experiencing 11.4 percent increases in international billings.[19] Two of the largest U.S.-based global agencies are Ogilvy & Mather Worldwide (part of the WPP Group, London), which has 270 offices in 59 countries, and the Omnicom Group headquartered in New York. Omnicom bills more than $2.5 billion annually through its worldwide agencies, which include BBDO Worldwide and DDB Needham Worldwide.

The great advantage of a global agency is that it will know the advertiser's products and current advertising programs (presuming it handles the domestic advertising duties). With this knowledge, the agency can either adapt domestic campaigns for international markets or launch entirely new campaigns. Another advantage is the geographic proximity of advertiser to the agency headquarters, which can often facilitate planning and the preparation of ads. The size of a global agency can be a benefit in terms of economies of scale and political leverage.

19.   R. Craig Endicott, "Shops Soar on Growth of 9.2%, to $17 Billion," *Advertising Age,* April 15, 1996, S-2.

EXHIBIT 9.16

Advertising regulations around the world.

United Kingdom	No television advertising for cigarettes, politics, hypnotists, gambling, religion, or charities. The Independent Broadcasting Authority (IBA) carefully monitors television advertising for "appropriateness." Recently, the major independent television network, ITV, has decided to start running liquor ads. This reverses a long-standing policy.[1]
France	No television advertising for tobacco, alcohol, margarine, or diet products. Tourism outside the country cannot be promoted. Children may be used only in ads for children's products. Supermarket advertising is discouraged (though not illegal) for fear that traditional food shops will suffer.
Germany	There are several volumes of regulation published by the German Advertising Federation (ZAW). Advertising cannot instill fear or promote superstition or discrimination. Children may not be used to promote products. Product claims must be carefully documented. No television advertising for cigarettes, religion, charities, narcotics, or prescription drugs. No advertising of any kind for war-related toys. The German regulatory system can act swiftly and effectively. An advertising campaign (for the Italian clothing firm Benetton) that featured child laborers and an oil-soaked seabird was deemed morally offensive because it exploited "pity for commercial purposes." The ads were immediately banned from print publication.[2]
Italy	Italy is one of the few international markets in which comparative ads are allowed. Testimonial statements must be authenticated. No television advertising for cigarettes, gambling, jewels, furs, clinics, or hospitals.
Sweden	Regulatory constraints in Sweden are hard to pin down. First, the two government-controlled television stations and the three government-controlled radio stations do not accept advertising. The independent media are just starting to evolve within the country, and cable broadcasts are being sent from outside the country. The Swedes do not allow the use of young, attractive models in cigarette advertising.
Brazil	Price advertising is carefully regulated by the Brazilian government. Restrictions on television advertising include no advertising for alcohol, cigarettes, or cigars until after 9 P.M. Nudity in Brazilian ads is unregulated. The Brazilian government is committed to economic growth, and the new, more stable currency is causing tremendous change in the consumption culture. While there are good markets for many U.S. goods, Brazilians frown on ads made by U.S. agencies.
Australia	Restrictions on Australian advertising are fairly basic, with one major exception—the Australian government has mandated that 80 percent of all advertising running in Australia must be created by Australian companies. Deception is subject to regulation. Cigarettes are banned from television advertising.
Japan	For a country of strict rules and regulations, there is much flexibility in the interpretation of advertising regulation—with the exception of comparison and hard-sell advertising. As long as good taste prevails, nudity is permitted. There are no laws governing the use of a product by a spokesperson. The one area of high scrutiny is exaggeration of claims.
China	As we have seen recently with copyright infringement and intellectual property disputes, the regulatory system for commercial transactions in China is still in a state of infancy. The "regulation" of advertising has much more to do with understanding traditions and complying with standard business practice. For example, many media organizations will discriminate against advertisers who use an agency, in an attempt to circumvent agency commissions. Some have been known to refuse to execute a media plan submitted by an agency. Specific restrictions are placed on comparative ads and "slanderous propaganda."

1. Laurel Wentz, "UK TV to Accept Liquor Ads," *Advertising Age,* June 5, 1995, 8.
2. Brandon Mitchener, "German Court Rules against Benetton," *International Herald Tribune,* July 7, 1995, 13.

Their greatest disadvantage stems from their distance from the local culture. Exporting meaning is never easy. This is no small disadvantage to agencies that actually believe they can do this. Most, however, are not that naive or arrogant, and they have procedures for acquiring local knowledge.

The International Affiliate

Many agencies do not own and operate worldwide offices, but rather have established foreign-market **international affiliates** to handle clients' international advertising needs. Many times these agencies join a network of foreign agencies or take minority ownership positions in several foreign agencies. The benefit of this arrangement is that the advertiser typically has access to a large number of international agencies that can provide local market expertise. These international agencies are usually well established and managed by foreign nationals, which gives the advertiser a local presence in the international market, while avoiding any resistance to foreign ownership. This was the reasoning behind Coca-Cola's recent decision to give local creative responsibility for advertising its Coke Classic brand in Europe to the French agency Publicis SA.[20] The agency is the French arm of the New York-based agency McCann-Erickson Worldwide. Although Coke Classic is a global brand, Coke felt that the French agency was better suited to adapt U.S. ad campaigns for European use.

The risk of these arrangements is that while an international affiliate will know the local market, it may be less knowledgeable about the advertiser's brands and competitive strategy. The threat is that the real value and relevance of the brand will not be incorporated into the foreign campaign.

The Local Agency

The final option is for an advertiser to choose a **local agency** in every foreign market where advertising will be carried out. Local agencies have the same advantages as the affiliate agencies just discussed: they will be knowledgeable about the culture and local market conditions. Such agencies tend to have well-established contacts for market information, production, and media buys. But the advertiser that chooses this option is open to administrative problems. There will be duplication of effort. There is less tendency for standardization of the creative effort; each agency in each market will feel compelled to provide a unique creative execution. This lack of standardization can be costly and potentially disastrous. Finally, working with local agencies can create communications problems, which increases the risk of delays and errors in execution.

Globalized versus Localized Campaigns

4 One additional issue must be resolved. This key issue involves the extent to which a campaign will be standardized versus localized across markets. In discussions of this issue, the question is often posed as, How much can the advertiser globalize the advertising? **Globalized campaigns** use the same message and creative execution across all (or most) international markets. Exhibits 9.17 and 9.18 show ads from Jack Daniel's globalized campaign. By contrast, **localized campaigns** involve preparing different messages and creative executions for each foreign market a firm has entered.

The issue is more complex than simply a question of globalized versus localized advertising. Both the brand and its overall marketing strategy must be examined. The marketer must first consider the extent to which the brand can be standardized across markets, and then the extent to which the advertising can be globalized across markets. The degree to which advertising in international markets can use a common appeal, versus whether the ads prepared for each market must be customized, has been a widely debated issue.

20. Daniel Tilles, "Publicis Gets a Sip of Coke Account," *International Herald Tribune,* July 7, 1995, 13.

WEB SIGHTING

Clockwise from top left, that's Jack Daniel, Jess Motlow, Lem Tolley, Frank Bobo and Jess Gamble. (Jimmy's in the middle).

JACK DANIEL'S HEAD DISTILLER, Jimmy Bedford, has lots of folks looking over his shoulder.

Since 1866, we've had only six head distillers. (Every one a Tennessee boy, starting with Mr. Jack Daniel himself.) Like those before him, Jimmy's mindful of our traditions, such as the oldtime way we smooth our whiskey through 10 feet of hard maple charcoal. He knows Jack Daniel's drinkers will judge him with every sip. So he's not about to change a thing. The five gentlemen on his wall surely must be pleased about that.

SMOOTH SIPPIN'
TENNESSEE WHISKEY

Tennessee Whiskey • 40-43% alcohol by volume (80-86 proof) • Distilled and Bottled by Jack Daniel Distillery, Lem Motlow, Proprietor, Route 1, Lynchburg (Pop 361), Tennessee 37352
Placed in the National Register of Historic Places by the United States Government.

飲酒は20歳を過ぎてから

洞穴に湧くこの水と樽を世話するリチャード・マッギー。

それは、テネシーの自然が育んでくれた2つの驚異だ。
ジャック・ダニエル蒸溜所の谷間では、ピュアで鉄分を含まない水が、洞穴の泉から
何百万年もの間、湧き続けている。ウイスキーづくりに理想的なその水を
すくっているのが、マッギー。洞穴の泉ばかりではないが、誰よりも古くから、
誰よりも多く、樽をころがし、ウイスキーの世話を続けている名人だ。
まだ、味わっていない方は、ぜひ、ご一飲を。
テネシーの2つの驚異なしには生まれなかったジャック・ダニエルの
格別な滑らかさを、きっと確かめていただけるに違いない。

JACK DANIEL'S
TENNESSEE WHISKEY
テネシーウイスキー ジャック・ダニエル
容量750㎖・4,600円 希望小売価格(消費税込み) 輸入・販売サントリー株式会社

EXHIBIT 9.17 AND 9.18

Globalized advertising campaigns maintain a highly similar look and feel across international markets. These Jack Daniel's ads from the United States and Japan demonstrate how a global brand can use a global campaign. Can you identify the common themes used in these two ads? The Web site for the company, www.jackdaniels.com/, *continues the same singular theme of focus on the product and company as appropriate for all markets. For more information on how one agency has set up a separate Internet-based division to deal with global brands and campaigns, see Ogilvy & Mather at* www .ogilvy.com/english/index.html.

Those who favor the globalized campaign assume that similarities as well as differences between markets should be taken into account. They argue that standardization of messages should occur whenever possible, adapting the message only when absolutely necessary. For example, Mars's U.S. advertisements for Pedigree dog food use golden retrievers, while poodles are more effective for the brand's positioning and image in Asia. Otherwise, the advertising campaigns are identical in terms of basic message appeal.[21]

Those who argue for the localized approach see each country or region as a unique communication context, and they claim that the only way to achieve advertising success is to develop separate campaigns for each market.

The two fundamental arguments for globalized campaigns are based on potential cost savings and creative advantages. Just as organizations seek to gain economies of scale in production, they also look for opportunities to streamline the communication

---

21.   Zachary Schiller and Rischar A. Melcher, "Marketing Globally, Thinking Locally," *International Business Week,* May 13, 1991, 23.

process. Having one standard theme to communicate allows an advertiser to focus on a uniform brand or corporate image worldwide, develop plans more quickly, and make maximum use of good ideas. Thus, while Gillette sells over 800 different products in more than 200 countries around the world, its corporate philosophy of globalization is expressed in its "Gillette, the Best a Man Can Get" theme. This theme is attached to all ads for men's toiletry products, wherever they appear.[22]

In recent years, several aspects of the global marketplace have changed in such a way that the conditions for globalized campaigns are more favorable. Specifically, these conditions fostering the use of such campaigns are as follows:[23]

- *Global communications.* Worldwide cable networks have resulted in television becoming a truly global communications medium. MTV's 200 European advertisers almost all run English-language-only campaigns in the station's 28-nation broadcast area. These standardized messages will themselves serve to homogenize the viewers within these market areas.
- *The global teenager.* Global communications, global travel, and the demise of communism are argued to have created common norms and values among teenagers around the world. One advertising agency videotaped the rooms of teenagers from 25 countries, and it was hard to tell if the room belonged to an American, German, or Japanese teen. The rooms had soccer balls, Levi's jeans, NBA jackets, and Doc Marten shoes.[24] In response to such similarity, Swatch has created a worldwide campaign aimed at teenagers that uses the same image in all international markets and merely changes the copy in print ads to adapt to language differences.
- *Universal demographic and lifestyle trends.* Demographic and lifestyle trends that emerged in the 1980s in the United States are manifesting themselves in markets around the world. More working women, single-person households, increasing divorce rates, and fewer children per household are now global demographic phenomena that are affecting lifestyles. The rising number of working women in Japan caused Ford Motor Company to prepare ads specifically targeted to this audience.
- *The Americanization of consumption values.* Perhaps of greatest advantage to U.S. advertisers is

REGULATORY ISSUES

DON'T MENTION IT: POSTREVOLUTIONARY REGS RULE IRAN

How do you promote products in a nation that bars women, jokes, English, celebrities, product claims, and any hint of sex whatsoever from its advertising? Marketers in Iran are still trying to figure out how; most current ads have nothing to do with the products, and ads tend to confuse more than promote. "We can't really give information about the products, only the name," says Kamran Katouzian, the managing director of Karpay, Iran's largest advertising firm. "It makes our tasks a bit delicate." Delicate, indeed; Iranian ads for soaps and shampoos show babbling brooks and waterfalls, without a hint of people or product demonstrations. One refrigerator manufacturer, Damavand, took a similar approach to exhibit its wares. "Only nature makes cold like Damavand" was summarily rejected because all things natural are "God's territory." The fix: animated characters featuring a mommy, a daddy, and a baby fridge. The ad copy read, "Like a member of your household."

While the Farsi spoken in Iran is Indo-European in nature, the predominant cultural influence is Islam, and pan-European advertising must be heavily revised to pass the Iranian censors. For instance, an ad for France's Alcatel telephones featuring a man wearing a necktie had to be altered; ties are decidedly unorthodox in Iran. Another advertisement, a public service spot for the National Statistics Center, failed to make it past the censors because the man lacked a mustache and therefore looked Kurdish. All things American are banned by the censors, although teenagers can't get enough of heavy metal and rap music. Without a hint of promotion, naturally.

Source: "Please Don't Show Your Lingerie in Iran, Even If It's for Sale," *Wall Street Journal*, June 21, 1995, A1.

22.   Bill Saporito, "Where the Global Action Is," *Fortune,* Autumn/Winter 1993, 63.
23.   This list is adapted from Henry Assael, *Consumer Behavior and Marketing Action,* 5th ed. (Cincinnati, Ohio: South-Western/International Thomson Publishing, 1995), 491–94.
24.   Shawn Tully, "Teens: The Most Global Market of All," *Fortune,* May 16, 1994, 90.

the Americanization of consumption values around the world. Images of America and American values are gaining popularity worldwide. Europeans find the rugged American image appealing. Russian consumers are eating hamburgers and drinking Budweiser. Japanese consumers are starting to insist on American labels. L. L. Bean shipped more than $100 million of merchandise to Japan in 1994.[25]

All of these forces are creating a communication environment where a common message across national boundaries becomes more valid. To the extent that consumers in various countries hold the same interests and values, standardized images and themes can be effective in advertising.

Arguments against globalization tend to center on issues relating to local market requirements and cultural constraints within markets. The target audiences in different countries must understand and place the same level of importance on brand features or attributes for a globalized campaign to be effective. In many cases, different features are valued at different levels of intensity, making a common message inappropriate. Also, if a globalized campaign defies local customs, values, and regulations, or if it ignores the efforts of local competition, then it has a reduced chance of being successful.

It is sometimes the case that local managers do not appreciate the value of globalized campaigns. Since they did not help create the campaign, they may drag their feet in implementing it. Without the support of local managers, no globalized campaign can ever achieve its potential.

Developing global brands through standardized campaigns can be successful only when advertisers can find similar needs, feelings, or emotions as a basis for communication across cultures. Creating culture-free ads is an impossibility, but the global marketer may be able to draw upon enough commonality to be effective.

Finally, global marketers need to distinguish between strategy and execution when using a global approach to advertising. The basic need identified may well be universal, but communication about the product or service that offers satisfaction of the need may be strongly influenced by cultural values in different markets and thus may work against globalization. Recall the example of AT&T's "Reach Out and Touch Someone" campaign. The campaign was highly successful in the United States in communicating the universal need to keep in touch with loved ones, but it was viewed by European audiences as too sentimental in style and execution. For another example, take a look at Exhibit 9.19. What do you think of this Italian ad for Yokohama tires? Would it play in Peoria?

25.   Sheryl WuDunn, "Japanese Take to Package Deals," *International Herald Tribune,* July 4, 1995, 11.

EXHIBIT 9.19

Using standardized campaigns for global brands is difficult. This Italian Yokohama ad is well received in Italy, but would it communicate well in the United States, where high-performance tire ads are information intensive?

SUMMARY

1 Explain the types of audience research that are useful for understanding cultural barriers that can interfere with effective communication.

All of us wear cultural blinders, and as a result we must overcome substantial barriers in trying to communicate with persons from other countries. This is a major problem for international advertisers as they seek to promote their brands around the world. To overcome this problem and avoid errors in advertising planning, cross-cultural audience analysis is needed. Such analyses involve evaluation of economic conditions, demographic characteristics, customs, values, rituals, and product use and preferences in the target countries.

2 Identify three distinctive challenges that complicate the execution of advertising in international settings.

Worldwide advertisers face three distinctive challenges in executing their campaigns. The first of these is a creative challenge that derives from differences in experience and meaning among cultures. Even the pictures featured in an ad may be translated differently from one country to the next. Media availability, media coverage, and media costs vary dramatically around the world, adding a second complication to international advertising. New media options continue to evolve globally. Finally, the amount and nature of advertising regulation vary dramatically from country to country and may force a complete reformulation of an ad campaign.

3 Describe the three basic types of advertising agencies that can assist in the placement of advertising around the world.

Advertising agencies provide marketers with the expertise needed to develop and execute advertising campaigns in international markets. Marketers can choose to work with global agencies, local agencies in the targeted market, or an international affiliate of the agency they use in their home country. Each of these agency types brings different advantages and disadvantages on evaluative dimensions like geographic proximity, economies of scale, political leverage, awareness of the client's strategy, and knowledge of the local culture.

4 Discuss the advantages and disadvantages of globalized versus localized advertising campaigns.

A final concern for international advertising entails the degree of customization an advertiser should attempt in campaigns designed to cross national boundaries. Globalized campaigns involve little customization among countries, whereas localized campaigns feature heavy customization for each market. Standardized messages bring tremendous cost savings and create a common brand image worldwide, but they may miss the mark with consumers in different nations. As consumers around the world become more similar, globalized campaigns are likely to become more prevalent. Teenagers in many countries share similar values and lifestyles and thus make a natural target for globalized campaigns.

KEY TERMS

international advertising (236)
ethnocentrism (239)
self-reference criterion (SRC) (239)
less-developed countries (240)
newly industrialized countries (240)
highly industrialized countries (241)

picturing (246)
global agencies (251)
international affiliates (253)
local agency (253)
globalized campaigns (253)
localized campaigns (253)

QUESTIONS FOR REVIEW AND CRITICAL THINKING

1. Coca-Cola is one of the world's best-known brands and most successful global marketers. Given this state of affairs, why would Pepsi challenge Coke's dominant position in Brazil? Is Pepsi using a globalized or localized campaign in Brazil?

2. Explain the difference between individualism and collectivism as core values. Pick up a recent issue of your favorite magazine and see if it contains any advertisements that appeal to the values of individualism or collectivism.

3. If you were creating a media strategy for a global advertising campaign, what emphasis would you put on newspapers in executing your strategy? What factors complicate their value for achieving broad market coverage?

4. Explain the appeal of new media options like direct broadcast by satellite and the World Wide Web for marketers who have created globalized advertising campaigns.

5. Compare and contrast the advantages of global versus local ad agencies for implementing international advertising.

6. Identify several factors or forces that make consumers around the world more similar to one another. Conversely, what factors or forces create diversity among consumers in different countries?

7. Teens and retired persons are two market segments found worldwide. If these two segments of European consumers were each being targeted for new advertising campaigns, which one would be most responsive to a globalized ad campaign? Why?

EXPERIENTIAL EXERCISE

As discussed in the chapter, it is extremely important to understand cultural differences before developing advertising for foreign countries. For example, personal care products seem to be a preoccupation of consumers in the United States. Write a report on how consumers in Russia, Brazil, and France appear to differ from their U.S. counterparts when it comes to the use of personal care products. Explain how these differences will affect American advertisers developing ads for personal care products in these countries. You may wish to talk with someone who is familiar with advertising in these countries or go to the university or local library and browse through consumer magazines published in these countries to see which products are being advertised and which are not.

USING THE INTERNET

A company's advertising efforts may be globalized or largely localized. Visit the European sites for O'Neill (www .oneill.jsi.nl) and Plymouth Voyager (www.rdc.nl/voyager).

1.   Where would you place each site on a spectrum ranging from global to local in nature? Which site attributes give you this impression?

2.   What aspects of each site would appeal to a person living in the Netherlands? What aspects of each site would appeal to a person living in China?

Advertising agencies also operate on both global and local scales. Visit the sites for Gitam International (www.gitam .co.za) and Chiat/Day (www.chiatday.com).

3.   Which agency appears to be more global? What aspects of each site give you this impression?

4.   If you owned a business that operates exclusively in South Africa and were seeking an advertising agency, which would you choose? What is it about the agency that has influenced your decision? How would your answers change if your South African–based business operated on a global scale?

Visit the IBM site (www.ibm.com).

5.   How is this site both globalized and localized?

6.   Are all messages communicated in English, or in other languages as well? What effect do you think the Web will have on English as the universal language?

▲ Delta Air Lines

Planning Integrated Marketing Communications

There is nothing new about planning promotional efforts around a mix of different promotional tools. Depending on a firm's communications objectives, different tools and different combinations of tools are used for different purposes. For example, advertising is relied on more heavily for long-term, image-building purposes, sales promotions are used to cause short-term spikes in demand, direct marketing is used to communicate with narrowly defined target audiences, and public relations can help a firm manage media reports about its activities.

This range of promotional devices and their application under different conditions is common. But the planning of integrated marketing communications goes beyond merely using the right tool under the right conditions. Strategic planning of IMC is distinguished from the traditional use of multiple promotional tools by four important factors:[1]

- *An outside-in approach is used to plan communications.* Traditionally, communications have been planned from the inside out; that is, firms have historically begun the planning process by setting communications goals that fulfill brand and/or corporate information or differentiation objectives. In planning IMC, a firm starts with the customer or prospect and works backward, identifying what the customer deems important information. This outside-in approach helps ensure that the customer gets information when and how she or he wants it, rather than when and in what form the firm deems appropriate.
- *IMC planning requires comprehensive and detailed knowledge about customers and prospects.* IMC programs are much more database driven than traditional promotional programs. This feature is highlighted by American Express. With its huge database of cardholders and travelers, AmEx has detailed information on tens of millions of people. So detailed, in fact, that it can send out special promotions in monthly bills to as few as 20 people.[2]
- *An IMC plan is built around brand contacts.* Brand contacts are all the ways in which customers or prospective customers come in contact with the organization: packaging, employee contacts, in-store displays, sales literature, and media exposure. Each contact must be evaluated for clarity and consistency with the overall IMC program.
- *Control of an IMC plan is highly centralized.* The effectiveness of an IMC program is greatly increased by appointing a single person or a group to control and evaluate all communications contacts with customers and prospects and manage the overall plan.

A Model for Planning Integrated Marketing Communications

Integrated marketing communications takes a truly systems-oriented approach to the planning process; all communications components in the system are designed to maximize overall communications impact, not the impact of an individual component. IMC implementation shares database information with the marketing program. This database foundation is considered critical to the success of IMC programs by 9 out of 10 marketing and advertising agency people questioned in a recent survey.[3]

A general planning model for IMC is shown in Exhibit IMC 2.1. Notice that customer/prospect databases relating to demographics, psychographics, purchase history, and category network are the foundation of the planning. Demographics, psychographics, and purchase history help profile current and potential customers. A category network is the way a consumer mentally sorts through all the information available about a product in a particular category.

From these databases, various market segments can be identified. The model shows three basic segments: loyal users, competitive users, and swing users. Swing users are those consumers who are prone to brand switching. Each of these segments, of course, has a different set of contacts with the firm's brand. Consequently, different communications objectives and strategies and different brand networks will be set for these segments.

Finally, notice at the bottom of the model that a firm must decide which communications tools to use to cultivate each broad segment—direct marketing (DM), advertising (ADV), sales promotion (SP), public relations (PR), and event marketing (EV). Decisions must also be made regarding how heavily to invest in the tools chosen.

While the tools of IMC can be clearly identified, it is less clear how these various ways of communicating with segments can be *truly* integrated. Recent industry studies of IMC show that firms believe an IMC approach will be valuable because the process helps focus messages on key target audiences

EXHIBIT IMC 2.1

An integrated marketing communications planning model.

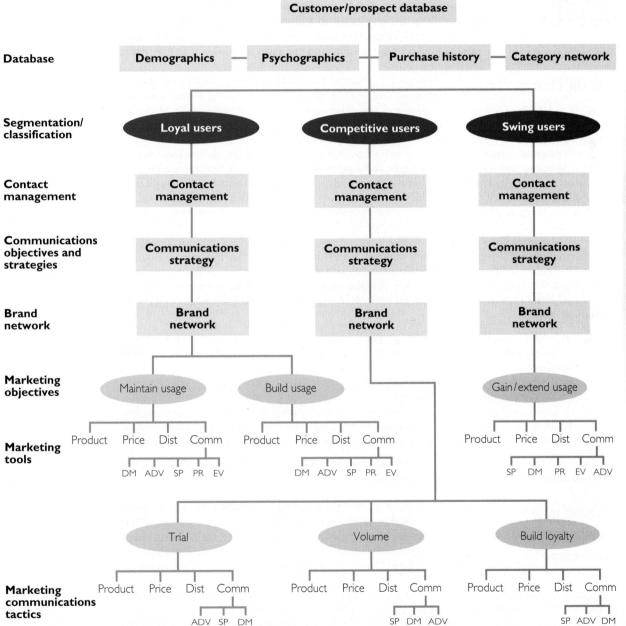

DM = Direct marketing   ADV = Advertising   SP = Sales promotion   PR = Public relations   EV = Event marketing

Source: Don E. Schultz, Stanley I. Tannenbaum, and Robert F. Lauterborn, *Integrated Marketing Communications* (Lincolnwood, Ill.: NTC Business Books, 1993) 54. Used with permission.

and reduces wasted circulation. But these same firms express concern that ego conflicts and turf battles within the firm and among the many specialty communications agencies that serve the firm could undermine the process.[4] And there is disagreement about who is responsible for the integration and coordination. Some firms feel it is their own responsibility, while others believe the outside agencies should make it their business to integrate their individual communications efforts. Perhaps the best solution is as Schultz, Tannenbaum, and Lauterborn suggest: The IMC program in a firm should have a designated manager or team to evaluate and control communications contacts and manage the overall plan.[5]

Planning Integrated Marketing Communications at Delta Air Lines

As we saw in Part 1, Delta Air Lines has developed an organizational structure for coordinating and integrating its many communications programs. This section will highlight how Delta's Marketing Division and Advertising and Creative Services department, in conjunction with its general agency, BBDO South, plans the integrated marketing communications effort. We will first examine the overall inputs to the planning process. Then we will begin to focus on a particular Delta campaign known as the "Cincinnati Instead" campaign, which grew out of strategic planning and has been executed successfully in the market as an IMC effort.

The IMC Planning Process at Delta

At the outset, let's examine the overall planning process used at Delta to develop its communications programs. Planning begins with corporate goals and objectives communicated directly to the Marketing Division. These corporate-level goals and objectives address major initiatives that pervade all areas of operations, from human resource management to route scheduling to marketing and communications. For example, a specific corporate goal might identify improving performance with the premium-level business segment. This is the high-frequency, high-yield business traveler and is identified within the frequent flyer database that Delta has developed in its SkyMiles program. Each division of the organization plays a major role in serving this segment, and the communications program must follow through with messages that attract and retain this type of traveler.

The Marketing Division takes corporate goals and objectives and develops sales, marketing, and communications programs—including support materials to address the initiatives identified. Remember that at this point in the communications process, an organization determines consumer behavior issues that affect its market, identifies market segments, differentiates and positions the brand, conducts research, and then sets the advertising plan. There are three stages to the basic planning process:

1. Delta's Advertising department is responsible for setting forth the initiatives, timing, and priorities for communications. This department is also responsible for setting the communications budget and statements of strategic intent.
2. BBDO South is responsible for providing strategic research insights, media plans, strategic planning documents, and creative solutions.
3. Both Delta and BBDO South contribute research information to the planning process. Secondary sources of information and primary data are both used in planning. Delta has an internal research group, and BBDO South conducts extensive proprietary research for Delta.

Let's turn our attention now to the extensive research that Delta and BBDO South conduct in planning integrated marketing communications.

Analyzing Delta's Communications Environment

As a major part of the strategic planning process for Delta, BBDO South provides a number of research tools and studies for its client. While many of the studies are conducted to address and identify specific marketing opportunities, much of the value of the research is in the accumulation of knowledge across a number of important areas for strategic planning.

The list of specific studies conducted by Delta and BBDO South that are an integral part of the planning process at Delta is impressive. A short description of each major study follows. Once again, the main purpose is to identify the important information regarding consumer behavior, market segmentation, differentiation and positioning, competitive intelligence, and communications effectiveness:

1. *Major-market tracking study.* This study is executed twice a year in Delta's seven primary markets, and once a year in five secondary markets. A phone survey is conducted among a random sample of fre-

quent business travelers (six or more trips per year). The purpose is to measure changes in awareness, attitudes, and perceptions of Delta and its major competitors. This study provides information on business traveler preferences and priorities and how well Delta and its competitors are addressing those preferences and priorities. The study also provides information on advertising effectiveness.

2. *Customer satisfaction study.* This is a continuous customer tracking study conducted by Delta. A sample of Delta passengers is called each week after they have completed trips, and they are questioned about their experiences. The questions evaluate all aspects of travel, from reservations to check-in, flight, in-flight service, and baggage claim. The data can be examined based on length of trip, class of service (Coach, Business, or First Class), connecting versus nonstop flight, or a variety of other partitioning variables.

3. *Brand Fitness Study.*™ This is a proprietary technique used by BBDO to profile competing brands in a visual manner. The study measures Delta and competing airlines on the following:
   a. *Brand imagery.* What characteristics and attributes are most associated with a brand in the respondent's mind?
   b. *User imagery.* What sort of people use a particular product? What do they look like? How much does the respondent like these people or want to be like them?
   c. *Personal drive imagery.* What motivates people that use a particular product?

   The methodology used to gather data allows the construction of perceptual maps that identify areas of unmet customer needs. These unmet needs provide opportunities for brand positioning. A Brand Fitness Study™ was conducted for Delta in 1992 in the Los Angeles and New York markets and was the basis for Delta's newest slogan, "You'll Love the Way We Fly."

4. *Precision Media.*™ This is another BBDO proprietary research tool. It is designed to provide a more efficient and effective media plan. For Delta, Precision Media™ is used for targeting the frequent business traveler segment. The technique uses standard media-tracking tools, like age and income characteristics available from Simmons or ABC Audit, and combines these data with geodemographic segmentation data. The result is a more efficient media plan for television and magazine placement.

5. *Copy testing.* When Delta launches major campaigns, quantitative copy testing is sometimes used to evaluate the creative concept. Once a campaign is initiated, new creative executions are tested in focus group settings to ensure that the creative concept continues to deliver on the objectives set with the original work.

6. *Segmentation studies.* Studies are regularly conducted to identify segments and traveler values within target segments. Travelers are segmented based on geographic and demographic characteristics, attitudes, and travel frequency. Delta and BBDO have identified at least 20 different target segments, with some travelers fitting into multiple segments. Delta concentrates on the high-value segments—segments that offer superior revenue opportunities. The following are some examples of these high-value segments and the ads targeted to them:
   a. *Frequent business traveler:* This segment is 70 percent male and 30 percent female and includes travelers who take six or more business trips a year. The average number of trips for travelers in this segment is 18. This is a high-revenue segment with specific and very demanding values. Exhibit IMC 2.2 shows an ad designed for this segment.
   b. *International business traveler.* Travelers in this segment take at least one international business trip per year. The ad shown in Exhibit IMC 2.3 targets these customers.
   c. *Delta Shuttle passenger.* The northeastern U.S. shuttle passenger has the highest income among all segments and takes the most flights per year at a high yield.
   d. *Travel trade customer.* Approximately 80 percent of Delta's travelers use an agent to book their flights.
   This is an extremely important segment and requires its own specialized communications program. Other segments include children 2 to 12, college students, senior citizens, and, of course, domestic and international leisure travelers. Delta and BBDO are sensitive to these segments and prepare communications specifically designed for them. Exhibit IMC 2.4 shows a direct mail promotion aimed at families in the leisure travel segment.

7. *Focus groups and the Business Traveler Advisory Committee.* The last two forms of research used are more qualitative in nature. Both Delta and BBDO regularly conduct focus group studies to explore travelers' feelings on issues related to travel. Focus groups are particularly useful for evaluating creative strategies.

   The Business Traveler Advisory Committee (BTAC) is a group of high-mileage Delta passengers with whom Delta management meets quarterly. The BTAC is extremely important to the planning process; this group represents the feelings and values of an important segment in the industry.

EXHIBIT IMC 2.2

The frequent business traveler is a demanding segment of the airline travel market. This ad is aimed specifically at this type of traveler and touts Delta's ability to provide service equal to the traveler's demanding values.

EXHIBIT IMC 2.3   *The international business traveler is an important segment for Delta Air Lines. This ad was designed to communicate Delta's wide range of international destinations compared to those of competitors.*

As you can see, Delta and BBDO South combine to produce an enormous amount of information upon which marketing strategy and ultimately communications programs are built. It was from the diligent analysis of the communications environment that the "Cincinnati Instead" campaign was launched. We will examine this integrated marketing communications effort now.

Planning the "Cincinnati Instead" Integrated Marketing Communications

On December 1, 1994, Delta celebrated the opening of its new $375 million facility at the Cincinnati/Northern Kentucky International Airport (CVG). Over several years, Delta has consistently added new routes to and through this Cincinnati hub. The new facilities and routes resulted in CVG becoming the number-two hub in Delta's system, behind Atlanta.

The new facilities in Cincinnati were important, but findings from the Delta and BBDO planning research revealed that a major competitive opportunity existed related to these facilities. First, general industry research suggested that the midwestern hub cities used by competitors—Chicago O'Hare, Detroit, St. Louis, Minneapolis, and Pittsburgh—had major problems. Travel to these airports was difficult. The airports themselves were congested and some tended to have weather delays, so many travelers were experiencing delays during their travel. In addition, several of these major metropolitan airports were in need of renovation—both structural and cosmetic. Second, an important finding emerged from a major-market tracking study. A key decision criterion in airline choice among frequent business travelers is convenience. In view of the congestion and delays at competitors' hubs, this key traveler segment was likely less than totally satisfied with travel on competing airlines. Third, a customer satisfaction study found that Delta's operations at CVG were rated very high by passengers in the tracking study.

Using these basic analyses of market information, Delta and BBDO discovered the following:

- Competitors' midwestern hubs were dated and were providing deteriorating service to travelers.
- A key market segment, frequent business travelers, placed a premium on convenience.
- Delta's newly renovated Cincinnati hub was rated highly by passengers on all dimensions of customer satisfaction, including the key criterion of convenience.

These findings produced the following strategic plan: Delta would begin to promote Cincinnati, with its new facilities and additional routes, as a major marketing initiative. The positioning strategy would feature the campaign slogan "Cincinnati Instead." But since the current year's budget did not have incremental funds available for this campaign, Delta and BBDO developed an integrated marketing communications plan to use ad dollars in the most efficient way. The campaign would ultimately feature the use of advertising, direct marketing, promotions, and public relations. One of the primary advertising pieces from this campaign is shown in Exhibit IMC 2.5.

In Part 3, "Preparing the Integrated Marketing Communications Message," we will look at the creative process used to develop the messages associated with the "Cincinnati Instead" program.

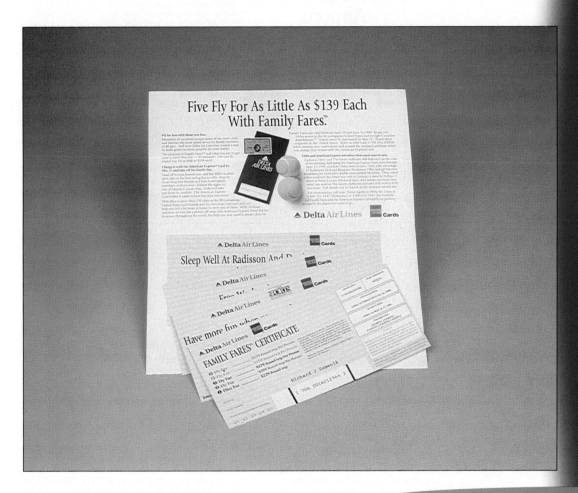

EXHIBIT IMC 2.4

While the business traveler is critical to Delta's success, leisure travelers are an important segment as well. Delta's Family Fares™ program is one of many advertising and promotional efforts developed for the leisure travel segment.

IMC EXERCISES

1. Pick a major national or multinational organization you are interested in—Coca-Cola, Ford Motor Company, Fidelity Investments, or Nike, as examples. Go to the library and examine national magazines and newspapers. What types of ads for the firm you have chosen are running in these print media? Have you seen television ads or heard radio ads for the firm? Have you ever received direct mail from the firm? Have you seen this firm's name or brands associated with events?

2. In Chapter 5, we learned that attitude affects consumer decision making. If a firm creates highly integrated communications messages, what effect do you think this has on consumer attitude? If the messages are not integrated, would this necessarily adversely affect attitude?

3. One of the ways Delta and BBDO gather data is through focus group research. Develop a list of 10 questions you would use in a focus group of international travelers to identify their preferences and values related to traveling.

4. Delta and BBDO have identified approximately 20 different segments in the travel market. Some of them were identified in the discussion of Delta's research programs. Develop a list of segments you believe exist in the air travel market. Can you identify 20 or more? Which of the Delta or BBDO research efforts would provide information on each of the segments you have identified?

ENDNOTES

1. Don E. Schultz, "Maybe We Should Start All Over with an IMC Organization," *Advertising Age,* October 25, 1993, 8.

2. Jonathan Berry, "Database Marketing," *Business Week,* September 5, 1994, 56.

3. Adrienne Ward Fawcett, "Integrated Marketing Door Open for Experts," *Advertising Age,* November 8, 1993, S2.

4. Thomas R. Duncan and Stephen E. Everett, "Client Perceptions of Integrated Marketing Communications," *Journal of Advertising Research* (May/June 1993): 30–39.

5. Don E. Schultz, Stanley Tannenbaum, and Robert Lauterborn, *Integrated Marketing Communications* (Lincolnwood, Ill.: NTC Business Books, 1993).

Part 3 | Preparing the Message

This part, "Preparing the Message,"
marks an important passage in our
study of advertising. The topics to this
point have raised the essential process
and planning issues that make advertising what it is as a communication
and business tool. Now we need to
take the plunge into the actual
preparation of advertising. Gone is
the comfort of merely thinking
about the process or extolling
how useful advertising can be
because market insights have produced a sound strategy. Now we
must take on the challenging—
but greatly rewarding—tasks of
preparing the message that will be
directed to a target audience.
One of the most insightful observa-
tions on the creative process in
advertising was made by Jim Nelson, a
well-seasoned advertising executive:
"Creativity is a misunderstood phenomenon. The key isn't simply brilliant
insight from above, but hard work here
below. For my money, you need two things:
tough, analytical thinking and intuitive,
creative imagination. Rubbing them together
may cause friction, but it may also set fire to
a real people-moving idea." (A. Jerome Jewler,
Creative Strategy in Advertising, 3rd ed. (Belmont,
Calif.: Wadsworth Publishing, 1989), 61.)
The valuable insight in this comment is that creativity
and the creative process should not be totally sepa-
rated from the analytical, strategic marketing-planning
effort. Rather, when they are rubbed together, the result
can be advertising that has impact and the power to move
people. This section of the text will explore aspects of how
messages get created and how creativity plays an important role
in effective advertising.

Chapter 10, "Message Development," begins by describing how creativity in the process of message development often begins with the big idea. The big idea is a key message appeal that has the power to move people. You will also learn in this chapter that effective message development is not just creativity. A wide range of message objectives and strategies, which require astute insights from consumer and market analysis, can be used to develop messages effectively. In the end, you will see that what ultimately communicates to a target audience is what that audience finds relevant and interesting.

Chapter 11, "Copywriting," focuses on the enormous challenge of writing the descriptions that accompany print and broadcast advertising. This chapter explores the development of copy from the creative plan through dealing with the constraints and opportunities of the medium that will carry the message. This chapter also highlights guidelines for writing effective copy and common mistakes in copywriting. A full discussion of radio and television advertising formats, which provide the context for copy development, is also provided. At the end of this chapter is a discussion of a typical copy approval process used by advertisers and agencies.

In Chapter 12, "Art Direction and Production in Print Advertising," you will learn about creating effective print advertisements destined for magazines, newspapers, or direct-marketing promotions. The nature of the illustration, design, and layout components of print advertising are considered first. Then, illustration components and formats as well as the creative impact of illustrations are discussed. The principles of design and the components of effective design are considered next. Layout, which is the process of positioning all the pictorial and word elements in an ad, is discussed with an emphasis on the layout process. A final section on the technical aspects of production in print advertising is included.

Finally, the exciting and complex process of creating broadcast advertising is discussed. Chapter 13, "Art Direction and Production in Broadcast Advertising," describes the people and techniques involved in creating television and radio ads. The emphasis in this chapter is on the creative team and how creative concepts are brought to life. The chapter follows a preproduction, production, and postproduction sequence. Also highlighted in this chapter are the large number of people outside the agency who facilitate the production effort.

Chapter 10

Message

Development

After reading and thinking about this chapter, you will be able to do the following:

1 Recognize the impact of creativity in the development of advertising.

2 Describe the essential characteristics of the advertising message.

3 Identify nine types of message strategies and several methods for executing each of them.

There are those who say it was brilliant and inspired. Others argue it was a capricious and expensive exercise in grandstanding. In January of 1984, during the third quarter of the Super Bowl, Apple Computer introduced the Macintosh computer with a 60-second spot. The ad known as "1984," seen in Exhibit 10.1, climaxed with a young athletic woman hurling a mallet through a huge projection screen in a monochromic vision of a hypercorporate and ugly future.[1] On the big screen was an Orwellian Big Brother instructing the masses. As the ad closed, with the near soulless masses chanting a mantra in the background, the following simple statement appeared on the television screen of millions of viewers: "On January 24th, Apple Computer will introduce Macintosh. And you'll see why 1984 won't be like 1984."

What made this advertisement particularly newsworthy is that it cost $400,000 (very expensive for its day) to produce, another $500,000 to broadcast, and it was broadcast only *once*. It was a creative super event. The three major networks covered the event on the evening news, and the ad went on to become *Advertising Age*'s Commercial of the Decade for the 1980s. But why? It wasn't just its high cost and single play. It was that the ad seemed to capture and articulate something important lying just below the surface of mid-1980s American culture. It was about us versus them, threatened individuals versus faceless corporations. It was about the defiant rejection of sterile corporate life, and the celebration of individuality through, of all things, a computer. Arch rival IBM was implicitly cast as the evil Big Blue (i.e., Big Brother), and Apple as the good anticorporate corporation. The ad captured the moment and, most critically, served up a consumer product as popular ideology. Apple became the hip, the young, the cool, the democratic, the populist, the antiestablishment computer. It was the computer of the nonsellout.

As we've said before, you can rarely go wrong by emphasizing individuality in the United States. Likewise, if you can link your product to a strong social movement, so much the better, as long as the trend lasts. Steve Hayden, the "1984" copywriter, described the ad this way: "We thought of it as an ideology, a value set. It was a way of letting the whole world access the power of computing and letting them talk to one another. The democratization of technology—the computer for the rest of us."[2]

With "1984," Apple and its advertising agency Chiat/Day wanted to focus attention on the new product and absolutely distinguish Apple and the Macintosh from Big Blue, IBM. Macintosh was going to offer computing power to the people. This declaration of computing independence was made on the most-watched broadcast of the year. Forty-six percent of all U.S. households watched the 1984 Super Bowl. Apple offered a cyberethos for those who felt alienated or intimidated by the IBM world. The "1984" ad offered a clear choice, a clear instruction: Buy a Mac.

Of course, there is another lesson here: Nothing lasts forever, not even a great creative idea. Things change. Apple effectively cultivated an us-versus-them ethic, and this worked well for quite a while. But then, the message became something of a problem. Jump back to the present. Today, Apple's future is threatened, some believe, by a failure to recognize and adapt to changes in the marketplace. Because Apple refused to license its operating system until 1995, Macs became a relatively expensive alternative. Coupled to a premium price, the idea of being the "rest of us" came to be regarded by some as evidence of Apple's snooty and elitist attitude. The "rest of us" seemed to think they were better than us—not a desirable product attribute if a company hopes to sell a lot of computers. Still, in 1984, Apple's advertising was superior. It was truly creative, and for this the company and their agency deserve a great deal of credit.

1.   The term "ugly future" was first used in this context by Connie Johnson, University of Illinois, in the late 1970s.
2.   This quote appears in Bradley Johnson, "10 Years after 1984: The Commercial and the Product That Changed Advertising," *Advertising Age,* January 10, 1994, 12.

EXHIBIT 10.1

What is the message or messages communicated in this ad? How is message development influenced by the product, the audience, and the competitive situation? This 1984 ad that launched the Apple Macintosh computer was enormously successful for Apple and is now a legend in the advertising industry. Compare this groundbreaking advertisement with the image of the company found on its home page at **www.apple.com/**. *Is this the same type of approach to innovation and new technology? Examine the two different advertising approaches that Apple is using to educate markets about the future of personal computing at* **opendoc.apple.com/users/users.html** *(for real-time, on-screen information) and at* **product.info.apple .com/productinfo/tech/** *(for Apple White Papers on key technologies issues).*

Creativity in Message Development

❶ Let's be honest. No one knows exactly how advertising creativity works. That's because no one knows exactly how any form of creativity works. So we won't kid you; we don't know, either. But what the remainder of this chapter will do is discuss how creative messages are developed. We'll talk about some aspects of the process that experience tells us are particularly important, and we'll try to explain why.

As long as we're being honest, you might as well know something else: Some of the best advertising ever done wasn't done by-the-book. Of course, since this is a textbook, we're supposed to tell you how to do it the right way. The "right way" of message development is supposed to follow a very orderly progression that eventually leads to a very orderly production of the actual creative product, the ad. The refined analysis of relevant information is supposed to lead to a beautifully crafted advertising strategy, which is then taken by the creatives and turned into a perfectly logical extension of that strategy. The truth is, a lot of times the process works in reverse, or even in seemingly random sequence. A creative is walking down the street, playing volleyball, drinking some pop, or whatever, and says something like, "Ah, I've got it!" and turns an idea into advertising. Sometimes when that happens, the creative hasn't even talked to the account executive or brand manager or any of the other strategists on the job. He or she just dreams the idea up. Then, the people in charge of the strategic process must go back and refit their facts to the creative's vision (and claim it as a product of their brilliant strategy, or at least tell the client it is). Following the standard how-to, top-down management flowchart certainly has a lot to recommend it, but successful management also allows creativity to emerge, to simply happen. As long as the creative message is consistent with the managerial facts and circumstances, exactly how it occurs is irrelevant.

One of the most difficult transitions for a marketing strategist is to abandon the measured comfort of product/market analysis and step into the seemingly chaotic world of creative execution. Marketing strategists often have a hard time understanding and accepting the nature and process of creativity and the important role it plays in message development. The typical reaction is confusion or bewilderment. But the truth is that creativity is what separates the highly effective message from the mediocre message. Creativity is essential to the process: "Knowledge is the stuff from which good ideas are made. Nonetheless, knowledge alone won't make a person creative. I think we've all known people who knew lots of stuff and nothing happened. Their knowledge just sat in their crania because they didn't think about what they knew in any new ways. Thus, the real key to being creative lies in what you do with your knowledge."[3] This quote from Roger von Oech, creative consultant to major corporations, highlights a critical component in message development: using the knowledge base creatively to develop effective advertisements. The creatives in advertising agencies will offer creative concepts in ways that may differ greatly from the recommended and highly structured sequence.

The Big Idea

The **big idea** is the creative concept behind an advertisement that attracts attention and creates a distinctive impression for the advertised brand in the mind of receivers. The big idea has been described as "that flash of insight that synthesizes the purpose of strategy, joins the product benefit with consumer desire in a fresh, involving way, brings the subject to life, and makes the reader or audience stop, look, and listen."[4]

---

3.   Roger von Oech, *A Whack on the Side of the Head: How to Unlock Your Mind for Innovation* (New York: Warner Books, 1983), 6.
4.   John O'Toole, *The Trouble with Advertising,* 2nd ed. (New York: Random House Publishers, 1985), 131.

The big idea is the kind of creative concept that makes the average, uninitiated marketing strategist nervous. It is bold, powerful, and distinctive. But the big idea is actually an outstanding execution of the message strategy. The big idea is also referred to as the key selling idea in an advertisement or advertising campaign—its guiding light.[5] It is a brand claim with meaningful appeal to the target audience. Few advertisements or advertising campaigns have ever achieved truly outstanding big ideas. But like Apple's "1984," Nike's "Just Do It," or Coca-Cola's "Always Coca-Cola," shown in Exhibit 10.2, it is a creative aspiration.

Whether the creative impetus is the big idea or something else, the goal is always the same: a message that attracts attention and creates a positive, memorable identity for a brand. This goal is hopefully shared by both the marketing strategists and the creatives. As you will see throughout this chapter, there are many ways the big idea can become an advertising message—from functional appeals to transformational ads to infomercials.

EXHIBIT 10.2

The big idea in an advertisement attracts attention and gives a brand a distinctive presence in the market. Few ad campaigns ever truly achieve a big idea. The "Always Coca-Cola" campaign, however, has indeed found a big idea and made it into a long-lasting and successful campaign.
www.cocacola.com/

Message Development

❷ Message development signals a major shift in our perspective on advertising. To this point in the book, the emphasis has been on the *process* of advertising and *planning* the advertising effort: identifying and synthesizing pertinent information. Now, our perspective turns to the *preparation* itself. Developing a message presents the challenge of actually articulating advertising strategy.

When advertisers refer to a **message,** they are referring to what is said and/or shown in an advertisement or advertising campaign. Message components are often referred to as copy and art:

• **Copy**—the verbal or written part of a message. Copy includes headlines, subheads, and all verbal descriptions to communicate information to a receiver.

• **Art**—any graphics, photography, film, or video that offers visual information to a receiver. In some advertisements, particularly image-oriented ads, the visual component is the primary way in which meaning is conveyed.

As you might guess, the advent of new media options like the World Wide Web has forced advertisers to revisit their definition of the advertising message. This point is developed more fully in the New Media box on page 276.

Traditional ad message development involves both copy and art, and it must result in a message with a reasonably clear intended meaning for the advertiser's audience. But remember, audience members are active interpreters. Each member adapts and

---

5.   A. Jerome Jewler, *Creative Strategy in Advertising,* 3rd ed. (Belmont, Calif.: Wadsworth Publishing Company, 1989), 46.

negotiates the meaning of an ad, rather than merely accepting it whole. Each person's unique background and experience results in a personalized interpretation of the message. Still, it is the goal of advertisers to place those individualized interpretations within reasonable bounds. Good creative messages permit each individual to personalize the message by linking it to his or her own experiences and likes and dislikes, while keeping the vast majority of interpretations similar enough that the advertiser's intended meaning is generally communicated.

The goal of the advertiser is to strive for clarity in the meaning of the message, in all its component parts, so that consumers understand what the firm is offering and why it is valuable. Each consumer can then determine the appropriateness of the product for her or him. In the "1984" ad created by Apple, an eerie, subdued atmosphere disrupted by a rebellious young woman represented independence and personal power—a meaning Apple hoped to create with the message. Although every consumer remembered the ad just a little differently, made different connections, the interpretations were similar enough that Apple's main idea got across. The power of an ad is not found in its absolutely faithful reproduction in the mind of a consumer, but in its shared interpretation by consumers.

NEW MEDIA

IS THE MEDIUM THE MESSAGE?

The traditional challenge in developing a potent advertising message is to identify an appeal that is relevant and meaningful to consumers and then weave a message for a brand around that appeal. The main appeal is reinforced by the visuals or the audio accompaniment. The final goal has always been to create a total impression with a message that first attracts the receiver and then leaves her or him with positive feelings for a brand. This is a tough assignment in an environment cluttered with relevant, entertaining messages.

But what about cybermessages? Do advertisers take the same approach in new media? Not quite. In these early stages of cybercommunication, advertisers believe that consumers search the Internet expecting information—not advertising about brands. In fact, advertisers are creating Web sites that offer information first, and only incidentally tout their brands. For example, if you go to site www.leggs.com, you'll find a lot more than information about panty hose. This is the Web site created by L'eggs Products. Information about nylons and tights takes a backseat to discussions about fashion trends and career advice. Similarly, www.womenslink.com offers a lot of information about women's issues and almost nothing about the site creator—Bristol-Myers Squibb, the pharmaceutical conglomerate.

The theory behind these sites and dozens of others set up by big advertisers is that no consumer will visit a marketer's site if it just contains messages about products and brands. In other words, consumers will avoid sites if they are just advertising messages. The fact is that messages in traditional media—television, radio, newspapers, magazines—appear whether consumers want them to or not. New media, like the World Wide Web, offer a communications environment where the consumer chooses to be exposed to information. A new twist and new challenge for advertisers—getting consumers to seek out ads.

To meet this message challenge of the new media, advertisers like L'eggs, Toyota, and Bridgestone-Firestone are offering information-intensive sites to attract consumers and fulfill their WWW expectations. This puts advertisers in the business of creating editorial content on the Web—not just persuasive messages—in order to attract consumer attention. As the director of interactive marketing at one New York agency put it, "Nobody is going to wake up in the morning and say, 'Gotta go to that Bridgestone-Firestone site today.'"

Message Strategy

❸ An advertising strategy is the summary statement of all the essential and defining planning, preparation, and placement decisions. One major component of an advertising strategy is the **message strategy.** The message strategy consists of objectives and methods. It defines the goals of the advertiser and how those goals will be achieved. This section of the chapter offers nine message strategy objectives and the methods often

Sources: Debra Aho Williamson and Jan Hodges, "Editorial Lines Blur As Advertisers Create Sites," *Advertising Age*, February 26, 1996, S9; and Chuck Ross, "TCI and P&G in Cyber-Huddle," *Advertising Age*, April 1, 1996, 1, 60.

used to satisfy these objectives. This is not an exhaustive list, but it covers many of the most important message strategy objectives. Exhibit 10.3 summarizes the nine message strategies presented here, and the Contemporary Issues box on page 279 illustrates a rather unconventional message strategy.

Objective: Promote Brand Recall

Since the very beginning, a major goal of advertisers has been to get consumers to remember their name. This is typically referred to as the brand recall objective. Advertisers not only want consumers to remember their name, but also want that name to be the first name consumers remember. Advertisers want their brand name to be "top of mind." In the case of parity products and other low-involvement goods and services, the first brand remembered is often the most likely to be purchased. First-remembered brands are often the most popular brands. Sometimes, advertisers want consumers to remember a single attribute along with the brand name. Examples are "All-Temp-a-Cheer" and the wholly affirming message "Coke Is It."

EXHIBIT 10.3

Message strategy objectives and methods.

Objective: What the Advertiser Hopes to Achieve	Method: How the Advertiser Plans to Achieve the Objective
Promote brand recall: To get consumers to recall its brand name(s) first; that is, before any of the competitors' brand names	Repetition ads Slogan ads
Instill brand preference: To get consumers to like or prefer its brand above all others	Feel-good ads Humor ads Light Fantasy ads Sexual-appeal ads
Scare the consumer into action: To get consumers to buy a product or service by instilling fear	Fear-appeal ads
Change behavior by inducing anxiety: To get consumers to make a purchase decision by playing to their anxieties; often, the anxieties are social in nature	Anxiety ads
Transform consumption experiences: To create a feeling, image, or mood about a brand that is activated when the consumer uses the product or service	Transformational ads
Situate the brand socially: To give the brand meaning by placing it in a desirable social context	Slice-of-life ads
Define the brand image: To create an image for a brand by relying predominantly on visuals rather than discourse	Image ads
Persuade the consumer: To convince consumers to buy a product or service through high-engagement discourse	Benefit-appeal ads Unique selling proposition ads Reason-why ads Hard-sell ads Comparison ads Information-only ads Testimonial ads Demonstration ads Advertorial ads Infomercials
Invoke a direct response: To get consumers to take immediate buying action, typically by providing a toll-free number	Direct response ads

Method: Repetition. As simple as it sounds, repetition is the tried-and-true way of gaining easy retrieval from memory. This is done not only through buying a lot of ads, but also through repeating the brand name within the ad copy itself. The example from Kibbles 'n Bits®, shown in Exhibit 10.4, may have set the record.

EXHIBIT 10.4

Repeating the brand name in an ad can help establish the name in receivers' memory. This ad for Kibbles 'n Bits® may have established a record for brand name repetition in a 30-second ad.

Method: Slogans. Slogans are rhetorical devices that link a brand name to something memorable, due either to the slogan's simplicity, meter, rhyme, or some other factor. Examples are numerous: "Bud-Weis-Er"; "You Deserve a Break Today"; "Tide's In, Dirt's Out"; "The Best Part of Waking Up Is Folgers in Your Cup"; "You're in Good Hands with All-state"; "Like a Good Neighbor, State Farm Is There"; "We Love to Fly and It Shows"; "Two, Two, Two Mints in One"; "Get Met, It Pays"; and "It Keeps on Going and Going and Going." No doubt you've heard a few of these before.

Objective: Instill Brand Preference

The brand-preference objective is fairly universal. Advertisers want consumers to like or prefer their brand. Liking is different from awareness or top-of-mind recall. Liking is measured in attitudes and is expressed as a feeling. You know what it means to like something, don't you?

Method: Feel-Good Ads. Feel-good ads work by positive affective association. They link the good feeling elicited by the ad with the brand. While the actual theory and mechanics of this are more complex than you might think, the basic idea is that by creating ads with positive feelings, consumers will associate those positive feelings with the advertised brand, leading to a higher probability of purchase. The evidence on how well this method works is debated. It may be that positive feelings are transferred to the brand, or it could be that they actually interfere with remembering the message or the brand name. Liking the ad doesn't necessarily mean liking the brand. But message strategy development is a game of probability, and liking may, more times than not, lead to a higher probability of purchase. There are certainly many practitioners who continue to believe in the method's intuitive appeal.

What creates a good feeling is a product of interpretation on the part of the audience member. For example, the long-running and apparently successful Chevrolet truck television campaign "Like a Rock" features the music of Bob Seger and scenes of hard-working, patriotic Americans and their families. The good feeling it produces may be the result of the patriotic associations and the celebration of working-class Americans.

Other feel-good ads make a much more explicit connection for the audience. For example, Delta Air Lines could show how often its planes depart and arrive on schedule. Instead, it shows the happy reunion of family members and successful business meetings, which create a much more emotional message. Here, the emotions become the product attribute and are linked to the brand. Consider Kodak's highly successful print and television campaign that highlighted the "Memories of Our Lives" with powerful scenes: a son coming home from the military just in time for Christmas dinner, and a father's reception dance with his newly married daughter. Here, Kodak makes it clear that it is in the memory business, and Kodak memories are good memories. Good feelings are a desirable product attribute.

Method: Humor Ads.   The goal of humor in advertising is to create in the receiver a pleasant and memorable association with the product. Recent advertising campaigns as diverse as those for Miller Lite beer ("Can Your Beer Do This?"), Magnavox consumer electronics (the disappearing remote control), and Little Caesar's ("Pizza-Pizza") have all successfully used humor as the primary message theme. But research suggests that the positive impact of humor is not as strong as the intuitive appeal of the approach. Quite simply, humorous versions of advertisements often do not prove to be more persuasive than nonhumorous versions of the same ad—or research is simply inadequate to detect the difference.

How many times have you been talking to friends about your favorite ads, and you say something like, "Remember the one where the guy . . . ," and then you can't remember what brand the ad is for? You remember the gag but not the brand. Yet with other ads, you can recall the brand. The difference may be that ads in which the payoff for the humor is an integral part of the message strategy ensure the memory link between humor and brand. If the ad is merely funny and doesn't link the joke to the brand name, then the advertiser may have bought some very expensive laughs.

An example of an explicitly linked payoff is the Bud Light "Give Me a Light" campaign of the early 1980s. Miller Lite was quickly becoming the generic term for light beer. To do something about this, Bud Light came up with the series

---

CONTEMPORARY ISSUES

OKAY, HERE'S THE ADVERTISING MESSAGE STRATEGY: NONE

Adidas sales jumped 80 percent to $340 million for its 1960s-era sneakers with the trademark stripes on the side. The advertising message strategy? None.

Puma watched consumers snap up 1 million pairs of its 1960s-style basketball shoes priced at $55 and dubbed the Clyde after New York Knicks basketball legend Walt "Clyde" Frazier. The advertising message strategy? None.

Converse, a perennial also-ran in the athletic footwear market (with a 4.6 percent market share), saw a 7 percent gain in annual sales mostly due to a huge jump in demand for its $50 canvas sneakers designed in the 1970s and called the One Star. The advertising message strategy? Small ads in Gen X magazines like *Thrasher* and *Dirt*.

No multimillion-dollar sports celebrities? No $120 million advertising budget? No $150-per-pair price tag? How could these sneakers possibly sell? Marketing strategists put it this way: "It's an anti-sneaker sneaker kind of thing." And: "The best advertising strategy is, you don't."

In the ever-fickle athletic shoe market, the newest, hottest trend is retro sneakers. Nostalgic styles from the sixties and seventies are enjoying runaway sales without carefully crafted advertising message strategies. In fact, the agency that represents Converse shoes believes that the Gen X'ers that are driving the sales "don't like being over-marketed to, they don't like hype, and they're wise to paying a premium for celebrity-endorsed shoes."

Well, if advertising is not getting the word out, then how is the word getting out? The influence is much more fundamental—the sneakers became part of the Gen X culture. First, the retro shoes caught on with skateboarders and hip-hop dancers. Then, Hollywood got hip—Madonna wore Adidas on the MTV video awards show. When it comes to a contest pitting the influences of culture versus advertising, bet on culture every time.

Source: Geoffrey Smith, "Sneakers That Jump into the Past," *Business Week*, March 13, 1995, 71.

---

of "Give Me a Light" ads to remind light beer drinkers that they had to be a little more specific in what they were ordering. The ads showed customers ordering "a light" and getting spotlights, landing lights, searchlights, and other types of lights. The customer would then say, "No, a Bud Light." The ads not only were funny, but also made the point perfectly: Say "Bud Light," not just "a light," when ordering a beer. In addition, the message allowed thousands and thousands of customers and would-be comedians in bars and restaurants to repeat the line in person, which amounted to a lot of free advertising.

Miller Brewing is an advertiser that has both reaped the benefits of humor in its recent ad campaigns and suffered from its risks. The original "Less Filling—Tastes Great" campaigns that pitted famous retired athletes against one another rose to great prominence in the late 1970s and through nearly the entire decade of the 1980s. Sports fans could hardly wait for the next installment of the campaign. But the campaign, while highly successful overall, ultimately ran into the problem of wearout. The brand began to lose market share and is still struggling to regain past glories.

In light of research findings, there are several cautions associated with the use of humor as a message tactic:

- Humorous messages may adversely affect comprehension.
- Humorous messages can wear out as quickly as after three exposures, leaving no one laughing, especially the advertiser.[6]
- Humorous messages may attract attention but may not increase the effectiveness or persuasive impact of the advertisement.

Method: Light Fantasy. Some ads make use of a form of light fantasy. These ads allow receivers to pretend a little and think about themselves in the position of the rich, the famous, or the accomplished. For example, the average guy wearing a particular athletic shoe can feel like an NBA all-star. The advertisement in Exhibit 10.5 appeals to the fantasies of just about anyone who has ever played in a garage band. Becoming a rock star is not likely, but it's fun to think about.

Method: Sex Appeal. Because they are directed toward humans, ads tend to focus on sex from time to time. Not a big surprise.[7] But does sex sell? In a literal sense, the answer is no, because nothing, not even sex, makes someone buy something. However, sexual appeals are attention getting and occasionally arousing, which may affect how consumers feel about a product. Context is extremely important in sexual-appeal messages. Knowing just what constitutes sex appeal is not easy. Is it showing skin? How much skin? What's the difference between the celebration of a beautiful body and its objectification? Motive? Politics? In 1993, the print ads rated most successful in *Starch Tested Copy* were ads using muted sexual appeal.[8] The ads shown in Exhibits 10.6 and 10.7 use a sexual-appeal message to one degree or another. How effective do you think these ads are in fulfilling the objective of creating brand preference?

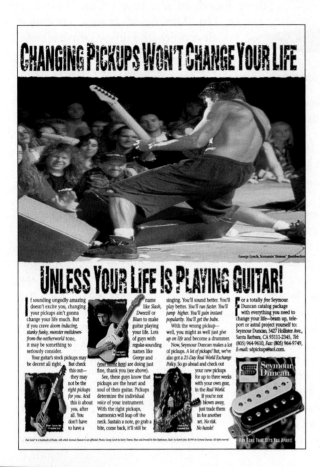

EXHIBIT 10.5

Some ads are referred to as light fantasy ads, which allow receivers to think about themselves as rich, famous, or accomplished. This ad for guitar pickups is a good example. www.seymourduncan.com

---

6.   This claim is made by Video Storyboards Tests, based on its extensive research of humor ads, and cited in Kevin Goldman, "Ever Hear the One about the Funny Ad?" *Wall Street Journal,* November 2, 1993, B11.

7.   The political left often complains about exploitation, objectification, and the oppressive patriarchy found in advertising. The right, on the other hand, sees sexual ads as evidence of moral decay and the excesses of secular humanism. While some of these charges are regrettably true, to both the right and left the sin is really often nothing more than that it's advertising, low culture and commercial at that. If the images were from the seventeenth century and hung in a museum, they would be okay, but because they are popular culture and commercial, they must approach pornography. Go figure.

8.   Leah Richard, "Basic Approach in Ads Looks Simply Superior," *Advertising Age,* October 10, 1994, 30.

EXHIBITS 10.6 AND 10.7

A popular advertising method is to use sexual-appeal messages. These ads for Dewar's Scotch and Tabu perfume use light sexual content in an attempt to attract attention and affect receivers' feelings toward these brands. Ads that use muted sex appeal often test very high on recall. What about their effect on brand preference?

Objective: Scare the Consumer into Action

Sometimes the idea is simply to scare the consumer. Again, this not a difficult concept. You've probably heard of fear; perhaps you've even experienced it yourself. Sometimes advertisers adopt the scare-the-consumer-into-action objective using fear appeals. Fear is an extraordinarily powerful emotion and may be successfully used to get consumers to take some very important action. However, it must be used strategically and judiciously to work well in advertising.

Method: Fear-Appeal Ads.

A fear appeal highlights the risk of physical harm or the negative consequences of not using the advertised brand or taking some recommended action. The intuitive belief about fear as a message tactic is that fear will motivate the receiver to buy a product that will reduce or eliminate the portrayed threat. For example, Radio Shack spent $6 million to run a series of ads showing a dimly lit unprotected house, including a peacefully sleeping child, as a way to raise concerns about the safety of the receiver's valuables, as well as his or her family. The campaign used the theme "If security is the question, we've got the answer." The ad closed with the Radio Shack logo and the National Crime Prevention Council slogan, "United Against Crime."[9] Similarly, Portland General Electric suggested leaving a light on for uninvited, unwanted guests, as seen in Exhibit 10.8.

EXHIBIT 10.8

How does this ad for Portland GE embody the scare-the-consumer-into action-objective? Does this ad have ethical implications? How so? For more information on fear appeal go to **carmen.artsci.washington.edu/propaganda/fear.htm**.

WEB SIGHTING

9.   Jeffery D. Zbar, "Fear!" *Advertising Age,* November 14, 1994, 18.

The contemporary social environment has provided advertisers with an ideal context for using fear appeals. In an era of drive-by shootings, car-jackings, and gang violence, Americans fear for their personal safety. Manufacturers of security products like alarm and lighting security systems play on this fearful environment.[10] Other advertisers as well have recently tried fear as an appeal. One such advertiser, the Asthma Zero Mortality Coalition, urges people suffering from asthma to seek professional help and uses a fear appeal in its ad copy: "When those painful, strained breaths start coming, keep in mind that any one of them could easily be your last." The creator of the ad states, "Sometimes you have to scare people to save their lives."[11]

Unfortunately, research does not offer such an absolute conclusion on the effectiveness of fear as a message tactic. Fear as a tactic in advertising has generated controversy. Social psychologists and marketing researchers have disagreed on the effectiveness of a fear-based appeal. Traditional research wisdom indicates that intense fear appeals actually short-circuit persuasion and result in a negative attitude toward the advertised brand.[12] It seems that receivers get so anxious about the fear-inducing message that they focus on the fear and not on overcoming it. Other researchers argue that the tactic is beneficial to the advertiser.[13] More-recent research on fear appeals suggests that the effectiveness of this method is difficult to evaluate. Still, it stands to reason that too much fear may occupy so much cognitive work space that the types of inferences needed to take action may never occur. It may also come down to how explicit the suggestions for avoiding the harm are made. Using fear messages without offering a way out seems likely to fail.

Objective: Change Behavior by Inducing Anxiety

Feeling anxious is not pleasant. In fact, it's pretty awful. Most people try to avoid feeling anxious. They try to minimize, moderate, and alleviate anxiety. Often people will buy or consume things to help them in their continuing struggle with anxiety. They might watch television, exercise, eat, or take medication. They might also buy mouthwash, deodorant, condoms, a safer car, or even a retirement account, and advertisers know this. Advertisers pursue a change-behavior-by-inducing-anxiety objective by playing on consumer anxieties.

Method: Anxiety Ads.

There are many things to be anxious about. Advertisers realize this and use many settings to demonstrate why you should be anxious and what you can do to alleviate the anxiety. Social, medical, and personal care products frequently use anxiety ads. The message conveyed in anxiety ads is that (1) there is a clear and present danger, and (2) the way to avoid this danger is to buy the advertised brand. When Head and Shoulders dandruff shampoo is advertised with the theme "You only have one chance to make a first impression," the audience realizes the power of Head and Shoulders in saving them the social embarrassment of having dandruff.

Other anxiety ads tout the likelihood of being stricken by gingivitis, athlete's foot, calcium deficiency, body odor, and on and on. The idea is that these anxiety-producing conditions are out there, and they may affect you unless you take the appropriate action. The danger is often social judgment. Procter & Gamble has long relied on such presentations for its household and personal care brands. In fact, Procter & Gamble has used this approach so consistently over the years that in some circles the anxiety tactic is referred to as the P&G approach. One of the more memorable P&G social anxiety ads is the scene where husband and wife are busily cleaning the spots off the water glasses

10.   Ibid.

11.   Emily DeNitto, "Healthcare Ads Employ Scare Tactics," *Advertising Age,* November 7, 1994, 12.

12.   Irving L. Janis and Seymour Feshbach, "Effects of Fear Arousing Communication," *Journal of Abnormal Social Psychology* 48 (1953): 78–92.

13.   Michael Ray and William Wilkie, "Fear: The Potential of an Appeal Neglected by Marketing," *Journal of Marketing* 34, no. 1 (January 1970): 54–62.

before dinner guests arrive because they didn't use P&G's Cascade dish-washing product, which, of course, would have prevented the glasses from spotting. Most personal care products have used this type of appeal.

Objective: Transform Consumption Experiences

Advertisers also use a transform-consumption-experiences objective by creating a mood, image, or feeling about a brand. You know how sometimes it's hard to explain to someone else just exactly why a certain experience was so special, why it felt so good? It wasn't just this thing, or that thing; it was that the entire experience was somehow better than the sum of the individual facets. Sometimes, that feeling is at least partly due to your expectations of what something will be like, your positive memories of previous experiences, or both. Sometimes, advertisers try to provide that very anticipation and/or familiarity, bundled up in a positive memory of an advertisement, activated during the consumption experience itself.

Method: Transformational Ads. The idea behind transformational advertising is that it can actually make the consumption experience better. For example, after years of advertising by McDonald's, the experience of eating at a McDonald's is actually transformed or made better by virtue of what you know and feel about McDonald's each time you walk in. Transformational advertising messages attempt to create a brand feeling, image, and mood that is activated when the consumer uses the product or service. Transformational ads that are acutely effective are said to connect the experience of the advertisement so closely with the brand that consumers cannot help but think of the advertisement when they think of the brand.

Objective: Situate the Brand Socially

Maybe you haven't given it much thought, but if you're ever going to understand advertising, you have to get this: Objects have social meanings. While it applies to all cultures, this simple truth is at the very center of consumer cultures. In consumer cultures such as ours, billions of dollars are spent in efforts to achieve specific social meanings for advertised brands. Advertisers have long known that by placing their product in the right social setting, their brand takes on some of the characteristics of its surroundings. These social settings are created in advertising. In advertising, a product is placed into a custom-created social setting perfect for the brand, a setting in which the brand excels. Hopefully, this becomes the way in which the consumer remembers the brand, as fitting into this manufactured social reality. Advertisers often set a situate-the-brand-socially objective by creating an ad that places a brand in a socially desirable context.

Method: Slice-of-Life Ads. By placing a brand in a social context, it gains social meaning by association. Slice-of-life advertisements depict an idealized user in a typical usage situation gaining benefits and satisfaction from using the brand, as the Swisher Sweets ad in Exhibit 10.9 shows. The social context surrounding the brand rubs off and gives the brand social meaning. Receivers may, of course, reject that meaning.

Objective: Define the Brand Image

Madonna has an image; Michael Jordan has an image; so do Saab and Pepsi. Just like people, brands have images. Images are the most apparent and most prominently associated characteristics of a brand. They are the thing consumers most remember or associate with a brand. Advertisers are in the business of creating, adjusting, and maintaining images—in other words, they often engage in the define-the-brand-image objective.

Method: Image Ads. Image advertising means different things to different people. To some, it means the absence of hard product information. To others, it refers to advertising that is almost exclusively visual. This is an oversimplification, but it is true that most image advertising tends toward the visual. In both cases, it means an attempt to link certain attributes to the brand, rather than to engage the consumer in any kind of discourse. Sometimes these linkages are quite explicit, such as using a tiger to indicate the strength of a brand. Other times, the linkages are implicit and subtle, such as the colors and tones associated with a brand.

EXHIBIT 10.9

Slice-of-life ads depict an idealized user in a typical setting, with the user benefiting from a brand. Receivers are then supposed to identify with the user or scene, and the brand acquires social meaning for receivers.

Objective: Persuade the Consumer

Advertising that attempts to persuade is high-engagement advertising. Its goal is to convince the consumer, through a form of commercial discourse, that a brand is superior. The persuasion objective requires a significantly high level of cognitive engagement with the audience. The receiver has to think about what the advertiser is saying. The receiver must engage in a form of mental argument with the commercial. For example, an ad says, "In a Mercedes, you wouldn't get stuck behind a Lexus on the road. . . . Why would you get stuck behind one at your dealer?" You might read that and say to yourself, "Hey, what's wrong with Lexus? I think Lexus is great. Forget this." Or you might say, "Yeah, if I could afford a Mercedes, I'd buy a really great car." Or maybe you would say to yourself, "Hey, that's right. . . . You know, maybe I should consider a Mercedes next time. They're probably not much more than a Lexus." The point is that in a persuasion ad, there is an assumed dialogue between the ad and the receiver.

Method: Benefit-Appeal Ads. Benefit-appeal ads focus the consumer's attention on the benefit or benefits of using a product or service. For example, an advertiser might rely on the functional features of its brand as the basis for its message strategy, emphasizing those tangible attributes of the brand that can be measured in some standardized fashion. Examples are the fuel economy of an automobile, the watts-per-channel output of a stereo receiver, the on-time performance of an airline company, or the annual rate of return of a mutual fund. Price, warranty, and performance attributes are other prominent features on which a benefit message strategy can be based. Many household consumers and most business buyers emphasize these criteria in their evaluation of products and services. An advertiser is more likely to rely on functional features when its brand has a competitive advantage based on a unique and tangible feature or when the target audience is oriented to judging products in the category based on such functional features. When Casterol introduced Syntec synthetic motor oil, the firm was able to show how synthetic additives increased the heat protection capability of the oil compared to standard motor oils. When CNS introduced Breathe Right nasal strips, one of the functional benefits it espoused was the strips' ability to alleviate snoring, as seen in the ad in Exhibit 10.10.

A benefit, however, does not have to be tangible. In many cases, the target audience has little interest in or ability to evaluate a product's functional features, but the advertiser can demonstrate important benefits from its use. Potential buyers may have little appreciation for the horsepower, construction, or blade width of a riding lawn mower, but the benefits of using such a product are easy to envision. The speed and convenience of a riding lawn mower allow the user to spend more time with family, watch television, or simply relax instead of laboring over the lawn. The product provides the benefit of increased discretionary time. Life insurance companies often use this copy method. Rather than run an ad that describes the mysterious and mundane differences between term and whole life insurance, insurance firms show how a comfortable retirement or funding for children's education is the result of wise insurance investments. The ad for Putnam Investments shown in Exhibit 10.11 is a good example of an intangible benefit-appeal message.

Method: Unique Selling Proposition.

A **unique selling proposition (USP)** is a promise contained in an advertisement in which the advertised brand offers a specific, unique, and relevant benefit to the consumer. This method was championed by Rosser Reeves at the Ted Bates agency in the 1950s. The idea is simply to find a unique benefit and then sell it,

EXHIBIT 10.10

A straightforward advertising approach is the benefit-appeal technique. This method focuses consumer attention on the main benefit of using a brand. Brands with unique performance capabilities, like the Breathe Right nasal strip, can use a benefit-appeal ad effectively. **www2 .breatheright.com/breatheright/html/breathe1.html**

EXHIBIT 10.11 *For brands whose primary value is intangible, the benefit-appeal method is often an ideal way to communicate with receivers. A good night's sleep, as this ad for Putnam Investments suggests, exemplifies the benefits of using the firm's financial-planning services.*

sell it, sell it. The unique feature may be apparent or created. In the case of the former, when Rayovac introduced the Renewal alkaline battery that was reusable "25 times or more," it offered consumers unique and relevant benefits over both standard alkaline batteries and traditional rechargeable batteries: lower initial cost and quicker recharging. Rayovac's USP message strategy is shown in Exhibit 10.12.

In the case of created USPs, a beer drinker, when blindfolded, may not be able to tell the difference between brands, but one advertiser emphasizes its use of "pure Canadian spring water." It may be that several Canadian beers use spring water, but this beer has staked out that attribute as its own. The implication to consumers is that other beers don't have this quality. Many USPs are created.

Method: Reason-Why.
In a reason-why ad, the advertiser reasons with the potential consumer. The ad points out to the receiver that there are reasons why this brand will be satisfying and beneficial. Advertisers are usually relentless in their attempt to reason with consumers when using this method. They begin with some claim, like "Seven great reasons to buy Brand X," and then proceed to list all seven, finishing with the conclusion (implicit or explicit) that only a moron would, after such compelling evidence, do anything other than purchase Brand X. The biggest task to this method is making sure that the reason why makes sense and that consumers care. Consumer research is important before this appeal is attempted.

Method: Hard-Sell.
Hard-sell ads are characteristically high pressure and urgent. Phrases like "act now," "limited time offer," "your last chance to save," and "one-time-only sale" are representative of this method. The idea is to create a sense of urgency so consumers will act impulsively. Of course, many consumers have learned how to decode and otherwise discount these messages, decreasing their effectiveness and persuasive ability.

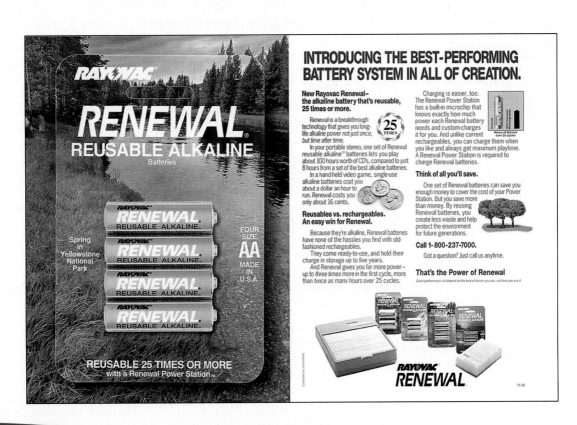

EXHIBIT 10.12

The unique selling proposition (USP) method offers consumers a specific and unique benefit from using the advertised brand. The introductory advertising campaign for Rayovac's reusable alkaline batteries employed the USP method. **www.rayovac.com**

Method: Comparison Ads. **Comparison advertisements** are ads in which a brand's ability to satisfy consumers is demonstrated by comparing its features to those of competitive brands.

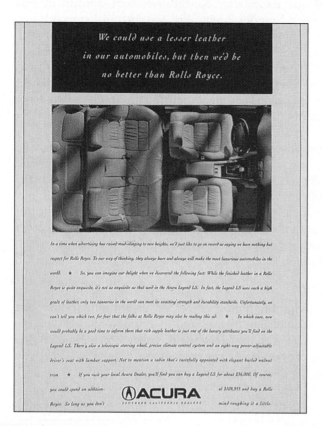

Comparisons can be an effective and efficient means of communicating a large amount of information in a clear and interesting way, or they can be extremely confusing. Comparison as a technique has traditionally been used by marketers of convenience goods, such as pain relievers, laundry detergents, and household cleaners. More recently, advertisers in a wide range of product categories have tried comparison as their main message method. AT&T and MCI have had a long-running feud over whose rates are lower for household consumers, which may have completely confused everyone. Even luxury carmakers BMW and Lexus have recently targeted each other with comparative claims.[14] In one ad, BMW attacks the sluggish performance of Lexus with the message "According to recent test results, Lexus' greatest achievement in acceleration is its price." Not to be left out of the luxury car comparative advertising skirmish, the Acura dealers of Southern California took on Rolls-Royce, as shown in the ad in Exhibit 10.13.

Using comparison in an advertisement can be direct and name competitors' brands, or it can be indirect and refer only to the "leading brand" or "Brand X." The following are conclusions about the use of comparison as a message tactic:

EXHIBIT 10.13

Comparison ads compare the advertiser's brand to one or more competitors. Here, Acura is comparing the quality of its leather interior to that of Rolls-Royce. Copy research suggests that making a feature-specific comparison to a leading competitor and naming the competitor is the most effective way to use the comparison method. **www.acura.com/**

- Direct comparison by a low-share brand to a high-share brand increases the attention on the part of receivers and increases the purchase intention of the low-share brand.
- Direct comparison by a high-share brand to a low-share brand does not attract additional attention and increases awareness of the low-share brand.

- Noncomparative claims by high-share brands are more effective at enhancing purchase intention than either direct or indirect comparison.
- Indirect comparison by moderate-share brands to either high- or low-share brands is more effective at enhancing the purchase intention of moderate-share brands than direct comparison.
- Direct comparison is more effective if members of the target audience have not demonstrated clear brand preference in their product choices.
- Direct comparison is more effective if the television medium is employed to make the comparison.[15]

There is also evidence that comparison advertising is not appropriate and will not be effective when one or more of the following are true:

14. Jim Henry, "Comparative Ads Speed Ahead for Luxury Imports," *Advertising Age,* September 12, 1994, 10.
15. Conclusions in this list are drawn from William R. Swinyard, "The Interaction between Comparative Advertising and Copy Claim Variation," *Journal of Marketing Research* 18 (May 1981): 175–86; Cornelia Pechmann and David Stewart, "The Effects of Comparative Advertising on Attention, Memory, and Purchase Intentions," *Journal of Consumer Research* (September 1990): 180–91; and Sanjay Petruvu and Kenneth R. Lord, "Comparative and Noncomparative Advertising: Attitudinal Effects under Cognitive and Affective Involvement Conditions," *Journal of Advertising* (June 1994): 77–90.

- The fundamental brand appeal is emotional rather than logical.
- The brand is a new product in the product category.
- The product category is characterized by insignificant functional differences between brands, thus making comparisons trivial.
- The competition has powerful counterclaims that can be made in retaliation to the original comparison.
- The brand has distinctive features that can differentiate it from the competition in the absence of comparison.[16]

There are some risks to the advertiser with the use of the comparison tactic. The firm sponsoring a comparative ad is sometimes perceived as less trustworthy, and comparative ads are sometimes evaluated as more offensive and less interesting than noncomparative ads.

Method: Information-Only Ads.

An information-only ad simply presents the facts about a product or service. Of course, these facts are not randomly selected but are chosen for persuasive reasons, which means there is no such thing as a purely information-only ad. A brand with distinctive features can use the information-only message tactic to great advantage. These ads often use a visual to help the audience identify the product features being highlighted. For example, Fidelity Investments can show with straight information the performance of its popular Magellan mutual fund by showing the one-year, five-year, and ten-year investment returns the fund has produced.

Method: Testimonial Ads.

A frequently used message tactic is to have a spokesperson who champions the brand in an advertisement, rather than simply providing information. When an advocacy position is taken by a spokesperson in an advertisement, this is known as a **testimonial.** The value of the testimonial lies in the authoritative presentation of a brand's attributes and benefits by the spokesperson. There are three basic versions of the testimonial message tactic.

The most conspicuous version is the *celebrity testimonial.* Sports stars like Michael Jordan (McDonald's) and Arnold Palmer (Pennzoil, Cadillac) are favorites of advertisers. Actresses like Candice Bergen (Sprint) and supermodels such as Cindy Crawford (Pepsi) are also widely used. The belief is that a celebrity testimonial will increase an ad's ability to attract attention and produce a desire in receivers to emulate or imitate the celebrities they admire.

Whether this is really true or not, the fact remains that a list of top commercials is dominated by ads that feature celebrities.[17] Of course, there is the ever-present risk that a celebrity will fall from grace, as several have in recent years, and potentially damage the reputation of the brand for which he or she was once the champion.

Expert spokespersons for a brand are viewed by the target audience as having expert product knowledge. The GM Parts Service Division created an expert in Mr. Goodwrench, who was presented as a knowledgeable source of information. A spokesperson portrayed as a doctor, lawyer, scientist, gardener, or any other expert relevant to a brand is intended to increase the credibility of the message being transmitted. There are also real experts. Advertising for The Club, a steering-wheel locking device that deters auto theft, uses police officers from several U.S. cities to demonstrate the effectiveness of the product. Some experts can also be celebrities. This is the case when Michael Jordan gives a testimonial for Nike basketball shoes.

---

16.   In general, comparative advertisements are not more effective than noncomparative ads when the intention is to affect brand attitude. For a current review of literature on conditions related to the effectiveness of comparative advertising, see Cornelia Pechmann and David Stewart, "The Psychology of Comparative Advertising," in *Attention, Attitude and Affect in Response to Advertising,* ed. E. M. Clark, T. C. Brock, and D. W. Steward (Hillsdale, N.J.: Lawrence Erlbaum Associates, 1994), 79–96.

17.   Kevin Goldman, "Year's Top Commercials Propelled by Star Power," *Wall Street Journal,* March 16, 1994, B1.

There is also the *average user testimonial*. Here, the spokesperson is not a celebrity or portrayed as an expert but rather as an average user speaking for the brand. The philosophy is that the target market can relate to this person. Solid theoretical support for this testimonial approach comes from reference group theory. An interpretation of reference group theory in this context suggests that consumers may rely on opinions or testimonials from people they consider similar to themselves, rather than on objective product information. Simply put, the consumer's logic in this situation is "That person is similar to me and likes that brand; therefore, I will also like that brand." In theory, this sort of logic frees the receiver from having to scrutinize detailed product information by simply substituting the reference group information. Of course, in practice, the execution of this strategy is nowhere near that easy. Consumers are very sophisticated at detecting this attempt at persuasion.

EXHIBIT 10.14

Demonstrating a brand's performance helps receivers appreciate the satisfaction the brand has to offer. Here, the traction of a Ford Explorer is demonstrated as the sport-utility vehicle is driven on an ice rink—right alongside the Zamboni ice-cleaning machine. **www.ford.com/**

Method: Demonstration.

How close an electric razor shaves, how green a fertilizer makes a lawn, or how easy an exercise machine is to use are all product features that can be demonstrated by using a method known simply as the demonstration ad. "Seeing is believing" is the motto of this school of advertising. When Ford rolled one of its Explorers onto a hockey rink, for example (see Exhibit 10.14), it provided the ideal setting for demonstrating the sport-utility vehicle's superior traction.

Method: Advertorial.

An **advertorial** is a special advertising section designed to look like the print publication in which it appears. Advertorials are so named because they have the look of the editorial content of a magazine or newspaper but really represent a long and involved advertisement for a firm and its product or service. The *Wall Street Journal, Redbook,* and *New York Magazine* have all carried advertorials. *Sports Illustrated* has inserted advertorials for the Kentucky Derby and the Indianapolis 500. The potential effectiveness of this technique lies with the increased credibility that comes from the look and length of the advertisement. These features have, however, raised controversy. Some critics believe that most readers aren't even aware they're reading an advertisement because of the similarity in appearance to the publication.[18]

Method: Infomercials.

With the **infomercial,** an advertiser buys from 5 to 60 minutes of television time and runs a documentary/information/entertainment program that is really an extended advertisement. An infomercial is the television equivalent of an advertorial.

18. Cynthia Crossen, "Proliferation of 'Advertorials' Blurs Distinction between News and Ads," *Wall Street Journal,* April 21, 1988, 33.

Real estate investment programs, weight-loss and fitness products, motivational programs, and cookware have dominated the infomercial format. A 30-minute infomercial can cost from $50,000 to $1.2 million to put on the air. The program usually has a host who is providing information about a product and typically brings on guests to give testimonials about how successful they have been using the featured product. Most infomercials run on cable stations, although networks have sold early-morning and late-night time as well. Recently, big firms have used infomercials. Philips Electronics has had great success with a 30-minute adventure-like infomercial for its compact disc interactive (CD-I) player. Philips spent nearly $20 million to produce and buy prime-time media for the infomercial but contends the infomercial has much more impact than the print advertising it replaced.[19] Apple Computer also ran a 30-minute infomercial as part of the advertising campaign to introduce its new lower-priced Macintosh, called the Performa. The ad was targeted to families looking to buy their first computer and was a huge success. The infomercial generated four times as many telephone inquiries as Apple anticipated.[20]

Not all advertisers have had such good success with infomercials. After spending nearly half a million dollars to produce and air a 30-minute infomercial promoting a Broadway show, the producers pulled the ad after three weeks. The toll-free number to order tickets drew an average of only 14 calls each time the ad ran.[21] But Exhibit 10.15 shows the tremendous sales impact some infomercials can have. Notice that many of these leading infomercials relied on celebrity spokespersons as part of the program. Also see the Global Issues box on page 292 for an update on the worldwide prospects for the infomercial.

Objective: Invoke a Direct Response

A direct response advertising appeal implores the receiver to act immediately. It's a blend of hard selling and impulse buying. Price appeals associated with special sales or the convenience of ordering from the

EXHIBIT 10.15

Infomercials generating the greatest sales in 1994.

Infomercial Program	Product	Host	Estimated Gross Sales ($ in millions)
Psychic Friends Network	900 toll number	Dionne Warwick	$100
Dura-Lube	Engine treatment	Jim Caldwell	210
Fitness Tread	Manual treadmill	Jane Fonda	130
Making Love Work	Relationship video series	Barbara DeAngelis	24
Popeil Automatic Pasta Maker	Kitchen appliance	Ron Popeil	80
Komputer Tutor	PC videos	Mike Levey	15
The Principal Secret	Skin-care system	Victoria Principal	85
Gravity Edge	Exercise machine	Lorenzo Lamas	n.a.
Hip & Thigh Machine	Exercise machine	Jake Steinfeld	50
Personal Power	Motivational tapes	Tony Robbins	140

Source: Jacqueline M. Graves, "The Fortune 500 Opt for Infomercials," *Fortune*, March 6, 1995, 20. Reprinted with permission.

19.   Kevin Goldman, "Philips Infomercial Does Its Thing in Popular TV Watching Hours," *Wall Street Journal*, September 23, 1993, B6.
20.   Kevin Goldman, "Apple Plans Infomercial Aimed at Families," *Wall Street Journal*, January 4, 1994, B3; and Jacqueline M. Graves, "The Fortune 500 Opt for Infomercials," *Fortune*, March 6, 1995, 20.
21.   Kevin Goldman, "Broadway Hopeful Flops with Debut of Infomercial," *Wall Street Journal*, April 29, 1994, B3.

comfort of one's home form the basis of the direct response objective. Local retailers and national direct merchants like L. L. Bean and J. Crew are the most frequent users of this message strategy. In some cases, organizations use more feature-laden appeals in their direct response advertising, as does the FannieMae Foundation in its informational guides on the home-buying process (see Exhibit 10.16). The main characteristic of such ads, however, is encouraging the audience to respond immediately by calling a toll-free number.

GLOBAL ISSUES

AMERICA'S NEWEST CONTRIBUTION TO WORLD CULTURE: INFOMERCIALS GO GLOBAL

France offers the world haute cuisine and fine wine. Italy gives the world high fashion and fast cars. The Swiss give us elegant timepieces. And America comes through with—the infomercial! U.S.-based National Media has gone global. The leading infomercial marketer now sells media space and products to more than 215 million households in 56 countries worldwide. Over the past three years, National Media has acquired several infomercial production companies and produced some of the most successful infomercials in the United States, including *Psychic Friends Network* and *Making Love Work.*

But the infomercial's role in global markets is somewhat different from its role in the United States. Domestic infomercials represent a low-cost alternative to expensive mass media options. Also, the vast majority of infomercial users in the United States are direct marketers. In global markets, the infomercial is seen as a way to create brand awareness, whether the product is direct marketed or not.

Infomercials have met with great success in Japan and Europe. HSN (the international subsidiary of Home Shopping Network) runs pan-European infomercials that air simultaneously in 14 countries. In less than one year, 11 Japanese television stations have agreed to air infomercials to an audience reaching 26 million homes, or more than half of Japan's total population. One large marketer that places infomercials with National Media says, "For some reason, U.S.-produced infomercials work in Japan at staggering levels."

The products that sell on global TV fall into familiar categories like cosmetic, personal care, fitness, and cooking items. And there is no lack of enthusiasm for the future from the president of National Media, who says, "Down the road, we'll be able to put a product simultaneously into the homes of 300 to 500 million people around the globe. Now that's powerful."

Source: Kim Cleland, "Infomercial Audience Crosses over Cultures," *Advertising Age International,* January 15, 1996, 1-8.

Method: Direct Response. Direct response ads have become more prevalent in recent years for several reasons. First, many direct response messages feature a price-oriented appeal. In today's era of value-oriented, price-conscious consumers, direct response messages provide an ideal opportunity for offering consumers a discount via a mail-in coupon or special television offer that is a price-based appeal. Second, firms have developed sophisticated databases that allow them to specifically target well-defined customer groups. Such databases can be tailored to geographic areas, demographic characteristics of audiences, or past product use as ways to target different audiences. The firm can then send a specific and different message to each target audience. Thirdly, advertisers are demanding more evidence that the dollars they spend on advertising are having an impact. Ad agencies have found that direct response messages offer the most tangible evidence of advertising impact, and they are using the technique as a means of accountability.

Message development is where the advertising battle is usually won or lost. It's where real creativity exists. It's where the agency has to be smart and figure out just how to turn the wishes of the client into effective advertising. It is where the creatives have to get into the minds of consumers, realizing that the advertisement will be received by different people in different ways. Great messages are developed by people who can put themselves into the minds of their audience members and anticipate their response, leading to the desired outcomes.

Ads with the objective of invoking a direct response from receivers, like this ad from the FannieMae Foundation, implore consumers to take action immediately. Providing a toll-free number for receivers to call is a common method of facilitating direct response. **www.fanniemae.com/**

SUMMARY

❶ Recognize the impact of creativity in the development of advertising.

Detailed planning and analysis are important to advertising success. However, truly great advertising has a dramatic creative insight, or what is often referred to as a big idea, at the core of its message strategy. Creativity is not a process that can be managed in a step-by-step fashion to generate predictable results. To derive the benefits of the big idea, marketing managers must learn to accommodate, or better yet, inspire, the creative process.

❷ Describe the essential characteristics of the advertising message.

An advertising message is the heart of any advertising campaign. A message is composed of copy and art, and it must do the actual work of communicating with the audience. The message communicated by an ad may derive from any of its verbal or nonverbal elements. Since audience members are active interpreters, advertisers can never take for granted the true meaning an audience will derive from their message.

❸ Identify nine types of message strategies and several methods for executing each of them.

Advertisers can choose from a wide array of message strategy objectives as well as methods for implementing these objectives. Two fundamental message objectives are brand recall and brand preference. The advertiser may also seek to activate negative emotive states like fear or anxiety as the means to motivate brand purchase. Transformational advertising seeks to influence the nature of the consumption experience. A message may also feature the brand in an important social context to heighten the brand's appeal. Enhancing brand imagery is another common message objective and can be contrasted with designing messages to produce immediate action. Finally, many advertising messages are designed with the primary intent of persuading the customer. A wealth of approaches are used to effect persuasion, including comparison ads, testimonials, and infomercials.

KEY TERMS

big idea (274)

message (275)

copy (275)

art (275)

message strategy (276)

unique selling proposition (USP) (286)

comparison advertisements (288)

testimonial (289)

advertorial (290)

infomercial (291)

QUESTIONS FOR REVIEW AND CRITICAL THINKING

1. Review the chapter opener about the success of Apple's "1984" commercial. What was the big idea at the heart of this ad that helped make the Macintosh computer a success? A decade later, Apple's big idea had worn out. What went wrong?

2. Once again, reflect on the "1984" commercial. As this chapter suggested, consumers are active interpreters of ads, and one of the virtues of the "1984" ad was that it invited the audience to become involved and make an interpretation. Thinking about the "1984" ad, what sorts of interpretations could a consumer make that would benefit the brand? Conversely, what sorts of interpretations might a person make, after a single exposure to this ad, that would be detrimental to Macintosh?

3. Think back to the last time you leafed through your favorite magazine. Can you remember reading any of the copy in any of the ads in this magazine? Can you remember any copy that you have ever read in a magazine ad? From your experience, what conclusions would you draw about the importance of art and copy in magazine advertisements?

4. Explain the difference between brand recall and brand preference as message objectives. Which of these objectives do you think would be harder to achieve, and why?

5. Procter and Gamble has had considerable success with the message strategy involving anxiety arousal. How does P&G's success with this strategy refute the general premise that the best way to appeal to American consumers is to appeal to their pursuit of personal freedom and individuality?

6. Compare and contrast the notions of the big idea and the unique selling proposition (USP). Are these two notions referring to the same thing? Is it possible to have a USP that is not the big idea for an ad campaign? How about the other way around—is it possible to have a big idea that is not a USP?

7. Review the do's and don'ts of comparison advertising and then think about each of the brand pairs listed below. Comment on whether you think comparison ads would be a good choice for the product category in question, and if so, which brand in the pair would be in the most appropriate position to use comparisons: Ford versus Chevy trucks; Coors Light versus Bud Light beer; Nuprin versus Tylenol pain reliever; Brut versus Obsession cologne; Wendy's versus McDonald's hamburgers.

EXPERIENTIAL EXERCISE

Describe one of your favorite feel-good ads, print or broadcast. Are you a loyal purchaser of the brand being promoted? If so, what is it about the ad that leads you to purchase the product? If not, what feel-good ads do promote brands you are loyal to? What is your conclusion about the effectiveness of feel-good ads?

USING THE INTERNET

Advertisers use a variety of message strategies and methods for accomplishing their strategic goals. Visit the following sites:

Clinique: www.clinique.com

Ragu: www.eat.com

Sprint: www.sprint.com/college/

For each site, answer the following questions:

1.   Is there a big idea behind the site?

2.   What is the fundamental message objective?

3.   How have the site designers used creativity to achieve this objective?

4.   How is the site designed relative to the message issues raised in the New Media box on page 276?

Chapter 11

Copywriting

After reading and thinking about this chapter, you will be able to do the following:

1 Explain the need for a creative plan in the copywriting process.

2 Detail the components of print copy, along with important guidelines for writing effective print copy.

3 Describe various formatting alternatives for radio ads and articulate guidelines for writing effective radio copy.

4 Describe various formatting alternatives for television ads and articulate guidelines for developing effective television copy.

We live in an age when just about everything carries a warning label of some sort. Objects in rearview mirrors may be closer than they appear. Hair dryers should be kept away from water. Using a lawn mower to trim the hedge may result in injury.

In this spirit, the authors of this book urge you to read the warning label in Exhibit 11.1. It's far too simplistic to state that copywriters are responsible for the verbal elements in an ad and art directors are responsible for the visual elements. In fact, copywriters and art directors function as partners and are referred to as the **creative team** in agencies. The creative team is first and foremost responsible for coming up with the **creative concept.** The creative concept, which can be thought of as the unique creative thought behind a campaign, is then turned into individual advertisements. During this process, copywriters often suggest the idea for magnificent, arresting visuals. Likewise, art directors often come up with killer headlines.

As you can see in Exhibits 11.2 and 11.3, some ads have no headlines at all. Some have no visuals. Still, in most cases, both a copywriter and an art director are equally involved in creating an ad. This doesn't mean that copywriting and art directing are one and the same. The following two chapters will show that the talent and knowledge needed to excel in one area differ in many ways from those needed to excel in the other. Still, one must recognize that not all copywriting is done by copywriters and not all art directing is done by art directors.

Understanding copywriting is as much about the people who write copy as it is about the product research, audience research, and other information that copywriters use to create effective copy. This is what some of the most influential people in the history of advertising have said:

As I have observed it, great advertising writing either in print or television is disarmingly simple. It has the common touch without being or sounding patronizing. If you are writing about baloney, don't try to make it sound like Cornish hen, because that is the worst kind of baloney. Just make it darned good baloney.[1]

—Leo Burnett, founder of the Leo Burnett agency, Chicago

Why should anyone look at your ad? The reader doesn't buy his [her] magazine or tune his [her] radio and TV to see and hear what you have to say. . . . What is the use of saying all the right things in the world if nobody is going to read them? And, believe me, nobody is going to read them if they are not said with freshness, originality and imagination.[2]

—William Bernbach, cofounder of one of the most influential agencies during the 1960s, Doyle, Dane, Bernbach

Never write an advertisement which you wouldn't want your family to read. Good products can be sold by honest advertising. If you don't think the product is good, you have no business to be advertising it. If you tell lies, or weasel, you do your client a disservice, you increase your load of guilt, and you fan the flames of public resentment against the whole business of advertising.[3]

—David Ogilvy's ninth of eleven commandments of advertising

If you think you have a better mousetrap, or shirt, or whatever, you've got to tell people, and I don't think that has to be done with trickery, or insults, or by talking down to people. . . . The smartest advertising is the advertising that communicates the best and respects consumers' intelligence. It's advertising that lets them bring something to the communication process, as opposed to some of the more validly criticized work in our profession which tries to grind the benefits of a soap or a cake mix into a poor housewife's head by repeating it 37 times in 30 seconds.[4]

—Lee Clow, creator of the Apple Macintosh "1984" advertisement

1.   Leo Burnett, "Keep Listening to That Wee, Small Voice," in *Communications of an Advertising Man* (Chicago, Ill.: Leo Burnett, 1961), 160.
2.   Cited in Martin Mayer, *Madison Avenue, U.S.A.* (New York: Pocket Books, 1954), 66.
3.   David Ogilvy, *Confessions of an Advertising Man* (New York: Atheneum, 1964), 102.
4.   Jennifer Pendleton, "Bringing New Clow-T to Ads, Chiat's Unlikely Creative," *Advertising Age*, February 7, 1985, 1.

EXHIBIT 11.1

While copywriters are primarily responsible for writing the verbal descriptions in ads and art directors are primarily responsible for the visuals, they act as partners and often come up with great ideas outside their primary responsibility.

> # WARNING: The Difference Between Copywriters And Art Directors May Not Be As Great As You Think.

Finally, the following observation on the power of a good advertisement, brilliant in its simplicity, is offered by one of the modern-day geniuses of advertising:

Imagination is one of the last remaining legal means to gain an unfair advantage over your competition.[5]

—Tim McElligott, cofounder of a highly creative and successful Minneapolis advertising agency

Good copywriters must always bring spirit and imagination to advertising. Leo Burnett, William Bernbach, David Ogilvy, and Lee Clow have created some of the most memorable advertising in history: the "We're Number 2, We Try Harder" Avis campaign (William Bernbach); the Hathaway Shirt Man ads (David Ogilvy); the Jolly

Lesson one: How to avoid getting a nickname like Lefty, Stumpy or Knuckles.

CARPENTRY/CABINET MAKING CLASSES THE RICHMOND TECHNICAL CENTER
CALL 780-6237 OR ASK YOUR GUIDANCE COUNSELOR FOR DETAILS.

ACE WINDOW CLEANERS

EXHIBITS 11.2 AND 11.3

While most effective ads use multiple copy components—headline, subhead, body copy, visual—some ads excel by focusing on a single component. The Richmond Technical Center ad in Exhibit 11.2 succeeds without the use of an illustration. Similarly, the Ace Window Cleaners ad in Exhibit 11.3 uses no copy or headline, but the illustration communicates brilliantly.

5.   Tim McElligott is credited with making this statement in several public speeches during the 1980s.

Green Giant ads (Leo Burnett); and the "1984" Apple Macintosh ad (Lee Clow). See Exhibits 11.4 and 11.5 for samples of their work. When these advertising legends speak of creating good ads that respect the consumer's intelligence and rely on imagination, they count copywriting as a central dimension in the process.

Copywriting and the Creative Plan

❶ **Copywriting** is the process of expressing the value and benefits a brand has to offer, via written or verbal descriptions. Copywriting requires far more than the ability to string product descriptions together in coherent sentences. One apt description of copywriting is that it is a never-ending search for ideas combined with a never-ending search for new and different ways to express those ideas.

Effective copywriters are well-informed and astute advertising decision makers with creative talent. Copywriters are able to comprehend and then incorporate the complexities of marketing strategies, consumer behavior, and advertising strategies into a brief, yet powerful communication. They must do so in such a way that the copy does not interfere with but rather enhances the visual aspects of the message.

An astute advertiser will go to great lengths to provide copywriters with as much information as possible about the objectives for a particular advertising effort. The responsibility for keeping copywriters informed lies with the client's marketing managers in conjunction with account executives and creative directors in the ad agency. For a firm with an in-house advertising department, the marketing managers and the creative

When you're only No.2, you try harder. Or else.

Avis can't afford to relax.

Little fish have to keep moving all of the time. The big ones never stop picking on them.

Avis knows all about the problems of little fish.

We're only No.2 in rent a cars. We'd be swallowed up if we didn't try harder.

There's no rest for us.

We're always emptying ashtrays. Making sure gas tanks are full before we rent our cars. Seeing that the batteries are full of life. Checking our windshield wipers.

And the cars we rent out can't be anything less than spanking new Plymouths.

And since we're not the big fish, you won't feel like a sardine when you come to our counter.

We're not jammed with customers.

Hathaway and the Duke's stud groom

EXHIBIT 11.4

One of the great names in advertising is William Bernbach, and the memorable and highly effective "We Try Harder" campaign for Avis Rent a Car was produced by his agency, Doyle, Dane, Bernbach.
www.avis.com/

EXHIBIT 11.5 *David Ogilvy, to many a guru in advertising, created the Hathaway Shirt Man (complete with an eye patch) as a way to attract attention and create an image for the Hathaway brand many years ago.*

people in the department must communicate the foundations and intricacies of the firm's marketing strategies to the copywriters. Without this information, copywriters are left without guidance and direction, and they must rely on intuition about what sorts of information are relevant and meaningful to a target audience. Sometimes that works; most of the time, it does not.

Depending on the assignment, the client, and the traditions of the agency, the creative team may also rely on various forms of copy research. Typically, copy research is either developmental or evaluative. **Developmental copy research** can actually help copywriters at the early stages of copy development by providing audience interpretations and reactions to the proposed copy. **Evaluative copy research** is used to judge copy only after the fact. Here, the audience expresses its approval or disapproval of the copy used in an ad. Copywriters are not fond of these evaluative report cards.

A **creative plan** is a guideline used during the copywriting process to specify the message elements that must be coordinated during the preparation of copy. These elements include main product claims, creative devices, media that will be used, and special creative needs a product or service might have. One of the main challenges faced by a copywriter is to make creative sense out of the maze of information that comes from the message development process. Part of the challenge is creating excitement around what can otherwise be dull product features. For example, the challenge for the copywriter responsible for the ad in Exhibit 11.6 was to express the expected feature of toughness in a pickup truck in an unexpected fashion.

Another aspect of the challenge is bringing together various creative tools (such as illustration, use of color, and use of sound and action) in conjunction with the copy. Finally, copy must be coordinated with the media that will be used. All of these factors

Pit Bull Meets Moose.

WEB SIGHTING

Chevy S-Series ZR2 Pickup. What a confrontation. Two serious off-roaders. One with a stance that'd make a cougar turn tail. The guts to track a grizzly bear where he lives. And the brute strength to pull a yak. Of course the other one can grow pretty neat antlers. If you want to meet him, just get yourself a ZR2 and go. But remember whose backyard you're visiting. Don't spoil it.

Chevy S-Series LIKE A ROCK

EXHIBIT 11.6

What is the creative concept behind this Chevrolet ad? Can you articulate the creative plan that guides the copy in the ad? Does the creative plan as seen in the exhibit also guide the Chevrolet Web site at www.chevrolet.com? Does the Ford site at www.ford.com/ have the same overall creative guidance?

are coordinated through the use of a creative plan. Some of the elements considered in devising a creative plan are

- the product features to be emphasized
- the benefits a user receives from these features
- the media chosen for transmitting the information and the length of time the advertisement will run
- the suggested mood or tone for the ad

- the ways in which mood and atmosphere will be achieved in the ad
- the production budget for the ad[6]

These considerations can be modified or disregarded entirely during the process of creating an ad. For example, sometimes a brilliant creative execution demands that television, rather than print, be the media vehicle of choice. Occasionally, a particular creative thought may suggest a completely different mood or tone than the one listed in the creative plan. A creative plan is best thought of as a starting point, not an end point, for the creative team. Like anything else in advertising, the plan should evolve and grow as new insights are gained.

Once the creative plan is devised, the creative team can get on with the task of creating the actual advertisement. The creative plan provides a blueprint from which the team can work. Because writing copy for a print advertisement and writing copy for a broadcast advertisement entail vastly different challenges, we will consider each type of copywriting effort separately. The New Media box on this page raises yet another challenge: writing copy for cyberspace.

NEW MEDIA

WRITING CYBERCOPY: DON'T ABANDON ALL THE OLD RULES

Writing effective copy for print and broadcast media is difficult enough, but what kind of copy does the average Net surfer find appealing? No one really knows, but we do know a few things about early users of the Internet and World Wide Web. First, users of the Internet are there first and foremost because it is an information environment. It is hard to imagine someone getting up in the morning, turning on the computer, and seeking out ads. Quite to the contrary, the beauty of the Internet in the minds of many has been its freedom from advertising.

Second, when Internet users visit a site, that visit may last only a few seconds. *HotWired* magazine says that on a good day, it can have 600,000 "hits," or visits, some lasting only a few seconds—just long enough for the visitor to quickly scan what is available and then, if not intrigued, move on to another site. The chance to communicate online thus may be even more fleeting than the opportunity offered by radio or television. Third, advertisers have to accept that cyberspace may soon become just as cluttered with competing ads as the traditional media.

In the end, the rules for writing effective copy in cyberspace may not be all that different from the general rules for copywriting. Once a browser is attracted to a site for the information it offers, she or he will, oh by the way, bump into ads. The new opportunity is to make these ads and their copy interactive according to an individual consumer's interest. If an IBM advertisement can lead a consumer through a series of alternative click-and-proceed paths, then customization of ads is the new copywriting opportunity offered by the interactive environment.

Sources: "Cerfin' the Net," *Sales and Marketing Management*, March 1995, 18–23; Julie Chao, "Tallies of Web-Site Browsers Often Deceive," *Wall Street Journal*, June 21, 1995, B1; and Bruce Judson, "Luring Advertisers' Prospects to Web," *Advertising Age*, August 7, 1995, 16.

Copywriting for Print Advertising

2 In preparing copy for a print ad, the first step in the copy development process is deciding how to use (or not use) the three separate components of print copy: the headline, the subhead, and the body copy. Be aware that the full range of components applies most directly to print ads that appear in magazines, newspapers, or direct mail pieces. These guidelines also apply to other "print" media like billboards, transit advertising, and specialty advertising, but in a more limited way. Because of the size and presentation constraints imposed by the

6.   The last two points in this section were adapted from A. Jerome Jewler, *Creative Strategy in Advertising,* 3rd ed. (Belmont, Calif.: Wadsworth Publishing Company, 1989), 196.

formats of these other media, there is a limit to the range of copywriting possibilities. More detail on support media is presented in Chapter 16.

The Headline

The **headline** in an advertisement is the leading sentence or sentences, usually at the top or bottom of the ad, that attract attention, communicate a key selling point, or achieve brand identification. Many headlines fail to attract attention, and the ad itself then becomes another bit of clutter in consumers' lives. Lifeless headlines do not compel the reader to examine other parts of the ad. Simply stated, a headline can either motivate a reader to move on to the rest of an ad, or lose the reader for good.

Purposes of a Headline. In preparing a headline, a copywriter begins by considering the variety of purposes a headline can have in terms of gaining attention or actually achieving persuasion. In general, a headline can be written to pursue the following purposes:

- *Give news about the brand.* A headline can proclaim a newsworthy event focused on the brand. "Champion Wins Mt. Everest Run" and "25 of 40 Major Titles Won with Titleist" are examples of headlines that communicate newsworthy events about Champion spark plugs and Titleist golf balls. The Red Dog ad in Exhibit 11.7 uses this approach quite cleverly.
- *Emphasize a brand claim.* A primary and perhaps differentiating feature of the brand is a likely candidate for the headline theme. "30% More Mileage on Firestone Tires" highlights durability.

EXHIBIT 11.7

How does this headline attract attention or arouse interest in the audience to read the copy? Is this an effective way to give news about the brand? At the Web site **www.reddog.com:443***, what headline do you find? Does it convey as much news about the brand as the headline in this ad? In contrast, check out Budweiser's home page at* **www.budweiser .com/***. Can you think of ways in which the Web lets advertisers expand the use of headlines to supply news about brands?*

- *Give advice to the reader.* A headline can give the reader a recommendation that (usually) is followed by results provided in the body copy. "Increase Your Reading Skills" and "Save up to 90% on Commissions" both implore the reader to take the advice of the ad. The headline in Exhibit 11.8 advises readers to call mom this Mother's Day.

- *Select Prospect.* Headlines can attract the attention of the intended audience. "Good News for Arthritis Sufferers" and "Attention June Graduates" are examples of headlines designed to achieve prospect selection. The headline in the recruiting ad shown in Exhibit 11.9 is designed to attract the attention of college students.

- *Stimulate the reader's curiosity.* Posing a riddle with a headline can serve to attract attention and stimulate readership. Curiosity can be stimulated with a clever play on words or a contradiction. Take, for example, the headline "With MCI, Gerber's Baby Talk Never Sounded Better." The body copy goes on to explain that Gerber Products (a maker of baby products) uses the high technology of MCI for its communication needs. Does the headline in the ad shown in Exhibit 11.10 get your attention? It was written for that purpose.

- *Set a tone or establish an emotion.* Language can be used to establish a mood that the advertiser wants associated with its product. Teva sports sandals has an ad with the headline "When you die, they put you in a nice suit and shiny shoes. As if death

EXHIBIT 11.8

Giving readers advice in a headline can attract attention and stimulate interest in the body copy. MCI's 1-800-COLLECT uses just such an approach in this Mother's Day ad. **www.mci.com/**

EXHIBIT 11.9 *This ad uses its headline to succinctly select a prospect. Does it get the attention of the intended audience? At the Web site* **www.army.mil/,** *do you find the same approach? How is it different? How is it alike?*

A headline can create curiosity. The headline in this Intel ad is intriguing and stimulates the reading of the entire advertisement. **www.intel .com/**

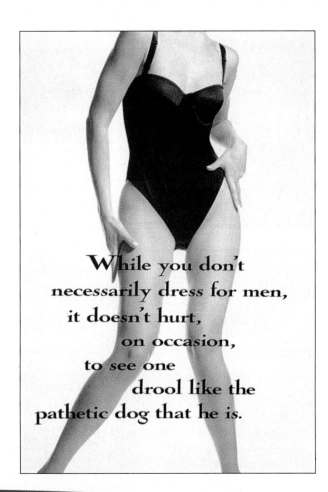

Headlines can set a tone and establish a mood that the advertiser desires for a brand. This ad for Bodyslimmers women's apparel does just that.

didn't suck enough already." Even though there is no direct reference to the product being advertised, the reader has learned quite a bit about the company doing the advertising and the types of people expected to buy the product. The headline in the ad shown in Exhibit 11.11 accomplishes the same objective.

- *Identify the brand.* This is the most straightforward of all headline purposes. The brand name or label is used as the headline, either alone or in conjunction with a word or two. The goal is to simply identify the brand and reinforce brandname recognition. Advertising for Brut men's fragrance products often uses merely the brand name as the headline.

Guidelines for Writing Headlines. Once a copywriter has firmly established the purpose a headline will serve in an advertisement, several guidelines can be followed in preparing the headline. The following are basic guidelines for writing a good headline for print advertisements:

- Make the headline a major persuasive component of the ad. Five times as many people read the headline as the body copy of an ad. If this is your only opportunity to communicate, what should you say? The headline "New Power. New Comfort. New Technology. New Yorker" in a Chrysler ad communicates major improvements in the product quickly and clearly.

- Appeal to the reader's self-interest with a basic promise of benefits coming from the brand. For example, "The Temperature Never Drops Below Zerex" promises engine protection in freezing weather from Zerex antifreeze.
- Inject the maximum information in the headline without making it cumbersome or wordy.
- Limit headlines to about five to eight words.[7] Research indicates recall drops off significantly for sentences longer than eight words.
- Include the brand name in the headline.
- Entice the reader to read the body copy.
- Entice the reader to examine the visual in the ad. An intriguing headline can lead the reader to carefully examine the visual components of the ad.
- Never change the typeface in a headline. Changing the form and style of the print can increase the complexity of visual impression and negatively affect the readership.
- Never use a headline whose persuasive impact depends on reading the body copy.
- Use simple, common, familiar words. Recognition and comprehension are aided by words that are easy to understand and recognize.

This set of guidelines is meant only as a starting point. A headline may violate one or even all of these basic premises and still be effective. And, it is unrealistic to try to fulfill the requirements of each guideline in every headline. This list simply offers general safeguards to be considered. Test the list for yourself using the ads in Exhibits 11.12 through 11.14. Which, if any, of these ten guidelines do these ads comply with? Which of these guidelines would you say are most important for creating effective headlines?

EXHIBITS 11.12, 11.13, AND 11.14

There are ten general guidelines for writing headlines. How do you rate the headlines in these ads relative to the guidelines? **www.mot .com/** *and* **www.purethrill.com/**

---

7.   Based in part on Jewler, 232–33; and Albert C. Book, Norman D. Cary, and Stanley I. Tannenbaum, *The Radio and Television Commercial* (Lincolnwood, Ill.: NTC Business Books, 1984), 22–26.

The Subhead

A **subhead** consists of a few words or a short sentence and usually appears above or below the headline. It includes important brand information not included in the headline. The subhead in the ad for Clorox in Exhibit 11.15 is an excellent example of how a subhead is used to convey important brand information not communicated in the headline. A subhead serves basically the same purpose as a headline—to communicate key selling points or brand information quickly. A subhead is normally in print larger than the body copy, but smaller than the headline. In many cases, the subhead is more lengthy than the headline and can be used to communicate more-complex selling points. The subhead should reinforce the headline and, again, entice the reader to proceed to the body copy.

Subheads can serve another important purpose: stimulating a more complete reading of the entire ad. If the headline attracts attention, the subhead can stimulate movement through the physical space of the ad, including the visual. A good rule of thumb is the longer the body copy, the more appropriate the use of subheads. Most creative directors try to keep the use of subheads to the barest minimum, however. They feel that if an ad's visual and headline can't communicate the benefit of a product quickly and clearly, the ad isn't very good.

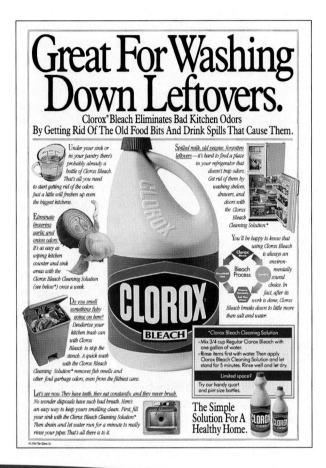

EXHIBIT 11.15

Subheads include important brand information not included in the headline. Where is the subhead in this Clorox ad? What does the subhead accomplish that the headline does not? **www.clorox.com/**

The Body Copy

Body copy is the textual component of an advertisement and tells the complete story of a brand. Effective body copy is written in a fashion that takes advantage of and reinforces the headline and subhead, is compatible with and gains strength from the visual, and is interesting to the reader. Whether or not body copy is interesting is a function of how accurately the copywriter and other decision makers have assessed various components of message development. The most elaborate body copy will probably be ineffective if it is "off strategy."

There are several standard techniques for preparing body copy. The **straight-line copy** approach explains in straightforward terms why a reader will benefit from use of a brand. This technique is used many times in conjunction with a benefits message strategy. Body copy that uses **dialogue** delivers the selling points of a message to the audience through a character or characters in the ad. The Prudential ad shown in Exhibit 11.16 is an example of the dialogue technique. A **testimonial** uses dialogue as if the spokesperson is having a one-sided conversation with the reader through the body copy. Dialogue can also depict two people in the ad having a conversation, a technique often used in slice-of-life messages.

Narrative as a method for preparing body copy simply displays a series of statements about a brand. A person may or may not be portrayed as delivering the copy. It is difficult to make this technique lively for the reader, so the threat of writing a dull ad using this technique is ever present. **Direct response copy** is, in many ways, the least complex of the copy techniques. In writing direct response copy, the copywriter is trying to highlight the urgency of acting immediately. Hence, the range of possibilities for direct response copy is severely limited. In addition, many direct response advertisements rely on sales promotion devices, like coupons, contests, and rebates, as a means of stimulating action. Giving deadlines to the reader is also a common approach in direct response advertising.

These techniques for copywriting establish a general set of styles that can be used as the format for body copy. Again, be aware that any message objective can be employed within any particular copy technique. There are a vast number of compatible combinations.

Guidelines for Writing Body Copy.
Regardless of the specific technique used to develop body copy, the probability of writing effective body copy can be increased if certain guidelines are followed. However, guidelines are meant to be just that—guidelines. Copywriters have created excellent ads that violate one or more of these recommendations. Generally, however, body copy for print ads has a better chance of being effective if these guidelines are followed:

- *Use the present tense whenever possible.* Casting brand claims in the past or future reduces their credibility and timeliness. Speaking to the target audience about things that have happened or will happen sounds like hollow promises.
- *Use singular nouns and verbs.* An ad is normally read by only one person at a time, and that person is evaluating only one brand. Using plural nouns and verbs simply reduces the focus on the item or brand attribute being touted and makes the ad less personal.
- *Use active verbs.* The passive form of a verb does little to stimulate excitement or interest. The use of the active verb in Pontiac's "We Build Excitement" slogan suggests something is happening, and it's happening *now.*
- *Use familiar words and phrases.* Relying on familiar words and phrases to communicate in an interesting and unique way poses a formidable challenge for a copywriter. Familiar words can seem common and ordinary. The challenge is to creatively stylize what is familiar and comfortable to the reader so that interest and excitement result.
- *Vary the length of sentences and paragraphs.* Using sentences and paragraphs of varying lengths not only serves to increase interest but also has a visual impact that can make an ad more inviting and readable.
- *Involve the reader.* Talking *at* the receiver or creating a condescending mood with copy results in a short-circuited communication. Copy that impresses the reader as having been written specifically for him or her reduces the chances of the ad being perceived as a generalized, mass communication.
- *Provide support for the unbelievable.* A brand may have features or functions that the reader finds hard to believe. Where such claims are critical to the brand's positioning in the market and value to the consumer, it is necessary to document (through test results or testimonials) that the brand actually lives up to the claims made. Without proper support of claims, the brand will lose its credibility and therefore its relevance to the consumer. As noted in the Contemporary Issues box on page 310, documented claims are especially important for persuading aging baby boomers.

The real hero here is a guy who got his wings long before I did. When my father died I was only twelve. Mom had a pretty good life insurance policy to fall back on, thanks to Phil Saggese—one of the best Prudential Reps ever. But to make that benefits check last, she had to invest it. Then, six years later, I hit her with the big one: I wanted to go to aeronautical school, where a single course can cost $3000! Well, she not only had the money— she had enough to put herself through college, too. Today Mom's a teacher. And I fly planes for a living. It all came back to me when my Aunt Sandy was congratulating me for getting my Captain's wings. "Now you can pay back all those college loans," she said. "What loans?" I asked. "There aren't any." That's the beauty of it. 'Course, if we had it to do over again, I'd much rather have loans to pay and my father back. See, Phil Saggese was not only our Prudential Rep—he was my Dad.

Prudential

Printed with permission of Michael Saggese, Minneapolis, MN. Photo and expenses for Michael were paid for by Prudential. © 1996 The Prudential Insurance Company of America, Prudential Plaza, Newark, NJ 07102-3777, http://www.prudential.com

EXHIBIT 11.16

In this testimonial ad from Prudential, a spokesperson tells his story directly to the reader. **www.prudential.com**

- *Avoid clichés and superlatives.* Clichés are rarely effective or attention getting. The average consumer assumes that a brand touted through the use of clichés is old-fashioned and stale. Even though the foundation for puffery as a message method is the use of superlatives (*best, superior, unbeatable*), it is wise to avoid their use. These terms are worn out and can signal to the consumer that the brand has little new or different to offer.[8]

Copywriting for Broadcast Advertising

Relative to the print media, radio and television present totally different challenges for a copywriter. It is obvious that the audio and audiovisual capabilities of radio and television provide different opportunities for a copywriter. The use of sound effects and voices on radio and the ability to combine copy with color and motion on television provide vast and exciting creative possibilities.

Compared to the print media, however, the broadcast media have inherent limitations for a copywriter. In the print media, a copywriter can write the long and involved copy necessary to communicate complex brand features. For consumer shopping goods like automobiles or VCRs, a brand's basis for competitive differentiation and positioning may lie with complex, unique functional features. In this case, the print media provide a copywriter the time and space to communicate these details, complete with illustrations. In addition, the printed page allows a reader to dwell on the copy and process the information at a personalized, comfortable rate.

These advantages do not exist in the broadcast media. Radio and television offer a fleeting exposure. In addition, introducing sound effects and sight stimuli through these media can distract the listener or viewer from the copy of the advertisement. Despite the additional creative opportunities radio and television offer, the essential challenge of copywriting remains. We will consider the copywriting task in each of these broadcast media separately.

Writing Copy for Radio

3 Some analysts consider radio the ultimate forum for copywriting creativity. While the radio is restricted to an audio-only presentation, a copywriter is free from the realities of visuals and illustrations. The creative potential of radio rests in its ability to stimulate a theater of the mind, which allows a copywriter to create images and moods for an audience that transcend those created in any other medium.

Despite these creative opportunities, the drawbacks of this medium should never be underestimated. Few radio listeners ever actively listen to radio programming, much less the commercial interruptions. (Talk radio is something of an exception.) Radio may be viewed by some as the theater of the mind, but others have labeled it verbal wallpaper—wallpaper in the sense that radio is used as filler or unobtrusive accompaniment to reading, driving, household chores, or homework. If it was absent, the average person would miss it in many contexts. On the other hand, the average person would be hard-pressed to recall the radio ads aired during dinner last evening.

The most reasonable view of copywriting for radio is to temper both the enthusiasm of the theater-of-the-mind perspective and the pessimism of the verbal-wallpaper view. A radio copywriter should recognize the unique character of radio and exploit the opportunities it offers. First, radio adds the dimension of sound to the copywriting task, and sound (other than voices) can become a primary tool in creating copy. Second, radio can conjure images in the mind of the receiver that extend beyond the starkness of the information actually being provided. Radio copywriting should, therefore, strive to stimulate each receiver's imagination.

8.   The last three points in this section were adapted from Kenneth Roman and Jan Maas, *The New How to Advertise* (New York: St. Martin's Press, 1992), 18–19.

Writing copy for radio should begin in the same way writing copy for print begins. The copywriter must review components of the creative plan so as to take advantage of and follow through on the marketing and advertising strategies specified and integral to the brand's market potential. Beyond that fundamental task, there are particular formats for radio ads and guidelines for copy preparation the writer can rely on for direction and stimulation.

Radio Advertising Formats

There are four basic formats for radio advertisements, and these formats provide the structure within which copy is prepared: the music format, dialogue format, announcement format, and celebrity announcer format. Each of these formats is discussed here.

Music. Since radio provides audio opportunities, music is often used in radio ads. One use of music is to write a song or jingle in an attempt to communicate in an attention-getting and memorable fashion. Songs and jingles are generally written specifically to accommodate unique brand copy. On occasion, an existing tune can be used, and the copy is fit to its meter and rhythm. This is especially true if the music is being used to capture the attention of a particular target segment. Tunes popular with certain target segments can be licensed for use by advertisers. Advertisements using popular tunes by Green Day and Barry Manilow would attract two very different audiences simply by virtue of the music.

Singing and music can do much to attract the listener's attention and enhance recall. How many of us had difficulty getting McDonald's "Two all-beef patties, special sauce, lettuce, cheese, pickles, onions on a sesame seed bun" jingle out of our minds? Singing can also create a mood and image with which the product is associated. Modern scores can create a contemporary mood, while sultry music and lyrics create a totally different mood.

There are some hazards in the use of singing or jingles. Few copywriters are trained lyricists or composers. The threat is ever present that a musical score or a jingle will strike receivers as amateurish and silly. To avoid this, expert songwriters are often used. Further, ensuring that the copy information dominates the musical accompaniment takes great skill. The musical impact can easily overwhelm the persuasion and selling purposes of an ad.

CONTEMPORARY ISSUES

WHAT DO BOOMERS WANT FOR THEIR 50TH BIRTHDAY? INFORMATION!

Market researchers are busy trying to find out what baby boomers want for their 50th birthday. This huge generation of consumers is, indeed, growing older. Currently, 68 million boomers are 50 years old and older, and the number is expected to grow to 115 million by the year 2025. Because of the size and spending power of this group, Roper Starch Worldwide Research was commissioned by *Modern Maturity* magazine to find out what kind of information boomers find appealing in print ads. The research focused specifically on automobile, food, and health and beauty advertising.

The results of the Roper study are somewhat surprising. The over-50 market is best addressed with information-intensive ads that identify a brand's benefits, rather than image-oriented advertising. Copywriting for this group needs to be developed with a recognition of the following:

- Successful auto print ads featured third-party endorsements and a tone that respected the audience's intelligence.
- High-scoring health and beauty ads emphasized positive and specific product benefits, like keeping skin soft. Young models in ads didn't affect responses, but age-neutral or older models were viewed positively. High-price brands were more preferred if their benefits were made explicit.
- Food ads that were well received featured recipes, coupons, ingredient information, or 1-800 information lines. High-scoring food ads also used enlarged product photos.

Whether all advertising to the aging baby boomers should be information intensive remains to be seen. The study did not address the issue of what copy format might be most successful in broadcast advertising. It is interesting to note, though, that a generation of consumers that has had a steady diet of image advertising for many decades now appears to prefer informative print ads.

Source: Jane Hodges and Jennifer DeCoursey, "Aging Boomers Like 'Info' Ads," *Advertising Age*, April 1, 1996, 47.

Another use of music in radio commercials is to open the ad with a musical score and/or have music playing in the background while the copy is being read. The role of music here is generally to attract attention. This application of music, as well as music used in a song or jingle, is subject to an ongoing debate. If a radio ad is scheduled for airing on music-format stations, should the music in the ad be the same type of music the station is noted for playing, or should it be different? One argument says that if the station format is rock, for example, then the ad should use rock music to appeal to the listener's taste. The opposite argument states that using the same type of music simply buries the ad in the regular programming and reduces its impact. There is no good evidence to suggest that music similar to or different from station programming is superior.

Dialogue. The dialogue technique, described in the section on print copywriting, is commonly used in radio. There are difficulties in making narrative copy work in the short periods of time afforded by the radio medium (typically 15 to 60 seconds). In addition, dialogue copy has no inherent attention-getting capabilities. The threat is that dialogue will result in a dull drone of two or more people having a conversation. To reduce the threat of boredom, many dialogues are written with humor, like the one in Exhibit 11.17.

Announcement. Radio copy delivered by an announcer is similar to narrative copy in print advertising. The announcer reads important product information as it has been prepared by the copywriter. Announcement is the prevalent technique for live radio spots delivered by disc jockeys or news commentators. The live setting leaves little opportunity for much else. If the ad is prerecorded, sound effects or music may be added to enhance the transmission.

Celebrity Announcers. Having a famous person or persons deliver the copy is alleged to increase the attention paid to a radio ad. Most radio ads that use celebrities do not fall into the testimonial category. The celebrity is not expressing his or her satisfaction with the product, but merely acting as an announcer. Some celebrities (such as James Earl Jones) have distinctive voice qualities or are expert at the emphatic delivery of copy. It is argued that these qualities, as well as listener recognition of the celebrity, increase attention to the ad.

EXHIBIT 11.17

Dialogue ads prepared for radio often use humor as a way to attract and hold attention. Here is the script for a dialogue ad prepared for Toyota. **www.toyota .com/**

ENGINEER:	Um, before we start, the advertising guys have had to take out a few things for legal reasons.
ANNCR:	Well, read them out and I'll cross them off the script.
ENGINEER:	Okay, delete line one where it says that the hot Toyota Corolla SX is faster than an F18 fighter.
ANNCR:	Yeah, I wondered about that.
ENGINEER:	Then the next bit, where it says this Hot Hatch is so hot it comes with a free date with Kim Basinger.
ANNCR:	Shame, big selling point I thought.
ENGINEER:	And they had a few problems with promising that the Corolla Hot Hatch can seat a whole football team in comfort.
ANNCR:	Right.
ENGINEER:	Then that whole section from "By Royal Command" to "You'll get an infectious disease if you don't buy one."
ANNCR:	Including, um, "Guaranteed to increase your IQ by twenty points?"
ENGINEER:	Just a sec', I'll check.
CLIENT:	No, lose it.
ANNCR:	It's lost.
ENGINEER:	Right, what does that leave us with?
ANNCR:	The 100kW Toyota Corolla SX. This Hot Hatch is really hot…
ENGINEER:	Nothing else.
ANNCR:	Just the usual music at the end.
(MUSIC:	OH WHAT A FEELING, COROLLA)

Guidelines for Writing Radio Copy

The unique opportunities and challenges of the radio medium warrant a set of guidelines for the copywriter to increase the probability of effective communication. The following are a few suggestions for writing effective radio copy:

- *Use common, familiar language.* The use of words and language easily understood and recognized by the receiver is even more important in radio than in print copy preparation.
- *Use short words and sentences.* The probability of communicating verbally increases if short, easily processed words and sentences are used. Long, involved, elaborate verbal descriptions make it difficult for the listener to follow the copy.
- *Stimulate the imagination.* Copy that can conjure up concrete and stimulating images in the receiver's mind can have a powerful impact on recall.
- *Repeat the name of the product.* Since the impression made by a radio ad is fleeting, it may be necessary to repeat the brand name several times before it will register. The same is true for location if the ad is being used to promote a retail organization.
- *Stress the main selling point or points.* The premise of the advertising should revolve around the information that needs to be presented. If selling points are mentioned only in passing, there is little reason to believe they'll be remembered.
- *Use sound and music with care.* By all means, a copywriter should take advantage of all the audio capabilities afforded by the radio medium, including the use of sound effects and music. While these devices can contribute greatly to attracting and holding the listener's attention, care must be taken to ensure that the devices do not overwhelm the copy and therefore the persuasive impact of the commercial.
- *Tailor the copy to the time, place, and specific audience.* Take advantage of any unique aspect of the advertising context. If the ad is specified for a particular geographic region, use colloquialisms unique to that region as a way to tailor the message. The same is true with time-of-day factors or unique aspects of the audience.[9]

Writing Copy for Television

4 From the standpoint of broadcast communication opportunities, television has a tremendous (and obvious) advantage over radio in that action as well as sound can be used in the message. The ability to create a mood or demonstrate a brand in use gives television a superior capability compared to all other media. But this also changes the whole concept of copy for the copywriting effort. Copy for television must be highly sensitive to the ad's visual aspects as envisioned and specified by the creative director.

The opportunities inherent to television as an advertising medium represent challenges for the copywriter as well. Certainly, the inherent capabilities of television can do much to bring a copywriter's words to life. But the action qualities of television can create problems. First, the copywriter must remember that words do not stand alone. Visuals, special effects, and sound techniques may ultimately convey a message far better than the cleverest turn of phrase. Second, television commercials represent a difficult timing challenge for the copywriter. It is necessary for the copy to be precisely coordinated with the video. If the video portion were one continuous illustration, the task would be difficult enough. Modern television ads, however, tend to be heavily edited (that is, they use several different scenes), and the copywriting task can be a nightmare. The copywriter not only has to fulfill all the responsibilities of proper information inclusion (based on creative platform and strategy decisions), but also has to carefully fit all the information within, between, and around the visual display taking place. To make sure this coordination is precise, the copywriter, producer, and director assigned to a television advertisement work together closely to make sure the copy supports and enhances the video element. The road map for this coordination effort is known as a storyboard.

---

9.   Book, Cary, and Tannenbaum.

A **storyboard** is a frame-by-frame sketch depicting in sequence the visual scenes and copy that will be used in a television advertisement. The procedures for coordinating audio and visual elements through the use of storyboards will be presented in Chapter 13, when television production is discussed.

Television Advertising Formats

Because of the broad creative capability of the television medium, there are several alternative formats for a television ad: demonstration, problem and solution, music and song, spokesperson, dialogue, vignette, and narrative. Each is discussed here. Again, this is not an exhaustive list, but rather a sampling of popular forms.

Demonstration. Due to television's abilities to demonstrate a brand in action, demonstration is an obvious format for a television ad. Brands whose benefits result from some tangible function can effectively use this format. Copy that accompanies this sort of ad embellishes the visual demonstration. The copy in a demonstration is usually straight-line copy, but drama can easily be introduced into this format, such as with the Radio Shack home security system that scares off a burglar, or the Fiat braking system that saves a motorist from an accident. Demonstration with sight and sound lets viewers appreciate the full range of features a brand has to offer.

Problem and Solution. In this format, a brand is introduced as the savior in a difficult situation. This format often takes shape as a slice-of-life message, in which a consumer solves a problem with the advertised brand. Dishwashing liquids, drain openers, and numerous other household products are readily promoted with this technique. A variation on the basic format is to promote a brand on the basis of problem prevention. A variety of auto maintenance items and even insurance products have used this approach.

Music and Song. Many television commercials use music and singing as a creative technique. The various beverage industries (soft drinks, beer, and wine) frequently use this format to create the desired mood for their brands. Additionally, the growth of image advertising has resulted in many ads that show a product in action accompanied by music and only visual overlays of the copy. This format for television advertising tends to restrict the amount of copy and presents the same difficulties for copywriting as the use of music and song in radio copywriting. The "Uh-huh" Diet Pepsi commercials with Ray Charles and the Chevrolet truck ads with the song "Like a Rock" are examples of campaigns that rely on music and song.

Spokesperson. The delivery of a message by a spokesperson can place a heavy emphasis on the copy. The copy is given precedence over the visual and is supported by the visual, rather than vice versa. Expert, average-person, and celebrity testimonials fall into this formatting alternative. An example of the effective use of an expert spokesperson is the long-running Sprint campaign with Candice Bergen.

Dialogue. As in a radio commercial, a television ad may feature a dialogue between two or more people. Dialogue format ads pressure a copywriter to compose dialogue that is believable and keeps the ad moving forward. Most slice-of-life ads in which a husband and wife or friends are depicted using a brand employ a dialogue format.

Vignette. A vignette format uses a sequence of related advertisements as a device to maintain viewer interest. Vignettes also give the advertising a recognizable look, which can help achieve awareness and recognition. The Taster's Choice couple featured in a series of advertisements in the United States and Great Britain is an example of the vignette format.

Narrative. A narrative is similar to a vignette but is not part of a series of related ads. Narrative is a distinct format in that it tells a story, like a vignette, but the mood of the ad is highly personal, emotional, and involving. A narrative ad often focuses on storytelling and only indirectly touches on the benefits of the brand. Many of the "heart-sell" ads by McDonald's, Kodak, and Hallmark use the narrative technique to great effect.

Guidelines for Writing Television Copy

Writing copy for television advertising has its own set of unique opportunities and challenges. The following are some general guidelines:

- *Use the video.* Allow the video portion of the commercial to enhance and embellish the audio portion. Given the strength and power of the visual presentation in television advertising, take advantage of its impact with copy.
- *Support the video.* Make sure that the copy doesn't simply hitchhike on the video. If all the copy does is verbally describe what the audience is watching, an opportunity to either communicate additional information or strengthen the video communication has been lost.
- *Coordinate the audio with the video.* In addition to strategically using the video, it is essential that the audio and video do not tell different stories or rely on different types of persuasion. Dual purposes for audio and video can serve only to confuse the audience.
- *Sell the product as well as entertain the audience.* Television ads can sometimes be more entertaining than television programming. A temptation for the copywriter and art director is to get caught up in the excitement of a good video presentation and forget that the main purpose is to deliver persuasive communication.
- *Be flexible.* Due to media-scheduling strategies, commercials are produced to run as 15-, 20-, 30-, or 60-second spots. The copywriter may need to ensure that the audio portion of an ad is complete and comprehensive within varying time lengths.
- *Use copy judiciously.* If an ad is too wordy, it can create information overload and interfere with the visual impact. Ensure that every word is a working word and contributes to the impact of the message.
- *Reflect the brand personality and image.* All aspects of an ad, copy and visuals, should be consistent with the personality and image the advertiser wants to build or maintain for the brand.
- *Build campaigns.* When copy for a particular advertisement is being written, evaluate its potential as a sustainable idea. Can the basic appeal in the advertisement be developed into multiple versions that form a campaign?[10]

Slogans

Copywriters are often asked to come up with a good slogan or tag line for a product or service. A **slogan** is a short phrase in part used to help establish an image, identity, or position for a brand or an organization, but mostly used to increase memorability. A slogan is established by repeating the phrase in a firm's advertising and other public communication as well as through salespeople, event promotions, and rocket launches. Yes, we did say rocket launches, per the Global Issues box on page 316. Slogans are often used as a headline or subhead in print advertisements, or as the tag line at the conclusion of radio and television advertisements. Slogans typically appear directly below the brand or company name, as in all Toyota advertising: "I Love What You Do for Me." Some of the more memorable and enduring ad slogans are listed in Exhibit 11.18.

A good slogan can serve several positive purposes for a brand or a firm. First, a slogan can be an integral part of a brand's image and personality. BMW's slogan, "The Ultimate Driving Machine," does much to establish and maintain the personality and image of the brand. Second, if a slogan is carefully and consistently developed over time, it can

---

10.   The last three points in this section were adapted from Roman and Maas.

EXHIBIT 11.18

Slogans used for brands and organizations.

Brand/Company	Slogan
Allstate Insurance	You're in Good Hands with Allstate.
American Express	Don't Leave Home without It.
American Stock Exchange	The Smarter Place to Be.
AT&T (consumer)	Reach Out and Touch Someone.
AT&T (business)	AT&T. Your True Choice.
Beef Industry Council	Real Food for Real People.
BMW	The Ultimate Driving Machine.
Budweiser	This Bud's for You.
Chevrolet trucks	Like a Rock.
Cotton Industry	The Fabric of Our Lives.
DeBeers	Diamonds Are Forever.
Delta Airlines	You'll Love the Way We Fly.
Ford	Have You Driven a Ford Lately?
Gemini Consulting	Worldwide Leader in Business Transformation.
Goodyear	The Best Tires in the World Have Goodyear Written All over Them.
Lincoln	What a Luxury Car Should Be.
Microsoft (online)	Where Do You Want to Go Today?
Northwestern Mutual	The Quiet Company.
Panasonic	Just Slightly Ahead of Our Time.
Prudential Insurance	Get a Piece of the Rock.
Saturn	A Different Kind of Company. A Different Kind of Car.
Sharp	From Sharp Minds Come Sharp Products.
Smith Barney	We Make Money the Old-Fashioned Way. We Earn It.
Toshiba	In Touch with Tomorrow.
Toyota	I Love What You Do for Me.
Visa	It's Everywhere You Want to Be.

act as a shorthand identification for the brand and provide information on important brand benefits. The long-standing slogan for Allstate Insurance, "You're in Good Hands with Allstate," communicates the benefits of dealing with a well-established insurance firm. A good slogan also provides continuity across different media and between advertising campaigns. Nike's "Just Do It" slogan has given the firm an underlying theme for a wide range of campaigns and other promotions throughout the 1990s. In this sense, a slogan is a useful tool in helping to bring about thematic integrated marketing communications for a firm.

Common Mistakes in Copywriting

The preceding discussions have shown that print, radio, and television advertising present the copywriter with unique challenges and opportunities. Copy in each arena must be compatible with the various types of ads run in each medium and the particular capabilities and liabilities of each medium and format. Beyond the guidelines for effective copy in each area, there are common mistakes made in copywriting that can and should be avoided:

- *Vagueness.* Avoid generalizations and words that are imprecise in meaning. To say that a car is stylish is not nearly as meaningful as saying it has sleek, aerodynamic lines.
- *Wordiness.* Being economical with descriptions is paramount. Copy has to fit in a limited time frame (or space), and receivers bore easily. When boredom sets in, effective communication often ceases.
- *Triteness.* Using clichés and worn out superlatives was mentioned as a threat to print copywriting. The same threat (to a lesser degree, due to audio and audiovisual capabilities) exists in radio and television advertising. Trite copy creates a boring, outdated image for a brand or firm.
- *Creativity for creativity's sake.* Some copywriters get carried away with a clever idea. It's essential that the copy in an ad remain true to its primary responsibility: communicating the selling message. Creativity is the hallmark of a good ad that attracts and holds attention. However, copy that is extraordinarily funny or poses an intriguing riddle yet fails to register the main selling theme will simply produce another amusing advertising failure.

The Copy Approval Process

The final step in copywriting is getting the copy approved. For many copywriters, this is the most dreaded part of their existence. During the approval process, the proposed copy is likely to pass through the hands of a wide range of client and agency people, many of whom are ill-prepared to judge the quality of the copy. The challenge at this stage is to keep the creative potency of the copy intact. As David Ogilvy suggests in his commandments for advertising, "Committees can criticize advertisements, but they can't write them."[11]

The copy approval process usually begins within the creative department of an advertising agency. A copywriter submits draft copy to either the senior writer or the creative director, or both. From there, the redrafted copy is forwarded to the account management team within the agency. The main concern at this level is to evaluate the copy on legal grounds. After the account management team has made recommendations, a meeting is likely held to present the copy, along with proposed visuals, to the client's product manager, brand manager, and marketing staff. Inevitably, the client representatives feel compelled to make recommendations for altering the copy. In some cases, these recommendations realign the copy in accordance with important marketing strategy objectives. In other cases, the recommendations are amateurish and problematic.

GLOBAL ISSUES

FORGET CYBERSPACE—WE'RE TALKING OUTER SPACE HERE

Cyberspace is all right for all those earthbound advertisers. But outer space, now there's an opportunity—global marketing at its pinnacle! For an entry-level price of a mere $1 million, an advertiser can buy space in the final frontier.

Swedish Space, Daimler-Benz's Deutsch Aerospace, and the European Space Agency are offering the highest-bidding advertiser the chance to plaster logos and the company slogan on an unmanned commercial rocket. The five-story rocket will be launched from a remote site in northern Sweden.

There are a few drawbacks to the opportunity, though. First, the rocket will spend just 15 minutes in space before crashing back to earth. Second, it's hard to find advertisers with a target segment in outer space. As the senior copywriter at Saatchi & Saatchi in London said, "Are we aiming the ads at Martians?"

Despite the drawbacks, the aerospace organizations point out the unique opportunities that rocket-powered slogans represent. First, film footage of the takeoff can be used in brand advertising and promotions in more traditional media. Second, publicity for the launch will be widespread, thereby justifying the high price. Some advertisers share the enthusiasm of the aerospace organizations. An executive vice president of the Swedish ad agency, Gazolin & S, describes it this way: "It's a small step for the people behind the project. And it's a giant leap for marketing."

Source: Tara Parker-Pope, "Will a New Promotional Vehicle Send Sales into the Stratosphere?" *Wall Street Journal*, August 8, 1995, B1.

11. Ogilvy, 101.

EXHIBIT 11.19

The copy approval process.

Finally, copy should always be submitted for final approval to the advertiser's senior executives. Many times, these executives have little interest in evaluating advertising plans, and they leave this responsibility to middle managers. In some firms, however, top executives get very involved in the approval process. The various levels of approval for copy are summarized in Exhibit 11.19. For the advertiser, it is best to recognize that copywriters, like other creative talent in an agency, should be allowed to exercise their creative expertise with guidance but not overbearing interference. Copywriters seek to provide energy and originality to what might otherwise be a mundane marketing strategy. To override their creative effort violates their reason for being.

SUMMARY

❶ Explain the need for a creative plan in the copywriting process.

Effective ad copy must be based on a variety of individual inputs and information sources. Making sense out of these diverse inputs and building from them creatively is a copywriter's primary challenge. A creative plan is used as a device to assist the copywriter in dealing with this challenge. Key elements in the creative plan include product features and benefits that must be communicated to the audience, the mood or tone appropriate for the audience, and the intended media for the ad.

❷ Detail the components of print copy, along with important guidelines for writing effective print copy.

The three unique components of print copy are the headline, subhead, and body copy. Headlines need to motivate additional processing of the ad. Good headlines communicate information about the brand or make a promise about the benefits the consumer can expect from the brand. If

the brand name is not featured in the headline, then that headline must entice the reader to examine the body copy or visual material. Subheads can also be valuable in helping lead the reader to and through the body copy. In the body copy, the brand's complete story can be told. Effective body copy must be crafted carefully to engage the reader, furnish supportive evidence for claims made about the brand, and avoid clichés and exaggeration that the consumer will dismiss as hype.

❸ Describe various formatting alternatives for radio ads and articulate guidelines for writing effective radio copy.

There are four basic formats that can be used to create radio copy. These are the music format, dialogue format, announcement format, and celebrity announcer format. Guidelines for writing effective radio copy start with using simple sentence construction and language familiar to the intended audience. When the copy stimulates the listener's imagination, the advertiser can expect improved results as long as the brand name and the primary selling points don't get lost. When using music or humor to attract and hold the listener's attention, the copywriter must take care not to shortchange key selling points for the sake of simple entertainment.

4 Describe various formatting alternatives for television ads and articulate guidelines for developing effective television copy.

Several formats can be considered in preparing television ad copy. These are demonstration, problem and solution,

music and song, spokesperson, dialogue, vignette, and narrative. To achieve effective copy in the television medium, it is essential to coordinate the copy with the visual presentation, seeking a synergistic effect between audio and video. Entertaining to attract attention should again not be emphasized to the point that the brand name or selling points of the ad get lost. Developing copy consistent with the heritage and image of the brand is also essential. Finally, copy that can be adapted to various time lengths and modified to sustain audience interest over the life of a campaign is most desirable.

KEY TERMS

creative team (298)
creative concept (298)
copywriting (300)
developmental copy research (301)
evaluative copy research (301)
creative plan (301)
headline (303)
subhead (307)

straight-line copy (307)
dialogue (307)
testimonial (307)
narrative (307)
direct response copy (307)
storyboard (313)
slogan (314)

QUESTIONS FOR REVIEW AND CRITICAL THINKING

1.   Explain the applications for copy research in the copywriting process. What other forms of consumer or market research might be particularly helpful in developing effective ad copy?

2.   Pull ten print ads from your favorite magazine. Using the classifications offered in this chapter, what would you surmise was the copywriter's intended purpose for each of the headlines in your ten print ads?

3.   Discuss the advantages and disadvantages of music as a tool for constructing effective radio ads.

4.   Listen with care to the radio ads in 30 minutes of programming on your favorite radio station. Then do the same for 30 minutes of programming on a parent's or grandparent's favorite station. Identify ads that did the best job of using terms and jargon familiar to the target audience of each station. What differences in mood or tone did you detect among ads on the two stations?

5.   Compare and contrast the dialogue and narrative formats for television ads. What common requirement must be met to construct convincing TV ads using these two formats?

6.   Entertainment is both the blessing and the curse of a copywriter. Is it conceivable that ads that merely entertain could actually prove valuable in stimulating sales? If so, how so?

7.   Describe the four common categories of mistakes that copywriters must avoid. From your personal experience with all types of ads, are there other common mistakes that you believe copywriters are prone to make on a regular basis?

8.   Everyone has their own opinion on what makes advertisements effective or ineffective. How does this fundamental aspect of human nature complicate a copywriter's life when it comes to winning approval for his or her ad copy?

EXPERIENTIAL EXERCISE

Divide into groups. Your team assignment is to study and improve upon local car dealer television advertising. Watch two or three television commercials by local car dealers. Discuss what you found good or bad about the ads. Seize upon the worst commercial and develop a list of suggestions to improve it. Apply your thoughts to the generation of a storyboard for a much-improved commercial.

USING THE INTERNET

There are several major elements used when producing advertising copy. Visit the following sites:

Leggs: www.leggs.com

Valvoline: www.valvoline.com

Pontiac: www.pontiac.com

1.   What is the creative concept behind each site?

2.   Which of the headlines is the most appealing? What features are most effective in a headline for a Web page?

3.   Do you think that the body copy for each site supports the headline? What aspects of the body copy do you think are most effective? Least effective?

4.   Which site exhibits the most unity between headline, subhead, and body copy? How does this unity support the creative concept?

Part 3 | Preparing the Message

What's on your PowerBook?

Gene Shalit
Movie Critic

Transcripts of 30 years of
my movie reviews
Material for three books
I'm currently writing
Form letter declining
invitations to speak
Microsoft Word
MacEnvelope
Details of consequences
(medical, legal) of being
hit by a car
List of movie producers
who may have
been driving that car
Letters to write, calls to make
this month (87 items)
Form letter explaining
how to tie a bow tie
Form letter explaining
why I wear a bow tie
Form letter explaining
why I do not fly
Catalogue of 371 CDs
Catalogue of 5477 books
Notes for an essay on
procrastination
Letters to people disagreeing
with my reviews
Letters to people
praising my reviews
My will

Linda Fetters-Howard
Stuntwoman

Meeting schedule for
the Stuntwomen's Association
of Motion Pictures
Ideas for the new SWAMP
brochure
PGA Tour Golf game
Stunt coordinators'
phone numbers
Burn specialists' phone numbers
Birthday list
Anniversary list
Medical emergency file for
SWAMP members
Microsoft Word
Now Up-to-Date
Now Contact
A fax modem
My personalized fax cover sheet
My résumé and bio
My husband Ken's résumé
and bio
Women in Film contacts
Directors' phone numbers
My florist's phone number
A dictionary
An alarm clock
My Christmas card list
Phone number
of Dr. Richard Fleming,
reconstructive surgeon

Chapter 12

Art Direction

and Production

in Print

Advertising

After reading and thinking about this chapter, you will be able to do the following:

1 Identify the basic purposes for, and components and formats of, print ad illustrations.

2 Describe the principles and components that help ensure the effective design of print ads.

3 Detail the stages that art directors follow in developing the layout of a print ad.

4 Discuss the activities and decisions involved in the final production of print ads.

The $90 million consumer home electronics market is one of the most competitive in the world. Sony, Toshiba, Hitachi, Philips, Matsushita, and Sharp are the major players.[1] In the late 1980s and early 1990s, just when this market was realizing dynamic change and burgeoning growth, the firm responsible for the commercial introduction of the television—Radio Corporation of America (RCA)—was being left behind. RCA had a reasonable market share in color televisions, but it had not kept pace with the desires of young, affluent consumers who were buying VCRs, camcorders, and CD players.

A large part of the problem was the image of RCA and its products. The company's illustrious heritage, forged in the 1950s and 1960s, was out of touch with modern tastes. Young consumers of the '90s associated the RCA name with the ornate wooden-cabinet televisions their grandparents owned. This outdated image was aggravated by a lack of advertising support for the brand name. While competitors like Sony and Philips were spending around 3 percent of annual sales on advertising support, RCA was investing an anemic 0.6 percent of sales. This not only affected awareness in the consumer market, but also turned off retailers, who themselves began to ignore the brand.

When Thomson Electronics bought the RCA brand from General Electric in 1987, these problems with image and advertising became painfully clear. Thomson immediately set its agency, Ammirati & Purvis/Lintas, to the task of reviving, reinventing, and reestablishing the RCA name in the critical videophile market. Thomson would invest $300 million to develop contemporary, competitive products, and Ammirati & Purvis/Lintas was challenged to overcome the severe image handicap that the RCA name presented.

The agency decided that competing head-on with the Japanese brands would be difficult because of the well-established high-technology perception of these brands. Furthermore, such a dramatic shift in emphasis for the RCA brand would forsake the brand's long and valuable heritage and a substantial group of loyal consumers. The strategy chosen to balance the history of the brand with the image of change was the reintroduction of Nipper, the loyal dog who had been a symbol of the RCA brand for more than 100 years. Nipper did not take on this image challenge alone, however. To communicate a sense of change, Nipper was given a son, Chipper, to communicate the modern rebirth of RCA. The new slogan—"Changing Entertainment. Again."—supported the notion of change.

As important as the strategic decisions were to repositioning RCA, the media chosen for the new campaign were just as important. Television was a major component because competitive spending was heavy in television. The RCA television ads with Nipper and Chipper positioned side by side in front of a big-screen TV were highly effective. But Ammirati & Purvis/Lintas had to make a relatively small budget go a long way, and the message of contemporary technology needed to be communicated to the well-defined and highly important target segment of videophiles.

Magazine ads reach a highly targeted audience better than television ads, and one of the real advantages of print advertising is the ability to use high-quality reproduction, which could do justice to the new and stylish designs of the televisions, VCRs, and camcorders the firm was producing. For the RCA brand, this meant using photographic and print production techniques to show the contemporary design and styling of a full range of RCA products in the most favorable manner. Exhibit 12.1 is an example of the type of print advertising used as part of the media strategy for the RCA image campaign.[2]

The strategy and execution of the RCA campaign were a huge success. As the campaign unfolded, market tests showed that three out of four receivers claimed their opinion of RCA had improved. The campaign also affected retailers positively. Dealers invested approximately $15 million in the early part of the campaign on local spot advertising, both print and television ads that featured RCA-brand merchandise.[3]

---

1.   "The World Market for Consumer Audiovisual Products, 1994," *Wall Street Journal Europe,* September 20, 1995, 6.
2.   Information for the RCA campaign was drawn from Nicholas Ind, *Great Advertising Campaigns* (Lincolnwood, Ill.: NTC Business Books, 1993), 97–108.
3.   "RCA's Old Dog Learns New Tricks," *Advertising Age,* September 24, 1990, 53.

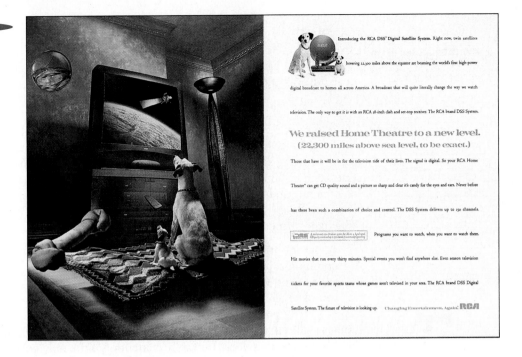

Illustration, Design, and Layout

Just as RCA found print advertising to be integral to its image campaign, many advertisers realize that print advertising offers tremendous opportunities for creative expression. In Chapter 11 we concentrated on the verbal components of a print ad: headline, subhead, and body copy. But often it is the visual that marks a successful ad. We now turn to the visual aspect of the creative mission: art direction.

The illustration, design, and layout of an ad bring to the forefront the role of art direction in print advertising. Initially, the art director and copywriter decide on the content of an illustration. Then the art director, often in conjunction with a graphic designer, takes this raw idea for the visual and develops it further. These creatives, with their specialized skills and training, coordinate the design and illustration components of a print ad. The creative director oversees the entire process.

This chapter will consider each of the three primary visual elements of a print ad: illustration, design, and layout. We will identify those aspects of each that must be specified, or at least considered, as a print ad is being prepared. An advertiser must appreciate the technical aspects of coordinating the visual elements in an ad with the mechanics of the layout and ultimately with the procedures for print production. The last section of the chapter discusses issues and procedures related to the print production process.

Be aware that it is not absolutely necessary that print advertising contain any visuals whatsoever. Louis Engle of Merrill Lynch once wrote an ad that contained 6,540 words with no illustration![4] The ad appeared in the *New York Times* and stimulated 10,000 inquiries for a booklet mentioned near the end of the ad. Artistic design and illustration may not be required in print advertising, but the tremendous opportunities offered by a visual impression make the issues of illustration, design, and layout critical to the process of print ad preparation.

---

4.   This unusual ad began with the headline "What everybody ought to know…about this stock and bond business," then proceeded to fill an entire newspaper page. A reproduction of this unique ad appears in David Ogilvy, *Ogilvy on Advertising* (New York: Vintage Books, 1985), 85.

Illustration

❶ Illustration, in the context of print advertising, is the drawing, painting, photography, or computer-generated art that forms the picture in an advertisement. Illustrations serve several important purposes.

Illustration Purposes

Few copywriters can accomplish the feat that Louis Engle managed for Merrill Lynch: a highly successful, full-page, multithousand-word newspaper ad without an illustration of any kind. Modern consumers would likely not tolerate such an ad. A print ad without illustration generally has a much lower probability of attracting and holding a receiver's attention. There are several specific, strategic purposes for illustration, which can greatly increase the chances of effective communication. The basic purposes of an illustration are to

- attract the attention of the target audience
- communicate product features and benefits
- create a mood, feeling, or image
- stimulate reading of the body copy

Attract the Attention of the Target Audience.

One of the primary roles of an illustration is to attract and hold attention. This doesn't mean that attention is the only goal, however. An advertisement is made to communicate information to a particular target audience. While the illustration can do much to attract and hold the attention of that audience, it must support other components of the ad to achieve the intended communication impact.

Communicate Product Features or Benefits.

Perhaps the most straightforward illustration is one that simply displays brand features, benefits, or both. A picture can stimulate future recognition of the brand in the market. Prominently picturing a product in a print ad will likely increase brand name and package recognition. David Ogilvy suggests that if you don't have a particular story to tell in the ad, then make the package the subject of the illustration.[5]

There are opportunities beyond simple recognition of the brand and the package, however, when product benefits are highlighted. Even though a print ad is static, the product can be shown in use through an actionlike scene or even a series of illustrations. These types of illustrations can emphasize specific brand features or benefits. The benefits of product use can be demonstrated with before-and-after shots, or by demonstrating the result of having used the product. Household items, such as decor pieces, are ideally suited for such an illustration. Diet programs, fashion items, and cosmetics focusing on style and attractiveness can all be effectively displayed with illustration.

Create a Mood, Feeling, or Image.

Another goal is to create a mood, feeling or image around a product or service with the illustration. Pursuing these purposes with a print ad depends on the technical execution of the illustration. The lighting, color, tone, and texture of the illustration have a huge impact on these goals. The photograph used as the illustration in the print ad for Prudential in Exhibit 12.2 captures a feeling of tenderness and security with its tone and texture. Recent research described in the Contemporary Issues box on page 326 suggests that print ads may be an advertiser's best option for shaping a brand's image.

Stimulate Reading of the Body Copy.

Just as a headline can stimulate examination of the illustration, the illustration can stimulate reading of the body copy. Since body copy generally carries the essential selling message, any tactic that encourages reading is useful. Illustrations can

---

5.   Ogilvy, *Ogilvy on Advertising,* 77.

EXHIBIT 12.2

How does the illustration in this ad help create a mood or feeling? Is this an appropriate choice for the product/service advertised by Prudential? At the Web site **www .prudential.com/**, *what illustration does Prudential use to get your attention? Do these illustrations create the same kind of mood as the ad in Exhibit 12.2? Contrast this approach with the use of illustrations at the Web site for State Farm Insurance* **www .statefarm.com/**. *Are these illustrations as evocative as the Prudential site?*

WEB SIGHTING

Live well.
"I always tell newlyweds that if you're willing to go halfway, it's not enough. You have to go beyond. The basic idea in a happy marriage is the basic idea in life. The decision to be happy."

Make a plan.
"We always had a five-year plan. I think life is like an ocean, and the waves go up and down and no wave stays up forever."

Be your own rock.
Prudential offers life insurance, investments, real estate and health care that can help you manage your life. And live well.

The Prudential

http://www.prudential.com

create curiosity and interest in readers. To satisfy that curiosity, readers will proceed to the body copy for clarification. Normally, an illustration and headline need to be fully coordinated and play off each other for this to occur. One caution is to avoid making the illustration too clever as a stimulus for motivating copy reading. Putting cleverness ahead of clarity in choosing an illustration can confuse the receiver and cause the body copy to be ignored. As one expert puts it, such ads will win awards but can camouflage the benefit offered by the product.[6]

Illustration Components

Various factors contribute to the overall visual presentation and impact of an illustration. The components of size, color, and medium can effect different impressions in the viewer. Individual decisions regarding size, color, and medium are a matter of artistic discretion and creative execution. There is some evidence of the differing effects of various decisions made in each of these areas. But remember, the interpretation and meaning of any visual representation cannot be explained completely by a series of rules or prescriptive how-tos. Thankfully, it's not that simple. Art is still a little magic.

Size. Does doubling the size of an illustration double the probability that the illustration will achieve its intended purpose? The answer is probably no. There is no question that greater size in an illustration may allow an ad to more successfully compete for the reader's attention, especially in a cluttered media environment. Recall, however, that simply attracting attention is only a first step in successful communication.

Generally speaking, regardless of the size of an illustration, the clarity of visual impression is the most important factor with respect to effectiveness. Illustrations with a focal point immediately recognizable by the reader are more likely to be noticed and comprehended. Conversely, illustrations that arouse curiosity or incorporate action score high in attracting attention but have been found to score low in inducing the reading of the total ad.[7]

6. Tony Antin, *Great Print Advertising* (New York: John Wiley & Sons, 1993), 38.
7. Daniel Starch, *Measuring Advertising Readership and Results* (New York: McGraw-Hill, 1966), 83.

Color. While not every execution of print advertising allows for the use of color (either because of expense or the medium being employed), color is a creative tool with important potential. Some products (such as furniture, floor coverings, or expensive clothing) may be dependent on color to accurately communicate a principal value. Color can also be used to emphasize a product feature or attract the reader's attention to a particular part of an ad, as shown in Exhibit 12.3. Color has no set or fixed meaning, so no hard rules can be offered. Context is everything. Saying that red always means this or blue always means that is a silly and uninformed generalization.

Medium. The choice of a **medium** for an illustration is the decision regarding the use of drawing, photography, or computer graphics.[8] Drawing represents a wide range of creative presentations, from cartoons to pen-and-ink drawings to elaborate watercolor and oil paintings. Photography can emphasize detail, which is often the desired visual impression, especially for unique product features. Photos also have an element of believability as representations of reality. Further, photos can often be prepared more quickly and at much less expense than art. There are photographers all over the world who specialize in different types of photography: landscape, seascape, portrait, food, and architecture, for example. The American Society of Magazine Photographers is a clearinghouse for nearly 5,000 photographers whose work is available as off-the-shelf photography.[9] Photographs can be cropped to any size or shape, retouched, color corrected, and doctored in a number of ways to create the desired effect. Exhibit 12.4 offers an example of the highly effective use of photography as the focal point of the ad. The choice of drawings over photography must be considered carefully. Some advertising analysts feel that photography increases recall and communicates more effectively than artwork.[10]

With the advancement of technology, artists have discovered the application of computer graphics to advertising illustrations. Computer graphics specialists can create and manipulate images for both print and broadcast production. With respect to illus-

CONTEMPORARY ISSUES

EVEN $6 BILLION DOESN'T IMPRESS CONSUMERS

Despite the fact that advertisers spend $6 billion for time on the major television networks, a new study shows that consumers consider print ads more entertaining and less offensive than television commercials. The study, conducted by Video Storyboard Tests in New York, showed that more consumers considered print ads "artistic" and "enjoyable."

The 2,000 consumers surveyed blasted TV ads compared to their print counterparts: 34 percent of respondents thought print ads were artistic, compared with 15 percent for television ads; 35 percent thought print ads were enjoyable, compared to 13 percent for television; and, most surprising, 33 percent of consumers felt print ads were entertaining, compared to only 18 percent for TV ads. Much of the artistic impact and positive reaction to print ads comes from the illustrations used. The illustration is primary in creating the mood for a print ad, which ultimately affects consumers' feelings about and image of a brand.

While the study's sponsors were somewhat surprised by the survey results, some industry executives felt that print ads were finally getting the credit they deserve. Richard Kirshenbaum, chair and chief creative officer of Kirshenbaum, Bond & Partners, a New York advertising and public relations firm, is one such believer. In fact, Kirshenbaum says that when he looks to hire a new person for a creative position in his agency, "I always look at the print book first because I think it is harder to come up with a great idea on a single piece of paper."

But as impressed as consumers say they are by the aesthetics and style of print ads, television executives (as you might expect) dismiss the findings. One network official said, "Nothing will replace the reach and magnitude of an elaborately produced television spot. TV ads get talked about. Print ads don't." This executive must have missed the Benetton and Absolut print campaigns.

Source: Kevin Goldman, "Consumers Like Print Ads Better Than Those on TV, Study Says," *Wall Street Journal,* June 6, 1995, B13.

8.   This section is adapted from Sandra E. Moriarty, *Creative Advertising: Theory and Practice,* 2nd ed. (Englewood Cliffs, N.J.: Prentice-Hall, 1991), 139–41.
9.   G. Robert Cox and Edward J. McGee, *The Ad Game: Playing to Win* (Englewood Cliffs, N.J.: Prentice-Hall, 1990), 44.
10.   Kenneth Ramon and Jane Maas, *The New How to Advertise* (New York: St. Martin's Press, 1992), 44.

trations for print advertising, the most important development in computer graphics in the last five years is the ability to digitize images. Digitizing is a computer process of breaking an image (illustration) into a grid of small squares. Each square is assigned a computer code for identification. With a digitized image, computer graphics specialists can break down an illustration and reassemble it or import other components into the original image. Age can be added or taken away from a model's face, or the Eiffel Tower can magically appear on Madison Avenue. The creative possibilities are endless with computer graphics. Exhibit 12.5 is an example of an ad with multiple images imported through computer graphics.

The size, color, and medium decisions regarding an illustration are difficult ones. It is likely that strategic and budgetary considerations will heavily influence choices in these areas. Once again, an advertiser should not constrain the creative process too severely.

Illustration Formats

The just-discussed components represent a series of decisions that must be made in conceiving an illustration. Another important decision is how the product or brand will appear as part of the illustration. **Illustration format** refers to the choices the advertiser has for displaying its product. Here is a list of several possible illustration formats:

- The product alone
- A part of the product
- The product ready for use
- The product in use, as illustrated in Exhibit 12.6

EXHIBIT 12.5

WEB SIGHTING

- The product being compared to the competition
- The product in a test situation
- The product being used by typical product users, as illustrated in Exhibit 12.7
- The happy results of using the product, as Exhibit 12.7 also shows
- The unhappy results of not using the product[11]

This list of possible formats for illustration should be self-explanatory. Obviously, the illustration format must be consistent with the copy strategy set for the ad. The creative department and the marketing planners must communicate with one another so that the illustration format selected helps pursue the specific objectives set for the ad campaign.

The Strategic and Creative Impact of Illustration

Defining effectiveness is a matter of first considering the basic illustration purposes, components, and formats we've just discussed on the preceding pages. Next, these factors need to be evaluated in the context of marketing strategy, campaign planning, consumer behavior, and, in general, all the knowledge bases used in message development. Combining the characteristics of illustrations considered here and the discussions in preceding chapters, we can conclude that an effective illustration achieves one or more of the following strategic goals:

- It attracts the attention of the target segment and initiates information processing by the receivers.
- It communicates the brand's value relative to the target audience's established or emerging decision-making criteria in the product category.
- It visually represents the creative strategy established for the brand's advertising.
- It associates a particular mood or feeling with the brand.
- It creates a particular image for the brand.
- It makes concrete those values or benefits of a brand that may be intangible or hidden.

---

11.   Based in part on a typology offered by A. Jerome Jewler, *Creative Strategy in Advertising,* 3rd ed. (Belmont, Calif.: Wadsworth Publishing, 1989), 19–101.

The illustration format used in this ad helps involve the audience in the ad's copy. Would other formats work as well? How does Cannondale use illustrations at its Web site **www.cannondale.com/**? *What is Cannondale's communications strategy for its Web site? Compare Cannondale's format with that of Wheelworks, a bicycle maker in Davis, California, at* **dcn.davis.ca.us/~bicycles**. *Which format do you think is most effective?*

WE CREATED A SUSPENSION BIKE SO QUICK AND AGILE, WE HAD TO DESIGN A WHOLE NEW BRAKING SYSTEM TO STOP IT.

Mountains divide countries. Separate nations. Even alter climates. But they are no longer an obstacle to those who possess the Cannondale E.S.T. Short for Elevated Suspension Technology, the E.S.T. is a radical departure in bicycle design that lets you attack the most unsettling terrain as if it were paved.

The secret is the spring-supported, oil-dampened shock absorber. Once calibrated to your weight and the terrain, the E.S.T. soaks up all of the shock that's normally absorbed by you. And like a true suspension system, it holds the wheel to the road over

bumps, ruts and rocks. So you can put less effort into controlling the bike, and more energy into something else. Going faster. In fact, the E.S.T. can increase your speed so dramatically, we had to devise a more efficient way to stop it. Force 40 braking. A cable routing system that increases stopping power by 40% over conventional cantilevers. And like every Cannondale, the E.S.T. is distinguished by its ultralight, hand-welded and heat-treated aluminum frame.

Maybe you can't move mountains. But with the Cannondale E.S.T., you can level them.

WEB SIGHTING

DON'T JUST DO SOMETHING. SIT THERE.

Sometimes, the most important thing you can do for yourself is to *do nothing at all*. Simply take a few minutes to unwind from the busy, non-stop, responsibility-filled adventure you call your everyday life.

It's easy when you have the warm, swirling waters of a Hot Spring to come home to. Hot Spring® Portable Spas — the world's number one selling brand — are self-contained, so there are no plumbing or other installation hassles to worry about. With a Hot Spring, you can order a spa one day and have it delivered and running the next. Hot Spring Spas are always hot and ready to enjoy 365 days a year, in any kind of weather.

They're also extremely energy efficient — costing just pennies a day to operate. And Hot Spring Spas are also the most dependable, backed by a five year parts and labor warranty — the best in the business — and the largest dealer network in America.

So if you want to relax, ease your aches and pains, or spend quality time with friends and loved ones, there's nothing to do. Except call 1-800-468-2656 for the Hot Spring Spa Dealer near you.

HotSpring *Portable Spas*

A picture of a typical user can say a great deal about the value of a brand.

Design

❷ **Design** is "the structure itself and the plan behind that structure" for the aesthetic and stylistic aspects of a print advertisement.[12] Design represents the effort on the part of creatives to physically arrange all the components of a printed advertisement in such a way that order and beauty are achieved—order in the sense that the illustration, headline, body copy, and special features of the ad are easy to read; beauty in the sense that the ad is visually pleasing to a reader.

Certainly, not every advertiser has an appreciation for the elements that constitute effective design, nor will every advertiser be fortunate enough to have highly skilled designers as part of the team creating a print ad. As you will see in the following discussions, however, there are aspects of design that directly relate to the potential for a print ad to communicate effectively based on its artistic form. As such, design factors are relevant to creating effective print advertising. The New Media box on page 330 makes clear that this is a lesson yet to be learned by many advertisers on the World Wide Web.

Principles of Design

Principles of design govern how a print advertisement should be prepared. The word *should* is carefully chosen in this context. It is used because just as language has rules of grammar and

12.   This discussion is based on Roy Paul Nelson, *The Design of Advertising,* 5th ed. (Dubuque, Iowa: Wm. C. Brown Publishers, 1985), 126.

syntax, visual presentation has rules of design. The **principles of design** relate to each element within an advertisement *and* to the arrangement of and relationship between elements as a whole.[13] Principles of design suggest that

- a design must be in balance
- the proportion within an advertisement must be pleasing to the viewer
- the components within an advertisement will have an ordered and directional pattern
- there should be a unifying force within the ad
- one element of the ad should be emphasized above all others

We will consider each of these principles of design and how they relate to the development of an effective print advertisement. Of course, as sure as there are rules, there are occasions when the rules need to be broken. An experienced designer knows the rules and follows them, but is also prepared to break the rules to achieve a desired outcome.

Balance. **Balance** in an ad is an orderliness and compatibility of presentation. Balance can be either formal or informal. As shown in Exhibit 12.8, **formal balance** emphasizes symmetrical presentation—components on one side of an imaginary vertical line through the ad are repeated in approximate size and shape on the other side of the imaginary line. Formal balance creates a mood of seriousness and directness and offers the viewer an orderly, easy-to-follow visual presentation.

Informal balance emphasizes asymmetry—the optical weighing of nonsimilar sizes and shapes. Exhibit 12.9 shows an advertisement using a range of type sizes, visuals, and colors to create a powerful visual effect that achieves informal balance. Informal balance in an ad should not be interpreted as imbalance. Rather, components of different size, shape, and color are arranged in a more complex relationship providing asymmetrical balance to an ad. Informal balance is more difficult to manage in that the placement of unusual shapes and sizes must be precisely coordinated.

Proportion. Proportion has to do with the size and tonal relationships between different elements in an advertisement. Whenever two elements are placed in proximity, proportion results. In a printed advertisement, proportional considerations

NEW MEDIA

WEB ADS FLUNK DESIGN TEST

In its short history, the Internet's World Wide Web has attracted thousands of companies. Marketers of goods and services, from Acura to Zima, all want to take advantage of snazzy graphics and color photos to parade their wares before millions of computer users.

How good are the home pages created by these new cyberspace advertisers? Not so good. The judgment is that many of them serve up the online equivalent of junk mail. In the words of an executive vice president at MCI Communications, "It's hideous."

The problem seems to be that little design creativity, the hallmark of outstanding print advertising, is finding its way to Web sites. The typical home page is filled with turgid company profiles, hokey product pitches, and bland marketing material. One Web user wrote in an Internet posting, "Too many Web pages are designed like drive-by billboards that are about as interesting and informative as rocks in the road."

The explanation for firms flunking the Web design test so badly seems to be a combination of lack of experience, premature posting on the Web, and limited funds to create a more aesthetically pleasing site. Marketers, in their urgency to set up a Web storefront, simply dump online whatever text-based marketing materials are on hand. Many firms simply scan in their print ads or photos from annual reports and let those materials form the visual foundation for the site. A spokesperson for Boeing said of his firm's online effort, "We aren't inventing anything new." In terms of Boeing's future efforts to spiff up its site, he said, "That takes some resources. The times are such that that's not in the cards."

In the view of one expert, the lack of attention to design could ultimately undermine a firm's success on the Web. Bob O'Keefe, a professor at Rensselaer Polytechnic Institute who tracks business use of the Internet, believes that if a firm's site lacks style and sophistication, Internet users "may subconsciously dismiss [the firm] and never have anything to do with [it] down the road."

Source: Bart Ziegler, "In Cyberspace the Web Delivers Junk Mail," *Wall Street Journal*, June 13, 1995, B1.

13. Ibid., 129–36.

EXHIBIT 12.8

Using similarly sized objects, Apple achieves formal visual balance in this ad. **www.apple.com/**

EXHIBIT 12.9

Informal balance is achieved through the use of many objects of different sizes. **www.digital.com**

are the relationship of the width of an ad to its depth; the width of each element to the depth of each element; the size of one element relative to the size of every other element; the space between two elements and the relationship of that space to a third element; and the amount of light area as opposed to the amount of dark area.

Ideally, factors of proportion vary so as to avoid monotony in an ad. Further, the designer should pursue pleasing proportions, which means the viewer will not detect mathematical relationships between elements. In general, unequal dimensions and distances make for the most lively designs in advertising.

Order. Order in an advertisement is also referred to as sequence or, in terms of its effects on the reader, gaze motion. The designer's goal is to establish a relationship among elements that leads the reader through the ad in some controlled fashion. A designer can create a logical path of visual components to control eye movement. The eye has a natural tendency to move from left to right, from up to down, from large elements to small elements, from light to dark, and from color to noncolor. Exhibit 12.10 is an example of an ad that induces the reader's eye to move from the upper left to the lower right based on the elements of order.

Order also includes inducing the reader to jump from one space in the ad to another, creating a sense of action. The essential contribution of this component is to establish a visual format that results in a focus or several focuses.

Unity. Ensuring that the elements of an advertisement are tied together and appear to be related is the purpose of unity. Considered the most important of the design principles, unity results in harmony among the diverse components of print advertising: headline, subhead, body copy, and illustration. Several design techniques contribute to unity. The **border** surrounding an ad keeps the ad elements from spilling over into other ads or into the printed matter next to the ad. **White space** at the outside edges creates an informal border effect. The indiscriminate use of white space within an ad can separate elements and give an impression of disorder. The proper use of white space can be dramatic and powerful and draw the receiver's attention to the most critical elements of an ad. Exhibit 12.11 shows a classic example of the effective use of white space.

The final construct of unity is the axis. In every advertisement, an axis will naturally emerge. The **axis** is a line, real or imagined, that runs through an ad and from which the elements in the advertisement flare out. A single ad may have one, two, or even three axes running vertically and horizontally. An axis can be created by blocks of copy, by the placement of illustrations, or by the items within an illustration, such as the position and direction of a model's arm or leg. Elements in an ad may violate the axes, but when two or more elements use a common axis as a starting point, unity is enhanced.

A design can be more forceful in creating unity by using either a three-point layout or a parallel structure. A **three-point layout structure** establishes three elements in the ad as dominant forces. The uneven number of prominent elements is critical to creating a gaze motion in the viewer. **Parallel layout structure** employs art on the right-hand side of the page and repeats the art on the left-hand side. This is an obvious and highly structured technique to achieve unity.

Emphasis. At some point in the decision-making process, someone needs to decide which major component—the headline, subhead, body copy, or illustration—will be emphasized. The key to good design relative to emphasis is that one item is the primary but not the only focus in an ad. If one element is emphasized to the total exclusion of the others, then a poor design has been achieved, and ultimately a poor communication will result.

Balance, proportion, order, unity, and emphasis are the basic principles of design. As you can see, the designer's objectives go beyond the strategic and message development elements associated with an advertisement. Design principles relate to the aesthetic impression an ad produces. Once a designer has been informed of the components that will comprise the headline, subhead, body copy, and illustration to be included in the

EXHIBIT 12.10

Manipulating the order of elements to control the reader's eye.
www.ford.com/

EXHIBIT 12.11   *The effective use of white space to highlight the critical aspect of the ad: the product.* **www.vw.com/**

ad, then advertising and marketing decision makers *must* allow the designer to arrange those components according to the principles of creative design. At some point, however, creativity and effective selling must come together.

Components of Effective Design

The principles of design suggest there are artistic ideals to be pursued in the design of print advertising. But an art director should always recognize that the design of a print advertisement must first and foremost fulfill the commercial purposes for the piece. In this sense, effective design relates directly to the persuasion and communication goals for the advertising, in addition to the artistic and creative principles of design just discussed. The following are the components of effective design in the context of commercial communication. These factors have proved to be related to the ability of an advertisement to communicate effectively to a target audience.

Focus. Focusing a receiver's attention on a particular component of an advertisement can be achieved through various principles of design. Most directly applicable to advertising is the emphasis principle. The **emphasis principle** states that effective design focuses attention on and emphasizes the key value or selling point of a brand. This can be achieved by focusing the reader on the headline, subhead, body copy, or illustration, depending on which component is carrying the burden of the persuasive message. In Exhibit 12.12, the designer added rectangular lines to the visual to focus the reader's attention on the underside of the car.

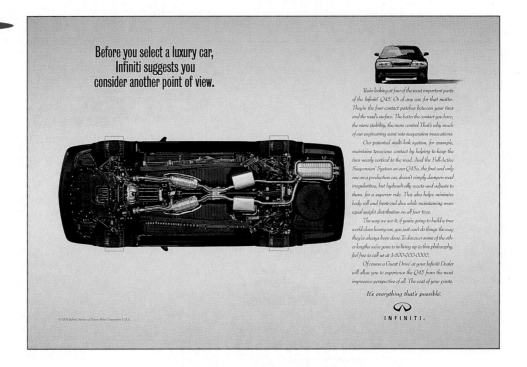

Before you select a luxury car, Infiniti suggests you consider another point of view.

You're looking at four of the most important parts of the Infiniti Q45. Or of any car, for that matter. They're the four contact patches between your tires and the road's surface. The better the contact you have, the more stability, the more control. That's why much of our engineering went into suspension innovations.

Our patented multi-link system, for example, maintains tenacious contact by helping to keep the tires nearly vertical to the road. And the Full-Active Suspension™ System on our Q45a, the first and only one on a production car, doesn't simply dampen road irregularities, but hydraulically reacts and adjusts to them, for a superior ride. This also helps minimize body roll and front-end dive while maintaining more equal weight distribution on all four tires.

The way we see it, if you're going to build a true world-class luxury car, you just can't do things the way they've always been done. To discover some of the other lengths we've gone to in living up to this philosophy, feel free to call us at 1-800-000-0000.

Of course a Guest Drive® at your Infiniti Dealer will allow you to experience the Q45 from the most impressive perspective of all. The seat of your pants.

It's everything that's possible.

INFINITI.

© 2004 Infiniti Division of Nissan Motor Corporation, U.S.A.

Movement and Direction. Ideally, an advertisement is designed to encourage eye movement through all parts of the ad and in a particular sequence. The designer can use the principles of proportion and order to achieve a desired eye movement by a receiver. What is desired in any particular ad with regard to movement and direction will vary. In general, an advertiser wants a reader to begin with major selling points and move to supportive information in the ad, including the body copy and illustration. One primary component of proper movement is to lead the reader's eyes to the copy. Movement should also ensure that the reader stays on the page rather than being led off the top, bottom, or sides.

Clarity and Simplicity. The printed page should strike the viewer as simple to read and easy to comprehend. Advertisements perceived as complex and chaotic deter careful inspection. The designer's main tools to achieve clarity and simplicity are balance, proportion, and order.

The discussions of design presented here are not meant to teach design or instantly create the ability to effectively design print ads. Rather, by understanding the principles and components of effective design, we can gain an appreciation for the goals of the art director and the potent role design can play in the preparation of print ads.

Layout

3 In contrast to design, which emphasizes the concept behind a print ad, layout is the mechanical aspect of design—the physical manifestation of the design concepts. A **layout** is a drawing of a proposed print advertisement, showing where all the elements in the ad are positioned. An art director uses a layout to work through various alternatives for visual presentation and sequentially develop the print ad to its final stages. It is part and parcel of the design process and inextricably linked to the development of an effective design. Many art directors still work with a layout pad, T-square, triangle, pens, pencils, and pasteup supplies. Others have adopted the technology of computer-aided design and paint-brush software.

An art director typically proceeds through various stages in the construction of a final design for an ad. The following are the different stages of layout development, in order of detail and completeness, that an art director typically uses.

Thumbnails

Thumbnails, or thumbnail sketches, are the rough first drafts of advertising design. It is likely that the designer will produce several sketches in an attempt to work out the general presentation of the ad. Thumbnails are rarely drawn to actual size. One-quarter the size of the finished ad is typical for a sketch. While the designer is simply beginning to work out design details, the thumbnail sketch will represent final proportions between elements as well as the relative placement of elements in the ad. Additionally, the designer will begin to pursue emphasis with shades and half shades, gray areas and white areas. Headlines are often represented with zigzag lines, and body copy with straight parallel lines. An example of a thumbnail is shown in Exhibit 12.13.

Rough Layout

The second stage is the **rough layout,** in which greater detail is worked into the design. A rough layout is done in the actual size of the proposed ad, and the headline is lettered in. Type styles and weight are not yet decided on, but the illustration is more carefully drawn, and a greater commitment to positioning the elements is made. The main purpose of a rough layout is to further refine the size and positioning of various elements in the ad. Exhibit 12.14 features a rough layout.

Semicomp

The next step in the layout process is the semicomp. A **semicomp** is one step more refined than a rough layout. In a semicomp, the **display type** (larger-size copy in the headline and subhead) is lettered in so it closely resembles the type that will be used in the final ad. A semicomp is often prepared for preliminary presentation by the advertising agency to the client.

Comprehensive

In many cases, a comprehensive, or comp, layout is the next stage in the evolution of a print ad. A **comp layout** is a polished, drawn version of the ad. In cases where advertising decision makers demand final approval, a comp layout is produced to give strategists as close an approximation to the final product as possible. The display type in headlines is carefully lettered, illustrations are painted in, and copy may actually be set in place (usually in the proper type style and length, but in nonsense type called Greeking type). Comprehensives are an expensive interim step, but they are often a critical stage in layout. A comp layout is featured in Exhibit 12.15.

EXHIBIT 12.13

A thumbnail showing the transition from idea to advertisement.

EXHIBIT 12.14 *A rough layout.*

EXHIBIT 12.15 *A comp layout.*

Mechanicals

The last stage of the layout process is referred to as the mechanicals stage. Mechanicals are also called the keyline or pasteup. The **mechanicals** are carefully prepared pasteups of the exact components of an advertisement, prepared specifically for the printer. The mechanicals are given to the printer to be photographed on a printing plate. Mechanicals are used strictly as preparation for print production.

Computers have changed the process of preparing mechanicals. With the advent of computerized layout, art directors can communicate via computerized files with printers, often eliminating the need to photograph the final layout. Once all the elements of an ad are scanned into computer memory, the process of designing alternative versions of the ad can be completed in just a few minutes. Before computer technology, each new mechanical could take over an hour to prepare at a cost of $50 to $100 per version.

The stages of layout development discussed here provide the artistic blueprint for a print advertisement (see Exhibit 12.16). At this point, the practical matters of choosing the look and style of a print ad can be considered. We now turn our attention to the matter of print production.

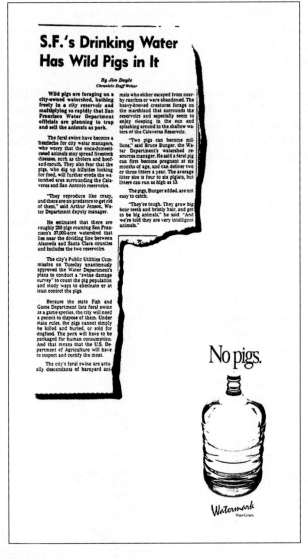

EXHIBIT 12.16

The finished ad.

Production in Print Advertising

❹ The production process in print advertising represents the technical and mechanical activities that transform a creative concept and rough layout into a finished print advertisement. While the process is fundamentally technical, some aspects of print production relate to the strategic and design goals of the print ad. Different type styles can contribute to the design quality, readability, and mood in an advertisement. Our purpose in this section, however, is to provide a basic familiarity with production details. It is our goal to outline the sequence of activities and proper time frame related to print production and the various options available for print preparation.

The Print Production Schedule

An advertiser is only partly in control of the timing of the appearance of a print advertisement. While plans can be made to coordinate the appearance of the ad with overall marketing strategies, it must be recognized that the print media will have specifications regarding how far in advance and in what form an ad must be received to appear in print. The deadline for receipt of an ad is referred to as the **closing date.** Closing dates for newspapers can be one or two days before publication. For magazines, the closing date may be months ahead of publication. Exhibit 12.17 describes the sequence of events and the amount of time between

Preparation and production schedule for a magazine advertisement.

Stage	Time
Creative work begins	Copy platform approved
Creative work completed and approved	2 weeks
Artwork ordered (photography or art)	1 day
Artwork completed	2 weeks
Working layout ordered	1 day
Working layout including art complete	1 week
Finished materials to printer (engraver)	5 days
First proof from printer	2 weeks
Final proof from printer	5 days
Printer (engraver) to plate preparation	5 days
Plates shipped to publication	5 days
Publication date of issue	4 to 12 weeks
Total time	13 to 21 weeks

stages for a typical magazine ad production schedule. The schedule for a newspaper ad can be significantly shorter.

As you can see from this typical schedule, from the time design work begins until the ad appears in magazine publication, 13 to 21 weeks' time can be involved. For newspaper advertising, the time is typically much shorter, perhaps 6 to 12 weeks, but this still represents a fairly long planning and execution period. Advertisers must be aware that such advance planning is necessary to accommodate the basic nature of print production.

Print Production Processes

Seven major processes can be used in print production.[14] Depending on the medium (newspaper, magazine, direct mail, or specialty advertising), the length of the print run (quantity), the type of paper being used, and the quality desired in reproduction, one of the following processes is used: letterpress, gravure, offset lithography, flexography, screen printing, electronic and inkjet printing, or computer print production. Advances in technology have made computer print production an ideal alternative under certain conditions.

Letterpress is the oldest and most versatile method of printing. Text and images are printed from a plate or mat. Printing presses are available for production runs of vastly different quantities. Letterpress is the only process that uses type directly. Letterpress production is capable of high-quality color reproduction when high-quality paper is used. As discussed in the Contemporary Issues box on page 338, this turns out to be a major concern given today's high prices for quality paper.

Gravure is a print production method that also uses a plate or mat. It is excellent for reproducing pictures, but the high costs associated with plate making limits its use to large-quantity production runs. Gravure printing is often used for Sunday newspaper supplements and magazine sections.

14.   This discussion is based in part on Michael H. Bruno, ed., *Pocket Pal: A Graphic Arts Production Handbook,* 13th ed. (New York: International Paper, 1983), 24–31.

Offset lithography is a process that prints from a flat, chemically treated surface that attracts ink to the areas to be printed and repels ink from other areas. The inked image is then transferred to a rubber blanket on a roller, and from this roller the impression is carried to paper. Offset lithography is still a widely used form of print production. It can create a clearer impression on a wider range of paper surfaces than any other production technique. Because of the versatility of this method, it is often used for catalogs and direct mail promotional pieces.

Flexography is a printing technique similar to offset lithography because it also uses a rubber blanket to transfer images to paper. It differs from offset in that the process uses water-based ink, and printing can be done on any surface. Many newspapers have started to use flexography because the image tends to be sharper and less ink rubs off on the reader.

Screen printing, also known as silk screening, is a process that employs a stencil produced on a screen. This method has traditionally been limited to small-quantity print runs, but the recent introduction of rotary screen presses allows a continuous printing process, thus greatly increasing capacity.

Electronic and inkjet printing uses computers, electronics, electrostatics, and special toners and inks to produce images. These are plateless printing processes in which images are stored in digital form in computers. Since the image in these processes must be produced each time a print is made, there is greater chance of variability between impressions. As such, these techniques are better suited to computer letters—which are the mainstay of direct mail print advertising. Another application of inkjet printing is the printing of subscribers' names and addresses on magazines. *Time* and *Fortune* are two prominent publications that use inkjet printing for this purpose.

Computer print production is a printing process whereby computerized typesetting combined with digitized art and fiber-optic communication replace traditional printing processes. Using desktop publishing programs on powerful PCs, computer print production is now a reality. Computers are used to set type, digitized artwork is incorporated into the pages, and the pages are sent via phone lines or satellite to printing facilities. Such print production may be of relatively low quality, but

CONTEMPORARY ISSUES

SKYROCKETING PAPER COSTS THREATEN PRINT ADS

Magazine publishers should be rejoicing. Recent years have provided them with not only all-time-record ad revenues, but also double-digit growth. But the mood is subdued. Skyrocketing paper costs are threatening the ability of the industry to continue to grow. As paper price pressures mount, publishers are raising ad rates and cutting back on circulation. Both moves are getting a less than enthusiastic response from advertisers and agencies.

The root of the problem is that as magazines have successfully sold more and more advertising pages, they've consumed more coated groundwood paper—the main grade used by magazines and catalogs. This jump in demand has dwindled supply of coated groundwood and sent prices soaring. In mid-1992, a ton of No. 5 34-pound groundwood cost about $750. Now that same 2,000-pound lot goes for more than $1,500. Since paper costs amount to about 10.3 percent of a consumer magazine publisher's overall costs, the impact is significant. Because of the effect, publishers feel they have little choice but to ask advertisers and readers to bear the cost through higher base rates and higher subscription and newsstand prices. Hearst Magazines has raised rates 5 percent to advertisers and has boosted subscription and newsstand prices from 7 percent to 33 percent.

Not surprisingly, many advertisers and their agencies aren't particularly interested in publishers' paper problems. An executive vice president at Ammirati & Purvis/Lintas advertising agency in New York says, "I'm not going to pay double-digit increases. My clients' budgets are not going up double digits." And the harsh words appear to be more than an idle threat. Hearst Magazines seems to have lost Kraft Foods advertising in its big magazines *Good Housekeeping* and *Redbook,* and both Clorox and Unilever are reevaluating their media buys.

The industry is still searching for the right way to deal with these problems. For its part, Hearst feels like it is acting in the best interests of both advertisers and readers. D. Claeys Bahrenburg, the president of Hearst Magazines, says, "It still comes down to this being a long-term strategy that involves quality brand-name magazines. In my view, we'll see in the year 2000 which magazines are healthy."

Sources: Keith J. Kelly, "Record Harvest Succumbs to High Price," *Advertising Age,* November 6, 1995, S-1; Keith J. Kelly, "Hearst's High-Stakes Gamble," *Advertising Age,* November 6, 1995, S-4; and Keith J. Kelly, "Publishers Get Econ 101 Lesson," *Advertising Age,* November 6, 1995, S-6.

EXHIBIT 12.18

An example of computer print production. **www.usatoday.com**

it is suitable for newspaper production. Regional editions of the newspaper *USA Today* are the most prominent examples of the use of computer print production, as shown in Exhibit 12.18.

As stated earlier, choice of the proper printing process depends on the requirements of the advertisement with regard to the medium being used, the quantity being printed, the type of paper being printed on, and the level of quality needed. With respect to magazines, the production process is mandated by the publisher of a particular vehicle within the medium. Print production processes are independent publishing decisions. From an advertising decision-making standpoint, the illustration and design of an ad should be planned with an awareness of the production process to be used so that the ad itself is compatible with the printing technique.

Typography

The issues associated with typography have to do with the typeface chosen for headlines, subheads, and body copy, as well as the various size components of the type (height, width, and running length). Designers agonize over the type to use in a print ad because decisions about type affect both the readability and the mood of the overall visual impression. For our purposes, some knowledge of the basic considerations of typography is useful for an appreciation of the choices that must be made.

Categories of Type. Typefaces have distinct personalities, and each can communicate a different mood and image. A **type font** is a basic set of typeface letters. For those of us who do word processing on computers, the choice of type font is a common decision. In choosing type for an advertisement, however, the art director has literally hundreds of choices based on typeface and type size.

There are four broad categories of type, distinguished by the thickness of the strokes and the presence or absence of **serifs,** the small lines that cross the ends of the main strokes. The most popular category of type is **roman.** There are several subcategories of roman type, all maintaining the basic character of a roman serif. **Sans serif** type, as the name implies, has no small lines crossing the ends of the main strokes, and the result is a block-lettered look. Sans serif type is popular for headlines because of its boldness. Its use is somewhat restricted for body copy because the even thickness throughout creates a monotony of impression. **Slab serif** type is often categorized with sans serif type because of the squareness of the type. However, this type does have serifs and does employ varying thicknesses of letters. Examples of these first three categories of type follow:

This line is set in roman type.

This line is set in sans serif type.

This line is set in slab serif type.

For purposes of organization, the fourth type category can be classified as miscellaneous. There are some commonly used groups in the miscellaneous category, such as Old English. **Old English** type is distinguished by its elaborate overlapping strokes. This feature can make it a difficult type to read. Script types are supposed to resemble handwriting but rarely achieve the effect. Italic types, distinguished by their slant to the right, can be considered a separate category, but they actually can be included in any of the main categories.

Type Measurement. There are two elements of type size. **Point** refers to the size of type in height. In the printing industry, type sizes run from 6 to 120 points. Exhibit 12.19 shows a range of type sizes for comparison purposes. **Pica** measures the width of lines. A pica is 12 points wide, and each pica measures about one-sixth of an inch. Therefore, it is possible to judge, based on the typeface chosen, the amount of running space occupied. There are copy-fitting charts available to facilitate this sort of calculation during the design and layout process.

EXHIBIT 12.19

A range of type point sizes.

This is 8 point type

This is 12 point type

This is 18 point type

This is 36 point type

This is 60 point type

Readability. It is critical in choosing type to consider readability. Type should facilitate the communication process. Some traditional recommendations when deciding on what type to use are as follows:

- Use capitals and lowercase, NOT ALL CAPITALS.
- Arrange letters from left to right, not up and down.
- Run lines of type horizontally, not vertically.
- Use even spacing between letters and words.

Different typefaces and styles also affect the mood conveyed by an ad. Depending on the choices made, typefaces can connote grace, power, beauty, modernness, simplicity, or any number of other qualities.

SUMMARY

❶ Identify the basic purposes for, and components and formats of, print ad illustrations.

With few exceptions, illustrations are critical to the effectiveness of print ads. Specifically, illustrations can serve to attract attention, communicate product features or benefits, create a mood and enhance brand image, or stimulate reading of the body copy. The overall impact of an illustration is determined in part by its most basic components: its size, use of color, and the medium used to create the illustration. Another critical aspect of the illustration's effectiveness has to do with the format chosen for the product in the illustration. Obviously, a print ad cannot work if the consumer doesn't easily identify the product or service being advertised.

❷ Describe the principles and components that help ensure the effective design of print ads.

In print ad design, all the verbal and visual components of an ad are arranged for maximum impact and appeal. Several principles can be followed as a basis for a compelling design. These principles feature issues like balance, proportion, order, unity, and emphasis. The first component of an effective design is focus—drawing the reader's attention to specific areas of the ad. The second component is movement and direction—directing the reader's eye movement through the ad. The third component is clarity and simplicity—avoiding a complex and chaotic look that will deter most consumers.

❸ Detail the stages that art directors follow in developing the layout of a print ad.

The layout is the physical manifestation of all this design planning. An art director uses various forms of layouts to bring a print ad to life. There are several predictable stages in the evolution of a layout. The art director starts with a thumbnail, proceeds to the rough layout, and continues with the semicomp. With each stage, the layout becomes more concrete, more expensive, and more like the final form of the advertisement. The comp layout is an interim stage that may be used before the mechanicals. Mechanicals represent the final stage in the evolution; from the mechanicals, the ad moves to final production.

❹ Discuss the activities and decisions involved in the final production of print ads.

Timing is critical to advertising effectiveness: advertisers must have a keen understanding of production cycles to have an ad in the consumer's hands at just the right time. In addition, there are many possible means for actually printing an ad. These range from the letterpress to screen printing to computer print production. As with many aspects of modern life, the computer has had a dramatic impact on print ad preparation and production. Before a print ad can reach its audience, a host of small but important decisions need to be made about the type styles and sizes that will best serve the campaign's purposes.

KEY TERMS

illustration (324)

medium (326)

illustration format (327)

design (329)

principles of design (330)

balance (330)

formal balance (330)

informal balance (330)

border (332)

white space (332)

axis (332)

three-point layout structure (332)

parallel layout structure (332)

emphasis principle (333)

thumbnails, or thumbnail sketches (335)

rough layout (335)

semicomp (335)

layout (334)

display type (335)

comp layout (335)

mechanicals (336)

closing date (336)

letterpress (337)

gravure (337)

offset lithography (338)

flexography (338)

screen printing (338)

electronic and inkjet printing (338)

computer print production (338)

type font (339)

serifs (340)

roman (340)

sans serif (340)

slab serif (340)

Old English (340)

point (340)

pica (340)

QUESTIONS FOR REVIEW AND CRITICAL THINKING

1. Is there anyone out there who would rather watch black-and-white television than color? If not, why would any advertiser choose to run a black-and-white print ad in a medium that supports color? Can you think of a situation where a black-and-white ad might be more effective than a color ad?

2. *Effective* turns out to be a very elusive concept in any discussion of advertising's effects. In what ways might an illustration in a print ad prove to be effective from the point of view of a marketer?

3. This chapter reviewed five basic principles for print ad design: balance, proportion, order, unity, and emphasis. Give an example of how each of these principles might be employed to enhance the selling message of a print ad.

4. Creativity in advertising is often a matter of breaking with conventions. Peruse an issue of your favorite magazine or newspaper to find examples of ads that violate the five basic principles mentioned in the previous question.

5. Why is it appropriate to think of print as a static medium? Given print's static nature, explain how movement and direction can be relevant concepts to the layout of a print ad.

6. For an art director who has reached the mechanicals stage of the ad layout process, explain the appeal of computer-aided design versus the old-fashioned pasteup approach.

7. Evaluate newspapers versus magazines as the media most appropriate for rapidly counterattacking a competitor's advances in the three cities of Miami, Baltimore, and Portland.

8. This chapter opened with an excellent example of an advertising campaign directed at reversing RCA's fortunes in the consumer electronics market. Given RCA's situation at the time the campaign was developed, list as many arguments as you can think of to support RCA's decision to feature magazine ads as part of its revival campaign.

EXPERIENTIAL EXERCISE

Find an ad that uses an effective illustration and explain what makes it effective. Find two other ads, one that uses formal balance, and one that uses informal balance. Do you find these ads equally appealing? Why or why not?

Finally, find an ad that seems to lack any good visuals, and explain whether is it good or bad advertising, and why. What conclusions can you draw about the use of illustrations in print ads?

USING THE INTERNET

When designing an advertisement, both the verbal and visual components of the ad are arranged to maximize impact and appeal. Visit the Internet Link Exchange site (www.linkexchange.com) and view the results of the most recent banner ad contest. Choose the three ads that you like the most.

For each ad, explain how the ad uses the principles of design to achieve its impact on the viewer:

1.   Which is more dominant, the illustration or the copy?

2.   What element receives the most emphasis?

3.   Does the ad use formal or informal balance?

4.   How would you characterize the typeface?

5.   Does the ad make effective use of white space?

6.   Which of these banner ads is most effective at influencing you to click on it? What aspects of the ad design are the most appealing?

Part 3 | Preparing the Message

Chapter 13

Art Direction

and Production

in Broadcast

Advertising

After reading and thinking about this chapter, you will be able to do the following:

1 Identify the various players who must function as a team to produce television ads.

2 Discuss the specific stages and costs involved in producing television ads.

3 Describe the major formatting options for TV ad production.

4 Explain the process of radio ad production and describe the formatting options for ads in this medium.

Warner-Lambert Company, the makers of personal care products including such widely known brands as Listerine, Certs, and Efferdent, and its advertising agency Young & Rubicam (Y&R) had a major challenge on their hands. One of Warner-Lambert's premier brands, Rolaids, had taken a major blow from its primary competitor, Tums. Tums's advertising had struck on a new and relevant benefit for the target audience. Tums was emphasizing the extra benefit of calcium in its antacid tablets. The timing of the Tums ad was perfect. Physicians had begun suggesting calcium as a dietary supplement for women, and the National Osteoporosis Foundation was promoting the use of calcium as well. As soon as the Tums calcium campaign was established, sales of Tums jumped 40 percent.

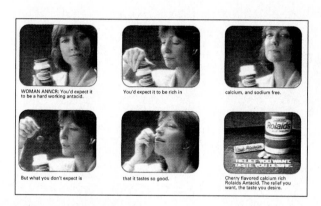

WOMAN ANNCR: You'd expect it to be a hard working antacid.

You'd expect it to be rich in

calcium, and sodium free.

But what you don't expect is

that it tastes so good.

Cherry flavored calcium rich Rolaids Antacid. The relief you want, the taste you desire.

EXHIBIT 13.1

To respond effectively to a competitor's advertising, Warner-Lambert and its agency Young & Rubicam created this ad for Rolaids antacid. Despite the fact that this ad is only 15 seconds long, it took four solid months of production and more than $500,000 to create. **www.warner-lambert.com/**

Warner-Lambert needed a response to the Tums surprise attack. The brand needed a strong, features-and-benefits-based advertising effort to recapture share of mind and hopefully some lost market share as well. For a six-month period, a team of more than 70 people from Warner-Lambert and Y&R set out to research the audience and then respond to Tums with new, different, and powerful television ads. The ads would highlight a new and previously unrecognized benefit for the target audience. The counterattack would be the result of three separate consumer surveys, 30 hours of brainstorming, 50 hours of revisions, and four solid months of production. The Rolaids response to Tums was embodied in the 15-second television commercial shown in Exhibit 13.1.

Some 3,500 feet of film, 72 takes, and 72 maraschino cherries later, the spot was finished and ready to air. The price tag for the Rolaids response to Tums: $500,000—not including the cost of the media time to run the spot.[1]

Art Direction in Television Advertising

● The essential creative responsibility for TV is the same as for other media: effective communication. Television presents some unique challenges, however. Due to its complexity, television production involves a lot of people. These people have different but often overlapping expertise, responsibility, and authority. This makes for a myriad of complications and calls for tremendous organizational skills. At some point, individuals who actually shoot the film or the tape are brought in to execute the copywriter's and art director's concepts. At this point, the creative process becomes intensely collaborative: the film director applies his or her craft and has responsibility for the actual production. But who really has ownership is often unclear. The creative team rarely relinquishes control of the project, even though the film director may prefer exactly that. Getting the various players to perform their particular specialty at just the right time, while avoiding conflict with other team members, is an ongoing challenge in TV ad production.

The Creative Team

The vast and ever-increasing capability of the broadcast media introduces new challenges and complexities to the production process. One aspect of these complexities is that aside from the creative directors, copywriters, and art

1.   Information regarding the Rolaids production was adopted from John Pfeiffer, "Six Months and Half a Million Dollars, All for 15 Seconds," *Smithsonian* (January 1988), 134–45.

directors who assume the burden of responsibility in the production of print advertising, we now encounter a host of new and irreplaceable creative and technical participants. The proper and effective production of broadcast advertising depends on a team of highly capable creative people: agency personnel, production experts, editorial specialists, and music companies. An advertiser and its agency must consider and evaluate the role of each of these participants. Descriptions of the roles played by the participants in television advertising are provided in Exhibit 13.2.

EXHIBIT 13.2

The creative team for television advertising production.

Agency Participants

Creative director (CD). The creative director manages the creative process in an agency for several different clients. Creative directors typically come from the art or copywriting side of the business. The main role of the CD is to oversee the creative product of an agency across all clients.

Art director (AD). The art director and the copywriter work together to develop the concept for a commercial. The AD either oversees the production of the television storyboard or actually constructs the storyboards. In addition, the AD works with the director of the commercial to develop the overall look of the spot.

Copywriter. The copywriter is responsible for the words and phrases used in an ad. In television and radio advertising, these words and phrases appear as a script from which the director, creative director, and art director work during the production process. Together with the AD, the copywriter also makes recommendations on choice of director, casting, and editing facility.

Account executive (AE). The account executive acts as a liaison between the creative team and the client. The AE has the responsibility for coordinating scheduling, budgeting, and the various approvals needed during the production process. The AE can be quite valuable in helping the advertiser understand the various aspects of the production process. Account executives rarely have direct input into either the creative or technical execution of an ad.

Executive producer. The executive producer in an agency is in charge of many line producers, who manage the production at the production site. Executive producers help manage the production bid process. They also assign the appropriate producers to particular production jobs.

Producer. The producer supervises and coordinates all the activities related to a broadcast production. Producers screen director reels, send out production bid forms, review bids, and recommend the production house to be used. The producer also participates in choosing locations, sets, and talent. Normally, the producer will be on the set throughout the production and in the editing room during postproduction, representing agency and client interests.

Production Company Participants

Director. The director is in charge of the filming or taping of a broadcast advertising production. From a creative standpoint, the director is the visionary who brings the copy strategy to life on film or tape. The director also manages the actors, actresses, musicians, and announcers used in an ad to ensure that their performances contribute to the creative strategy being pursued. Finally, the director manages and coordinates the activities of technical staff. Camera operators, sound and lighting technicians, and special effects experts get their assignments from the director.

Producer. The production company also has a producer present, who manages the production at the site. This producer is in charge of the production crew and sets up each shoot. The position of cameras and readiness of production personnel are the responsibility of this producer.

Production manager. The production manager is on the set of a shoot, providing all the ancillary services needed to ensure a successful production. These range from making sure that food service is available on the set to providing dressing rooms and fax, phone, and photocopy services. The production manager typically has a production assistant (PA) to help take care of details.

Camera department. Another critical part of the production team is the camera department. This group includes the director of photography, camera operator, and assistant camera operator. This group ensures that the lighting, angles, and movement are carried out according to the plan and the director's specification.

Art department. The art department that accompanies the production company includes the art director and other personnel responsible for creating the set. This group designs the set, builds background or stunt structures, and provides props.

Editors. Editors enter the production process at the postproduction stage. It is their job, with direction from the art director, creative director, producer, or director, to create the finished advertisement. Editors typically work for independent postproduction houses and use highly specialized equipment to cut and join frames of film or audiotape together to create the finished version of a television or radio advertisement. Editors also synchronize the audio track with visual images in television advertisements and perform the transfer and duplication processes to prepare a commercial for shipping to the media.

Creative Guidelines for Television

Just as for print advertising, there are general creative principles for television advertising.[2] These are not foolproof or definitive, but they certainly represent good advice. Again, truly great creative work has no doubt violated some or all of these.

- *Use an attention-getting and relevant opening.* The first few seconds of a television commercial are crucial. A receiver can make a split-second assessment of the relevance and interest a message holds. An ad can either turn a receiver off or grab her or his attention for the balance of the commercial with the opening. In Exhibit 13.3, Pepsi grabs the viewer with an older woman delivering a line that is unexpected and against type.
- *Emphasize the visual.* A picture can communicate a more rich and detailed message than copy alone. The video capability of television should be highlighted in every production effort. To some degree, this emphasis is dependent on the creative concept, but the visual should carry the selling message even if the audio portion is ignored by the receiver. In Exhibit 13.4, Nature's Course dog food tells its story with a minimum of words.
- *Coordinate the audio with the visual.* The images and copy of a television commercial must reinforce each other rather than pursue separate objectives. Such divergence between the audio and visual portions of an ad only serves to confuse and distract the viewer. In Exhibit 13.5, Portland General Electric uses both words and visuals to convince viewers of the dangers of downed power lines.
- *Persuade as well as entertain.* It is tempting to produce a beautifully creative television advertisement rather than a beautifully effective television advertisement. The vast

EXHIBIT 13.3

Good television ads grab the viewer's attention right away. Having an older woman deliver lines about her preference for rap music over rock 'n' roll helped gain and hold attention for this Pepsi ad.
www.pepsi.com

(MUSIC: UPBEAT)
OLD WOMAN 1:   Rock and roll is okay but I prefer rap.
OLD MAN 1:   Hey Joe.
OLD WOMAN 2:   Right on.
OLD MAN 2:   Hot, hey, hey.
OLD MAN 3:   Awesome.
OLD MAN 1:   This music is good but nobody can touch Hendrix.
OLD MAN 3:   Awesome.
DELIVERY MAN 1: Wait a second. Shady Acres was supposed to get the Coke and the frat house was supposed to get the Pepsi.
DELIVERY MAN 2: Coke, Pepsi, what's the difference?
(MUSIC: CLASSICAL)
FRAT BOY: I-24. [playing bingo]
(MUSIC: UPBEAT)
OLD WOMAN 3:   Do you like slam dancing?
OLD MAN 1:   Love it.
OLD MAN 3:   This is radical.
SUPER: PEPSI. THE CHOICE OF A NEW GENERATION.

2.   These guidelines were adapted from A. Jerome Jewler, *Creative Strategy in Advertising.* 3rd ed. (Belmont, Calif.: Wadsworth Publishing, 1989), 210–11; and Roy Paul Nelson, *The Design of Advertising,* 5th ed. (Dubuque, Iowa: Wm. C. Brown Publishers, 1985), 296.

Good television creative work emphasizes the visual component of an ad. Notice this Nature's Course ad needs only 17 words of copy to deliver its message. **www .purina.com**

ANNCR: Too many artificial colors in your dog's food? There are no artificial colors in new Nature's Course.

The audio and visual components of an ad must work together to effectively communicate. This Portland General Electric ad has well-coordinated audio and video components.

(MUSIC: MOODY, WIND INSTRUMENTS)
ANNCR: The frightening thing about downed power lines is that it's impossible to tell if they're dangerous or not. Just like it's hard to tell a harmless bull snake from a deadly cottonmouth. Now, would you pick one up . . . hoping it's the harmless snake? If you see a downed power line, don't touch it. Call PGE. We'll handle it.
SUPER: PORTLAND GENERAL ELECTRIC.

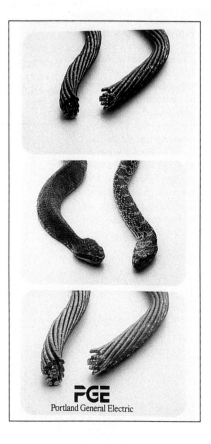

potential of film lures the creative urge in all the production participants. Creating an entertaining commercial is an inherently praiseworthy goal *except* when the entertainment value of the commercial completely overwhelms its persuasive impact. In Exhibit 13.6 Black & Decker sells the Cordless Power Pro with simple yet persuasive demonstrations of the strength of its suction.

- *Maintain continuity.* There are no hard-and-fast rules regarding the use of camera angles, but some commercials are awkward and difficult to watch because of inappropriate cuts, dissolves, fades, and distances. Every commercial must maintain a continuity in its technical execution and transitions, its pace, its rhythm, and its feel. In Exhibit 13.7, Sovran Bank maintains continuity by shooting the entire spot from the viewpoint of a video camera that has been dropped into a swimming pool.
- *Show the product.* Unless a commercial is using intrigue and mystery surrounding the product, the product should be highlighted in the ad. Close-ups and shots of the brand in action help receivers recall the brand and its appearance.

These recommendations go beyond the basics of copywriting and message development discussed in previous chapters. Each of these recommendations focuses on how the physical production of a television ad can affect communication.

The Television Production Process

2 The television production process can best be understood by identifying the activities that take place before, during, and after the actual production of an ad. These stages are referred to as preproduction, production, and postproduction. By breaking the process down into this sequence, we can appreciate both the technical and the strategic aspects of each stage.

SUPER:	BLACK & DECKER PRESENTS THE NEW, CORDLESS POWER PRO.
SUPER:	DEMONSTRATION 1.
SUPER:	DEMONSTRATION 2.
SUPER:	DEMONSTRATION 3.
ANNCR:	Power Pro. The most powerful dustbuster yet.
SUPER:	BLACK & DECKER.

WEB SIGHTING

Continuity in technical execution helps receivers follow the logic in an ad. Here, Sovran Bank communicates the Buyer's Coverage feature of its Sovran Select checking account by shooting the entire spot with a video camera that is underwater.

(SFX: GARBLED TALKING)
CHILD: Daddy!
ANNCR: Last week, the Hendersons bought a new video camera. It has all the latest features . . . Including a zoom lens and low light capabilities.
CHILD: I made the camera go splash.
ANNCR: In fact, the camera does just about every thing, except float.
FATHER: You what?!
ANNCR: Fortunately, the Hendersons paid for their new video camera with a check from their Sovran Select account, which has built-in Buyer's Coverage.
FATHER: Helen!!
ANNCR: So even though they sunk some money into it . . .
(SFX: BZZT OF PICTURE GOING OUT)
ANNCR: . . . They'll have no trouble getting it all back.
SUPER: INTRODUCING SOVRAN SELECT. SOVRAN BANK.

Preproduction

The **preproduction** stage is that part of the television production process in which the advertiser and the advertising agency (or in-house agency staff) carefully work out the precise details of how the creative planning behind an ad can best be brought to life with the opportunities offered by television. Exhibit 13.8 shows the sequence of six events in the preproduction stage.

Storyboard and Script Approval. As Exhibit 13.8 shows, the preproduction stage begins with storyboard and script approval. A **storyboard** is a frame-by-frame sketch depicting, in sequence, the visual scenes and copy that will be used in an advertisement. A **script** is the written version of an ad; it specifies the coordination of the copy elements with the video scenes. The script is used by the producer and director to set the location and content of scenes, by the casting department to choose actors and actresses, and by the producer in budgeting and scheduling the shoot.

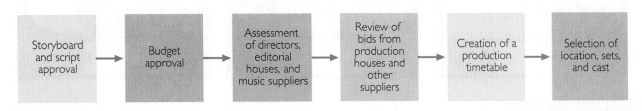

Sequence of events in the preproduction stage of television advertising.

Exhibit 13.9 is part of a storyboard from the Miller Lite "Can Your Beer Do This?" campaign, and Exhibit 13.10 shows the related script. This particular spot was entitled "Ski Jump" and involved rigging a dummy to a recliner and launching the chair and the dummy from a 60-meter ski jump.

The art director and copywriter are significantly involved at this stage of production. It is important that the producer has discussed the storyboard and script with the creative team and fully understands the creative concept and objectives for the advertisement before production begins. Since it is the producer's responsibility to solicit bids for the project from production houses, the producer must be able to fully explain to bidders the requirements of the job so that cost estimates are as accurate as possible.

Budget Approval. Once there is agreement on the scope and intent of the production as depicted in the storyboard and script, the advertiser must give budget approval. The producer needs to work carefully with the creative team and the advertiser to estimate the approximate cost of the shoot, including production staging, location costs, actors, technical requirements, staffing, and a multitude of other considerations. It is essential that these discussions are as detailed and comprehensive as possible because it is from this budget discussion that the producer will evaluate candidates for the directing role and solicit bids from production houses to handle the job.

WEB SIGHTING

EXHIBIT 13.9

How does this storyboard for a Miller Lite Beer ad help link the creative idea to the final ad during the preproduction process? Does the use of a storyboard help the advertiser save time and money during the television production process? Check out Miller's Web site **www.careermosaic.com/cm/miller/**. *Could Miller use more visuals along the lines of storyboards at its Web site? At the Web site for Canada's Molson Beer at* **www.molson.com**, *which is partly owned by Miller, do you find a similar approach to the use of visuals?*

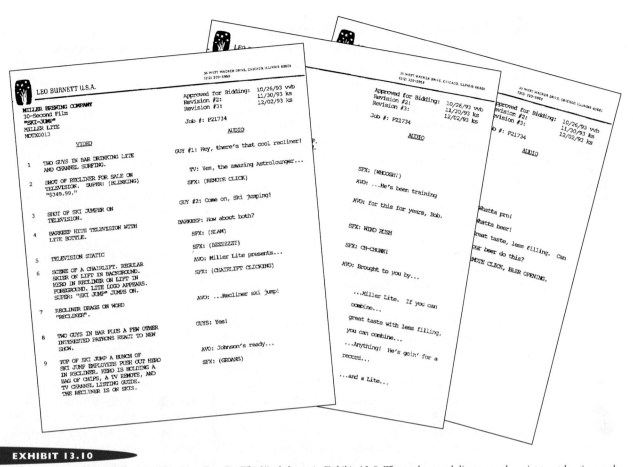

EXHIBIT 13.10

This is the script for the Miller Lite "Can Your Beer Do This?" ad shown in Exhibit 13.9. The producer and director use the script to set locations and the content of scenes and for budgeting and scheduling. The script is also used in choosing actors and actresses for the ad. **www.careermosaic.com/ cm/miller/**

Assessment of Directors, Editorial Houses, Music Suppliers. A producer has dozens (if not hundreds) of directors, postproduction editorial houses, and music suppliers from which to choose. An assessment of those well suited to the task must take place early in the preproduction process. Directors of television commercials, like directors of feature films, develop specializations and reputations. Some directors are known for their work with action or special effects. Others are more highly skilled in working with children, animals, or outdoor settings. The director of an advertisement is responsible for interpreting the storyboard and script and managing the talent to bring the creative concept to life. A director specifies the precise nature of a scene, how it is lit and how it is filmed. In this way, the director acts as the eye of the camera. Choosing the proper director is crucial to the execution of a commercial. Aside from the fact that a good director commands a fee anywhere from $8,000 to $25,000 per day, the director can have a tremendous effect on the quality and impact of the presentation. An excellent creative concept can be undermined by poor direction. The agency creative team should be intimately involved in the choice of directors.

Similarly, editorial houses (and their editors) and music suppliers (and musicians) have particular expertise and reputations. The producer, the director, and the agency creative team actively review the work of the editorial suppliers and music houses particularly well suited to the production. In most cases, geographic proximity to the agency facilities is important. As members of the agency team try to maintain a tight schedule, editorial and music services that are nearby facilitate the timely completion of an ad. Because of this need, editorial and music suppliers have tended to cluster near agencies in Chicago, New York, and Los Angeles.

Review of Bids from Production Houses and Other Suppliers. Production houses and other suppliers, such as lighting specialists, represent a collection of specialized talent and also provide needed equipment for ad preparation. The expertise in production houses relates to the technical aspects of filming a commercial. Producers, production managers, sound and art specialists, camera operators, and others are part of a production house team. The agency sends a bid package to several production houses. The package contains all the details of the commercial to be produced and includes a description of the production requirements and a timetable for the production. An accurate timetable is essential because many production personnel work on an hourly or daily compensation rate.

To give you some idea of the cost of the technical personnel and equipment available from production houses, Exhibit 13.11 lists some key production house personnel who would participate in shooting a commercial, and the typical daily rates (for a ten-hour day) for such personnel and related equipment. Also listed are the rental costs of various pieces of equipment. These costs vary from market to market, but it is obvious why production expenses can run into the hundreds of thousands of dollars. The costs listed in Exhibit 13.11 represent only the daily rates for production time or postproduction work. In addition to these costs are overtime costs, travel, and lodging (if an overnight stay is necessary).

Most agencies send out a bid package on a form developed by the agency. An example of such a bid form is provided in Exhibit 13.12. By using a standardized form, an agency can make direct comparisons between production house bids. A similar form can be used to solicit bids from other suppliers providing editorial or music services. The producer reviews each of the bids and revises them if necessary. From the production house bids *and* the agency's estimate of its own costs associated with production (travel, expenses, editorial services, music, on-camera talent, and agency markups), a production cost estimate is prepared for advertiser review and approval. Once the advertiser has approved the estimate, one of the production houses is awarded the job. The lowest production bid is not always the one chosen. Aside from cost, there are creative and technical considerations. A hot director costs more than last-year's model. The agency's evaluation of the reliability of a production house also enters into the decision.

Creation of a Production Timetable. In conjunction with the stages of preproduction just discussed, the producer will be working on a **production timetable.** This timetable projects a real-

Personnel	Cost
Director	$8,000–25,000/day
Director of photography	3,000/day
Producer	800/day
Production assistant	200/day
Camera operator	600/day
Unit manager	450/day

Equipment	
Production van (including camera, lighting kit, microphones, monitoring equipment)	$2,500–4,000/day
Camera	750–1,000/day
Grip truck with lighting equipment and driver	400–500/day
Telescript with operator	600–700/day
Online editing with editor and assistant editor	250–400/hour

<table>
<tr><td>CLIENT:</td><td>DATE:</td></tr>
</table>

NAME / LENGTH	TYPE	OC	EXT	VO

CLIENT:
PRODUCT:

DATE:
A. E.:
ACCT. SUP.:
WRITER:
A. D.:
C. D.:

TALENT COUNT

NAME / LENGTH	TYPE	OC	EXT	VO
1				
2				
3.				
4.				

	ESTIMATE	ACTUAL
PRODUCTION CO.		
EDITING		
MUSIC		
TALENT		
ARTWORK/CC PACKAGES		
RECORDING STUDIO		
VIDEOTAPE TRANSFERS		
ANIMATION		
CASTING		
SUB TOTAL NET		
% A. C.		
TRAVEL		
SHIPPING		
TOTAL GROSS COST		

NOTES:

EXHIBIT 13.12

Advertising agencies use a bid form to make comparisons between production house bids and provide the client with an estimate of production costs.

istic schedule for all the preproduction, production, and postproduction activities. To stay on budget and complete the production in time to ship the final advertisement to television stations for airing, an accurate and realistic timetable is essential. A timetable must allow a reasonable amount of time to complete all production tasks in a quality manner. Exhibit 13.13 is a timetable for a national 30-second spot, using location shooting.

Realize that a reasonable timetable is rarely achieved. Advertisers often request (or demand) that an agency provide a finished spot (or even several spots) in times as short as four or five weeks. Because of competitive pressures or corporate urgency for change, production timetables are compromised. Advertisers have to accept the reality that violating a reasonable timetable can dramatically increase costs and puts undue pressure on the creative process—no matter what the reason is for the urgency. In fact, a creative director at one agency often told clients that they could pick any two selections off the following list for their television commercials: good, fast, and reasonably priced.[3]

Selection of Location, Sets, and Cast.

Once a bid has been approved and accepted, both the production house and the agency production team begin to search for appropriate, affordable locations if the commercial is to be shot outside of a studio setting. Studio production warrants the design and construction of the sets to be used.

EXHIBIT 13.13

Example of a reasonable timetable for shooting a 30-second television advertisement.

Activity	Time
Assess directors/editorial houses/music suppliers	1 week
Solicit bids from production houses/other suppliers	1 week
Review bids, award jobs to suppliers, submit production estimate to advertiser	1 week
Begin preproduction (location, sets, casting)	1 to 2 weeks
Final preparation and shooting	1 to 2 weeks
Edit film	1 week
Agency/advertiser review of rough cut film	1 week
Postproduction (final editing, voice mix, record music, special effects, etc.) and transfer of film to video; ship to media	2 weeks
Transfer film to videotape; ship to stations	1 week
Total	10 to 12 weeks

3.   Peter Sheldon, former creative director and current doctoral student, University of Illinois.

A delicate stage in preproduction is casting. While not every ad uses actors and actresses, when an ad calls for individuals to perform roles, casting is crucial. Every individual appearing in an ad is, in a very real sense, a representative of the advertiser. This is another reason why the agency creative team stays involved. Actors and actresses help set the mood and tone for an ad and affect the image of the brand. The successful execution of various message strategies is dependent on proper casting. For instance, a slice-of-life message requires actors and actresses with whom the target audience can readily identify. Testimonial message tactics require a search for particular types of people, either celebrities or common folks, who will attract attention and be credible to the audience. The point to remember is that successfully casting a television commercial depends on much more than simply picking people with good acting abilities. Individuals must be matched to the personality of the brand, the nature of the audience, and the scene depicted in the ad. A young male actor who makes a perfect husband in a laundry detergent ad may be totally inappropriate as a rugged outdoorsman in a chainsaw commercial.

Production

The **production stage** of the process, or the **shoot,** is where the storyboard and script come to life and are filmed. The actual production of the spot may also include some final preparations before the shoot begins. The most common final preparation activities are lighting checks and rehearsals. An entire day may be devoted to prelight, which involves setting up lighting or identifying times for the best natural lighting to ensure that the shooting day runs smoothly. Similarly, the director may want to work with the on-camera talent along with the camera operators to practice the positioning and movement planned for the ad. This work, known as blocking, can save a lot of time on a shoot day, when many more costly personnel are on the set.

Lighting, blocking, and other special factors are typically specified by the director in the script. Exhibit 13.14 is a list of common directorial specifications that show up in a script and are used by a director to manage the audio and visual components of a commercial shoot.

Shoot days are the culmination of an enormous amount of effort beginning all the way back at the development of the copy platform. They are the execution of all the well-laid plans by the advertiser and agency personnel. The set on a shoot day is a world all its own. For the uninformed, it can appear to be little more than high-energy chaos. For the professionals involved, however, a shoot has its own tempo and direction.

Production activities during a shoot require the highest level of professionalism and expertise. A successful shoot depends on the effective management of a large number of diverse individuals—creative performers, highly trained technicians, and skilled laborers. Logistical and technical problems always arise, not to mention the ever-present threat of a random event (a thunderstorm or intrusive noise) that disrupts filming and tries everyone's patience. There is a degree of tension and spontaneity on the set that is a necessary part of the creative process but must be kept at a manageable level. Much of the tension stems from trying to execute the various tasks of production correctly and at the proper time.

Another dimension to this tension, however, has to do with expense. As pointed out earlier, most directors, technicians, and talent are paid on a daily rate plus overtime after ten hours. Daily shooting expenses, including director's fees, can run $80,000 to $120,000 for just an average production, so the agency and advertiser, understandably, want the shoot to run as smoothly and quickly as possible.

There is the real problem of not rushing creativity, however, and advertisers often have to learn to accept the pace of production. For example, a well-known director made a Honda commercial in South Florida, where he shot film for only one hour per day—a half-hour in the morning and a half-hour at twilight. His explanation? "From experience you learn that cars look flat and unattractive in direct light, so you have to

EXHIBIT 13.14

Instructions commonly appearing in television commercial scripts.

Script Specification	Meaning
CU	Close-up.
ECU	Extreme close-up.
MS	Medium shot.
LS	Long shot.
Zoom	Movement in or out on subject with camera fixed.
Dolly	Movement in or out on subject moving the camera (generally slower than a zoom).
Pan	Camera scanning right or left from stationary position.
Truck	Camera *moving* right or left, creating a different visual angle.
Tilt	Camera panning vertically.
Cut	Abrupt movement from one scene to another.
Dissolve	Smoother transition from one scene to another, compared to a cut.
Wipe	Horizontal or vertical removal of one image to replace it with a new image (inserted vertically or horizontally).
Split screen	Two or more independent video sources occupying the screen.
Skip frame	Replacement of one image with another through pulsating (frame insertion of) the second image into the first. Used for dramatic transitions.
Key insert, matte, chromakey	Insertion of one image onto another background. Often used to impose product over the scene taking place in the commercial.
Super title	Lettering superimposed over visual. Often used to emphasize a major selling point or to display disclaimers/product warnings.
SFX	Sound effects.
VO	Introducing a voice over the visual.
ANN	Announcer entering the commercial.
Music under	Music playing in the background.
Music down and out	Music fading out of commercial.
Music up and out	Music volume ascending and abruptly ending.

catch the shot when the angle [of the sun] is just right."[4] Despite the fact that the cameras were rolling only an hour a day, the $9,000-per-hour cost for the production crew was charged all day for each day of shooting. Advertisers have to accept, on occasion, that the television advertising production process is not like an assembly line production process. However, sweating the details to achieve just the right look can provoke controversy as well, as the production episodes discussed in the Ethical Issues box on page 358 demonstrate.

The Cost of Television Production. Coordinating and taking advantage of the skills offered by creative talent is a big challenge for advertisers. Another major challenge, as the Rolaids production clearly demonstrated, is the tremendous expense. The average 30-second television commercial prepared by a national advertiser can run up production charges from $100,000 to $500,000 and even more if special effects or celebrities are used in the spot.[5] The cost of making a television commercial increased nearly 400 percent

4.   Jeffrey A. Trachtenberg, "Where the Money Goes," *Forbes,* September 21, 1987, 180.
5.   Joe Mandese, "Study Shows Cost of TV Spots," *Advertising Age,* August 1, 1994, 32.

between 1979 and 1993.[6] Part of that increase is attributed to the escalating cost of creative talent, like directors and editors. Other aspects of the cost have to do with more and better equipment being used at all stages of the production process, and longer shooting schedules to ensure advertiser satisfaction.

ETHICAL ISSUES

DÉJÀ VU ALL OVER AGAIN?

In 1990, consumers marveled at how the Big Foot monster truck could mutilate an entire row of cars with its giant tires—an entire row except for the Volvo, that is. Well, the marveling turned into dismay and disbelief when Volvo's advertising agency was forced to admit that the roof of the Volvo used in the ad had been reinforced with steel and plywood while the other cars in the row had had their roof supports weakened. Volvo, long known for promoting the safety and durability of its automobiles, was humiliated—and fined. The deception, which Volvo blamed on its ad agency, cost the firm $150,000.

Fast-forward to 1995 and the controversy surrounding an ad for Czech automaker Skoda. The Skoda is an odd-looking little car with a reputation for being unreliable and poorly built. To overcome this image, Grey Advertising devised an ad that would demonstrate the car's sturdiness. In the ad, a Skoda Felicia is lifted by a crane and suspended by ropes tied to the car's open doors. When a Czech television crew tried to duplicate the demonstration, though, its car ended up with severe structural damage and doors that wouldn't shut. Was this the work of the ghost of Volvo past?

To vindicate itself, Grey responded by staging a public demonstration in front of hundreds of spectators and dozens of reporters in the center of Prague's Old Town Square. Using a crane imported from Germany, the agency suspended a car in the air for several minutes. Once lowered to the ground, the doors shut easily, and there appeared to be no damage. The real proof came, though, when Grey pulled a Felicia off the street and again successfully suspended it without damage. The car's owner? The Czech television crew.

Sources: Steven W. Coldford and Raymond Serafin, "Scali Pays for Volvo Ad: FTC," *Advertising Age*, August 26, 1991, 4; and Normandy Madden, "Demo Gives Lift to Skoda," *Advertising Age*, October 2, 1995, 17.

Exhibit 13.15 shows the average production costs in 1993 for national 30-second television ads of various types and in various industries. Notice that the average expense for a 30-second spot tends to be higher for commercials in highly competitive consumer markets, such as beer, soft drinks, autos, and banking, where image campaigns (which require high-quality production) are commonly used. Conversely, average production costs tend to be lower for advertisements in which functional features or shots of the product often dominate the spot, as with household cleansers and office equipment.

The high and rising cost of television production has created some tensions between advertisers and their ad agencies. Most agencies and production companies respond by saying that advertisers are demanding to stand out from the clutter, and to do so requires complex concepts and high-priced talent.[7] Conversely, as described in the Contemporary Issues box on page 361, when an advertiser is not image conscious, ways can be found to stand out without spending huge dollar amounts.

The important issue in the preparation of all television advertising, regardless of cost, is that the production process has direct and significant effects on the communication impact of a finished advertisement. A well-conceived copy strategy can fall flat if the execution at the point of production is poor. As one advertiser put it, "We don't want to be penny wise and pound foolish. If we're spending $10 million to buy TV time, we shouldn't threaten creative integrity just to cut production cost to $140,000 from $150,000."[8]

6.   Information for the average cost of a 30-second ad in 1979 was taken from Ronald Alsop, "Advertisers Bristle As Charges Balloon for Splashy TV Spots," *Wall Street Journal,* June 20, 1985, 29. Information for the average cost of a 30-second ad in 1993 was taken from Peter Caranicas, "4A's Survey Shows Double-Digit Hike in Spot Production Costs," *Shoot,* July 15, 1994, 1, 40–42.

7.   Caranicas, 42.

8.   Alsop.

EXHIBIT 13.15

Average production costs for national 30-second television spots.

Product Category	Average Cost for 30-Second Spot
Banking/financial/insurance	$535,000
Beer/wine	516,000
Corporate image	397,000
Soft drinks/snacks	332,000
Autos/trucks/motorcycles	323,000
Apparel/clothing	289,000
Beauty/fashion/cosmetics	257,000
Furniture/appliances	226,000
Consumer services/national retail stores	189,000
Drugs/toiletries	157,000
Gifts/toys/hobbies/recreation	154,000
Household products	145,000
Office equipment/computers	97,000
Type of Commercial	
Special effects	$254,000
Interview/testimonial (avg. person and celebrity)	249,000
Multistory/vignettes	246,000
Animation	210,000
Large-scale product performance (e.g., auto)	208,000
Song/dance	187,000
Monologue	172,000
Tabletop/food	111,000
Specific Length	
15 seconds	$100,000
30 seconds	257,000
45 seconds	271,000
60 seconds	589,000

Source: Data from American Association of Advertising Agencies (4As) survey of 1,864 national spots produced in 1993, cited in Peter Caranicas, "4A's Survey Shows Double-Digit Hike in Spot Production Costs," *Shoot*, July 15, 1994, 40.

Postproduction

Once filming is completed, several postproduction activities are required before the commercial is ready for airing. At this point, a host of additional professional talent enters the process. Film editors, audio technicians, voice-over specialists, and musicians may be contracted. Exhibit 13.16 shows the sequence of events in the postproduction phase.

The first step in postproduction is review of the **dailies**—scenes shot during the previous day's production. Such screening may result in reshooting certain segments of the ad. Once dailies are acceptable to the agency, the editing process begins. **Editing** involves piecing together various scenes or shots of scenes, called takes, to bring about the desired visual effect. Most editing involves making decisions about takes shot at different angles, or subtle differences in the performance of the talent. If music is to be

長

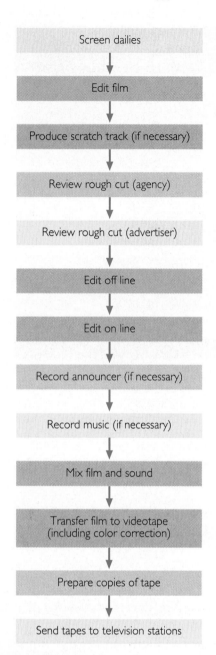

EXHIBIT 13.16

Sequence of events in television commercial postproduction.

included, it will be prepared at this point using a **scratch track,** which is a rough approximation of the musical score using only a piano and vocalists.

A rough cut of the commercial is then prepared by loading the video dailies into an AVID computer to digitize and time code the tape. The **rough cut** is an assembly of the best scenes from the shoot edited together using the quick and precise access afforded by digital technology. Using the offline AVID computer on the digitized rough cut, various technical aspects of the look of a commercial can be refined—color alterations and background images, for example. The final editing of the advertisement—which includes repositioning of elements, correcting final color, and adding fades, titles, blowups, dissolves, final audio, and special effects is done with online equipment in online rooms equipped for final editing. **Online editing** involves transferring the finalized rough cut onto one-inch videotape, which is on-air quality suitable for media transmission.

The personnel and equipment required for postproduction tasks are costly. Film editors charge about $150 to $200 per hour, and an editing assistant is about $50 per hour. An offline computer costs about $100 per hour. When online editing begins, the cost goes up with online rooms running about $700 per hour. The reason for the dramatic difference in cost between offline editing and online editing is that offline edits are done on a single machine to produce a rough, working version of an ad. The online room typically includes many specialized machines for all the final effects desired in the ad. Additionally, a mixing room for voice and music costs about $400 per day.

In all, it is easy to see why filmed television commercials are so costly. Scores of people with specialized skills and a large number of separate tasks are included in the process. The procedures also reflect the complexity of the process. Aside from the mechanics of production, a constant vigil must be kept over the creative concept of the advertisement. Despite the complexities, the advertising industry continues to turn out high-quality television commercials on a timely basis.

Television Production Options

❸ There are several production options available to an advertiser in preparing a television commercial. Eighty percent of all television commercials prepared by national advertisers use film as the medium for production. The previous discussion of production procedures, in fact, described the production process for a filmed advertisement. **Film** (typically 35 mm) is the most versatile medium and produces the highest quality visual impression. It is, however, the most expensive medium for production and is also the most time-consuming.

A less-expensive option is **videotape.** Videotape is not as popular among directors or advertisers for a variety of reasons. Tape has far fewer lines of resolution, and some say videotape results in a flatter image than film. Its visual impressions are more stark, have less depth, and less color intensity. While this can sometimes add to the realism of a commercial, it can also detract from the appearance of the product and the people in the ad. The obvious advantages of videotape—its lower costs, no need to process before viewing, and its flexibility—make it very appealing. New digital video formats may challenge film, however. These advantages have prompted production houses (especially television-station-based production facilities) to use videotape as the medium of choice in filming infomercials.[9] Infomercials can actually benefit from the starkness and realism of the videotape format.

There is always the choice of live television commercial production. **Live production** can result in realism and the capturing of spontaneous reactions and events that couldn't possibly be re-created in a rehearsed scene. It is clear, however, that the loss of control in live settings threatens the carefully worked out objectives for a commercial. On occasion, local retailers (such as auto dealers) use live commercials to execute direct response message strategies. Such a technique can capture the urgency of an appeal.

Two techniques that do not neatly fit the production process described earlier are animation and stills. **Animation** (and the variation known as claymation) is the use of drawn figures and scenes (like cartoons) to produce a commercial. Keebler cookie and the California Raisin commercials use characters created by animators and claymakers. Animated characters, like Tony the Tiger, are frequently incorporated into filmed commercials for added emphasis. A newer form of animation uses computer-generated images. Several firms, such as TRW, have developed commercials totally through the use of computers. The graphics capabilities of giant-capacity computers make futuristic, eye-catching animation ads an easy alternative.

Still production is a technique whereby a series of photographs or slides is filmed and edited so that the resulting ad appears to have movement and action. Through the use of pans, zooms, and dissolves with the camera, still photographs can be used to produce an interesting yet low-cost finished advertisement.

The production option chosen should always be justified on both a creative and a cost basis. The dominance of filmed commercials is explainable by the level of quality of the finished ad and the versatility afforded by the technique. A local retailer or social service organization may not need or may not be able to afford the quality of film. In cases where quality is less significant or costs are primary, other production techniques are available.

CONTEMPORARY ISSUES

IT DOESN'T ALWAYS HAVE TO BE EXPENSIVE

Big advertisers like Nike, IBM, and Coca-Cola are accustomed to spending big money on television production. Campaigns like Nike's "Just Do It" and IBM's "Solutions for a Small Planet" don't come cheap. Production tabs of $500,000, $1 million, or even $2 million can be racked up for a multispot campaign.

Not every advertiser has that kind of money to spend. Giant Carpet, a New York City–area carpet retailer, doesn't have a multimillion-dollar production budget, so it needed an agency to produce TV spots on a shoestring. Enter the agency of Dweck & Campbell, a small New York shop with some good clients, like Pepsi and Swatch, but with total billings less than $20 million. Michael Dweck and his partner Lori Campbell believe that when a client doesn't have a big production budget, then getting consumers to talk about the agency's clients is an important step in building brand identity. If this means producing spots that are a little outlandish, well, so be it.

Giant Carpet and Dweck & Campbell were made for each other. The first spot the agency produced for Giant Carpet was a Fourth of July sales ad that featured alternating red, white, and blue TV screens with goofy music and a funny voice-over. As Dweck describes it, "It cost us like 18 cents to produce and we did it in 4 hours, but everybody was yapping about it." The Fourth of July spot was followed by a New Year's sale ad that featured a shot of the White House, noisemaker sound effects, and a George Bush look-alike trashing the White House carpets. The voice-over offered the challenge, "Let's see Hillary clean that up." It was another good spot for a fraction of what the big advertisers spend.

Source: Anthony Vagnoni, "Dweck Humors Clients with Unique Attitude," *Advertising Age*, July 17, 1995, 30–31.

9.   Kevin Goldman, "CBS to Push Videotaping of Infomercials," *Wall Street Journal,* November 15, 1994, B6.

The Radio Production Process

❹ The other major broadcast option for advertisers is radio. Radio is referred to as the theater of the mind, which alludes to the power of radio advertising in creating vivid and powerful images in the mind of the receiver. Radio commercial production highlights the role of the copywriter. There is no art director involved in the process to specify visual components. Further, the writer is relatively free to plan nearly any radio production he or she chooses because of the significantly reduced costs of radio execution compared to television. In radio, there are far fewer expert participants than in television. Camera operators and lighting technicians are not required. This more streamlined form of production does not mean, however, that the process is more casual. Successful fulfillment of the objectives of an advertisement still requires the careful planning and execution of the production process.

Exhibit 13.17 lists the stages and timetable of a fairly complex radio production: a fully produced commercial. Again, this is a realistic and reasonable timetable once script and budget approval have been secured. The production process for radio is quite similar to the production process for television. Once the copy strategy and methods for the commercial are approved, the process begins with soliciting bids from production houses. Once again, the producer reviews bids and submits the best bid for advertiser approval. When the best bid (again, not always the lowest-priced bid) is identified, the agency submits an estimate to the advertiser for approval. The bid estimate includes both the production house bid and the agency's estimates of its own costs associated with production. When the agency and the advertiser are in agreement, then the producer can award the job to a production house.

After awarding the job to a production house, the next step is to cast the ad. A radio ad may simply have an announcer, in which case the casting job is relatively simple. If the dialogue technique is used, two or more actors and actresses may be needed. Additionally, musical scores often accompany radio ads, and either the music has to be recorded, which includes a search for musicians and possibly singers, or prerecorded music has to be obtained for use by permission. Securing permission for existing music, especially if it is currently popular, can be costly. Much music is considered in the public domain, that is, it is no longer rigidly protected by copyright laws and is available for far less cost. Closely following the casting is the planning of special elements for the ad, which can include sound effects or special effects, like time compression or stretching, to create distinct sounds.

EXHIBIT 13.17

Stages in radio commercial production, and a timetable.

Activity	Time
Solicits bids from production houses/other suppliers	1 week
Review bids, award job, submit production estimate to advertiser	1 week
Select a cast (announcer, singers, musicians)	1 week
Plan special elements (e.g., sound effects); make final preparations; produce tape	1 week
Edit tape	Less than 1 week
Review production (advertiser)	1 week
Mix sound	Less than 1 week
Duplicate tape; ship to stations	1 week
Total	6 to 7 weeks

Final preparation and production entails scheduling a sound studio and arranging for the actors and actresses to record their pieces in the ad. If an announcer is used in addition to acting talent, the announcer may or may not record with the full cast; her or his lines can be incorporated into the tape at some later time. Music is generally recorded separately and simply added to the commercial during the sound-mixing stage.

It is during the actual production of the ad that the copywriter's efforts become a reality. As in television production, the copywriter will have drawn on the copy platform plans approved in the message development stage to write copy for the radio spot. The script used in the production of a radio advertisement serves the same purpose that the storyboard does in television production. Exhibit 13.18 is a typical radio script.

Note that the copywriter must indicate the use of sound effects (SFX) on a separate line to specify the timing of these devices. Further, each player in the advertisement is listed by role, including the announcer (ANNCR), who may or may not be needed, depending on the commercial.

One important element of writing radio copy not yet discussed is the number of words of copy to use given the length of the radio ad. As a general rule, word count relative to airtime is as follows:

10 seconds	20 to 25 words
20 seconds	40 to 45 words
30 seconds	60 to 65 words
60 seconds	120 to 125 words
90 seconds	185 to 190 words [10]

The inclusion of musical introductions, special effects, or local tag lines (specific information for local markets) reduces the amount of copy in the advertisement. Special sound effects interspersed with copy also shorten copy length. The general rules for number of words relative to ad time change depending on the form and structure of the commercial.

EXHIBIT 13.18

A radio script, like this one, serves the same purpose as a storyboard in a television commercial—it allows the producer and director to plan the production and specify the talent and staff needed to produce the ad.

CLIENT: *King's Daughters' Medical Center*
PROJECT: *Family Care Radio (REV 3)*
JOB #: *4600–195*
DATE: *November 9, 1995*
JYG

Doctors :60 Radio

(MUSIC UP AND THROUGHOUT)

ANNCR: No wonder people hate to change doctors.

Your doctor has seen you at your absolute worst—when your eyes are all watery, your skin has turned that kind of sick, greenish color and your breath's so bad, you don't want to be in the same room with yourself. Worse yet, your doctor has seen you in one of those gown things that just doesn't cover you up as well as you'd like.

When you have a physician who knows you that well, the last thing you want is the new one who doesn't know you at all.

Well, King's Daughters' had that in mind when we opened our Family Care Centers in Grayson, Catlettsburg and South Shore. The doctor you see at your Family Care Center is also on staff at our medical center.

So, if you or anyone in your family ever needs hospital care, the same doctor who treats them here can treat them there. Not a doctor they don't know.

King's Daughters' wants to provide you more than a convenient, well-equipped facility. We want to make sure you have someone you can feel comfortable feeling bad around.

The Family Care Centers of King's Daughters' Medical Center. The right care. Right here.

10. Sandra E. Moriarty, *Creative Advertising: Theory and Practice,* 2nd ed. (Englewood Cliffs, N.J.: Prentice-Hall, 1991), 293.

After production, the tape goes through editing to create the best version of the production. Then, after advertiser approval, a sound mix is completed in which all music, special sound effects, and announcer copy are mixed together. The mixing process achieves proper timing between all audio elements in the ad and ensures that all sounds are at the desired levels. After mixing, the tape is duplicated and sent to radio stations for airing.

There are some significant differences between radio and television broadcast production. Most notably, radio production time is appreciably shorter than television production time. Overall, it is possible to produce the average radio ad in about half the time it takes for the average television ad. As already discussed, the number of participants in radio production, both agency personnel and external facilitators, is greatly reduced. Finally, the cost of radio production is radically less than television production. Expenses for a radio ad should be in the $30,000 to $50,000 range, although big-name talent can push that cost way up.

Elements of Effective Radio Production

The just-outlined production procedure for radio describes a radio commercial that is fully produced and sent to a station on tape and ready to air. There are, however, several options for radio production. Additionally, it should be recognized that various aspects of radio production can heighten the creative and strategic impact of an ad. Moreover, radio broadcasts on the World Wide Web may one day furnish dramatic new formats for the radio ad, as discussed in the New Media box on this page.

NEW MEDIA

RADIO GOES OFF AIR, ONLINE

Music, news, conversation—the silence of the Internet is being filled by a handful of online radio networks that are delivering live audio "webcasts." These new webcasts are not being offered by traditional radio stations and networks, though. Startups like AudioNet and Pseudo Online Network are providing the online audio to computer-bound listeners.

So far, even with the best equipment available, the fidelity is no better than on AM radio. But the providers believe what they have to offer will draw users and advertisers to their site. Mark Cuban, the president of AudioNet (www.audionet.com), believes that his Web site can truly become a "Net-work." His company, AudioNet, and Pseudo Online Network are taking different approaches to programming. AudioNet has offered live webcasts of the NCAA Final Four games and has provided feeds from the Super Bowl and National Hockey League. It has also provided simulcasts online of 25 traditional radio stations nationwide. By contrast, Pseudo Online Network (www.pseudo.com) is focusing on original content with Web-only daily and weekly programs. The programs, like CD-Mom Family Hour and African-American Stories Online, are targeted to very specific segments. The president of Pseudo verifies that Pseudo Online programming is different by stating, "We're not just repurposing radio."

The success of online radio remains to be seen. Marketers and broadcasters are waiting to see how these early attempts fare. The director of marketing for CBS verifies that "everybody is still evaluating the value of webcasting." As for listeners, the lack of portability is a big problem. Additionally, this new medium will have to achieve some comparative advantage, perhaps through interactivity, over a radio sitting on the tabletop *next* to a computer, if it is to flourish.

Source: Michael Wilke, "Online Radio Startups Music to Net User's Ears," *Advertising Age*, March 26, 1996, 40.

Radio Production Options. The most loosely structured production option essentially requires no production at all. It is called a fact sheet. A **fact sheet radio ad** is merely a listing of important selling points that a radio announcer can use to ad-lib a radio spot. This method works best with radio personalities who draw an audience because of their lively, entertaining monologues. The fact sheet provides a loose structure so the announcer can work in the ad during these informal monologues. The risk, of course, is that the ad will get lost in the chatter and the selling points will not be convincingly delivered. On the positive side, radio personalities many times go beyond the scheduled 30 or 60 seconds allotted for the ad.

Another loosely structured technique is the live script. The **live script radio ad** involves having an on-air radio personality, like a DJ or talk-show host, read the detailed script of an advertisement. Normally there are no sound effects, since such effects would require special production. The live script ensures that all the selling points are included when the commercial is delivered by the announcer. These scripts are not rehearsed, however, and the emphasis, tone, and tempo in the delivery may not be ideal. The advantage of a live script is that it allows an advertiser to submit a relatively structured commercial for airing in a very short period of time. Most stations can work in a live script commercial in a matter of hours after it is received. Exhibit 13.19 shows that a live script is, indeed, read right over the air.

The most controllable and expensive form of radio production is the fully produced commercial. The radio production process discussed earlier highlighted this method. A **fully produced radio ad** involves producing, directing, and recording a radio ad for taped transmission. Most advertisers go to the expense of fully producing a radio ad because this technique allows for the use of all possible creative devices, such as sound effects and music, as well as the assurance that the ad will air precisely as the advertiser wants.

The final technique is the combination produced-taped advertisement. With a **combination produced-taped radio ad,** the advertiser sends the radio station a tape that usually includes background music or special sound effects and a script that is to be read by the announcer. This technique allows an advertiser to take advantage of some of the more elaborate creative devices of radio production while keeping the commercial timely with a recently prepared script.

The choice of radio production method depends on the advertiser's desire for control over the quality of execution balanced against the costs of production. Using a fully produced radio advertisement increases the probability that creative execution and persuasive impact will be achieved. The pursuit of these objectives, though, increases both the cost and time commitment associated with preparing the ad.

EXHIBIT 13.19

A live script radio ad has an on-air personality read a detailed script over the air. Normally, there are no sound effects or music to accompany the ad—just the announcer's voice.

Radio Production Guidelines. Vigilance over several aspects of radio production can help ensure that a spot accomplishes all that the copy strategy intended. Factors ranging from creative strategy through copywriting and technical execution can affect the quality and impact of a radio commercial. Several of the essentials of good radio production are discussed here:

- *Alert production personnel to the time, place, and audience strategies associated with the commercial.* The type of commercial appropriate for morning scheduling on an all-news station is unlikely to be appropriate for mid-afternoon scheduling on an album rock station. Tailoring the message is a matter of creative concept, media strategy, *and* production. It is at the production stage where these factors come together. Minor changes in copy emphasis, the inclusion of local tag lines, and the choice of special sound effects can radically change the tone of an ad and, ultimately, its potential. These sorts of decisions may be made at the production level. Any and all efforts to alert production personnel to the strategic planning intentions for the commercial will ensure consistency.

- *Fully produce the commercial whenever possible.* Options other than full production of a radio ad drastically reduce the creative options available to an advertiser and signal significant loss of control over execution. Whenever it is feasible, a radio commercial should be fully produced, taped, and then sent to stations.

- *Use humor—with caution.* Humor is a popular copy tactic for radio. Many copywriters see the radio script as lifeless drone of selling points and are irresistibly drawn to humor as a way of injecting excitement into the commercial. The essence of humor is timing and tone. Radio production formats like the fact sheet and live script should avoid the use of humor; it simply is too delicate a tactic to effectively execute without rehearsal. Few radio ads can ever equal the brilliance of the Motel 6 ads by Tom Bodette or the outrageous humor of voice-over actor Stan Freberg.[11] Unless an advertiser can enlist comedic talent of this stature, humor is a risky technique.

- *Strive to make a single point.* As with all forms of advertising, a radio commercial must be restricted to a single, relevant point. Trying to crowd too much into a radio ad will be aggravating to the receiver.

- *Identify the sound effects.* Unless the advertiser makes clear what the sounds are in a radio ad, the audience will be confused and distracted. Unidentified sound effects can change the meaning of an ad. The sound of rain falling in a forest, for example, sounds exactly like bacon frying.

- *Use music to contribute to image.* The proper music mixed into an ad in the proper way can contribute to the image and mood.[12]

---

11.   Christy Fisher and Ira Teinowitz, "Budget Motels Take to Humor Ads," *Advertising Age,* November 14, 1988, 65.
12.   The last three points in this section were adapted from Jewler, 195–96.

SUMMARY

❶ Identify the various players who must function as a team to produce television ads.

The complexity of ad production for television is unrivaled and thus demands the inputs of a variety of functional specialists. From the ad agency come familiar players like the art director, copywriter, and account executive. Then there are a host of individuals who have special skills in various aspects of production for this medium. These include directors, producers, production managers, and camera crews. Editors will also be needed to bring all the raw material together into a finished commercial. Organizational and team management skills are essential to make all these people and pieces work together.

❷ Discuss the specific stages and costs involved in producing television ads.

The intricate process of TV ad production can be broken into three major stages: preproduction, production, and postproduction. In the preproduction stage, scripts and storyboards are prepared, budgets are set, production houses are engaged, and a timetable is formulated. Production includes all those activities involved in the actual filming of the ad. The shoot is a high-stress activity that usually carries a high price tag. The raw materials from the shoot are mixed and refined in the postproduction stage. Today's editors work almost exclusively with computers to create the final product—a finished television ad. If all this sounds expensive, it is!

❸ Describe the major formatting options for TV ad production.

Film is the preferred option for most TV ads because of the high-quality visual impression it provides. Videotape suffers on the quality issue, and live television is not practical in most cases. Animation is probably the second most popular formatting option. With continuing improvements in computer graphics, computer-generated images may one day become a preferred source of material for TV ad production. Still production can be an economical means to bring a message to television.

❹ Explain the process of radio ad production and describe the formatting options for ads in this medium.

A fully produced radio advertisement has many similarities to a television advertisement when it comes to production. Copywriters are at the heart of the process in the preproduction stage, but then budgets must be set, suppliers selected, and timetables established. Musical selections, special effects, or tag lines from local retailers may be integrated with the copy in the editing stage. While there are parallels with TV, a radio ad can be produced more quickly and at less cost. Other formatting options, like fact sheet or live script radio ads, provide even greater savings in terms of both time and money.

KEY TERMS

preproduction (351)
storyboard (351)
script (351)
production timetable (354)
production stage, or shoot (356)
dailies (359)
editing (359)
scratch track (360)
rough cut (360)
online editing (360)

film (360)
videotape (360)
live production (361)
animation (361)
still production (361)
fact sheet radio ad (364)
live script radio ad (364)
fully produced radio ad (365)
combination produced-taped radio ad (365)

QUESTIONS FOR REVIEW AND CRITICAL THINKING

1.   Explain the role of the production company in the evolution of a television commercial. As part of this explanation, be certain you have identified each of the unique skills and specialties that people in the production company bring to the ad development process.

2.   Compare and contrast the creative guidelines for TV offered in this chapter with those offered for magazine ads in the previous chapter. Based on this analysis, what conclusions would you offer about the keys to effective communication in these two media?

3.   Identify the six steps involved in the preproduction of a television ad and describe the issues that an art director must attend to at each step if his or her goals for the ad are to be achieved.

4.   Without a doubt, a television ad shoot is one of the most exciting and pressure-packed activities that any advertising professional can take part in. List the various factors or issues that contribute to the tension and excitement that surrounds an ad shoot.

5.   Review the formatting options that an art director can choose from when conceiving a television ad. Discuss the advantages of each option and describe the situation for which each is best suited.

6.   What are the important similarities and differences in the production processes of TV versus radio ads? In your analysis, make special note of those factors that have the greatest implications for the time and/or expense of the production process.

7.   Describe the risks associated with using a fact sheet radio ad instead of a fully produced ad. What advantages might an advertiser gain from the fact sheet format besides saving money on production costs? If you need some help thinking about the advantages of fact sheet ads, tune in to a popular AM radio talk show and listen while the host of the show delivers the day's fact sheet ads.

EXPERIENTIAL EXERCISE

Over the past decade the success of MTV has inspired a unique style of television ad. Watch an hour of programming on MTV, and list the ads shown in that hour. How would you describe the MTV-style commercial? How large a role does the video editor play in creating this style of commercial?

USING THE INTERNET

Many television networks have established a presence on the Web. Although the broadcasting of multimedia programming over the Internet is still in its infancy, these networks are using the Internet to offer their viewers more information. Explore the following sites:

MTV: www.mtv.com

Comedy Channel: www.comcentral.com

PBS: www.pbs.org

Discovery Channel: www.discovery.com

TV Food Network: www.foodtv.com

1.   If possible, view a video from MTV's site. Was the amount of time it took to download the video worthwhile? How does viewing the video clip compare with seeing a video on MTV itself?

2.   In what way does each site enhance the viewer's satisfaction? Would the site encourage someone to watch a show more or less? What factors on a site would increase a show's appeal to potential viewers?

3.   In what ways does each site reflect the programming style of each network? Are there ways the site could be improved to strengthen the fit between media?

▲ Delta Air Lines

Preparing the Integrated Marketing Communications Message

Developing an effective message for any of the IMC communications tools presents the same challenge as developing an effective advertising message: Information that is important to current and prospective customers must be turned into words, pictures, symbols, or images that attract and hold attention. The message must be interesting, relevant, and meaningful to a target audience. So, whether the message is presented through a mass media advertisement, direct marketing, sales promotion, public relations, sponsored event, or even a Web site, the challenge remains the same: Make it meaningful and forceful.

But with an IMC perspective, there are two additional issues. First, all the messages in the IMC program must be consistent with one another. What is said in advertising must be complemented by direct marketing, public relations, premiums, sponsored events, and so forth. Similarly, advertising can take advantage of potent communications in other areas. For example, Powerfoods, a marketer of nutrition products, runs print ads that feature photos from the firm's sponsorship of the renowned Women's International Challenge cycling race.[1] This firm's event sponsorship creates excellent visuals for its print advertising.

Second, messages for different IMC applications are best developed separately. Merely transferring the language from a sales promotion to a print ad does not take advantage of the unique opportunities offered by print media. Similarly, public relations press releases will be less credible if they use language that sounds too much like a firm's advertising appeals. Separate message development efforts do not mean, necessarily, that the messages prepared will be different. Different messages could easily violate the first goal, message consistency. But separate message preparation can ensure that each version of a firm's communications is best suited to the communications vehicle and the consumer's information desires.

As we saw in the chapters in this part of the text, developing effective messages requires insight and creativity. We will now consider the two major issues in preparing messages with an IMC perspective—message consistency and separate message development—in detail.

Message Consistency

When marketing communications are truly integrated, consumers begin to encounter messages from the same firm in a variety of different ways: The morning paper will have an ad showing that IBM ThinkPads are featured at the Circuit City outlet; during the evening news, the speed and power of the ThinkPad are compared to the most advanced jet fighter plane; and a brochure from IBM PC Direct (the direct-marketing arm of the firm) arrives at the potential customer's office, showing the full line of IBM ThinkPad options.

Each of these communications addresses a slightly different element of the consumer's information needs, and all contain relevant information. The most difficult task is to make these slightly different messages consistent with one another even though each may be touting different values of the brand or the firm. When a message is consistent across all forms of IMC, this is referred to as one-voice communications. One-voice communications ensures that messages sent to consumers through various IMC options have a consistency of tone and emphasize the same positioning for a brand. Contradictions between media advertising and brochures or direct-marketing efforts and public relations serve to confuse rather than enlighten consumers. Recall from Part 2 that consumers have multiple brand contacts that create their realm of exposure to information about a brand. When communications are developed with an emphasis on consistency and the goal of one-voice communications is achieved, then these brand contacts reinforce each other. This, in turn, achieves one of the fundamental goals of IMC: a synergistic effect for all the communications.

Developing Messages across IMC Options

One-voice communications is an obvious goal of integrated marketing communications, but achieving such consistency is complicated by two factors. First, messages in each area of IMC—media advertising, direct marketing, sales promotion, public relations, event sponsorship, new media—may be prepared by four or five different support agencies. The task of coordinating this message development structure falls squarely on the shoulders of the advertiser. The advertiser (often in conjunction with its general advertising agency) must ensure that everyone—in-house and in the support agencies—knows and understands that there is a one-voice goal with respect to the tone of the message and the positioning effect the message will have on the brand.

Second, different options for IMC have different inherent capabilities as communications tools. This means that the messages prepared for each option should emphasize the strengths of that particular communications option. Specifically, each IMC option excels in the following ways:

- *Advertising messages* are best suited for long-term, brand-image development and competitive positioning for a brand or a corporation as a whole.
- *Sales promotions* like coupons or other value-enhancing devices are designed to create short-term demand stimulation, attract attention, and stimulate trial use.
- *Direct-marketing efforts* like telemarketing and direct mail communications offer the opportunity for developing customized messages that can be sent to narrowly defined target audiences.
- *Public relations* uses the mass media to present newsworthy events of general interest about a firm or its brands. Public relations is also the main damage control device available to a firm should negative publicity appear in the media when unfavorable events occur.
- *Event sponsorship* creates an affinity with consumers. The affinity is based on the consumers' attraction to a sport, cause, or event and the resultant positive attitude toward the firm or brand associated with the sport, cause, or event.
- *New Media* environments should offer the information-intensive messages that consumers expect from the Web or other interactive media.

Given these inherent capabilities, the challenge of preparing messages across all IMC options is to use the option for its intended effect while sticking to the one-voice goal of the overall IMC program. This can be difficult. For example, if the goal of advertising is to develop a perception of quality, then sales promotions to attract new users could easily contradict the advertising message.

While it can be difficult, it is by no means impossible. Accomplishing the goal requires a clear statement of the one-voice communications intention of the marketer. Let's consider the way Delta Air Lines used various methods of communication for the "Cincinnati Instead" campaign to achieve a one-voice communications effect.

Delta Air Lines: Preparing the Message

Recall from Part 2 that Delta and its general agency BBDO South discovered that a major market opportunity existed to feature Delta's new Cincinnati hub (CVG) as a convenient alternative for the high-value frequent business traveler segment. The strengths of CVG combined with the inconveniences and other weaknesses of competitors' midwestern hubs spawned the "Cincinnati Instead" integrated marketing communications campaign.

The strategists at Delta and BBDO South knew from a major-market tracking study and a customer satisfaction study that featuring the convenience of CVG would appeal to the needs of the business traveler. Let's consider Delta's statements of strategic and creative intent, which led to the development of IMC messages:

- *Strategic initiative.* The main strategic intent of the communications program is to build high-value business traveler traffic to and through Cincinnati to support an enhanced schedule.
- *Competitive situation.* Other midwestern connecting hubs (Chicago, Detroit, St. Louis, Minneapolis, Pittsburgh) are larger and more established, but they are becoming dated, and travelers are experiencing hub delays. CVG is an emerging market that Delta dominates. The facility is new and functions smoothly.
- *Creative strategy.* The creative strategy is to position Delta and CVG as superior to competitors' hubs by communicating the benefits of connecting through CVG: fewer hassles, quick connections, less crowded and newer facilities.
- *Creative position.* The creative position is to embody the creative strategy of the communications with the campaign theme "Cincinnati Instead."

These statements of strategic initiative and creative strategy were captured in the main advertisement from the "Cincinnati Instead" campaign, shown in Exhibit IMC 3.1. Notice that everything about this ad communicates the creative intent: The visual communicates how travelers will be harried if they travel through competitors' hubs; the headline delivers the main positioning benefit immediately—fly through Cincinnati because it is convenient and fast; the subheads identify the target business traveler and lend support to the headline (connections to 300 cities).

The copy in the ad is particularly well written and follows through on the headline claims. Notice how the copy is specifically written to be relevant to the targeted audience—the frequent business traveler who needs to connect when flying east to west, or vice versa. The copy highlights that CVG offers the business traveler many values: "faster," "easier," "comfortable," "state-of-the-art," "300 cities," "400 daily departures." The advertisement concludes with the tag line slogan and logo "Cincinnati Instead." All of these copy points and the layout design support the main creative strategy of positioning Cincinnati as an alternative to competitors' midwestern hubs.

The advertisement in Exhibit IMC 3.1 was a building block for the overall integrated marketing communications campaign for "Cincinnati Instead." But advertising was by no means the only communications tool used in the campaign. The promotional tools used in the integrated plan were as follows:

- *Advertising.* The main "Cincinnati Instead" message was run as a print campaign. This ad was placed in national newspapers *(USA Today* and the *Wall Street Journal)* and in national magazines like *Fortune* and *Business Week.* In addition, the ad ran regularly in Delta's own in-flight magazine, *Sky Magazine.*

- *Direct marketing.* There were two separate direct-marketing campaigns. First, notice in the ad in Exhibit IMC 3.1 that the target audience is encouraged to check with a travel agent. Simultaneously, travel agents were targeted with a direct-marketing communication. Travel agents were mailed the promotional piece shown in Exhibit IMC 3.2. This promotion encourages agents to book clients through "Cincinnati Instead" and features a giveaway. The agents can win two first-class tickets to anywhere Delta flies in the United States—connecting, of course, through Cincinnati. The grand prize is a European vacation for two for the travel agent who books the most passengers through CVG in a designated three-month period. The mailer also included information on the new terminal facilities.

  A second direct-marketing promotion targeted consumers and, specifically, business travelers. The mailer featured incentives for travelers to connect through Cincinnati. These incentives included coupons for up to $199 off a connecting flight through CVG, a free day of rent on an Alamo rental car in Cincinnati, a free weekend night at a Radisson Hotel, and a 5,000-mile bonus to the traveler's SkyMiles account for connecting through Cincinnati. The materials in this direct-marketing piece are shown in Exhibit IMC 3.3.

- *Promotional event.* Delta sponsored a remote radio broadcast of popular morning disk jockeys from 18 cities across the United States. The radio show was broadcast live from the Cincinnati terminal for two days. The DJs interviewed travelers and asked for their opinion on the ease and convenience of connecting through Cincinnati.

- *Public relations.* Local newspapers in Cincinnati and northern Kentucky ran several articles on the new terminal. The features of the facility and its economic impact were highlighted.

- *Support media.* Premium items were prepared as supportive communications. These included banners, buttons, stickers, and pamphlets to help create awareness of the CVG hub.

In evaluating this campaign for consistency, several features of the creative execution are notable. In each of the communications components just listed, Delta ensured that the "ease and convenience" message was consistent and prominent—right down to the DJs doing live interviews. The look and feel of all the materials maintained a particular tone and emphasis. The "Cincinnati Instead" slogan and logo were prominent on all materials. Finally, the colors and hues were carefully coordinated to provide a similar look.

Overall, Delta accomplished a truly integrated communications campaign. Each of the messages maintained a consistency not only related to the strategic initiative—building traffic through CVG—but also with respect to business travelers' main values. This IMC campaign was synergistic in that each brand contact created in the campaign offered the same information.

The way in which the "Cincinnati Instead" campaign was delivered to target audiences is the topic of Part 4. In that section, we will examine the media schedule and timing of the program, and we will look at Delta's measures of success.

This advertisement formed the foundation for Delta's "Cincinnati Instead" integrated marketing communications campaign. The visual and copy contained in this ad effectvely communicate the main message of the campaign: Traveling on Delta and connecting through Cincinnati is faster and more convenient than traveling through competitors' midwestern hubs.

Why Crawl Through Some Airports When You Can Fly Through Cincinnati?

A quicker way to the world of business. Delta's Cincinnati terminal.

If business travel has you spending more time on the ground than in the air, on your next trip, fly through Cincinnati instead.

Delta's incomparable terminal at the Cincinnati/ Northern Kentucky International Airport is specifically designed to make getting where you're going faster and easier.

Or, if you have a few minutes between flights, Crown Room lounges and our comfortable International First/Business Class lounge let you get down to business.

Crossroads to over 300 cities.

But what good is a state-of-the-art airport without service to the cities you need?

Together with the Delta Connection, Delta gives you more than 400 daily departures from Cincinnati – including 16 new flights* – to major business centers throughout the United States, Canada, Mexico, Europe and Asia.

Fly through Cincinnati and see for yourself. For information or reservations, see **CINCINNATI INSTEAD** your Travel Agent. Or call Delta at 1-800-221-1212. And say you want Cincinnati instead.

▲ Delta Air Lines
You'll love the way we fly

*Includes four new nonstop flights to San Antonio, Austin, Scranton and Ontario, CA. *Based on cities served by Delta, Delta Connection and Delta's Worldwide Partners™ flights. Delta Connection flights operate with Delta flight numbers 3000-5999 and 7000-7999. ©1995 Delta Air Lines, Inc.

A key component of the "Cincinnati Instead" campaign was an effort to convince travel agents to book their clients on Delta through Cincinnati. The direct mail piece shown here provides information about the Cincinnati hub and offers travel agents an incentive for booking their clients through Cincinnati.

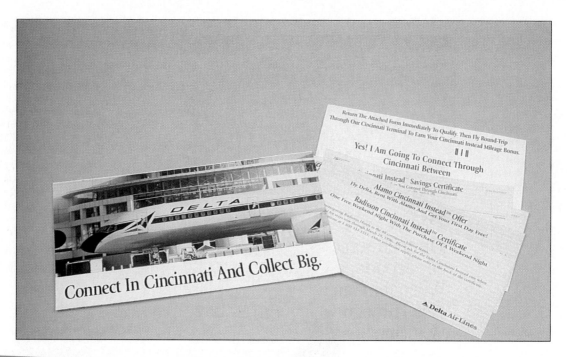

In addition to national advertising, Delta used several other forms of communication to get the "Cincinnati Instead" message to business travelers. The direct mail piece shown here encouraged business travelers to make connections through the Cincinnati hub by offering frequent flyer miles as an incentive.

IMC EXERCISES

1. Examine the print media—local and national newspapers and magazines. Look for a brand that you believe is not preparing its communications in an integrated manner. Why do you believe the different communications are inconsistent with one another? Redo this firm's communications using the original visuals but changing the headlines, subheads, and copy so that one-voice communications is achieved.

2. If it was your job to coordinate the specialty agencies that help an organization prepare advertising, sales promotions, direct marketing, and public relations, how would you manage the process? Draw an organizational chart that shows the relationship between your organization's marketing and advertising departments and four external specialty agencies.

3. Delta has just established a major hub operation in your city and wants to run a "[Your City] Instead" cam-

paign. The goal is the same as for the "Cincinnati Instead" campaign—draw travelers from competitors' hubs in close proximity. Delta has hired you to prepare all the materials to promote this new hub. What communications tools would you emphasize for the "[Your City] Instead" campaign? Write the copy that would feature why your city is the place to make connections. (Note: You can't emphasize convenience; that one's already claimed!)

4. Think of another special event Delta could have prepared for the "Cincinnati Instead" campaign. Think of an event that plays off the main values of the Cincinnati hub: ease and convenience.

ENDNOTE

1. "10 Steps to Evaluating an Event," *Promo,* November 1995, 61.

Part 4 | Placing the Message: Media and Supportive Communications

Once again we pass into a new and totally different area of advertising, "Placing the Message: Media and Supportive Communications." We are now at the point where reaching the target audience is the key issue. The challenge of message preparation gives way to that of message placement. Beyond the formidable challenge of effectively choosing media to reach the target audience, contemporary advertisers are demanding even more from the placement decision: synergy and integration. Throughout the first three parts of the text, the issue of integrated marketing communications was raised whenever the opportunity existed to create coordinated communications. Indeed, the Delta Air Lines sections at the end of each part are included to highlight the IMC issue. But nowhere is IMC more critical than at the media placement and supportive communications stage. Here, audiences may be exposed to the advertiser's messages through a wide range of different media. Each medium has a unique quality and tone for communications. The advertiser is challenged to ensure that if diverse communications options are chosen for placing the message, there is still a one-voice quality to the over-all communication program.

Maintaining integration is indeed a challenge in the contemporary media environment. Chapter 14, "Media Planning, Objectives, and Strategy," begins with an overview of major media options. The media-planning process is explored next, including a discussion of media objectives, strategies, choices, and scheduling issues. Next, the complexity of the current media environment is discussed. Finally, media choice is considered in the context of integrated marketing communications.

CHAPTER 14

Media Planning, Objectives, and Strategy

Chapter 15, "Media Evaluation: Print and Broadcast Media," offers an analysis of the major media options available to advertisers. The chapter follows a sequence in which the advantages and disadvantages of each medium are discussed first, then costs, buying procedures, and audience measurement techniques.

Chapter 16, "Media Evaluation: Traditional and Emerging Support Media," reflects the extraordinary range of options available to today's advertiser, from billboards and transit advertising through event sponsorship and the most elaborate online services. Special emphasis is placed here on a discussion of the new interactive media.

The newest and perhaps greatest challenge for advertisers has recently presented itself—the Internet. Chapter 17 describes this new and formidable technology available to advertisers. Basic terminology and procedures are described. A multitude of Web sites are offered for exploration.

Chapter 18, "Sales Promotion," describes the ways that games, contests, sweepstakes, and price incentives attract the attention of customers. The impact of many sales promotion techniques is much easier to measure than the impact of advertising, thus prompting some marketers to shift spending from advertising to promotion, and thus making promotion an important contemporary topic.

Consumers' desire for greater convenience and marketers' never-ending search for competitive advantage has spawned tremendous growth in direct marketing. Chapter 19, "Direct Marketing," considers this area, which is both marketing and promotion. With direct marketing, advertisers communicate to the target audience, but they also seek an immediate response.

Chapter 20, "Public Relations and Corporate Advertising," concludes the discussion of media and supportive communications. Public relations offers opportunities for positive communication but also provides damage control when negative events affect an organization. Corporate advertising can serve a useful role in supporting an advertiser's brand advertising programs.

Chapter 14

Media Planning,

Objectives,

and Strategy

After reading and thinking about this chapter, you will be able to do the following:

1 Describe the major media options available to advertisers.

2 Detail the important components of the media-planning process.

3 Explain the applications of computer modeling in media planning.

4 Discuss five additional challenges that complicate the media-planning process.

Ed Artzt, then the chair and CEO of Procter & Gamble, sent shock waves through the advertising industry in 1994 when he boldly proclaimed that "from where we stand today, we can't be sure that ad-supported TV programming will have a future in a world of video-on-demand, pay-per-view, and subscription TV. These are designed to carry no advertising at all."[1] Artzt followed that blast with another, just weeks before he stepped down as head of P&G in 1995. This time his point was that advertisers need to control the content of new media—like CD-ROMs, interactive television, and online information services—to better control the placement of their advertising. Specifically, he said that "content is king, and for advertisers, content is programming. We have to develop it. We have to share in its ownership, and we have to market it through whatever channels the new technologies deem most effective and most efficient for reaching consumers."[2] Exhibit 14.1 shows one form of the new media—a World Wide Web site—that Artzt is alluding to.

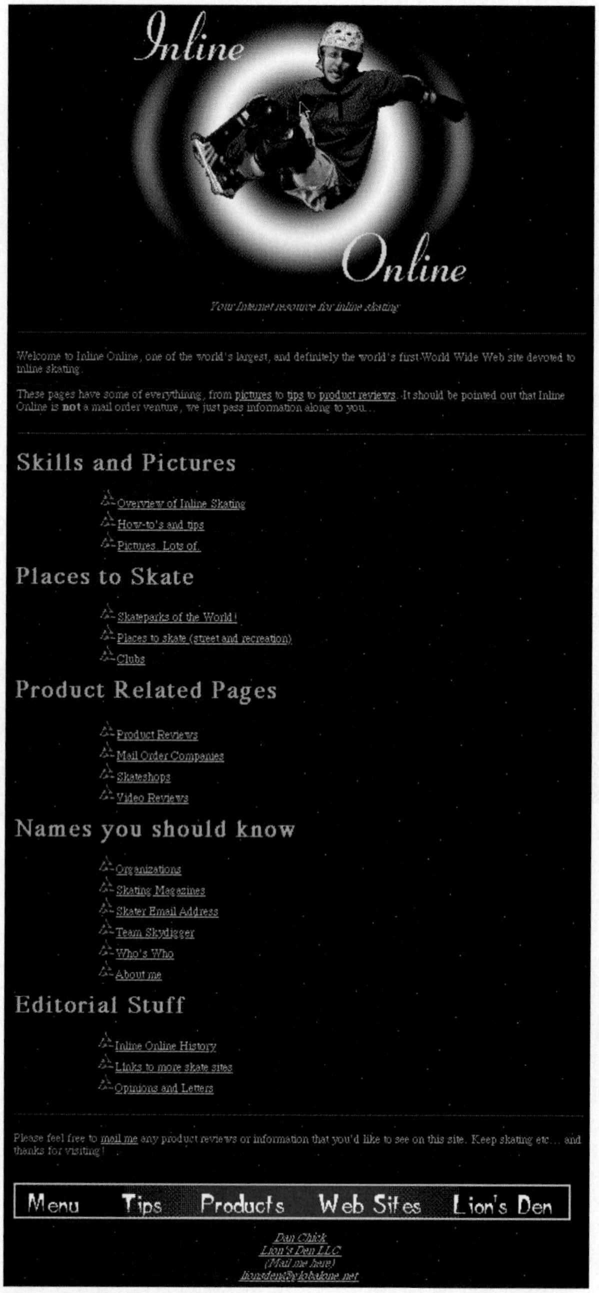

Artzt's vision for the control of media by P&G is far more than speculation and goes beyond just new media. The firm has already set up a budget for programming development as part of a major alliance with the Paramount Television Group. But while big advertisers like P&G respect the power and potential of new media, they also recognize the vast presence of traditional media. Artzt's position on television, for example, is that "broadcast television is still the best way to achieve the reach and frequency advertisers need to build consumers' loyalty to our products and services."[3] Ad-spending projections support this position, as discussed in the New Media box on page 385.

All this control-the-media philosophizing could be dismissed as ranting and raving if it was just one individual, like Artzt, from one company. But other large and influential advertisers are pursuing innovative media alternatives, perhaps more subtly than P&G, but just as actively. Philip Guarascio, vice president and general manager of marketing and advertising for General Motors, has also taken the position that advertisers need to be involved in developing the content of programming for traditional and new media. To further its programming efforts, GM has entered into an agreement with Time Warner to develop proprietary new media applications that will run on new media platforms, from CD-ROM to two-way television. Finally, Disney Company's $19 billion acquisition of the ABC television network gives the entertainment conglomer-

EXHIBIT 14.1

Advertisers are struggling with the choice between investing in traditional media and gaining control of new media options—like the World Wide Web. Some advertisers believe that controlling information in new media is the wave of the future. Notice that this WWW site devoted to inline skating features product information and links to mail-order companies.
bird.taponline.com/inline/

1.   Steve Yahn, "Advertising's Grave New World," *Advertising Age,* May 16, 1994, 1, 53.
2.   Scott Donaton and Pat Sloan, "Control New Media," *Advertising Age,* March 13, 1995, 1.
3.   Ibid., 8.

ate a broad foundation for controlling both traditional media and new media options being developed with ABC.[4] As many have said: "Someday we'll all be working for the mouse."

An Overview of the Major Media

To this point, we have studied advertising as a process that includes the planning and preparation of creative advertising materials. Placing the message is the next step. A well-planned and creatively prepared campaign needs to be placed in media to reach the target audience and stimulate demand for a brand. Have the activities of firms like P&G and General Motors changed the very nature of media placement decisions? The answer, simply, is no, not yet. What these firms see are new opportunities to shape the media environment to their advantage. For now the basic process of choosing channels through which a message can be sent is fundamentally the same: How can an advertisement or campaign be placed in media to reach a target audience effectively and efficiently? Recall that Artzt expressed P&G's desire for media control in almost precisely these words. What has changed is the speed at which media options are evolving; advertisers must sort out the best alternatives for effective and efficient media placement.

Through all the speculation about media one fact remains: No matter how great a marketing plan is and no matter how insightful or visionary advertising strategists are, poor message placement will undermine even the best-laid plans. Advertising placed in media that do not reach the target audience—whether via new media or traditional media—will be much like the proverbial tree that falls in the forest with no one around: Does it make a sound? From an advertising standpoint, it doesn't matter. Advertising placed in media that do not reach target audiences will not achieve the communications or sales impact an advertiser desires.

To gain perspective on media placement, we need to understand the opportunities for communicating with audiences and, as the opening discussion highlighted, the challenges of new media options. From both a global and domestic standpoint, the media industry is large and complex. From the mergers and acquisitions of large U.S. media firms like Disney/ABC, Warner Communications, and TCI, to the global communications possibilities of the Intelsat satellite project (undertaken by Motorola) and the World Wide Web, media options seem to be in a perpetual state of turmoil.

To begin to appreciate the nature of the media placement challenges and opportunities, let's consider the largest media organizations in the world, as shown in Exhibit 14.2. Notice that across the broad classes of newspapers, magazines, and television networks, firms headquartered in the United States are dominant players in the global media arena. From the 3.5 million daily readers of the *Wall Street Journal* around the world to the estimated 163 million viewers of MTV, global reach with highly accessible media is becoming a reality. Notice also that many of these global media organizations have large audiences outside of North America. BBC Worldwide TV based in London has more than 7.2 million viewers throughout Asia, and NBC has 70 million viewers in Europe.

The reach and power of the global print media are reflected in the advertising rates also listed in Exhibit 14.2. Note that a full-page black-and-white ad in the *Wall Street Journal* costs more than $170,000, and a four-color ad in *Reader's Digest* costs over half a million dollars for global distribution.

Another way to gain a perspective on the nature of message placement options is to examine the media environment in the United States. Exhibits 14.3 and 14.4 provide interesting information in this regard. In Exhibit 14.3, total media expenditures by media category are listed. Notice that less than half of media expenditures in the United States are made in what are referred to as measured media. The **measured media**—television, radio, newspapers, magazines, and outdoor media—are listed in detail in

4.   Joe Mandese, "Is It Magic Kingdom or an Evil Empire?" *Advertising Age,* August 7, 1995.

EXHIBIT 14.2

Global media circulation and advertising rates, 1994–1995.

Media and Location	Total Distribution		
	1995	1994	Change
DAILIES			
The Financial Times, London	294,217	292,248	+0.7%
International Herald Tribune, Neuilly-sur-Seine, France*	n/a	188,711	n/a
Nihon Keizai Shimbun, Tokyo	2,870,268	n/a	n/a
USA Today International, New York[†]	2,098,157	2,106,705	–0.4%
The Wall Street Journal, New York	3,563,811	2,937,059	+21.3%
The Yomiuri Shimbun, Tokyo	10,230,000	10,230,000	0%
WEEKLIES			
Business Week, New York[†]	993,000	987,000	+0.6%
ComputerWorld, Boston[‡]	1.7 million	n/a	n/a
The Economist, London	598,501	568,683	+5.2%
The Guardian Weekly, London	106,577	104,688	+1.8%
L'Express, Paris[§]	n/a	547,837	n/a
Le Point, Paris[§]	n/a	305,388	n/a
Madame Figaro, Paris	990,000	n/a	n/a
Time, New York	5,604,281	5,705,830	–1.8%
MONTHLIES			
Cosmopolitan, New York[‖]	4,700,597	5,755,795	–18.3%
Elle, Levallois Perret, France	4,819,899	4,788,843	+0.9%
Esquire, New York[‖]	683,143	1,207,478	–43.4%
Good Housekeeping, New York[‖]	6,052,577	5,715,865	+5.9%
MacWorld, Boston	860,000	n/a	n/a
Marie Claire, Issy-les–Moulineaux, France[‖]	2,795,633	n/a	n/a
National Geographic, Washington	8,812,000	9,138,000	–3.6%
Network World, Boston[#]	620,000	n/a	n/a
PC World, Boston	2.8 million	n/a	n/a
Reader's Digest, Pleasantville, New York	27,322,000	26,954,000	+1.4%
Redbook, New York[‖]	3,760,824	3,826,869	–1.7%
Scientific American, New York	733,716	755,138	–2.8%
The WorldPaper, Boston	776,000	262,000	+196.2%
OTHER PRINT			
Fortune, New York	878,822	917,921	–4.30%
TV			
CNN International, Atlanta[†]	133.4 million	118 million	+13.1%
Cartoon Network International, Atlanta[†]	58.9 million	34.4 million	+71.2%
CMT: Country Music Television, New York	41.3 million	34.8 million	+18.7%
The Discovery Channel, Bethesda, Md.	90 million	85 million	+5.9%
Dow Jones' ABN and EBN networks, New York	23 million	n/a	n/a
ESPN, New York	166,450,000	137,700,000	+20.9%
MTV: Music Television, New York[†]	163.8 million	134.1 million	+22.1%
NBC, New York**	231.5 million	212.5 million	+8.9%
TNT International, Atlanta[†]	100.6 million	84.5 million	+19.1%
USA Networks and the Sci-Fi Channel, New York[††]	108.9 million	82.9 million	+31.4%

Data unavailable from BBC Worldwide TV, GEMS TV, *Harper's Bazaar*, Middle East Broadcasting Centre, *Runner's World*.
*Latest circulation figures available are 1994.
[†]Europe and Middle East/Africa figures are combined. 1995 *USA Today International* worldwide circulation is an estimate.
[‡]Bi-monthly distribution in selected markets.
[§]North America figures include Latin America. Latest circulation figures available are 1994.
[‖]U.S. ad rates given. Rates vary by country.

North America	Latin America	Europe	Middle East/Africa	Asia/ Pacific	Ad Rates, 1996 (change from '95)
		Total Distribution			
30,786	1,395	250,862	2,905	8,269	B&w, $54,208 (+9.0%); 4C, $67,950 (+8.2%)
n/a	n/a	n/a	n/a	n/a	B&w, $56,758 (+7.5%); 4C, $78,045 (+6.4%)
13,348	886	10,385	739	2,844,910	B&w, $173,337 (+0%); 4C, $200,716 (+0%)
2,028,157	n/a	n/a	n/a	n/a	B&w: $79,350 weekend (+0%), $66,125, weekday (+0%); 4C, $117,760 weekend (+6.0%), $98,095 (+6.0%)
1,763,140	1,418,501	61,161	270,000	51,009	B&w, $170,468.48 (+6.4%); 4C, $208,226.66
20,000	n/a	3,000	n/a	10,000,000	B&w, $439,000 (+0%); 4C, $519,640 (+0%)
870,000	20,000	63,000	n/a	40,000	B&w, $64,200 (+7.7%); 4C, $97,200 (+7.6%)
—	—	—	—	—	
271,372	12,448	235,719	14,897	64,065	B&w, $15,800 (+6.8%); 4C, $49,100 (+7.0%)
26,052	1,660	22,350	33,090	23,425	B&w, $4,605 (+25%); 4C, $6,755 (+9.3%)
n/a	n/a	n/a	n/a	n/a	B&w, $26,800 (+0%); 4C, $41,200 (+0%)
n/a	n/a	n/a	n/a	n/a	4C, $32,200 (+0%)
n/a	n/a	570,000	n/a	420,000	n/a
4,429,993	92,858	556,385	84,174	440,871	B&w, $104,986 (+8.8%); 4C, $157,995 (+10.0%)
2,573,096	448,373	1,703,277	110,000	265,851	B&w, $67,215 (+5.0%); 4C, $90,465 (+5.0%)
963,030	390,292	2,504,648	n/a	961,929	n/a
710,555	n/a	115,412	n/a	88,000	B&w, $33,515 (+5.0%); 4C, $49,815 (+5.0%)
5,127,340	222,726	702,511	n/a	n/a	B&w, $128,250 (+5%); 4C, $60,930 (+5%)
—	—	—	—	—	n/a
600,000	346,740	1,115,213	12,000	721,680	B&w, $16,800 (n/a); 4C, $23,200 (n/a)
7,500,000	95,000	790,000	60,000	367,000	B&w, $156,200 (+6.3%); 4C, $206,180 (+6.3%)
—	—	—	—	—	n/a
—	—	—	—	—	n/a
16,527,200	1,085,000	7,451,000	403,000	1,855,800	B&w, $400,851 (+9.2%); 4C, $513,566 (+9.2%)
3,294,403	n/a	364,228	n/a	102,193	B&w, $69,570 (+5.0%); 4C, $91,990 (+5%)
619,303	9,973	74,841	3,774	25,825	B&w, $28,050 (+4.3%); 4C, $42,000 (+4.2%)
2,000	219,000	n/a	20,000	—	B&w, $39,900 (+2.3%)
752,320	9,165	43,393	14,544	59,400	B&w, $49,300 (+14.3%); 4C, $74,700 (+14.3%)
70 million	3.8 million	55.2 million	n/a	4.4 million	n/a
23.6 million	5.2 million	28 million	n/a	2.1 million	n/a
31.7 million	n/a	9.6 million	n/a	n/a	n/a
67 million	5 million	11 million	n/a	7 million	n/a
n/a	n/a	10 million	n/a	13 million	30-second spots: ABN: $375; EBN: $1,200
76 million	6.5 million	64 million	150,000	19.8 million	n/a
61.6 million	20.5 million	52 million	n/a	29.7 million	n/a
152.2 million	5.3 million	70 million	n/a	4 million	n/a
66 million	4.5 million	28 million	n/a	2.1 million	n/a
94.5 million	4.8 million	4.8 million	n/a	n/a	30-second prime-time spot: $6,500 (+30%)

#Weekly distribution in selected markets.
**Includes CNBC. Europe includes Middle East.
††Total gross buy across both networks.

Source: Advertising Age International, February 12, 1996, 1-10. Reprinted with permission from the February 12, 1996, issue of Advertising Age International. Copyright © Crain Communications Inc. 1996.

Exhibit 14.3. But notice that spending on these measured media, $70 billion, represents only about 43 percent of all U.S. expenditures for 1994–1995. **Unmeasured media,** which include direct mail, catalogs, special events, and other ways to reach business and household consumers, are estimated at nearly twice the measured media total.

The other noteworthy aspect of Exhibit 14.3 is the tremendous increase in expenditures in cable TV. This signals that advertisers are using specific programming to reach specific target audiences with more precision.

EXHIBIT 14.3

Advertising spending by media category in the United States, 1994–1995 ($ in millions).

Media	1995	1994	% change	Media as % of total 1995	1994
Magazines	$10,057.8	$ 8,463.0	12.0	6.3	6.0
Sunday magazines	955.5	999.9	–4.4	.06	.07
Local newspapers	13,338.6	11,774.6	13.6	8.3	7.8
National newspapers	1,136.5	1,092.1	4.1	0.7	0.7
Outdoor	1,114.9	909.8	22.5	0.7	0.6
Network TV	12,402.2	11,893.2	4.3	7.7	7.9
Spot TV	13,017.2	12,718.8	2.3	8.1	8.5
Syndicated TV	2,316.8	2,358.1	–1.8	1.4	1.6
Cable TV networks	3,418.8	2,970.2	15.1	2.1	2.0
Network radio	776.5	599.8	29.5	0.5	0.4
National spot radio	1,352.3	1,272.3	6.3	0.8	0.8
Yellow Pages	10,236.0	9,825.0	4.2	6.4	6.5
Total measured media	70,123.1	55,022.0	7.3	43.6	43.6
Estimated unmeasured media	90,796.8	84,666.0	7.2	56.4	56.4
Grand total	160,920.0	150,030.0	7.3	100.0	100.0

Source: "100 Leading National Advertisers," *Advertising Age,* September 30, 1996, 54. Reprinted with permission from the September 30, 1996, issue of *Advertising Age.* Copyright © Crain Communications Inc. 1996.

EXHIBIT 14.4

Media expenditures in the United States by selected product categories, 1995 ($ in millions).

Product Category	1995 Total Ad Spending	Leading Medium	
Automotive	$10,625.9	Network television	$2,937.1
Retail	8,781.4	Local newspapers	4,465.7
Foods	4,033.1	Network television	1,451.8
Toiletries and cosmetics	2,950.5	Network television	1,234.6
Direct response companies	1,633.0	Consumer magazines	919.4
Sporting goods, toys	1,177.5	Network television	211.7
Beer and wine	806.8	Network television	379.8
Soaps, cleansers, polishes	596.4	Network television	262.4
Household furnishings	340.5	Consumer magazines	169.9
Pets and pet food	273.4	Network television	95.1

Source: "100 Leading National Advertisers," *Advertising Age,* September 30, 1996, 54. Reprinted with permission from the September 30, 1996, issue of *Advertising Age.* Copyright © Crain Communications Inc. 1996.

Exhibit 14.4 reveals a different dimension of the media placement environment in the United States. Marketers in some product categories spend more on media and rely more on certain types of media than others. Notice that this media-spending list is headed by automobile marketers and then retailers, who each invested more than $8.5 billion in measured media in 1995. Not surprisingly, retailers relied most on local newspapers ($4.4 billion), while the auto advertisers spent most heavily for network television ads ($2.9 billion).

Another aspect of media placement revealed in Exhibit 14.4 is that those advertisers with the broadest consumer product lines, like food, cosmetics, and beverages, spend the most money placing their advertisements on network television—the medium with the broadest consumer market coverage. Direct response companies, on the other hand, invest most heavily in consumer magazines, which reach the most well-defined target audiences.

The Media-Planning Process

2 This wealth of media options demands incredible attention to detail in the media-planning process. Some basic terminology is essential to understanding this effort. A **media plan** specifies the media in which advertising messages will be placed to reach the desired target audience. A **media class** is a broad category of media, such as television, radio, or newspapers. A **media vehicle** is a particular option for placement within a media class. For example, *Newsweek* is a media vehicle within the magazine media class.

A media plan includes objectives, strategies, media choices, and a media schedule for placing a message. Exhibit 14.5 shows the specific components of a media plan. Recall from Chapter 8 that the advertising plan, developed during the planning stage of the advertising effort, is the driving force behind a media plan. Market and advertising research determines that certain media options hold the highest potential. Thus, in reality, the media-planning process takes place simultaneously with the overall development of the advertising plan.

Notice in Exhibit 14.5 that media planners set media objectives, identify strategies, make media choices, and finally set a media schedule, including the media-buying process. We will discuss each component of the media-planning process.

NEW MEDIA

SHOULD IT BE WWW OR www?

CEOs of huge companies like Procter & Gamble yearn to control its content, and media barons like John Malone of TCI and Rupert Murdoch of News Corporation ponder with delight the opportunities it presents. The World Wide Web (WWW) is arguably the most important of the new media that corporations and consumers alike are totally fascinated by. If a firm does not have a Web site, it runs the risk of being perceived as out-of-touch and out-of-date.

But just how important is the World Wide Web as a media option for advertisers, and what is its future? Does the WWW represent as attractive an alternative for effectively and efficiently reaching consumers as traditional media? The facts are that online advertising is not making much of a dent in traditional media spending—no matter how much CEOs or media barons ponder its potential. In 1995, $42.9 million was spent on advertising on the WWW, compared to $32 billion in television advertising and $10 billion for magazine advertising. These numbers suggest that there is not a mad rush to the WWW by advertisers, and future projections suggest there will never be a mad rush to the Net. While online spending will grow rapidly through the year 2000 to $5 billion, it will still represent a fraction of television spending, at $51.2 billion, and magazine spending, at $10 billion.

So, while the world seems totally taken with the World Wide Web, it appears that advertisers will continue to rely most heavily on traditional media to reach their target audiences.

Sources: "Malone Looks Ahead to More Deals," *Advertising Age*, January 22, 1996, 1; and "Marketers Link Up to Tune of $54.7 Mil," *Advertising Age*, January 22, 1996, 28.

Media Objectives

Media objectives set specific goals for a media placement: Reach the target audience, determine the geographic scope of placement, and identify the message weight, or the total mass of advertising delivered against a target audience.

The first and most important media objective is that the media

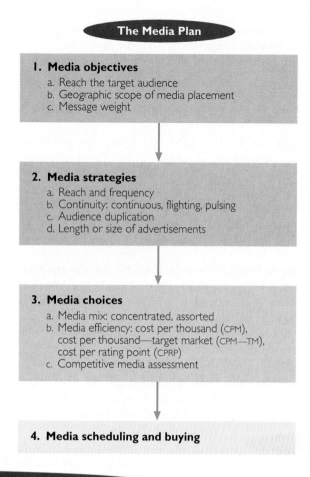

The Media Plan

1. Media objectives
   a. Reach the target audience
   b. Geographic scope of media placement
   c. Message weight

2. Media strategies
   a. Reach and frequency
   b. Continuity: continuous, flighting, pulsing
   c. Audience duplication
   d. Length or size of advertisements

3. Media choices
   a. Media mix: concentrated, assorted
   b. Media efficiency: cost per thousand (CPM),
      cost per thousand—target market (CPM—TM),
      cost per rating point (CPRP)
   c. Competitive media assessment

4. Media scheduling and buying

EXHIBIT 14.5

The media-planning process.

chosen *reach the target audience.* Recall that the definition of a target audience can be demographic, geographic, or based on lifestyle or attitude dimensions. Unfortunately, media planners are often put in the awkward position of trying to target a media effort based on weak secondary data from media organizations.

If advertisers are willing to spend extra money, however, there are media research organizations that provide detailed information on the media habits and purchase behaviors of target audiences; this information can greatly increase the precision with which media choices are made. The two most prominent providers of demographic information correlated with product usage data are Mediamark Research (MRI) and Simmons Market Research Bureau (SMRB). An example of the type of information supplied is shown in Exhibit 14.6, where market statistics for four brands of men's aftershave and cologne are compared: Mennen Skin Bracer, Obsession, Old Spice, and Paco Rabanne. The most-revealing data are contained in columns C and D. Column C shows each brand's strength relative to a demographic variable, like age or income. Column D provides an index indicating that particular segments of the population are heavier users of a particular brand. Specifically, the number expresses each brand's share of volume as a percentage of its share of users. An index number above 100 shows particular strength for a brand. The strength of Paco Rabanne is apparent in both the 18–24 and the 25–34 age cohorts.

Recently, even more sophisticated data have become available. Research services like A. C. Nielsen's *Home★Scan* and Information Resources' *BehaviorScan* are referred to as **single-source tracking services,** which offer information not just on demographics but also on brands, purchase size, purchase frequency, prices paid, and media exposure. BehaviorScan is the most comprehensive, in that exposure to particular television programs, magazines, and newspapers can be measured by the service. With demographic, behavioral, and media-exposure correlates provided by research services like these, advertising and media planners can address issues such as the following:

- How many members of the target audience have tried the advertiser's brand, and how many are brand loyal?
- What appears to affect brand sales more—increased amounts of advertising, or changes in advertising copy?
- What other products do buyers of the advertiser's brand purchase regularly?
- What television programs, magazines, and newspapers reach the largest number of the advertiser's audience?[5]

Another critical element in setting advertising objectives is determining the *geographic scope of media placement.* In some ways, this is a relatively easy objective to set. Media planners merely need to identify media that cover the same geographic area as the advertiser's distribution system. Obviously, spending money on the placement of ads in media that cover geographic areas where the advertiser's brand is not distributed is wasteful.

When factors such as brand performance or competitors' activities are taken into account, media objectives for geographic scope become more complicated. For example,

5.   Donaton and Sloan.

16   AFTERSHAVE LOTION & COLOGNE (MEN)

BASE: MEN	TOTAL U.S. '000	MENNEN SKIN BRACER A '000	B % DOWN	C % ACROSS	D INDEX	OBSESSION A '000	B % DOWN	C % ACROSS	D INDEX	OLD SPICE A '000	B % DOWN	C % ACROSS	D INDEX	PACO RABANNE A '000	B % DOWN	C % ACROSS	D INDEX
ALL MEN	85035	5069	100.0	6.0	100	1831	100.0	2.2	100	13724	100.0	16.1	100	1396	100.0	1.6	100
HOUSEHOLD HEADS	71432	4493	88.6	6.3	106	1559	85.1	2.2	101	11689	85.2	16.4	101	972	69.6	1.4	83
HOMEMAKERS	21060	1073	21.2	5.1	85	640	35.0	3.0	141	3272	23.8	15.5	96	•311	22.3	1.5	90
GRADUATED COLLEGE	17485	940	18.5	5.4	90	408	22.3	2.3	108	2400	17.5	13.7	85	378	27.1	2.2	132
ATTENDED COLLEGE	15427	735	14.5	4.8	80	•316	17.3	2.0	95	2153	15.7	14.0	86	•253	18.1	1.6	100
GRADUATED HIGH SCHOOL	30535	1961	38.7	6.4	108	772	42.2	2.5	117	5237	38.2	17.2	106	585	41.9	1.9	117
DID NOT GRADUATE HIGH SCHOOL	21587	1434	28.3	6.6	111	•335	18.3	1.6	72	3934	28.7	18.2	113	•181	13.0	.8	51
18-24	13250	•470	9.3	3.5	60	•334	18.2	2.5	117	1792	13.1	13.5	84	•423	30.3	3.2	194
25-34	21369	785	15.5	3.7	62	598	32.7	2.8	130	2751	20.0	12.9	80	442	31.7	2.1	126
35-44	16714	796	15.7	4.8	80	606	33.1	3.6	168	2762	20.1	16.5	102	•189	13.5	1.1	69
45-54	11289	830	16.4	7.4	123	•128	7.0	1.1	53	2073	15.1	18.4	114	•164	11.7	1.5	88
55-64	10660	1018	20.1	9.5	160	•94	5.1	.9	41	2359	17.2	22.1	137	•94	6.7	.9	54
65 OR OVER	11753	1170	23.1	10.0	167	•70	3.8	.6	28	1987	14.5	16.9	105	•86	6.2	.7	45
18-34	34618	1256	24.8	3.6	61	933	51.0	2.7	125	4543	33.1	13.1	81	864	61.9	2.5	152
18-49	57034	2605	51.4	4.6	77	1552	84.8	2.7	126	8382	61.1	14.7	91	1163	83.3	2.0	124
25-54	49372	2411	47.6	4.9	82	1333	72.8	2.7	125	7586	55.3	15.4	95	794	56.9	1.6	98
EMPLOYED FULL TIME	59836	2953	58.3	4.9	83	1591	86.9	2.7	123	9303	67.8	15.5	96	1239	88.8	2.1	126
PART-TIME	2980	•205	4.0	6.9	115	•40	2.2	1.3	62	•537	3.9	18.0	112	•16	1.1	.5	33
SOLE WAGE EARNER	22015	1143	22.5	5.2	87	555	30.3	2.5	117	3449	25.1	15.7	97	358	25.6	1.6	99
NOT EMPLOYED	22218	1911	37.7	8.6	144	•200	10.9	.9	42	3884	28.3	17.5	108	•141	10.1	.6	39
PROFESSIONAL	7683	•318	6.3	4.1	69	•188	10.3	2.4	114	1080	7.9	14.1	87	•180	12.9	2.3	143
EXECUTIVE/ADMIN./MANAGERIAL	8822	445	8.8	5.0	85	•284	15.5	3.2	150	1452	10.6	16.5	102	•154	11.0	1.7	106
CLERICAL/SALES/TECHNICAL	12287	605	11.9	4.9	83	•329	18.0	2.7	124	1720	12.5	14.0	87	•288	20.6	2.3	143
PRECISION/CRAFTS/REPAIR	12604	624	12.3	5.0	83	•376	20.5	3.0	139	2077	15.1	16.5	102	•281	20.1	2.2	136
OTHER EMPLOYED	21420	1165	23.0	5.4	91	•454	24.8	2.1	98	3511	25.6	16.4	102	•352	25.2	1.6	100
H/D INCOME $60,000 OR MORE	12618	659	13.0	5.2	88	•252	13.8	2.0	93	1783	13.0	14.1	88	378	27.1	3.0	182
$50,000 - 59,999	8293	459	9.1	5.5	93	•238	13.0	2.9	133	1368	10.0	16.5	102	•161	11.5	1.9	118
$35,000 - 49,999	19554	1053	20.8	5.4	90	530	28.9	2.7	126	2771	20.2	14.2	88	•424	30.4	2.2	132
$25,000 - 34,999	15891	928	18.3	5.8	98	•360	19.7	2.3	105	2754	20.1	17.3	107	•166	11.9	1.0	64
$15,000 - 24,999	15297	1064	21.0	7.0	117	•291	15.9	1.9	88	2759	20.1	18.0	112	•111	8.0	.7	44
LESS THAN $15,000	13382	907	17.9	6.8	114	•160	8.7	1.2	56	2290	16.7	17.1	106	•156	11.2	1.2	71

Source: Mediamark Research Inc., *Mediamark Research Men's, Women's Personal Care Products Report* (Mediamark Research Inc., Spring 1989), 16. Reprinted with permission.

EXHIBIT 14.6

Commercial research firms can provide advertisers with an evaluation of a brand's relative strength within demographic segments. Exhibit 14.6 is a typical data table from Mediamark Research showing how various men's aftershave and cologne brands perform in different demographic segments.

the strength of microbreweries in the northeastern and northwestern United States has forced major national brewers, like Miller Brewing and Anheuser-Busch, to not only develop specialty beers, like Red Wolf, but also alter their geographic media objectives to provide different coverage based on the competitive intensity of these markets. In markets where microbreweries are particularly strong, Miller and A-B buy extra media time or run special promotions to combat the competition.

Some analysts suggest that when certain geographic markets demonstrate unusually high purchasing tendencies by product category or by brand, then geo-targeting should be the basis for the media placement decision. **Geo-targeting** is the placement of ads in geographic regions where higher purchase tendencies for a brand are evident. For example, in one geographic area the average consumer purchases of Prego spaghetti sauce were 36 percent greater than the average consumer purchases nationwide. With this kind of information, media buys can be geo-targeted to reinforce high-volume users.[6]

The final media objective is *message weight,* the total mass of advertising delivered. **Message weight** is the gross number of advertising messages delivered by a vehicle in a schedule. An important issue in message weight is that the measurement includes duplication of exposure; that is, an individual may be counted more than one time in a message weight calculation. Unduplicated audience measurement, known as reach, is discussed in the next section, dealing with media strategies. Media planners are

6.   This section and the example are drawn from Erwin Ephron, "The Organizing Principle of Media," *Inside Media,* November 2, 1992.

interested in the message weight of a media plan because it provides a simple indication of the size of the advertising effort being placed against a specific market.

Message weight is typically expressed in terms of gross impressions. **Gross impressions** represent the sum of exposures to all the media placement in a media plan. (Of course, when we say *exposures,* we really mean opportunities to be exposed.) For example, consider a media plan that, in a one-week period, placed ads on three television programs and in two national newspapers. The sum of the exposures to the media placement might be as follows:

Television:	Program A audience	16,250,000
	Program B audience	4,500,000
	Program C audience	7,350,000
	Sum of TV exposures	28,100,000
Newspapers:	Newspaper 1	1,900,000
	Newspaper 2	450,000
	Sum of np exposures	2,350,000
	Total gross impressions	30,450,000

Of course, this does not mean that 30,450,000 separate people were exposed. Some people who watched TV Program A also saw Program B and read Newspaper 1, as well as all other possible combinations. This is called **between-vehicle duplication.** It is also possible that someone who saw the ad in Newspaper 1 on Monday saw it again in Newspaper 1 on Tuesday. This is **within-vehicle duplication.** That's why we say that the total gross impressions number contains audience duplication. Data available from services such as SMRB report both these types of duplication so that they may be removed from the gross impressions to produce the unduplicated estimate of audience called *reach.* The concept of reach is discussed in the next section.

The message weight objective provides only a broad perspective for a media planner. What does it mean that a media plan for a week produced more than 30 million gross impressions? Only that a fairly large number of people were potentially exposed to the advertiser's message. This does not mean that message weight is not important, however; it provides a general point of reference. When Toyota Motors introduced the Avalon in the U.S. market, the $40 million introductory ad campaign featured 30-second television spots, newspaper and magazine print ads (see Exhibit 14.7 for an example), and direct mail pieces. The highlight of the campaign was a nine-spot placement on a heavily watched Thursday evening TV show, costing more than $2 million. The message weight of this campaign in a single week was enormous—just the type of objective Toyota's media planners wanted for the brand introduction.[7]

Media Strategies

Media objectives provide the foundation for media selection. The true power of a media plan, though, is in media strategies: decisions made with respect to a media vehicle's reach and frequency, the continuity of media placement, the audience duplication, and the length and size of advertisements. Media strategy decisions help ensure that messages placed in chosen media have as much impact as possible.

Reach and Frequency. **Reach** refers to the number of people or households in a target audience that will be exposed to a media vehicle or schedule at least one time during a given period of time. It is often expressed as a percentage. If an advertisement placed on the hit network television program *ER* is watched at least once by 30 percent of the advertiser's target audience, then the reach is said to be 30 percent. Media vehicles with broad reach are ideal for consumer convenience goods, like toothpaste and cold remedies. These are

7.   Bradley Johnson, "Toyota's New Avalon Thinks Big, American," *Advertising Age,* November 14, 1994, 46.

EXHIBIT 14.7

What is the importance of message weight for the introduction of a new product like the Avalon? Is it important that the advertiser be able to distinguish between gross impressions and audience reach in this kind of campaign? At the Web site for Toyota **www.toyota.com**, *options include virtual show-rooms, feedback forms, and an owners-only link that may help the company measure advertising impact and reach. Compare the Toyota site to Nissan's at* **www.nissan.com**. *What is a striking difference between these two sites? Which site uses the new media most effectively? Why?*

products with fairly simple features, and they are frequently purchased by a broad cross section of the market. Broadcast television, cable television, and national magazines have the largest and broadest reach of any of the media, due to their national and even global coverage. For example, as explained in the Global Issues box on page 395, placing ads on cable TV is an excellent method to achieve broad reach across Latin America.

Frequency is the average number of times an individual or household within a target audience is exposed to a media vehicle in a given period of time (typically a week or a month). For example, say an advertiser places an ad on a weekly television show with a 20 rating (20 percent of households) four weeks in a row. The show has an (unduplicated) reach of 43 (percent) over the four-week period. Frequency is then equal to $(20 \times 4)/43$, or 1.9. This means that an audience member had the opportunity to see the ad an average of 1.9 times.

An important measure for media planners related to both reach and frequency is **gross rating points (GRP).** GRP is the product of reach times frequency ($GRP = r \times f$). When media planners calculate the GRP for a media plan, they multiply the rating (reach) of each vehicle in a plan times the number of times an ad will be inserted in the media vehicle. Exhibit 14.8 shows the GRP for a combined magazine and television schedule.

The GRP number is used as a relative measure of the intensity of one media plan versus another. Whether a media plan is appropriate or not is ultimately based on the judgment of the media planner.

Advertisers often struggle with the dilemma of increasing reach at the expense of frequency, or vice versa. At the core in this struggle are the concepts of effective frequency

EXHIBIT 14.8

Gross rating points (GRP) for a media plan.

Media Class/Vehicle	Rating (reach)	Number of Ad Insertions (frequency)	GRP
Television			
ER	25	4	100
Law & Order	20	4	80
Good Morning America	12	4	48
Days of Our Lives	7	2	14
Magazines			
People	22	2	44
Travel & Leisure	11	2	22
U.S. News and World Report	9	6	54
Total			**362**

and effective reach. **Effective frequency** is the number of times a target audience needs to be exposed to a message before the objectives of the advertiser are met—either communications objectives or sales impact. Many factors affect the level of effective frequency. New brands and brands laden with features may demand high frequency. Simple messages for well-known products may require less-frequent exposure for consumers to be affected. While most analysts agree that one exposure will typically not be enough, there is debate about how many exposures are enough. An old rule of thumb placed effective frequency at three exposures, but analysts argue that as few as two or as many as nine exposures are needed to achieve effective frequency.[8]

Effective reach is the number or percentage of consumers in the target audience that are exposed to an ad some minimum number of times. The minimum number estimate for effective reach is based on a determination of effective frequency. If effective reach is set at four exposures, then a media schedule must be devised that achieves at least four exposures over a specified time period within the target audience.

Continuity. The second important strategic decision in the media plan is about continuity. **Continuity** is the pattern of placement of advertisements in a media schedule. There are three strategic scheduling alternatives: continuous, flighting, and pulsing.

Continuous scheduling is a pattern of placing ads at a steady rate over a period of time. Running one ad each day for four weeks during the soap opera *General Hospital* would be a continuous pattern. Similarly, an ad that appeared in every issue of *Redbook* magazine for a year would also be continuous. **Flighting** is another media-scheduling strategy. Flighting is achieved by scheduling heavy advertising for a period of time, usually two weeks, then stopping advertising altogether for a period, only to come back with another heavy schedule.

Flighting is often used to support special seasonal merchandising efforts or new product introductions, or as a response to competitors' activities. The financial advantages of flighting are that discounts might be gained by concentrating media buys in larger blocks. Communication effectiveness may be enhanced because a heavy schedule can achieve the repeat exposures necessary to achieve consumer awareness.

Finally, **pulsing** is a media-scheduling strategy that combines elements from continuous and flighting techniques. Advertisements are scheduled continuously in media

8. For a complete discussion of the evolution of the concepts of effective reach and effective frequency, see Jack Z. Sissors and Lincoln Bumba, *Advertising Media Planning* (Lincolnwood, Ill.: NTC Business Books, 1993), 106–120.

over a period of time, but with periods of much heavier scheduling (the flight). Pulsing is most appropriate for products that are sold fairly regularly all year long but have, like clothing, certain seasonal requirements.

Length or Size of Advertisements. Beyond who to reach, how often to reach them, and in what pattern, media planners must make strategic decisions regarding the length of an ad in electronic media or the size of an ad in print media. Certainly, the advertiser, creative director, art director, and copywriter have made determinations in this regard as well.

Television advertisements (excluding infomercials) can range from 10 seconds to 60 seconds, and sometimes even two minutes, in length. Is a 60-second television commercial always six times more effective than a 10-second spot? Of course, the answer is no. Is a full-page newspaper ad always more effective than a two-inch, one-column ad? Again, not necessarily. Advertisers make use of full-page newspaper ads when a product claim warrants it. This was the case with Quaker Oats when the FDA determined that oatmeal had beneficial dietary effects, as shown in Exhibit 14.9.

The decision about the length or size of an advertisement depends on the creative requirements for the ad, the media budget, and the competitive environment within which the ad is running. From a creative standpoint, ads attempting to develop an image for a brand may need to be longer in broadcast media or larger in print media to offer more creative opportunities. On the other hand, a simple, straightforward message announcing a sale may be quite short or small, but it may need heavy repetition. From the standpoint of the media budget, shorter and smaller ads are, with few exceptions, much less expensive. If a media plan includes some level of repetition to accomplish its objectives, the lower-cost option may be mandatory. From a competitive perspective, matching a competitor's presence with messages of similar size or length may be essential to maintain the share of mind in a target audience. Once again, the size and length decisions are a matter of judgment between the creative team and the media planner, tempered by the availability of funds for media placement.

Why is this man smiling?

**FDA Proposes
First Food-Specific Health Claim:**

Diets high in oatmeal and low in saturated fat and cholesterol may reduce the risk of heart disease.

*The Food and Drug Administration has tentatively determined that there is enough scientific evidence to support the claim that a diet high in oatmeal and low in saturated fat and cholesterol may reduce the risk of heart disease. Through April 3, 1996, the FDA will be accepting comments from all interested parties before finalizing its decision.
Choosing a diet that is low in saturated fat and cholesterol and includes plenty of fruits, grains and vegetables may help lower your risk of heart disease. Other heart healthy steps to take include watching your weight and exercising regularly. And, of course, if you have elevated cholesterol levels, consult your physician.*   ©1996 Quaker Oats Co.

EXHIBIT 14.9

When the Food and Drug Administration announced that oatmeal might have several beneficial health effects, Quaker Oats took the opportunity to run full-page newspaper ads in USA Today.

Media Choices

The next stage of the media-planning process focuses on media selection. Exhibit 14.10 gives general ratings for the major media. The advertiser and the agency team determine which media class is appropriate for the current effort, based on criteria similar to those listed in Exhibit 14.10. These criteria give a general orientation to major media and the inherent capabilities of each media class.

Media choice addresses three distinct issues: media mix, media efficiency, and competitive media assessment.

Media Mix. In making specific media choices for placing advertisements, media planners have to decide what sort of media mix to use. The **media mix** is the blend of different media that will be used to effectively reach the target audience. There are two options for a media planner with respect to the media mix: a concentrated media mix or an assorted

EXHIBIT 14.10

Evaluation of traditional major media options.

Characteristics	Broadcast TV	Cable TV	Radio	News-paper	Maga-zines	Direct Mail	Outdoor	Transit	Directory
Reach									
Local	M	M	H	H	L	H	H	H	M
National	H	H	L	L	H	M	L	L	M
Frequency	H	H	H	M	L	L	M	M	L
Selectivity									
Audience	M	H	H	L	H	H	L	L	L
Geographic	L	M	H	H	M	H	H	H	H
Audience reactions									
Involvement	L	M	L	M	H	M	L	L	H
Acceptance	M	M	M	H	M	L	M	M	H
Audience data	M	L	L	M	H	H	L	L	M
Clutter	H	H	H	M	M	M	M	L	H
Creative flexibility	H	H	H	L	M	M	L	L	L
Cost factors									
Per contact	L	L	L	M	M	H	L	L	M
Absolute cost	H	H	M	M	H	H	M	M	M

H = High, M = Moderate, L = Low

media mix.[9] A **concentrated media mix** focuses all the media placement dollars in one medium. The rationale behind this option is that it allows an advertiser to have great impact on a specific audience segment. A highly concentrated media mix can give a brand an aura of mass acceptance, especially within an audience with restricted media exposure.[10] The full range of benefits possible from a concentrated media mix are as follows:

- It may allow the advertiser to be dominant in one medium relative to the competition.
- Brand familiarity might be heightened, especially within target audiences that have a narrow range of media exposure.
- Concentrating media buys in high-visibility media, like prime-time television or large advertising sections in premium magazines, can create enthusiasm and loyalty in a trade channel. Distributors and retailers may give a brand with heavily concentrated media exposure preferential treatment in inventory or shelf display.
- A concentration of media dollars may result in significant volume discounts from media organizations.

An **assorted media mix** employs multiple media alternatives to reach target audiences. The assorted mix can be advantageous to an advertiser because it facilitates communication with multiple market segments. By using a mix of media, an advertiser

9.   Arnold M. Barban, Steven M. Cristol, and Frank J. Kopec, *Essentials of Media Planning: A Marketing Viewpoint,* 3rd ed. (Lincolnwood, Ill.: NTC Business Books, 1993), 76–80.
10.   Leo Bogart, *Strategy in Advertising,* 2nd ed. (Lincolnwood, Ill.: NTC Business Books, 1984), 147.

can place different messages for different target audiences in different media. In general, the advantages of an assorted media mix are as follows:

- An advertiser can reach different target audiences with messages tailored to each target's unique interests in the product category or brand.
- Different messages in different media reaching a single target may enhance the learning effect.
- Assorted media placement will increase the reach of a message, compared to concentrating placement in one medium.
- The probability of reaching audiences exposed to diverse media is greater with an assorted media mix.

One caution should be offered with the assorted media mix approach. Since different media placements require different creative and production efforts, the cost of preparing advertisements can increase dramatically. Preparing both print and broadcast versions of an ad may draw funds away from media expenditures. Using funds for multiple preparations likely will come at the expense of other important goals, such as gross impressions or GRP.

Media Efficiency. Each medium under consideration in a media plan must be scrutinized for the efficiency with which it performs. In other words, which media deliver the largest target audiences at the lowest cost? The standard measure of media efficiency is cost per thousand. **Cost per thousand (CPM)** is the dollar cost of reaching 1,000 members of an audience using a particular medium. The CPM calculation can be used to compare the relative efficiency of two media choices within a media class (magazine versus magazine) or between media classes (magazine versus radio). The basic measure of CPM is fairly straightforward; the dollar cost for placement of an ad in a medium is divided by the total audience and multiplied by 1,000. Let's calculate the CPM for a full-page ad in *USA Today*:

$$\text{CPM} = \frac{\text{cost of media buy}}{\text{total audience}} \times 1{,}000$$

$$\text{CPM for } USA\ Today = \frac{\$66{,}100}{2{,}100{,}000} \times 1{,}000 = \$31.47$$

These calculations show that *USA Today* has a CPM of $31.47 for a full-page black-and-white ad. But this calculation shows the cost of reaching the entire readership of *USA Today*. If the target audience is restricted to male college graduates in professional occupations, then the **cost per thousand–target market (CPM–TM)** calculation might be much higher for a general publication like *USA Today* than for a more specialized publication like *Fortune* magazine:

$$\text{CPM–TM for } USA\ Today = \frac{\$66{,}100}{640{,}000} \times 1{,}000 = \$103.28$$

$$\text{CPM–TM for } Fortune = \frac{\$43{,}100}{740{,}000} \times 1{,}000 = \$58.24$$

You can see that the relative efficiency of *Fortune* is much greater than that of *USA Today* when the target audience is specified more carefully and a CPM–TM calculation is made. An advertisement for business services appearing in *Fortune* will have a better CPM–TM than the same ad appearing in *USA Today*. Information about gross impressions and target audience viewership or readership is usually available from the medium itself. Detailed information to make a cost per thousand–target market analysis is also available from media research organizations, like Simmons Market Research Bureau (for magazines) or A. C. Nielsen (for television).

The same sort of straightforward calculation is possible for television in the form of the cost per rating point. Like the CPM, a **cost per rating point (CPRP)** calculation provides a relative comparison between media options. In this calculation, the cost of a spot on television is divided by the program's rating (a rating point is equivalent to 1 percent of the television households in the designated rating area tuned to a specific program). Like the CPM calculation, the CPRP calculation gives a dollar figure, which can be used for comparing TV program efficiency. The calculation for CPRP is as follows:

$$\text{CPRP} = \frac{\text{dollar cost of ad placement on a program}}{\text{program rating}}$$

It is important to remember that these efficiency assessments are based solely on costs and coverage. They say nothing about the quality of the advertising and thus should not be viewed as indicators of advertising effectiveness. When media efficiency measures like CPM and CPM–TM are combined with an assessment of media objectives and media strategies, they can be quite useful. Taken alone and out of the broader campaign-planning context, such efficiency measures can cause ineffective media buying.

Competitive Media Assessment. While media planners never base an overall media plan on how much competitors are spending or where competitors are placing their ads, a competitive media assessment can provide a useful perspective. A competitive media assessment is particularly important for product categories in which all the competitors are focused on a narrowly defined target audience. This condition exists in several product categories in which heavy-user segments dominate consumption: snack foods, soft drinks, beer and wine, and chewing gum are examples. Brands of luxury cars and financial services also compete for common-buyer segments.

When a target audience is narrow and attracts the attention of several major competitors, an advertiser must assess the competitors' spending and the relative share of voice its brand is getting. **Share of voice** is a calculation of any one advertiser's brand expenditures relative to the overall spending in a category:

$$\text{share of voice} = \frac{\text{one brand's advertising expenditures in a medium}}{\text{total product category advertising expenditures in a medium}}$$

Research firms like Leading National Advertisers can provide an assessment of share of voice in various print media. A detailed report shows how much a brand was advertised in a particular issue of a magazine versus the combined total for all other products in the same category. Knowing what competitors are spending in a medium and how dominant they might be allows an advertiser to strategically schedule within a medium. Some strategists believe that scheduling in and around a competitor's schedule can create a bigger presence for a small advertiser.[11]

Consider how Leo Burnett scheduled advertising for Miller Lite on Super Bowl Sunday in 1994. Since the Super Bowl delivers such a high proportion of the beer-drinking target audience, strategists at Burnett were faced with the prospect of a very dense competitive environment—and a very expensive one, at $1 million for a 30-second spot. Anheuser-Busch had already scheduled its "Bud Bowl" spots during the Super Bowl. So, instead of going head-to-head with Anheuser-Busch in a cluttered, million-dollar environment, Miller bought heavily during the pregame show. In this way, the brand achieved good exposure in the target segment without extraordinary expense in a cluttered environment.

As with the media efficiency measures discussed in the previous section, a competitive media assessment should never be the foundation for media planning. A competitive media assessment contains valuable information; however, media objectives and media strategies should be the driving forces behind media planning.

---

11. Andrea Rothman, "Timing Techniques Can Make Small Ad Budgets Seem Bigger," *Wall Street Journal*, February 3, 1989, B4; also see Robert J. Kent and Chris T. Allen, "Competitive Interference Effects in Consumer Memory for Advertising: The Role of Brand Familiarity," *Journal of Marketing* (July 1994): 97–105.

Media Scheduling and Buying

Media scheduling and buying are activities that take place throughout the planning effort. Media scheduling focuses on several issues related to timing and impact.[12] All aspects of timing, reach, frequency, and competitive media assessment are evaluated during the scheduling phase. In addition, the total media schedule is evaluated with respect to CPM or gross impressions to gauge the impact the entire schedule delivers in each time frame. Seasonal buying tendencies in the target segment also have a major impact on scheduling. Scheduling media more heavily when consumers show buying tendencies is referred to as **heavy-up scheduling.**[13]

One of the most important aspects of the media-scheduling phase involves creating a visual representation of the media schedule. Exhibit 14.11 shows a media schedule flowchart that includes both print and electronic media placement. With this visual representation of the schedule, the advertiser has tangible documentation of the overall media plan.

Once an overall media plan and schedule are in place, the focus must turn to media buying. Media buying entails securing the electronic media time and print media space specified in the schedule. An important part of the media-buying process is the agency of record. The **agency of record** is the advertising agency chosen by the advertiser to purchase time and space. The agency of record coordinates media discounts and negotiates all contracts for time and space. Any other agencies involved in the advertising effort submit insertion orders for time and space within those contracts.

Rather than using an agency of record, some advertisers use a **media-buying service,** which is an independent organization that specializes in buying large blocks of media time and space and reselling it to advertisers. Some agencies have developed their own media-buying units to control both the planning and the buying process.[14] Regardless of the structure used to make the

GLOBAL ISSUES

REACHING THE LATIN AMERICAN CONSUMER: ADVERTISERS PLUG IN TO CABLE

With a potential audience of 470 million consumers, advertisers are keeping a keen eye on Latin America, including Mexico, Argentina, Venezuela, Chile, and Brazil. The traditional and emerging professional elite that occupies top professional and executive positions represents 14 percent of the population. In addition, the professional and skilled middle class represents 33 percent of the population. The size and growing professionalism of the population is just a foundation for advertisers' interest.

What makes Latin America an exciting prospect for U.S. advertisers is the ability to reach this huge potential audience with increased precision and efficiency. Culturally homogeneous and bonded by a single language (with the exception of Brazil, where Portuguese is the primary language), Latin America is increasingly the target of pan-regional advertising. Pan-regional ads are created for the entire Latin American market rather than for a single country. Satellite and cable television systems are reaching upscale consumers and raising the prospect of extended, multicountry reach for international advertisers. The unifying factor making pan-regional campaigns more effective and cost-efficient is that while fewer than 16 percent of the Latin American homes have cable or satellite access, these consumers control more than 50 percent of the region's disposable income.

Typical of the marketers who have adopted a pan-regional approach to reach their target markets are MasterCard International and FedEx. MasterCard uses neutral international images of ocean sunsets and urban energy to create a Latin American campaign around its tag line "One currency." The vice president of marketing for MasterCard says, "For us, it's pretty easy because it's international utility that we are selling." FedEx has advertised in Latin America since 1984 but broke its first pan-regional campaign in 1994. With the niche programming offered by cable, FedEx can hit specific demographic groups with ESPN and the Discovery Channel.

It remains to be seen how long it will take Latin American economies to fully recover from the devaluation of the Mexican peso in late 1994. But with the reach provided by cable and the growth of the upper and middle class, pan-regional campaigns by firms like MasterCard, FedEx, Coca-Cola, and Shell Oil have boosted advertising spending by 9 percent annually in the region, to nearly $20 billion. Overall, the future looks bright for reaching and selling to Latin American consumers.

Sources: Jeffery D. Zbar, "Latin America," *Advertising Age International*, March 11, 1996, I-19; and Jeffery D. Zbar, "Advertisers Drop Markets for Latin Buy," *Advertising Age International*, March 11, 1996, I-20.

---

12.   John J. Burnett, *Promotion Management* (Boston: Houghton Mifflin, 1993), 520–21.
13.   Sissors and Bumba, 257.
14.   Joe Mandese, "Ayer Adjusts to Complex Media Buys," *Advertising Age*, December 12, 1994, 6.

EXHIBIT 14.11

A media flowchart gives an advertiser a visual representation of the overall media plan.

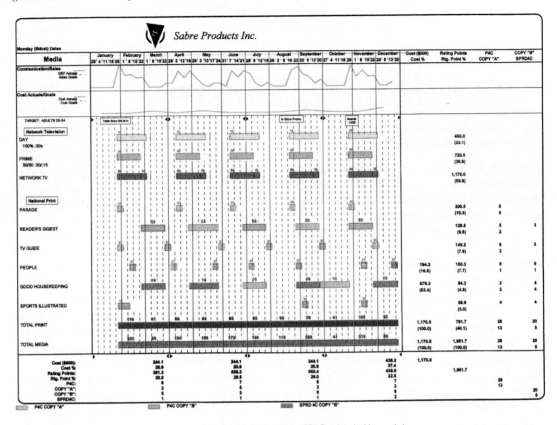

Source: Telmar Information Services Corp., *FlowMaster for Windows™*, New York, 1996. Reprinted with permission.

buys, media buyers evaluate the audience reach, CPM, and timing of each buy. The organization responsible for the buy also monitors the ads and estimates the actual audience reach delivered. If the expected audience is not delivered, then media organizations have to make good by repeating ad placements or offering a refund or price reduction on future ads. For example, making good to advertisers because of shortfalls in delivering certain age cohorts cost CBS an estimated $25 million in 1994.[15]

Computer Media-Planning Models

❸ The explosion of available data on markets and consumers has motivated media planners to rely more on computerization to assist with various parts of the media-planning effort. The most significant impact of computer technology has come in the development of three types of media-planning models: simulation models, media strategy models, and media scheduling and buying models.

Simulation models compare alternative media plans by computing the hypothetical effects of different plans on factors like reach, store traffic, information requests, and coupon redemption. The value of simulation models is that they allow media planners to quickly assess the effect of different media plans before making a decision about which plan to use. One of the problems with simulation models is that the data needed to run the models can be expensive and time-consuming to obtain.

15.   Kevin Goldman, "CBS Again Must Offer 'Make Good' Ads," *Wall Street Journal,* October 27, 1994, B6.

Media strategy models compare media plans by focusing on the issues of reach, frequency, and efficiency. With programs like Marketron and AdWare, media planners input various media class and media vehicle choices. The programs then estimate the reach and frequency capability for several different alternatives given specified budget parameters. The AdWare program uses syndicated data from Arbitron and A. C. Nielsen to calculate total media cost, GRP, and overall efficiency.

Finally, **media-scheduling and -buying models** allow media planners to develop and then evaluate alternative media schedules. Media Management Plus is one such program. It can be used to rank television stations according to target market delivery and cost for every market the media planner is considering. Then, by projecting ratings of programs, the media planner is provided with an estimate of total costs and efficiency on a market-by-market basis. Exhibit 14.12 shows typical screens from one such computer program. The first screen is reach and cost data for spot TV ads, and the second screen is the combined reach and cost data for spot TV and newspaper ads.

Computerization and modeling can never substitute for planning and judgment by media strategists. Computer modeling does, however, allow for the assessment of a wide range of possibilities before making costly media buys.

EXHIBIT 14.12

The explosion of data about markets and consumers has caused advertisers to rely more on computerized media-planning tools.

```
--------------------------------------------------------
ADplus(TM) RESULTS:  SPOT TV (30S)

Walt Disney World               Frequency (f) Distributions
Off-Season Promotion            ----------------------------
Monthly                            Vehicle          Message
                                   -------          -------
Target:   973,900        f    % f    % f+      % f    % f+
Jacksonville DMA Adults  ---  -----  -----    -----  -----
                          0    5.1    ---      9.1    ---
Message/vehicle = 32.0%   1    2.0   94.9      7.5   90.9
                          2    2.2   92.9      8.1   83.4
                          3    2.3   90.7      8.1   75.2
                          4    2.4   88.3      7.8   67.1
                          5    2.4   85.9      7.2   59.3
                          6    2.5   83.5      6.6   52.1
                          7    2.5   81.0      6.0   45.5
                          8    2.5   78.5      5.3   39.5
                          9    2.5   76.0      4.7   34.2
                         10+  73.5   73.5     29.5   29.5
                         20+  49.8   49.8      6.1    6.1

Summary Evaluation
------------------
Reach 1+ (%)                          94.9%           90.9%
Reach 1+ (000s)                       923.9           885.3

Reach 3+ (%)                          90.7%           75.2%
Reach 3+ (000s)                       882.9           732.8

Gross rating points (GRPs)          2,340.0           748.8
Average frequency (f)                  24.7             8.2
Gross impressions (000s)           22,789.3         7,292.6
Cost-per-thousand (CPM)                6.10           19.06
Cost-per-rating point (CPP)              59             186

Vehicle List  Rating  Ad Cost  CPM-MSG  Ads  Total Cost  Mix %
------------  ------  -------  -------  ---  ----------  -----
WJKS-ABC-AM     6.00     234    12.51    30     7,020      5.1
WJXT-CBS-AM     6.00     234    12.51    30     7,020      5.1
WTLV-NBC-AM     6.00     234    12.51    30     7,020      5.1
WJKS-ABC-DAY    5.00     230    14.76    60    13,800      9.9
WJXT-CBS-DAY    5.00     230    14.76    60    13,800      9.9
WTLV-NBC-DAY    5.00     230    14.76    60    13,800      9.9
WJKS-ABC-PRIM  10.00     850    27.27    30    25,500     18.4
WJXT-CBS-PRIM  10.00     850    27.27    30    25,500     18.4
WTLV-NBC-PRIM  10.00     850    27.27    30    25,500     18.4
                      --------  ------   ---  ----------  -----
              Totals:    19.06  360    138,960    100.0
--------------------------------------------------------
```

```
--------------------------------------------------------
ADplus(TM) RESULTS:  DAILY NEWSPAPERS (1/2 PAGE), SPOT TV (30S)

Walt Disney World               Frequency (f) Distributions
Off-Season Promotion            ----------------------------
Monthly                            Vehicle          Message
                                   -------          -------
Target:   973,900        f    % f    % f+      % f    % f+
Jacksonville DMA Adults  ---  -----  -----    -----  -----
                          0    1.2    ---      4.0    ---
Message/vehicle = 28.1%   1    0.8   98.8      4.9   96.0
                          2    0.9   98.0      5.9   91.1
                          3    0.9   97.2      6.5   85.2
                          4    1.0   96.2      6.7   78.7
                          5    1.1   95.2      6.8   72.0
                          6    1.1   94.2      6.6   65.2
                          7    1.2   93.0      6.3   58.6
                          8    1.3   91.8      5.9   52.4
                          9    1.3   90.6      5.5   46.5
                         10+  89.3   89.3     41.0   41.0
                         20+  73.3   73.3      9.6    9.6

Summary Evaluation
------------------
Reach 1+ (%)                          98.8%           96.0%
Reach 1+ (000s)                       962.6           934.6

Reach 3+ (%)                          97.2%           85.2%
Reach 3+ (000s)                       946.5           829.7

Gross rating points (GRPs)          3,372.0           948.0
Average frequency (f)                  34.1             9.9
Gross impressions (000s)           32,839.9         9,232.3
Cost-per-thousand (CPM)               10.96           38.99
Cost-per-rating point (CPP)             107             380

Vehicle List  Rating  Ad Cost  CPM-MSG  Ads  Total Cost  Mix %
------------  ------  -------  -------  ---  ----------  -----
1 DAILY NEWSPAPERS    Totals:  114.00    80   221,040     61.4

Times-Union    42.00   8,284   104.93    20   165,680     46.0
Record          4.00     866   115.18    20    17,320      4.8
News            3.20     926   153.95    20    18,520      5.1
Reporter        2.40     976   216.35    20    19,520      5.4

2 SPOT TV (30S)       Totals:   19.00   360   138,960     38.6

WJKS-ABC-AM     6.00     234    12.51    30     7,020      2.0
WJXT-CBS-AM     6.00     234    12.51    30     7,020      2.0
WTLV-NBC-AM     6.00     234    12.51    30     7,020      2.0
WJKS-ABC-DAY    5.00     230    14.76    60    13,800      3.8
WJXT-CBS-DAY    5.00     230    14.76    60    13,800      3.8
WTLV-NBC-DAY    5.00     230    14.76    60    13,800      3.8
WJKS-ABC-PRIM  10.00     850    27.27    30    25,500      7.1
WJXT-CBS-PRIM  10.00     850    27.27    30    25,500      7.1
WTLV-NBC-PRIM  10.00     850    27.27    30    25,500      7.1
                      --------  ------   ---  ----------  -----
              Totals:    38.99  440    360,000    100.0
--------------------------------------------------------
```

Source: Kent M. Lancaster, *ADplus™ with FlowMaster™: For Multi-Media Advertising Planning*, Windows™ edition. New York: Telmar Information Services Corp. and Media Research Institute, Inc., 1996. Reprinted with permission.

Other Ongoing Challenges in the Media Environment

4 Several additional challenges add to the complexity of media planning. To explain these additional complications, we will review five dynamic aspects of the media environment: the proliferation of media options; insufficient and inaccurate information; escalating media costs; interactive media; and the complications of media choice in the new era of integrated marketing communications.

The Proliferation of Media Options

One of the most daunting challenges for media placement is simply keeping track of the media options available. There are two areas where media proliferation is occurring. First, there has been an expansion of traditional media, both globally and in the United States. Where there were once just three broadcast television networks, there are now four, with a fifth prepared to debut. Cable television is also expanding rapidly, and the new smaller satellite dishes now offer consumers an even greater range of programming. New magazines are being launched at a rate of more than one per day.[16] Advertisers can reach older consumers with *Modern Maturity,* preschoolers with *Sesame Street Magazine,* and everyone in between with numerous other magazines.

Second, new media are being developed to reach consumers in more and different ways. Retailers mail videotapes to consumers in carefully designated geographic areas to entice a trip to their retail store. Interactive video kiosks in Minneapolis grocery stores dispense Minnesota Twins baseball tickets and advertise team merchandise.[17] Turner Broadcasting has developed the CNN Airport Network, one of many new place-based media that reach consumers when they're not at home. The Airport Network transmits advertising along with news and entertainment programming to airport terminal gates around the United States. Advertisers who market travel-related services, like American Express and AT&T, find this new media vehicle an ideal option. Exhibit 14.13 illustrates one of the new place-based media.

Interactive video kiosks, CD-ROM ads, online information services, movie theater ads—there is little left untouched by the long arm of advertising placement. Many of the players in new media are big names in traditional media as well. The trade association Magazine Publishers of America estimates that more than 200 magazines are already involved with new media distribution platforms. This includes some of the biggest names in magazine publishing, like *Newsweek* and *Time.*[18] *Newsweek* has attracted advertisers like Honda, Chrysler, and Fidelity Investments now that the magazine has an interactive version on the Prodigy online service. There are many new players in the new media environment as well. *Launch* is a CD-ROM music magazine that contains reviews of albums with three 30-second song clips from each album, full-motion video interviews with popular bands, and three-minute movie reviews. *Launch* has signed big advertisers like Reebok International, Janus Mutual Funds, and Sony Electronics to the inaugural issue at $12,000 apiece. Overall, new media advertising is still low priced because the new media, at this point, lack the broad reach of traditional media. The typical CD-ROM magazine has a total audience of 150,000, versus five to ten times that for a traditional magazine. Of course, the creative flexibility of interactive sound and motion available on the CD-ROM format far exceeds the capabilities of print magazines.

Finally, the evolution of what used to be called direct mail into a new form of direct marketing, which will be discussed in detail in Chapter 19, has also created new opportunities for advertisers. The evolution began with the airlines and their in-flight magazines, and now firms of all types have started to publish newsletters, news magazines, and catalogs targeted at their current customers. As a way to increase efficiency in

16.   Laura Loro, "Heavy Hitters Gamble on Launches," *Advertising Age,* October 19, 1992, S-13–S-14.
17.   Debra Aho, "Kiosks: The Good, The Bad & Ugly," *Advertising Age,* January 17, 1994, 13.
18.   Keith J. Kelly, "Publishers Pine for Cyber-Profits," *Advertising Age,* March 13, 1995, S-22.

How does the proliferation of media options, like CNN's Airport Network, affect strategic decisions about media scheduling and media buying? Can you think of other products or services that might benefit from an increased focus on place-based media? At the CNN Web site www .cnn.com/, *the news is more interactive, because CNN lets you choose the headlines and stories you want to learn about. How do you think this will affect advertisers? Will ads be scheduled by individual story themes or by categories of news? To see how another news organization is using new media options, visit ABC News online at* www.realaudio .com/contentp/abc.html *to sample audio files. Does the use of Internet audio have implications for media-scheduling and media-buying decisions?*

reaching target audiences, advertisers have essentially created their own in-house media options. For example, TIAA-CREF, the largest pension fund in the world, publishes a quarterly news magazine called *The Participant.* Similarly, Physicians Mutual Insurance has a quarterly publication called *Between Friends,* which is mailed to insureds and passes along safety information, household tips, comments from customers, and a short memo from the president of the firm. These created media are efficient in that current and past customers are reached. The probability that the receiver will pay attention to the message is greater because there is some affinity for the firm sending the message.

Insufficient and Inaccurate Information

Placing ads in media that reach the intended target audience and few nontarget audience members is a tremendous challenge. The truth is that much of the information advertisers must use to make media choices is either insufficient for identifying how to reach a target audience or simply inaccurate. All the information used to identify who is using what medium at what time and in what numbers is generated as secondary data by large commercial media research organizations. Secondary data are frequently out-of-date or do not provide the category of measurement the marketer or advertiser is interested in.

Many of the problems related to media information are unique to the measurement situation; others are simply a matter of lack of availability. For example, no media information service measures audience exposure to outdoor advertising. Nor does any service provide audience measures for both AM and FM listening for every market in the United States. Another frustrating problem for advertisers is the accuracy of the measurement of television audience size. A nagging concern exists about the way television audiences have been measured. All television audience measurement services provide information on either individuals or homes tuned in to programs. This measurement has been used as a surrogate for exposure for many years. But, as we all know from personal experience, the fact that a household is tuned in to a program (as measured by a device attached to the television set) does not mean that exposure to the ad or attention to the ad has been achieved.

Nielsen, which holds a virtual monopoly on national television ratings in the United States, has been under pressure to improve the accuracy of its ratings.[19] Indeed, several firms, including General Electric (the parent of NBC), Disney/ABC, and CBS have paid for a statistical analysis to examine ways of improving the ratings process. Some television stations have even dropped out of the Nielsen rating program, claiming that the measurement periods, known as sweep periods, create an artificial measurement context.[20] Nielsen has also come under fire for the accuracy of its methods in markets outside the United States. In Japan, Nielsen has been criticized for the way it breaks down the audiences for Japanese television broadcast programs.[21] Problems with media-audience measurement are why so much pretesting of messages is done. Pretesting provides a controlled measure of effectiveness. In an environment where measuring the actual audience is so imprecise, advertisers are opting for pretesting rather than posttesting.

Finally, media organizations often provide information to advertisers in ways that are only marginally useful. While it is possible to get detailed information on the age, gender, and geographic location of target audiences, these characteristics may not be relevant to audience identification. Not all brands show clear tendencies among consumer groups based on Simmons or MRI data. Rather, consumer behavior is much more often influenced by peer groups, lifestyles, attitudes, and beliefs—which don't show up on commercial research reports. If we base our target marketing on these behavioral and experiential factors, then we would logically want to choose our media in the same way. But such information is often not available from media organizations, nor is it likely to be forthcoming (due to the cost of gathering this information). In fairness, some media kits from magazines targeted to upper-income consumers (such as *Smithsonian Magazine*) provide fairly detailed information on past purchase behaviors and some leisure activities. This information is the exception rather than the rule, however.

Escalating Media Costs

While advertisers have always complained about media costs, the situation may be reaching a critical point. Over the ten-year period from 1984 to 1994, media costs (as measured by cost per thousand) have risen 68 percent—much faster than the rate of inflation for this period.[22] Exhibit 14.14 depicts this sharp percentage increase for the last half of the decade for all major media, in both unit-cost increases and CPM increases. As we saw earlier in this chapter, the cost of newspaper and magazine ads can reach into the hundreds of thousands of dollars for a single page. In 1995, the cost for a 30-second spot during the Super Bowl finally cracked the $1 million barrier, and in 1996 it escalated to $1.3 million for 30 seconds. Spots during prime-time network television programs cost $80,000 to $500,000 for 30 seconds.

These sorts of price increases, as well as the high absolute dollar amount for media placement, have made advertisers scrutinize their media costs. Some advertisers are questioning the wisdom of massive expenditures on media with broad reach, like network television. For the time being, big advertisers are still investing more in all forms of traditional mass media, but that might be changing with the growth of interactive media and the greater attention being paid to integrated marketing communications.

Interactive Media

Aside from the escalating cost of traditional mass media options, the media environment has gotten considerably more challenging as interactive media have been refined. **Interactive media** reach beyond television and include kiosks in shopping malls or student unions, as you can read in the Contemporary Issues

19. See Joe Mandese, "Rivals' Ratings Don't Match Up," *Advertising Age,* February 24, 1992, 50.
20. "TV Station Drops Nielsen," *Marketing News,* March 11, 1996, 1.
21. Jennifer Cody, "Broadcasters Pan Nielsen Japan's Ratings," *Wall Street Journal,* November 9, 1994, B8.
22. Robert J. Coen, "Look for Bid Up of Desirable Media," *Advertising Age,* November 7, 1994, S-20–S-22.

EXHIBIT 14.14

Advertisers are struggling with escalating media costs that have far outpaced inflation over the past 15 years. Here, you can see the increases in major media expense in both unit-cost increases and CPM increases from 1991 to 1995.

Media unit costs (percentage change from previous year)

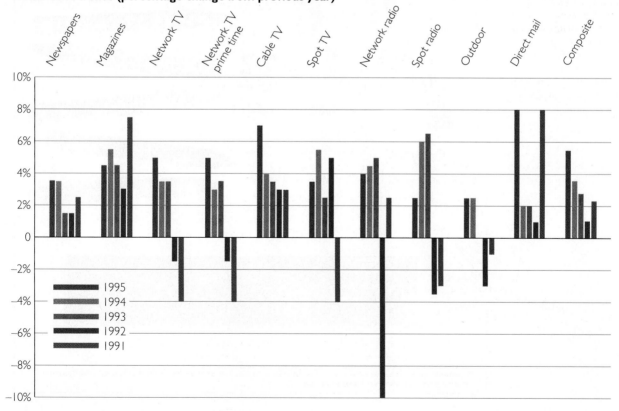

Media CPM trends (percentage change from previous year)

Source: Robert J. Coen, "Look for Bid Up of Desirable Media," *Advertising Age*, November 7, 1994, S-21. Reprinted with permission from the November 7, 1994, issue of *Advertising Age*. Copyright © Crain Communications Inc. 1994.

box on page 403. Also included are interactive telephones, interactive CDs, online services, the Internet, and online versions of magazines. Exhibit 14.15 shows an example of a home page on the Internet. The confounding factor for media placement decisions is that if consumers truly do begin to spend time with interactive media, they will have less time to spend with traditional media like television and newspapers. This will force advertisers to choose whether to participate in (or develop their own) interactive media.

In the beginning, a few shopping networks, like QVC, and a few retailers, like Macy's and Nordstrom, found interactive technology well suited to serving their customers with greater ease and convenience. But interactive media are growing beyond a few retail-shopping experiments. U.S. West has announced ambitious plans to invest several billion dollars to build multimedia networks in 20 cities in the United States through the year 1999.[23] Although no one knows for sure whether consumers will use interactive television for home shopping, education, games, movie rental, or other entertainment programming, the chair and CEO of U.S. West, Richard D. McCormick, says firmly, "We want consumers to have access to any piece of information in the multi-

EXHIBIT 14.15

Explain the seeming contradiction of how the Internet can be both a promising source of new advertising options and a threat to established advertising vehicles. What are the advantages of interactive media in terms of media planning, objectives, and strategy? Crayola at **www.crayola .com/** *offers an interactive Web site. Want your own interactive presence on the Web? Like many traditional advertising vehicles, individuals are also developing a Web presence. For example, America Online* **www.aol .com/** *subscribers can get their own free Web page with their membership.*

WEB SIGHTING

23.   Leslie Cauley, "U.S. West Prepares to Make a Big Splash in Multimedia," *Wall Street Journal,* January 10, 1994, B4.

media sense, anytime they want it."[24] Big players like Time Warner, Bell Atlantic, Tele-Communications, and Cablevision System see similar potential in interactive media, because they are all developing their own interactive options for advertisers.

Media Choice and Integrated Marketing Communications

A final complicating factor in the media environment is that more firms are adopting an integrated marketing communications (IMC) perspective, which relies on a broader mix of communication tools. IMC is the process of creating a comprehensive communication plan using a broad range of promotional options in a unified way. Promotional options such as event sponsorship, direct marketing, sales promotion, and public relations are drawing many firms away from traditional mass media advertising. But these new approaches still require coordination with the advertising that remains. Some of the more significant implications for media planning to achieve IMC are as follows:

- The reliance on mass media will be reduced as more highly targeted media are integrated into media plans. Database marketing programs and more sophisticated single-source data research will produce more tightly focused efforts through direct marketing and interactive media options.
- More-precise media impact data, not just media exposure data, will be needed to compare media alternatives. Advertisers will be looking for proof that consumers exposed to a particular medium are buyers, not just prospects.
- Media planners will need to know much more about a broader range of communication tools: event sponsorship, interactive media, direct marketing, and

---

CONTEMPORARY ISSUES

CHECK OUT THE LATEST ROCK VIDEO—AND YOUR GRADE IN ANTHRO

Marketers who want to reach college students don't have to get tangled up in the World Wide Web. A firm called Campus Interaction is setting up high-tech interactive kiosks that let students access university-related information, like their grades from last semester, as well as a few friendly words from corporate America, such as a clip from Natalie Merchant's CD *Tigerlily*.

The kiosks are slated for introduction on 135 college campuses throughout the United States and will reach nearly one million students. The eight-foot-tall and nine-foot-wide kiosk features three sections, each with one large screen and smaller touch-sensitive screens below the larger ones. The kiosk's middle section contains campus-related information, with a directory and a campus map. That section is flanked by two others devoted to advertisers' messages. The large screens play teaser reels, and students can use the smaller touch-sensitive screens to access information from marketers who are using the system. The *Wall Street Journal* and *huH Music Magazine* will use the system to accept online subscription applications; American Express will sign up new members electronically; Warner Music Group will use the system to show video clips of new groups.

Located in the student union, IKE (interactive kiosk experience) gives advertisers a way to break through the campus clutter. It meets students on their own terms in their own space. Jeff Scult, director of interactive marketing at Campus Interaction, says, "Today's students are the most techno-savvy consumers ever, and to talk to them with any success, marketers have to speak to them in their language, which is technology."

Source: Cyndee Miller, "Kiosk Targets Those Techno-Savvy Students," *Advertising Age*, October 23, 1995, 2.

public relations. They will need to know more about the impact and capability of these other forms of promotion to fully integrate communications.

- Central control will be necessary for synergistic, seamless communication. At this point, it is unclear who will provide this central control—the advertiser, the advertising agency, the copywriter, or the media planner. There is some reason to believe that, because of the need for integration and coordination, media planners will emerge as more critically important to the communications process than they have ever been in the past.[25]

---

24. Ibid.
25. Adapted from Sissors and Bumba, *Advertising Media Planning*, 4th ed. (Lincolnwood, Ill.: NTC Business Books, 1993) 26–29.

SUMMARY

1 Describe the major media options available to advertisers.

No advertising campaign can achieve its objectives without skillful use of one or several media vehicles. Poor media selection will in the end undermine any advertising campaign. Media planners today are faced with a wide variety of options for message placement. These options may be generally categorized as either measured or unmeasured media. Measured media include familiar alternatives like television, radio, magazines, and newspapers. Unmeasured media are more varied and include direct mail, store catalogs, and event sponsorship.

2 Detail the important components of the media-planning process.

A media plan specifies the media vehicles that will be used to deliver the advertiser's message. Developing a media plan entails setting objectives and determining strategies to achieve those objectives. Media planners use several quantitative indicators, such as CPM and CPRP, to help them judge the efficiency of prospective media choices. The media-planning process culminates in the scheduling and purchase of a mix of media vehicles expected to deliver the advertiser's message to specific target audiences at precisely the right time to affect their consumption decisions.

3 Explain the applications of computer modeling in media planning.

As is true in so many aspects of modern life, the computer has become an essential tool for the media planner. The detailed information available and the myriad of choices that must be made in working up a media schedule lend themselves to computer modeling. Modeling allows a planner to economically gauge the potential impact of alternative plans before making a media buy. Computer models can also be used to rate media vehicles in terms of their efficiency in reaching a target segment. These models are important decision-support tools in media planning.

4 Discuss five additional challenges that complicate the media-planning process.

Several additional factors complicate media planning. Simply keeping track of all the options is a challenge, given that new options are constantly being invented. Inadequate information and rising media costs are additional hurdles. The emergence of interactive media presents advertisers with new, untested vehicles. This incredible array of choices creates many dilemmas for the media planner who seeks to achieve integrated marketing communications.

KEY TERMS

measured media (381)
unmeasured media (384)
media plan (385)
media class (385)
media vehicle (385)
media objectives (385)
single-source tracking services (386)
geo-targeting (387)
message weight (387)
gross impressions (388)
between-vehicle duplication (388)
within-vehicle duplication (388)
reach (388)
frequency (389)
gross rating points (GRP) (389)
effective frequency (390)
effective reach (390)
continuity (390)

continuous scheduling (390)
flighting (390)
pulsing (390)
media mix (391)
concentrated media mix (392)
assorted media mix (392)
cost per thousand (CPM) (393)
cost per thousand–target market (CPM–TM) (393)
cost per rating point (CPRP) (394)
share of voice (394)
heavy-up scheduling (395)
agency of record (395)
media-buying service (395)
simulation models (396)
media strategy models (397)
media-scheduling and -buying models (397)
interactive media (400)

QUESTIONS FOR REVIEW AND CRITICAL THINKING

1.   Why have Ed Artzt and other senior business leaders been so outspoken in recent years about the need to influence content and programming in the mass media? What are Artzt and others seeking for their companies?

2.   Media plans should of course take a proactive stance with respect to customers. Explain how geo-targeting and heavy-up scheduling can be used in making a media plan more proactive with respect to customers.

3.   Carefully watch one hour of television and record the time length of each advertisement. Using your perceptions about the most and least persuasive ads during this hour of television, develop a hypothesis about the value of long versus short advertising messages. When should an advertiser use long instead of short ads, to accomplish what goals?

4.   Review the mathematics of the CPM and CPRP calculations, and explain how these two indicators can be used to assess the efficiency and effectiveness of a media schedule.

5.   Assume that you are advising a regional snack-food manufacturer whose brands have a low share of voice.

Which pattern of continuity would you recommend for such an advertiser? Would you place your ads in television programming that is also sponsored by Pringles and Doritos? Why or why not?

6.   Media strategy models allow planners to compare the impact of different media plans, using criteria like reach, frequency, and gross impressions. What other kinds of criteria should a planner take into account before deciding on a final plan?

7.   You have probably visited Web sites on the Internet for many different products and brands. How would you rate the World Wide Web as a medium for delivering commercial messages? Use the evaluative dimensions listed in Exhibit 14.11 as a guide for your assessment of the Web.

8.   Discuss the issues raised in this chapter that represent challenges for those who champion integrated marketing communications. Why would central control be required for achieving IMC? If media planners wish to play the role of central controller, what must they do to qualify for the role?

EXPERIENTIAL EXERCISE

Divide into teams. For one day have each member of the team record all the ways that marketers send messages about their goods or services. Discuss which messages, if any, you found yourselves taking in, and what it was about

those messages that made them effective. Think about a message that got through to you primarily because of repetition. What is your attitude and purchasing behavior toward such advertisers? Present your findings to the class.

USING THE INTERNET

Choose a company that currently has a Web site, and assume you are the Internet media planner for this company.

1.   What other Web sites would you suggest placing banner ads on?

2.   What combination of high-traffic or narrowly focused sites does your media plan consist of? What is it about your

company that makes it pay off to use a high-traffic site?

3.   Explain how these placements will reach people in your company's target market.

4.   What is the scheduling plan for each site you place banner ads on?

Chapter 15

Media Evaluation:

Print and

Broadcast Media

After reading and thinking about this chapter, you will be able to do the following:

1 Detail the advantages and disadvantages of newspapers as a media class, identify different types of newspapers, and describe buying and audience measurement for newspapers.

2 Detail the advantages and disadvantages of magazines as a media class, identify different types of magazines, and describe buying and audience measurement for magazines.

3 Detail the advantages and disadvantages of television as a media class, identify different types of television, and describe buying and audience measurement for television.

4 Detail the advantages and disadvantages of radio as a media class, identify different types of radio, and describe buying and audience measurement for radio.

In 1980, Absolut vodka was on the verge of extinction. The Swedish brand was selling only 12,000 cases a year in the United States—not enough to even register a single percentage point of market share. The U.S.-based importer of Absolut decided to invest in a marketing research study to assess the brand's future potential. The results of the research study tolled the death knell: American consumers almost exclusively associated vodka with Russia and Russian-sounding brand names like Stolichnaya and Popov. The name Absolut was seen as gimmicky; bartenders thought the bottle was ugly and hard to pour from. To top things off, consumers gave no credibility at all to a vodka produced in Sweden, which they knew as the land of boxy-looking cars and hot tubs.

Despite these devastating marketing research findings, Michel Roux, the president of Carillon Importers, thought the brand had promise if it had the right advertising to give it an appealing personality. The agency assigned to handle Absolut advertising was determined to give the brand a personality by making it distinctively upscale. This meant breaking from traditional liquor advertising and finding a way to communicate quality, style, and a premium image. This creative challenge was matched by an equally large media challenge. At that time spirits advertisers in the United States could not use television or radio advertising, which meant that Absolut advertisements would have to be placed in print media. This media limitation made the task of creating awareness and building brand preference a formidable one, indeed.

TBWA advertising in New York set about the task of developing magazine and newspaper ads that would build awareness, communicate quality, achieve credibility, and avoid Swedish clichés etched in the minds of American consumers. The firm came up with one of the most famous and successful print campaigns of all time. The concept was to feature the strange-shaped Absolut bottle as the hero of each ad, in which the only copy was a two-word line always beginning with *Absolut* and ending with a quality word like *perfection* or *clarity*. The campaign began with the "Absolut Perfection" copy and progressed through a series of popular and memorable print ads in leading magazines and newspapers. The two-word description evolved from the original quality concept to a variety of clever combinations. "Absolut Centerfold" appeared in *Playboy* and featured an Absolut bottle with all the printing removed, and "Absolut Wonderland" was a Christmas-season ad with the bottle in a snow globe like the ones that feature snowy Christmas scenes. Another extension of the campaign featured the bottle in locations such as "Absolut Manhattan," where the bottle became Central Park, and "Absolut LA," where the bottle was a swimming pool. While this ever-changing print campaign was creatively distinctive, it was also well financed. Absolut was outspending its rivals in the vodka market dramatically. At one point, Absolut was investing $10.68 per case in advertising, compared to Stolichnaya's $8.68 per case.

In the end, the Absolut campaign was not only a creative masterpiece, but also a resounding market success. By 1994, Absolut had become the leading imported vodka in the United States, selling nearly 2.4 million cases. The vodka with no credibility and the ugly bottle had become sophisticated and fashionable with a well-conceived and well-placed print campaign.[1] The campaign remains so potent that other vodka marketers have tried to mimic the style with their own print ads.[2] An ad for Smirnoff vodka appears in Exhibit 15.1.

This chapter focuses on evaluating print and broadcast media as important means for an advertiser to reach audiences. As the discussion of media planning in the previous chapter emphasized, even great advertising will not achieve communications and sales objectives if the media placement misses the target audience.

This evaluation of print and broadcast media will emphasize several key aspects of using these major media options. With respect to the print media—newspapers and magazines—we will first consider the advantages and disadvantages of the media them-

1.   Information about the Absolut vodka campaign was adapted from information in Nicholas Ind, "Absolut Vodka in the U.S.," in *Great Advertising Campaigns* (Lincolnwood, Ill.: NTC Business Books, 1993), 15–32.
2.   Eben Shapiro, "New Smirnoff Ads Are Similar to Absolut's," *Wall Street Journal,* November 4, 1993, B8.

EXHIBIT 15.1

The print advertising prepared for Absolut vodka has been so successful that other vodka marketers have begun to emulate it. Here, Smirnoff also features its bottle as the central element of the ad and uses the word pure *much like the word* Absolut *is used in that brand's ads.* www .purethrill.com/

selves. Both newspapers and magazines have inherent capabilities and limitations that advertisers must take into consideration in building a media plan. Next, we will look at the types of newspapers and magazines that advertisers have to choose from. Finally, we will identify buying procedures and audience measurement techniques.

The discussion of the broadcast media follows a similar sequence. First, advantages and disadvantages of television and radio are examined. Next, the types of television and radio options are described. Finally, the buying procedures and audience measurement techniques are identified.

Print and broadcast media represent the major alternatives available to advertisers for reaching audiences. While much has been said—and more will be said in the following chapters—about increased spending on new media and integrated marketing communications, about 35 percent of all advertising dollars spent in the United States still goes to traditional print and broadcast media.[3] In addition, the vast majority of creative effort is expended on print and broadcast advertising campaigns. Despite the many intriguing opportunities that new media options offer, print and broadcast media will likely form the foundation of most advertising campaigns for years to come. The discussions in this chapter will demonstrate why these media represent such rich communication alternatives for advertisers.

Print Media Evaluation

The great success of Absolut vodka demonstrates that not every brand needs a multimedia, new media, interactive, database-managed advertising effort to achieve outstanding communications and sales impact. The marketing and advertising strategists for Absolut used one media class—print—to bring the brand from near oblivion to market leadership. The reason print media alone was able to accomplish this task relates to some of the important inherent capabilities of print, which we will identify shortly. We will discuss the full range of issues in print advertising, beginning with newspapers and then turning our attention to magazines.

3.   "100 Leading National Advertisers," *Advertising Age,* September 30, 1996, 54.

Newspapers as an Advertising Medium

❶ Newspaper is the medium that is most accessible to the widest range of advertisers. Advertisers big and small—even you and I when we want to sell that old bike or snowboard—can use newspaper advertising. In fact, investment in newspaper advertising reached $34 billion in 1994.[4] Exhibits 15.2 and 15.3 show the top ten advertisers in national and local newspapers. Notice three features of the spending data in these exhibits. First, the list of national newspaper advertisers includes many business products and services. Several national newspapers reach primarily business audiences. Second, notice that the list of local newspaper advertisers is dominated by retailers. Newspapers are, of course, ideally suited to reaching a narrow geographic area—precisely the type of audience retailers want to reach. Finally, look at how much more money is spent by the top ten local advertisers than by the national advertisers. This is because the national advertisers use newspaper advertising as part of a multimedia plan, while local advertisers, even though they are national companies, often rely on newspapers as the primary medium for reaching their well-defined geographic target audiences.

There are some sad truths about the current status of newspapers as a medium. Since the early 1980s, newspapers across the United States have been suffering circulation declines, and the trend has continued into the mid-1990s.[5] What may be worse is that the percentage of adults reading daily newspapers is also declining. About 61 percent of adults in the United States read a daily newspaper, compared with about 78 percent in 1970.[6] Much of the decline in both circulation and readership comes from the fact that both morning and evening newspapers have been losing patronage to television news programs. While shows like *Good Morning America* and *20/20* cannot provide the breadth of coverage that newspapers can, they still offer news, and they offer it in a lively multisensory format.

Declining newspaper readership and circulation is not a problem in other parts of the world. In Japan, the average household subscribes to several newspapers. In England, newspaper readership has remained strong over many decades. And in several European markets, there is high newspaper circulation among households and businesses.

EXHIBIT 15.2

Top ten national newspaper advertisers.

Rank	Advertiser	National Newspaper Ad Spending ($ in millions)		
		1995	1994	% Change
1	IBM Corp.	$32.7	$22.5	45.4
2	General Motors Corp.	28.2	33.2	−15.0
3	Dow Jones & Co.	23.0	19.6	17.8
4	Ford Motor Co.	21.9	27.5	−20.3
5	Fidelity Investment Cos.	20.5	23.2	−11.3
6	Toyota Motor Corp.	16.8	17.6	−4.5
7	AT&T Corp.	14.4	30.2	−52.4
8	Charles Schwab	14.0	11.4	22.7
9	Chrysler Corp.	13.8	8.7	58.1
10	Washington Mint	13.0	5.4	143.4

Source: *Advertising Age*, September 30, 1996, 34. Reprinted with permission from the September 30, 1996, issue of *Advertising Age*. Copyright © Crain Communications Inc. 1996.

4. *Facts about Newspapers 1995* (Reston, Va.: Newspaper Association of America, 1995), 1.
5. Keith J. Kelly, "Newspapers See Decline Continue," *Advertising Age*, November 14, 1994, 41.
6. *Facts about Newspapers 1995*, 4.

EXHIBIT 15.3

Top ten local newspaper advertisers.

Rank	Advertiser	Local Newspaper Ad Spending ($ in millions)		
		1995	1994	% Change
1	Federated Department Stores	$340.1	$378.3	−12.2
2	May Department Stores Co.	279.6	278.4	0.4
3	Time Warner	231.6	126.5	83.1
4	Walt Disney Co.	219.9	117.9	86.4
5	Circuit City	206.2	239.3	−13.8
6	Sears	184.0	158.7	16.0
7	Dayton Hudson	154.9	137.1	13.0
8	Sony	125.9	65.9	91.1
9	Kmart	113.6	93.3	21.7
10	Viacom	110.2	58.9	87.2

Source: *Advertising Age*, September 30, 1996, 30. Reprinted with permission from the September 30, 1996, issue of *Advertising Age*. Copyright © Crain Communications Inc. 1996.

Advantages of Newspapers. Newspapers may have lost some of their impact and luster over the past two decades, but they do reach more than 50 percent of U.S. households, representing more than 132 million adults. And, as mentioned earlier, newspapers are still an excellent medium for retailers targeting local geographic markets. But broad reach isn't the only attractive feature of newspapers as a medium. Newspapers offer other advantages to advertisers.

- *Geographic selectivity.* Daily newspapers in cities and towns across the United States offer advertisers the opportunity to reach a well-defined geographic target audience. Some newspapers are beginning to run zoned editions, which target even more narrow geographic areas within a metropolitan market. Zoned editions are typically used by merchants doing business in the local area; national marketers like Kellogg and Colgate can use the paper carrier to deliver free samples to these zoned areas.
- *Timeliness.* The newspaper is one of the most timely of the major media. Because of the short time needed for producing a typical newspaper ad and the regularity of daily publication, the newspaper allows advertisers to reach audiences in a timely way. This doesn't mean on just a daily basis. Newspaper ads can take advantage of special events or a unique occurrence in a community—like the Infiniti ad in Exhibit 15.4, which ties into the popular Chicago Auto Show.
- *Creative opportunities.* While the newspaper page does not offer the breadth of creative options available in the broadcast media, there are things advertisers can do in a newspaper that represent important creative opportunities. Since the newspaper page offers a large and relatively inexpensive format, there is the opportunity to provide a lot of information to the target audience at relatively low cost. This is important for products or services with extensive or complex features that may need lengthy and detailed copy. The Tire America ad in Exhibit 15.5 needs just such a large format to provide detail about tire sizes and prices.
- *Credibility.* Newspapers still benefit from the perception that "if it's in the paper it must be the truth." This, combined with the community image of most newspapers, creates a favorable environment for an advertisement.
- *Audience interest.* Newspaper readers are interested in the information they are reading. While overall readership may be down in the United States, those readers that

remain are loyal and interested. Many readers buy the newspaper specifically to see what's on sale in the local area, making this an ideal environment for local merchants.

- *Cost.* In terms of both production and space, newspapers offer a low-cost alternative. The cost per contact may be higher than with the broadcast options, but the absolute cost for placing a black-and-white ad is still within reach of even a small advertising budget.

Disadvantages of Newspapers. Newspapers offer advertisers many good opportunities. Like every other media option, however, newspapers have some significant disadvantages.

- *Limited segmentation.* While newspapers can achieve good geographic selectivity, the ability to target a specific audience ends there. Newspaper circulation simply cuts across too broad an economic, social, and demographic audience to allow the isolation of specific targets. The placement of ads within certain sections can achieve minimal targeting by gender, but even this effort is somewhat fruitless. Some newspapers are developing special sections to enhance their segmentation capabilities. Many papers are offering kids news sections targeted at 9-to-13-year-olds.[7] An example is

EXHIBIT 15.4

One of the advantages of the newspaper as a medium is its timeliness. Ads can be timed with special events, like this ad for Infiniti timed to run with the Chicago Auto Show. www.infinitimotors.com/

EXHIBIT 15.5 The newspaper medium offers a large format for advertisers. This is important when an advertiser needs space to provide the target audience with extensive information, as Tire America has done with this ad featuring tire sizes and prices.

7.   Scott Hume and Ira Teinowitz, "KidNews Gets 'A' from Young Set," *Advertising Age,* October 5, 1992, S-6.

shown in Exhibit 15.6. In addition, more and more newspapers are being published to serve specific ethnic groups, which is another form of segmentation.

EXHIBIT 15.6

Many newspapers are trying to increase their target selectivity by developing special sections for advertisers, like this kid's section.

- *Creative constraints.* The opportunities for creative executions in newspapers are certainly outweighed by the creative constraints. First, newspapers have poor reproduction quality. Led by *USA Today,* most newspapers now print some of their pages in color. But even the color reproduction does not enhance the look of most products. For advertisers whose product images depend on accurate, high-quality reproduction (color or not), newspapers simply have severe limitations compared to other media options. Second, newspapers are a uni-dimensional medium—no sound, no action. For products that demand a broad creative execution, this medium simply cannot deliver.

- *Cluttered environment.* The average newspaper is filled with headlines, subheads, photos, and announcements—not to mention news stories. This presents a terribly cluttered environment for an advertisement. To make things worse, most advertisers in a product category try to use the same sections to target audiences. For example, all the home equity loan and financial services ads are in the business section, and all the women's clothing ads are in the local section.

- *Short life.* In most U.S. households, newspapers are read quickly and then discarded (or, hopefully, stacked in the recycling pile). The only way advertisers can overcome this limitation is to buy several insertions in each daily issue, buy space several times during the week, or both. In this way, even if a reader doesn't spend much time with the newspaper, at least multiple exposures are a possibility.

The newspaper has creative limitations, but what the average newspaper does, it does well. If an advertiser wants to reach a local audience with a simple black-and-white ad in a timely manner, then the newspaper is the superior choice.

Types of Newspapers. All newspapers enjoy the same advantages and suffer from the same limitations to one degree or another. But there are different types of newspapers from which advertisers can choose. Newspapers are categorized by target audience, geographic coverage, and frequency of publication.

- *Target audience.* Newspapers can be classified by the target audience they reach. The three primary types of newspapers serving different target audiences are general population newspapers, business newspapers, and ethnic newspapers. General population newspapers serve local communities and report news of interest to the local population. Newspapers like the *Kansas City Star, Dayton Daily News,* and *Columbus Dispatch* are examples. Business newspapers like the *Wall Street Journal* and *Investor's Business Daily* (United States) and the *Financial Times* (United Kingdom) serve a specialized business audience. Newspapers that target specific ethnic groups are growing in popularity. Most of these newspapers are published weekly. The *New York Amsterdam News* and the *Michigan Chronicle* are two of the more than 200 newspapers in the United States that serve African-Americans. The Hispanic community in the United States has more than 300 newspapers. One of the most prominent is *El Diario de las Americas* in Miami.

- *Geographic coverage.* As noted earlier, the vast majority of newspapers are distributed in a relatively small geographic area—either a large metropolitan area or a state. Newspapers like the *Tulsa World* and the *Atlanta Journal,* with a circulation of 170,000 and 140,000 respectively, serve a local geographic area. The other type of newspaper in the United States is a national newspaper. *USA Today* was, from its inception, designed to be distributed nationally, and it currently has a circulation of 1.4 million. The *New York Times, Los Angeles Times,* and *Christian Science Monitor,* each with a circulation of about 1 million, have evolved into national newspapers.

- *Frequency of publication.* The majority of newspapers in the United States are called dailies because they are published each day of the week, including Sunday. There are a smaller number of weeklies, and these tend to serve smaller towns or rural communities. Finally, another alternative for advertisers is the Sunday supplement, which is published only on Sunday and is usually delivered along with the Sunday edition of a local newspaper. The most widely distributed Sunday supplements— *Parade Magazine* and *USA Weekend*—are illustrated in Exhibit 15.7.

Categories of Newspaper Advertising. Just as there are categories of newspapers, there are categories of newspaper advertising: display advertising, inserts, and classified advertising.

- *Display advertising.* Advertisers of goods and services rely most on display advertising. **Display advertising** in newspapers includes the standard components of a print ad—headline, body copy, and often an illustration—to set it off from the news content of the paper. An important form of display advertising is co-op advertising sponsored by manufacturers. In **co-op advertising,** a manufacturer pays part of the media

EXHIBIT 15.7

Sunday supplements like Parade Magazine *and* USA Weekend *offer advertisers another alternative for placing newspaper ads.*

bill when a local merchant features the manufacturer's brand in advertising. Co-op advertising can be done on a national scale as well. Intel invested more than $200 million in 1994 in co-op advertising with PC manufacturers who featured the "Intel Inside" logo in their ads.[8]

- *Inserts.* There are two types of insert advertisements. Inserts do not appear on the printed newspaper page but rather are folded into the newspaper before distribution. An advertiser can use a **preprinted insert,** which is an advertisement delivered to the newspaper fully printed and ready for insertion into the newspaper, as shown in Exhibit 15.8. The second type of insert ad is a **free-standing insert (FSI),** which contains cents-off coupons for a variety of products and is typically delivered with Sunday newspapers. The Pizza Hut ad in Exhibit 15.9 is part of a free-standing insert.
- *Classified advertising.* **Classified advertising** is newspaper advertising that appears as all-copy messages under categories such as sporting goods, employment, and automobiles. Many classified ads are taken out by individuals, but real estate firms, automobile dealers, and construction firms also buy classified advertising.

Costs and Buying Procedures for Newspaper Advertising.

When an advertiser wishes to place advertising in a newspaper, the first step is to obtain a rate card from the newspaper. A **rate card** contains information on costs, closing times (when ads have to be submitted), specifications for submitting an ad, and special pages or features available in the newspaper. The rate card also summarizes the circulation for the designated market area and any circulation outside the designated area.

The cost of a newspaper ad depends on how large the advertisement is, whether it is black-and-white or color, how large the total audience is, and whether the newspaper has local or national coverage. Advertising space is sold in newspapers by the **column inch,** which is a unit of space one inch deep by one column wide. Each column is 2 1/16 inches wide. Most newspapers have adopted the **standard advertising unit (SAU)** system for selling ad space, which defines unit sizes for advertisements. There are 57 defined SAU sizes for advertisements in the system, so that advertisers can prepare ads to fit one of the sizes. Many newspapers offer a volume discount to

EXHIBIT 15.8

Advertisers like Kmart, Walgreens, and Target can deliver a fully printed advertisement ready for insertion into a newspaper. Ads like these are called preprinted inserts.

8.   Bradley Johnson, "Intel Co-op Boost Is Boon for TV, Radio," *Advertising Age,* April 3, 1995, 3.

EXHIBIT 15.9

This example of a free-standing insert (FSI) from Pizza Hut shows how an ad can be delivered via a newspaper distribution system without having to become part of the paper itself. What are the production and attention-getting advantages that this insert provides? Pizza Hut's Web site at **www.pizzahut.com/** *is serious business. Could the idea of the FSI be used here? At Apple Mountain Software* **www.apmtn soft.com***, an interactive brochure is inserted in the Web page for downloading and viewing separately, which functions much like an FSI in traditional advertising media.*

advertisers who buy more than one ad in an issue or buy multiple ads over some time period.

When an advertiser buys space on a **run-of-paper (ROP)** basis, which is also referred to as a run-of-press basis, the ad may appear anywhere, on any page in the paper. A higher rate is charged for **preferred position,** in which the ad is placed in a specific section of the paper. **Full position** places an ad near the top of a page or in the middle of editorial material. Exhibit 15.10 shows how a full-position ad looks in a newspaper.

Measuring Newspaper Audiences. There are several different dimensions to measuring newspaper audiences. The reach of a newspaper is reported as the newspaper's circulation. **Circulation** is the number of newspapers distributed each day (for daily newspapers) or each week (for weekly publications). **Paid circulation** reports the number of copies sold through subscriptions and newsstand distribution. **Controlled circulation** refers to the number of copies of the newspaper that are given away free. The Audit Bureau of Circulations (ABC) is an independent organization that verifies the actual circulation of newspapers.

Rates for newspaper advertising are not based solely on circulation numbers, however. The Newspaper Association of America estimates that 2.28 people read each copy of a daily newspaper distributed in the United States. **Readership** of a newspaper is a measure of the circulation multiplied by the number of readers of a copy. This number, of course, is much higher than the circulation number and provides a total audience figure on which advertisers base advertising rates. To give you some idea of costs, a full-page four-color ad in *USA Today* costs about $90,000, and a full-page black-and-white ad in the *Wall Street Journal* costs about $160,000.[9] A full-page ad in your local newspaper is, of course, considerably less—probably around $10,000 to $15,000. Remember, though, that few advertisers, national or local, purchase an entire page.

The Future of Newspapers. At the outset of this chapter, we talked about the fact that newspaper circulation has been in a long, sustained downward trend, and that readership is following the same pattern. To survive as a viable advertising medium, newspapers will have to evolve with the demands of both audiences and advertisers, who provide them with the majority of their revenue. One research study indicates that to compete in the future as a viable advertising medium, newspapers will have to do the following:

• Continue to provide in-depth coverage of issues that focus on the local community
• Increase coverage of national and international news
• Provide follow-up reports of news stories

9.   Rate information taken from Todd Purzan, "Global Media: Distribution Slows but Rates Climb," *Advertising Age International,* January 16, 1995, I-19.

- Maintain and expand their role as the best local source for consumers to find specific information on advertised product features, availability, and prices
- Provide the option of shopping through an online newspaper computer service[10]

Magazines as an Advertising Medium

② The marketing director for Schwinn Cycling & Fitness wanted to resurrect the company's bicycle division. Schwinn had been pummeled by worthy competitors like Trek and Specialized over the past decade, and he felt certain one of the underlying problems was that the image of the brand was outdated. To begin solving this image problem, the marketing director first instructed the firm's advertising agency to develop a $10 million magazine campaign. One of Schwinn's ads from this campaign is shown in Exhibit 15.11. The ads were placed in specialty biking magazines and aimed at mountain-biking and race-biking enthusiasts. Schwinn integrated the magazine campaign with a broad promotional strategy that

EXHIBIT 15.10

A full-position ad appears near the top of the page in a newspaper or is surrounded by editorial content, like this ad for a furniture retailer.

10.   Ronald Redfern, "What Readers Want from Newspapers," *Advertising Age,* January 23, 1995, 25.

We fell. We got up. End of apology.

When you're bleeding like we were, there's only one tourniquet: Clean, wicked new product. Survey this aluminum s[9s1x].10. Every millimeter is concepted and Ride-Tuned in Boulder. This is THE all-purpose ride. 4 times stiffer standing than seated. Single pivot sealed bearing means no stop and no creaks. Hey, it's Schwinn's 100th birthday. In bike years, you know what that means? Puberty, man. THE SECOND CENTURY.

EXHIBIT 15.11

Schwinn Cycling & Fitness relied on magazine ads like this one to upgrade its brand image and regain lost market share from Trek and Specialized.
www.schwinn.com

included event sponsorship and interactive mall kiosks. While Schwinn is still a distant third in the U.S. bike market, sales were up 18.4 percent in 1994.

Schwinn's emphasis on magazine advertising as part of its effort to upgrade the brand image was an excellent strategic decision. Magazines, more than any other media option, provide advertisers with a choice of highly selective alternatives that offer a wide variety of formats and contexts. The top ten magazines in the United States, based on revenue, are listed in Exhibit 15.12. This list suggests the diversity of magazines as a media class. Exhibit 15.13 shows the top ten advertisers in magazines.

Like newspapers, magazines have advantages and disadvantages, come in different types, offer various ad costs and buying procedures, and measure their audiences in specific ways. We will consider these issues now.

Advantages of Magazines. Magazines have many advantages relative to newspapers. These advantages make them more than just an ideal print medium—many analysts conclude that magazines are, in many ways, superior to even broadcast media alternatives.

- *Audience selectivity.* The overwhelming advantage of magazines relative to other media —print or broadcast—is the ability of magazines to attract, and therefore target, a highly selective audience. This selectivity can be based on demographics *(Woman's Day),* lifestyle *(Muscle & Fitness),* or special interests *(Mountain Biking)* as shown in Exhibit 15.14. The audience segment can be narrowly defined, as is the one that reads *Modern Bride,* or it may cut across a variety of interests, as does the one for *Newsweek.* Magazines also offer geographic selectivity on a regional basis, as does *Southern Living* or the city magazines like *Atlanta,* which highlight happenings in major metropolitan areas. Also, large national publications have multiple editions for advertisers to choose from. *Better Homes & Gardens* has 85 different specific market editions, and *Time* offers advertisers a different edition for each of the 50 states.

EXHIBIT 15.12

Top ten magazines by gross revenue, 1995.

Magazine	Total Revenue ($ in millions)	Ad Revenue ($ in millions)	Paid Circulation
TV Guide	$1,068,832	$406,945	13,175,549
People	801,153	437,663	3,321,198
Sports Illustrated	697,381	435,710	3,157,303
Time	672,626	404,462	4,083,105
Reader's Digest	529,742	186,588	15,103,830
Parade	515,591	515,591	37,268,000
Newsweek	480,535	331,853	3,155,155
Better Homes & Gardens	406,573	274,445	7,603,207
PC Magazine	391,341	331,072	1,107,187
Good Housekeeping	339,000	238,675	5,372,786

Source: *Advertising Age*, June 17, 1996, S-2. Reprinted with permission from the June 17, 1996, issue of *Advertising Age*. Copyright © Crain Communications Inc. 1996.

EXHIBIT 15.13

Top ten magazine advertisers.

Rank	Advertiser	Magazine Ad Spending ($ in millions)		
		1995	1994	% Change
1	General Motors Corp.	$412.0	$379.5	9.0
2	Philip Morris Cos.	373.8	294.0	27.1
3	Ford Motor Co.	254.3	241.9	5.1
4	Procter & Gamble Co.	251.5	197.3	28.0
5	Chrysler Corp.	231.1	148.9	55.2
6	Toyota Motor Corp.	121.1	128.2	–5.5
7	Time Warner	119.9	110.1	8.9
8	Unilever	109.5	113.4	–3.5
9	IBM	109.2	60.4	80.7
10	L'oreal	98.4	125.4	–21.5

Source: *Advertising Age*, September 30, 1996, 32. Reprinted with permission from the September 30, 1996, issue of *Advertising Age*. Copyright © Crain Communications Inc. 1996.

- *Audience interest.* Perhaps more than any other medium, magazines attract an audience because of content. While television programming can attract audiences through interest as well, magazines have the additional advantage of voluntary exposure to the advertising. Golfers are interested in golf equipment like that shown in Exhibit 15.15 and advertised in *Golf Digest,* while auto enthusiasts find the accessory equipment in *Car and Driver* appealing.

- *Creative opportunities.* Magazines offer a wide range of creative opportunities. Because of the ability to vary the size of an ad, use color, use white space, and play off the special interests of the audience, magazines represent a favorable creative environment. Also, because the paper quality of most magazines is quite high, color reproduction can be outstanding—another creative opportunity. In an attempt to expand

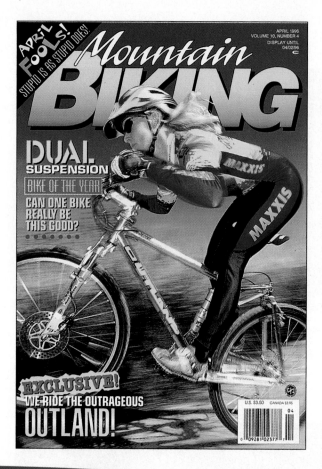

EXHIBIT 15.14

One distinct advantage of magazines over most other media options is the ability to attract and target a highly selective audience. Magazines like Mountain Biking *attract an audience based on special interests and activities.*

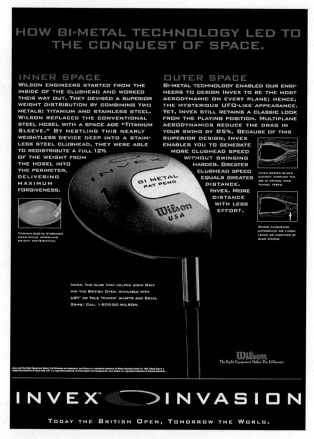

EXHIBIT 15.15 *Magazines can attract readers with specialized content, and in so doing, they attract advertisers. This ad by Wilson appeared in* Golf Digest.

the creative environment even further, some advertisers have tried various other creative techniques: pop-up ads, scratch-and-sniff ads, ads with perfume scent strips, and even ads with small computer chips that have flashing lights and play music. The ad in Exhibit 15.16 takes advantage of the creative opportunities offered by magazines.

- *Long life.* Many magazines are saved issue-to-issue by their subscribers. This means that, unlike newspapers, a magazine can be reexamined over a week or a month. Some magazines are saved for long periods for future reference, such as *Architectural Digest, National Geographic,* and *Travel & Leisure.* In addition to multiple subscriber exposure, this long life increases the chance of pass-along readership as people visit the subscriber's home (or professional offices) and look at magazines.

As opposed to newspapers, many magazines are realizing solid revenue and readership gains. Publications like *Sports Illustrated, Entertainment Weekly,* and *Parenting* have realized revenue gains in the 40 percent range. Overall, major magazines tracked by the Publishers' Information Bureau showed gains of 5.3 percent in ad pages and 10.9 percent in overall revenue.[11] Despite this growing popularity among advertisers, magazines are not without limitations.

11.   Patrick M. Reilly, "Magazine Firms Celebrate Ad-Page Gains," *Wall Street Journal,* October 24, 1994, B5; and Keith Kelly, "Magazines' Ad Pages Hit New Heights in '94," *Advertising Age,* January 25, 1995, 14.

EXHIBIT 15.16

Magazines offer unique creative opportunities to advertisers. Perfume marketers, like Clarins, include scent strips in their magazine ads for consumers to sample.

Disadvantages of Magazines. The disadvantages of magazines as a media choice have to do with their being too selective in their reach and with the recent proliferation of magazines.

- *Limited reach and frequency.* The tremendous advantage of selectivity discussed in the previous section actually creates a limitation for magazines. The more narrowly defined the interest group, the less overall reach a magazine will have. Since most magazines are published monthly or perhaps every two weeks, there is little chance for an advertiser to achieve frequent exposure using a single magazine. To overcome this limitation, advertisers often use several magazines targeted at the same audience. For example, many readers of *Better Homes & Gardens* may also be readers of *Architectural Digest.* By placing ads in both publications, an advertiser can increase both reach and frequency within a targeted audience.
- *Clutter.* Magazines are not as cluttered as newspapers, but they still represent a fairly difficult context for message delivery. The average magazine is about half editorial and entertainment content and half advertising material, but some highly specialized magazines contain as much as 80 percent advertising.[12] And this advertising, given the narrowly defined audiences, tends to be for brands in direct competition with each other. In addition to this clutter, there is another sort of clutter that has recently begun to plague magazines. As soon as a new market segment is recognized, there is a flood of "me-too" magazines. This may be good in terms of coverage, but it may devalue individual ads and the vehicles in which they appear. As an example, by mid-1995 there were 30 magazines aimed at Generation X, the highly sought-after segment of young adults. With names like *Blaster* and *Subnation,* these Gen X publications have circulations from less than 1,000 to about 350,000.[13]
- *Long lead times.* Advertisers are required to submit their ads as much as 90 days in advance of the date of publication. If the submission date is missed, there can be as much as a full month delay in placing the next ad. And once an ad is submitted, it cannot be changed during that 90-day period, even if some significant event alters the communications environment.
- *Cost.* While the cost per contact in magazines is not nearly as high as in some media (direct mail in particular), it is more expensive than most newspaper space, and many times the cost per contact in the broadcast media. The absolute cost for a single insertion can be prohibitive. For magazines with large circulation, like *Modern Maturity* and *Good Housekeeping,* the cost for a one-time four-color ad runs from $100,000 to about $250,000.

Types of Magazines. The magazine medium is highly fragmented, with more than 12,000 magazine titles published annually in the United States and literally hundreds of titles introduced every year. A useful classification scheme for magazines is to categorize them by major target audience: consumer, business, and farm publications.

12. Thomas R. King, "Bride's Magazine Takes Cake in Ad Clutter," *Wall Street Journal,* January 4, 1990, B8.
13. Todd Pruzan, "Advertisers Wary of Generation X Titles," *Advertising Age,* October 24, 1994, S-22.

- *Consumer publications.* Magazines that appeal to consumer interests run the gamut from international news to sports, education, age-group information, and hobbies. These include magazines written specifically for men *(Men's Journal),* women *(Woman's Day),* and ethnic groups *(Ebony).* Many new consumer magazines appeal to the lifestyle changes of the 1980s and 1990s: *New Woman, Men's Health.* Advertisers invested $8.5 billion in advertising in consumer magazines in 1994.[14] The top five magazines in this category are listed in Exhibit 15.17.
- *Business publications.* Business magazines come in many different forms. Each major industry has a trade publication, like *InfoWorld* in the computer industry, which highlights events and issues in that industry. Professional publications are written for doctors, lawyers, accountants, and other professional groups. *American Family Physician* publishes articles for family practitioners and carries advertising from many pharmaceutical manufacturers. General-interest business magazines like *Fortune* and *Forbes* cut across all trades, industries, and professions. The leading business magazine categories are listed in Exhibit 15.18.
- *Farm publications.* The three major farm publications in the United States and their approximate circulations are *Farm Journal* (800,000), *Successful Farming* (570,000), and *Progressive Farmer* (490,000). These magazines provide technical information about farming techniques as well as business management articles to improve farmers' profitability. In addition to national publications, there are regional farm magazines and publications that focus on specific aspects of the industry.

EXHIBIT 15.17

Top five consumer magazine categories, ranked by revenue, 1995.

Magazine Category	Total Revenue ($ in millions)	Ad Revenue ($ in millions)	Paid Circulation	Top Magazine in Classification
Newsweeklies	$ 4,321.5	$2,394.7	31,696,107	*TV Guide*
Women's	3,039.7	1,714.6	57,169,271	*Good Housekeeping*
General editorial	2,974.5	1,543.7	108,345,555	*Reader's Digest*
Home service and home	1,533.6	873.0	33,329,396	*Better Homes & Gardens*
Business and finance	1,182.3	909.2	6,730,712	*Business Week*

Source: *Advertising Age,* June 17, 1996, S-10. Reprinted with permission from the June 17, 1996, issue of *Advertising Age.* Copyright © Crain Communications Inc. 1996.

EXHIBIT 15.18

Top five business magazine categories, ranked by revenue, 1995.

Magazine Category	Total Revenue ($ in millions)	Ad Revenue ($ in millions)	Paid Circulation	Top Magazine in Classification
Computers	$2,276.0	$1,996.3	7,533,113	*PC Magazine*
Electronic engineering	200.9	200.9	0	*Electronic Engineering Times*
Travel, retail	174.0	172.7	49,737	*Travel Weekly*
Business	171.9	98.9	1,139,273	*Barron's*
Medical and surgical	95.8	63.3	633,293	*NE Journal of Medicine*

Source: *Advertising Age,* June 17, 1996, S-10. Reprinted with permission from the June 17, 1996, issue of *Advertising Age.* Copyright © Crain Communications Inc. 1996.

14. Kelly, "Magazines' Ad Pages Hit New Heights in '94."

Costs and Buying Procedures for Magazine Advertising.

The cost for magazine space varies dramatically. As with newspapers, the size of an ad, its position in a publication, its creative execution (black-and-white or color or any special techniques), and its placement in a regular or special edition of the magazine all affect costs. The main cost, of course, is based on the magazine's circulation. A full-page four-color ad in *Reader's Digest* costs $150,000; a full-page four-color ad in *People* costs about $106,000; a full-page ad in *Skiing* costs about $25,000; and a full-page ad in *Surreal,* a Gen X magazine with a paid circulation of 3,000, is only $500.

Each magazine has a rate card that shows the cost for full-page, half-page, two-column, one-column, and half-column ads. A rate card also shows the cost for black-and-white, two-color, and four-color ads. Rate cards for magazines, as with newspapers, have been the standard pricing method for many years. In recent years, however, more and more publishers have been willing to negotiate rates and give deep discounts for volume purchases—discounts as large as 20 to 30 percent off the published card rate.[15] The rate card in Exhibit 15.19 shows the kind of discount advertisers can get for volume purchases.

In addition to standard rates, there is an extra charge for a **bleed page.** On a bleed page, the background color of an ad runs to the edge of the page, replacing the standard white border. **Gatefold ads,** or ads that fold out of a magazine to display an extra-wide advertisement, also carry an extra charge. Gatefolds are often used by advertisers on the inside cover of upscale magazines. Nearly every issue of *Fortune* magazine begins with a gatefold ad, like the IBM ThinkPad 760 ad in Exhibit 15.20.

When buying space in a magazine, advertisers must decide among several placement options. A **run-of-press** advertisement can appear anywhere in the magazine, at the discretion of the publisher. The advertiser may pay for several preferred positions, however. **First cover page** is the front cover of a magazine; **second cover page** is the inside front cover; **third cover page** is the inside back cover; and **fourth cover page** is the back cover. When advertisers prepare **double-page spreads**—advertisements that bridge two facing pages—it is important that no headlines or body copy run through the gutter, which is the fold between the magazine pages.

Buying procedures for magazine advertising demand that an advertiser follow several guidelines and honor several key dates. A **space contract** establishes a rate for all advertising placed in a publication by an advertiser over a specified period. A **space order,** also referred to as an insertion order, is a commitment by an advertiser to advertising

---

Advertisers can earn large-volume discounts when they buy multiple insertions. Notice that when advertisers buy space in Marketing News, *a trade publication, the cost for eight insertions of a ½-page horizontal ad is about 12.5 percent less per insertion.*

Marketing News General Advertising Rates

	1x	4x	8x	14x	20x	26x	40x
Full Page	$2615	$2355	$2290	$2220	$2155	$2090	$1960
Full Spread	$4925	$4430	$4310	$4185	$4065	$3940	$3695
Pony Page	$2125	$1910	$1860	$1805	$1755	$1700	$1595
Pony Spread	$4050	$3645	$3545	$3440	$3340	$3240	$3040
4/7 Page (vert.)	$1950	$1755	$1705	$1655	$1610	$1560	$1460
1/2 Page (horiz.)	$1750	$1575	$1530	$1485	$1445	$1400	$1310
3/7 Page	$1570	$1415	$1375	$1335	$1295	$1255	$1175
2/5 Page	$1465	$1320	$1280	$1245	$1210	$1170	$1100
2/7 Page	$1090	$980	$955	$925	$900	$870	$815
1/4 Page	$985	$885	$860	$835	$815	$790	$740
1/5 Page	$775	$695	$680	$660	$640	$620	$580
1/7 Page	$545	$490	$475	$465	$450	$435	$410
1/10 Page	$415	$375	$365	$355	$345	$335	$310
1/14 Page	$305	$275	$265	$260	$250	$245	$230
Ads smaller than 5 col. in.	$90/col. in.	$80	$78	$76	$74	$72	$68

---

15.   Lisa I. Fried, "New Rules Liven Up the Rate-Card Game," *Advertising Age,* October 24, 1994, S-8.

EXHIBIT 15.20

This IBM gatefold ad attracts attention by its placement, size, and color. What do these characteristics say about the product and company to the target audience? Go to the IBM Web site **www.ibm.com/**. *Does any option or feature at the IBM Web site act like this? Compare this approach to the features of Compaq Computer's new line of notebook computers at* **www.compaq.com/**. *How are these Web-based ads similar to or different from the gatefold?*

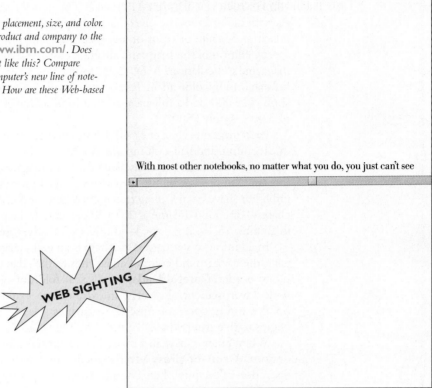

With most other notebooks, no matter what you do, you just can't see

space in a particular issue. It is accompanied by production specifications for the ad or ads that will appear in the issue. The dates that an advertiser must be aware of are as follows:

- **Closing date:** The date when production-ready advertising materials must be delivered to a publisher for an ad to make an issue.
- **On-sale date:** The date on which a magazine is issued to subscribers and for newsstand distribution. Most magazines put issues on sale far in advance of the cover date.
- **Cover date:** The date of publication appearing on a magazine.

Measuring Magazine Audiences. Most magazines base their published advertising rates on **guaranteed circulation,** which is a stated minimum number of copies of a particular issue that will be delivered to readers. This number guarantees for advertisers that they are achieving a certain, minimum reach with an ad placement. In addition, publishers estimate **pass-along readership,** which is an additional number of people, other than the original readers, who may see a publication. Advertisers can verify circulation through the Audit Bureau of Circulations, which reports total and state-by-state circulation for magazines, as well as subscriber versus newsstand circulation. When an advertiser wants to go beyond basic circulation numbers, the syndicated magazine research services like Simmons Market Research Bureau and Mediamark Research can provide additional information. Through the use of personal interviews and respondent-kept diaries, these services provide advertisers with information on reader demographics, media use, and product usage.

The Future of Magazines. Magazines have had a roller-coaster history over the past 10 to 15 years. Currently, revenues and ad pages are up, and advertisers are finding the advantages of magazines well suited to their current needs. Magazines will, like other media options,

have to determine how to adapt to new media options. More than 200 magazines now offer online versions with computer services like America Online, CompuServe, and Prodigy. Examples are discussed in the New Media box on page 427. To date, these digizines have attracted minimal ad spending. Some analysts feel that for online advertising to be successful, it must be unintrusive. Such ads will have to be interactive, educational, or entertaining.[16] Until online magazine publication proves viable, advertisers are likely to stay with traditional formats.

Broadcast Media Evaluation

When you say the word "advertising," the average person thinks of *television* advertising. It's easy to understand why. Television advertising can be advertising at its very best. With the full benefit of sight and sound, color and music, action and special effects, television advertising can be the most powerful advertising of all. It has some other advantages as well. In many parts of the world, particularly in the United States, television is the medium most widely used by consumers for entertainment and information.

Advertisers readily appreciate the power of television advertising and invest billions of dollars a year in the medium. Television has broad reach and crosses all demographic, socioeconomic, and ethnic lines. But television is not the only medium capable of broadly disseminating a message. Radio has, in some ways, even greater power for widely disseminating an advertiser's message.

16. Scott Donaton, "New Creative Tools Give Online Titles Hope for Bolstering Ad Revenues," *Advertising Age*, October 24, 1994, S-18.

This section of the chapter will describe the nature of the television and radio broadcast media. First, we will look at the options available to advertisers. Next, as with the print media, we'll consider the inherent advantages and disadvantages of the broadcast media. Finally, each evaluation concludes with a discussion of buying procedures and techniques for audience measurement.

Television as an Advertising Medium

3 To many, television is the medium that defines what advertising is. With its multisensory stimulation, television offers the chance for advertising to be all that it can be. Television presents two extraordinary opportunities to advertisers. First, the breadth of communication possibilities allows for outstanding creative expression of a brand's value. Dramatic color, sweeping action, and spectacular sound effects can cast a brand in an exciting and outstanding light. Second, once this expressive presentation of a brand is prepared, it can be disseminated to millions of consumers, often at a fraction of a penny per contact.

These opportunities have not been lost on advertisers. In the United States in 1995, advertisers invested more than $31 billion in television advertising for media time alone—this does not include the many billions of dollars spent on production costs. And advertisers are finding television more and more to their liking. The $31 billion was a full 6 percent increase over the prior year's spending.[17] To fully appreciate all that television means to advertisers, we need to understand much more about this complex medium.

Television Categories. Without careful evaluation, the natural tendency is to classify television as a single type of broadcast medium. When we turn on the television, we simply decide what program we find interesting and then settle in for some entertainment. The reality is that over the past 15 to 20 years, several distinct versions of television have evolved, from which consumers can choose for entertainment and advertisers can choose for reaching those consumers. There are four different alternatives: network, cable, syndicated, and local television. Exhibit 15.21 shows the spending in these television categories for 1994 and 1995.

Notice that while all the options showed solid growth in advertising receipts, the fastest growth was in cable television. Let's examine the nature of each of these four options for television advertising.

- *Network television.* **Network television** broadcasts programming over airwaves to affiliate stations across the United States under a contract agreement. Advertisers can buy time within these programs to reach audiences in hundreds of markets. There are currently four major broadcast television networks in the United States: Disney/ABC (ABC), Columbia Broadcasting System (CBS), Fox Network (FOX) and National Broadcasting Company (NBC). Two additional competitors in network television have only recently begun to broadcast. WB, a new network financed by

EXHIBIT 15.21

Spending by advertisers in the four television categories.

	Total Measured Advertising Spending ($ in millions)		
	1995	1994	% Change
Local TV	$13,338.6	$12,718.8	3.3
Network TV	12,402.2	11,893.2	8.5
Cable TV	3,418.8	2,970.2	14.0
Syndicated TV	2,316.8	2,358.1	8.5

Source: "The Top 200 Brands," *Advertising Age*, May 6, 1996, 34. Reprinted with permission from the May 6, 1996, issue of *Advertising Age*. Copyright © Crain Communications Inc. 1996.

17. R. Craig Endicott, "Top 200 Brands," *Advertising Age,* May 6, 1996, 34.

NEW MEDIA

DIGIZINES: DON'T LOOK FOR ONE WHILE YOU WAIT FOR THE DENTIST

Blender. Trouble & Attitude. Launch. Sound like names for the latest, hippest magazines? They are. But don't look for one the next time you go to the dentist. These new magazines can be found only in cyberspace. In fact, they are so hip, they're not even called magazines— they've been dubbed digizines. These three digizines, along with dozens of others, are published only online or on CD-ROM. Several publishers with good ideas for new magazines are skipping the cost, risk, and clutter of the newsstand and going straight to cyberspace.

While content and advertising look a bit like that in a traditional magazine, a digizine is not confined by traditional print media rules. Michael Rogers, executive producer of broadband products for the *Washington Post,* says, "There are no preconceptions on the part of the audience. They're not going to expect things to be in the electronic magazine that are in the print magazine and then be disappointed." The opportunities and capabilities of cyberspace make this digizine option a truly new medium.

The rush to electronic magazine publishing was more like a crawl in 1993. A few big-name publications with lots of brand awareness and loyal readers were put online first by America Online. Publications like *Time* and *Car and Driver* offered a low-risk way for consumers to venture into cyberspace. But the lukewarm response to such trusted publications opened the door to a swarm of newcomers. In addition to *Blender, Trouble & Attitude,* and *Launch*—aimed primarily at Gen X'ers— humor, music, business, and men's magazines are being published or planned for online or CD-ROM distribution. Their ranks include titles like *Urban Desires, Word, Melvin, Nautilus,* and *eGG (electronic Gourmet Guide).*

Attracting advertisers will, of course, be a key to the success of digizines. Most online publications charge by the megabyte, although some seem to be dreaming up space charges just to see where the cost limits for advertisers might be. Rates range from $500 per megabyte for an audio trade digizine called *Control,* to $2,500 per meg for *Launch,* which guarantees advertisers a circulation of 150,000 discs priced at $8.95 and distributed through music and software retailers. *Launch* has been the most successful digizine at attracting mainline advertisers. The first issue included ads by Reebok, Dewar's Scotch, Cadbury, Schweppes, Warner Brothers, and Levi Strauss. *Launch* uses a cityscape internal design throughout the disc that allows readers to access ads in interesting and entertaining ways. For example, the Dewar's ads can be accessed by clicking on billboards in the city. The reader can enter a movie theater to view a trailer for Warner Brothers' *Batman Forever.*

The brightest future for digizines may actually lie with the pioneers like *Launch.* As one digizine publisher put it, "We don't look anything like a print magazine. A print magazine couldn't do what we're doing. You have to find something compelling for the consumer. *Newsweek Interactive* is just not compelling."

Source: Scott Donaton, "Not Your Father's Magazine," *Advertising Age,* April 10, 1995, 18, 20.

Time Warner, started with 50 affiliate stations and four programs on Wednesday nights. The network estimates it will reach about 80 percent of U.S. households. The other new network is United Paramount Network (UPN), which began broadcasting in January of 1995 with only five shows over two nights of programming. Exhibit 15.22 displays the top ten network television advertisers.

- *Cable television.* From its modest beginnings as community antenna television (CATV) in the 1940s, cable television has grown into a worldwide communications force. **Cable television** transmits a wide range of programming to subscribers through wires rather than over airwaves. In the United States, more than 60 million households (65 percent of all U.S. households) are wired for cable reception and receive on average more than 30 channels of sports, entertainment, news, music video, and home-shopping programming. Cable's power as an advertising option has grown enormously over the past decade. During 1994, cable's share of prime-time ratings in the United States had risen to 30 percent of the viewing audience—an 18 percent increase over the previous year.[18] Exhibit 15.23 shows the global reach of the largest cable networks.[19] Cable now reaches hundreds of millions of viewers worldwide, making it a truly global medium for multinational firms to reach their audiences.

- *Syndicated television.* Television syndication is either original programming or programming that first appeared on network television. It is then rebroadcast on either network or cable stations. Syndicated programs provide advertisers with proven programming that typically attracts a well-defined, if not enormous,

18.   "Ratings Race," *Advertising Age,* May 1, 1995, 35.
19.   "Cable Penetration Reaches 65% of All Television Homes," *Advertising Age,* February 22, 1993, C-4.

Top ten network TV advertisers.

Rank	Advertiser	Network TV Ad Spending ($ in millions)		
		1995	1994	% Change
1	Procter & Gamble Co.	$684.3	$680.9	–5.8
2	General Motors Corp.	500.9	509.4	–1.0
3	Philip Morris Cos.	475.3	424.3	13.3
4	Johnson & Johnson	388.6	297.6	30.6
5	PepsiCo	362.1	349.6	3.6
6	Ford Motor Co.	360.3	349.0	3.2
7	McDonald's Corp.	322.4	227.5	41.7
8	Kellogg Co.	271.7	270.2	0.6
9	Chrysler Corp.	239.7	207.5	15.5
10	Unilever	232.6	213.8	8.8

Source: *Advertising Age*, September 30, 1996, 38. Reprinted with permission from the September 30, 1996, issue of *Advertising Age*. Copyright © Crain Communications Inc. 1996.

audience. There are several types of television syndication. **Off-network syndication** refers to programs that were previously run in network prime time. Some of the most popular off-network syndicated shows are *M*A*S*H* and *The Cosby Show*. **First-run syndication** refers to programs developed specifically for sale to individual stations. The most famous first-run syndication show is *Star Trek: The Next Generation*. **Barter syndication** takes both off-network and first-run syndication shows and offers them free or at a reduced rate to local television stations, with some national advertising presold within the programs. Local stations can then sell the remainder of the time to generate revenues. This option allows national advertisers to participate in the national syndication market conveniently. Some of the most widely recognized barter syndication shows are *Jeopardy* and *Wheel of Fortune*.

- *Local television.* **Local television** is the programming other than the network broadcast that independent stations and network affiliates offer local audiences. Completely independent stations broadcast old movies, sitcoms, or children's programming. Network affiliates get about 90 hours of programming a week from the major networks, but they are free to broadcast other programming beyond that provided by the network. News, movies, syndicated programs, and community interest programs typically round out the local television fare.

As you can see, while all television looks the same to the average consumer, advertisers actually have four distinct options to consider. Regardless of which type of television transmission advertisers choose, television offers distinct advantages to advertisers as a way to communicate with target audiences.

Advantages of Television. Throughout the book, we have referred to the unique capability of television as an advertising medium. There must be some very good reasons why advertisers like AT&T, General Motors, and Procter & Gamble invest hundreds of millions of dollars annually in television advertising. The specific advantages of this medium are as follows:

- *Creative opportunities.* The overriding advantage of television compared to other media is, of course, the ability to send a message using both sight and sound. With recent advances in transmission and reception equipment, households now have brilliantly clear visuals and stereo-enhanced audio to further increase the impact of television advertising. In addition, special effects perfected for films like *Mask* are now making their way into advertising prepared for television.

EXHIBIT 15.23

Cable television's global reach.

Cable Network	Sample Regions	Reach (millions of homes)	Programming
MTV	North America	59.4	Music television
	Europe	61.0	
	Latin America	3.0	
	Brazil	7.5	
CNN	North America	69.5	News/information
	Europe	66.9	
	South Asia	6.5	
	Far East	4.2	
TNT/Cartoon Network	North America	71.5	Entertainment
	Europe	22.3	
	Latin America	6.1	
ESPN	North America	81.0	Sports
	Europe	58.2	
	Asia	8.0	
	Latin America	4.5	
Discovery Channel	North America	67.1	Education/entertainment
	Europe	8.6	
	Latin America	5.0	
	Asia	2.8	

Source: Elena Bowes, "Culture Gap in Tykes' TV Slows Regional Expansion," *Advertising Age*, March 20, 1995, 1-18. Reprinted with permission from the March 20, 1995, issue of *Advertising Age*. Copyright © Crain Communications Inc. 1995.

- *Coverage, reach, and repetition.* Television, in one form or another, reaches more than 98 percent of all households in the United States—an estimated 250 million people. These households represent every demographic, economic, and ethnic segment in the United States, which allows advertisers to achieve broad coverage. We have also seen that the cable television option provides reach to hundreds of millions of households throughout the world. Further, no other medium allows an advertiser to repeat a message as frequently as television.
- *Cost per contact.* For advertisers that sell to broadly defined mass markets, television offers a cost-effective way to reach millions of members of a target audience. The average prime-time television program reaches 11 million households, and top-rated shows can reach more than 20 million households. This brings an advertiser's cost-per-contact figure down to an amount unmatched by any other media option.[20]
- *Audience selectivity.* Television programmers are doing a better job of developing shows that attract well-defined target audiences. **Narrowcasting** is the development and delivery of specialized programming to well-defined audiences. Cable television is far and away the most selective of the television options. Cable provides not only well-defined programming, but also entire networks—like MTV and ESPN—built around the concept of attracting selective audiences.

Disadvantages of Television. Television has great capabilities as an advertising medium, but it is not without limitations. Some of these limitations are serious enough to significantly detract from the power of television advertising.

20.   Patricia Sellers, "The Best Way to Reach Buyers," *Fortune*, Autumn/Winter 1993, 14–17.

- *Fleeting message.* One problem with the sight and sound of a television advertisement is that it is gone in an instant. The fleeting nature of a television message, as opposed to a print ad (which a receiver can contemplate), makes message impact difficult. Some advertisers invest huge amounts of money in the production of television ads to overcome this disadvantage.

- *High absolute cost.* While the cost per contact of television advertising is the best of all media, the absolute cost may be the worst. The average cost of airtime for a single 30-second television spot during prime time is just over $100,000. The average cost of producing a 30-second television spot is around $200,000. These costs make television advertising prohibitively expensive for many advertisers. Of course, large, national, consumer products companies—for which television advertising is best suited anyway—find the absolute cost acceptable for the coverage, reach, and repetition advantages discussed earlier.

- *Poor geographic selectivity.* While programming can be developed to attract specific audiences, program transmission cannot target geographic areas nearly as well. For a national advertiser that wants to target a city market, the reach of a television broadcast is too broad. Similarly, for a local retailer that wants to use television for reaching local segments, the television transmission is likely to reach a several-hundred-mile radius—which will increase the advertiser's cost with little likelihood of drawing patrons.

- *Poor audience attitude and attentiveness.* Since the inception of television advertising, consumers have bemoaned the intrusive nature of the commercials. Just when a movie is reaching its thrilling conclusion—on come the ads. The involuntary and frequent intrusion of advertisements on television has made television advertising the most distrusted form of advertising among consumers.[21]

  Along with—and perhaps as a result of—this generally bad attitude toward television advertising, consumers have developed ways of avoiding exposure. Making a trip to the refrigerator or conversing with fellow viewers are the preferred low-tech ways to avoid exposure. On the high-tech side, **channel grazing,** or using a remote control to monitor programming on other channels while an advertisement is being broadcast, is the favorite way to avoid commercials. When programs have been videotaped for later viewing, zapping and zipping are common avoidance techniques. **Zapping** is the process of eliminating ads altogether from videotaped programs. **Zipping** is the process of fast-forwarding through advertisements contained in videotaped programs.

- *Clutter.* All the advantages of television as an advertising medium have created one significant disadvantage: clutter. The major television networks run about 13 minutes of advertising during each hour of prime-time programming, and cable broadcasts carry about 17 minutes of advertising per hour.[22] Aside from the sheer number of intrusive minutes of advertising, these minutes are jammed with messages. In 1980, 96 percent of all television ads were 30 seconds in length. In 1992, only 63 percent of all ads were 30 seconds long, and 32 percent were the newer 15-second ads.[23] This has significantly increased the number of messages audiences are exposed to, and it has caused a much more cluttered environment for communication and persuasion.

Buying Procedures for Television Advertising. Discussions in Chapters 13 and 14 as well as in this chapter have identified the costs associated with television advertising from both a production and a space standpoint. Here we will concentrate on the issue of buying time on television. Advertisers buy time for television advertising through sponsorship, participation, and spot advertising.

- *Sponsorship.* In a **sponsorship** arrangement, an advertiser agrees to pay for the production of a television program and for most (and often all) of the advertising that

21.   Ernest F. Larkin, "Consumer Perceptions of Media and Their Advertising Content," *Journal of Advertising* 8 (1979): 5–7.
22.   Kevin Goldman, "TV Promotional Clutter Irks Ad Industry," *Wall Street Journal,* February 11, 1994, B6.
23.   Wayne Walley, "Popularity of :15s Falls," *Advertising Age,* January 14, 1994, 41.

appears in the program. Sponsorship is not nearly as popular today as it was in the early days of network television. Contemporary sponsorship agreements have attracted big-name companies like AT&T and IBM, who often sponsor sporting events, and Hallmark, known for its sponsorship of dramatic series.

- *Participation.* The vast majority of advertising time is purchased on a participation basis. **Participation** means that several different advertisers buy commercial time during a specific television program. No single advertiser has a responsibility for the production of the program or a commitment to the program beyond the time contracted for.
- *Spot advertising.* **Spot advertising** refers to all television advertising time purchased from and aired through local television stations. Spot advertising provides national advertisers the opportunity to either adjust advertising messages for different markets or intensify their media schedules in particularly competitive markets. Spot advertising is the primary manner in which local advertisers, like car dealers, furniture stores, and restaurants, reach their target audiences with television.

A final issue with respect to buying television advertising has to do with the time periods and programs during which the advertising will run. Once an advertiser has determined that sponsorship, participation, or spot advertising (or, more likely, some combination of the last two) meets its needs, the time periods and specific programs must be chosen. Exhibit 15.24 shows the way in which television programming times are broken into **dayparts** that represent segments of time during a television broadcast day.

The dayparts are important to advertisers because the size and type of audience varies by daypart. Morning audiences tend to be predominantly made up of women and children. The daytime daypart is dominated by women. Prime time has the largest and most diverse audiences. Once dayparts have been evaluated, specific programs within dayparts are chosen. As we have discussed, programs are developed and targeted to specific audiences, and advertisers match their ad buying to the program audience profiles. Let's turn our attention to these television audience issues.

Measuring Television Audiences. Television audience measurements identify the size and composition of audiences for different television programming. Advertisers choose where to buy time in television broadcasts based on these factors. These measures also set the cost for television time. The larger the audience or the more attractive the composition, the more costly the time will be.

The only source for *both* network and local audience information is A. C. Nielsen. Arbitron is another source for network measurement, but it abandoned local measurement in 1993.

The following are brief summaries of the information used to measure television audiences.

- *Television households.* **Television households** is an estimate of the number of households that are in a market and own a television. Since more than 98 percent of all households in the United States own a television, the number of total households and

EXHIBIT 15.24

Television broadcast day-parts (in eastern time zone segments).

Morning	7:00 A.M. to 9:00 A.M., Monday through Friday
Daytime	9:00 A.M. to 4:30 P.M., Monday through Friday
Early fringe	4:30 P.M. to 7:30 P.M., Monday through Friday
Prime-time access	7:30 P.M. to 8:00 P.M., Sunday through Saturday
Prime time	8:00 P.M. to 11:00 P.M., Monday through Saturday 7:00 P.M. to 11:00 P.M., Sunday
Late news	11:00 P.M. to 11:30 P.M., Monday through Friday
Late fringe	11:30 P.M. to 1:00 A.M., Monday through Friday

the number of television households is virtually the same, at about 95.9 million. Markets around the world do not have the same level of television penetration.

- *Households using television.* **Households using television (HUT),** also referred to as sets in use, is a measure of the number of households tuned to a television program during a particular time period.
- *Program rating.* A **program rating** is the percentage of television households that are in a market and are tuned to a specific program during a specific time period. Expressed as a formula, program rating is

$$\text{program rating} = \frac{\text{TV households tuned to a program}}{\text{total TV households in the market}}$$

A **ratings point** indicates that 1 percent of all the television households in an area were tuned to the program measured. If an episode of *Seinfeld* is watched by 19.5 million households, then the program rating would be calculated as follows:

$$\textit{Seinfeld} \text{ rating} = \frac{19{,}500{,}000}{95{,}900{,}000} = 20 \text{ rating}$$

The program rating is the best known of the television audience measures, and it is the basis for the rates television stations charge for advertising on different programs. Recall that it is also the way advertisers develop their media plans from the standpoint of calculating reach and frequency estimates, like gross rating points.

- *Share of audience.* **Share of audience** provides a measure of the proportion of households that are using television during a specific time period and are tuned to a particular program. If 65 million households are using their televisions during the *Seinfeld* time slot, the share of audience measure is:

$$\textit{Seinfeld} \text{ share} = \frac{\text{TV households tuned to a program}}{\text{total TV households using TV}} = \frac{19{,}500{,}000}{65{,}000{,}000} = 30 \text{ share}$$

The Future of Television. The future of television is exciting for two reasons. First, the emerging interactive era will undoubtedly affect television as an advertising medium. Prospects include viewer participation in mystery programs and game shows in which household viewers play right along with studio contestants. While this interactivity is intriguing, there are varying opinions about how popular it might be. Early experiments with interactivity have been met with a less than enthusiastic response from consumers.[24]

The other major change that will affect the future of television is emerging transmission technology. **Direct broadcast satellite (DBS)** is a program delivery system whereby television (and radio) programs are sent directly from a satellite to homes equipped with small receiving dishes. This transmission offers the prospect of hundreds of different channels. While advertisers will still be able to insert advertising in programs, the role of networks and cable stations in the advertising process will change dramatically.

While it is hard to predict what the future will hold, one thing seems sure—television will continue to grow as an entertainment and information medium for households. The convenience, low cost, and diversity of programming make television an ideal medium for consumers. Additionally, as detailed in the Global Issues box on page 435, television's expansion around the world will generate access to huge new markets. Television, despite its limitations, will continue to be an important part of the integrated communications mix of many advertisers.

---

24. William M. Buckeley and John R. Wilke, "Can the Exalted Vision Become a Reality? Early Attempts Show Viewers May Be Leery," *Wall Street Journal*, October 14, 1993, B1.

Radio as an Advertising Medium

4 Radio may seem the least glamorous and most inconspicuous of the major media. This perception does not jibe with reality. Radio plays an integral role in the media plans of some of the most astute advertisers. Because of the unique features of radio, advertisers invested $10.7 billion in the medium in 1994.[25] There are good reasons why retailers turn to radio as a means to reach their target audiences. Let's turn our attention to the different radio options available to advertisers.

Radio Categories. Radio offers an advertiser several options for reaching target audiences. The basic split of national and local radio broadcasts presents an obvious, geographic choice. More specifically, though, advertisers can choose among the following categories, each with specific characteristics: networks, syndication, and AM versus FM.

- *Networks.* **Radio networks** operate much like television networks in that they deliver programming via satellite to affiliate stations across the United States. Network radio programming concentrates on news, sports, business reports, and short features. Some of the more successful radio networks that draw large audiences are ABC, CNN, and AP News Network.
- *Syndication.* **Radio syndication** provides complete programs to stations on a contract basis. Large syndicators offer stations complete 24-hour-a-day programming packages that totally relieve a station of any programming effort. Aside from full-day programming, they also supply individual programs, like talk shows. Large syndication organizations like Westwood One and Satellite Music Network place advertising within programming, making syndication a good outlet for advertisers.
- *AM versus FM.* AM radio stations send signals that use amplitude modulation (AM) and operate on the AM radio dial at signal designations 540 to 1600. AM was the foundation of radio until the 1970s. Today, AM radio broadcasts, even the new stereo AM transmissions, cannot match the sound quality of FM. Thus, most AM stations focus on local community broadcasting or news and talk formats that do not require high-quality audio. Indeed, as described in the Contemporary Issues box on page 437, talk radio has been the salvation of AM radio. FM radio stations transmit using frequency modulation (FM). FM radio transmission is of a much higher quality. Because of this, FM radio has attracted the wide range of music formats that most listeners prefer.

Types of Radio Advertising. Advertisers have three basic choices in radio advertising: local spot radio advertising, network radio advertising, or national spot radio advertising. Spot radio advertising attracts 80 percent of all radio advertising dollars in a year—about $9.5 billion. In **local spot radio advertising,** an advertiser places advertisements directly with individual stations rather than with a network or syndicate. Spot radio dominates the three classes of radio advertising because there are more than 9,000 individual radio stations in the United States, giving advertisers a wide range of choices. And, spot radio reaches well-defined geographic audiences, making it the ideal choice for local retailers.

Network radio advertising is advertising placed within national network programs. Since there are few network radio programs being broadcast, only about $600 million a year is invested by advertisers in this format.

The last option, **national spot radio advertising,** offers an advertiser the opportunity to place advertising in nationally syndicated radio programming. The leading national spot radio advertisers are listed in Exhibit 15.25. An advertiser can reach millions of listeners by contracting with Westwood One for *Casey Kasem's Top 40 Countdown,* which is carried by thousands of stations across the United States. National spot radio advertising accounted for about $1.2 billion in radio revenues in 1994.[26]

25.   Michael Wilke, "Y&R's New Buying Plan Jolts Radio," *Advertising Age,* May 1, 1995, 28.
26.   Ibid.

EXHIBIT 15.25

Top ten national spot radio advertisers.

Advertiser	National Spot Radio Ad Spending, 1995 ($ in millions)
News Corp.	$30.8
AT&T Corp.	25.3
Montgomery Ward & Co.	21.3
General Motors	20.9
Walt Disney	20.3
MCI Communications Corp.	18.8
US West	18.5
CompUSA	18.0
7-Eleven	16.9
Tandy Corp.	16.4

Source: *Advertising Age*, September 30, 1996, 47. Reprinted with permission from the September 30, 1996, issue of *Advertising Age*. Copyright © Crain Communications Inc. 1996.

Advantages of Radio. While radio may not be the most glamorous or sophisticated of the major media options, it has some distinct advantages over newspapers, magazines, and television.

- *Cost.* From both a cost-per-contact and absolute-cost basis, radio is often the most cost effective medium available to an advertiser. A full minute of network radio time can cost between $5,000 and $10,000—an amazing bargain compared to the other media we've discussed. In addition, production costs for preparing radio ads are quite low; an ad often costs nothing to prepare if the spot is read live during a local broadcast.
- *Reach and frequency.* Radio has the widest exposure of any medium. It reaches consumers in their homes, cars, offices, and backyards, and even while they exercise. The wireless and portable features of radio provide an opportunity to reach consumers that exceeds all other media. The low cost of radio time gives advertisers the opportunity to frequently repeat messages affordably.
- *Target audience selectivity.* Radio can selectively target audiences on a geographic, demographic, and psychographic basis. The narrow transmission of local radio stations gives advertisers the best opportunity to reach narrowly defined geographic audiences. For a local merchant with one store, this is an ideal opportunity. Radio programming formats and different dayparts also allow target audience selectivity. CBS Radio recently converted 4 of 13 stations to a rock 'n' roll oldies format to target 35-to-49-year-olds—in other words, the baby boomers.[27] Hard rock, new age, easy-listening, country, classical, and talk radio formats all attract different audiences. Radio dayparts, shown in Exhibit 15.26, also attract different audiences. Morning and afternoon/evening drive times attract a male audience. Daytime attracts predominantly women, and nighttime, teens.

EXHIBIT 15.26

Radio dayparts.

Morning drive time	6:00 A.M. to 10:00 A.M.
Daytime	10:00 A.M. to 3:00 P.M.
Afternoon/evening drive time	3:00 P.M. to 7:00 P.M.
Nighttime	7:00 P.M. to 12:00 A.M.
Late night	12:00 A.M. to 6:00 A.M.

27.   Kevin Goldman, "CBS Radio Retunes to Music of the '70s," *Wall Street Journal,* December 30, 1993, B5.

GLOBAL ISSUES

GAINING A GLOBAL FOOTHOLD: MUSIC AND NEWS TELEVISION WORLDWIDE

MTV took the first step in 1986, selling a few hours of programming to Japan's Asahi network. Now, MTV is available as a television channel on every continent in the world. Deregulation in countries that once had only government-controlled television stations has made global expansion possible.

MTV was the first, but is by no means the only, U.S. network striving for global reach. Disney/ABC has investments in the Scandinavian Broadcasting System, which operates four stations in Norway, Sweden, and Denmark, and additional investments in Eurosport, a European cable sports network. In 1993, NBC acquired the Super Channel, with broadcast reach to 35 countries and nearly 100 million viewers. Other NBC ventures include Canal de Noticias NBC, a 24-hour Spanish-language news service that reaches Latin America and Spain.

Most recently, fierce competition has erupted among the worldwide media giants in launching news channels in Europe. The players are Turner Broadcasting's CNN International, the first and leading news channel in Europe; Dow Jones and Tele-Communications' 24-hour business news channel called European Business News; British Broadcasting Corporation and Cox Communications' BBC World, a 24-hour news and current events channel; British Sky Broadcasting and Reuters Holdings' Sky News, providing international news coverage; and NBC Super Channel's CNBC Money Wheel, a 4-hour live news show. At stake is the dominant position in one of the most lucrative global markets. Currently, 75 million European households have cable or satellite service, and the market is poised for major expansion. The winner of this scramble will likely become the dominant provider of programming for Europe's information superhighway.

Markets like China and India are, of course, a high priority for U.S. broadcasters. In 1987, there were only 30 million Chinese households with televisions; now there are more than 200 million. Turner Broadcasting is paying $1.5 million to the state broadcasting system to get an early and dominant position in the fledgling Indian cable television market. Over the next ten years, international deals will account for the bulk of market development for networks like MTV, CNN, Nickelodeon, and CNBC. In a mature domestic market with limited opportunities for growth, U.S. broadcasters relish the thought of an emerging global market with an estimated 1.2 billion television households.

While the prospects are great, not everyone thinks this global expansion by U.S. networks will work. Some believe that there will be a nationalistic backlash to outside ownership of television resources. As one analyst put it, "Americans are going to lose tons of money. People want to watch programming in their own language, about their own countries." In response, the manager of one of the ventures said simply, "We fully understand the magnitude of the challenge."

Sources: Paula Dwyer and Gail Edmondson, "CNN Copycats Get Set for a Catfight," *Business Week*, March 6, 1995; Lynn Elber, "U.S. TV Networks Expand Interests Overseas," *Marketing News*, November 11, 1994; and Sally D. Goll, "Turner Accord to Boost Reach of CNN in India," *Wall Street Journal*, July 3, 1995.

- *Flexibility and timeliness.* Radio is the most flexible medium because of very short closing periods for submitting an ad. This means an advertiser can wait until close to an air date before submitting an ad. With this flexibility, advertisers can take advantage of special events or unique competitive opportunities in a timely fashion.
  - *Creative opportunities.* While radio may be unidimensional in sensory stimulation, it can still have powerful creative impact. Recall that radio has been described as the theater of the mind. Ads like the folksy tales of Tom Bodett for Motel 6 or the eccentric humor of Stan Freberg are memorable and can have tremendous impact on the attitude toward a brand. In addition, the musical formats that attract audiences to radio stations can also attract attention to radio ads. Audiences that favor certain music may be more prone to an ad that uses recognizable, popular songs.[28]

Disadvantages of Radio.

As good as radio can be, it also suffers from some severe limitations as an advertising medium. Advertising strategists must recognize these disadvantages when deciding what role radio can play in an integrated marketing communications program.

- *Poor audience attentiveness.* Just because radio reaches audiences almost everywhere doesn't mean that anyone is paying attention. Remember that radio has also been described as verbal wallpaper. It provides a comfortable background distraction while a consumer does something else—hardly an ideal level of attentiveness for advertising communication. When a consumer is listening

28.   Kevin Goldman, "Hot Songs Are Wooing Younger Ears," *Wall Street Journal*, January 2, 1993, B1.

and traveling in a car, she or he often switches stations when an ad comes on and divides her or his attention between the radio and the road.

- *Creative limitations.* While the theater of the mind may be a wonderful creative opportunity, taking advantage of that opportunity can be difficult, indeed. The audio-only nature of radio communication is a tremendous creative compromise. An advertiser whose product depends on demonstration or visual impact is at a loss when it comes to radio. And like its television counterpart, a radio message creates a fleeting impression that is often gone in an instant.

- *Fragmented audiences.* The large number of stations that try to attract the same audience in a market has created tremendous fragmentation. Think about your own local radio market. There are probably four or five different stations that play the kind of music you like. Or, consider that in the past few years, more than 1,000 radio stations in the United States have adopted the talk radio format. This fragmentation means that the percentage of listeners tuned to any one station is likely very small.

- *Chaotic buying procedures.* For an advertiser that wants to include radio as part of a national advertising program, the buying process can be sheer chaos. Since national networks and syndicated broadcasts do not reach every geographic market, an advertiser has to buy time in individual markets on a station-by-station basis. This could involve dozens of different negotiations and individual contracts.

Buying Procedures for Radio Advertising. While buying procedures to achieve national coverage may be chaotic, this does not mean they are completely without structure. Although the actual buying may be time-consuming and expensive if many stations are involved, the structure is actually quite straightforward. Advertising time can be purchased from networks, syndications, or local radio stations. Recall that among these options, advertisers invest most heavily in local placement. About 80 percent of annual radio advertising is placed locally. About 15 percent is allocated to national spot placement, and only 5 percent is invested in network broadcasts.

The other factor in buying radio time relates to the time period of purchase. Refer again to Exhibit 15.26. This shows the five basic daypart segments from which an advertiser can choose. The time period decision is based primarily on a demographic description of the advertiser's target audience. Recall that drive-time dayparts attract a mostly male audience, while daytime is primarily female, and nighttime is mostly teen. This information, combined with programming formats, guides an advertiser in a buying decision.

As with magazine buying, radio advertising time is purchased from rate cards issued by individual stations. Run-of-station ads—ads that the station chooses when to run—cost less than ads scheduled during a specific daypart. The price can also increase if an advertiser wants the ad read live on the air by a popular local radio personality hosting a show during a daypart.

The actual process of buying radio time is relatively simple. A media planner identifies the stations and the dayparts that will reach the target audience. Then the rates and daypart availabilities are checked to be sure they match the media-planning objectives. At this point, agreements are made regarding the number of spots to run in specified time frames.

Measuring Radio Audiences. There are two primary sources of information on radio audiences. Arbitron ratings cover 260 local radio markets. The ratings are developed through the use of diaries maintained by listeners who record when they listened to the radio and to what station they were tuned. The *Arbitron Ratings/Radio* book gives audience estimates by time period and selected demographic characteristics. Several specific measures are compiled from the Arbitron diaries:

- **Average quarter-hour persons:** The average number of listeners tuned to a station during a specified 15-minute segment of a daypart.

CONTEMPORARY ISSUES

THE RUSH TO TALK RADIO

In the colorful and storied history of radio, there has never been anything like talk radio. And the reason there has never been anything like talk radio is because there has never been anyone like Rush Limbaugh. As one beneficiary of Limbaugh's power over audiences put it, "If Rush Limbaugh says to try something, there are a lot of people who will try it." This is from the inventor of Breathe Right Nasal Strips, Daniel Cohen. When Limbaugh told his audience of 20 million to try the product, sales of Breathe Right went crazy—sales increased 470 percent.

Beyond host celebrities like Rush Limbaugh and Howard Stern, talk radio has a thriving life of its own. In reality, talk has saved AM radio from extinction. Since 1990, the number of radio stations that devote the bulk of their programming day to talk has almost tripled, from 405 to 1,130 stations. Almost 10 percent of adults over 18 listen to talk radio, and advertising revenues from this format industrywide reached $1.4 billion in 1994. Advertising on Limbaugh's show costs $10,000 a minute, and he generates $30 million in annual revenue for his syndicator, EFM Media.

The trade-off for advertisers, Rush or not, is that the talk can be too hot. National advertisers like IBM, Maxwell House Coffee, and Snapple advertise on talk radio—but very carefully. They will buy time sporadically or purchase time around the show. The reason for this gingerly buying behavior is that radical talk show hosts can create controversy that spills over to the advertiser's brand. When shock-jock Howard Stern offended most of the Hispanic community with disparaging remarks about the slain singer Selena, Gatorade ended up on a boycott list and had its products pulled from some store shelves.

But the risks may be worth the payoff. Syndicated talk shows reach large, loyal audiences with well-defined demographic profiles—music to advertisers' ears. Perhaps more importantly, radio listeners are actively involved with the show. They phone in, offer their opinions, and almost never switch channels during a listening time period. This kind of involvement is usually achieved only with television. And, most important of all, talk radio listeners seem to be influenced by the advertising they hear. As Daniel Cohen says, "It's nice to pay for advertising you can count on."

Sources: Kelly Shermach, "Talk Radio Attracts Ads As Well As Listeners," *Marketing News*, January 30, 1995, 8; and Michael Oneal et al., "Everybody's Talkin' at Us," *Business Week*, May 22, 1995, 104–108.

- **Average quarter-hour share:** The percentage of the total radio audience that was listening to a radio station during a specified quarter-hour daypart.
- **Average quarter-hour rating:** The audience during a quarter-hour daypart expressed as a percentage of the population of the measurement area. This provides an estimate of the popularity of each station in an area.
- **Cume:** The cumulative audience, which is the total number of different people who listen to a station for at least five minutes in a quarter-hour period within a specified daypart. Cume is the best estimate of the reach of a station.

RADAR is the other major measure of radio audiences. Sponsored by the major radio networks, RADAR collects audience data twice a year based on interviews with radio listeners. Designated listeners are called daily for a one-week period and asked about their listening behavior. Estimates include measures of the overall audience for different network stations and audience estimates by market area. The results of the studies are reported in an annual publication, *Radio Usage and Network Radio Audiences*. Media planners can refer to published measures like Arbitron and RADAR to identify which stations will reach target audiences at what times across various markets.

SUMMARY

❶ Detail the advantages and disadvantages of newspapers as a media class, identify different types of newspapers, and describe buying and audience measurement for newspapers.

Newspaper types cluster into three categories, by target audience, geographic coverage, and frequency of publication. As a media class, newspapers provide an excellent means for reaching local audiences with informative advertising messages. Precise timing of message delivery can be achieved at modest expenditure levels. But for products that demand creative and colorful executions, this medium simply cannot deliver. Newspaper costs are typically transmitted via rate cards and are primarily a function of a paper's readership levels.

❷ Detail the advantages and disadvantages of magazines as a media class, identify different types of magazines, and describe buying and audience measurement for magazines.

Three important magazine types are consumer, business, and farm publications. Because of their specific editorial content, magazines can be effective in attracting distinctive groups of readers with common interests. Thus, magazines can be superb tools for reaching specific market segments. Also, magazines facilitate a wide range of creative executions. Of course, the selectivity advantage turns into a disadvantage for advertisers trying to achieve high reach levels. Costs of magazine ad space can vary dramatically because of the wide array of circulation levels achieved by different types of magazines.

❸ Detail the advantages and disadvantages of television as a media class, identify different types of television, and describe buying and audience measurement for television.

The four basic forms of television are network, cable, syndicated, and local television. Television's principal advantage is obvious: because it allows for almost limitless possibilities in creative execution, it can be an extraordinary tool for affecting consumers' perceptions of a brand. Also, it can be an efficient device for reaching huge audiences; however, the absolute costs for reaching these audiences can be staggering. Lack of audience interest and involvement certainly limit the effectiveness of commercials in this medium. The three ways that advertisers can buy time are through sponsorship, participation, and spot advertising. As with any medium, advertising rates will vary as a function of the size and composition of the audience that is watching.

❹ Detail the advantages and disadvantages of radio as a media class, identify different types of radio, and describe buying and audience measurement for radio.

Advertisers can choose from three basic types of radio advertising: local spot, network radio, or national spot advertising. Radio can be a cost-effective medium, and because of the wide diversity in radio programming, it can be an excellent tool for reaching well-defined audiences. Poor listener attentiveness is problematic with radio, and the audio-only format places obvious constraints on creative execution. Radio ad rates are driven by considerations like the average number of listeners tuned to a station at specific times throughout the day.

KEY TERMS

display advertising (414)
co-op advertising (414)
preprinted insert (415)
free-standing insert (FSI) (415)
classified advertising (415)
rate card (415)
column inch (415)
standard advertising unit (SAU) (415)
run-of-paper (ROP) (416)
preferred position (416)
full position (416)
circulation (416)
paid circulation (416)
controlled circulation (416)
readership (416)
bleed page (423)
gatefold ads (423)
run-of-press (423)
first cover page (423)
second cover page (423)

third cover page (423)
fourth cover page (423)
double-page spreads (423)
space contract (423)
space order (423)
closing date (424)
on-sale date (424)
cover date (424)
guaranteed circulation (424)
pass-along readership (424)
network television (426)
cable television (427)
off-network syndication (428)
first-run syndication (428)
barter syndication (428)
local television (428)
narrowcasting (429)
channel grazing (430)
zapping (430)
zipping (430)

sponsorship (430)
participation (431)
spot advertising (431)
dayparts (431)
television households (431)
households using television (HUT) (432)
program rating (432)
ratings point (432)
share of audience (432)
direct broadcast satellite (DBS) (432)
radio networks (433)
radio syndication (433)
local spot radio advertising (433)
network radio advertising (433)
national spot radio advertising (433)
average quarter-hour persons (436)
average quarter-hour share (437)
average quarter-hour rating (437)
cume (437)

QUESTIONS FOR REVIEW AND CRITICAL THINKING

1. Magazines certainly proved to be the right media class for selling Absolut vodka. Why are magazines a natural choice for vodka advertisements? What has Absolut done with its advertising to take full advantage of this medium?

2. Reach and frequency can be perceived as conflicting goals in media planning. Evaluate each of the four major media classes discussed in this chapter in terms of how well they would serve reach versus frequency objectives.

3. Peruse several recent editions of your town's newspaper and select three examples of co-op advertising. What objectives do you believe the manufacturers and retailers are attempting to achieve in each of the three ads you've selected?

4. Place your local newspaper and an issue of your favorite magazine side by side and carefully review the content of each. From the standpoint of a prospective advertiser, which of the two publications has a more dramatic problem with clutter? Identify tactics being used by advertisers in each publication to break through the clutter and get their brands noticed.

5. The costs involved in preparing and placing ads in television programming like the Super Bowl broadcast can be simply incredible. How is it that advertisers like PepsiCo or Apple can justify the incredible costs that come with this media vehicle?

6. Think about the television viewing behavior you've observed in your household. Of the four means for avoiding TV-ad exposure discussed in this chapter, which have you observed in your household? What other avoidance tactics do your friends and family use?

7. The choice between print and broadcast media is often portrayed as a choice between high- and low-involvement media. What makes one medium inherently more involving than another? How will the characteristics of an ad's message affect the decision to employ an involving versus an uninvolving medium?

8. For an advertiser that seeks to achieve nationwide reach, can radio be a good buy? What frustrations are likely to be encountered in using radio for this purpose?

EXPERIENTIAL EXERCISE

Buy a weekday copy of your local daily newspaper. About what portion of the newspaper is devoted to advertising? What types of local advertisers are dominant? About how many national advertisers appear in the issue? Are there any two-color or four-color ads? Finally, describe the extent to which preprints or inserts are included in the paper.

USING THE INTERNET

The impact of ads placed in print media can depend on the editorial content and style of the publication within which the ad is placed. Visit the following newspaper and magazine sites and find one banner ad on each:

Boston Globe: www.boston.com

New York Times: www.nytimes.com

Pathfinder: www.pathfinder.com

U.S. News & World Report: www.usnews.com

Elle: www.ellemag.com

1. Evaluate the fit between the advertiser and Web publication. Does the style of the publication match the corporate image of the advertiser?

2. Give a general description for the type of people that would visit each publication's site. What type of people would be interested in what is being advertised? How similar are your descriptions?

3. Which banner ad had the most impact? How does the effectiveness of a banner ad depend on how long it takes the banner ad to appear on your screen and where the banner ad is positioned on the page?

Chapter 16

Media Evaluation:

Traditional and

Emerging Support

Media

After reading and thinking about this chapter, you will be able to do the following:

1 Describe the traditional support media and the role they can play in a media plan.

2 Explain the growing popularity of event sponsorship as another supportive component of a media plan.

3 Distinguish when and how the interactive, or new, media are best employed as advertising and marketing tools.

4 Discuss the challenges presented by the ever-increasing variety of media for achieving integrated marketing communications.

There have always been signs and billboards in sports stadiums. (See Exhibit 16.1.) By 1993, signage had become a pervasive aspect of professional sports. The accounting firm Ernst & Young reported in 1993 that there were an average of 77 signs in National Hockey League arenas, 59 in National Basketball Association arenas, 25 in Major League Baseball parks, and 23 in National Football League stadiums.[1] But in that year, the Detroit Tigers and Milwaukee Brewers set off a signage revolution at the baseball park.

In 1993 the Tigers and Brewers became the first teams to sell rotating billboard space behind home plate. This space has tremendous appeal to advertisers for one reason —it is always in view of the television camera that focuses from center field on the batter.[2] A sign picked up by a television camera can expose a brand name to the viewing audience at a fraction of the cost of traditional television ads, without the problems of channel surfing or zipping and zapping that accompany the typical commercial break. Additionally, since advertisers share the space on these rotating billboards over the course of a game, they become an affordable option for many different types of businesses. Fans soon saw traditional sports sponsors like Budweiser and Pizza Hut on this new signage option, along with the Metro Detroit Ford Dealers and Duraflame firelogs. The Tigers' and Brewers' home-plate signage proved to be an instant hit with advertisers of all types.

But not everyone was happy with these made-for-TV signs. Baseball purists complained that the signage damaged the appeal of the game, infielders complained that the baseball was hard to see coming out of the signage background, and advertisers began to worry that too many signs in the ballpark would create commercial overload in sign-infested stadiums.

What is one to do when reality becomes unbearable? Invent a new reality! In this case, that new reality involves the virtual billboard. Virtual billboards appear real to the viewer watching the game on television, but they are only an electronic mirage that does not contribute to the clutter problem in the ballpark.

In the future, advertisers will be able to choose from both real and virtual billboards in creating their media mix.[3] A fan watching the telecast at home won't be able to tell

EXHIBIT 16.1

Signage and advertiser slogans are standard fare at all professional sporting events. This example is from Fenway Park in Boston.

1.   John Helyar, "Signs Sprout at Sports Arenas as a Way to Get Cheap TV Ads," *Wall Street Journal,* March 8, 1994, B1.
2.   Ibid.
3.   Skip Wollenberg, "Virtual Ads to Hit Baseball," *Cincinnati Enquirer,* June 17, 1994, B8.

the difference. A computerized system will insert the signage in the television picture just where it would appear in the ballpark if it was real, and ballplayers will appear to walk in front of this signage from cyberspace on their way to the batter's box. Since the sign is just an electronic image, it can be changed easily from inning to inning, and different signs could be sent over cable to different households viewing the same game. Once these virtual delivery systems are perfected, the advertising options for ballparks, arenas, and all varieties of sports stadiums will become virtually limitless.

The virtual billboard example is a nice prelude to this chapter because it illustrates several of the chapter's basic themes. It makes the point that advertisers are constantly on the lookout for new, cost-effective ways to break through the clutter of competitors' advertisements to register their appeals with consumers. Of course, as soon as a new vehicle begins to deliver results, many will make it part of their media plans, and the clutter problem returns. This example also illustrates the interdependent nature of different media options, and in it we see the potential offered by new technologies for reshaping the advertising landscape of the future. Technological change can create new media options that may fundamentally alter the way advertising and marketing dollars are allocated. Integrating the new media options with traditional and established performers will be one of the great advertising challenges of the next decade.

Although print and broadcast media continue to draw the lion's share of advertising expenditures, many other options exist for communicating with consumers. This chapter will examine a set of options commonly referred to as support media. Traditional support media like signs and billboards have been around for many years. However, advertisers are constantly experimenting with new ways to get their messages into the marketplace, and we will also look at several options referred to as the emerging support media. As we have seen at the ballpark, technology dictates constant change. Deciding which new media bandwagon to jump on represents a real quandary for advertisers.

Traditional Support Media

① This section will discuss **traditional support media:** outdoor billboard advertising, transit and aerial advertising, specialty advertising, point-of-purchase advertising, and directory advertising. **Support media** are used to reinforce a message being delivered via some other media vehicle; hence the name *support media*. They can be especially productive when used to deliver a message near the time or place where consumers are actually contemplating product selections. Since these media can be tailored for local markets, they can have value to any organization that wants to reach consumers in a particular venue, neighborhood, or metropolitan area.

Outdoor Billboard Advertising

Billboards, posters, and outdoor signs are perhaps the oldest advertising form.[4] Posters first appeared in North America when they were used during the Revolutionary War to keep the civilian population informed about the war's status. In the 1800s they became a promotional tool, with circuses and politicians being among the first to adopt this new medium. With the onset of World War I, the U.S. government turned to posters and billboards to call for recruits, encourage the purchase of war bonds, and cultivate patriotism. Exhibits 16.2 and 16.3 show some of these early uses of outdoor advertising. By the 1920s outdoor advertising also enjoyed widespread commercial applications and, until the invention of television, was the medium of choice when an advertiser wanted to communicate with imagery.

While the rise of television stifled the growth of outdoor advertising, the federal highway system that was laid across the nation in the sixties pumped new life into billboards. The 40-foot-high burgers and pop bottles were inevitable, but throughout the seventies and eighties billboards became an outlet for great advertising innovation. One

---

4.   Ann Cooper, "All Aboards," *Adweek,* May 9, 1994, 3–10.

EXHIBIT 16.2

Advertising in the United States began with posters and billboards. Circuses were the early pioneers in this medium.

EXHIBIT 16.3 *Public service announcements also got their start in posters and billboards. Here we see an appeal to patriotism featuring the potent combination of the Boy Scouts and the U.S. government.* **www .publicdebt.treas.gov/sav/sav.htm**

exceptional example of using the medium to its fullest was a Nike campaign run in the mid-eighties featuring high-profile athletes, like Olympian Carl Lewis, performing their special artistry.[5] In the nineties the creative challenge posed by outdoor advertising is as it has always been—to grab attention and communicate with minimal verbiage and striking imagery, as do the billboards in Exhibits 16.4 and 16.5.

In excess of $1.5 billion was spent to deliver advertiser's messages on the 390,000 billboards in the United States in 1993.[6] Outdoor advertising offers several distinct advantages.[7] This medium provides an excellent means to achieve wide exposure of a message in specific local markets. Size is, of course, a powerful attraction of this medium, and when combined with special lighting and moving features, billboards can be captivating. Billboards also offer around-the-clock exposure for an advertiser's message and are well suited to showing off a brand's distinctive packaging or logo.

Billboards are especially effective when they reach passers by with a message that speaks to a need or desire that is immediately relevant. For example, British Airways runs a single billboard in Manhattan along the freeway to JFK and LaGuardia airports,

5.   Ibid.

6.   Kevin Goldman, "Spending on Billboards Is Rising; Video Tool Makes Buying Easier," *Wall Street Journal,* June 27, 1994, B6.

7.   Jack Z. Sissors and Lincoln Bumba, *Advertising Media Planning* (Lincolnwood, Ill.: NTC Business Books, 1993).

EXHIBIT 16.4

Minimal verbiage is one key to success with billboard advertising. This example easily satisfies the minimal-verbiage rule.

EXHIBIT 16.5

As with all media, creativity is a must in making effective use of billboards. Soaring above the clutter to grab the attention of passing motorists is the goal of this execution.

featuring a spectacular shot of its *Concorde* jet at takeoff.[8] The board simply reads "London Bridge" and provides a constant reminder that British Airways should be in one's consideration set when traveling to Europe from New York City. This strategic reinforcement of a brand's presence and relevance represents the best that outdoor advertising has to offer. Another example of the successful mating of brand presence and relevance is shown in Exhibit 16.6.

Billboards have their drawbacks. Long and complex messages simply make no sense on billboards; some experts suggest that billboard copy should be limited to no more than six words.[9] Also, the impact of billboards can vary dramatically depending on their location, and assessing locations is tedious and time-consuming. To assess locations, companies typically must send individuals to the site to see if the location is desirable.[10] This activity, known in the industry as **riding the boards,** can be a major investment of time and money. Moreover, the Institute of Outdoor Advertising rates billboards as expensive in comparison to several other media alternatives.[11] Considering that billboards are constrained to short messages, are often in the background, and are certainly not the primary focus of a driver's attention, their costs may be prohibitive for many advertisers.

Despite the costs, and the criticism by environmentalists that billboards represent a form of visual pollution, spending on outdoor advertising has increased every year since 1970 except for 1992, when revenues fell 4.3 percent.[12] Because of some important technological advances, the future looks secure for outdoor billboards. The first of these advances combines the videotaping of billboard sites and their surroundings with software from International Outdoor Systems of London.[13] This tool reduces the amount of time and money that executives must spend riding the boards, and it helps them design boards to fit in with the surroundings at a particular location. The software package not only allows advertisers to view billboard sites via videotape, but also

EXHIBIT 16.6

This sign uses the perfect slogan for a sports venue. Has there ever been a referee who didn't need glasses?

8.   Cooper.
9.   *Yellow Pages and the Media Mix* (Troy, Mich.: Yellow Pages Publishers Association, 1990).
10. Goldman, "Spending on Billboards Is Rising."
11. Sissors and Bumba.
12. Goldman, "Spending on Billboards Is Rising."
13. Ibid.

allows them to insert mock-ups of different billboard executions into the specific location pictured on their computer screen. This design tool and time-saving system should make outdoor advertising a more attractive option for many advertisers.

Perhaps even more important to the future of billboard advertising is the development of computer-aided production technology for board facings.[14] Until recently, billboard painting was a labor-intensive process that could take a crew of workers several days to complete, and quality control from board to board was always problematic. Now, thanks to computer graphics, board facings can be produced in unlimited quantities with complete quality control, which ensures consistent color from Providence to Portland. The advent of computer-directed painting brings magazine-quality reproduction to billboards in any market, making them a more effective medium and a more appealing alternative for diverse marketers.

Transit and Aerial Advertising

Transit advertising is a close cousin to billboard advertising, and in many instances it is used in tandem with billboards. The phrase **out-of-home media** is commonly used to refer to the combination of transit and billboard advertising. Transit ads appear as both interior and exterior displays on mass transit vehicles and at terminal and station platforms, as exemplified in Exhibit 16.7. Some cash-strapped cities and towns now even allow transit advertising on police cars, school buses, and garbage trucks.[15] As suggested by the Ethical Issues box on page 448, some of these new options make for tough choices.

Transit advertising can be valuable when an advertiser wishes to target adults who live and work in major metropolitan areas.[16] The medium reaches people as they travel to and from work, and because it taps into daily routines repeated week after week, transit advertising offers an excellent means for repetitive message exposure. In large metro areas such as New York—with its 200 miles of subways and 3 million subway riders—transit ads can reach large numbers of individuals in a cost-efficient manner.

When working with this medium, an advertiser may find it most appropriate to buy space on just those trains or bus lines that consistently haul persons from the demographic segment being targeted. This type of demographic matching of vehicle with target is always preferred as a means of deriving more value from limited ad budgets. Transit advertising can be appealing to local merchants because their message may reach a passenger as he or she is traveling to a store to shop. For some consumers, transit ads are the last medium they are exposed to before making their final product selection.

There are times when the particular advantages of transit advertising fit a marketer's communication objectives so perfectly that this medium will not be used merely as a support medium, but instead as the primary means for reaching customers. For example,

EXHIBIT 16.7

Transit advertising has much in common with billboard advertising. In this case we see a nice illustration of the six-word rule.

14.   Cyndee Miller, "Outdoor Gets a Makeover," *Marketing News,* April 10, 1995, 26.
15.   Douglas A. Blackmon, "New Ad Vehicles: Police Car, School Bus, Garbage Truck," *Wall Street Journal,* February 20, 1996, B1.
16.   Sissors and Bumba.

Donna Karan's DKNY line of clothing, accessories, and cosmetics has relied heavily on transit advertising to reach its target audience in Manhattan.[17] For starters, the firm bought out the ten-car subway train that runs under Lexington Avenue on Manhattan's East Side and filled it with sophisticated image ads for DKNY. Not coincidentally, this particular subway train runs under the Bloomingdale's store on 59th Street, where DKNY has a supershop featuring all the products in its extensive line. DKNY ads have also appeared on the shuttles from Times Square to Grand Central Terminal, and at subway stations in the city. For DKNY, extensive advertising on and under the streets of New York City reflects its general strategy of using unconventional locations to create awareness and distinctive imagery for the DKNY product line.

Transit advertising works best for building or maintaining brand awareness; as is the case with outdoor billboards, lengthy or complex messages simply cannot be worked into this medium. Also, transit ads can easily go unnoticed in the hustle and bustle of daily life. People traveling to and from work via a mass transit system are certainly one of the hardest audiences to engage with an advertising message. They can be bored, exhausted, absorbed by their thoughts about the day, or occupied by some other media. Given the static nature of a transit poster, breaking through to a harried commuter can be a tremendous challenge.

When an advertiser can't break through on the ground or under the ground, it may have to look skyward. **Aerial advertising** can involve airplanes pulling signs or banners, skywriting, or those majestic blimps. For several decades, Goodyear had blimps all to itself; however, in the early nineties, new blimp vendors came to the market with smaller, less-expensive blimps that made this medium surge in popularity with other advertisers.[18] Virgin Lightships now flies a fleet of small blimps that measure 70,000 cubic feet in size and can be rented for advertising purposes for around $200,000 per month. Not to be outdone, Airship International flies full-size blimps, about 235,000 cubic feet in size, which it promotes as offering 200 percent more usable ad space than the competition's mini-blimps.

Compared to other out-of-home media, blimps are expected to deliver better results because they are less widespread than transit posters and billboards. The Family

---

ETHICAL ISSUES

THE FOUR RS: READIN', 'RITIN', 'RITHMETIC, AND (AD) REVENUE

The El Paso County School District in Colorado Springs is going way beyond the traditional three Rs to help ensure an education for the 32,000 students in 53 district schools. They've added a fourth R to the program: revenue. Specifically, revenue generated from selling advertising space on the district's school bus fleet and in newsletters, calendars, and staff magazines. So far, 12 of the buses carry advertising, and other specialty ads have generated more than $100,000 in revenue—about half of which goes directly into district coffers. Advertisers include the local Burger King franchise, an electric utility, a 7-Up bottler, King Soopers Grocery Stores, a children's hair salon, and a day care provider. Some are spending up to $15,000 a year in various specialty media available from the district.

School administrators expected an outcry from a community already concerned about their children being media blitzed. What are the ethical issues surrounding the placement of commercial messages in and around a learning environment? Parents demanded an answer to this question. But when parents and community leaders found out that the revenue generated would help fund endangered programs like arts activities and sports, they were more understanding and supportive. Furthermore, most of the ads are targeted at adults who see the buses passing by or receive the school newsletter or events calendar. When ads are aimed at the students, like a Pepsi-Cola Bottling ad, the message encourages educational achievement by adding the phrase "Insure your tomorrow with good decisions today" to the standard Pepsi tag line.

Source: Tammy Parker, "Schools Learning New Ad Lessons," *Advertising Age*, February 13, 1995, 27.

---

17.   Fara Warner, "DKNY Takes Upscale Ads Underground," *Wall Street Journal*, October 6, 1994, B5.
18.   Fara Warner, "More Companies Turn to Skies as Medium to Promote Products," *Wall Street Journal*, January 5, 1995, B6.

Channel has been a frequent user of Virgin Lightships' mini-blimps over sporting events like the Daytona 500 car race. A recall study done after one such event showed that 70 percent of target consumers remembered The Family Channel as a result of the blimp flyovers.[19] Blimps carrying television cameras at sporting events also provide game coverage that can result in the blimp's sponsor getting several on-air mentions. This brand-name exposure comes at a small fraction of the cost of similar exposure through television advertising. With these kinds of benefits and a growing number of affordable options, turning skyward may be the answer for breaking through the clutter of ordinary earthbound advertising.

Specialty Advertising

No one can say for sure, but it is believed that modern-day specialty advertising came into being around 1840. An insurance salesperson in Auburn, New York, wanted local businesses to post information about his insurance offerings. When the owners declined to help, he bought calendars, attached the information he had wanted to post, and presented the wall calendars as gifts. The local business owners were pleased with the gift, hung the calendars in their stores, and the rest, as they say, is history.

The insurance salesperson's wall calendar illustrates the essence of all modern specialty advertising. **Specialty-advertising items** have three defining elements: (1) they contain the sponsor's logo and perhaps a related promotional message; (2) this logo and message appear on a useful or decorative item; and (3) the item is given freely, as a gift from the sponsor. This third element distinguishes specialty-advertising items from those referred to as premiums.[20] **Premiums** are items that feature the logo of a sponsor and that must be paid for through some means. For example, the next time you receive a "free" Batman glass with the purchase of a large Coke at McDonald's, you're taking home a premium.

Literally thousands of different items have been used for specialty-advertising purposes, but the majority of these fall into five broad categories: wearables, writing instruments, desk or office accessories, calendars, and glassware or ceramics.[21] Bumper stickers, coffee mugs, matchbooks, ashtrays, cups and glasses, buttons, decals, clocks, pens and pencils, kitchen magnets, balloons, litter bags, coin holders, note pads, rulers, and yardsticks are all examples of specialty-advertising items. Samples are shown in Exhibit 16.8.

Using such items to carry a brand name has several appealing aspects for organizations.[22] First, specialty-advertising items can be made available on a selective basis. Whether they are sent by direct mail, distributed only in a local trading area, or passed out by salespeople to target customers, the dispensing of these items can be carefully monitored. This ensures cost effectiveness and literally puts a message into the hands of prospective customers. Second, unlike other media options, specialty-advertising items can hang around for long periods of time. For example, a Friskies wall calendar will reinforce the virtues of Friskies cat food day in and day out

EXHIBIT 16.8

People like to receive gifts. This simple premise is a big part of the appeal of specialty-advertising items.

19. Ibid.
20. Dan S. Bagley, *Understanding Specialty Advertising* (Irving, Tex.: Specialty Advertising Association International, 1990).
21. Ibid.
22. Ibid.

for at least a year. Third, specialty advertising can help build goodwill. Young or old, people like to receive free gifts. When executed with good taste, specialty-advertising programs can generate the goodwill that is an important asset for any brand.

Specialty advertising shares the space limitation problems of many other support media. Coffee mugs, coin holders, and the like provide little space for detailing the virtues of a brand; relative to the vast array of information that people are exposed to on a daily basis, what can be said on the back of a matchbook is easily overlooked. In addition, the mind-boggling variety of items to choose from for specialty advertising makes selection complex and time-consuming. This decision must be made carefully, because associating a brand name with items that some might see as junk or trinkets always has the potential of backfiring by cheapening the brand's image.

Point-of-Purchase Advertising

From 1981 to 1994, marketers' annual expenditures on point-of-purchase (P-O-P) advertising rose from $5.1 to $17.0 billion per year.[23] Why this dramatic growth in expenditures on P-O-P advertising? First, consider that P-O-P is the only medium that places advertising, products, and a consumer together in the same place at the same time. Then, think about these results. Research conducted by the P-O-P Advertising Institute indicates that 66 percent of all product selections involve some final deliberation by consumers at the point of purchase. (Perhaps true, but consider the source.) Additionally, a joint study sponsored by Kmart and Procter & Gamble found that P-O-P advertising boosted the sales of coffee, paper towels, and toothpaste by 567 percent, 773 percent, and 119 percent, respectively.[24] With results like these, it is plain to see why P-O-P advertising is one of the fastest-growing categories in today's marketplace. Still, like any other form of promotion, most P-O-P is ignored.

P-O-P advertising can take many forms. In-store displays, banners, shelf signs, wall units, and floorstands are traditional and economical means of drawing attention to a brand in a retail setting. A corrugated cardboard dump bin and an attached header card featuring the brand logo or related product information can be produced for pennies per unit. When filled with a product and placed as a free-standing display in a retail outlet, sales gains follow. A typical P-O-P display is shown in Exhibit 16.9.

Technological developments may only add to the appeal of P-O-P options for the future. Interactive electronic displays, like on-shelf computers and stand-alone kiosks, remain expensive relative to traditional low-tech options, but as their costs come down, they are likely to see broad application. Warner-Lambert has shown good results from on-shelf computers placed in 600 Canadian drugstores.[25] At

EXHIBIT 16.9

Point-of-purchase advertising is meant to be at the right place at the right time. When these placement and timing objectives are met, P-O-P advertising can turn out to be a powerful sales stimulator.

23. Data cited in Lisa Z. Eccles, "P-O-P Scores with Marketers," *Advertising Age,* September 26, 1994, P1–P4; and Leah Haran, "Point of Purchase: Marketers Getting with the Program," *Advertising Age,* October 23, 1995, 33.
24. Ibid.
25. Lisa Z. Eccles, "Technology Gives P-O-P a New Look," *Advertising Age,* September 26, 1994, P6.

$250 per unit, these computers help consumers sort through the maze of over-the-counter cough, cold, and allergy remedies, leading them to select from Warner-Lambert brands like Actifed and Benadryl. In the United States, interactive kiosks provide a similar function in 2,900 pharmacies across the country, generating 33 million customer contacts in 1995.[26] Advances in the materials used to construct traditional displays, like new powder coatings that can give a cardboard display the look of chrome, zinc, or brass plating, will also keep the dollars flowing to P-O-P advertising.[27] Additional possibilities are featured in the New Media box on this page.

Directory Advertising

The last time you reached for a phone directory to appraise the local options for Chinese or Mexican food, you probably didn't think about it as a traditional support medium. However, yellow pages advertising plays an important role in the media mix for many types of organizations, as is evidenced by the $10.2 billion that was spent in this medium in 1995.[28]

A phone directory can play a unique and important role in consumers' decision-making processes. While most support media keep a brand name or key product information in front of a consumer, yellow pages advertising helps people follow through on their decision to buy. By providing the information that consumers need to actually find a particular product or service, the yellow pages can serve as the final link in a buying decision. Because of their availability and consumers' familiarity with this advertising tool, yellow pages directories provide an excellent means to support awareness-building and interest-generating campaigns that an advertiser might be pursuing through other media vehicles.

On the downside, the proliferation and fragmentation of phone directories can make this a difficult medium to work in.[29] Many metropolitan areas are covered by multiple directories, some of which are specialty directories designed to serve specific neighborhoods, or ethnic or interest groups. Selecting the right set of directories to get full coverage of large sections of the country can be a daunting task. Additionally, working in this medium requires

NEW MEDIA

P-O-P GOES H-I-G-H T-E-C-H

Traditionally, point-of-purchase displays have offered customers an easy-to-spot, attractive product display or featured a two-for-one offer or perhaps even dispensed a money-saving coupon. Well, P-O-P has leaped into the future with high-tech displays that not only make shopping more interesting for consumers, but also can generate valuable data for advertisers.

Everbrite of Greenfield, Wisconsin, has introduced a line of interactive P-O-P units that provide a variety of services to both consumers and marketers. One unit prints coupons, product use recommendations, and prescription drug information. The real power of this type of Everbrite unit lies in the fact that the display is linked to information sources by telephone lines. This means an advertiser can change or update the unit's output daily to provide unique and timely information to consumers.

Another high-tech P-O-P unit can link together as many as 30 microcomputers. A host PC supplies the entire network with a database containing product information and graphic displays. When a customer interacts with the computer (which looks like a video display unit), the printer is programmed to print a coupon for the specific product in which the consumer is interested.

These new P-O-P units can also be used to gather information *from* consumers. A Toyota dealership in San Diego ran a direct mail game. To find out if they won a prize, consumers had to visit the dealership and swipe the bar code of their game piece on a bar code reader P-O-P display. The display also asked consumers, now identified by name and zip code location, their impressions of various Toyota products and programs. These data then are fed into the dealership's database for future direct mail campaigns.

P-O-P displays are no longer the lifeless pyramid of products stacked at the end of an aisle. They can interact with consumers and gather data for advertisers to produce better-integrated promotional programs.

Source: Kelly Shermach, "Great Strides Made in P-O-P Technology," *Marketing News*, January 2, 1995.

26. Kelly Shermach, "New CD Products Show Times Are a Changin'," *Marketing News*, March 27, 1995, 11.
27. Lisa Z. Eccles, "Technology Gives P-O-P a New Look."
28. "Yellow Pages Revenues up 4.2 Percent in 1995," *Link*, March 1996, 5.
29. *Yellow Pages and the Media Mix*.

long lead times, and over the course of a year information in a yellow pages ad can easily become dated. There is also limited flexibility for creative execution in the traditional paper format.

Again, because of emerging technologies, the phone directory of the future may evolve into a form that allows advertisers considerably more room for creative execution. Regional Bell companies like Bell Atlantic and Nynex are developing interactive directory options that could one day contribute to a paperless society.[30] The Nynex approach is a joint venture with Prodigy. This system would allow consumers with personal computers to search for Chinese restaurants in Boston and retrieve current menu information online, along with photographs of the dining room and service staff.

Bell Atlantic is working with CD technology to deliver directory listings on television sets. The CD-based system can offer full-motion video and stereo sound, along with an interactive capability that could allow a customer to create a personalized map from home to the restaurant or retailer selected. In addition, many World Wide Web sites are building yellow page–style databases that allow for highly individualized searches. Exhibit 16.10 illustrates this alternative. Clearly, future-thinking marketers are preparing to travel the information superhighway to reach sophisticated consumers with information they want and can use.

Emerging Support Media: Event Sponsorship

When we add the traditional support media to the many options that exist in print and broadcast media, we have an incredible assortment of choices for delivering messages to a target audience. And it doesn't stop there. As you have seen, marketers and advertisers are constantly searching for new, cost-effective ways to break through the clutter and reach consumers. Important developments in information technologies will only accelerate this search for new options as the traditional mass media undergo profound changes.

Consider the fragmentation taking place in television. In the 1960s the three major TV networks had a 100 percent share of the viewing audience, so an advertiser could

EXHIBIT 16.10

The World Wide Web has tremendous potential for changing the way information gets disseminated. The Virtual Yellow Pages is one of many possibilities. **www.vyp.com/**

30.   Leslie Cauley, "Nynex and Prodigy Team Up on Yellow Pages That Will Provide On-Line Listings and Ads," *Wall Street Journal,* December 10, 1993, B1.

have easy access to large viewing audiences by sponsoring popular programs. In 1980 the three networks still attracted 87 percent of the viewing audience, but by 1990 their audience had slipped to 62 percent.[31] The culprit, of course, is cable television, with its growing list of options for the viewer. As we move closer and closer to the projected 500-channel television environment, the fragmentation of the television-viewing audience will only accelerate. As it does, advertisers will accelerate their search for new options to reach their potential customers.

In the remainder of this chapter we will examine several emerging ways to communicate with customers. Although they all are in use currently, it is appropriate to distinguish them as **emerging support media** because they all play a support role, and they all are likely to grow in their importance to advertisers. The first of these options will be familiar to you if you have ever gone to Florida for spring break, watched a college bowl game on New Year's Day, or attended a rock 'n' roll concert. This option is event sponsorship. The second option is often referred to generally as the new media and will also be familiar to you if you are an experienced Web surfer. Methods like advertising on the Internet may one day become major components in an advertising campaign.

Who's Using Event Sponsorship?

❷ Event sponsorship is a special and increasingly popular way to reach consumers. **Event sponsorship** involves a marketer providing financial support to help fund an event, like a rock concert or golf tournament (see Exhibit 16.11). In return, that marketer acquires the rights to display a brand name, logo, or advertising message on-site at the event. If the event is covered on TV, the marketer's brand and logo may also receive exposure with the television audience. In 1994 expenditures on event marketing exceeded $4 billion, with about two-thirds of this total coming from sports sponsorship.[32]

Event sponsorship can take many forms. The events can be international in scope, like the Olympics, or they may have a local flavor, like a chili cook-off in Amarillo, Texas. The events may have existed on their own, with marketers offering funding after the fact, or marketers may create an event they can sponsor, in hopes of engaging a segment of their customers. An example of a created event is described in the Contemporary Issues box on page 455. Events provide a captive audience, may receive live coverage by radio and television, and often are reported in the print media. Hence, event sponsorship can both yield face-to-face contact with real consumers and receive simultaneous and follow-up coverage in the mass media.

The list of companies participating in event sponsorships seems to grow with each passing year. Sears Roebuck, Levi Strauss, Anheuser-Busch, and a host of other companies have sponsored touring rock 'n' roll bands like the Spin Doctors, Boston, and the Rolling Stones. To capitalize on the growing popularity of women's NCAA college basketball, State Farm Insurance began hosting the Hall of

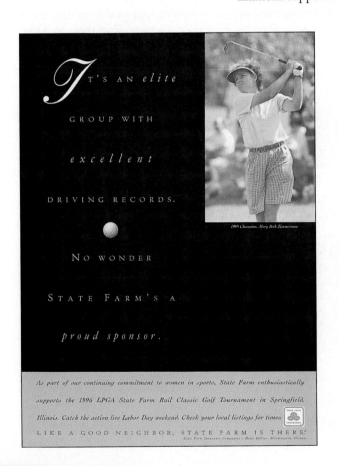

EXHIBIT 16.11

Sports sponsorship continues to grow in popularity as an advertising tool. Here, State Farm uses a clever play on words to validate its association with the LPGA. **www.statefarm.com/**

---

31.   Roland T. Rust and Richard W. Oliver, "The Death of Advertising," *Journal of Advertising* (December 1994): 71–77.
32.   William M. Bulkeley, "Sponsoring Sports Gains in Popularity; John Hancock Learns How to Play to Win," *Wall Street Journal*, June 24, 1994, B1.

Fame Tip-Off Classic in 1993.[33] If you have ever hit the beaches for spring break, you already know that companies like Coca-Cola and Chevrolet's Geo division will be there to greet you. In 1995 corporate sponsors like these spent $20 million trying to get their messages across to college students on the beach.[34] With the growing interest in stock-car racing and an expanded NASCAR circuit that includes races all over the United States, major brands like Canon, Tide, Gillette, Winston, McDonald's, and Kodak are scrambling for the privilege to spend $4 million a year to sponsor a car like the one shown in Exhibit 16.12.[35] Also in 1995, Stroh Brewery's Old Milwaukee brand landed the rights for 147 bass-fishing tournaments run by an organization named Operation Bass.[36] There can be little doubt that more marketers of all types will pursue event sponsorship in the future.

The Appeal of Event Sponsorship

In the early days of event sponsorship, it often wasn't clear what an organization was receiving in return for its sponsor's fee. Even today, many critics contend that sponsorship, especially of sporting events, can be ego-driven and thus a waste of money.[37] Company presidents are human, and they like to associate with sports stars and celebrities. This is fine, but when sponsorship of a golf tournament, for example, is motivated mainly by a CEO's desire to play in the same foursome as Jack Nicklaus or Michael Jordan, the company is really just throwing away advertising dollars.

One of the things fueling the growing interest in event sponsorship is that many companies now are finding ways to make a case for the effectiveness of their sponsorship dollars. Boston-based John Hancock Mutual Life Insurance has been a pioneer in

EXHIBIT 16.12

Automobile racing attracts big crowds with lots of purchasing power. Is it any surprise that advertisers want to be part of the action?

33.   Joan O'C. Hamilton, "The Hoopla over Women's Hoops," *Business Week,* April 10, 1995, 46.
34.   Bruce Horovitz, "Students Get Commercial Crash Course," *USA Today,* March 22, 1995, B1–B2.
35.   Chris Roush, "Red Necks, White Socks, and Blue-Chip Sponsors," *Business Week,* August 15, 1994, 74; and Alex Taylor III, "Can NASCAR Run in Bigger Circles?" *Fortune,* February 5, 1996, 38.
36.   "Marketers Push into New Venues Event-ually," *Advertising Age,* March 13, 1995, 1.
37.   Bulkeley.

developing detailed estimates of the advertising equivalencies of its sponsorships.[38] John Hancock began sponsoring a college football bowl game in 1986 and soon after had a means to judge the value of its sponsor's fee. Hancock employees scoured magazine and newspaper articles about their bowl game to determine name exposure in print media. Next they'd factor in the exact number of times that the John Hancock name was mentioned during television broadcast of the game, along with the name exposure in pregame promos. In 1991, Hancock executives estimated that they received the equivalent of $5.1 million in advertising exposure for their $1.6 million sponsorship fee. One John Hancock executive called this result "an extraordinarily efficient media buy."[39] As the television audience for the John Hancock bowl dwindled in subsequent years, however, Hancock's estimates of the bowl's value also plunged. By 1994, Hancock had moved its sports sponsorship dollars into other events, like the winter Olympics from Lillehammer, Norway.

Other research is also providing hard evidence for the value of sponsorship. Studies conducted with various types of sports fans by Performance Research of Newport, Rhode Island, indicate that fan loyalty can be converted to sales. Among stock-car racing fans, 70 percent say they frequently buy the products they see promoted at the race track. (Of course, they could have been purchasing those products prior to attending the event.) For baseball, tennis, and golf, these commitment levels run at 58 percent, 52 percent, and 47 percent, respectively.[40] These findings suggest that racing fans in particular have specific product preferences that advertisers can identify and appeal to, and explain why marketers are flocking to the race track to get their brand names on the hood of a stock car or on the cap of a stock-car driver.

Event sponsorship can also furnish a unique opportunity to foster brand loyalty with an event's devout attendees. When a marketer connects a brand with the potent emotional experiences often found at rock concerts, race tracks, and sport stadiums or

CONTEMPORARY ISSUES

CHEVY MEDIA EVENT TARGETS WOMEN

In an interesting twist on the concept of event sponsorship, the Chevrolet division of General Motors sponsored a four-day women-only press conference. Sixty journalists, editors, and publishers from automotive and women's publications across the United States were treated to seminars about GM's products and test drives in Chevy cars and trucks on mountain highways and specially prepared off-road courses. Of course, the event was well stocked with Chevy logo merchandise for journalists to take home.

The conference, called "Women of Influence," was the latest and most creative effort by Chevrolet to target women and convince them that its vehicles are made with a sensitivity toward women's automobile needs and desires. The event was part of an ongoing effort by Chevrolet to recognize the power of women in the auto market. Women spent $85 billion in 1995 buying 50 percent of all the new cars sold in the United States.

From a strategic standpoint, the event was well conceived. Chevrolet could use the event not only to introduce influential journalists to Chevrolet products, programs, and policies, but also to get important feedback—and sister, did they get feedback! Journalists argued that while there may be a commitment to women at the corporate level, dealers ignore the female segment. Critics at the conference suggested that Chevrolet dealers "have a targeted market that they're not taking advantage of. You've got the dealership, and then you've got the corporate organization. If it were up to the organization, there wouldn't be problems with women buying cars." Members of the Chevrolet team at the meeting generally agreed. Chuck Hip, regional marketing manager for Chevrolet, said, "It's a challenge. Dealers are trying to drive and stimulate traffic, but by not advertising to specific niches, they send the wrong message to consumers."

Chevrolet used this event to gain direct contact with influential journalists who can write about Chevy products and influence the female market, but they also gathered valuable insights from the women in attendance—members of the target market themselves. No word yet on whether there will be a second annual conference.

Source: Julie Ralston, "Chevy Targets Women," *Advertising Age*, August 7, 1995, 24.

38.   Michael J. McCarthy, "Keeping Careful Score on Sports Tie-Ins," *Wall Street Journal*, April 24, 1991, B1.
39.   Ibid.
40.   Roush.

on Fort Lauderdale beaches in mid-March, positive feelings may be attached to that brand. Likewise, the brand may serve as a lasting reminder that links an individual to a special experience. Additionally, since various types of events attract well-defined target audiences, marketers can choose to sponsor just those events that help them reach a desired target.

For instance, a who's who of the European brewing industry lines up to sponsor professional soccer teams like Britain's Chelsea football club. Brewers such as Bass PLC and Carlsberg AS want to reach beer-drinking soccer fans in hopes that the fans will become as loyal to their beers as they are to their favorite soccer team. This union of beer sponsors, soccer clubs, and emotional, unruly fans has created a backlash in countries such as France, who now ban club sponsorship by alcohol companies. Other brewers have made the decision to avoid the rowdy image of European soccer. Heineken, based in the Netherlands, has a multiyear deal with the International Tennis Federation both because its managers want the international exposure and because they believe that perceptions of tennis as a more civilized sport better match the refined image they want for Heineken.[41]

Seeking a Synergy around Event Sponsorship

As we have seen, one way to justify event sponsorship is to calculate the number of viewers who will be exposed to a brand either at the event or through media coverage of the event, and then assess whether the sponsorship provides a cost-effective way of reaching the target segment. This approach assesses sponsorship benefits in direct comparison with traditional advertising media. Some experts now maintain, however, that the benefits of sponsorship can be fundamentally different from anything that traditional media might provide. These additional benefits can take many forms.

Events can be leveraged as ways to entertain important clients, recruit new customers, motivate the firm's salespeople, and generally enhance employee morale. Events provide unique opportunities for face-to-face contact with key customers. Marketers commonly use this point of contact to distribute specialty-advertising items so that attendees will have a branded memento to remind them of the rock concert or soccer match. Marketers may also use this opportunity to sell premiums like T-shirts and hats; administer consumer surveys as part of their marketing research efforts; or distribute product samples.

As part of its spring break promotion, Coca-Cola sponsors dance contests on the beach, where it hands out thousands of cups of Coke and hundreds of Coca-Cola T-shirts each day. The goal is to build brand loyalty with those 18-to-24-year-old students who've come to the beach for fun and sun. As assessed by one of Coke's senior brand managers, "This is one of the best tools in our portfolio."[42]

John Hancock Mutual Life has shown remarkable creativity in maximizing the benefits it derived from the $24 million it spent for its five-year sponsorship of the Olympic Games.[43] Of course, association with a high-profile event like the 1996 summer games in Atlanta yields broad exposure for the John Hancock name, but Hancock has also been skillful in taking advantage of its sponsor status with local programs. For instance, in conjunction with the winter games, Hancock sponsored hockey clinics featuring Olympians from the 1980 gold-medal-winning team. Children and their parents turned out in droves. While the clinics were designed for children, the parents who brought them became immediate prospects for Hancock sales representatives. It is this sort of synergy between sponsorship and local selling efforts that organizations often fail to strive for in maximizing the benefits of their sponsorship expenditures.

41. Tara Parker-Pope, "Brewers' Soccer Sponsorships Draw Fire," *Wall Street Journal,* February 27, 1995, B1.
42. Horovitz.
43. Bulkeley.

Emerging Support Media: The New Interactive Media

❸ Technological change will make the nineties one of the most exciting and unpredictable of any era in the history of advertising. At the heart of this revolution are the new interactive media. James Cantalupo, CEO of McDonald's International, puts it this way: "Understanding the new media is the single largest business challenge that marketers have faced since the creation of TV."[44]

In the mid-1990s the state of interactive media paralleled the early years of TV.[45] The technology was cumbersome, and the pictures were simplistic. Only a tiny fraction of households were willing to invest in the equipment—the computers, modems, CD-ROM drives, and interactive television converters—that allowed full interactive access. Even though new media and information superhighway hype were everywhere, most marketers saw little value in placing messages on the 1990s equivalent of a wooden box with a nine-inch black-and-white picture.

But as was the case at the inception of television in the 1950s, new media pioneers emerged to experiment and refine the emerging technologies. Future-thinking marketers began to conceive a place for interactive television, online services, the Internet, and CD-ROMs in their long-range marketing strategies. Although advancements in technology will have a major influence on which new-media options move from hype to hard-core use, advertisers must keep in mind that the challenge is not just about technology. The challenge of the new media also entails learning how to initiate and sustain a true interactive dialogue with individual customers.

The eminent appeal of the new media is not a matter of futuristic technology—it's a matter of interactivity.[46] Traditional media are basically one-way streets: an advertiser presents a message, and the audience may accept or ignore what's offered. In the new media, consumers choose the programming and advertising they are exposed to; advertising and product information will be furnished on request from the consumer. Additionally, marketers will be in a position to get online feedback from a customer and promote a two-way interface that allows relationship building at an individual level.

In the brave new world of interactivity, advertisers will need to tap into a whole new set of skills for communicating with consumers. For example, to create an advertisement that consumers will want to interact with as they are surfing the World Wide Web, skills like those traditionally used in the creation of video games will be needed.[47] Few consumers will choose to download and view a conventional ad like one they might see on their television or in a magazine.

Ameritech's Web site is a study in how to use interactive capabilities. With the click of a mouse, a visitor can learn about new products, determine which of these products may be helpful, visit a special section dealing with slamming (being tricked into changing long-distance phone companies), and even find links to other Web sites. Ameritech's home page is shown in Exhibit 16.13.

Traditional advertising agencies have scrambled to develop the internal expertise needed to provide their clients with this interactive capability, but not all have been successful. Small, more-nimble multimedia production shops have emerged to place major clients in the new media.[48]

Projected revenues for 1996 from interactive television, commercial online services, Internet uses, and CD-ROM applications are shown in Exhibit 16.14. As with event

44. Patricia Sellers, "The Best Way to Reach Your Buyers," *Fortune,* Autumn/Winter 1993, 14.
45. Katy M. Bachman, "Brave New World," *Marketing Tools,* March/April 1995, 54–62.
46. Ibid.
47. Ibid.
48. See Kim Cleland, "Fear Creates Strange Bedfellows," *Advertising Age,* March 13, 1995, S-16; and Joan E. Rigdon, "Hip Advertisers Bypass Madison Avenue When They Need Cutting-Edge Web Sites," *Wall Street Journal,* February 28, 1996, B1.

WEB SIGHTING

What's New?

This page contains links to recently posted content on the Ameritech server. Today, check out our Library of Congress Grant information and our First Quarter Earnings . Also, visit our special section to inform customers about slamming.

Products & Services

As a full-service communications company, Ameritech provides a wide variety of products and services for use at home, at work, and on the go.

News & Information

This is where you'll find almost everything you would ever want to know about Ameritech and the rapidly changing communications industry.

WebLink Center

Here's a direct link to a number of interesting destinations on the World Wide Web.

Search | Feedback | Text Version

Copyright © 1995, 1996 Ameritech

EXHIBIT 16.13

The home page of Ameritech (formerly Illinois Bell Telephone) shows some of the potential for interactive media. In the future, will this form of support media take the place of more traditional forms of advertising? When you visit this page online at **www.ameritech.com/**, *try out some of the choices provided. Do these choices make it easier for Ameritech to provide advertising support? Compare this approach to that of Southwestern Bell at* **www .swbell.com/**.

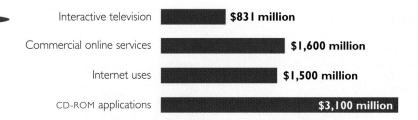

EXHIBIT 16.14

Projected new media revenues, 1996.

Interactive television   **$831 million**

Commercial online services   **$1,600 million**

Internet uses   **$1,500 million**

CD-ROM applications   **$3,100 million**

Source: "Building a New Industry," *Advertising Age,* March 13, 1995, S-3, S-4. Reprinted with permission from the March 13, 1995, issue of *Advertising Age.* Copyright © Crain Communications Inc. 1995.

sponsorship, it is appropriate to view these options as emerging support media. Before consumers will choose to engage with any form of interactive advertising, they must be aware that a brand exists and have developed an interest in finding out more about that brand. Awareness building and interest generation will continue to be executed through traditional means, like print and broadcast media. Hence, as marketers move forward and attempt to interact with consumers via the new media, it is imperative that this effort be coordinated with and support other, more conventional advertising. We will now describe several of the new media options.

Interactive Television and Commercial Online Services

Interactive television holds the greatest potential for altering the advertising business, but the future of interactive television remains clouded as cable and telecommunication companies struggle to find feasible technological solutions.[49] Interactive television would work like this: Say cable customer Mary Peterson missed *Sixty Minutes* at 7:00 on Sunday evening. In the interactive future, she can call up the show on Tuesday morning at 6:36 (or any other time) and have it appear on her television. The show costs Mary nothing if she watches it with commercials, or perhaps a dollar if she chooses to watch with no commercials. Obviously, in a media environment where the consumer makes all the choices, many will choose a world without advertising. This outcome could have devastating consequences for today's mass media advertisers.

While interactive television will not become a dominant medium before the next millennium, many organizations are currently experimenting to find the right mix of content and pricing that would make interactive television a viable commercial endeavor. One such experiment involved Bell Atlantic's Stargazer.[50] This video-on-demand service began by offering about 700 video titles, including classic movies, television sitcoms, news documentaries, and children's programming. The initial pricing of the service attempted to make the cost of the programming competitive with videotape rentals. Significant advertising dollars are likely to be shifted to such interactive systems once the service providers work through their experiments to resolve technological, content-related, and pricing issues. No one can say for sure when this new era of television will actually begin.

Computer online services have matured more rapidly than interactive television, with three major players becoming dominant. You probably recognize their names—America Online, Prodigy, and CompuServe—and their trial kits pictured in Exhibit 16.15. These subscription services offer a variety of programming choices that households can tap into via a PC and modem. Entertainment, games, bulletin boards, news services, and electronic shopping malls are common fare in this interactive medium. ABC's Super Bowl site on America Online has been a record setter, drawing in excess of 250,000

49.   Lindsey Kelly, "Interactive TV's Rough Road," *Advertising Age,* March 13, 1995, S-12–S-14.
50.   Ibid.

EXHIBIT 16.15

America Online, Prodigy, and CompuServe have been the early leaders in online computer services. Their trial kits were instrumental in linking many households to the information superhighway.

visitors in 1995.[51] Of course, when consumers visit, advertisers will be there to greet them. For example, *Newsweek*'s multimedia magazine on Prodigy has attracted interactive advertisements from companies like Chrysler, Honda, and Fidelity Investments.

The online services have offered marketers one of the best early opportunities for experimentation with interactive media. However, there are those who now question the long-term viability of these services as more and more advertisers flock to the Internet and its user-friendly constituent, the World Wide Web.[52] Preparing for the ascendance of the Web will be critical to the survival of online services in the late nineties and beyond. America Online has made ready for this challenge through partnership agreements with Microsoft, Netscape Communications, and AT&T.[53]

Advertising on the Internet

Of all the creations of modern global society, the Internet certainly is among the most intricate and fascinating. The **Internet** is a vast global network of scientific, military, and research computers that allows people inexpensive access to the largest storehouse of information in the world. Skillful users can send and receive files across oceans at no cost. Currently there are at least 8 million users, perhaps as many as 20 million users worldwide, and the number of users continues to grow.[54]

Until recently, the Internet has not been user friendly. Accessing it was like trying to find a book in a library that had no card catalog or filing system. Only those who were proficient in the Net's arcane computer codes were able to use the full potential of the system. Many users were content to tap the Internet as an inexpensive way to send electronic mail.

51. Joe Mandese, "Snags Aside, Nets Enamored of 'Net," *Advertising Age,* March 13, 1995, S-20.
52. Debra Aho Williamson, "Building a New Industry," *Advertising Age,* March 13, 1995, S-3–S-8.
53. Jared Sandberg, "America Online Stars in Soap-Opera-Like Internet Action," *Wall Street Journal,* March 18, 1996, B4.
54. Cyndee Miller, "Marketers Find It's Hip to Be on the Internet," *Marketing News,* February 27, 1995, 2.

But the Internet's unfriendly constitution was changed forever with the invention of software programs like Netscape and Mosaic, which allow Net novices to navigate using point-and-click operations. (See Exhibit 16.16 for Netscape's Web site.) This new software also allows graphical interfaces with a growing subcomponent of the Internet called the World Wide Web. The World Wide Web refers to the hundreds of computers around the world programmed to serve information specifically for Internet users.[55] The Web offers a great deal of graphical and audio data that can furnish a true interactive experience. For marketers, the Web quickly emerged as one of the hottest new media options of the 1990s.

EXHIBIT 16.16

Netscape is another key player in the new media revolution. Netscape software makes the World Wide Web accessible to millions of Web surfers.
home.netscape.com/

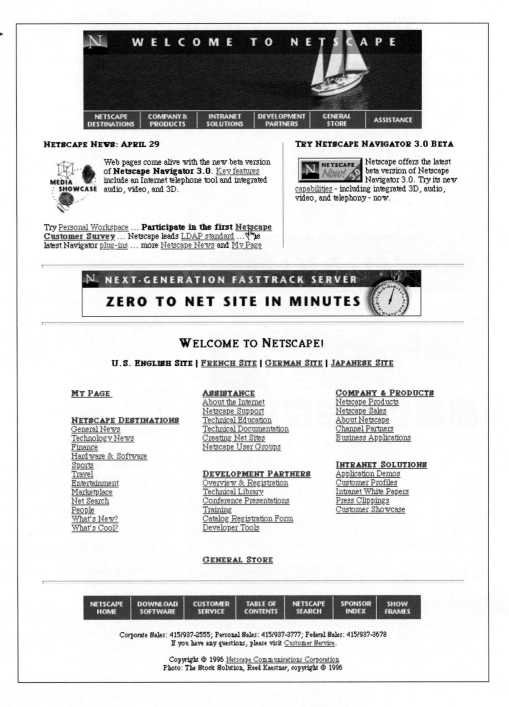

55. Larry Chase, "Crossroads: Advertising on the Internet," *Marketing Tools,* July/August 1994, 60–68.

The primary method of advertising on the Internet has involved establishing sites on the World Wide Web. A decent Web site, or home page, in cyberspace can be established for around $150,000.[56] Thousands of advertisers, like Volvo, Royal Caribbean, and Burlington Coat Factory, have set up on the Web with product information, snazzy graphics, and downloadable audio and visual materials. Examples are shown in Exhibits 16.17 through 16.19. The critical point to remember about a Web site is that the consumer is in control, so entertainment and services are critical to a successful site. If consumers don't like what they find at a site, they won't linger, and they certainly won't come back.

Recently, advertising space has also been offered for sale on the World Wide Web. Time Warner was among the first to sell online ads on the Web as part of its Pathfinder electronic newsstand. Pathfinder is one of the most popular sites on the Web, attracting several hundred thousand users each week to discuss current news stories or sample the latest edition of *Sports Illustrated*. Sponsors like AT&T and Saturn pay approximately $30,000 per quarter to test their interactive advertisements with Pathfinder's audience.[57]

Advertising on the Web is certainly not mass marketing. In 1995 there were fewer than 3 million Web visitors; this number is expected to grow to between 12 and 22 million by the year 2000.[58] That's a lot of people, but keep in mind that a highly rated

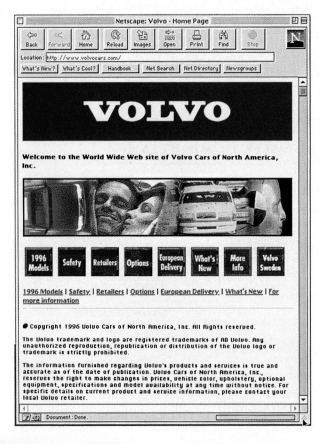

EXHIBIT 16.17

With the advent of the World Wide Web, corporate home pages have proliferated. Automobile companies were among the first to join the new media revolution. **www.volvo.se/**

EXHIBIT 16.18 Many companies flocked to the Internet initially to experiment and learn about its potential for interacting with customers. Burlington Coat Factory is candid with customers about its desire to experiment and learn from their feedback. **www.coat.com/**

56.   Mary Kuntz, "Burma Shave Signs on the I-way," *Business Week,* April 17, 1995, 102–104.
57.   Jared Sandberg, "Time Warner Sells Ads in Cyberspace via Its Pathfinder Service on Internet," *Wall Street Journal,* April 10, 1995, B6.
58.   Projections about future Web usage rates vary dramatically. For example, compare estimates in Williamson versus those in Miller.

EXHIBIT 16.19

The map at Royal Caribbean's Web site at **www.royalcaribbean.com/** *lets customers control the information they receive from the advertiser. Are there both good and bad implications of this kind of interactive control for advertisers? In contrast, see how rival Carnival Cruise Lines at* **firstct .com/carnival.html** *uses its Web site to support its advertising campaigns.*

WEB SIGHTING

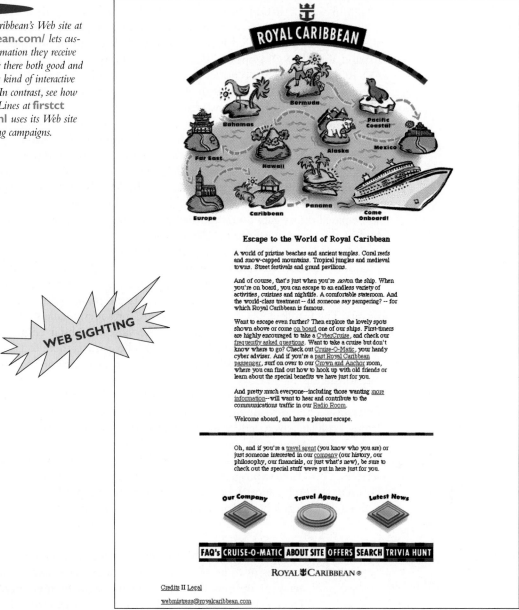

television program can easily attract in excess of 30 million viewers each week. But Web users are a well-defined segment of young, college-educated, affluent individuals —a group that many marketers constantly want more contact with.[59] Also, advertising on the Web can lend a brand a modern, distinctive image. A marketing manager for Coors' Zima clear malt beverage called the cutting-edge Web subculture the perfect place for a brand that defies categorization and comparison to other alcoholic beverages.[60]

Thus, in this decade, advertising on the Internet has been about experimenting with interactivity, reaching a well-defined target segment, and creating contemporary imagery for a brand. Five years from now, as the user base expands and more companies find secure means to execute purchase transactions on the Web, the Internet may shed its support media status to become a dominant element in the marketing programs of many organizations. Chapter 17 will provide a more in-depth assessment of the opportunities and obstacles to advertising on the Internet.

59. Kuntz.
60. Ibid.

CD-ROM Applications   CD-ROM technology provides marketers with a vehicle for offering consumers a tremendous amount of product information on a small shiny disk. As the installed base of CD-ROM drives in household PCs continues to expand, the CD-ROM option becomes more and more attractive for marketers. While CD-ROM applications do not have interactive television's or the Internet's potential for effecting fundamental changes in the ad business, they are likely to serve as a potent support media option for many years to come.

CD-ROM technology can be applied by an advertiser to replace or supplement many conventional printed media. As noted earlier in this chapter, phone companies are experimenting with CD products as alternatives to the traditional yellow pages. CDs have also been used as interactive catalogs: dozens of catalogers commonly join forces to offer their wares on CDs like Magellan's "The Merchant" and Redgate's "2Market."[61] An inventive CD-ROM magazine industry is also emerging to sell its interactive ad space based on megabytes rather than pages. The CD magazine *Launch* devotes 180 of its 650 megabytes per issue to advertisements.[62]

Marketers are also developing their own CDs as interactive brochures for their products. Cadillac was one of the pioneers in this application.[63] In trying to attract the next generation of Cadillac owners, Cadillac's marketing plan called for heavy use of the new media to establish a contemporary brand image with younger, more affluent buyers. The Cadillac CD, titled "Impressions," provides detailed information on everything from trunk dimensions to the V-8, 32-valve Northstar engine. It also includes a nine-hole golf game hosted by Lee Trevino. The game is there to take advantage of the interactive technology in a way that promotes repeated use and increases the pass-along rate for the disc.

From its experimentation, Cadillac executives learned that to get maximum value from this technology, the disc had to be marketed aggressively. To get it into customers' hands, Cadillac advertised the disc in magazines like *Home Office Computing* and sent it free to those who called an 800 number. Subscribers to CompuServe and Prodigy were also able to order the disc online as part of their visit to Cadillac's posting on these services. This Cadillac program is an excellent example of how new and old media can be used in combination to deliver helpful, engaging product information to a well-defined target segment. Is that not the essence of effective, modern advertising?

The Coordination Challenge

4 In concluding this chapter, a critical point about the media explosion needs to be reinforced. Advertisers have a vast and ever-expanding array of options for delivering messages to their potential customers. From cable TV to national newspapers, from virtual billboards to home pages on the World Wide Web, the variety of options is staggering. The keys to success for any advertising campaign are choosing the right set of options to engage a target segment and then coordinating the placement of messages to ensure coherent and timely communication. Achieving this coordination is easier said than done.

Many factors work against coordination. As advertising has become more complex, organizations often become reliant on functional specialists. For example, an organization might have separate managers for advertising, event sponsorship, and direct marketing. Specialists, by definition, focus on their specialty and can lose sight of what others in the organization are doing.[64] Specialists also want their own budgets and typically argue for more funding for their particular area. Internal competition for budget dollars often yields rivalries and animosities that work against coordination.

61. Bachman.
62. Kevin Goldman, "Firms Click on Ads in CD-ROM Magazines," *Wall Street Journal,* February 27, 1995, B8.
63. Raymond Serafin, "Discs Drive Cadillac Target Marketing," *Advertising Age,* December 5, 1994, 24.
64. Don E. Schultz, Stanley I. Tannenbaum, and Robert F. Lauterborn, *Integrated Marketing Communications* (Lincolnwood, Ill.: NTC Business Books, 1993).

Coordination is also complicated by the fact that few ad agencies have all the internal skills necessary to fulfill clients' demands for integrated marketing communications.[65] The interactive media discussed in this chapter often require special skills that are not the forte of traditional ad agencies. For example, to develop and continuously upgrade its Zima Web site, Coors Brewing employed Modem Media, an interactive-only ad agency based in Norwalk, Connecticut.[66] Coors' traditional advertising agency, Foote, Cone & Belding, was not involved in this Internet project. With each additional external organization employed to help deliver messages to customers, coordination problems become more complicated.

Remember from the discussion of IMC in previous chapters that the objective underlying this coordination is to achieve a synergistic effect. Individual media can work in isolation, but advertisers get more from their advertising dollars if various media build on one another and work together. A recent campaign for L.A. Gear's Flak Tech impact-protection, high-performance athletic shoes nicely illustrates an integrated communications strategy.[67] To introduce the new shoe L.A. Gear made certain that its P-O-P display units for Flak Tech reflected images from its television, print, and out-door ads. Its interactive P-O-P displays also included push-button access to recorded messages from celebrity endorsers Joe Montana and Wayne Gretzky that encouraged shoppers to feel an attached Flak Pad to appreciate the cushioning benefits offered by the new shoe. The objectives of this integrated campaign were to build consumer awareness of the new Flak Tech brand and drive home its unique selling proposition—the cushioning benefits of Flak technology.

The coordination challenge does not end here. Chapters that follow will add more levels of complexity to this challenge, as well as simplify strategies. Topics to come include sales promotion, direct marketing, and public relations. These activities entail additional contacts with a target audience and should reinforce the messages being delivered through broadcast, print, and support media. Integrating these efforts to speak with one voice represents a marketer's best strategy for breaking through the clutter of competitive advertising to engage with a target segment or customer.

65.   Don E. Schultz, "Why Ad Agencies Are Having So Much Trouble with IMC," *Marketing News,* April 26, 1993, 12.
66.   For an in-depth description of the Zima Internet campaign, see Cathy Taylor, "Z Factor," *Adweek,* February 6, 1995, 14–16.
67.   Lisa Z. Eccles, "Plan P-O-P at the Start," *Advertising Age,* September 26, 1994, P-4–P-6.

SUMMARY

1 Describe the traditional support media and role they can play in a media plan.

The traditional support media include out-of-home media along with specialty, P-O-P, and directory advertising. Billboards and transit advertising are excellent means for carrying simple messages into specific metropolitan markets. Aerial advertising is becoming more prevalent and can be a great way to break through the clutter. Specialty-advertising items and premiums are useful for getting and keeping a brand name in front of a customer. Expenditures on P-O-P advertising continue to grow at a rapid pace because P-O-P can be an excellent sales generator when integrated with an overall advertising campaign. Finally, directory advertising can be a sound investment because it helps a committed customer locate an advertiser's product.

2 Explain the growing popularity of event sponsorship as another supportive component of a media plan.

The list of companies sponsoring events grows with each passing year, and the events include a wide variety of activities. Of these various activities, sports attract the most sponsorship dollars. Sponsorship can help in building brand familiarity; it can promote brand loyalty by connecting a brand with powerful emotional experiences; and in most instances it allows a marketer to reach a well-defined target audience. Events can also facilitate face-to-face contacts with key customers and present opportunities to distribute product samples, sell premiums, and conduct consumer surveys.

3 Distinguish when and how the interactive, or new, media are best employed as advertising and marketing tools.

The new media present a tremendous challenge for advertisers over the next decade. Forward-thinking advertisers will learn how to use these media to promote an ongoing dialogue with key customers. Important applications are being realized today through the commercial online services, through Web site development on the Internet, and in CD-ROM applications. The Web has emerged as one of the hottest new media options of the 1990s. As the user base for these new media expands, they ultimately may shed their status as support media and become dominant components in advertising campaigns of the future.

4 Discuss the challenges presented by the ever-increasing variety of media for achieving integrated marketing communications.

The tremendous variety of media options we have seen thus far represents a monumental challenge for an advertiser who wishes to speak to a customer with a single voice. Achieving this single voice is critical for breaking through the clutter of the modern advertising environment. However, the functional specialists required for working in the various media have their own biases and subgoals that can get in the way of IMC. We will return to this issue in subsequent chapters as we explore other options available to marketers in their quest to persuade customers.

KEY TERMS

traditional support media (443)
support media (443)
riding the boards (446)
transit advertising (447)
out-of-home media (447)
aerial advertising (448)

specialty-advertising items (449)
premiums (449)
P-O-P advertising (450)
emerging support media (453)
event sponsorship (453)
Internet (460)

QUESTIONS FOR REVIEW AND CRITICAL THINKING

1.   Explain three important advancements in technology that are likely to contribute to the appeal of billboards as an advertising medium.

2.   Critique the out-of-home media as tools for achieving reach versus frequency objectives in a media plan.

3.   During your next visit to the grocery store, identify three examples of P-O-P advertising. How well were each of these displays integrated with other aspects of a more comprehensive advertising campaign? What would you surmise are the key factors in creating effective P-O-P displays?

4.   Present statistics to document the claim that the television-viewing audience is becoming fragmented. What are the causes of this fragmentation? Develop an argument that links this fragmentation to the growing popularity of event sponsorship.

5.   Event sponsorship can be valuable for building brand loyalty. Search through your closets, drawers, or cupboards and find a premium or memento that you acquired at a sponsored event. Does this memento bring back fond memories? Would you consider yourself loyal to the brand that sponsored this event? If not, why not?

6.   This chapter featured discussions of the new media applications developed for two very different products—Zima and Cadillac. How could either of these advertisers justify their investments in the new media? Are their applications consistent with the overall marketing strategies of each brand? Why or why not?

7.   Do you agree with this chapter's characterization of advertising on the Internet as an emerging support medium? In your opinion, will the Internet ever evolve into a true mass medium? What conditions must change to foster this evolution?

8.   Explain why the new media contribute to the need for functional specialists in ad preparation. What problems do these and other functional specialists create for the achievement of integrated marketing communications?

EXPERIENTIAL EXERCISE

In this chapter you learned about traditional support media. Driving down a busy street, what types of commercial messages do you see? Which ones do you think are most effective, and why? How could an advertiser conduct formal, systematic research to determine if its outdoor advertising messages are effective? What other traditional support media alternatives are available in your town? The next time you go to a movie, record the ways in which an advertiser could get a message to you. How much influence does support media advertising have on your purchasing decisions?

USING THE INTERNET

Choose three Web addresses you either remember from or can find in traditional advertising media. Visit these three sites.

For each site, answer the following questions:

1.   In what way is the Web address placed within the advertisement? How do the characteristics of the Web address within the advertisement make it more memorable and encourage you to actually visit the site?

2.   Does the Web site communicate the same message or messages that the traditional media advertisement is attempting to communicate? Does the content of the site tend to reinforce or detract from the image of the product advertised?

3.   How effectively does the site use new media marketing tools such as interactivity and visual imagery?

Open all night. Come as you are. Because our new office isn't on the Interstate. It's on the Internet.

With 24-hour INTERNET access
We're ALWAYS *with* you.℠

Chapter 17

Advertising on

the Internet

After reading and thinking about this chapter, you will be able to do the following:

1 Describe who uses and the ways they are using the Internet.

2 Identify the advertising and marketing opportunities presented by the Internet.

3 Discuss fundamental requirements for establishing viable sites on the World Wide Web.

4 Explain the challenges inherent in measuring the cost-effectiveness of the Internet versus other advertising media.

Up until the summer of 1996, two of the three World Wide Web (WWW) home pages of consumer products giant Procter & Gamble were for Sunny Delight orange drink (www.sunnyd.com) and Hugo cologne (wordslam.hugo.com). Given that the Internet's audience has been young and male, this made sense. It was good advertising.

Very recently, the demographics of the Internet have started to diversify a bit, and an enormous bandwagon phenomenon has occurred as well. Justified by data or not, major advertisers are jumping in. Now, there are several P&G sites. In addition to an informational site for the fat substitute Olestra (www.olean.com), sites for Tide, Pampers, and Covergirl were introduced in the summer of 1996. From that point forward, you could go right to the source for advice on stain removal or mascara application from the comfort of your own home computer, or for that matter, anywhere you could plug in.[1]

But P&G has done something very smart beyond merely establishing a home page. P&G is putting forth a near seamless link between advertising and actual product use through easy and inexpensive contact with the manufacturer. P&G's commitment to Internet advertising is evidenced by the way in which it links its Internet addresses to its advertising, its packaging, and ultimately the consumption experience itself. If carried through consistently, this makes the distance between company and consumer much smaller. It also facilitates contact between consumers of the same brands, thus contributing to a sense of shared experience with a common brand. This contributes to actually producing not only brand images, but communities of brand users as well.[2]

From an advertiser's perspective, Internet advertising offers several advantages. One advantage is cost. For now, Internet advertising can be done relatively inexpensively. However, the actual cost per thousand can be high compared with traditional media, so an advertiser can get into Internet advertising for fewer total dollars yet actually spend more to reach each consumer. But the bottom line is that the Internet reaches an audience long seen as attractive to advertisers: educated, upscale, and young.

There is also the potential advantage of accountability. At least in some Internet setups, such as the Yahoo!/P&G relationship discussed later in this chapter, advertisers pay only for demonstrated consumer interest in the advertised good or service, rather than for mere exposure. Yet, even this is still a speculative, or potential, advantage.

From the consumer's perspective, Internet advertising has the advantage of convenience. Consumers can browse, order, and receive products without ever leaving their homes. The headline in the ad shown in Exhibit 17.1, "I marched on Washington and never left home," shows how the times are changing. Internet advertising also provides a significant savings to the advertiser in terms of costs normally associated with retail operations (for example, sales staff, health insurance, and parking). For the consumer, there is the further advantage of around-the-clock access, shown in the ad in Exhibit 17.2. There is also the simple advantage of novelty. For the time being, Internet advertising involves the thrill of discovery. But that thrill will, like that of all new discoveries, diminish with time. When the thrill is gone, will there be enough left to sustain the online advertising movement? On this, no one is sure, but we think so.

An Overview of Cyberspace

❶ The **Internet** is a global collection of computer networks linking both public and private computer systems. It was originally designed by the U.S. military to be a decentralized, highly redundant, and thus reliable communications system in the event of a national emergency. Even if some of the military's computers crashed, the Internet would continue to perform. Today the Internet is comprised of a combination of computers from governmental, educational, military, and commercial sources. In the past few years the number of computers connected to the Internet has approximately doubled every year, from 2 million in 1994 to 5 million in 1995 to about 10 million in 1996. One source predicts

---

1.   R. Narisetti, "P&G Steps Up Ad Cyber-Surfing; Tide Could Have a Major Effect," *Wall Street Journal,* April 18, 1996, B10.
2.   H. Rheingold, *Virtual Community: Homesteading on the Electronic Frontier* (Reading, Mass.: Addison-Wesley, 1993).

more than 30 million computers online by 1998.[3] Exhibit 17.3 provides other indicators of activity on the Internet.

There are four main components of the Internet: electronic mail, the IRC, Usenet, and the World Wide Web. Electronic mail (E-mail) allows people to send messages to one another. The **Internet relay chat (IRC)** makes it possible for people to "talk" electronically with each other, despite their geographical separation. For people with common interests, the Usenet provides a forum for them to share their knowledge. Finally, the World Wide Web (WWW) gives people access to an immense database of information in a graphical environment. Most Web sites are listed with the prefix *http://*. While this is the technical address, most Web browsers don't require the user to type it out, so it has been dropped from the sites in this book.

For people to use the Internet, their personal computer must be connected to the network in some way. The most common way to access the Internet is by using a modem to call a host computer, which then provides the client computer access to the Internet. The four most common access options are through a commercial online service, such as CompuServe; a corporate gateway; a local Internet service provider; or an educational institution. In addition to using one of these networks, a personal computer needs software to communicate and move around while online. For example, if one is interested in the graphic-oriented World Wide Web, then something like Netscape's Navigator software is needed.

3.   "Web Cruisers Proliferate," *Wall Street Journal,* March 28, 1996, R6.

EXHIBIT 17.3

Web cruisers proliferate as content explodes.

Source: For "Growth in U.S. consumers with Internet access," the source is Lycos Inc. For "Growth in pages of information on the World Wide Web," the source is Forrester Research, Inc. Reprinted with permission of Lycos Inc. and Forrester Research, Inc.

Growth in U.S. consumers with Internet access, in millions

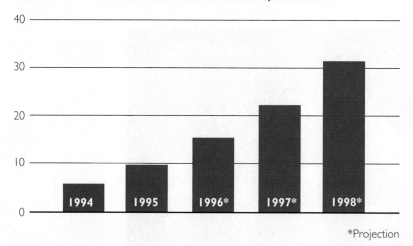

*Projection

Growth in pages of information on the World Wide Web, in millions

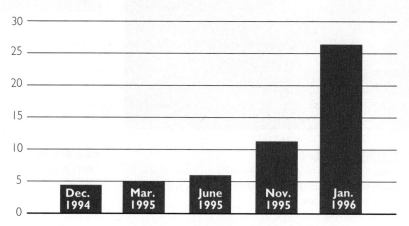

Who Uses the Internet?

At this point, no one knows exactly how many people use the Internet. The numbers vary depending on who is counting, how the counting is done, and the definition of an Internet user. A conservative estimate is somewhere between 8 and 15 million users, but it could be higher. The number of users is growing so fast that by the time the ink is dry on this page, the number will have changed significantly. In terms of who Internet users are, a telephone survey conducted by CommerceNet and Nielsen Media Research finds that of all Web users, 37 percent are professional workers, 12 percent are in technical fields, and 14 percent are managers; two-thirds are male.[4] At present, the Internet is also disproportionately white. Women's Web representation is discussed in the New Media box on page 473.

As more people use the Internet for longer periods, it is becoming a viable advertising medium. Based on a study of marketers, Jupiter Communications estimates that in 1995, $54.7 million was spent advertising on the Internet. Spending in 1996 was around $300 million. *Advertising Age* predicts spending in 1997 will be $500 million.[5] As a point of comparison, consider that in 1995, television advertising was $31.15 billion. In other words, at present, Internet advertising is small potatoes. As one researcher said, "For AT&T, the Web budget is a rounding error."[6] Still, Internet advertising growth is substantial; Jupiter Communications estimates a figure of $7 billion in Inter-

4.   "More Web Demographics from CommerceNet Nielsen," *Advertising Age,* November 27, 1995, 32.
5.   adage.com/interactive/articles/19961223/article1.html.
6.   Josh Bernoff, a senior analyst at Forrester Research, quoted in K. Hafner and J. Tanaka, "This Web's for You," *Newsweek,* April 1, 1996, 75.

EXHIBIT 17.4

Comparing costs for Internet and traditional advertising media.

Type	Cost	Total Exposures	Cost per Thousand
TV: 30-second, network news	$ 85,000	12,000,000	$ 5.42
Magazine: full-color, national weekly+	$185,000	8,100,000	$43.55
Newspaper: full-page, midsize city	$ 81,000	514,000	$60.31
World Wide Web: online magazine, one-month placement	$ 15,000	200,000	$75.00

Source: Forrester Research, from *Newsweek*, April 1996, 76. Reprinted with permission of Forrester Research, Inc.

NEW MEDIA

WOMEN WOULD RATHER NOT BE SHOPPING ON THE WEB

Finding women prospects on the World Wide Web is getting easier, but understanding what they want from this new medium is still unclear. A study conducted by Nielsen Media Research and CommerceNet found that 34 percent of Internet users are women. The firms that have targeted women at this early stage are clothing retailers like Express (express.style.com), packaged goods manufacturers like Kellogg (www.kelloggs.com), and personal care products companies like Bristol-Myers Squibb (www.womenslink.com).

But many analysts are saying that the sites being developed are not what women want. The Nielsen survey and others have found that shopping online ranks low in interest among both sexes, but particularly so for women. Further, some analysts claim it is sexist for men to develop shopping sites. What is more sexist and offensive to women is the development of chat rooms for women. Judith Broadhurst, author of *The Women's Guide to Online Services,* claims that online services have "done some damage in saying chat rooms are where it's at—it's really backfired in terms of women's perceptions about online."

The real concern women have is with the security of online use. Women are put off by the technology of online services. There is also a fear factor: fear of harassment, pornography, or even being stereotyped as a techno-geek. The firm that can overcome any resistance women feel may find a potent way to reach an expanding female market. The director of interactive marketing for CompuServe believes that "women online are probably in higher positions and [earning greater] incomes than men online—you're getting influencers." Microsoft Network product manager Jodi DeLeon argues that what women want from a Web site is efficiency, time savings, and relevancy.

Here are three media companies trying to attract women to their Web sites without using a shopping lure:

* Lang's Women's Web (www.womweb.com) focuses on business and networking advice.
* iVillage (www.ivillage.com/) is creating content devoted to parenting.
* Women's Wire (www.women.com) features information on health and fitness, fashion, and finance.

Source: Jane Hodges, "What Women Want Online," *Advertising Age,* November 6, 1995, 30.

net advertising by 2000.[7] Other estimates are much lower. No one is sure how blue the sky is.

On a cost-per-thousand basis, Web ads are fairly pricey. Exhibit 17.4 compares Web advertising costs with other traditional sources.

The real attraction of the Internet is not found in huge numbers and low costs per thousand, but in terms of highly desirable and segmentable audiences. The Internet is great for niche marketing, that is, for reaching only those consumers most likely to buy what the advertiser is selling.

Internet Media

There are several ways for advertisers to communicate with consumers using the Internet. Four will be discussed here: E-mail, LISTSERV, Usenet, and the World Wide Web.

E-Mail. **E-mail** is an Internet function that allows users to communicate much as they do using standard mail. Some marketers have used this function of the Internet to communicate their messages. A variety of companies are collecting E-mail addresses and profiles that will allow advertisers to direct E-mail to a specific group. The DM Group (www.dm1.com) maintains a list of E-mail groups and has reportedly collected up to 250,000 E-mail addresses. However, widespread E-mail advertising has not yet materialized due to significant consumer resistance to marketers' direct mailings to personal

7.   Kathy Balog, "On-Line Shoppers Post Record Buying," *USA Today,* December 24, 1996, B1.

E-mail addresses.[8] As techniques and guidelines are better established for direct E-mail advertising, it may become more accepted in the future. Many believe it's only a matter of time; historically, advertisers have rarely worried about being too intrusive.

LISTSERV. LISTSERV is another option for advertisers. People who wish to discuss specific topics through the Internet often join electronic mailing lists, or **LISTSERVs.** There are thousands of mailing lists available on an incredible variety of topics. By sending a message to the list's E-mail address, the message is then re-sent to everybody on the mailing list. A niche for commercial services that collect and sell LISTSERVs certainly exists and is already attracting attention. Still, advertisers need to be cautious here since it is currently considered in very bad taste to openly sell products via LISTSERVs, particularly when there is no apparent connection between the mailing list's theme and the advertised product. Product information shared through these mailing lists can be likened to traditional word-of-mouth communications and is, at the moment, still in the hands of users. Again, it's likely the temptation to defy the current taboo will be too strong for advertisers to resist for much longer.

Usenet. **Usenet** is a collection of more than 17,000 discussion groups in cyberspace. People can read messages pertaining to a given topic, post new messages, and answer messages. For advertisers, this is an important source of consumers who care about certain topics. For example, the Usenet group alt.beer is an excellent place for a new microbrewery to promote its product. Advertisers can also use Usenet as a source of unobtrusive research, getting the latest opinions on their products and services. Television shows, such as *The X-Files,* often monitor Usenet groups, such as alt.tv.x-files, to find out what people think about the show. Usenet is also used as a publicity vehicle for goods and services.[9] Usenet represents a great word-of-mouth channel.

One notorious practice is to **spam,** or post messages to many unrelated newsgroups. For example, more than 6 million people have been spammed at a cost of only $425. For an ambitious and gutsy advertiser, such a tactic could prove an enormously cost-effective advertising buy, or it could provoke a great deal of hate mail, resentment, or even more dire consequences, including a loss of business reputation.[10] Again, the point is for Usenet advertisers to make sure they are at least wanted guests, and not despised intruders into what often amount to virtual communities.

World Wide Web. The **World Wide Web (WWW)** is a universal database of information available to most Internet users, and its graphical environment makes navigation simple and exciting. Of all the options available for Internet advertisers, the WWW holds the greatest potential. It allows for detailed and full-color graphics, audio transmission, the delivery of in-depth messages, 24-hour availability, and two-way information exchanges between the advertiser and customer. For some people, surfing the Web is replacing time spent viewing other media, such as print, radio, and television. There is one great difference between the Web and other cyberadvertising vehicles: It is the consumer who actively searches for the advertiser's home page. In contrast, E-mail advertising, for example, is sent from the advertiser to the consumer.

Surfing the World Wide Web

By using software such as Netscape, consumers can simply input the addresses of Web sites they wish to visit and directly access the information available there. However, the Web is a library with no card catalog. There is no central authority that lists where specific sites are located. This condition leads to surfing—gliding from home page to home page. Users can seek and find different sites in a variety of ways: through search engines, through direct links with other

8.   R. L. Bruno, "Net.News," *Netguide,* February 1996, 16.
9.   M. Slatalla, "Net.Media," *Netguide,* February 1996, 32.
10.   S. Garfinkel, "Spam King! Your Source for Spams Netwide!" *Wired,* February 1996, 84.

sites, and by word of mouth. Some functions previously allowed only to librarians are now granted to Internet users.

To use a **search engine,** a user types in a few keywords, and the search engine then finds all sites that correlate with the keywords. Search engines all have the same basic user interface but differ in how they perform the search and in the amount of the WWW accessed. There are three distinct styles of search engines: hierarchical, collection, and concept.

Hierarchical Search Engines. Yahoo!, as shown in Exhibit 17.5, is an example of a search engine built on a hierarchical, subject-oriented guide. All sites have to fit into a certain category. For example, Stolichnaya vodka is indexed as Business and Economy/Companies/Drinks/ Alcoholic/ Vodka. Users are thus able to find and select a category as well as all the relevant Yahoo! sites. Going to Business and Economy/Companies/Sports/Snowboarding/ Board Manufacturers, for instance, gives a list of all the companies that sell snowboards on the Web, as shown in Exhibit 17.6.

By checking these sites, a person could find a snowboard company and even buy a snowboard over the Web. Although hierarchical sites like Yahoo! are great for doing general searches, they do have some significant limitations. For example, Yahoo!'s database of Web sites contains only submissions; that is, Yahoo! does not actually perform a search of the Web for sites but only contains sites that users tell it about. Because of this, Yahoo! omits a significant portion of the vast information available on the Web.

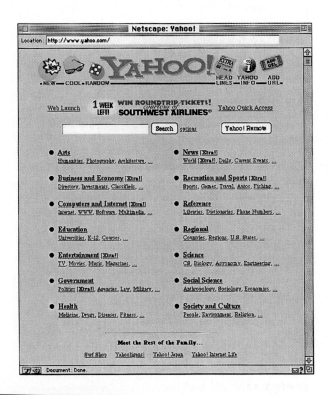

EXHIBIT 17.5

Search engines are familiar to any accomplished Web user. Among the most familiar of these engines is Yahoo! **www.yahoo.com/**

EXHIBIT 17.6 *Yahoo! is hierarchical by design. This search result for snowboard manufacturers provides a nice illustration of the hierarchical format of Yahoo!* **www.yahoo.com/**

Collection. This second type of search engine is exemplified by AltaVista, shown in Exhibit 17.7. AltaVista uses a spider, which is an automated program that crawls around the Web and collects information. As of May 1996, the collection of Web pages indexed by AltaVista stood at more than 30 million on 225,000 servers. With AltaVista, a person can perform a text search on all of these sites, resulting in access to approximately 10 billion words. For example, the search *vampire books,* shown in Exhibit 17.8, finds 30,000 Web pages that contain both terms.

Because of the sheer quantity of Web pages, AltaVista ranks the best matches first. The relatively large amount of information available on AltaVista mandates that users know what they are really interested in; otherwise, they will be flooded with information.

Concept Search Engines. The newest technique in search engines is a concept search service, such as Excite. Here, a concept rather than a word or phrase is the basis for the search. Back to the vampire example, the top ten sites with the concept *vampire books* are shown in Exhibit 17.9. To narrow the search, simply clicking on one of the sites found in the original search with the Excite icon enables another search based on the selected link. The % key gives the user an idea of how close a particular site is to his or her concepts. This is a very efficient way of searching, producing relatively focused results compared to AltaVista and with the added ability to use the results of a search to further modify the search. The downside is that concept search engines like Excite lack the comprehensiveness of collection search engines like AltaVista.

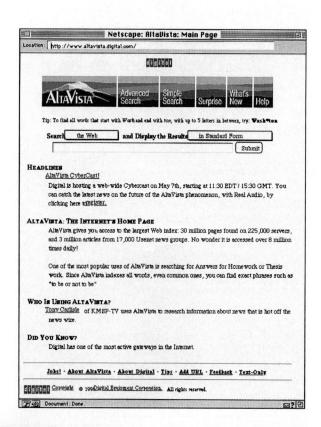

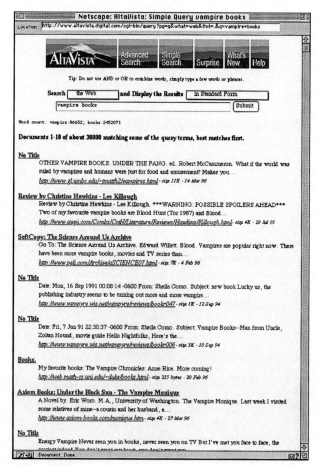

EXHIBIT 17.7

AltaVista is another popular Web search engine. By design, it provides access to more of the Web's content than does Yahoo! **www.altavista .digital.com/**

EXHIBIT 17.8 *This result from AltaVista illustrates the vast content available on the World Wide Web. This search turned up 30,000 Web pages containing the terms* vampire *and* books. **www.altavista .digital.com/**

Other Ways to Find Sites. Many people have created their own Web pages, which list their favorite sites. This is a fabulous way of finding new and interesting sites—as well as feeding a person's narcissism. For example, here is our Web address: www.swcollege.com/oguinn .html. Since this page is maintained, updated, and checked regularly, it is a good resource for someone interested in advertising. Of course, sites can also be discovered through traditional word-of-mouth communications. Internet enthusiasts tend to share their experiences on the Web through discussions in coffeehouses, reading and writing articles, Usenet, and other non-Web venues.

Advertising and Marketing on the Internet

⓶ Most of the largest companies now have a presence on the WWW or plan one in the near future. The list includes consumer-product companies, service providers, retailers, major television networks, major newspapers, and movie studios. An *Advertising Age* survey of advertising agencies found that 90 percent of their clients have home pages but only 39 percent advertise on other commercial online sites. At the end of 1996, 14 percent of all retailers, large and small, had an Internet presence.[11] Interestingly, advertising agencies actually express a degree of pessimism concerning the effectiveness of advertising on the Internet, due to the many questions that exist concerning measurement and efficiency. They're also not sure how *they* will make more money on the Internet. Still, a large majority of the agencies noted interactive advertising as a valuable part of the media mix of the future.[12] At present, it costs relatively little to hop on the bandwagon, and has relatively high upside potential. So, why not?

Regardless of the lack of effective measurement and evaluation of reach, the narrow audience composition, and the unknown impact of Web advertising, companies seem to be afraid of being left behind. Apparently, there is a great amount of prestige attached to advertising on the WWW. In response, many agencies have established their own home pages, are making strong efforts at gaining expertise with the Web, and are even establishing separate departments to handle interactive media, as discussed in the New Media box on page 480. Agencies have also emerged that specialize in Internet advertising (see Exhibit 17.10), and most agency reviews now include a presentation of Internet credentials. See Exhibit 17.11 for some agency Internet sites.

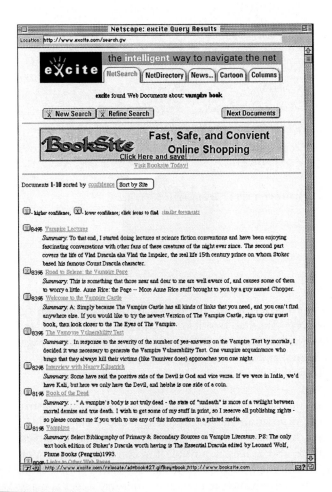

Excite represents yet another option for searching the WWW. Excite executes a concept search that allows the user to converge quickly on a concept of particular interest. **www.excite.com/**

Product versus Content Advertising

There are two essential ways for advertisers to post advertising messages on the Web. The basic route is by establishing a corporate home page. These home pages clearly identify the company and brand that supports the site. The style of sites ranges from those explicitly focused on the presentation of specific product benefits to those based on special interests or lifestyle topics, which indirectly push the product.

11. Balog.
12. K. Cleland, "Technology Agency Media Marketing Survey," *Advertising Age,* September 4, 1995, A6.

Sure you can host
your own Web site,
assuming you have an endless supply
of money, time
and hair.

Why go through the aggravation of hosting your company's Web site internally when you can turn the job over to BBN Planet, a company with unparalleled Internet experience? Just think. No late-night maintenance emergencies, no phone calls from customers annoyed by access problems, no staffing headaches. With Web Advantage, you get high-end UNIX™ servers running Netscape™ software, high-speed T3 Internet connections and round-the-clock service and support – all without losing control over your site's content. For a free Cost Justification Analysis, visit http://www.bbn.com/webadvantage or call (800) 472-4565.

BBN PLANET
How Business Does Business On The Internet

EXHIBIT 17.10

Advertising on the Internet requires a special set of skills. This has fostered the development of agencies, like BBN Planet, that specialize in creating and maintaining Web sites for clients. **www.near.net/**

The Ad Store	www.the-adstore.com/
Chiat Day	www.chiatday.com/factory/
Ted Bates-Dublin	www.iol.ie/resource/bates/index.html
DDB-Europe	www.globalnews.com/bmp
Dentsu Japan	www.dentsu.co.jp/DHP
Fallon McElligott	www.fallon.com/
Green Light Interactive	www.grnlt.com/
JWT San Francisco	www.jwtsf.com
Ketchum	www.ketchum.com/catalyst.html
McMann and Tate	www.mcmann-tate.com/
Ad Kingdom	uts.cc.utexas.edu/~ccho/adworld.html
Advertising Graveyard	www.zeldman.com/ad.html
Project 2000	www2000.ogsm.vanderbilt.edu/
Blue Marble	www.bluemarble.com/
Cyclops	www.cyclops.com/
KVO-Portland	www.kvo.com
Ogilvy	www.ogilvy.com
Winkler McManus	www.winklermcmanus.com/
Welinder-Stockholm	www.welinder.se/
Pete Smith Advertising	www.winternet.com/~smithads/

EXHIBIT 17.11   *Twenty interesting ad sites.*

The other way for marketers to advertise on the Web is through banner ads on entertainment, media, or online corporate sites. Besides the actual banner ad purchased on a media company's Web site, the advertiser can also get a link to its own home page. So, a consumer is browsing on Yahoo! and sees a Toyota banner ad. He or she clicks on the ad and is taken straight to Toyota's home page.

Corporate Home Pages. The Saturn site shown in Exhibit 17.12 is an example of a **corporate home page** that focuses on the Saturn corporation and its products. The Saturn site allows people to find out about the line of Saturn cars, pricing, specifications, and the closest dealers. This product-oriented site also makes it possible for consumers to request brochures and communicate their comments and questions to the Saturn corporation. Kelloggs Corn Pops has a truly interactive game site in which surfers try to get as many Corn Pops in their cereal bowl as possible while grandma tries to steal the bowl of Pops. See www.cornpops.com/granny/playpop.html. The site was developed by Giant Step, a Leo Burnett subsidiary.[13]

13. Thom Forbes, "Techies and Creatives Meld Their Skills: Interactive Ads Gain from the Marriage," *Agency,* Fall 1996, 18–21.

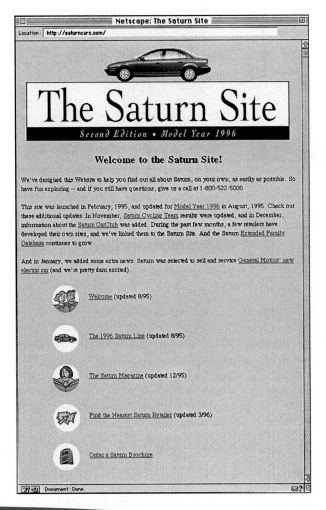

Saturn's home page provides the surfer with a vast array of information about the Saturn line. It also takes advantage of the Web's interactive capability by encouraging questions and comments from those who visit the site. **www.saturncars.com/index/html**

A corporate site that falls toward the lifestyle end of the spectrum is the Reebok site displayed in Exhibit 17.13. The Planet Reebok site contains information about human rights, sports, and fitness, and it offers links to other sports-related sites. Although the Planet Reebok site provides a starting point to browsing the Net on various lifestyle topics (the site even provides a "gymbag" of software that can be downloaded to aid in surfing the Web), the company name is displayed and the content of the site helps to build a positive image for Reebok.

Banner Ads. **Banner ads** are paid placements on other sites that contain editorial material. An additional feature of banner ads is that consumers not only see the ad but also can make a quick trip to the advertiser's home page by clicking on the ad. Thus, the challenge of creating and placing banner ads is not only to catch people's attention but also to entice them to visit the advertiser's home page and stay for a while. Many of the high-traffic Web sites that provide information content have started to rely on advertisers to support their services. Sites such as Yahoo! and HotWired often have banner advertisements. Exhibit 17.14 shows three banner ads across the bottom of the HotWired Web page.

A high-traffic site offers a relatively high level of exposure to an advertising message. Much like placing advertisements within traditional print media such as newspapers and magazines, advertisers can purchase space on sites providing a diversity of editorial content, such as the *New York Times, Chicago Tribune, Los Angeles Times, Wall Street Journal, USA Today, Newsweek, U.S. News & World Report, Car and Driver, Atlantic Monthly,* Time-Warner Communications, and ESPN.

A more targeted option is to place banner ads on sites that attract specific market niches. For example, a banner ad for running shoes would be placed on a site that offers information related to running. This option is emerging as a way for advertisers to focus more tightly on their target audiences. Currently, advertisers consider WWW users to be a focused segment of its own. However, as the Web continues to blossom, marketers will begin to realize that even across the entire Web, there are sites that draw specific subgroups of Web users. These niche users have particular interests that may represent important opportunities for the right advertiser.

A pricing evaluation service for banner ads is offered by Interactive Traffic. The I-Traffic Index computes a site's advertising value based on traffic, placement and size of ads, ad rates, and evaluations of the site's quality.[14] Forrester Research assesses the costs of banner ads on a variety of sites and what advertisers get for their money, as shown in Exhibit 17.15.

14. K. Cleland, "SRDS, I-Traffic Join Interactive Frenzy," *Advertising Age,* October 16, 1995, 22.

Other Types of Cybermarketing

Virtual Malls. Setting up a Web site and placing it inside a virtual mall is another strategy useful to Web marketers. A **virtual mall** is a gateway to a group of Internet storefronts that provide access to mall sites by simply clicking on a storefront, as shown in the Internet Mall ad in Exhibit 17.16. The nature of virtual malls varies widely from mall to mall.

NEW MEDIA

CYBERAGENCIES FOR CYBERSPACE?

Traditional, full-service advertising agencies helped build only 26 percent of the advertiser sites on the World Wide Web in 1995. According to a survey conducted by Forrester Research, traditional agencies are slow to make a commitment to helping clients move into cyberspace. In the same survey, 51 percent of the site managers interviewed said that they implemented their own online strategies without any help at all.

But advertisers interested in the Internet don't have to go it alone. While early sites may not have been developed by agencies, cyberagencies are starting to gain prominence. One small but fast-growing cyberagency that has landed big-name accounts is Modem Media. Modem Media has developed brand sites for AT&T and Adolph Coors. Most recently, Modem media was named interactive agency of record for Delta Air Lines. Organic Online in San Francisco developed GM's Saturn site, and Strategic Interactive Group in Boston developed sites for big-name marketers like L. L. Bean, Seagram's, and Kraft Foods.

Analysts suggest that these new cyberagencies have made inroads with major advertisers because large ad agencies have been slowed by cautious clients and layers of bureaucracy. And some large agencies just aren't believers. A creative director for a London-based agency said, "People are rushing in [to the Internet] thinking they know what consumers want, when, in reality, no one has any idea yet. I'm constantly saying what communicates is ideas—it's not the media that communicates."

But not all big agencies are sluggish or skeptical. Bozell, Jacobs, Kenyon & Eckhart has developed dozens of sites for clients including Chrysler, Toshiba, and Valvoline. Grey Advertising is developing online communications for Procter & Gamble brands, and Ogilvy & Mather, through its O&M Interactive division, is serving the new media needs of its clients IBM and American Express.

While some think the emergence of cyberagencies is bad news for traditional shops, some industry insiders don't see it that way. Doug Ryan, vice president of Leo Burnett's Interactive Marketing Group, which has developed online areas for Oldsmobile, McDonald's, Maytag, and United Airlines, sees the major agencies as easily having the upper hand. Ryan believes, "When you marry the technical expertise with the knowledge of and essence of the brand, that's when the magic is going to happen." It's the big agencies that have the brand knowledge—and they have, traditionally, made the magic.

Sources: Daniel Tilles, "Upstart Ad Firms Win in Cyberspace," *International Herald Tribune*, September 6, 1995, 13; Sally Goll Beatty, "Cyberagencies Outflank Old-Line Shops," *Wall Street Journal*, December 27, 1995, 17; and Mark Gleason and Debra Aho Williamson, "The New Interactive Agency," *Advertising Age*, February 26, 1996, S1, S6.

Compared to the Internet Mall with more than 11,000 stores, the Issaquah online site shown in Exhibit 17.17 features a more local orientation from the city of Issaquah, Washington. The advantage of malls for an advertiser is the opportunity to attract browsers to its site, much like the way window shopping works in the physical world.

Coupons. Coupons Online is a New York–based company that distributes coupons via the Internet and commercial online services for packaged goods, fast-food, and travel companies. A consumer simply prints the coupons on her or his home printer and then takes them to the store for redemption. The company charges clients anywhere from $3 to $15 per thousand coupons distributed. The average cost to manufacturers for coupons distributed via free-standing inserts is $7 per thousand. However, only a small portion of those coupons are even clipped (2 to 3 percent redemption rate), whereas with online coupons, the manufacturer is paying only per thousand clipped, or in this case printed, by consumers.[15]

Event Marketing. The Web is also an avenue for ties to event and sports marketing. For instance, both the Super Bowl and the Oscars had Web sites in 1996. For the Super Bowl site, sponsorships ranged in price from $100,000 to $225,000. The site is promoted during the program, and sponsors get their logos on the site, have links to their own home pages, and have an opportunity to provide editorial content for the event site.[16]

---

15.   M. Wilke, "Catalina, Coupons Online in Tests," *Advertising Age*, August 28, 1995, 15.
16.   B. Johnson, "Microsoft Developing Oscar's Web Site," *Advertising Age*, January 22, 1996, 2.

The Reebok site is less about product information than sites like Saturn's, and more about entertainment. Providing an entertaining encounter is one of the ways that advertisers can promote repeat visits and favorable word of mouth for their sites. **planetreebok .com/**

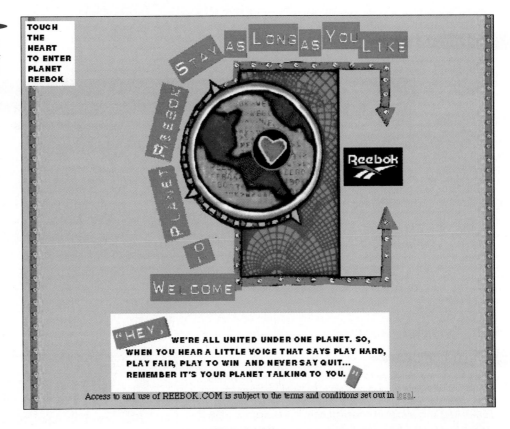

The use of banner ads on this page shows some of the potential for leveraging advertising formats on the Web. When you visit HotWired |at **www.hotwired.com/**, click on one or more of the banner ads shown. How effective are banner ads for a Web site? Or for the advertiser sponsoring them? Banner ads can also be used to link to strategic partners, as Microsoft **www.microsoft.com/sitebuilder/** does with banners for its partners in developing Internet products such as Macro-Media and Adobe.

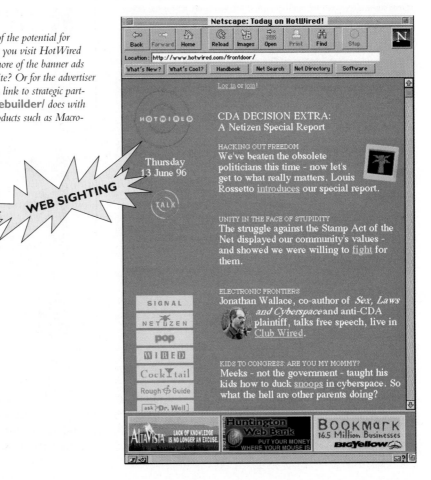

EXHIBIT 17.15

Advertising costs on the Web.

Site	Rate	Deliverables
ESPN SportZone	$100,000/quarter $300,000/year	Estimated 542,000 users/week; 20.5 million hits/week; exclusive and rotating placement
HotWired	$13,000–$15,000/month	Minimum 100,000 banner views guaranteed; weekly traffic reports; discounts for "Wired" advertisers
Netscape	$30,000/month	Estimated 1 million impressions; estimated CPM of $25–$30
Pathfinder	$30,000/quarter	Free position in Pathfinder marketplace; weekly tracking reports
Yahoo! search page	$20,000/1 million impressions	Estimated 2.9 million hits/month; 135 million search results (cumulative)

Source: Forrester Research and *Advertising Age*, January 8, 1996, 25. Reprinted with permission of Forrester Research, Inc.

EXHIBIT 17.16

This example of a virtual mall provides a cyberspace version of a familiar form of retail shopping. In what ways can virtual mall advertisers take advantage of this familiarity to promote their products? When you visit the Internet Mall at **www.internet-mall.com/**, *you may notice a different look than in the exhibit. This ability to update message components is a real advantage of virtual malls. Contrast the presentation of information here with the kind you get from a standard search engine, such as Yahoo!* **www.yahoo.com/**, *Lycos* **home.netscape.com/escapes/ search/netsearch3.html**, *or Magellan* **home.netscape.com/ escapes/search/netsearch4.html**. *You might also check out Dreamshop at* **www.dreamshop.com**, *World Avenue Mall at* **www.worldavenue.com**, *and Beers Across America at* **www.beer .com**.

Sales Support. The Internet equivalent to response vehicles such as 800 numbers and postcards is E-mail. Home pages have the ability to provide an E-mail option for those who visit the site to respond to the advertiser and ask for further information. As with 800 numbers, an advertiser has to make sure that the E-mail account is adequately staffed to respond to queries.

Establishing a Site on the World Wide Web

❸ Setting up a Web site can be done quite easily. A Web site can be boot-strapped onto an existing site for less than $20 a month, thus allowing the new site to take advantage of the current site's hardware, software, and Internet connection. However, the actual designing of the Web site's pages will still need to be done. More-complex sites and heavily trafficked sites can be implemented for $1,000 and a $200 monthly charge. Setting up an attractive site costs more because of the need for specialized designers to create the site and, most importantly, constantly update the site. The basic hardware for a site can be a personal computer, and the software to run the site ranges from free to several thousand dollars, depending on the number of extras needed. A site anticipating considerable traffic will need to plan for higher-capacity phone lines—and hence, a bigger phone bill. Heavily trafficked sites often pay more than $1,000 a month for high-capacity phone lines. Forrester Research reports the costs of creating various commercial sites as follows:

Corporate promotional site	$ 304,000
Online publication	$1,300,000
Catalog shopping	$3,400,000[17]

Getting Surfers to Come Back

For advertisers, getting people to come back to their site is a primary concern. A site with pages showing the product and its specifications may have no appeal beyond attracting a single visit. There may be little or no entertainment value to bring people back again and again. Surfing various business home pages reveals countless boring corporate Web pages. To attract and capture the interest of people simply browsing the Web, a good idea for advertisers is to be sure to learn about their customers before setting up a site. Good consumer and communications research can be useful in this context.

A well-developed site can keep customers coming back for more. A good example is Women's Link by Bristol-Myers Squibb, illustrated in Exhibit 17.18. Besides information on how to use the company's wide variety of products, the site offers information on such topics as health and fitness and the latest books, and it also offers a resource center for women to discuss various topics. These features give people multiple reasons to continue to visit the site.

A popular content-oriented Web site is HotWired. The site is continually updated with information on a wide variety of topics, from arts and music to commentary on the Internet and politics. It is not focused on selling a product per se; instead, it is an entertainment site. Like a good corporate site, the HotWired site is continually changing to appeal to repeat users. Another site of this style is SportsLine USA, shown in Exhibit 17.19. It allows users to check out continuously updated exclusive coverage, enter contests, and chat with sports superstars. If persons stumble on these sites and like them, chances are they will be return visitors.

Thus, the objective of having repeat customers depends on both substance and entertainment. Web surfers are discriminating, in that while nice pictures are interesting, sites that have considerable repeat users offer something more. This can be product information and ongoing technical support, or it can be general news about a product, or original writing, or the latest or most comprehensive information about just about anything. Above all, it has to be fun—pure and simple.

Purchasing Keywords on Search Engines

Online search engines such as Yahoo! sell keywords. If a keyword has been purchased by an advertiser, when users select that word for a

---

17. *New York Times,* February 12, 1996, C1.

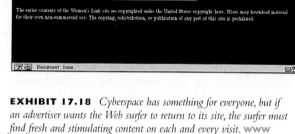

EXHIBIT 17.17

The chamber of commerce for Issaquah, Washington, took an innovative approach for bringing visitors to Issaquah. If you build it, will they come to small-town America on the Internet? **www2.issaquah.com/iol/**

EXHIBIT 17.18 *Cyberspace has something for everyone, but if an advertiser wants the Web surfer to return to its site, the surfer must find fresh and stimulating content on each and every visit.* **www .womenslink.com/**

search, the advertiser's banner ad will appear. For example, when a user searches for a keyword such as *inn* on the search engine Lycos, he or she will see an ad from a directory for bed and breakfast inns, as shown in Exhibit 17.20.

Keyword sponsorship on Lycos costs $750 per month, or five cents per impression. Sponsorship on Yahoo! costs $1,000 per month, or two to five cents per impression.[18] Note that search engines let advertisers pay a flat monthly fee or a per-impression fee (based on how many people see the ad). Thus, getting a popular word may result in a considerable number of impressions and a higher bill. The other factor is effectiveness. The Infoseek search engine claims buy rates from 2 to 36 percent, while other engines claim that keyword ads do not significantly differ from the banner ads in effectiveness. However, keyword ads are a great way to get a product in front of someone interested in the general category.

Registering

Currently, most Internet users are quite wary about providing personal information or registering with a site sponsor. Forcing people to register to gain access to a site may discourage potential visitors, but the information gained from this process can be valuable to an advertiser. Combining user profiles with records on each person's activities while browsing the site allows advertisers to determine what

18.   J. Hodges, "Words Hold the Key to Web Ad Packages," *Advertising Age,* January 15, 1996, 38.

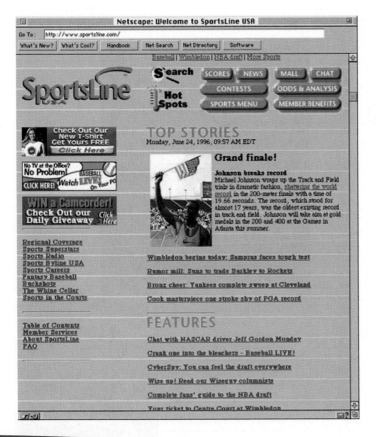

Sports fans have also taken to the Web. Entertainment sites like SportsLine tap into fans' seemingly insatiable desire for the inside scoop on their favorite athletes.
www.sportsline.com/

aspects of both the site and the product appeal to each type of consumer. Requesting people to register for access to additional information, as C:Net and HotWired do, is becoming increasingly common. Another way of obtaining visitor information is a cookie. A **cookie** is a coded identifier that is downloaded to the visitor's computer, where it resides, often undetected, but not really hidden. A cookie allows the Internet server to both keep track of a client or user throughout their visit to a site and collect a surprising amount of data on the user.[19] Cookie (or *persistent client state*) technology offers both a benefit for advertisers wishing to know their clients better, and obvious privacy concerns for the clients. The visitor is typically unaware of the downloaded cookie.

Promoting Web Sites

Building a Web site is only the first step; the next is promoting it. There are several firms that specialize in promoting Web sites, such as WebStep (www.mmgco.com/webstep.html). The quickest and most effective route is to notify appropriate Usenet groups. The other key method is to register the site with search engines such as Yahoo! and AltaVista. With Yahoo!, because it is a hierarchical search engine, it is important to pick keywords that are commonly chosen yet describe and differentiate that site. Other places to register are with the growing yellow pages on the Internet (www.bigyellow.com) and with appropriate LISTSERV groups. It is also important to send out press releases to Internet news sites. E-mail as a form of direct mail is another method to promote the site. Conventional media can be effective as well; a well-placed address for a Web site in a printed publication can draw considerable business. An example of this is the UPS ad in Exhibit 17.21.

If an advertiser wants to draw people to its Web site as one of the goals of a television commercial, the address should be visible on the screen long enough for viewers to capture and actually remember the site address. The necessary length of time can range from 3 to 5 seconds, depending on the length and memorability of the address.

Measurement and Security Issues

For the Web to become a truly competitive advertising medium, an accurate way to measure site traffic is needed. In addition, exposure or traffic measures should be linked to essential demographics for the information to be most useful. Currently, there are no clear industry standards monitored by third parties, as in conventional media. Sites that require registration (along with a few demographic questions) are able to get a clearer picture of their audience,

19. "Persistent Client State HTTP Cookies," home.netscape.com/newsref/std/cookie_spec.html; and Donna Hoffman and Thomas Novak, "Commercialization of the World Wide Web: The Role of Cookies," www2000.ogsm.vanderbilt.edu.

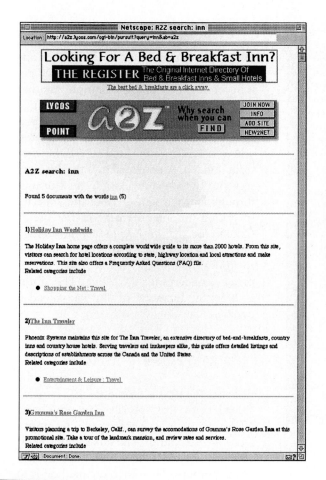

EXHIBIT 17.20

Search engine providers generate part of their operating revenue by selling keywords. Keyword sponsorship can be an excellent means for building brand awareness with those who have a special interest in the product category. For example, for your next stay in Berkeley, California, why not consider Gramma's Rose Garden Inn? **www.lycos.com/**

EXHIBIT 17.21 *All an advertiser's efforts in developing an engaging and informative Web site will go for naught if the consumer cannot find the site. Advertisers shouldn't overlook the important synergy that can occur between advertising in traditional media and advertising on the World Wide Web.* **www.ups.com/**

but registration sites are clearly in the minority. There are third-party companies, such as I/Pro, moving into Web measurement as independent verifiers. However, these services are not widespread and have not won the confidence of the industry as of this writing.

Procter & Gamble has reportedly entered into an agreement with Yahoo! that may prove to be more than controversial, perhaps even revolutionary. P&G will supposedly pay Yahoo! only for those that actually click through to a P&G site rather than those who merely eyeball a P&G banner ad on Yahoo!. Some have even argued for cost-per-lead or cost-per-sale systems.[20] This is a fundamentally different way of counting than has been the practice in advertising over the past century. About this method of compensation, Jeffery O'Brien of *Marketing Computers* magazine said, "In a way, [this practice] holds the Internet to a higher standard than other advertising media out there, but the Internet has something that none of those have—inherent accountability."[21]

Needless to say, other Internet providers and vehicles were not happy about this deal between these two important players. Still, it should be noted that the issue is far from resolved.

20.   adage.com/interactive/articles/19961223/article1.html.
21.   E. Weise, "P&G Changes Way Ads Paid For," *Cincinnati Enquirer*, April 29, 1996, A3.

Technical Aspects of the Measurement Problem

When a computer is connected to the Internet, it has a unique IP address, such as 204.17.123.5. When a link to a Web site, such as www.yahoo.com, is clicked on, a computer converts this textual representation into a number that is the unique IP address for Yahoo!. This computer then requests from Yahoo! its home page, and in return it gives Yahoo! its unique IP address so Yahoo! knows the address of the requester. Thus the only information a computer at a site such as Yahoo! receives is an IP address, along with the material the user is actually requesting. Note that a textual IP address is not the same thing as an E-mail address. E-mail addresses are similar but follow a different protocol on the Internet.

A Web site log file contains the IP addresses of the computers requesting information. However, an IP address does not usually correspond to just one person. Many systems dynamically assign IP addresses to computers connected to the Internet. Therefore a person visiting a site in two different sessions may have a different IP address each time. For an advertiser, this means it is unclear exactly how many different people visited the site. Even if a requesting computer has a permanent static address, thus allowing a site to keep track of a specific computer, the site still doesn't know who is actually using the computer. The computer could be used by one graduate student in his or her apartment, or it could be in a computer lab where hundreds of different people have access to the same computer.

A Web site can track how many machines accessed the site, but this does not correspond to how many people actually visited the Web site. One estimate is that the number of visitors exceeds IP addresses by about 15 percent.[22] Thus it is currently difficult to know exactly who is visiting a site, and if the visitors are revisiting. The only obvious enhancement would be implementing unique IDs in Web browsers. This would identify a specific computer visiting the site. However, this has not been seen as feasible due to current privacy concerns. It also leaves the possibility of many different people using the same computer, such as would occur in a computer lab.

The Caching Complication

To conserve resources on the Web, there is a system known as **caching.** Caching is a kind of active memory. Once a page is downloaded, the cache on the computer saves that page so it can be immediately accessed. Commercial online services such as America Online cache heavily trafficked sites on their computers so users get quicker response times when they request that page. Suppose a person first goes to a Web site's home page. After clicking on a link to go somewhere else, the user decides to go back to the home page. Instead of asking the Web site again for that home page, the cache will have stored it in anticipation of the user wanting it again. This conserves Internet resources, commonly called **bandwidth,** because the user is not needlessly requesting the same material twice. However, this complicates matters in measuring activity at the site because once a person has cached a page, the Web site has no idea whether the user repeatedly and prolongedly visited the page, or whether the user immediately moved on.

Technological solutions can reduce the amount of caching, thus allowing sites better data on how often a page is viewed, but it comes with the cost of additional bandwidth for the site and a slower response time for the person viewing the site. Caching may result in fewer page requests to a Web site than have actually occurred. Moreover, if a person hits the reload button, a Web site will register more traffic than there actually is.

Measurement Terminology

The information a Web site typically gets when a user connects with a site is the IP address of the Internet site that is requesting the page, what page is requested, and the time this is requested. This is the minimum amount of information available to a Web site. If a site requires registration, the additional information is requested directly from the user.

22. J. Udell, "Damn Lies," *Byte,* February 1996, 137.

Several terms, such as *hits, pages, visits,* and *users,* are used in Web audience measurement. **Hits** provide almost no indication of actual Web traffic. When a user requests a page with four graphical images, it counts as five hits. Thus by inflating the number of images, a site can quickly pull up its hit count. An example of this is *Penthouse*'s site. The *Penthouse* site gets 3 million hits a day, placing it among the top Web sites. However, this 3 million hits translates into only 80,000 people daily. (You do the math.)

Thus, hits do not translate into the number of people visiting a site.

Pages are defined as the pages sent to the requesting site. However, if a downloaded page occupies several screens, there is no indication that the requester examined the entire page. **Visits** are the number of occasions on which a user X looked up Y site during Z time. **Users** are the number of different people visiting X site during Y time.

Besides the address, page, and time, a Website can find out the referring link address. This allows a Web site to discover what links people are taking to the site. Thus, a site can analyze which links do in fact bring people to the site. This can be helpful in Internet advertising planning.

Log analysis software is measurement software that not only provides information on hits, pages, visits, and users but also lets a site track audience traffic within the site. A site could determine which pages are popular and expand on them. It is also possible to track the behavior of people as they go through the site, thus providing inferential information on what people find appealing and unappealing. An example of this software is MaxInfo's WebC, which allows advertisers to track what information is viewed, when it is viewed, how often it is viewed, and where users go within a site.[23] An advertiser can then modify the content and structure accordingly. It can also help advertisers understand how buyers make purchase decisions in general.[24] It still isn't possible, however, to know what people actually do with Web site information.

NEW MEDIA

USING THE NET TO RESEARCH AUDIENCES

One of the new media challenges for advertisers is understanding Internet users. Finding out who Net users are is a first step, and finding out what they value about the Internet is another important task. Crimson Communications of Menlo Park in California recently gained valuable insights for strategic decision making by gathering information from Internet users. The managing director of Crimson, Glenn Gow, offers these guidelines for gathering information about Internet audiences:

- *Target the right audience.* Gather names from people visiting your Web site. They already have an interest in your company or brand and will be more responsive. Crimson Communications realized a 45 percent response rate by tapping site visitors for information.
- *Pretest the survey.* As with any survey instrument, test the questionnaire first. A short online test is necessary since this is the context within which the survey will be administered.
- *Personalize the survey.* Personalization, to the extent possible, will increase response rates.
- *Mix in open-ended questions.* Use check boxes and rating scales to make responding easy. But also mix in open-ended questions to allow respondents to express their thoughts. Such open-ended responses often yield valuable copy points or tag line opportunities.
- *Follow up.* The proliferation of E-mail has created E-mail limbo for many messages. Follow up the original request with reminder messages. One reminder is probably appropriate. Harassing a potential customer with multiple requests for a response will accomplish nothing.
- *Ask for permission, online, to contact respondents offline.* Include in the survey a request to telephone the respondent. Phone interviews can yield much richer information than structured surveys.
- *Be prepared for all types of responses.* Some people use these kinds of opportunities to vent their frustrations. Be prepared for some nasty messages, particularly since some users think it is poor "netiquette" to conduct research on the Internet.
- *Recognize biases.* Conducting research on the Internet has at least two inherent biases. First, you can only contact active users—nonusers may hold the key to critical understanding. Second, like any survey, there will be some self-selection biases in those who choose to respond.

Source: "Eight Tips for Conducting Research over the Net," *Promo,* December 1995, 23.

23.   A. Cuneo, "BBDO West Links with 'Net Developer," *Advertising Age,* December 18, 1995, 28.
24.   E. Johnson, Marketing Doctoral Consortium, Wharton Business School, August 1995.

There are plenty of companies offering measurement services such as I/PRO, Net-Count, and Interse for interactive media. And, as exemplified in the New Media box on page 488, plenty of advice is available on how to do research on the Net. Yet there is no industry standard for measuring the effectiveness of one interactive ad placement over another. There also is no standard for comparing Internet with traditional media placements. Moreover, demographic information on who is using the WWW is severely limited. Until these limitations are overcome, many advertisers will remain hesitant about spending substantial dollars for advertising on the World Wide Web.

Security and Privacy   Any Web user can download text, images, and graphics from the World Wide Web. Although advertisers place trademark and copyright disclaimers on their online displays, advertisers on the Web have to be willing to accept the consequence that their trademarks and logos can be copied without authorization. Currently, there is no viable policing of this practice by users. Thus far, advertisers have taken legal action only against users who have taken proprietary materials and blatantly used them in a fashion that is detrimental to the brand or infringes on the exclusivity of the advertiser's own site. This may change.

With respect to consumer privacy, the Coalition for Advertising Supported Information & Entertainment (CASIE) has suggested five goals for advertisers:

- Consumers should be educated about electronic marketing.
- Marketers should clearly identify themselves in electronic communications.
- Marketers should respect the privacy of personal information.
- Consumers should be informed if personal information will be shared with others.
- Consumers should be able to request a summary of information that a marketer has obtained from them.[25]

Striving for these goals will certainly contribute to the loyalty and confidence that consumers possess for a brand. Privacy is a legitimate concern for Internet users, and will likely be one for civil libertarians and regulators as well.

25.   "CASIE Lists Goals for Interactive Privacy," *Advertising Age,* February 12, 1996, 26.

SUMMARY

1 Describe who uses and the ways they are using the Internet.

The Internet is a network of public and private computer systems. Millions of computers around the world are interconnected, in this modern-day wonder. No one knows for sure how many people are using the Net, but everyone projects that the number of users will continue to grow. The characteristics of those who do use the Internet make them an attractive audience for advertisers. To reach this audience, advertisers have four vehicles: E-mail, LISTSERVs, Usenet, and the World Wide Web. Of these, the World Wide Web clearly holds the greatest potential for advertisers. The WWW is a remarkable information resource, and surfing the Web using one of several search engines allows one to tap the resource. Web surfing is also emerging as a form of personal entertainment and thus represents a threat to traditional print and broadcast media.

2 Identify the advertising and marketing opportunities presented by the Internet.

Facing uncertainty about what they might hope to gain, advertisers and marketers nevertheless have flocked to the WWW. This interest by their clients has naturally forced ad agencies to develop expertise in Internet advertising. The two primary ways that advertisers establish themselves on the Web are by developing corporate home pages or placing banner ads. Other forms of marketing activity observed on the Web include participation in virtual malls, online coupon distribution, support for event marketing, and sales support that promotes one-to-one contact between marketers and their customers.

3 Discuss fundamental requirements for establishing viable sites on the World Wide Web.

Establishing a presence on the Web is relatively inexpensive when compared to the costs involved in mass media advertising, but updating and servicing a site are critical to its value and demand a continuing investment of time and money. In establishing and maintaining a site, one of the key goals must be to build in sources of information and entertainment that will keep surfers coming back to the site. Plain product information and promotion are not going to yield repeat visits. Also, to make a site valuable, an advertiser has to get a surfer to the site in the first place. This is no small undertaking in the chaotic order of the WWW. Purchasing keywords that connect a site to appropriate points of departure on a search engine like Yahoo!, or promoting the site via any number of other media, is necessary to get surfers to make an initial visit. Once there, they must find a reason to come back.

4 Explain the challenges inherent in measuring the cost-effectiveness of the Internet versus other advertising media.

To fulfill the Net's potential as an advertising medium, measurement tools must be developed that allow comparisons of the cost-effectiveness of the Internet versus traditional media. Better descriptive information on who is actually using the Net is also needed. Not surprisingly, current tracking mechanisms tally how often other computers have visited a particular Web site, but they cannot tell who the people were that operated the visiting computer. A memory technique known as caching adds further complications for tracking the frequency of visits to Web sites. Finally, privacy and anonymity have been characteristics highly valued by Internet users. If these are things that an audience values, getting detailed descriptions of such an audience will be a challenge.

KEY TERMS

Internet (470)
Internet relay chat (IRC) (471)
E-mail (473)
LISTSERVs (474)
Usenet (474)
spam (474)
World Wide Web (WWW) (474)
search engine (475)
corporate home page (478)
banner ads (479)

virtual mall (480)
cookie (485)
caching (487)
bandwidth (487)
hits (488)
pages (488)
visits (488)
users (488)
log analysis software (488)

QUESTIONS FOR REVIEW AND CRITICAL THINKING

1.   In the face of considerable uncertainty about audience size, audience composition, and cost-effectiveness, advertisers have nonetheless been flocking to the World Wide Web. What is it about the Web that advertisers have found so irresistible?

2.   How can an understanding of search engines and how they operate benefit an organization initiating an ad campaign on the WWW?

3.   Explain the two basic strategies for developing corporate home pages, exemplified in this chapter by Saturn and Reebok.

4.   Niche marketing will certainly be facilitated by the WWW. What is it about the WWW that makes it such a powerful tool for niche marketing?

5.   Visit some of the corporate home pages described in this chapter, or think about corporate home pages you have visited previously. Of those you have encountered, which would you single out as being most effective in giving the visitor a reason to come back? What conclusions would

you draw regarding the best ways to motivate repeat visits to a Web site?

6.   Visit www.zima.com, and you will find a site that asks the visitor to register to gain full access to the site. What incentive does Zima provide for registration? Would you be reluctant to register at this site? Why? In general, why would people be reluctant to register at this or other Web sites?

7.   Why is an agreement between Yahoo! and P&G such big news for advertisers with an interest in the WWW? Regarding the agreement between the two described in this chapter, in what sense did it hold Internet advertising to a higher standard than that used for print or broadcast media?

8.   The Internet was obviously not conceived or designed to be an advertising medium. Thus, some of its characteristics have proven perplexing to advertisers. If advertising professionals had the chance to redesign the Internet, what single change would you expect they would want to make to enhance its value from an advertising perspective?

EXPERIENTIAL EXERCISE

Television commercials often end with a Web site address. After viewing a television ad, go to the Web site address given. Are the television and Web site messages coordinated? Is there a synergy between the two messages? Does the

Web site refer to the television ad or to any print ads? Find a print ad for the same brand. Does the print ad include the Web site address? What does this exercise tell you about the coordination of advertising for the brand you selected?

USING THE INTERNET

There are three basic types of search engines, based on their classification schemes. Your task is to use the following search engines to find sites of interest to you:

Yahoo!: www.yahoo.com

Alta Vista: www.altavista.digital.com

Excite: www.excite.com

Based on your experiences with the search engines, answer the following questions:

1.   What are the unique advantages that each search engine offers?

2.   What are the disadvantages of each search engine?

3.   What type of search best takes advantage of each search engine's unique characteristics?

4.   Which of the search engines do you prefer to use? Why?

Chapter 18

Sales

Promotion

After reading and thinking about this chapter, you will be able to do the following:

1 Explain the popularity and rationale for different forms of sales promotions.

2 Describe the purposes and characteristics of sales promotions directed at consumers.

3 Describe the purposes and characteristics of sales promotions directed at the trade.

4 Discuss the risks and coordination issues associated with sales promotion.

Since the 1960s, 007 had always driven an Aston-Martin, the ultimate British performance sports car for the ultimate British spy. But in the newest James Bond movie, *GoldenEye,* Bond switched brands. 007's new vehicle of choice for daring chases and prestigious parties is the BMW Z3 roadster, shown in Exhibit 18.1. What would motivate a supersleuth to switch getaway cars? Performance? Styling? Status? No, what got James Bond to retire the Aston-Martin and roll out the Z3 was a product placement deal negotiated by a 34-year-old worldwide promotions vice president at MGM/United Artists.

This is the way the deal came about. MGM/UA needed to launch a new James Bond film featuring a new actor playing James Bond. BMW was launching its first true sports car for the commercial market in the Z3 roadster. Karen Sorito, senior vice president of worldwide promotions for MGM/UA, saw the partnership as a natural. The studio needed a new look and energy for the new James Bond, and BMW needed to create exposure and excitement for its new product. So a product placement deal was cut: The BMW Z3 would be prominently displayed as 007's new ride. In return, Munich-based BMW agreed to a media blitz promoting both the film and the car. BMW initiated an extensive campaign that hyped the film in television ads, BMW dealer showrooms, and even on airplanes. The impact of the promotion for BMW was swift and powerful. During the first two weeks, the company received 6,000 predelivery orders for the roadster. A spokesperson for BMW verified that the company "never had pre-order numbers like this before."[1]

Product placement (now, often referred to as brand placement) is another of the many tools that marketers can use to give visibility to a brand and support the advertising process. Until recently, product placement was simply considered a means to brand exposure. But with the immediate sales impact of programs like the one for the Z3, product placement takes a position alongside more traditional sales promotion tactics, like coupons, sampling, and sweepstakes.

Sales promotion is a multibillion-dollar business in the United States and is emerging as a global force as well. The message in a sales promotion typically features price reduction, a prize, or an incentive to visit a retailer. Sales promotions have proven to be popular alternatives to mass media advertising.

EXHIBIT 18.1

The BMW Z3 became James Bond's vehicle of choice after a product placement deal between MGM/UA and BMW.

1.   Blair R. Fischer, "Making Your Product the Star Attraction," *Promo,* January 1996, 88.

Basic Forms of Sales Promotion

Mass media advertising suffers from having effects that are hard to measure in the short run. This is not the case with sales promotion. Sales promotion is a conspicuous activity undertaken to make things happen in a hurry, as they did for BMW with the Z3 promotion. Used properly, sales promotion is capable of almost instant demand stimulation.

Formally defined, **sales promotion** is the use of incentive techniques that create a perception of greater brand value among consumers or distributors. The intent is to create a short-term increase in sales by motivating trial use or encouraging larger purchases or repeat purchases. **Consumer-market sales promotion** includes coupons, price-off deals, premiums, contests and sweepstakes, sampling and trial offers, product placements, refunds, rebates, and frequency programs. All are ways of inducing household consumers to purchase a firm's brand rather than a competitor's brand. Notice that some incentives reduce price, offer a reward, or encourage a trip to the retailer. **Trade-market sales promotion** uses point-of-purchase displays, incentives, allowances, trade shows, or cooperative advertising as ways of motivating distributors, wholesalers, and retailers to stock and feature a firm's brand in their merchandising programs.

The Importance and Growth of Sales Promotion

● Sales promotion is designed to affect demand differently than advertising. As we have learned throughout the text, most advertising is designed to have awareness-, image-, and preference-building effects for a brand over the long run. The role of sales promotion, on the other hand, is primarily to elicit an immediate purchase from a customer. Coupons, samples, rebates, sweepstakes, and similar techniques offer a consumer an immediate incentive, as exemplified in Exhibit 18.2.

EXHIBIT 18.2

Some forms of sales promotion turn the consumer into a walking billboard for the brand. Do you have your Pepsi Stuff? **www.pepsi.com/**

Other sales promotions like product placements and frequency programs provide an affiliation value with a brand. Sales promotions featuring price reductions are effective in the convenience-good category, where frequent purchases, brand switching, and a perceived homogeneity among brands characterize consumer behavior.

Sales promotions are used across all consumer goods categories and in the trade market as well. When a firm determines that a more immediate response is called for— whether the target customer is a household, business buyer, distributor, or retailer— sales promotions are designed to provide the incentive. The goals for sales promotion versus advertising are compared in Exhibit 18.3.

The Importance of Sales Promotion

The importance of sales promotion in the United States should not be underestimated. Sales promotion may not seem as stylish and sophisticated as mass media advertising, but expenditures on this tool are impressive. During the 1980s, sales promotion expenditures grew at an annual rate of 12 percent, compared to a 9 percent rate for advertising.[2] In 1995, the investment by marketers in sales promotions topped $70 billion.[3] Add to that figure consumer savings by redeeming promotions, and the figure exceeds $150 billion.[4]

It is important to recognize that advertising agencies specializing in advertising planning, creative preparation, and media placement typically do not prepare sales promotion materials for clients. These activities are delegated either to a subsidiary of the main agency or to specialized sales promotion agencies. A list of the top ten sales promotion agencies is shown in Exhibit 18.4.

The development and management of an effective sales promotion program requires a major commitment by a firm. Procter & Gamble estimates that during any given year, 25 percent of sales force time and 30 percent of brand management time is spent on designing, implementing, and overseeing sales promotions.[5] The rise in the use of sales promotion and the enormous amount of money being spent on various programs makes it one of the most prominent forms of marketing activity. But again, it must be undertaken only under certain conditions and then carefully executed for specific reasons.

Growth in the Use of Sales Promotion

Marketers have shifted the emphasis of their promotional spending over the past decade. Most of the shift has been away from mass media advertising and toward consumer and trade sales promotions. In 1981, the budget for promotions among packaged goods companies in the United States averaged 43 percent for advertising, 34 percent for trade promotions, and 23 percent for consumer

EXHIBIT 18.3

The purposes of sales promotion versus advertising.

Purpose of Sales Promotion	Purpose of Advertising
Stimulate short-term demand	Cultivate long-term demand
Encourage brand switching	Encourage brand loyalty
Induce trial use	Encourage repeat purchases
Promote price orientation	Promote image/feature orientation
Obtain immediate, often measurable results	Obtain long-term effects, often difficult to measure

2.   Russ Brown, "Sales Promotion," *Marketing and Media Decisions,* February 1990, 74.
3.   Statistic cited in Kerry E. Smith, "Another Great Year to Look Forward To," *Promo,* January 1996, 6.
4.   Kenneth Wylie, "Marketing Services," special report, *Advertising Age,* July 11, 1994, S1–S10.
5.   Robert D. Buzzell, John A. Quelch, and Walter J. Salmon, "The Costly Bargain of Sales Promotion," *Harvard Business Review* (March/April 1990): 141–49.

EXHIBIT 18.4

Largest sales promotion agencies in the United States, ranked by revenue.

Agency	U.S. Sales Promotion Revenue, 1994 ($ in thousands)	Percentage Change '93 to '94
1. Gage Marketing Group	$95,704.00	21.6%
2. Alcone Simes O'Brian	59,796.00	12.9
3. Frankel & Co.	31,591.00	19.2
4. Marketing Corp. of America	30,990.00	−3.5
5. Ross Roy Communications	30,043.00	5.3
6. D. L. Blair	25,544.00	−24.0
7. Ryan Partnership	21,322.00	−6.8
8. HMG Worldwide Corp.	20,000.00	NA
9. Flair Communications Agency	17,694.00	7.3
10. Clarion Marketing & Communications	16,387.00	15.2

Source: "Top Agencies by U.S. Sales Promotion Revenue," *Advertising Age,* July 10, 1995, S-2. Reprinted with permission from the July 10, 1995, issue of *Advertising Age.* Copyright © Crain Communications Inc. 1995.

promotions. By 1993, the budget allocation had shifted to 25 percent for advertising, 47 percent for trade promotions, and 28 percent for consumer promotions.[6] There are several reasons why some marketers have shifted their funds from mass media advertising to sales promotions. These reasons are discussed in the following sections.

Demand for Greater Accountability. In an era of cost cutting and downsizing, companies are demanding greater accountability across all functions, including marketing, advertising, and promotions. When activities are evaluated for their contribution to sales and profits, it is often difficult to draw specific conclusions regarding the effects of advertising. Conversely, the immediate effects of sales promotions are typically easier to document.

Short-Term Orientation. Several factors have created a short-term orientation among managers. Pressures from stockholders to produce better quarter-by-quarter revenue and profit per share is one factor. A bottom-line mentality is another factor. Many organizations are developing marketing plans—with rewards and punishments for performance—based on short-term revenue generation.[7] This being the case, tactics that can have short-term effects are sought. Thus the increased popularity of sales promotion.

Consumer Response to Promotions. The precision shopper of the nineties is demanding greater value across all purchase situations, and the trend is "battering overpriced brands."[8] These precision shoppers search for extra value in every product purchase. Coupons, premiums, price-off deals, and other sales promotions increase the value of a brand in these shoppers' minds. This positive response goes beyond value-oriented consumers. For consumers who are not well informed about the average price in a product category, a brand featuring a coupon or price-off promotion is sensed to be a good deal and will likely be chosen over competitive brands.[9]

Proliferation of Brands. Each year literally thousands of new brands are introduced into the consumer market. The drive by marketers to design products for specific market segments to satisfy ever more narrowly defined needs has caused a proliferation of brands that

6.   *16th Annual Survey of Promotional Practices* (Stamford, Conn.: Donnelley Marketing, 1994), 6.
7.   "What Happened to Advertising," *Business Week,* September 23, 1991, 66.
8.   Rahul Jacob, "Beyond Quality and Value," *Fortune,* Autumn/Winter 1993, 8–11.
9.   Leigh McAlister, "A Model of Consumer Behavior," *Marketing Communications,* April 1987, 26–28.

creates a mind-dulling maze for consumers. At any point in time, consumers can choose from approximately 64 spaghetti sauces, 103 snack chips, 54 laundry detergents, 91 cold remedies, and 69 disposable diaper varieties.[10] As you can see in Exhibit 18.5, gaining attention in this blizzard of brands is no easy task. Oftentimes marketers turn to sales promotions—product placements, contests, coupons, and premiums—to gain some recognition in a consumer's mind and stimulate a trial purchase.

Increased Power of Retailers.

Retailers like Home Depot, The Gap, Toys "Я" Us, and the most powerful of all, Wal-Mart, now dominate in the United States. These powerful retailers have responded quickly and accurately to the new environment for retailing, where consumers are demanding more and better products and services at lower prices. Because of the lower-price component of the retailing environment, these retailers are demanding more deals from manufacturers. Many of the deals are delivered in terms of trade-oriented sales promotions: point-of-purchase displays, slotting fees (payment for shelf space), case allowances, and cooperative advertising allowances. In the end, manufacturers use more and more sales promotion devices to gain and maintain good relations with the new, powerful retailers—a critical link to the consumer.

Media Clutter.

A nagging and traditional problem in the advertising process is clutter. Many advertisers target the same customers because their research has led them to the same conclusion about who to target. The result is that advertising media are cluttered with ads all seeking the attention of a common target. One way to break through the clutter is to feature a sales promotion. In print ads, the featured deal is often a coupon. In broadcast advertising, sweepstakes and premium offers can attract listeners' and viewers' attention. The combination of advertising and creative sales promotions can be a good way to break through the clutter, as suggested by the New Media box on page 502.

EXHIBIT 18.5

Marketers commonly turn to sales promotion in an effort to stand out from the crowd at the point of purchase. This exhibit nicely illustrates what the marketer (and the consumer!) is faced with in the cluttered retail environment.

10. Gabriella Stern, "Multiple Varieties of Established Brands Muddle Consumers, Make Retailers Mad," *Wall Street Journal,* January 24, 1992, B1, B9.

Sales Promotion Directed at Consumers

❷ It is clear that U.S. consumer-product firms have made a tremendous commitment to sales promotion in their overall marketing plans. During the 1970s, marketers allocated only about 30 percent of their budgets to sales promotion, with about 70 percent allocated to mass media advertising. Today, some estimate the percentages as just the opposite, with nearly 75 percent being spent on sales promotions.[11] Although the fundamental goal of sales promotion is to generate a sharp increase in short-term demand, there are some marketing strategists who also believe that proper application of these techniques can make a long-term contribution.[12]

Objectives for Consumer-Market Sales Promotion

To help ensure the proper application of sales promotion, specific strategic objectives should be set. The following are basic objectives that can be pursued with sales promotion in the consumer market:

- *Stimulate trial purchase.* When a firm wants to attract new users, sales promotion tools can reduce the consumer's risk of trying something new. A reduced price or offer of a rebate may stimulate trial purchase. When Keebler wanted to attract trial use in eight key Hispanic markets, it created the Keebler Kids Club, which featured giveaways and the *Keebler Kids Quiz Show,* which gave Spanish-speaking youngsters the chance to win college scholarships.[13]

- *Stimulate repeat purchases.* In-package coupons good for the next purchase, or the accumulation of points with repeated purchases, can keep consumers loyal to a particular brand. The most prominent frequency programs are found in the airline industry, where competitors like Delta, American, and United try to retain their most lucrative customers by enrolling them in frequency programs. Frequent flyers can earn free travel, hotel stays, gifts, and numerous other perks through the programs. Hyatt Hotels successfully launched a frequent-stay program much like the airlines' frequent-flyer programs. Hyatt's Gold Passport program rewards business travelers with discounts, room upgrades, free luggage tags, and other premiums if they stay at Hyatt Hotels.[14]

- *Stimulate larger purchases.* Price reductions or two-for-one sales can motivate consumers to stock up on a brand, thus allowing firms to reduce inventory or increase cash flow. Shampoo is often double-packaged to offer a value to consumers. Exhibit 18.6 is a sales promotion aimed at stimulating a larger purchase.

- *Introduce a new brand.* Because sales promotion can attract attention and motivate trial purchase, it is commonly used for new brand introduction. When the makers of Curad bandages wanted to introduce their new kid-size bandage, 7.5 million sample packs were distributed in McDonald's Happy Meal sacks. The promotion was a huge success, with initial sales exceeding estimates by 30 percent.[15]

- *Combat or disrupt competitors' strategies.* Because sales promotions often motivate consumers to buy in larger quantities or try new brands, they can be used to disrupt competitors' marketing strategies. If a firm knows one of its competitors is launching a new brand or initiating a new advertising campaign, a well-timed sales promotion offering deep discounts or extra quantity can disrupt the competitors' strategy. Add to the original discount an in-package coupon for future purchases, and a marketer

11. *15th Annual Survey of Promotional Practices* (Stamford, Conn.: Donnelley Marketing, 1993), 6.
12. B. Spethmann, "Money and Power," *Brandweek,* March 15, 1993, 21.
13. "Best in the World," *Promo,* November 1995, 39.
14. Constanza Montana, "Hotels Offer 'Frequent Stay' Plans to Lure Repeat Business," *Wall Street Journal,* January 6, 1987, 31.
15. Glen Heitsmith, "Still Bullish on Promotion," *Promo,* July 1994, 40.

can severely compromise competitors' efforts. *TV Guide* magazine used a sweepstakes promotion to combat competition. In an effort to address increasing competition from newspaper TV supplements and cable-guide magazines, *TV Guide* ran a Shopping Spree Sweepstakes in several regional markets. Winners won $200 shopping sprees in grocery stores—precisely the location where 65 percent of *TV Guide* sales are realized.[16]

• *Contribute to integrated marketing communications.* In conjunction with advertising, direct marketing, public relations, and other programs being carried out by a firm, sales promotion can add yet another type of communication to the mix. Sales promotions suggest an additional value, with price reductions, premiums, or the chance to win a prize. This is an additional and different message within the overall communications effort.

EXHIBIT 18.6

Sales promotions are commonly used to encourage consumers to stock up. In this exhibit, multiple incentives are being offered to promote larger and repeat purchases.

Consumer-Market Sales Promotion Techniques

There are several techniques used to stimulate demand and attract attention in the consumer market. Some of these are coupons, price-off deals, premiums, contests and sweepstakes, samples and trial offers, product placement, rebates, and frequency programs.

Coupons. A **coupon** entitles a buyer to a designated reduction in price for a product or service. Coupons are the oldest and most widely used form of sales promotion. The first use of a coupon is traced to around 1895, when the C. W. Post Company used a penny-off coupon as a way to get people to try its Grape-Nuts cereal. Annually, about 300 billion coupons are distributed to American consumers, with redemption rates ranging from 2 percent for gum purchases to nearly 45 percent for disposable diaper purchases. Exhibit 18.7 shows coupon redemption rates for several product categories. In 1995, consumers in the United States saved nearly $4 billion through coupon use.[17]

There are five advantages to the coupon as a sales promotion tool. First, the use of a coupon makes it possible to give a discount to a price-sensitive consumer while still selling the product at full price to other consumers. A price-sensitive customer takes the time to clip the coupon and carry it to the store; a regular consumer merely buys the product at full price.

Second, the coupon-redeeming customer is often a competitive-brand user, so the coupon can induce brand switching. Third, a manufacturer can control the timing and distribution of coupons. This way a retailer is not implementing price discounts inappropriately.

Fourth, a coupon is an excellent method of stimulating repeat purchases. Once a consumer has been attracted to a brand, with or without a coupon, an in-package coupon can induce repeat purchase. There is evidence that in-package coupons stimu-

16.   "*TV Guide* Tunes in Sweepstakes," *Promo,* November 1995, 1, 50.
17.   "Targeted Couponing Slows Redemption Slide," *Marketing News,* February 12, 1996, 11.

Product category   **Percentage of Purchases with Coupons**

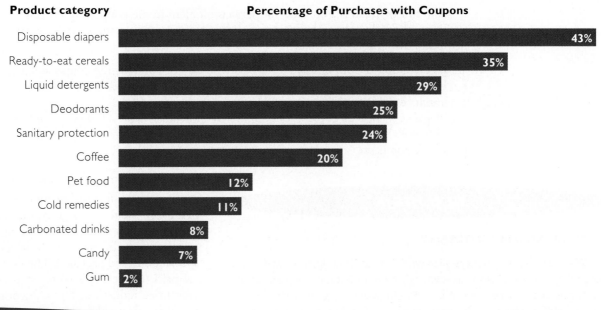

Product category	
Disposable diapers	43%
Ready-to-eat cereals	35%
Liquid detergents	29%
Deodorants	25%
Sanitary protection	24%
Coffee	20%
Pet food	12%
Cold remedies	11%
Carbonated drinks	8%
Candy	7%
Gum	2%

EXHIBIT 18.7

Product categories with the highest percentage of purchases made with coupons.

late greater brand loyalty than media-distributed coupons.[18] While an in-package coupon is designed to encourage repeat purchase and brand loyalty, retailers believe that coupons attached to the store shelf and distributed at the point of purchase are the most effective.[19]

And fifth, coupons can get regular users to trade up within a brand array. For example, users of low-price disposable diapers may be willing to try a premium variety with a coupon.

The use of coupons is not without its problems. First, while coupon price incentives and the timing of distribution can be controlled by a marketer, the timing of redemption cannot. Some consumers redeem coupons immediately; others hold them for months. Expiration dates printed on coupons help focus the redemption time but may compromise the impact of the coupons.

Second, coupons do attract competitors' users and some nonusers, but there is no way to prevent current users from redeeming coupons with their regular purchases. Heavy redemption by regular buyers merely reduces a firm's profitability. This has led some firms to consider eliminating coupons from their arsenal of marketing tools.[20] The Contemporary Issues box on page 504 describes one company's approach to coupon cutbacks.

Third, couponing entails administration. Coupon programs include much more than the cost of the face value of the coupon. There are costs for production and distribution and for retailer and manufacturer handling. In 1994, Procter & Gamble distributed 773 million coupons for its Folgers coffee brand, costing more than $14 million.[21] Marketers need to track these costs against the amount of product sold with and without coupon redemption.

18. Joe A. Dodson, Alice M. Tybout, and Brian Sternthal, "The Impact of Deals and Deal Retraction on Brand Switching," *Journal of Marketing Research* 15 (February 1978): 72.
19. Data displayed in *Advertising Age,* May 10, 1993, S–5.
20. "P&G to Experiment with Ending Coupons," *Marketing News,* February 12, 1996, 11.
21. "Coffee's On," *Promo,* February 1996, 48–49.

And fourth, fraud is a chronic and serious problem in the couponing process. The problem relates directly to misredemption practices. There are three types of misredemption that cost firms money:

- Redemption of coupons by consumers who do not purchase the couponed brand.
- Redemption of coupons by salesclerks and store managers without consumer purchases.
- Illegal collection or copying of coupons by individuals who sell them to unethical store merchants, who in turn redeem the coupons without the accompanying consumer purchases.

NEW MEDIA

A SCREAMING DEAL—LITERALLY

In 1994, parents and teachers alike were baffled when kids started screaming the word "Sega" in seemingly random fashion. The genesis of the Sega scream turned out to be a TV commercial tag line that caught on like wildfire with kids. But Sega wasn't satisfied to merely have kids all over the United States shrieking the brand name at the top of their lungs. Sega cleverly leveraged the phenomenon into a series of promotions and turned the scream into a marketing mantra.

Among a series of integrated promotions that included events, product tie-ins, on-pack promotions, and multimedia efforts, Sega developed an online contest to let Sega screamers test their howl against the experts. Specifically, visitors to Sega's Web site could upload to Sega to compare their screaming against that of Tom Kalinske—the company president. Then, users could download his version to be played back on their home computer system.

Tom Abramson, vice president of marketing and promotions, is the architect of Sega's award-winning promotional programs. *Advertising Age* named Sega the 1994 Promotional Marketer of the Year. Abramson came to Sega after working with the Ice Capades, Harlem Globetrotters, and Walt Disney World. Aside from the Sega Screaming Contest, he has conceived of such popular promotions as the Sega Worldwide Video Tournament (the finals of which took place at Alcatraz Prison) and special, limited flavors of Lifesavers candy to promote Sega's new Sonic 3 game.

But for all the creativity and aggressiveness of Abramson's promotions, he puts a premium on coordinating the promotional activities at Sega with the company's advertising. In his view, "Advertising sets the stage for our attitude and gets us into the heads of our users. But we use promotions and events to get Sega into the hands of consumers every day, by reaching into their school notebooks, lunch boxes, Little League and football practices, and their weekend parties."

Source: Kate Fitzgerald, "Sega 'Screams' Its Way to the Top," *Advertising Age*, March 20, 1995, S-2.

Price-Off Deals. The price-off deal is another straightforward technique. A **price-off deal** offers a consumer cents or even dollars off merchandise at the point of purchase through specially marked packages. The typical price-off deal is a 10 to 25 percent price reduction. The reduction is taken from the manufacturer's profit margin rather than the retailer's. Manufacturers like the price-off technique because it is controllable. Plus, the price off, judged at the point of purchase, can effect a positive price comparison against competitors. Consumers like a price-off deal because it is straightforward and automatically increases the value of a known brand. Regular users tend to stock up on an item during a price-off deal. Retailers are less enthusiastic about this technique. Price-off promotions can create inventory and pricing problems for retailers. Also, most price-off deals are snapped up by regular customers, so the retailer doesn't benefit from new business.

Premiums. **Premiums** are items offered free, or at a reduced price, with the purchase of another item. Many firms offer a related product free, such as a free granola bar packed inside a box of granola cereal. Service firms, like a car wash or dry cleaner, may use a two-for-one offer to persuade consumers to try the service.

There are two options available for the use of premiums. A **free premium** provides consumers with an item at no cost; the item is either included in the package of a purchased item or mailed to the consumer after proof of purchase is verified. The most frequently used free premium is an additional package of the original item or a free related item placed in the package. Some firms do offer unrelated free premiums, like balls, toys, and trading cards. These types of premiums are particularly popular with cereal manufacturers.

A **self-liquidating premium** requires a consumer to pay most of the cost of the item received as a premium, as shown in Exhibit 18.8. Cigarette brands, like Camel and Marlboro, have their own catalog of items from which consumers can order brand-logo products. A manufacturer may offer these items at or below cost to maintain visibility and brand loyalty.

Self-liquidating premiums are particularly effective with loyal customers. However, these types of premiums must be used cautiously. Unless the premium is related to a value-building strategy for a brand, it can, like other sales promotions, serve to focus consumer attention on the premium rather than on the benefits of the brand. Such an outcome could cause erosion of brand equity.

EXHIBIT 18.8

Premiums take many shapes and sizes. What is it about this premium offer that makes it self-liquidating?

Contests and Sweepstakes. Contests and sweepstakes can draw attention to a brand like no other sales promotion technique. Technically, there are important differences between the two. A **contest** has consumers compete for prizes based on skill or ability. Winners in a contest are determined by a panel of judges or based on which contestant comes closest to a predetermined criterion for winning, such as picking the total points scored in the Super Bowl. Contests tend to be somewhat expensive to administer because each entry must be judged against winning criteria.

A **sweepstakes** is a promotion in which winners are determined purely by chance. Consumers need only to enter their names in the sweepstakes as a criterion for winning. Sweepstakes often use official entry forms as a way for consumers to enter the sweepstakes. Publishers Clearing House has run a high-profile sweepstakes in the United States over the past ten years. Other popular types of sweepstakes use scratch-off cards. Instant-winner scratch-off cards tend to attract customers. Gasoline retailers, grocery stores, and fast-food chains commonly use scratch-off cards as a way of building and maintaining store traffic. Sweepstakes can also be designed so that repeated trips to the retail outlet are necessary to gather a complete set of winning cards. Research indicates that for contests and sweepstakes to be effective, marketers must design them in such a way that consumers perceive value in the prizes and find playing the games intrinsically interesting.[22]

Contests and sweepstakes can span the globe. British Airways ran a contest with the theme "The World's Greatest Offer," in which it gave away thousands of free airline tickets to London and other European destinations. While the contest increased awareness of the airline, a spokesperson said there was definitely another benefit: "We're creating a database with all these names. All those people who didn't win will be getting mail from us with information on other premium offers."[23]

Contests and sweepstakes often create excitement and generate interest for a brand, but the problems of administering these promotions are substantial. Primary among the problems are the regulations and restrictions on such promotions. Advertisers must

22.   James C. Ward and Ronald Paul Hill, "Designing Effective Promotional Games: Opportunities and Problems," *Journal of Advertising* 20, no. 3 (September 1991): 69–81.
23.   Thomas R. King, "Marketers Bet Big with Contests to Trigger Consumer Spending," *Wall Street Journal,* April 4, 1991, B8.

be sure that the design and administration of a contest or sweepstakes complies with both federal and state laws. Each state may have slightly different regulations. The legal problems are complex enough that most firms hire agencies that specialize in contests and sweepstakes to administer the programs.

CONTEMPORARY ISSUES

MAJOR MARKETER SAVING ON COUPONS

Procter & Gamble, considered by many the top marketing organization in the world, is testing a program of major cutbacks in coupon use. P&G has eliminated couponing for all its brands in the Buffalo, Rochester, and Syracuse markets and plowed the savings into value pricing and brand building. Early test results suggest that supermarkets in the area are reporting solid gains in the sales of P&G brands.

P&G's test is the latest step in a downward trend in coupon distribution and consumer redemption of coupons. In 1992, consumers redeemed 7.7 billion cents-off coupons at grocery and drug retail outlets. In 1995, that number had fallen to 5.8 billion (a 20 percent decline). In addition, coupon distribution by marketers fell 6 percent in 1995, to 291.1 billion. There is no doubt that Procter & Gamble is leading the way in this decline. Within its $5 billion annual marketing and promotions budget, P&G has reduced national coupon expenditures by 50 percent since 1990.

The success of the P&G test has led other marketers, also disenchanted with the drawbacks of couponing, to consider a similar cutback. As the discussion in this chapter points out, while coupons can attract attention and have positive effects on short-term demand, the liabilities of couponing can be troublesome. A spokesperson has said that P&G's own studies show that coupons are an "inherently inefficient way to promote products." Further, retailers are tired of the time and expense of handling manufacturer coupons that don't address their local market needs or strategic agendas.

This move away from broad national couponing should not be interpreted as a death knell for coupons as a promotional tool, however. Analysts following the P&G test agree that the coupon remains an important tool when used strategically for new-product trial and brand-switching programs.

Sources: Pat Sloan, "P&G Tops Rivals in No-Coupon Push," *Advertising Age,* January 15, 1996, 3; and Kate Fitzgerald, "P&G's Zero-Coupon Move Sparks Related Cutbacks by Competitors," *Advertising Age,* March 18, 1996, 3.

Another problem is that the game itself may become the consumer's primary focus, while the brand becomes secondary. The technique thus fails to build long-term consumer affinity for a brand. This problem is inherent to most forms of sales promotion, not just contests and sweepstakes.

The final problem with contests and sweepstakes relates to the IMC effort a firm may be attempting. It is hard to get any message across in the context of a game. The consumer's interest is focused on the game, rather than on any feature or value message included in the contest or sweepstakes communication. A related problem is that if a firm is trying to develop a quality or prestige image for a brand, contests and sweepstakes may contradict this goal.

Sampling and Trial Offers. Getting consumers to simply try a brand can have a powerful effect on future decision making. **Sampling** is a technique designed to provide a consumer with a trial opportunity, as Exhibit 18.9 illustrates. Saying that sampling is a popular technique is an understatement. Estimates suggest that nearly 90 percent of consumer-product companies use sampling and invest approximately 15 percent of their total promotional budget in the technique.[24] A recent survey shows that consumers are very favorable toward sampling; 92 percent of consumers surveyed preferred a free sample to a coupon.[25] Sampling is particularly useful for new products but should not be reserved for new products alone. It can be used successfully for established brands with weak market share in specific geographic areas. Through sampling, some firms have experienced immediate sales increases five to ten times normal rates, with lasting effects on volume in the 10 to 15 percent range.[26]

24. "Sampling Continues to Be a Popular Choice," *Advertising Age,* May 16, 1993.
25. Kate Fitzgerald, "Survey: Consumers Prefer Sampling over Coupons," *Advertising Age,* January 29, 1996, 9.
26. Alix M. Freedman, "Use of Free Product Samples Wins New Favor as Sales Tool," *Wall Street Journal,* August 28, 1986, 19.

EXHIBIT 18.9

Sampling is a potent tactic when just getting a brand into the hands of consumers is the best way to win them over. Upmann, anyone?

There are five techniques used in sampling. **In-store sampling** is popular for food products and cosmetics. This is a preferred technique for many marketers because the consumer is at the point of purchase and may be swayed by a direct encounter with the brand. Increasingly, in-store demonstrators are handing out coupons as well as samples. **Door-to-door sampling** is extremely expensive because of labor costs, but it can be effective if the marketer has information that locates the target segment in a well-defined geographic area. Some firms enlist the services of newspaper delivery people, who pack the sample with daily or Sunday newspapers as a way of reducing distribution costs. **Mail sampling** allows samples to be delivered through the postal service. Again, the value here is that certain zip-code markets can be targeted. A drawback is that the sample must be small to be economically feasible. Specialty-sampling firms, like Alternative Postal Delivery, provide targeted geodemographic door-to-door distribution as an alternative to the postal service.

On-package sampling, a technique in which the sample item is attached to another product package, is useful for brands targeted to current customers. Attaching a small bottle of Ivory conditioner with a regular-sized container of Ivory shampoo is a logical sampling strategy. Finally, **mobile sampling** is carried out by logo-emblazoned vehicles that dispense samples, coupons, and premiums to consumers at malls, shopping centers, fairgrounds, and recreational areas. Marketers like Kodak and Clairol are finding that intercepting prospects while they're at play or engaged in activities that complement product use is a good way to influence awareness, use, and preference.[27]

Of course, sampling has its critics. Unless the product has a clear value and benefit over competition, simple trial of the product is unlikely to convince a consumer to switch brands. This is especially true for convenience goods because consumers perceive a high degree of similarity among brands, even after trying them. The perception of benefit and superiority may have to be developed through advertising in combination with sampling. In addition, sampling is expensive. This is especially true in cases where a sufficient quantity of a product, like shampoo or laundry detergent, must be given away for a consumer to truly appreciate a brand's values. Finally, sampling can be a very imprecise process. Despite the emergence of special agencies to handle sampling programs, a firm can never completely ensure that the product is reaching the targeted audience.

Trial offers have the same goal as sampling—to induce consumer trial use of a brand—but they are used for more expensive items. Exercise equipment, appliances, watches, hand tools, and consumer electronics are typical of items offered on a trial basis. Exhibit 18.10 shows an offer, aimed at sales managers, to try a $199 package of computer software free for a limited time. Trials are offered for as little as 1 day to as long as 90 days. The expense to the firm, of course, can be formidable. Segments chosen for this promotional device must have high sales potential.

27.   Carolyn Shea, "Going Mobile," *Promo,* February 1996, 41–42.

EXHIBIT 18.10

For expensive products like exercise equipment or computer software, sampling is impractical. The familiar alternative is the 30-day, risk-free trial offer.

Product Placement. As we saw at the outset of the chapter, product placements in films, movies, and television shows can create a positive sales impact for a brand. Marketers and advertisers used to think product placements affected only consumers' perceptions of a brand, more like advertising. But recent product placements show that the technique can have a sales impact like a traditional sales promotion. For example, consider these results:

- Sales of Nike sneakers and apparel jumped after the release of the hit movie *Forrest Gump*. The film featured the star Tom Hanks getting a pair of Nike running shoes as a gift, which his character, Gump, believes is "the best gift anyone could get in the whole wide world." Later in the film, Gump wears a Nike T-shirt during a cross–country run.
- When Jennifer Gray danced in retro oxford sneakers in the film *Dirty Dancing,* the shoe's manufacturer, Keds, saw a huge increase in sales.
- One of the biggest beneficiaries of a product placement was Bausch and Lomb. Tom Cruise wore distinctive Bausch and Lomb Ray Ban sunglasses in the film *Risky Business* and the glasses were featured on the movie poster as well. Ray Ban sales rocketed to all-time highs after the film's release.[28]

The newfound power of product placement has been surprising, but the process is relatively simple. Once a movie studio or television production team approves a script and schedules production, product placement specialists, either in-house or working for specialty agencies, go to work. They send the script to targeted companies in an effort to sell product placement opportunities. If a company agrees, then little more is involved than having the product sent to the studio for inclusion in the film or program. Marketers like BMW and Coke play a more formative role, but they are exceptions.

Product placement, like any other communications effort, shows varying results. If the brand name is spoken aloud, such as Gene Hackman telling Tom Cruise to help himself to a Red Stripe beer during the film *The Firm,* the impact can be dramatic.

28. Examples found in Fischer.

Similarly, prominent use by a celebrity of a featured brand, such as Mel Gibson clearly drinking a Dr. Pepper or Dennis Quaid eating at McDonald's, can achieve 40 to 50 percent recognition within an audience. Less obvious placements, referred to as background placements, are considered by some a waste of money.[29]

Rebates. Rebates started in the mid-1970s when auto dealers feared price freezes would be imposed by the government as a means to curb inflation. Auto dealers discovered that a rebate on the purchase price of a car was a way around the impending freeze. The price freeze never materialized, but rebates have been a fixture in sales promotion ever since. The rebate technique has been refined over the years and is now used by a wide variety of marketers. Rebates are particularly well suited to increasing the quantity purchased by consumers, so rebates are commonly tied to multiple purchases.

Frequency Programs. In recent years, one of the most popular sales promotion techniques among consumers has been frequency programs. **Frequency programs,** also referred to as continuity programs, offer consumers discounts or free product rewards for repeat purchase or patronage of the same brand or company. These programs were pioneered by airline companies. Frequent-flyer programs like Delta Air Lines's SkyMiles, frequent-stay programs like Marriott's Honored Guest Award program, and frequent-renter programs like Hertz's #1 Club are examples of such loyalty-building activities. But frequency programs are not reserved for big national airline and auto-rental chains. Chart House Enterprises, a chain of 65 upscale restaurants, successfully launched a frequency program for diners, who earned points for every dollar spent. Frequent diners were issued "passports," which were stamped with each visit. Within two years, the program had more than 300,000 members.[30] Exhibit 18.11 features Marriott's frequency program.

EXHIBIT 18.11

The use of frequency programs can help build a sustained customer base. The reference to the frequency program in this Marriott ad closely ties the sales promotion to the advertising campaign. Two of the most successful frequency programs are those of Delta Air Lines and Marriott. At their Web sites **www.delta-air.com/index.html** *and* **www .marriott.com/**, *compare how they cater to their most important customers. Is one approach more effective than the other? Why?*

WEB SIGHTING

"WHY IS OUR AWARD PROGRAM SO POPULAR WITH FREQUENT TRAVELERS? WE'RE IN EVERY CITY THEY FREQUENT."

Bill Marriott

As a business traveler you earn free vacations faster with Marriott's Honored Guest Award program. With over 250 locations worldwide, we're doing business wherever you're doing business. To join the program call 1-800-648-8024. For reservations, call your travel agent or 1-800-228-9290.

Marriott
HOTELS·RESORTS·SUITES

WE MAKE IT HAPPEN FOR YOU

29.   "Motion Pictures, Moving Brands," *Promo,* January 1996, 44.
30.   Kerry J. Smith, "Building a Winning Frequency Program—The Hard Way," *Promo,* December 1995, 36.

Sales Promotion Directed at the Trade

3 Sales promotions directed at members of the trade—wholesalers, distributors, and retailers—are designed to stimulate demand in the short term and help push the product through the distribution channel. Effective trade promotions can generate enthusiasm for a product and contribute positively to the loyalty distributors show for a brand. With the massive proliferation of new brands and brand extensions, manufacturers need to stimulate enthusiasm and loyalty among members of the trade.

Objectives for Trade Promotions

As in the consumer market, trade-market sales promotions should be undertaken with specific objectives in mind. Four primary objectives can be identified for these promotions:

- *Obtain initial distribution.* Because of the proliferation of brands in the consumer market, there is fierce competition for shelf space. Sales promotion incentives can help a firm gain initial distribution and shelf placement. Like consumers, members of the trade need a reason to choose one brand over another when it comes to allocating shelf space. A well-conceived promotion incentive may sway them.

- *Increase order size.* One of the struggles in the channel of distribution is over the location of inventory. Manufacturers prefer that members of the trade maintain large inventories so the manufacturer can reduce inventory-carrying costs. Similarly, members of the trade would rather make frequent, small orders and carry little inventory. Sales promotion techniques can encourage wholesalers and retailers to order in large quantities, thus shifting the inventory burden to the channel.

- *Encourage cooperation with consumer-market sales promotions.* It does a manufacturer little good to initiate a sales promotion in the consumer market if there is little cooperation in the channel. Wholesalers may need to maintain larger inventories, and retailers may need to provide special displays or handling during consumer-market sales promotions. To achieve synergy, marketers often run trade promotions simultaneously with consumer promotions. This is precisely what Stroh Brewery did with its "Schlitz WWII 50th Anniversary" campaign. To commemorate the men and women who served in World War II, Strohs offered Schlitz Beer in a replica of its 1945 can. Consumers could also order a commemorative Schlitz beer tray or enter a sweepstakes to win a leather bomber jacket. The campaign included newspaper ads featuring the sweepstakes and point-of-purchase displays. Trade members contributed to an immediate 12 percent increase in sales.[31]

- *Increase store traffic.* Retailers can increase store traffic through special promotions or events. Door-prize drawings, parking lot sales, or live radio broadcasts from the store are common sales promotion traffic builders. Burger King has become a leader in building traffic at its 6,500 outlets with special promotions tied to Disney movie debuts. Beginning in 1991 with a *Beauty and the Beast* tie-in promotion, Burger King has set records for generating store traffic with premium giveaways. The *Pocahontas* campaign distributed 55 million toys and glasses. Most recently, a promotion tie-in with Disney's huge success *Toy Story* resulted in 50 million toys, based on the film's characters, being given away in $1.99 Kid Meals.[32]

Trade-Market Sales Promotion Techniques

When marketers devise incentives to encourage purchases by members of the trade, they are executing a **push strategy;** that is, sales promotions directed at the trade help push a product into the distribution channel until it ultimately reaches consumers. The sales promotion techniques used with the

---

31. "Best in the World," 40.
32. Editors' Special Report, "Having It Their Way," *Promo,* December 1995, 79–80.

trade are point-of-purchase displays, incentives, allowances, trade shows, sales training programs, and co-op advertising.

Point-of-Purchase Displays.
Product displays and information sheets are useful in reaching the consumer at the point of purchase and often encourage retailers to support one's brand. P-O-P promotions can help win precious shelf space and exposure in a retail setting. From a retailer's perspective, a P-O-P display should be designed to draw attention to a brand, increase turnover, and possibly distribute coupons or sweepstakes entry forms. Exhibit 18.12 shows a typical P-O-P display. Advertisers invested $17 billion in P-O-P materials in 1994. This is more than was spent on either magazine or radio advertising.[33]

Incentives.
Incentives to members of the trade include a variety of tactics not unlike those used in the consumer market. Awards in the form of travel, gifts, or cash bonuses for reaching targeted sales levels can induce retailers and wholesalers to give a firm's brand added attention. The incentive does not have to be large or expensive to be effective. Weiser Lock offered its dealers a Swiss Army knife with every dozen cases of locks ordered. The program was a huge success. A follow-up promotion featuring a Swiss Army watch was an even bigger hit.

One risk with incentive programs for the trade is that salespeople can be so motivated to win an award that they may try to sell the brand to every customer, whether it fits that customer's needs or not. Also, a firm must carefully manage such programs to minimize ethical dilemmas. An incentive technique can look like a bribe unless it is carried out in a highly structured and open fashion.

Allowances.
There are various forms of allowances offered to retailers and wholesalers with the purpose of increasing the attention given to a firm's brands. **Merchandise allowances,** in the form of free products packed with regular shipments, are payments to the trade for setting up and maintaining displays. The payments are typically far less than manufacturers would have to spend to maintain the displays themselves. Shelf space has

EXHIBIT 18.12

As noted by Exhibit 18.5, the point of purchase is an important competitive battleground. Here we see an excellent illustration of one marketer's effort to take control of that battleground.

33.   Data cited in Leah Haran, "Point of Purchase: Marketers Getting with the Program," *Advertising Age,* October 23, 1995, 33.

become so highly demanded, especially in supermarkets, that manufacturers are making direct cash payments, known as **slotting fees,** to induce food chains to stock an item. The proliferation of new products has made shelf space such a precious commodity that these fees now run in the hundreds of thousands of dollars per product.

Trade Shows. **Trade shows** are events where several related products from many manufacturers are displayed and demonstrated to members of the trade. Company representatives are on hand to explain the products and perhaps make an important contact for the sales force. The use of trade shows must be carefully coordinated and can be an important part of trade-oriented promotional programs. Trade shows can be critically important to a small firm that cannot afford advertising and has a sales staff too small to reach all its potential customers. Through the trade-show route, salespeople can make far more contacts than would be possible with direct sales calls. Several excellent trade-show tips are presented in the Contemporary Issues box on page 514.

Sales-Training Programs. An increasingly popular trade promotion is to provide training for retail store personnel. This method is used for consumer durables and specialty goods, like personal computers, home theater systems, heating and cooling systems, security systems, and exercise equipment. The increased complexity of these products has made it important for manufacturers to ensure that the proper factual information and persuasive themes are reaching consumers at the point of purchase. For personnel at large retail stores, manufacturers can hold special classes that feature product information, demonstrations, and training about sales techniques.

Another popular method for getting sales-training information to retailers is the use of videotapes and brochures. Manufacturers can also send sales trainers into retail stores to work side by side with store personnel. This is a costly method, but it can be very effective because of the one-on-one attention it provides.

Cooperative Advertising. As we have seen previously, cooperative advertising refers to joint advertising efforts between retailers and manufacturers. The manufacturer shares the cost of media—usually on a 50–50 basis—with the retailer. Exhibit 18.13 presents an example of a cooperative advertising program.

Cooperative advertising as a trade promotion technique is referred to as **vertical cooperative advertising.** (Such efforts are also called vendor co-op programs.) Manufacturers try to control the content of this co-op advertising in two ways. They may set strict specifications for the size and content of the ad and then ask for verification that such specifications have been met. Alternatively, manufacturers may send the template for an ad, into which retailers merely insert the names and locations of their stores.

EXHIBIT 18.13

Retailers and manufacturers often team up in creating sales promotion programs. These cooperative efforts can generate synergies that benefit both parties. **www.ariens.com**

Aside from co-op programs with individual retailers, some manufacturers sponsor advertising with dealer associations. One of the most successful programs of this type is the Rocky Mountain Chevy Dealers co-op program. Chevrolet has had a co-op advertising program for many years with this dealer association. The association runs a series of television ads featuring the popular celebrity Merlin Olsen as a spokesperson for both Chevrolet and the ten Chevrolet dealers that make up the association. One of their ads is shown in Exhibit 18.14.

The Risks of Sales Promotion

4 Sales promotion can be used to pursue important sales objectives. As we have seen, there are a wide range of sales promotion options for both the consumer and trade markets. But there are also significant risks associated with sales promotion, and these risks must be carefully considered.

Creating a Price Orientation

Since most sales promotions rely on some sort of price incentive or giveaway, a firm runs the risk of having its brand perceived as cheap, with no real value or benefits beyond low price. Creating this perception in the market contradicts the concept of integrated marketing communication. If advertising messages highlight the value and benefit of a brand only to be contradicted by a price emphasis in sales promotions, then a confusing signal is being sent to the market.

Borrowing from Future Sales

Management must admit that sales promotions are typically short-term tactics designed to reduce inventories, increase cash flow, or show periodic boosts in market share. The downside is that a firm may simply be borrowing from future sales. Consumers or trade buyers who would have purchased the brand anyway may be motivated to stock up at the lower price. This results in reduced sales during the next few time periods of measurement. This can cause havoc with the desire to measure and evaluate the effect of advertising campaigns or other image-building communications. If consumers are responding to sales promotions, it may be impossible to tease out the effects of advertising.

Alienating Customers

When a firm relies heavily on sweepstakes or frequency programs to build loyalty among customers, particularly their best customers, there is the

EXHIBIT 18.14

Here again we see an example of cooperation between a manufacturer and retailers. In this case the manufacturer is General Motors and the retailers are its Rocky Mountain Chevy Dealers.
www.chevrolet.com/

risk of alienating these customers with any change in the program. Airlines suffered just such a fate when they tried to adjust the mileage levels needed for awards in their frequent-flyer programs. Ultimately, many of the airlines had to give concessions to their most frequent fliers as a conciliatory gesture.

Time and Expense

Sales promotions are both costly and time-consuming. The process is time-consuming for the marketer and the retailer in terms of handling promotional materials and protecting against fraud and waste in the process. As we have seen in recent years, funds allocated to sales promotions are taking dollars away from advertising. Advertising is a long-term, franchise-building process that should not be compromised for short-term gains.

Legal Considerations

With the increasing popularity of sales promotions, particularly contests and premiums, there has been an increase in legal scrutiny at both the federal and state levels. Legal experts recommend that before initiating promotions that use coupons, games, sweepstakes, and contests, a firm check into lottery laws, copyright laws, state and federal trademark laws, prize notification laws, right of privacy laws, tax laws, and FTC and FCC regulations.[34] The best advice for staying out of legal trouble with sales promotions is to carefully and clearly state the rules and conditions related to the program so that consumers are fully informed.

The Coordination Challenge

There is an allure to sales promotion that must be put in perspective. Sales promotions can make things happen—quickly. While managers often find the immediacy of sales promotion valuable, particularly in meeting quarterly sales goals, sales promotions are rarely a viable means of long-term success. But when used properly, sales promotions can be an important element in a well-conceived IMC campaign. Key to their proper use is coordinating the message emphasis and the placement of sales promotions with the advertising effort. When advertising and sales promotion are well coordinated, the impact of each is enhanced—a classic case of synergy.

Message Coordination

The typical sales promotion should either attract attention to a brand or offer consumers and the trade greater value: reduced price, more product, or the chance to win a prize or award. In turn, this focused attention and extra value act as an incentive to choose the promoted brand over other brands. One of the coordination problems this presents is that advertising messages, designed to build long-term loyalty, may not seem totally consistent with the extra-value signal of the sales promotion.

This is the classic problem that advertisers face in coordinating sales promotion with an advertising campaign. First, advertising messages tout brand features or emotional attractions. Then, the next contact a consumer may have with the brand is an insert in the Sunday paper offering a cents-off coupon. These mixed signals can be damaging for a brand.

Increasing the coordination between advertising and various sales promotion efforts requires only the most basic planning. First, when different agencies are involved in preparing sales promotion materials and advertising materials, those agencies need to be kept informed by the advertiser regarding the maintenance of a desired theme. Second, simple techniques can be used to carry a coordinated theme between promotional tools. The use of logos, slogans, visual imagery, or spokespersons can create a consistent

34. Maxine S. Lans, "Legal Hurdles Big Part of Promotions Game," *Marketing News,* October 24, 1994, 15.

EXHIBIT 18.15

One simple principle for enhancing the impact of any sales promotion is to feature logos or visual imagery common in the brand's advertising. These examples from Progresso illustrate the common-look principle.
info.pillsbury.com/tpc/progresso.html

presentation. As illustrated in Exhibit 18.15, even if advertising and sales promotion pursue different purposes, the look and feel of both efforts may be coordinated. The more the theme of a promotion can be tied directly to the advertising campaign, the more impact these messages will generally have on the consumer.

Media Coordination

Another key in coordination involves timing. Remember that the success of a sales promotion depends on the consumer believing that the chance to save money or receive more of a product represents enhanced value. If the consumer is not aware of a brand and its features and benefits, and does not perceive the brand as a worthy item, then there will be no basis for perceiving value—discounted or not. This means that appropriate advertising should precede price-oriented sales promotions for them to be effective. The right advertising can create an image for a brand that is appropriate for a promotional offer. Then, when consumers are presented with a sales promotion, the offer will impress the consumer as an opportunity to acquire superior value.

Conclusions from Recent Research

The synergy theme prominent in the preceding discussion is not just a matter of speculation. Recent research using single-source data generated by A. C. Nielsen reaffirms many of the primary points of this chapter.[35] John Philip Jones has reported the major conclusions of this research:

- The short-term productivity of promotions working alone is much more dramatic than that of advertising. Promotions that involve price incentives on average yield a

---

35. John Philip Jones, *When Ads Work* (New York: Lexington Books, 1995).

CONTEMPORARY ISSUES

WINNING BUSINESS AT TRADE SHOWS

While many aspects of business-to-business marketing might not seem glamorous, the trade show is one activity that can equal any glamor or hype that consumer goods marketers can dream up. And nowhere is the spending and hype greater than at the Comdex annual trade show in Las Vegas. Every year hundreds of exhibitors and hundreds of thousands of conventioneers converge on Las Vegas for Comdex. Comdex is not just the largest computer hardware and software trade show, it is the largest trade show in America.

Trade shows have been a fixture in the trade market for many years. Despite years of experience, marketers still have trouble making a lasting impression and building strong relationships at these trade-market sales promotion events. Part of the problem is the intense competition for recognition. Aside from the huge numbers of exhibitors at many shows, the big-name companies spend lavishly on booths and special attractions. The editors at *Sales & Marketing Management*, a leading trade publication, offer some tips on getting the most out of a trade show:

- *Create moving billboards.* Smart exhibitors try to capture attendees' attention all over the trade show and the trade show city—not just at their booth. Give booth visitors handouts that create what amount to moving billboards. The most popular device is a tote bag with your company name and logo that gets carried around the show. Also try sponsoring bus boards and cab boards that cruise the city during the trade show.
- *Make the booth interactive.* Games, contests, tests of skill, trivia challenges, and other interactive activities are effective ways of getting people to and into the booth. Make sure the prizes are worth winning, or the encounter can create a lasting negative impression.
- *Qualify leads immediately.* Ask every booth visitor to fill out a qualification card that includes questions on their interest in your product. If they stopped by the booth out of curiosity or simply to enter a drawing, that's fine. You just don't want to waste time following up on those who have no real interest in your product.
- *Create a presence on the show floor.* While this may be easier said than done, standing out in the crowd is a must. Some exhibitors hire celebrities, others run exciting games. Whatever the technique, work hard at breaking from the ordinary.
- *Plan ahead.* Just showing up isn't good enough. Use the trade show as an opportunity to spend time with particularly important customers or prospects. This means planning well in advance to have the customer or prospect meet at the booth for a special presentation or demonstration. Since major trade shows attract a large number of interested prospects, book as many meetings and contacts as possible.
- *Get in people's faces.* Make sure your marketing and sales people don't stand around the booth talking to each other. Get them out in the aisles. Have them roam the convention hall passing out tote bags, buttons, or other premiums. Have them recruit people into the booth for a serious demonstration.

1.8 percent increase in sales for each 1 percent price reduction. A 1 percent increase in advertising yields just a 0.2 percent sales increase on average.

- The average cost of a 1 percent reduction in price is always far greater than the cost of a 1 percent increase in advertising. Thus, more often than not, sales promotions featuring price incentives are actually unprofitable in the short term.
- It is rare that a sales promotion generates a long-term effect. Hence, there are no long-term revenues to offset the high cost of promotions in the short run. Successful advertising is much more likely to yield a profitable return over the long run, even though its impact on short-run sales may be modest.
- While both advertising and sales promotions may be expected to affect sales in the short run, the evidence suggests that the most powerful effects come from a combination of the two. The impact of advertising and promotions working together is dramatically greater than the sum of each sales stimulus working by itself.
- According to Jones, "The strong synergy that can be generated between advertising and promotions working together points very clearly to the need to integrate the planning and execution of both types of activity: the strategy of Integrated Marketing Communications."[36]

36. Ibid., 56.

SUMMARY

1 Explain the popularity and rationale for different forms of sales promotions.

Sales promotions make use of diverse incentives to motivate action on the part of consumers or distributors. They serve different purposes than mass media advertising, and for many companies, sales promotions receive substantially more funding than does mass media advertising. The growing dependence on these promotions can be attributed to the heavy pressures placed on marketing managers to account for their spending and meet sales objectives in short time frames. Deal-prone shoppers, brand proliferation, the increasing power of large retailers, and media clutter have also contributed to the rising popularity of sales promotion.

2 Describe the purposes and characteristics of sales promotions directed at consumers.

Sales promotions directed at consumers can serve various goals. For example, they can be employed as means to stimulate trial, repeat, or large-quantity purchases. They are especially important tools for introducing new brands or for reacting to a competitor's advances. Coupons, price-off deals, and premiums provide obvious incentives for purchase. Contests, sweepstakes, and product placements can be excellent devices for stimulating brand interest. A variety of sampling techniques are available to get a product into the hands of the target audience. Rebates and frequency programs provide rewards for repeat purchase.

3 Describe the purposes and characteristics of sales promotions directed at the trade.

Sales promotions directed at the trade can also serve multiple objectives. They are a necessity in obtaining initial distribution of a new brand. For established brands, they can be a means to increase distributors' order quantities or obtain retailers' cooperation in implementing a consumer-directed promotion. P-O-P displays can be an excellent tool for gaining preferred display space in a retail setting. Incentives and allowances can be offered to distributors to motivate support for a brand. Trade shows, sales training, and cooperative advertising programs are additional devices for effecting retailer support.

4 Discuss the risks and coordination issues associated with sales promotion.

There are important risks associated with heavy reliance on sales promotion. Offering constant deals for a brand is a good way to erode brand equity, and it may simply be borrowing sales from a future time period. Constant deals can also create a customer mindset that leads consumers to abandon a brand as soon as a deal is retracted. Sales promotions are expensive to administer and fraught with legal complications. Sales promotions yield their most positive results when carefully integrated with the overall advertising plan.

KEY TERMS

sales promotion (495)
consumer-market sales promotion (495)
trade-market sales promotion (495)
coupon (500)
price-off deal (502)
premiums (502)
free premium (502)
self-liquidating premium (503)
contest (503)
sweepstakes (503)
sampling (504)
in-store sampling (505)

door-to-door sampling (505)
mail sampling (505)
on-package sampling (505)
mobile sampling (505)
trial offers (505)
frequency programs (507)
push strategy (508)
merchandise allowances (509)
slotting fees (510)
trade shows (510)
vertical cooperative advertising (510)

QUESTIONS FOR REVIEW AND CRITICAL THINKING

1. Compare and contrast sales promotion and mass media advertising as marketing tools. In what ways do the strengths of one make up for the limitations of the other? What specific characteristics of sales promotions account for the high levels of expenditures that have been allocated to them in recent years?

2. What is brand proliferation and why is it occurring? Why do consumer sales promotions become more commonplace in the face of rampant brand proliferation? Why do trade sales promotions become more frequent when there is excessive brand proliferation?

3. Pull all the preprinted and free-standing inserts from the most recent edition of your Sunday newspaper. From them find an example of each of these consumer-market sales promotions: coupon, free premium, self-liquidating premium, contest, sweepstakes, and trial offer.

4. In developing an advertising plan, synergy may be achieved through careful coordination of individual elements. Give an example of how mass media advertising might be used with on-package sampling to effect a positive synergy. Give an example of how event sponsorship might be used with mobile sampling to achieve a positive synergy.

5. Consumers often rationalize their purchase of a new product with a statement like, "I bought it because I had a 50-cent coupon and our grocery was doubling all manufacturers' coupons this week." What are the prospects that such a consumer will emerge as a loyal user of the product? What must happen if he or she is to become loyal?

6. Early in the chapter, it was suggested that large retailers like Wal-Mart are assuming greater power in today's marketplace. What factors contribute to retailers' increasing power? Explain the connection between merchandise allowances and slotting fees and the growth in retailer power.

7. In your opinion, are ethical dilemmas more likely to arise with sales promotions directed at the consumer or at the trade? What specific forms of consumer or trade promotions seem most likely to involve or create ethical dilemmas?

8. Many marketers argue that consumer sales promotions do not work unless a great deal of time and money are first invested in advertising. What logic might you offer to support this contention? Why would advertising be required to make a sales promotion work?

EXPERIENTIAL EXERCISE

Buy a Sunday newspaper. Make a list of the sales promotions offered by manufacturers, and attach a few examples. Make a second list of the sales promotions offered by retailers, and attach a few examples. Are there any other types of organizations that use sales promotion offers within the newspaper?

USING THE INTERNET

Sales promotions attempt to motivate consumers to take action. Some Web sites encourage people to visit and use what the site has to offer through promotions. Visit the following sites:

www.yoyo.com

www.couponsdirect.com

www.pch.com

www.shareware.com

For each site, answer the following questions:

1.   What type of promotional tool is the site using?

2.   Is the promotion easy to understand? What does it offer?

3.   How much effort on your part does the promotion require?

4.   What action does the promotion encourage?

5.   Is the promotion effective?

Chapter 19

Direct

Marketing

After reading and thinking about this chapter, you will be able to do the following:

1 Identify the three primary purposes served by and explain the growing popularity of direct marketing.

2 Distinguish a mailing list from a marketing database and review the many applications of each.

3 Describe the prominent media used by direct marketers in delivering their messages to the customer.

4 Articulate the added challenge created by direct marketing for achieving integrated marketing communication.

Book clubs, cable TV, magazines, software, videotapes, credit cards, life insurance, kitchen knives, and Tony Bennett CDs—ads for these and many other products and services fill the mailboxes of America with an endless stream of enticements and special offers. But did you get the letter from the mayor of Beverly Hills, promoting the virtues of her fair city for your next vacation? If you are part of the mayor's target segment, then you received her letter espousing the magic of Beverly Hills:

I think one of the most distinctive aspects of Beverly Hills is its atmosphere: the welcome comfort of a small community, combined with the dynamic energy of a big city. Beverly Hills plays host to the finest shopping and dining the world has to offer—all within walking distance from your hotel. And to top it off, the city is bathed in almost year-round sunshine.

The mayor closed with this promise about the magic of Beverly Hills: "I'm sure you will find that Beverly Hills is more than a city. It is a feeling."[1]

More than 12 million tourists visit Beverly Hills each year and spend about 60 million dollars just in the city's elegant hotels.[2] Thus it is easy to understand that the mayor would have a marketing budget of about $1.5 million to get her message out to affluent travelers that might be considering Southern California as a vacation destination. Additionally, as is the case in many direct-marketing campaigns these days, the mayor's letter contains an offer that allows readers to quickly learn more about the product she is selling.[3] Her letter offers a free videotape titled *The Review,* which takes viewers on a leisurely tour around town as seen through the eyes of a film critic and his wife. This tape, of course, turns out to be the Beverly Hills highlight package—the posh shops on Rodeo Drive, gourmet restaurants, exclusive homes and gardens, and plush hotel accommodations. You know—the lifestyles of the rich and famous. Beauty, glamour, prestige, and security are the selling points that the mayor communicates with the videotape.

Do you remember receiving such a letter (see Exhibit 19.1) from the mayor of Beverly Hills? Probably not, we would guess, unless you have a very wealthy aunt, or one incredible part-time job. The mayor's direct mail campaign was precisely targeted. Her letter with its offer of the free video was mailed to just 100,000 households with incomes in excess of $100,000. This direct mail campaign was supplemented with ads in elite magazines like *Conde Nast Traveler* and *The New Yorker.* The mayor's marketing plan appears sound, but you've got to wonder—did she sign all those letters herself?

The Evolution of Direct Marketing

❶ Like the mayor of Beverly Hills, marketers in all types of organizations large and small are allocating larger chunks of their budgets to direct-marketing activities. In this chapter we will examine the growing field of direct marketing and explain how it may be used to both complement and supplant other forms of advertising. Carefully coordinated advertising campaigns and direct-marketing programs produce the synergy that spells the difference between success and failure in the marketplace. Before we examine the evolution of direct marketing and look at the many reasons for its growing popularity, we need a better appreciation for what people mean when they use the phrase *direct marketing.* The "official" definition of direct marketing from the Direct Marketing Association (DMA) provides a starting point:

Direct marketing *is an interactive system of marketing which uses one or more advertising media to effect a measurable response and/or transaction at any location.*[4]

When examined piece by piece, this definition furnishes an excellent basis for understanding the scope of direct marketing.[5]

---

1.   Laura Loro, "Beverly Hills' Inviting Idea," *Advertising Age,* March 20, 1995, 24.
2.   Ibid.
3.   Junu Bryan Kim, "Marketing with Video," *Advertising Age,* May 22, 1995, S1.
4.   Bob Stone, *Successful Direct Marketing Methods* (Lincolnwood, Ill.: NTC Business Books, 1994), 5.
5.   The discussion to follow builds on that of Stone.

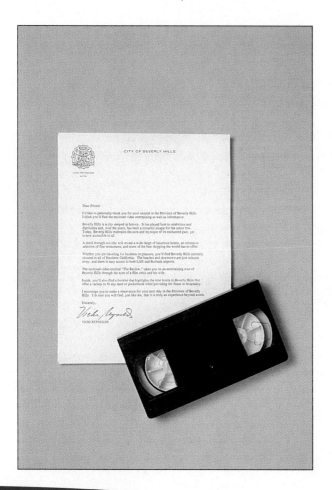

EXHIBIT 19.1

In direct marketing, it is common to seek a dialogue with the target customer. In this example the mayor pursues that dialogue with a letter and video about her "Province of Beverly Hills."

Direct marketing is interactive in that the marketer is attempting to develop an ongoing dialogue with the customer. Direct-marketing programs are commonly planned with the notion that one contact will lead to another and then another, so that the marketer's message can become more focused and refined with each interaction. In the Beverly Hills example, the mayor started the dialogue with her letter to 100,000 potential customers, who were offered a chance to respond by requesting *The Review* videotape. Those requesting the video would go on the mayor's hot-prospect list; hot prospects might be targeted for future mailings or even telephone contacts. The mayor might also turn over the hot-prospect list to local hotels or restaurants to let them furnish information requested by the customer.

The DMA's definition also notes that multiple media can be used in direct-marketing programs. This is an important point for two reasons. First, we do not want to equate direct mail and direct marketing. Any media can be used in executing direct-marketing programs, not just the mail. Second, as we have noted before, a combination of media is likely to be more effective than any one medium used by itself.

Another key aspect of direct-marketing programs is that they almost always are designed to produce some form of immediate, measurable response.[6] In the mayor's case, the immediate response to her letter could be measured by how many requests for the videotape were received. Direct-marketing programs may also be designed to produce an immediate sale. The customer might be asked to return an order form with $49.99 to get a copy of *The Lion King* Super Nintendo game, or to call a 1–800 number with a credit card handy to get 22 timeless hits on *The Very Best of Tony Bennett* compact disc. Because of this emphasis on immediate response, direct marketers are always in a position to judge the effectiveness of a particular program. As we shall see, this ability to gauge the immediate impact of a program has great appeal to marketers.

The final phrase of the DMA's definition notes that a direct-marketing transaction can take place anywhere. The key idea here is that customers do not have to make a trip to a retail store for a direct-marketing program to work. Follow-ups can be made by mail, over the telephone, through a modem linked to a customer's computer, and, in the future, via interactive television systems.

Direct Marketing— A Look Back

From Johannes Gutenberg to Benjamin Franklin to Richard Sears, Alvah Roebuck, and Lillian Vernon, the evolution of direct marketing has involved some of the great pioneers in business. As Exhibit 19.2 shows, the practice of direct marketing today is shaped by the successes of many notable mail-order companies and catalog merchandisers.[7] Among these there is none more exemplary than L. L. Bean. Bean founded his company in 1912 on his integrity and $400. His first

---

6.   Don E. Schultz and Paul Wang, "Real World Results," *Marketing Tools,* April/May 1994, 40–47.
7.   See also Edward Nash, "The Roots of Direct Marketing," *Direct Marketing Magazine,* February 1995, 38–40.

EXHIBIT 19.2

Direct-marketing milestones.

c1450	Johannes Gutenberg invents moveable type.
1667	The first gardening catalog is published by William Lucas, an English gardener.
1744	Benjamin Franklin publishes a catalog of books on science and industry and formulates the basic mail-order concept of customer satisfaction guaranteed.
1830s	A few mail-order companies began operating in New England, selling camping and fishing supplies.
1863	The introduction of penny postage facilitates direct mail.
1867	The invention of the typewriter gives a modern appearance to direct-mail materials.
1872	Montgomery Ward publishes his first "catalog," selling 163 items on a single sheet of paper. By 1884 his catalog grows to 240 pages, with thousands of items and a money-back guarantee.
1886	Richard Sears enters the mail-order business by selling gold watches and makes $5,000 in his first six months. He partners with Alvah Roebuck in 1887, and by 1893 they are marketing a wide range of merchandise in a 196-page catalog.
1912	L. L. Bean founds one of today's most admired mail-order companies on the strength of his Maine Hunting Shoe and a guarantee of total satisfaction for the life of the shoe.
1917	The Direct Mail Advertising Association is founded. In 1973 it becomes the Direct Mail/Direct Marketing Association.
1928	Third-class bulk mail becomes a reality, offering economies for the direct-mail industry.
1950	Credit cards first appear, led by the Diners' Club travel and entertainment card. American Express enters in 1958.
1951	Lillian Vernon places an ad for a monogrammed purse and belt and generates $16,000 in immediate business. She reinvests the money in what becomes the Lillian Vernon enterprise. Vernon recognizes early on that catalog shopping has great appeal to time-pressed consumers.
1953	Publishers' Clearinghouse is founded and soon becomes a dominant force in magazine subscription.
1955	Columbia Record Club is established, and eventually becomes Columbia House—the music-marketing giant.
1967	The term *telemarketing* first appears in print, and AT&T introduces the first toll-free 1-800 service.
1983	The Direct Mail/Direct Marketing Association drops *Direct Mail* from its name to become the DMA, as a reflection of the multiple media being used by direct marketers.
1984	Apple introduces the Macintosh personal computer.
1992	The number of persons who shop at home surpasses 100 million in the United States.

Source: Adapted from the DMA's "Grassroots Advocacy Guide for Direct Marketers" (1993). Reprinted with permission of the Direct Marketing Association, Inc.

product was a unique hunting shoe made from a leather top and rubber bottom sewn together. Other outdoor clothing and equipment soon followed in the Bean catalog.

A look at the L. L. Bean catalog of 1917 (black-and-white, just 12 pages) reveals the fundamental strategy underlying Bean's success. It featured the Maine Hunting Shoe and other outdoor clothing with descriptive copy that was informative, factual, and low-key. On the front page was Bean's commitment to quality. It read: *"Maine Hunting Shoe—guarantee. We guarantee this pair of shoes to give perfect satisfaction in every way. If the rubber breaks or the tops grow hard, return them together with this guarantee tag and we will replace them, free of charge. Signed, L. L. Bean."* [8] Bean realized that long-term relationships with customers must be based on trust, and his guarantee policy was aimed at developing and sustaining that trust.

8.   Allison Cosmedy, *A History of Direct Marketing* (New York: Direct Marketing Association, 1992), 6.

As an astute direct marketer, Bean also showed a keen appreciation for the importance of building a good mailing list. For many years he used his profits to promote his free catalog via advertisements in hunting and fishing magazines. Those replying to the ads received a rapid response and typically became Bean customers. Bean's obsession with building mailing lists is nicely captured by this quote from his friend, Maine native John Gould: "If you drop in just to shake his hand, you get home to find his catalog in your mailbox."[9]

By 1967 Bean sales approached $5 million, and by 1990 they had exploded to $600 million, as the product line was expanded to include more apparel and recreation equipment.[10] Today, L. L. Bean is still a family-operated business that emphasizes the basic philosophies of its founder. Quality products, understated advertising, and sophisticated customer-contact and distribution systems still drive the business. Additionally, L. L.'s 100 percent satisfaction guarantee can still be found in every Bean catalog, and it remains at the heart of the relationship between Bean and its customers. Bean's modern-day guarantee is shown in Exhibit 19.3.

EXHIBIT 19.3

Direct marketing pioneer L. L. Bean has always relied on its ability to track customer orders to advertising media. How does this kind of effectiveness create advantages for the company? L. L. Bean at **www.llbean.com:80/** *uses its own internal search engine by keyword to help customers quickly find the product or information they want. Competitor Lands' End at* **www.landsend.com/** *uses an in-house Internet store to process orders.*

From L.L. Bean to You—Fast FedEx® Delivery on Most Orders

Order Anytime Call us at **1-800-221-4221** toll free. Our representatives are available 24 hours a day, 365 days a year.

Fast, Reliable Shipping We send out in-stock items within 24 hours of receiving your order.
- **Fast Delivery** Most customers in the contiguous U.S. receive their orders just 2 to 4 days after we send it out. (For monogrammed items or alterations, please add an extra 1 to 2 days.)
- **Low Shipping Charge** You pay a flat rate of $4.50 per shipping address on most orders (unless noted otherwise). Check the Order Form for shipments to Alaska, Hawaii, Canada and overseas.
- **Need It Even Faster?** For an additional $6 per address, you can send your order by FedEx Standard Overnight® Service. For most addresses in the contiguous U.S., delivery will be the day after we process your order.
- **Reliable Tracking** We track your order all the way from our door to yours, and can tell you when your order will arrive.

We Honor Most Major Credit Cards MasterCard, VISA, Optima, American Express and the NOVUS Brand Cards. To help us serve you better, please have your card handy when ordering.

Easy Customer Service, 24 Hours a Day For information on your order, repairs, exchanges or returns call **1-800-341-4341** anytime.

International Shipping Product prices and delivery charges will vary when you request shipping to another country. Call for further information: **1-800-559-4288.**

We guarantee prices and terms in this catalog through **July 14, 1996.**

Our cover: "Katahdin Spring" by James Linehan Selection Consultant: Barridoff Galleries, Portland, Maine Courtesy of Sherry French Gallery, New York

Our Guarantee
Our products are guaranteed to give 100% satisfaction in every way. Return anything purchased from us at any time if it proves otherwise. We will replace it, refund your purchase price or credit your credit card, as you wish. We do not want you to have anything from L.L. Bean that is not completely satisfactory.

WEB SIGHTING

9.   Ibid.
10.   Ibid.

Direct Marketing Today

Direct marketing today is rooted in the legacy of mail-order giants and catalog merchandisers like L. L. Bean, Lillian Vernon, Publishers' Clearinghouse, and JCPenney. However, in the nineties, direct marketing has broken free from its mail-order heritage to become a tool used by all types of organizations throughout the world. Although many types of businesses and not-for-profit organizations are making use of direct marketing, it is common to find that such direct-marketing programs are not carefully integrated with an organization's other advertising efforts. Integration should be the goal for advertising and direct marketing; impressive evidence supports the thesis that integrated programs are more effective than the sum of their parts.[11]

Because many different types of activities are now encompassed by the label *direct marketing,* it is important to remember the defining characteristics spelled out in the DMA definition given earlier. Direct marketing involves an attempt to interact or create a dialogue with the customer; multiple media are often employed in the process, and direct marketing is characterized by the fact that a measurable response is immediately available for assessing a program's impact. With these defining features in mind, we can see that direct-marketing programs are commonly used for three principal purposes.

As you might imagine, the most common use of direct marketing is as a tool to close a sale with a customer. This can be done as a stand-alone program, or it can be carefully coordinated with a firm's other advertising. Telecommunications companies like AT&T, MCI, and Sprint make extensive use of the advertising/direct-marketing combination.[12] For example, MCI has spent heavily on TV advertising to promote its Friends & Family discount-calling program. This advertising is used to acquaint and justify the program for consumers and is followed up through both direct-mail and telemarketing campaigns to convert customers to the program. In response, AT&T has used TV advertising to mock the calling-circle concept at the heart of MCI's program, while promoting its own discount plan, known as True Savings. AT&T also makes extensive use of direct-marketing follow-ups to close sales.

A second purpose for direct-marketing programs is to identify prospects for future contacts and, at the same time, provide in-depth information to selected customers. This of course was the purpose of the Beverly Hills program discussed at the beginning of the chapter, and it was also the purpose of Cadillac's campaign to distribute its *Impressions* CD. As described in a previous chapter, Cadillac used the online services CompuServe and Prodigy and magazine ads with a 1-800 number to initiate its dialogue with customers. In the first year of this program, Cadillac had inquiries from 20,000 prospects and mailed them the *Impressions* CD.[13] These 20,000 persons can expect to hear from Cadillac many more times in the future.

Direct-marketing programs are also initiated as a means to engage customers, seek their advice, furnish helpful information about using a product, reward customers for using a brand, or in general foster brand loyalty, as the direct mail promotion for Infiniti in Exhibit 19.4 shows. As another example, the manufacturer of Valvoline motor oil seeks to build loyalty for its brand by encouraging young car owners to join the Valvoline Performance Team.[14] To join the team, young drivers just fill out a questionnaire that enters them into the Valvoline database. Team members receive posters, special offers on racing-team apparel, news about racing events in which Valvoline has provided sponsorship, and promotional reminders at regular intervals that reinforce the virtues of Valvoline for the driver's next oil change.

If you're still not convinced that everyone is getting on the direct-marketing bandwagon, consider the example of Kraft General Foods. Using the names and addresses

11.   Ernan Roman, *Integrated Direct Marketing* (Lincolnwood, Ill.: NTC Business Books, 1995).
12.   Kate Fitzgerald, "AT&T, MCI Ringing Up Bigger Cash Lures," *Advertising Age,* May 8, 1995, 6.
13.   Jean Halliday, "Cadillac Finds Second Home on the Internet," *Adweek,* May 8, 1995, 4.
14.   Nash.

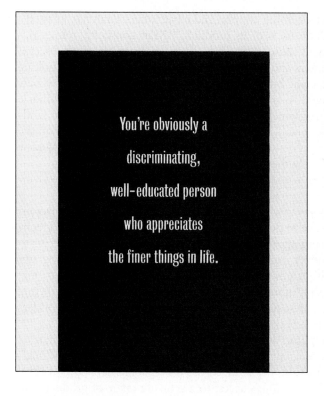

EXHIBIT 19.4

The distinguishing feature of a marketing database is direct input from the customer. This advertisement for Infiniti seeks to gather information and initiate a dialogue with the target customer. Do you see any parallels here vis-à-vis the approach used by the mayor of Beverly Hills? **www .infinitimotors.com/**

that consumers provide when redeeming coupon and rebate offers, Kraft has amassed a database of more than 30 million users of its products.[15] Kraft constantly refines this massive file by sending surveys to those on the list. From these surveys, Kraft discerns the interests of different customers and responds with nutrition information, cooking tips, recipes, and coupons for specific brands that the person has used in the past or new brands that they are encouraged to try. (Here's your sample tip: Use Kraft Miracle Whip rather than butter or margarine the next time you make grilled cheese sandwiches, and don't forget the Velveeta!) Kraft's direct-marketing strategy is based on the premise that the more information consumers have about its various brands like Miracle Whip and Velveeta, the more likely they are to remain loyal to those brands.

What's Driving the Growing Popularity of Direct Marketing?

The growth in popularity of direct marketing is due to a number of factors. Some of these have to do with changes in consumer lifestyles and technological developments that in effect create a climate more conducive to the practice of direct marketing. In addition, direct-marketing programs offer unique advantages vis-à-vis conventional mass media advertising, leading many organizations to shift more of their marketing budgets to direct-marketing activities. Direct marketing also presents interesting opportunities around the world, as exemplified in the Global Issues box on page 530.

From the consumer's standpoint, direct marketing's growing popularity might be summarized in a single word—*convenience.* Dramatic growth in the number of dual-income and single-person households has reduced the time people have to visit retail stores. Direct marketers provide consumers access to a growing range of products and services in their homes, thus saving many households' most precious resource—time.

More liberal attitudes about the use of credit and the accumulation of debt have also contributed to the growth of direct marketing. Credit cards are the primary means of payment in most direct-marketing transactions. The widespread availability of credit cards makes it evermore convenient to shop from the comfort of one's home.

Developments in telecommunications have also facilitated the direct-marketing transaction. After getting off to a slow start in the late sixties, toll-free 1-800 numbers have exploded in popularity to the point where one can hardly find a product or a catalog that does not include an 800 number for interacting with the manufacturer. And whether one is requesting that videotape about Beverly Hills, ordering a twill polo shirt from Eddie Bauer, or inquiring about an OzziRoo mountain bike like the one shown in Exhibit 19.5, the preferred mode of access for most consumers has become the 1-800 number.

Another technological development having a huge impact on the growth of direct marketing is the computer. Did you know that your parents' new Buick has more computer power than the Apollo spacecraft that took astronauts to the moon? The incredible diffusion of computer technology sweeping through all modern societies has been a tremendous boon to direct marketers. The computer now allows firms to track, keep records on, and interact with something like 5 million customers for what it cost to track a single customer in 1950.[16] Kraft General Foods obviously could not track and interact with 30 million of its customers without computer technology. As we will see in an upcoming discussion, the computer power now available for modest dollar amounts is fueling the growth of direct marketing's most potent tool—the marketing database.

Technology never stands still; future developments in the new media will also add to the prevalence of direct marketing. Pursuing customers through any of the interactive media is likely to become the preferred mode for direct marketers in the future. Already, shopping opportunities have become widely available on the online services

---

15.   Jonathan Berry, "Database Marketing," *Business Week,* September 5, 1994, 56–62.
16.   Don Peppers and Martha Rogers, "The End of Mass Marketing," *Marketing Tools,* March/April 1995, 42–51.

Convenience for the customer is a major factor driving the popularity of direct marketing. A key contributor to that convenience is the omnipresent 1-800 number.

like Prodigy and CompuServe. Many traditional catalog merchandisers can now be found on these systems and are even experimenting with them to expand their markets globally. For example, the Metropolitan Museum of Art in New York City is using CompuServe's growing base of subscribers in Europe as a test market for its broad line of jewelry, books, and art reproductions.[17] European subscribers just type "Go MMA" to hook up to the online store and get a $25 credit against their CompuServe fee for every $100 in purchases. Not surprisingly, very few orders are received by the Met for under $100.

Interactive television also promises to be an attractive vehicle for intensified direct marketing. Companies like Time Warner, Spiegel, Sharper Image, The Nature Company, Warner Brothers Studio Store, Williams Sonoma, and Chrysler are working together to develop the technical capabilities to deliver a wide array of interactive services through consumers' TV sets.[18] The day is coming when marketers of all sorts will be able to carry on interactive dialogues with consumers in their homes via the television.

Direct-marketing programs also offer some unique advantages that make them appealing compared with what might be described as conventional mass marketing. A general manager of marketing communications with AT&T's consumer services unit put it this way: "We want to segment our market more; we want to learn more about individual customers; we want to really serve our customers by giving them very specific products and services. Direct marketing is probably the most effective way in which we

17.   Matthew Rose, "Met Store DM Expands on CompuServe," *Direct Marketing News,* August 8, 1994, 23.
18.   Lindsey Kelly, "Interactive TV's Rough Road," *Advertising Age,* March 13, 1995, S12–S16.

can reach customers and establish a relationship with them."[19] As you might expect, AT&T is one of those organizations shifting more and more of its marketing dollars into direct-marketing programs.

The appeal of direct marketing is enhanced further by the persistent emphasis on producing measurable effects. For instance, in direct marketing, it is common to find calculations like **cost per inquiry (CPI)** or **cost per order (CPO)** being featured in program evaluation.[20] These calculations simply divide the number of responses to a program by that program's cost. When calculated for each and every program an organization conducts over time, CPI and CPO data quickly help an organization appreciate what works and what doesn't work in its competitive arena.

This emphasis on producing and monitoring measurable effects is realized most completely through an approach referred to as database marketing. Working with a database, direct marketers can target specific customers, track their actual purchase behavior over time, and experiment with different programs for affecting the purchasing patterns of these customers.[21] Obviously, those programs that produce the best outcomes become the candidates for increased funding in the future. Let's look into database marketing.

Database Marketing

22 If any ambiguity remains about what makes direct marketing different from marketing in general, that ambiguity can be erased by the database. The one characteristic of direct marketing that distinguishes it from marketing more generally is its emphasis on database development.[22] Knowing who the best customers are along with what and how often they buy is a direct marketer's secret weapon. This knowledge accumulates in the form of a marketing database.

Databases used as the centerpieces in direct-marketing campaigns take many forms and can contain many different layers of information about customers. At one extreme is the simple mailing list that contains nothing more than the names and addresses of possible customers; at the other extreme is the customized marketing database that augments names and addresses with various additional information about customers' characteristics, past purchases, and product preferences. Understanding this distinction between mailing lists and marketing databases is important in appreciating the scope of database marketing.

Mailing Lists

A **mailing list** is simply a file of names and addresses that an organization might use for contacting prospective or prior customers. Mailing lists are plentiful, easy to access, and inexpensive.[23] For example, CD-ROM phone directories now available for less than $200 provide a cheap and easy way to generate mailing lists.[24] More-targeted mailing lists are available from a variety of suppliers. These suppliers offer lists such as the 107,521 active members of the Association of Catholic Senior Citizens; the 174,600 Kuppenheimer male-fashion buyers; the 825,000 subscribers to *Home* magazine; and the 189,000 buyers of products from the Smith & Hawken gardening catalog.[25] Each time you subscribe to a magazine, order from a catalog, register your automobile, fill out a warranty card, redeem a rebate offer, apply for credit, or join a professional society, your name and address goes on another mailing list. These lists are freely bought and sold and, as suggested by Exhibit 19.6, can be applied rather carelessly at times.

19.   Gary Levin, "AT&T Exec: Customer Access Goal of Integration," *Advertising Age*, October 10, 1994, S1.
20.   Stone, 620.
21.   Schultz and Wang.
22.   Stone, Chapter 2.
23.   John Kremer, *The Complete Direct Marketing Sourcebook* (New York: John Wiley & Sons, 1992).
24.   Ira Teinowitz, "Let Your Keyboard Do the Walking," *Advertising Age*, February 20, 1995, 22.
25.   Kremer.

EXHIBIT 19.6

Attention to detail is an ever-present challenge when working with mailing lists. Can you identify any flaws in this offer to Peter Sheldon?

Two broad categories of lists should be recognized: the internal, or house, list versus the external, or outside, list. **Internal lists** are simply an organization's records of its customers, subscribers, donors, and inquirers. **External lists** are purchased from a list compiler or rented from a list broker. At the most basic level, internal and external lists facilitate the two fundamental activities of the direct marketer: Internal lists are the starting point for developing better relationships with current customers, whereas external lists help an organization cultivate new business.

List Enhancement

Name-and-address files, no matter what their source, are merely the starting point for database marketing. The next step in the evolution of a database is mailing-list enhancement. Typically this involves augmenting an internal list by combining it with other, externally supplied lists or databases. External lists can be appended or integrated with a house list.

One of the most straightforward list enhancements entails simply adding or appending more names and addresses to an internal list. Proprietary name-and-address files may be purchased from other companies that operate in noncompetitive businesses.[26] With today's computer capabilities, adding these additional households to an existing mailing list is simple. Many well-known companies, like Sharper Image, Bloomingdale's, and Hertz, sell or rent their customer lists for this purpose.

A second type of list enhancement involves incorporating information from external databases into a house list. Here the number of names and addresses remains the same, but an organization ends up with a more complete description of who its customers are. Typically, this kind of enhancement includes any of four categories of information:

- *Demographic data*—the basic descriptors of individuals and households available from the Census Bureau.
- *Geodemographic data*—information that reveals the characteristics of the neighborhood in which a person resides.
- *Psychographic data*—data that allows for a more qualitative assessment of a customer's general lifestyle, interests, and opinions.
- *Behavioral data*—information about other products and services a customer has purchased; prior purchases can help reveal a customer's preferences.[27]

List enhancements that entail merging existing records with new information rely on software that allows the database manager to match records based on some piece of information the two lists share. For example, matches might be achieved by sorting on zip codes and street addresses.

Many suppliers gather and maintain databases for the sole purpose of list enhancement. Infobase Premier is an enhancement file offered by Infobase Services and is particularly notable for its size and array of available information. Infobase Premier contains 170 different pieces of information about 200 million American consumers. Because of its massive size, this database has a very high match rate (60 to 80 percent) when it is merged with clients' internal lists.[28] A more common match rate between internal and external lists is 45 to 60 percent. A file like this also illustrates the critical nature of inexpensive computer power to the database marketer, since simple multiplication tells us that in Infobase Premier, a marketer is managing some 34 billion pieces of customer information.

26. Terry G. Vavra, "The Database Marketing Imperative," *Marketing Management* 2, no. 1 (1993): 47–57.
27. Ibid.
28. Ibid.

The Marketing Database

Mailing lists come in all shapes and sizes, and by enhancing internal lists they obviously can become rich sources of information about customers. But to qualify as a marketing database, one important additional type of information is required. Although a marketing database can be viewed as a natural extension of an internal mailing list, a **marketing database** also includes information collected directly from individual customers.[29] Developing a marketing database involves pursuing dialogues with customers and learning about their individual preferences and behavioral patterns. This can be potent information for hatching marketing programs that will hit the mark with consumers.

State-of-the-art direct marketing today has database development as its defining feature. According to a recent survey of marketing practices, 56 percent of retailers and manufacturers have database development under way, another 10 percent will soon begin development, and a whopping 85 percent believe that a marketing database will be a requirement to remain competitive after the year 2000.[30] As suggested by the New Media box on page 532, the World Wide Web is likely to be a focal point for much of this activity.

Aided by the dramatic escalation in processing power that comes from every new generation of computer chip, marketers see the chance to gather and manage more information about every individual who buys, or could buy, from them. Their goal might be portrayed as an attempt to cultivate a kind of cybernetic intimacy with the customer. A marketing database represents an organization's collective memory, which allows the organization to give customers the personalized attention that once was characteristic of the corner grocer in small-town America. For example, using its database of millions of cardmembers, American Express generates specific marketing programs almost person by person; some of the offers that

GLOBAL ISSUES

NAFTA—NEW APPROACH FOR TARGETING (LATIN) AMERICANS

With all due respect to the North American Free Trade Agreement, the big news for advertisers is the New Approach for Targeting (Latin) Americans. In other words, the current success and future prospects for direct marketing in Latin America are exciting indeed. The list of companies instructing their staffs to increase direct-marketing efforts in Latin America reads like a who's who of marketing—American Express, IBM, Nestle, Microsoft, and Time Warner. Sophisticated companies like these are realizing that infrastructure limitations in Latin American countries —like deficiencies in wholesale and retail distribution—make direct marketing a more efficient and effective method of reaching potential customers. By early 1996, this region housed 100 direct-marketing agencies, 80 telemarketing firms, and dozens of list brokers.

Certain characteristics of Latin America make the future prospects for direct marketing quite exciting. The literacy rate in Argentina, Chile, and Peru is over 90 percent, the economies in the region are beginning to show signs of permanent and steady growth, and early efforts in direct marketing have realized extremely high response rates. Latin Americans are responding not only because of the weaknesses in existing retail services but also because of the novelty of direct-marketing appeals.

But direct marketing in Latin America is not without formidable challenges. The ability to use some direct-marketing techniques is limited by consumers who lack sophistication and household income. Other issues for advertisers to consider are that credit card usage is still low, mailing lists are expensive, and the phone system is poor, but improving. Finding enough well-trained personnel to execute a direct-marketing effort can also be difficult.

Fernando Peydro, president and founder of the Clienting Group, an Argentine direct-marketing agency, and Steve Carr, manager of a Spanish-language business monthly, offer these tips to firms interested in trying direct marketing in Argentina, Brazil, Chile, and Peru:

- Engage a local partner in the direct-marketing effort. Local agencies have staffers that understand local market conditions.
- Global strategies seem to be less successful than local strategies. Adaptation and customization of marketing and advertising is a requirement.
- Direct mail campaigns need to be more eye-catching and colorful than U.S. campaigns, with more image and less verbiage.
- Offering consumers memberships and club privileges is popular and effective.
- Honor strongly felt Latin American traditions like respect for elders, family, and local authority.

Source: Lauro Loro, "New Ways to Reach Customers," *Ad Age International*, March 11, 1996, 1-30.

29. Herman Holtz, *Databased Marketing* (New York: John Wiley & Sons, 1992).
30. Berry.

AMERICAN EXPRESS®

Presents

SONY MAXIMUM TELEVISION™

Once you've experienced it,
you'll never want to watch TV any other way.

Price
Guarantee
Plus

FOR CARDMEMBERS ONLY

Smart, Simple Price
Guarantee *Plus*...
• **Free** Shipping and Handling
• **Interest-Free**
  Monthly Payments
• **Free** 1,000 Bonus
  Membership Rewards℠ Points
• **Free** Return Pick Up

SONY.

EXHIBIT 19.7

The ability to tailor a specific program or campaign based on how a target market has behaved in the marketplace is a distinct advantage of a marketing database. In this exhibit, how do you think Sony and American Express select card members as good targets for this ad? At the American Express Web site www.americanexpress.com/, *you might visit the small-business exchange where the company shares information useful to small-business owners while gathering more information for its databases in return. To see how a competitor can build its databases by recording site visits, check out some of the services at the home page for VISA International at* www.visa.com/.

AmEx sends out with its bill statements each month go to as few as 20 people.[31] This remarkable capability to sort through millions and speak to individuals is made possible by a marketing database. One of American Express's recent cardmember offers is shown in Exhibit 19.7.

While you might find this concept of cybernetic intimacy a bit far-fetched, it certainly is the case that a marketing database can have many valuable applications. Before we look at some of these applications, let's review the terminology introduced thus far. We now have seen that direct marketers use mailing lists, enhanced mailing lists, and/or marketing databases as the starting points for developing many of their programs. The crucial distinction between a mailing list and a marketing database is that the latter includes direct input from customers. Building a marketing database entails pursuing an ongoing dialogue with customers and continuous updating of records with new information. While mailing lists can be rich sources of information for program development, a marketing database has a dynamic quality that sets it apart. A marketing database can be an organization's living memory of who its customers are and what they want from the organization.

Marketing Database Applications

Many different types of customer-communication programs are driven by marketing databases. One of the greatest benefits of a database is that it allows an organization to quantify how much business the organization is actually doing with its current best customers. A good way to isolate the best customers is with a recency, frequency, and monetary (RFM) analysis.[32] An **RFM analysis** asks how recently and how often a specific customer is buying from a company, and how much money he or she is spending per order and over time. With this transaction data, it is a simple matter to calculate the value of every customer to the organization and identify those customers that have given the organization the most business in the past. Past behavior is an excellent predictor of future behavior, so yesterday's best customers are likely to be any organization's primary source of future business.

RFM analysis allows an organization to spend marketing dollars to achieve maximum return on those dollars. Promotions targeted at best customers will typically pay off with handsome returns. For example, Claridge Hotel & Casino uses its frequent-gambler card—CompCard Gold—to monitor the gambling activities of its 350,000 active members.[33] Promotions like free slot-machine tokens, monogrammed bathrobes, and door-to-door limo services are targeted to best customers. Such expenditures pay for themselves many times over because they are carefully targeted to people who spend freely when they choose to vacation at Claridge's resort hotels.

31. Ibid.
32. Rob Jackson and Paul Wang, *Strategic Database Marketing* (Lincolnwood, Ill.: NTC Business Books, 1994).
33. Berry.

A marketing database can also be a powerful tool for organizations that seek to create a genuine relationship with their customers. The makers of Ben & Jerry's® ice cream use their database for two things: to find out how customers react to potential new flavors and product ideas, and to involve their customers in social causes.[34] In one recent program, their goal was to find 100,000 people in their marketing database who would volunteer to work with Ben & Jerry's® to support the Children's Defense Fund. Jerry Greenfield, cofounder of Ben & Jerry's®, justifies the program as follows: "We are not some nameless conglomerate that only looks at how much money we make every year. I think the opportunity to use our business and particularly the power of our business as a force for progressive social change is exciting."[35] Of course, when customers feel genuine involvement with a brand like Ben & Jerry's®, they also turn out to be very loyal customers.

Reinforcing and recognizing preferred customers can be another valuable application of the marketing database. This application may be nothing more than a simple follow-up letter that thanks customers for their business or reminds them of the positive features of the brand to reassure them that they made the right choice. As reflected in Exhibit 19.8, GM's Saturn division has been an active user of this tactic.

To recognize and reinforce the behaviors of preferred customers, marketers in many fields are experimenting with frequency-marketing programs that provide concrete rewards to frequent customers. **Frequency-marketing programs** have three basic elements: *a database,* which is the collective memory for the program; *a benefit structure,* which is designed to attract and retain customers; and *a communication strategy,* which emphasizes a regular dialogue with the organization's best customers.[36]

Spectrum Foods, a San Francisco–based company with 15 upscale restaurants in California, has had considerable success with its frequency-marketing program known by diners as Table One.[37] Table One members earn points each time they

---

NEW MEDIA

BUILDING MARKETING DATABASES IN CYBERSPACE

While some marketers and advertisers are struggling with the concept of database marketing itself, others have taken the concept to the World Wide Web in the unending search for more-targeted communications. The arrival of database marketing to the World Wide Web offers the payoff of more-personalized—and presumably more-memorable—information experiences for Internet travelers. The payoff for the marketer is a chance to get information on the names, demographics, and habits of their online visitors.

Silicon Graphics was one of the first firms to build a database through Web sites when it ran a contest over the Internet to generate interest in a new product. Visitors to the Silicon Graphics site could enter to win $50,000 in computer paraphernalia by providing their name and E-mail address, answering six questions about their computer use, and writing a short essay. The contest attracted 5,600 entrants. When the new product hit retailers' shelves, Silicon Graphics could send tailored information directly to site users from the newly created database.

Chrysler Corporation used a more entertaining approach to coax information out of visitors to its Web site. When users log on to the Chrysler site, they are asked to fill out an information form for an "identification badge." The badge is needed for a virtual tour of the Chrysler Technology Center. Throughout the ensuing tour, the visitor is addressed by name. At the end of the tour, Chrysler has another E-mail address to add to its cyberdatabase.

Implementing database-marketing systems on the Web will only get easier. IBM has released DB2, a database system that offers a direct and transparent link to the Web for data exchange. And developing a database from Web contacts doesn't have to be just for the giant corporations. Borland International's Delphi program and O'Reilly & Associates Web Site Software have made it possible to create a database system on the Web for as little as $500. Such simple databases allow marketers to track how many times customers visit a page and how much time they spend there. That information can then be used to determine consumers' interests, and the firm can develop and deliver targeted messages and promotional offers based on the information.

Source: Charles Waltner, "Tell Us a Little about Yourself," *Advertising Age,* July 17, 1995, 13.

---

34.   Murray Raphel, "What's the Scoop on Ben & Jerry?" *Direct Marketing Magazine,* August 1994, 23–24.
35.   Ibid.
36.   Richard Barlow, "Starting a Frequency Marketing Program," *Direct Marketing Magazine,* July 1994, 35.
37.   Greg Gattuso, "Restaurants Discover Frequency Marketing," *Direct Marketing Magazine,* February 1995, 35–36.

Building relationships with existing customers is a key application of the marketing database. No company does this better than Saturn. www .saturncars.com/index.html

dine. They can earn $25 award certificates, $250 shopping sprees at Nordstrom, or, for really frequent diners, trips to Italy and Mexico. Spectrum's program also includes free benefits like valet parking, preferred reservations, and exclusive invitations to wine tastings and special dinners. Spectrum Foods has received a positive response to this program. Table One members now dine at Spectrum's restaurants more often, spend more money each time they dine, and recommend the program to their friends—which has helped Spectrum grow its business at twice the industry average.

Another common application for the marketing database is cross-selling.[38] Since most organizations today have many different products or services they hope to sell, one of the best ways to build business is to identify customers who already purchase some of a firm's products and create marketing programs aimed at these customers and featuring other products. If they like our ice cream, perhaps we should also encourage them to try our frozen yogurt. If they have a checking account with us, can we interest them in a credit card? If customers dine in our restaurants on Fridays and Saturdays, with the proper incentives perhaps we can get them to dine with us midweek, when we really need the extra business. A marketing database can provide a myriad of opportunities for cross-selling.

A final application for the marketing database is a natural extension of cross-selling. Once an organization gets to know who its current customers are and what they like about various products, it is in a much stronger position to go out and seek new customers. Knowledge about current customers is especially valuable when an organization is considering purchasing external mailing lists to append to its marketing database. If a firm knows the demographic characteristics of current customers—knows what they like about products, knows where they live, and has insights about their lifestyles and general interests—then the selection of external lists will be much more efficient. The basic premise here is simply to try to find prospects that share many of the same characteristics and interests with current customers. And what's the best vehicle for coming to know the current best customers? Marketing-database development is that vehicle.

The Privacy Concern

One big dark cloud looms on the horizon for database marketers, and that cloud is consumer concern about invasion of privacy. It is easy for marketers to gather a wide variety of information about consumers, and this is making the general public nervous. In a recent Harris poll, 83 percent of those contacted expressed concerns about invasion of privacy.[39] Many Americans are uneasy about the way their personal information is being gathered and exchanged by businesses and the government without their knowledge, participation, or consent.

38.   Jackson and Wang.
39.   William Dunn, "Ready, Set, Grow," *Marketing Tools,* July/August 1994, 56–57.

From time to time, state and federal lawmakers have proposed legislation to limit businesses' access to personal information, but not much has been accomplished. Direct marketers have been effective in blocking regulation by convincing lawmakers that they can police themselves. For example, the Direct Marketing Association has a toll-free hotline that consumers can call to have their names removed from mailing lists. However, it is not widely used by consumers. Privacy advocates contend that the hotline is primarily a public relations tool used by industry lobbyists to convince lawmakers that legislation is unnecessary.[40]

Individual organizations can address their customers' concerns about privacy if they remember two fundamental premises of database marketing. First, a primary goal for developing a marketing database is to get to know customers in such a way that an organization can offer them products and services that better meet their needs. The whole point of a marketing database is to keep junk mail to a minimum by targeting only exciting and relevant programs to customers. If customers are offered something of value, they will welcome being in the database.

Second, developing a marketing database is about creating meaningful, long-term relationships with customers. If you want someone's trust and loyalty, would you collect personal information from them and then sell it to a third party behind their back? We hope not! When collecting information from customers, an organization must help them understand why it wants the information and how it will use it. If the organization is planning on selling this information to a third party, it must get customers' permission. If the organization pledges that the information will remain confidential, it must honor that pledge. Integrity is fundamental to all meaningful relationships, including those involving direct marketers and their customers.

Media Applications in Direct Marketing

❸ While mailing lists and marketing databases are the focal point for originating most direct-marketing programs, information and arguments need to be communicated to customers in implementing these programs. As we saw in the definition of direct marketing offered earlier in this chapter, multiple media can be deployed in program implementation, and some form of immediate, measurable response is typically an overriding goal. The immediate response desired may be an actual order for services or merchandise, or it may be a free trial offer, like the CompuServe ad shown in Exhibit 19.9. Because advertising conducted in direct-marketing campaigns is typified by this emphasis on immediate response, it is commonly referred to as **direct response advertising.**

As you probably suspect, **direct mail** and **telemarketing** are the direct marketer's prime media. However, all conventional media, like magazines, radio, and television, can be used to deliver direct response advertising. One dramatic transformation of the television commercial—the infomercial—has become especially popular in direct marketing. Let's begin our examination of these media options by considering the advantages and disadvantages of the dominant devices—direct mail and telemarketing.

Direct Mail

Direct mail has some notable faults as an advertising medium, not the least of which is cost. It can cost 15 to 20 times more to reach a person with a direct mail piece than it would to reach that person with a television commercial or newspaper advertisement.[41] Additionally, in a society where people are constantly on the move, mailing lists are commonly plagued by bad addresses. Each bad address represents advertising dollars wasted. And direct mail delivery dates, especially for bulk, third-class mailings, can be unpredictable. When the timing of an advertising message is critical to its success, direct mail can be the wrong choice.

40. Mark Lewyn, "You Can Run, but It's Tough to Hide from Marketers," *Business Week,* September 5, 1994, 60–61.
41. Stone, 362.

Direct mail's advantages stem from the selectivity of the medium. When an advertiser begins with a database of prospects, direct mail can be the perfect vehicle for reaching those prospects with little waste. Also, direct mail is a flexible medium that allows message adaptations on literally a household-by-household basis.[42] For example, direct mail is often used by political candidates for fund-raising. Oliver North made heavy use of direct mail in his campaign for the U.S. Senate in 1994, and it proved to be a record-breaking effort that raised roughly $20 million.[43] North's marketing consultants were careful to calibrate their requests for donations by household, using automobile registrations as their key indicator. Hence, the owner of a $35,000 Lexus was asked to contribute $500 to the North campaign, while the owner of a $9,500 Hyundai across the street was asked for only $100. Few media offer such flexibility to tailor messages for individual households.

Direct mail as a medium also lends itself like no other to testing and experimentation. For example, with direct mail it is common to test two or more different appeal letters using a modest budget and small sample of households.[44] The goal is to establish which version effects the largest response. When a winner is decided, that form of the letter is backed by big-budget dollars in launching the organization's primary campaign.

In addition, with direct mail, the choice of formats an organization can send to customers is virtually limitless. It can mail large, expensive brochures, videotapes, computer disks, or CDs. It can use pop-ups (per Exhibit 19.10), foldouts, scratch-and-sniff strips, or just simple postcards. If a product can be described in a limited space with minimal graphics, there really is no need to get fancy with the direct mail piece. The double postcard (DPC) format has an established track record of outperforming more expensive and elaborate direct mail packages.[45] Moreover, if an organization follows U.S. Postal

EXHIBIT 19.9

How does CompuServe elicit an immediate response in this example of direct response advertising? At the CompuServe Web site at www.compuserve.com/, there is an opportunity for immediate direct response. Is it effective? Why or why not? How does this compare to the GNN site at gnn.com?

42. Jack Z. Sissors and Lincoln Bumba, *Advertising Media Planning* (Lincolnwood, Ill.: NTC Business Books, 1994).
43. Steven W. Colford, "Direct Mail Sophistication Aids Political Solicitations," *Advertising Age,* October 10, 1994, S10.
44. Pamela Sebastian, "Charity Tries Two Letters to Melt Cold Hearts," *Wall Street Journal,* November 22, 1994, B1.
45. Michael Edmondson, "Postcards from the Edge," *Marketing Tools,* May 1995, 14.

Service guidelines carefully in mailing DPCs, the pieces can go out as first-class mail for reasonable rates. Since the Postal Service supplies address corrections on all first-class mail, using DPCs usually turns out to be a winner on either CPI or CPO measures, and DPCs can be an effective tool for cleaning up the bad addresses in a mailing list!

Telemarketing

Telemarketing is probably the direct marketers' most potent tool. As with direct mail, contacts can be selectively targeted, the impact of programs is easy to track, and experimentation with different scripts and delivery formats is simple and practical. And because telemarketing involves real, live, person-to-person dialogue, there is no medium that produces better response rates.[46] Unfortunately, the power of this tool has been abused, which has brought about aggressive action by federal lawmakers. See the Regulatory Issues box on page 537 for an update.

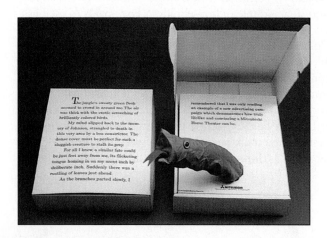

EXHIBIT 19.10

Direct mail is a versatile medium. Everything from a simple postcard to a pop-up snake can be delivered through the mail. **www.mitsucars.com/**

Telemarketing shares many of direct mail's limitations. Telemarketing is very expensive on a cost-per-contact basis, and just as names and addresses go bad as people move, so too do phone numbers. It is typical in telemarketing programs to find that 15 percent of the numbers called are inaccurate.[47] Further, telemarketing does not share direct mail's flexibility in terms of delivery options. When you reach people in their home or workplace, you have a limited amount of time to convey information and request some form of response.

If you have a telephone, you already know the biggest concern with telemarketing. It is a powerful yet highly intrusive medium that must be used with discretion. High-pressure telephone calls at inconvenient times can alienate customers. Telemarketing gives its best results over the long run if it is used to maintain constructive dialogues with existing customers and qualified prospects.[48]

For example, Kayla Cosmetics of Burbank, California, uses telemarketing to generate 93 percent of its sales from a marketing database of 19,000 customers.[49] Kayla's phone operators maintain ongoing dialogues with customers, and even though it may be months between contacts, each customer always works through the same personal operator when placing orders with Kayla. When that customer calls or is contacted by Kayla, her records, with purchase histories and personal details, appear immediately on the operator's computer screen. The first comment the customer hears from a Kayla operator is not "What item did you want to buy today?" but something like "What did you name your new baby?" Using technology and well-trained employees to add a personal touch to telemarketing efforts is a good way to get the most from this medium. Of course, such a personal response might make some people uncomfortable.

Direct Response Advertising in Other Media

The high costs associated with direct mail and telemarketing have led direct marketers to experiment with nearly every other medium as a way to deliver their requests for customer response. Using magazines, a popular device for executing a direct marketer's agenda is the bind-in insert card.[50] Thumb through a copy of any magazine and you will see how effective these light-cardboard inserts are in stopping the reader and calling attention

46.   Sissors and Bumba.
47.   Ibid.
48.   Stone, Chapter 14.
49.   William Dunn, "Building a Database," *Marketing Tools,* July/August 1994, 52–59.
50.   Stone, 250–52.

to themselves. Insert cards not only promote their products but also offer the reader an easy way to order a pair of Optek sport sunglasses, request a free sample of Skoal smokeless tobacco, or select those five free CDs that will make the reader a member of the BMG Music Club. In a recent bind-in insert that America Online ran in *Newsweek* magazine, the reader was invited to respond to an offer of ten free hours of online service either by returning a business-reply postcard or calling a 1-800 number. In either case, America Online added the respondent to its marketing database and pursued follow-up programs at a later date to try to convert the first-time user to a permanent subscriber.

When AT&T introduced the first 1-800 service in 1967, it simply could not have known how important this service would become to direct marketers. Newspaper ads from the *Wall Street Journal* provide 1-800 numbers for requesting Chrysler's Eagle Vision ESi test-drive kit. If you watch late-night TV, you may know the 1-800 number to call to order the Grammy-winning CD by Walter Ostanek and his polka band. IDS Financial Services, a division of American Express, features its 1-800 number in radio ads as part of a two-step offer designed to generate prospects for its financial-planning business. IDS operators take a caller's name, address, phone, and age to input into a marketing database, and they offer to book the caller for a consultation. IDS found this radio-based campaign to be more than twice as profitable as the direct mail campaigns it had used previously.[51] And as illustrated in Exhibit 19.11, magazine ads can also be used to

REGULATORY ISSUES

THE FED'S CRACKDOWN ON FRAUDULENT TELEMARKETERS

The Federal Trade Commission (FTC) has had it with telemarketing fraud and abuse. In December of 1995, FBI agents arrested 422 people in 15 states on fraud charges related to telemarketing operations that victimized the elderly. Congressional data suggests that Americans lose more than $40 billion a year to telemarketing fraud, most through phony contests and investment scams. More than 50 percent of the complaints to the FTC in 1995 were related to prize promotions.

The FTC is compelled to take consumer complaints seriously because the stakes in the industry are so high. In 1990, sales of goods and services through telemarketing totaled around $272 billion. In 1995, that figure increased to $385 billion; by the year 2000, sales are estimated to reach $599 billion.

Because of the large dollar amounts involved and consumers' apparent susceptibility to fraudulent practices, the FTC will administer the Telemarketing Sales Rule (TSR) passed by Congress in 1994. Key features of the TSR require that telemarketers

- promptly tell consumers they are making a sales call;
- reveal that, in the case of prize promotions, no purchase is necessary;
- disclose all cost information before asking consumers for money;
- must have verifiable authorization before debiting a consumer's checking accounts;
- not make sales calls before 8 A.M. and after 9 P.M. local time.

The new guidelines are welcomed by the American Telemarketers Association. A spokesperson for the group said that the new rules will "put additional burdens on legitimate businesses. But it will be worth the effort to go after the bad guys."

Source: Chad Rubel, "Stiffer Rules for Telemarketers As U.S. Cracks Down on Fraud," *Marketing News*, February 26, 1996, 1, 8.

provide a 1-800 number for starting a conversation with a customer. As these examples indicate, a 1-800 number makes it possible to use nearly any medium for direct response purposes.

Infomercials

The infomercial, discussed in Chapter 10 as one of the basic message tactics available to advertisers, is a novel form of direct response advertising that merits special mention. An **infomercial** is fundamentally just a long television advertisement made possible by the lower cost of ad space on many cable and satellite channels. They range in length from 3 to 60 minutes, but the common length is 30 minutes. Although producing an infomercial is more like producing a television program than it

51. Nancy Coltun Webster, "Radio Tuning In to Direct Response," *Advertising Age*, October 10, 1994, S14–S15.

Every spring the breathtaking sight of millions of tulip blooms emblazon Canada's capital, Ottawa, and grace the banks of the historic Rideau Canal. (During Winterlude, the canal becomes the world's longest skating rink.)

Immerse yourself in the pageantry and grandeur. Tour the majestic Parliament Buildings, or the skylit, colour-

It's here.

splashed National gallery. Visit historic Upper Canada Village in Morrisburg, take a cruise through the spectacular Thousand Islands or see split-second military manoeuvres performed at Fort Henry in Kingston, complete with fife, drum and cannon fire.

It's all just across the border, and with the favourable exchange rate, a trip to Eastern Ontario is an incredible deal. For your free vacation kit just give us a call.

The world's largest tulip festival isn't in Holland.

ONTARIO
CANADA
1-800-ONTARIO (668-2746)

EXHIBIT 19.11

Here again we see the direct marketer's favorite tool. Look for the World Wide Web to replace the 1-800 number as the direct marketer's favorite tool, say by the year 2001.

is like producing a 30-second commercial, infomercials are about selling. There appear to be several keys to successful use of this unique vehicle.

A critical factor is testimonials from satisfied users. Celebrity testimonials can help catch a viewer as he or she is channel surfing by the program, but celebrities aren't necessary, and, of course, they add to the production costs. Whether testimonials are from celebrities or from folks just like us, one expert summarizes matters this way: "Testimonials are so important that without them your chances of producing a profitable infomercial diminish hugely."[52]

Another key point to remember about infomercials is that viewers are not likely to stay tuned for the full 30 minutes. An infomercial is a 30-minute direct response sales pitch, not a classic episode of *Seinfeld* or *Happy Days*. The implication here is that the call to action should come not just at the end of the infomercial; most of the audience could be long gone by minute 28 into the show. A good rule of thumb in a 30-minute infomercial is to divide the program into 10-minute increments and close three times.[53] Each closing should feature the 1-800 number that allows the viewer to order the product or request more information. And an organization should not offer information to the customer unless it can deliver speedy follow-up; same-day response should be the goal in pursuing leads generated by an infomercial.

Many different types of products and services have been marketed using infomercials. CD players, self-help videos, home-exercise equipment, kitchen appliances, and hair-restoration treatments have all had success with the infomercial. The state of Ohio has run a 30-minute infomercial with its 1-800-BUCKEYE phone number to promote tourist destinations in the state.[54] Companies like Avon, KitchenAid, Mattel, Rayovac, and Whirlpool have all used infomercials to help inform consumers about their products.

While the infomercial has become a versatile tool, one final point needs to be made about making profitable use of this tool. If the primary goal in running infomercials is order solicitation, it is difficult to generate a profit for any item priced below $40 or $50.[55] The costs to produce and air an infomercial make it almost impossible to generate adequate cash flow from an item that can support a price of, say, only $19.95. If a firm is working with moderately priced items, the solution may be to bundle them together. If the product can justify a price of only $19.95, sell it in sets of three for $49.99, or, better yet, offer two for $49.99 with a third item free for those who call the 1-800 line immediately. Then, the firm must be prepared: 80 percent of all calls generated by infomercials occur within five minutes of the focal call to action.[56]

52.   Herschell Gordon Lewis, "Information on Infomercials," *Direct Marketing Magazine,* March 1995, 30–32.
53.   Ibid.
54.   Jim Kirk, "Ohio Joins Infomercial Parade," *Adweek,* May 9, 1994, 4.
55.   Lewis.
56.   Paul Kerstetter, "When Consumers Actually Respond to Infomercial Airings," *Adweek Infomercial Sourcebook,* 1994, 12–15.

The Coordination Challenge Revisited

4 As you have seen in the previous four chapters, the wide variety of media available to an advertiser poses a tremendous challenge with respect to coordination and integration. Organizations are looking to achieve the synergy that can come when various media options reach the consumer with a common and compelling message. However, to work in various media, functional specialists both inside and outside an organization need to be employed. It then becomes a very real problem to get the advertising manager, special events manager, sales promotion manager, and new media manager to work in harmony. And now we must add to the list of functional specialists the direct-marketing manager.

The evolution and growing popularity of direct marketing raises the challenge of achieving integrated marketing communications to new heights. In particular, the development of a marketing database commonly leads to interdepartmental rivalries and can create major conflicts between a company and its advertising agency. The marketing database is a powerful source of information about the customer; those who do not have direct access to this information will be envious of those who do. Additionally, the growing use of direct-marketing campaigns must mean that someone else's budget is being cut. Typically, direct-marketing programs come at the expense of conventional advertising campaigns that might have been run on television, in magazines, or in other mass media.[57] Since direct marketing takes dollars from those activities that have been the staples of traditional ad agency business, it is easy to see why advertising agencies view direct marketing with some resentment.[58] Similarly, it is easy to see why large advertising agencies are interested in buying up smaller, fast-growing direct-marketing companies.[59] If you can't beat 'em, buy 'em!

There are no simple solutions for achieving integrated marketing communications, but one approach that many organizations are experimenting with is the establishment of a marketing-communications manager, or a marcom manager for short.[60] A **marcom manager** plans an organization's overall communications program and oversees the various functional specialists inside and outside the organization to ensure that they are working together to deliver the desired message to the customer.

One company that has recently moved to this marcom manager system is AT&T. As mentioned, AT&T, like its telecommunications rivals, makes heavy use of both direct-marketing programs and mass media advertising to reach out and touch its customers. George Burnett, the marcom manager for AT&T, explains the value of integrating direct mail and advertising this way: "Honestly, I think it is simplicity and clarity. . . . That is one of the goals of integrated communications, because in this complicated world, adding complication on top of the competitiveness is really not in our customers' interest."[61]

Burnett adds emphasis to a theme we have developed throughout this book. Perhaps the major challenge in the world of advertising today is to find ways to break through the clutter of competitors' ads—and really all advertising in general—to get customers' attention and make a point with them. If the various media and programs an organization employs are sending different messages or mixed signals, the organization is only hurting itself. To achieve the synergy that will allow it to overcome the clutter of today's marketplace, an organization has no choice but to pursue integrated marketing communications.

57.   Scott Hample, "Fear of Commitment," *Marketing Tools,* January/February 1995, 6–10.
58.   Jim Osterman, "This Changes Everything," *Adweek,* May 15, 1995, 44–45.
59.   Sally Goll Beatty, "Interpublic Group Considers Move into Hot Field of Direct Marketing," *Wall Street Journal,* April 19, 1996, B3.
60.   Don E. Schultz, Stanley I. Tannenbaum, and Robert F. Lauterborn, *Integrated Marketing Communications* (Lincolnwood, Ill.: NTC Business Books, 1993).
61.   Levin.

SUMMARY

1 Identify the three primary purposes served by and explain the growing popularity of direct marketing.

Many types of organizations are increasing their expenditures on direct marketing. These expenditures serve three primary purposes: direct marketing offers potent tools for closing sales with customers, for identifying prospects for future contacts, and for offering information and incentives that help foster brand loyalty. The growing popularity of direct marketing can be attributed to several factors. Direct marketers make consumption convenient: credit cards and 1-800 numbers take the hassle out of shopping. Additionally, today's computing power, which allows marketers to build and mine large customer-information files, has enhanced direct marketing's impact. The emphasis on producing and tracking measurable outcomes is also well received by marketers in an era when everyone is trying to do more with less.

2 Distinguish a mailing list from a marketing database and review the many applications of each.

A mailing list is a file of names and addresses of current or potential customers, like those lists that might be generated by a credit card company or a catalog retailer. Internal lists are valuable for creating relationships with current customers, and external lists are useful in generating new customers. A marketing database is a natural extension of the internal list but includes information about individual customers and their specific preferences and purchasing patterns. A marketing database allows organizations to identify and focus their efforts on their best customers. Recognizing and reinforcing preferred customers can be a potent strategy for building loyalty. Cross-selling opportunities also emerge once a database is in place. In addition, as one gains keener information about the motivations of current best customers, insights usually emerge about how to attract new customers.

3 Describe the prominent media used by direct marketers in delivering their messages to the customer.

Direct-marketing programs emanate from mailing lists and databases, but there is still a need to deliver a message to the customer. Direct mail and telemarketing are the most common means used in executing direct-marketing programs. Infomercials are another prominent tool. Because the advertising done as part of direct-marketing programs typically requests an immediate response from the customer, it is known as direct response advertising. Conventional media like television, newspapers, magazines, and radio can also be used to request a direct response by offering a 1-800 number or a World Wide Web address to facilitate customer contact.

4 Articulate the added challenge created by direct marketing for achieving integrated marketing communication.

Developing a marketing database, selecting a direct mail format, or producing an infomercial are some of the new tasks attributable to direct marketing. These and other related tasks require more functional specialists, who further complicate the challenge of presenting a coordinated face to the customer. Some organizations are now experimenting with marcom managers, who are assigned the task of coordinating the efforts of various functional specialists working on different aspects of a marketing communications program. To achieve an integrated presence that will break through in a cluttered marketplace, this coordination is essential.

KEY TERMS

direct marketing (520)
cost per inquiry (CPI) (528)
cost per order (CPO) (528)
mailing list (528)
internal lists (529)
external lists (529)
marketing database (530)

RFM analysis (531)
frequency-marketing programs (532)
direct response advertising (534)
direct mail (534)
telemarketing (534)
infomercial (537)
marcom manager (539)

QUESTIONS FOR REVIEW AND CRITICAL THINKING

1.   Direct marketing is defined as an interactive system of marketing. Explain the meaning of the phrase *interactive system*. Give an example of a noninteractive system. How would an interactive system be helpful in the cultivation of brand loyalty?

2.   Start a collection of the direct mail pieces you receive at your home or apartment. After you have accumulated at least ten pieces, review the three main purposes for direct marketing discussed in this chapter. For each piece in your collection, what would you surmise is the direct marketer's purpose?

3.   Review the major forces that have promoted the growth in popularity of direct marketing. Can you come up with any reasons why its popularity might be peaking? What are the threats to its continuing popularity as a marketing tool?

4.   Describe the various categories of information that a credit card company might use to enhance its internal mailing list. For each category, comment on the possible value of the information for improving the company's market segmentation strategy.

5.   What is RFM analysis, and what is it generally used for? How would RFM analysis allow an organization to get more impact from a limited marketing budget? (Keep in mind that every organization views its marketing budget as too small to accomplish all that needs to be done.)

6.   Compare and contrast frequency-marketing programs with those tools described in Chapter 18 under the heading "Sales Promotion Directed at Consumers." What common motivators do these two types of activities rely on? How are their purposes similar or different? What goal is a frequency-marketing program trying to achieve that would not be a prime concern with a sales promotion?

7.   There's a paradox here, right? On the one hand, it is common to talk about building relationships and loyalty with the tools of direct marketing. On the other hand, it is also true that direct-marketing tools like junk mail and telephone interruptions at home during dinner are constant irritants. How does one build relationships with irritants? In your opinion, when is it realistic to think that the tools of direct marketing could be used to build long-term relationships with customers?

8.   What is it about direct marketing that makes its growing popularity a threat to the traditional advertising agency?

EXPERIENTIAL EXERCISES

Spend an hour watching television with the goal of viewing an advertisement by a direct marketer. What product was offered? Was the offer unique? Can the product be found in stores in your area? Describe what immediate action the advertiser wants you to take.

Describe one direct-marketing promotion you have responded to, print or broadcast. What made you respond to the offer? Were you satisfied with the product after receiving it? Have you made additional purchases from the same direct marketer? Explain why or why not.

USING THE INTERNET

Several merchandisers have established Web sites that serve as direct-marketing vehicles. Visit the following sites:

Sharper Image: www.sharperimage.com

Fingerhut: www.fingerhut.com

Lands' End: www.landsend.com

Spiegel: www.spiegel.com

Virtual Vineyard: www.virtualvin.com

For each site, answer the following questions:

1.   How attractive is the online catalog? Is it easy or difficult to navigate within the site and place an order? Make

some suggestions on how the online version can be improved.

2.   How does the shopping experience compare to more traditional ways of shopping? How does this site make it easier or less expensive for the company to sell and distribute its products?

3.   Are any specials offered? Do you think the specials are effective tools for getting people to purchase products on this site?

4.   Does the site adequately address the issue of security for those providing credit card numbers when placing orders?

Chapter 20

Public Relations

and Corporate

Advertising

After reading and thinking about this chapter, you will be able to do the following:

1 Explain the role of public relations as part of an organization's overall IMC strategy and detail the objectives and tools of public relations.

2 Describe two basic strategies for motivating an organization's public relations activities.

3 Discuss the applications and objectives of corporate advertising.

Intel is one of the great success stories of American industry. In the mid-1980s, only the most ardent computer users were aware of the Intel microcomputer processor—then called the 286. Through the late 1980s and early 1990s, the 386 and then the 486 became common language around offices and schools. The firm has gone on to dominate the PC processor market and has amassed a 70 percent worldwide market share. The "Intel Inside" advertising campaign, which turned a computer component part into a widely recognized brand name, may be the most successful original-equipment-manufacturer advertising campaign in history. Intel's, "What's the big attraction?" ad is shown in Exhibit 20.1. Odds are good that if you stop the average person on the street, they can tell you what "Intel Inside" means. Even a formidable chip design and manufacturing consortium of IBM, Apple Computer, and Motorola has had little effect on Intel's complete dominance of the microprocessor market. During this time, Intel has risen from relative techno-obscurity as an innovative computer technology company to number 60 on the Fortune 500 list. Sales have grown from $1.3 billion to more than $16.2 billion in just ten years.[1]

But all this success, market dominance, product innovation, and savvy advertising did not prepare Intel for the public relations challenge it faced in late 1994. Even Intel's creative and astute CEO, Andy Grove, who had handled huge challenges from aggressive competitors like Advanced Micro Devices and the IBM consortium, was overmatched. What was this public relations event that turned out to be more potent than Intel itself? In early 1994, Intel introduced its new-generation chip, the Pentium, as the successor to the widely used line of X86 chips. The Pentium processor was another leap forward in computing speed and power. But in November 1994, Pentium users were discovering a flaw in the chip. During certain floating-point operations, some Pentium chips were actually producing erroneous calculations—albeit the error showed up in only the fifth or sixth decimal place. While this might not affect the average consumer who's trying to balance a checkbook, power users in scientific laboratories require absolute precision and accuracy in their calculations.

Having a defect in a high-performance technology product like the Pentium chip was one thing; how Intel handled the problem was another. Intel's initial "official"

FIGURE 20.1

Intel's advertising helped it to dominate the microprocessor market. **www.intel.com/**

What's the big attraction?

1.   "The Fortune 500," *Fortune,* April 29, 1996, F3; and *Intel Annual Report 1995.*

response was that the flaw in the chip was so insignificant that it would produce an error in calculations only once in 27,000 years. Some users who had called Intel's customer service line to report processing flaws claimed to have been rebuffed by Intel customer reps.[2] Annoyed, the power users took their complaint to the Internet and warned PC users of the possible errors in processing caused by the Pentium. Then, IBM, which had shipped thousands of PCs with Pentium chips, challenged the assertion that the flaw was insignificant, claiming that processing errors could occur as often as every 24 days. IBM announced that it would stop shipment of all Pentium-based PCs immediately.[3]

From this point on, the Pentium situation became a runaway public relations disaster. Every major newspaper, network newscast, and magazine carried the story of the flawed Pentium chip. Even the cartoon series *Dilbert* got in on the act, running a whole series of cartoon strips that spoofed the Intel controversy. One of these *Dilbert* cartoons can be seen in Exhibit 20.2. One observer characterized it this way: "From a public relations standpoint, the train has left the station and is barreling out of Intel's control."[4] Many of the stories characterized Intel as arrogant or uncaring or both. Another analyst assessed the situation as follows: "Intel squandered the opportunity to take decisive action during the critical two-week period between receiving bona fide user complaints of processing flaws and IBM's preemptive announcement of its decision to withhold shipments."[5] But instead of decisive action, for weeks Intel publicly argued that the flaw would not affect the vast majority of users, and the firm did nothing.

Ultimately, public pressure and user demands forced Intel to change its position. Consumers were outraged at Intel's initial policy of refusing to replace Pentium chips unless Intel thought the user needed one. Finally, in early 1995, Intel decided to provide a free replacement chip to any user who believed he or she was at risk. Exhibit 20.3 shows a news story released over the Internet announcing the replacement program. Andy Grove, in announcing the $475 million program to replace customers' chips, admitted publicly that "the Pentium processor divide problem has been a learning experience for Intel."[6]

WEB SIGHTING

Source: DILBERT reprinted by permission of United Features Syndicate, Inc.

EXHIBIT 20.2

The importance of public relations to a company is underscored in this exhibit. A cartoon character can make fun of your company's problems and there isn't much you can do about it. In checking out the Dilbert Web site at **www.unitedmedia.com/comics/dilbert/**, *you can see that the "everyman" of corporate America has grown into quite a commercial enterprise. Does this site use public relations for comic strip author Scott Adams? How?*

2.   Alex Stanton, "Pentium Brouhaha a Marketing Lesson," *Advertising Age,* February 20, 1995, 18.

3.   Barbara Grady, "Chastened Intel Steps Carefully with Introduction of New Chip," *Computerlink,* February 14, 1995, 11.

4.   James G. Kimball, "Can Intel Repair the Pentium PR?" *Advertising Age,* December 19, 1994, 35.

5.   Stanton.

6.   Grady.

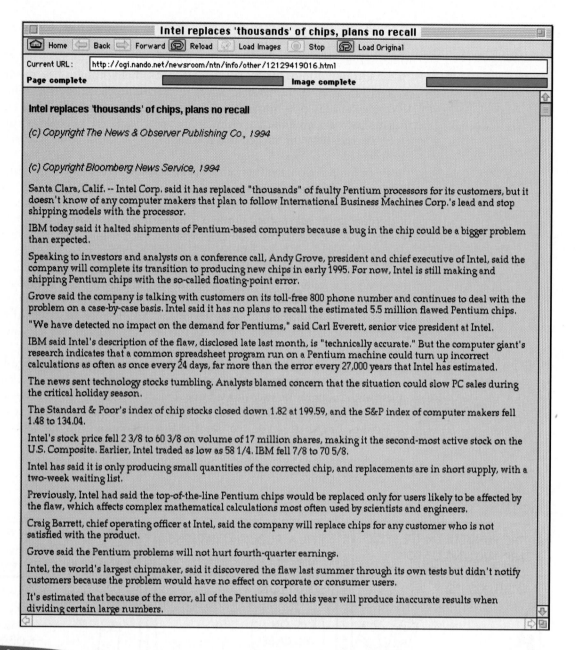

FIGURE 20.3

Intel admits its mistake and agrees to replace faulty Pentium chips.

Indeed, Intel had learned that public relations action can be a supportive communication that maintains the goodwill and good image of the firm developed through other communications. Just such good public relations support is in evidence in the *U.S. News & World Report* article shown in Exhibit 20.4. Since Intel had created a widely recognized brand with its broad-based advertising, the firm's image was vulnerable to strategic missteps, as in the case of the Pentium flaw. As we will see in this chapter, public relations efforts can make a major contribution to the integrated marketing communications program of a firm. Beyond the messages contained in public relations communications themselves, the damage control provided by public relations can salvage years of effective communication and preserve the effects of millions of dollars invested in advertising.

Good public relations are essential for a firm to be successful.

Intel Loses Few Chips on Pentium

Rumors of Pentium's death, to paraphrase Mark Twain, have been greatly exaggerated. Since mid-November, Intel Corp. has weathered a furious controversy over its handling of a tiny flaw in its top-of-the-line personal computer chip. First came the attacks on the world's No. 1 chip maker for failing to disclose the glitch as soon as the company learned of it this past summer. But the real trouble, according to industry analysts, came when Intel refused to offer wholesale replacement of the small silicon brain, which currently powers an estimated 5 million personal computers. Pentium owners across the nation were irate that they would have to prove that their calculations were complex enough to warrant replacement.

Strong sales. So far, the Pentium problem has not inflicted major financial damage on Intel's very solid bottom line. Sales of Pentium-based personal computers jumped more than 80 percent from October to December, according to ARS Inc., a market research firm located in Irving, Texas. These numbers reflect sales up until late December, when Intel announced that it would replace the faulty PC processors on request. Nearly half of all personal computers sold from mid-November through Christmas were Pentium-based, according to Channel Marketing, a Dallas-based research firm. In addition, Intel's stock price, which dropped to just under $58 a share during the Pentium flap, has regained its upward momentum and is currently trading at around $64.

It also appears that Intel's rivals have failed to capitalize on the big chip maker's recent stumble. Hordes of prospective Pentium customers did not defect to the PowerPC chip from IBM and Apple, according to ARS, although Apple's recent sales were very healthy. Consumers, it seems, simply weren't as nervous about Intel's prize product as analysts believed. And they showed it by giving Intel, and the computer industry in general, a very Merry Christmas.

Source: Amy Bernstein, *U.S. News & World Report*, January 9, 1995, 44. Copyright, January 9, 1995, *U.S. News & World Report*. Used with permission.

This chapter will consider in detail the role of two separate and important areas that must be part of a firm's overall integrated marketing communications effort: public relations and corporate advertising. Each of these areas has the potential to make a distinct and important contribution to the single and unified message and image of an organization, which is the ultimate goal of IMC. Each area has the potential for effective and supportive communication, but they achieve this in different ways. Public relations is a marketing and management function that deals with the public issues encountered by firms across a wide range of constituents. An important component of public relations is publicity—news media coverage of events related to a firm's products or activities. Publicity presents both challenges and opportunities. News reports about problems, like those Intel had to deal with, represent challenges. Large investment projects in facilities or new product discoveries represent opportunities for positive publicity. In contrast, corporate advertising serves a well-defined purpose in building an image for a firm above and beyond the image of its individual brands. So, while these areas of communication are, indeed, quite different, they share the same agenda of contributing to the meaning a firm and its products have in the marketplace. In other words, both fulfill a role in achieving integrated marketing communications.

Public Relations

Intel's public relations and publicity problems were of its own doing. But in many cases, firms are faced with public relations crises that are totally beyond their control. In 1993, Pepsi had just such a public relations nightmare on its hands. Complaints were coming in from all over the United States that cans of Pepsi, Diet Pepsi, and Caffeine Free Diet Pepsi had syringes inside them (see Exhibit 20.5). Other callers claimed their cans of Pepsi contained such things as a screw, a crack vial, a sewing needle, and brown goo in the bottom. Unlike Intel, Pepsi assembled a management team that was mobilized to handle the crisis. The team immediately considered a national recall of all Pepsi products—no matter what the cost. The Food and

Syringes Found in Two Cans
Of Cola in Washington State

SEATTLE, June 13 (Reuters) — Hypodermic needles were found in two cans of Diet Pepsi in Washington State this week, prompting a Federal investigation and a warning from a bottling company that Pepsi drinkers should rattle their cans before taking a sip.

Preliminary Food and Drug Administration tests of the two cans revealed no contamination, the regional Pepsi bottler Alpac Corporation said. Alpac has not issued a recall.

The first syringe was found in a Diet Pepsi by an elderly couple in Tacoma. Earl and Mary Tripplett discovered the syringe and bent needle Wednesday rattling around in an empty can of Diet Pepsi which they had opened and drunk. They reported no illness.

Alpac said the second can was found by a resident of Federal Way, about 18 miles south of Seattle. It was collected Friday and turned over to the F.D.A.

In a television interview on Saturday, the president of the bottler, Karl Behnke, urged consumers to "rattle the cans a little bit" before drinking. Alpac supplies Pepsi to Washington, Alaska, Oregon, Hawaii and Guam.

Source: *New York Times*, June 14, 1993, A-11.

FIGURE 20.5

Pepsi faced a potential public relations nightmare. **www.pepsi.com**

Drug Administration (FDA) told Pepsi there was no need for such action since no one had been injured and there was no health risk. The Pepsi team was sure that this was not a case of tampering in the production facility. A can of Pepsi is filled with cola and then sealed in nine-tenths of a second—making it virtually impossible for anyone to get anything in a can during production.[7]

The president of Pepsi went on national television to explain the situation and defend his firm and its products. Pepsi enlisted the aid of a powerful and influential constituent at this point—the Food and Drug Administration. The commissioner of the FDA, David Kessler, said publicly that many of the tampering claims could not be substantiated or verified. A video camera in Aurora, Colorado, caught a woman trying to insert a syringe in a Pepsi can. Pepsi was exonerated in the press, but the huge public relations problem had significantly challenged the firm to retain the stature and credibility of a truly global brand.

What happened to Intel and Pepsi highlights why public relations is such a difficult form of communication to manage. In many cases, a firm's public relations program is called into action for damage control, as the Pepsi ad in Exhibit 20.6 illustrates. Intel and Pepsi had to be totally reactive to the situation rather than strategically controlling it, as with the other tools in the integrated communications process. But while many episodes of public relations must be reactive, a firm can be prepared with public relations materials to conduct an orderly and positive goodwill and image-building campaign among its many constituents.

This section of the chapter will consider several aspects of that area of communications known as **public relations,** a marketing and management function that focuses on communications that foster goodwill between a firm and its many constituent groups. The constituent groups on which public relations efforts focus include customers, stockholders, suppliers, employees, government entities, educators, citizen action groups, the local communities where a firm has operations, and the general public. Public relations can be used to highlight positive events in an organization, like quarterly sales and profits or noteworthy community service programs. Conversely, public relations can be used strategically for damage control when adversity strikes. To fully appreciate the role and potential of public relations in the broad communications efforts of a firm, we will consider the objectives of public relations, the tools of public relations, the role of publicity, and basic public relations strategies.

Objectives of Public Relations

The public relations function in a firm, usually handled by an outside agency, is prepared to engage in positive public relations efforts and to deal with any negative events related to a firm's activities. Within the broad

---

7.   Annette Miller, Daniel Glick, and Sherry Keen-Osborn, "The Great Pepsi Panic," *Newsweek,* June 28, 1993, 32.

Pepsi engages in public relations damage control.
www.pepsi.com

Pepsi is pleased to announce...
...nothing.

As America now knows, those stories about Diet Pepsi were a hoax. Plain and simple, not true. Hundreds of investigators have found no evidence to support a single claim.

As for the many, many thousands of people who work at Pepsi-Cola, we feel great that it's over. And we're ready to get on with making and bringing you what we believe is the best-tasting diet cola in America.

There's not much more we can say. Except that most importantly, we won't let this hoax change our exciting plans for this summer.

We've set up special offers so you can enjoy our great quality products at prices that will save you money all summer long. It all starts on July 4th weekend and we hope you'll stock up with a little extra, just to make up for what you might have missed last week.

That's it. Just one last word of thanks to the millions of you who have stood with us.

**Drink All The Diet Pepsi You Want.
Uh Huh®.**

DIET PEPSI and UH HUH are registered trademarks of PepsiCo Inc.

guidelines of image building and establishing relationships with constituents, it is possible to identify six primary objectives for public relations:

- *Promoting goodwill.* This is an image-building function of public relations. Industry events or community activities that reflect favorably on a firm are highlighted. When employees of General Electric participate in the Habitat for Humanity program, this event is newsworthy in a public relations sense.
- *Promoting a product or service.* Press releases or events that increase public awareness of a firm's brands can be pursued through public relations. Large pharmaceutical firms like Merck and Glaxo issue press releases when new drugs are discovered or FDA approval is achieved.
- *Preparing internal communications.* Disseminating information and correcting misinformation within a firm can reduce the impact of rumors and increase employee support. For events like reductions in the labor force or mergers of firms, internal communications can do much to dispel rumors circulating among employees and in the local community.
- *Counteracting negative publicity.* This is the damage control function of public relations. The attempt here is not to cover up negative events, but rather prevent the negative publicity from damaging the image of a firm and its brands. When a lawsuit was filed against NEC alleging that one of its cellular phones had caused cancer, McCaw Cellular Communications used public relations activities to inform the

public and especially cellular phone users of scientific knowledge that argued against the claims in the lawsuit.[8]

- *Lobbying.* The public relations function can assist a firm in dealing with government officials and pending legislation. Industries maintain active and aggressive lobbying efforts at both the state and federal levels. As an example, the beer and wine industry has lobbyists monitoring legislation that could restrict beer and wine advertising.
- *Giving advice and counsel.* Assisting management in determining what (if any) position to take on public issues, preparing employees for public appearances, and helping management anticipate public reactions are all part of the advice and counsel function of public relations.

Tools of Public Relations

There are several vehicles through which a firm can make positive use of public relations and pursue the objectives just cited. The goal is to gain as much control over the process as possible. By using the methods discussed in the following sections, a firm can integrate its public relations effort with other marketing communications.

Press Releases. Having a file of information that makes for good news stories puts the firm in a position to take advantage of free press coverage. Press releases allow a firm to pursue positive publicity from the news media. Items that make for good public relations include

- new products
- new scientific discoveries
- new personnel
- new corporate facilities
- innovative corporate practices, like energy-saving programs or employee benefit programs
- annual shareholder meetings
- charitable and community service activities

The only drawback to press releases is that a firm often doesn't know if or when the item will appear in the media. Also, the news media are free to edit or interpret a news release, which may alter its meaning.

Feature Stories. While a firm cannot write a feature story for a newspaper or televise a story over the local television networks, it can invite journalists to do an exclusive story on the firm when there is a particularly noteworthy event. A feature story is different from a press release in that it is more controllable. A feature story, as opposed to a news release, offers a single journalist the opportunity to do a fairly lengthy piece with exclusive rights to the information.

Company Newsletters. In-house publications, like a newsletter, can disseminate positive information about a firm through its employees. As members of the community, employees are proud of achievements by their firm. Newsletters can also be distributed to important constituents in the community, like government officials, the Chamber of Commerce, or the Tourist Bureau. Suppliers often enjoy reading about an important customer, so newsletters can be mailed to this group as well. Exhibit 20.7 is an example of a company newsletter.

Interviews and Press Conferences. As in the Pepsi tampering crisis, interviews and press conferences can be a highly effective public relations tool. Often, interviews and press conferences are warranted in a crisis management situation. But firms have also successfully called press

8.   John J. Keller, "McCaw to Study Cellular Phones As Safety Questions Affect Sales," *Wall Street Journal,* January 29, 1993, B3.

FIGURE 20.7

A company newsletter for the University of Illinois, Urbana-Champaign.

Volume 15
Number 15   March 7, 1996

For Faculty and Staff, University of Illinois at Urbana-Champaign

Faulkner's first two years as provost provide challenges

By Nancy Koeneman

Budget reform. Competitive salary structures. Preservation and enhancement of quality in the UI's programs. Technology. These and other issues have been on the agenda of Larry Faulkner since he became provost and vice chancellor for academic affairs Jan. 1, 1994.

He's shepherded these issues to various levels of discussion, inquiry and resolution through task forces and work groups. Some topics were being examined as he took his office; others became a focal point due to his efforts over the past two years. Recently Faulkner shared his thoughts on the progress made during his tenure as provost and of the challenges that lie ahead.

Budget Reform

"I think there is a certain amount of apprehension about what might take place, but the main thing is that we are proceeding in a careful way through the Budget Strategies Committee to address a budget-making strategy that can meet the real needs of the campus in the years ahead," Faulkner said.

"In the past, habits have built up in an environment where the mechanisms for state funding were very different from the way they are now and [in that time] the university has become larger and more complex," he said.

The current budget system makes it difficult for the deans to understand "the larger implications" of how they allocate their money. Complicating the situation, he said, is the fact that "the system forces too many

decisions at too high a level." What the UI needs and what Faulkner wants to see is a "system that allows genuine empowerment of colleges and departments to direct programs," he said.

Subcommittees of the Budget Strategies Committee have been working on these issues, and members were expected to report back this month. The report will be made available to the campus, Faulkner said. Once the report is in hand, he and others on the committee will meet with the major decision-making groups on campus – including the Senate and its principal committees and the representatives of every college – to answer questions and "look at ways to refine this proposal," he said.

"This is a major initiative and it has involved a lot of people," Faulkner said. "I hope to move forward with some early elements [of the reform] in fiscal year 1996-97."

Undergraduate Education

A major theme in the orchestrated efforts to improve the UI is enhanced undergraduate education.

"We have, under the chancellor's leadership, put a strong focus on improving the students' first year here," Faulkner said. "The Discovery Program has received a great deal of attention. We have been working with colleges to provide a stable appropriations base and to increase capacity so that students who desire a course of this kind can get one."

Also, David Liu was appointed associ-

ate provost to focus on undergraduate education. "He's a leading faculty member and he will provide strong and more focused leadership in this area," Faulkner said.

Liu is involved in creating a Teaching Advancement Board, one of the recommendations in the Framework for the Future, and in a number of other undergraduate projects.

Salaries and Compensation

Faulkner said with the many topics under consideration, one that remains at the top of his list is improving the salaries for faculty and staff members and graduate assistants. "We're maintaining focus on this with hopes of making progress on an annual basis," he said.

A related issue – tuition and fee waivers for graduate students – has received a lot of attention lately.

"[The proposal] was developed to allow colleges to make their own decisions about support structures suited to their own programs," Faulkner said. "Proposals have been [made] to do that, within a framework governed with fairness by the Graduate College. Some colleges feel they don't have a support program that serves their needs within the competitive context that they face nationally." (For more information about tuition and fee

Enhanced undergraduate education, improving salaries and budget reform are among the items on provost Larry Faulkner's agenda.

waivers, see the Office of the Provost Web page, which is accessible under Administrative and Support Services on the UI's Web page.)

(See Faulkner, page 16)

Fans to honor Henson in post-game tribute

By Nancy Koeneman

Lou Henson's retirement announcement last month set off fireworks in the college sports media, but the real fireworks will be in his honor Saturday at Assembly Hall during post-game ceremonies on Lou Henson Fan Appreciation Day.

Saturday's program concludes with indoor fireworks; the event will sparkle with luminaries from the UI and the sports world as well.

Chancellor Michael Aiken, UI President James Stukel and Ron Guenther, UI's athletic director, are all expected to attend and comment at the post-game bash. Big 10 Commissioner Jim Delany also is expected to attend.

Several former Illini who are now playing in the NBA are sending videotaped tributes for the occasion.

Henson will be featured on the game program cover, commemorative T-shirts will be sold at the game and in the community (with proceeds going to the Fighting Illini Scholarship Fund), and a four-page pamphlet describing Henson's accomplishments in his 21-year history at the UI will be distributed to fans attending the March 9 game.

The last home game of the season, this is the fans' chance to give Henson a warm send-off, said Tom Porter, associate director of athletics in the UI's division of intercollegiate athletics.

"There are very few major NCAA basketball coaches who have an opportunity to retire," Porter said. "With the number of years he's coached and his success, I feel it's fitting to pay him a special tribute."

Guenther added, "We're pleased to honor Lou Henson following the Minnesota game. Henson has done a terrific job representing not only Fighting Illini basketball, but the UI through the last two decades. He is a true gentleman and has been a wonderful role model for our young men on and off the court. We're extremely proud of his accomplishments and delighted we have the opportunity to present him with a big send-off."

An eight-minute video highlighting Henson's UI career will be shown, along with the interviews with former UI athletes now in the NBA. The Rebounders, a basketball booster club, and the Alumni Association will make presentations to Henson, in addition to those by the chancellor, the UI president and the athletic director. Henson also will comment.

Former letterwinners from Henson's teams over the past two decades have been invited, Porter said, and many are expected to attend.

Since Henson's announcement, the game has sold out, Porter said. But those who want to see the celebration can hear it on WDWS-AM (1400) or watch it on WCIA Channel 3.

Head basketball coach Lou Henson retires after this season, his 21st at the UI.

Inside

2   Plans are under way for Cyberfest '97, a celebration of the birth of HAL from "2001: A Space Odyssey."

6   Recipients of the Chancellor's Academic Professional Excellence awards are announced.

---

conferences to announce important scientific breakthroughs or explain the details of a corporate expansion. The press conference has an air of importance and credibility because it uses a news format to present important corporate information.

Sponsored Events. Sponsored events were discussed as a form of emerging support media in Chapter 16. Sponsoring events can also serve as an important public relations tool. A firm can become involved in local community events through sponsorships. The Contemporary Issues box on page 554 provides several screening questions for selecting events to sponsor. With the prominent display of the corporate name and logo, local residents will recognize the community involvement of an organization, as illustrated in Exhibit 20.8. Fund-raisers of all sorts for nonprofit organizations give positive visibility to

FIGURE 20.8

Oscar Mayer participates in community events to generate favorable public relations. **www.oscar-mayer.com**

corporations. Chevrolet has for many years sponsored college scholarships through the NCAA by choosing the offensive and defensive player of a game. The scholarships are announced weekly at the conclusion of televised games. This sort of notoriety for Chevrolet creates a favorable image for viewers.

Publicity. **Publicity** is unpaid-for media exposure about a firm's activities or its products and services. Publicity is handled by the public relations function but cannot, with the exception of press releases, be strategically controlled like other public relations efforts. Public relations professionals can react swiftly to publicity, but rarely can they totally control the information. Despite the lack of control, publicity can build an image and heighten consumer awareness of brands and organizations. An organization needs to be prepared to take advantage of events that make for good publicity and to counter events that are potentially damaging to the firm's reputation. Moreover, as described in the Ethical Issues box on page 557, ad campaigns themselves may generate substantial publicity.

One major advantage of publicity—when the information is positive—is that it has credibility. Publicity carried as news stories on television and radio and in newspapers and magazines assumes an air of believability because of the credibility of the media context. Not-for-profit organizations often use publicity in the form of news stories and public interest stories as ways to gain widespread visibility at little or no cost.

Basic Public Relations Strategies   ❷ Given the breadth of possibilities for using public relations as part of a firm's overall integrated marketing communications effort, it is worth identifying basic public relations strategies. Public relations strategies can be categorized as either proactive or reactive. **Proactive public relations strategy** is dictated by marketing objectives, seeks to publicize a company and its brands, and takes the offensive rather than the defensive. **Reactive public relations strategy** is dictated by influences outside the control of a company, focuses on problems to be solved rather than opportunities, and requires a company to take defensive measures.[9] The two strategies involve different orientations to public relations.

Proactive Public Relations Strategy. In developing a proactive public relations strategy, a firm acknowledges opportunities for it to use public relations efforts to accomplish something positive. In many firms, the positive aspects of employee achievements, corporate contributions to the community, or the organization's social and environmental programs go unnoticed by important constituents. To implement a proactive public relations strategy, a firm needs to develop a comprehensive public relations program. The key components of a such a program are as follows:

1. *A public relations audit.* A **public relations audit** identifies the characteristics of a firm or the aspects of the firm's activities that are positive and newsworthy. Information is gathered in much the same way as information related to advertising strategy is gathered. Corporate personnel and customers are questioned to provide information. The type of information gathered in an audit includes descriptions of company products and services, market performance of brands, profitability, goals for products, market trends, new product introductions, important suppliers, important customers, employee programs and facilities, community programs, charitable activities, and the like.

2. *A public relations plan.* Armed with information from a public relations audit, the next step is a structured public relations plan. A **public relations plan** identifies the objectives and activities related to the public relations communications issued by a firm. The components of a public relations plan include the following:

   • *Current situation analysis.* This section summarizes the information obtained from the public relations audit. Information contained here is often broken down by category, such as product performance or community activity.

   • *Program objectives.* Objectives for a proactive public relations program stem from the current situation. Objectives should be set for both short-term and long-term opportunities. Public relations objectives can be as diverse and complex as advertising objectives. And, as with advertising, the focal point is not sales or profits. Rather, factors like the credibility of product performance (that is, placing products in verified, independent tests) or the stature of the firm's research and development efforts (highlighted in a prestigious trade publication article) are legitimate statements of objective.

   • *Program rationale.* In this section, it is critical to identify the role the public relations program will play relative to all the other communication efforts—particularly advertising—being undertaken by a firm. This is the area where an integrated marketing communications perspective is clearly articulated for the public relations effort.

   • *Communications vehicles.* This section specifies precisely what means will be used to implement the public relations plan. The public relations tools discussed earlier in the chapter constitute the communications vehicles through which program objectives can be implemented. There will likely be discussion of precisely how press releases, interviews, and company newsletters can be used.[10]

A proactive public relations strategy has the potential for making an important supportive contribution to a firm's IMC effort. Carefully placing positive information

---

9.   These definitions were developed from discussions offered by Jordan Goldman, *Public Relations in the Marketing Mix* (Lincolnwood, Ill.: NTC Business Books, 1992), xi–xii.
10. Ibid., 4–14.

targeted to important and potentially influential constituents—like members of the community or stockholders—supports the overall goal of enhancing the image, reputation, and perception of a firm and its brands.

CONTEMPORARY ISSUES

TO BE OR NOT TO BE A SPONSOR—THAT IS THE QUESTION

Many successful, well-respected organizations are besieged with requests to act as an official sponsor of an event. Most managers, sensing an opportunity for good exposure for their firms, are at a loss as to when and whether to sponsor events. While the event promoters make it sound like a good idea, how is a manager to know if the opportunity is a good one? The International Events Group, publisher of the *IEG Sponsorship Report,* offers these ten factors to use as criteria to evaluate sponsorship opportunities:

*   *Audience composition.* First and foremost, does the audience for the event represent an audience with whom the firm wants to communicate?
*   *Image compatibility.* Is the stature of the event consistent with the stature of the firm? This is particularly important for firms that want to develop or protect an upscale image.
*   *Exclusivity.* Can the event promoters offer exclusivity of sponsorship in the product category, or will competitors also be sponsoring the event? Being the "official airline" or "official beverage" of an event creates a positive impression.
*   *Media coverage.* Will the event be covered by television? Will the firm's brand be prominently displayed in the coverage area?
*   *Administrative ease.* Will the sponsor handle all administrative details, or will the organization have to allocate staff to the event?
*   *Leverageability.* Is the event sponsorship easily promotable in other ways? For example, Powerfoods's print ads feature the PowerBar Women's International Challenge cycling race.
*   *Measurability.* Who measures the attendance and media coverage of the event? If the sponsor doesn't, the firm will incur costs.
*   *Continuity.* Is this a one-time sponsorship, or is the event annual? Long-term association with an event can create relationships with target markets.
*   *Efficiency.* Are the terms of the sponsorship offering everything, or only what the firm needs? If the conditions include an official event auto or sponsor's tent and the firm will not use them, the costs are superfluous.
*   *Trade and employee tie-ins.* Will the event excite trade partners and employees? Exciting events are all the more potent for an organization.

Source: "Ten Steps to Evaluating an Event," *Promo,* November 1995, 61.

Reactive Public Relations Strategy. A reactive strategy seems a contradiction in terms. As stated earlier, firms must implement a reactive public relations strategy when events outside the control of the firm create negative publicity or circumstances. For firms like Johnson & Johnson, swift and effective public relations can save an important brand from disaster. The makers of Tylenol had to rely on reactive public relations heavily in the famous 1982 product-tampering case. Extra-Strength Tylenol brand had been tampered with and caused the death of several people. Within a week after the incident, Tylenol's market share had dropped from 35 percent to about 6 percent of the market. Public relations people handled literally hundreds of inquiries from the public, distributors, the press, and police. The firm then quickly and carefully issued coordinated statements to the general public, the press, and government authorities to provide clarification wherever possible. The result was that through conscientious and competent public relations activities, the firm came through the disaster viewed as a credible and trustworthy organization, and the brand regained nearly all of its original market share within a year.

It is much more difficult to organize for and provide structure around reactive public relations. Since the events that trigger the public relations effort here are unpredictable as well as uncontrollable, a firm must simply be prepared to react quickly and effectively. Two steps help firms implement reactive public relations strategy:

1. *The public relations audit.* Part of the preparation will occur during the public relations audit prepared for the proactive public relations strategy. The information provided by the audit gives a firm what it needs to issue public statements based on current and accurate data. For the Tylenol case and for Pepsi in the syringe scare, a

current list of distributors, suppliers, and manufacturing sites allowed the firms to quickly determine that the problems were not production issues.

2. *The identification of vulnerabilities.* In addition to preparing current information, the other key step in reactive public relations strategy is to recognize areas where the firm has weaknesses in its operations or products that can negatively affect its relationships with important constituents. These weakness are called **vulnerabilities** from a public relations standpoint. If a firm has aspects of its operations vulnerable to criticism, such as environmental issues related to manufacturing processes, then the public relations function should be prepared to discuss the issues in a broad range of forums with many different constituents.

Public relations is an prime example of how a firm can identify and then manage all aspects of communication in an integrated and synergistic manner. Without recognizing public relations activities as a component of the firm's overall communication effort, misinformation or disinformation could compromise more mainstream communications like advertising. The coordination of public relations into an integrated program is a matter of recognizing and identifying the process as an information source in the overall IMC effort.

Corporate Advertising

3 As we learned in Chapter 1, **corporate advertising** is not designed to promote a specific brand but rather is intended to establish a favorable attitude toward a company as a whole. A variety of highly regarded and highly successful firms use corporate advertising to enhance the image of the firm and affect consumers' attitudes. Toyota, Hewlett-Packard, Rockwell, and Coopers & Lybrand have recently invested in corporate advertising campaigns. The Coopers & Lybrand campaign was conceived to show how the firm helps manage change in a fast-changing world. The goal is to establish the image of Coopers & Lybrand as a contemporary and visionary organization.[11] Exhibit 20.9 is an example of a corporate ad that touts the firm as a whole rather than product features or a specific brand.

The Scope and Objectives of Corporate Advertising

Corporate advertising is a significant force in the overall advertising carried out by organizations in the United States. The best estimates are that about 65 percent of all service companies, 61 percent of business goods manufacturers, and 41 percent of consumer goods manufacturers employ some form of corporate advertising as part of their overall marketing communications.[12] Billions of dollars are invested annually in media for corporate advertising campaigns. Interestingly, the vast majority of corporate campaigns run by consumer goods manufacturers are undertaken by firms in the shopping goods category, like appliance and auto marketers. Studies have also found that larger firms (in terms of gross sales) are much more prevalent users of corporate advertising than smaller firms. Presumably, these firms have broader communications programs and more money to invest in advertising, which allows the use of corporate campaigns.

In terms of media use, firms have found both the magazine and television media to be well suited to corporate advertising efforts.[13] Corporate advertising appearing in magazines has the advantage of being able to target particular constituent groups with image- or issue-related messages. Magazines also provide the space for lengthy copy, which is often needed to achieve corporate advertising objectives. Television is a popular

11. Kevin Goldman, "Coopers & Lybrand TV Ads Paint Inspirational Image for Accounting," *Wall Street Journal,* January 3, 1994, 12.
12. David W. Schumann, Jan M. Hathcote, and Susan West, "Corporate Advertising in America: A Review of Published Studies on Use, Measurement and Effectiveness," *Journal of Advertising* 20, no. 3 (September 1991): 38.
13. Ibid., 40.

WEB SIGHTING

Risks can be managed

with foresight.

Damage can be controlled

with hindsight.

Your choice.

Coopers & Lybrand L.L.P.

Not Just Knowledge. Know How.℠

Our profession-leading standards for assessing, measuring and controlling risks protect billions of dollars in reputational value for our clients. This proactive, preventive approach to risk is at the heart of our audit and assurance services. Which lets your senior management spend more time building your business and less time putting out fires. It's your call. 1-800-340-5524.

Coopers & Lybrand | Coopers & Lybrand L.L.P.
| a professional services firm

choice for corporate campaigns, especially image-oriented campaigns, because the creative opportunities provided by television can deliver a powerful, emotional message.

The objectives for corporate advertising are well focused. In fact, corporate advertising shares similar purposes with proactive public relations when it comes to what firms hope to accomplish with the effort. While corporate managers can be somewhat vague about the purposes for corporate ads, the generally agreed-upon objectives are

- to build the image of the firm among customers, shareholders, the financial community, and the general public;
- to boost employee morale or attract new employees;
- to communicate an organization's views on social, political, or environmental issues;
- to better position the firm's products against competition, particularly foreign competition, which is often perceived to be of higher quality;
- to play a role in the overall integrated marketing communications of an organization as support for main product or service advertising.

Types of Corporate Advertising

There are three basic types of corporate advertising that dominate the campaigns run by organizations. These three types are image advertising, advocacy advertising, and cause-related advertising. Each is discussed in the following sections.

Corporate Image Advertising. The majority of corporate advertising efforts focus on enhancing the overall image of a firm among important constituents—typically customers, employees, and the general public. When IBM promotes itself as the firm providing "Solutions for a small planet" or when Toyota uses the slogan "Investing in the things we all care about" to promote its five U.S. manufacturing plants, the goal is to enhance the broad image of the firm. Bolstering a firm's image may not result in immediate effects on sales, but as we saw in Chapter 5, attitude can play an important directive force in consumer decision making. When a firm can enhance its overall image, it may well affect consumer predisposition in brand choice.[14] Exhibit 20.10 is an example of an image-oriented corporate ad. Here, Ford Motor Company is associating its vision of the organization's future products with a cleaner, healthier environment.

Not all image advertising is designed to directly or immediately influence consumer brand choice. In the case of Bayer Corporation, its corporate advertising campaign launched in 1995 had two specific goals: first, to announce its name change from Miles Inc. to Bayer Corporation, and second, to change the perception of the company from that of an aspirin-product firm to that of a diverse, research-based international company with businesses in health care, chemicals, and imaging technologies. The ads show a wide range of nonaspirin and often nonconsumer products to demonstrate how Bayer regularly touches people's lives in meaningful ways. The target audience is business decision makers and opinion leaders. The media schedule reflects this nonconsumer target: the *Wall Street Journal* and *Business Week* in print;

ETHICAL ISSUES

WITH FRIENDS LIKE THESE, WHO NEEDS ENEMIES?

The Italian sportswear retailer Benetton is no stranger to controversy. Throughout its history, the firm's leaders have thrived on developing an avant garde image for the firm. Typically, Benetton's ads generate attention and controversy, and cofounder Luciano Benetton likes to get into the act himself—like the time he posed nude for a charity ad campaign for the homeless.

But the most recent public relations controversy generated by Benetton ads caught the retailer off guard. While Benetton ads have been criticized by the conservative press for years, this time it was Benetton's own retailers who cried foul—and they did more than cry. In the summer of 1995, German and Spanish retailers withheld payment for merchandise, claiming that Benetton's controversial advertising campaign was destroying their businesses.

The controversy centers on two ads released by Benetton as part of its ongoing "United Colors of Benetton" campaign. The first depicted a white child wearing angel's wings alongside a black child sporting devil's horns. The second, meant to be a statement on the Bosnian war, showed a soldier's torn and blood-soaked uniform. The problem with these ads spreads beyond the financial discontent of the retailers, though. Trade and industry associations are criticizing the ads on an ethical basis. A spokesperson for the German ad agency association said that "Benetton's ad strategy is morally condemnable, legally untenable and economically extremely damaging." A German trade association spokesperson said, "They [Benetton] have ruined their own brand with the tasteless ads."

But Benetton is not letting up. A new $27 million print campaign for the firm's three-year-old SportSystem Division is sure to raise more ethical questions. The campaign includes Jesus being crucified by Roman soldiers and a crying Madonna; a pack of sperm heading toward an egg; German Olympians during the Third Reich giving the Nazi salute; and a Cuban refugee boat. The ads were created in-house by the Benetton Group creative director, Oliviero Toscani.

Sources: Dagmar Mussey, "Benetton, German Retailers Squabble," *Advertising Age*, February 6, 1995, 46; John Rossant, "The Faded Colors of Benetton," *Business Week*, April 10, 1995, 87, 90; and Jennifer DeCoursey, "Benetton Illustrates New Battles on Ads," *Advertising Age*, July 24, 1995, 26.

---

14.   For a recent, exhaustive assessment of the benefits of corporate advertising, see David M. Bender, Peter H. Farquhar, and Sanford C. Schulert, "Growing from the Top," *Marketing Management* 4, no. 4 (Winter/Spring 1996): 10–19.

Face the Nation and *Meet the Press* in television. Exhibit 20.11 shows a print ad from this campaign.

While most image advertising intends to communicate a general, favorable image, several corporate image advertising campaigns have been quite specific. When PPG Industries undertook a corporate image campaign to promote its public identity, the firm found that over a five-year period the number of consumers who claimed to have heard of PPG increased from 39.1 percent to 79.5 percent. The perception of the firm's product quality, leadership in new products, and attention to environmental problems were all greatly enhanced over the same period.[15] Another organization that has decided that image advertising is worthwhile is the national newspaper *USA Today*.[16] The newspaper has spent $1 million on print and outdoor ads that highlight the four color-coded sections of the newspaper: National, Money, Sports, and Lifestyle. McGraw-Hill has also run very specific image ads like the one in Exhibit 20.12.

Advocacy Advertising. Advocacy advertising attempts to establish an organization's position on important social, political, or environmental issues. **Advocacy advertising** is defined as "advertising that addresses and attempts to influence public opinion on issues of con-

FIGURE 20.10

Enhancing the corporate image for Ford. **www.ford.com/**

FIGURE 20.11 *Bayer changes names and repositions the company in this corporate ad.*

15. Schumann, Hathcote, and West, 43, 49.
16. Keith J. Kelly, "'USA Today' Unveils Image Ads," *Advertising Age,* February 6, 1996, 8.

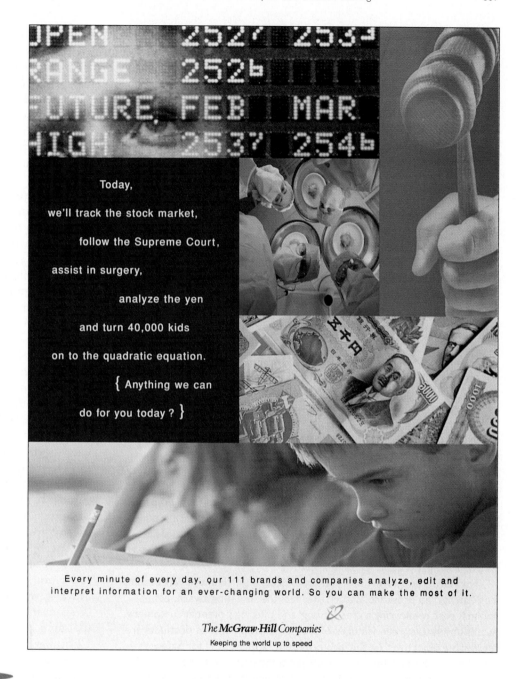

Today,

we'll track the stock market,

follow the Supreme Court,

assist in surgery,

analyze the yen

and turn 40,000 kids

on to the quadratic equation.

{ Anything we can

do for you today ? }

Every minute of every day, our 111 brands and companies analyze, edit and interpret information for an ever-changing world. So you can make the most of it.

The **McGraw·Hill** Companies

Keeping the world up to speed

EXHIBIT 20.12

Image advertising for McGraw-Hill. **www.mcgraw-hill.com**

cern to the sponsor."[17] Typically, the issue is directly relevant to the business operations of the organization. Cigarette companies have run advocacy advertising that supports commercial free speech. This position supports the industry's desire to maintain free speech in regard to advertising tobacco products through the mass media—a right often threatened by proposed legislation. W. R. Grace, a conglomerate in a variety of businesses, often runs advocacy ads warning the public about the disastrous effects of an ongoing federal government budget deficit. After one such campaign, the firm received 50,000 requests for its booklet on the issue.[18]

17.   Adapted from a definition offered by Karen Fox, "The Measurement of Issue/Advocacy Advertising Effects," *Current Issues and Research in Advertising* 9, no. 1 (1986): 62.
18.   Bob Dietrich, "Mr. Nice Guy," *Madison Avenue* 26 (September 1984): 82.

Cause-Related Advertising. Cause-related advertising takes place as part of cause-related marketing efforts undertaken by a firm. Firms often affiliate themselves with worthwhile social causes—reducing poverty, increasing literacy, or curbing drug abuse. The idea behind cause-related marketing is that a firm donates money to a nonprofit organization in exchange for using the company name in connection with a promotional campaign.

The purpose of cause-related marketing is that a firm's association with a worthy cause enhances the image of the firm in the minds of consumers.

Cause-related advertising is thus advertising that identifies corporate sponsorship of philanthropic activities. Each year, *Promo* magazine provides an extensive list of charitable, philanthropic, and environmental organizations that have formal programs for corporations to participate in.[19] Most of the programs suggest a minimum donation for corporate sponsorship and specify how the organization's resources will be mobilized in conjunction with the sponsor's other resources. Exhibit 20.13 is an example of a cause-related corporate advertisement. Here, Chevron is touting its commitment to a clean environment.

Some high-profile firms have participated in cause-related marketing programs and made extensive use of cause-related advertising. American Express first sponsored a major campaign as part of the restoration of the Statue of Liberty.[20] Next, it was the sole sponsor of a program in which the firm donated to a fight against hunger during the Christmas holidays each time an American Express card was used for a purchase. Another cause-related advertiser is Avon, the cosmetics firm, which has distributed more than 15 million brochures on breast cancer and underwritten a PBS special on the topic—all designed to encourage early detection of the disease.[21] And, as exemplified in the New Media box on this page, cause-related advertising can also be found on the World Wide Web.

While much good can come from cause-related marketing, there is some question as to whether consumers see this in a positive light. In a study by Roper Starch World-

NEW MEDIA

TURNING GREEN IN THE CYBERMALL

For marketers who have environmental causes as part of their corporate advertising agenda, the World Wide Web offers another opportunity to get their green message to consumers through new media. A large percentage of the 24 million Web users earn a median income of $50,000 to $60,000 and are highly educated. These demographics match the profile of environmentally aware consumers. Many of these consumers got started on the Web by looking for global environmental information. Now they are surfing the Net for green products and business opportunities.

Two well-known green advertisers who turned to the Web early on are Ben & Jerry's® Homemade Ice Cream (www.benjerry.com) and Annie's All Natural Pasta (www.annies.com). Both firms maintain Web sites that offer up-to-date environmental and social information, green games and activities, and ordering information.

In addition to setting up and maintaining a Web site, one of the best ways for an organization to establish a green presence on the Web is to join an online green cybermall. For as little as $500, green mall operators will create and maintain a Web listing for a company and its products. The listing is positioned with other green advertisers and is accompanied by tips on green living, discussion of green issues, and listings of green organizations. Three green mall operators who offer such services are Eco Expo (ecoexpo.com), Envirolink (envirolink.com), and GreenMarket (www.greenmarket.com/GreenMarket).

For now, green advertisers are not expecting much in the way of sales from their Web presence. Rather, they feel that creating awareness at minimal cost, reinforcing a green image, and offering potential customers details about the green features of the organization and its products are reasonable objectives. As the vice president of marketing for Safecoat paints put it, "It's another way for us to communicate with people and to get our message out there. It lets our competitors know we're the first and helps us promote an image of cutting edge."

Source: Jacquelyn Ottman, *Marketing News,* February 26, 1996, 7.

19.   For example, see the 1996 listing: "Causes That Move Cases," *Promo,* February 1996, 34–38.
20.   Bill Kelley, "Cause Related Marketing: Doing Well While Doing Good," *Sales & Marketing Management,* March 1991, 60.
21.   Sue Hwang, "Linking Products to Breast Cancer Fight Helps Firms Bond with Their Customers," *Wall Street Journal,* September 21, 1993, B1.

FIGURE 20.13

Cause-related advertising for Chevron.
www.chevron.com/

wide, 58 percent of consumers surveyed believed that the only reason a firm was supporting a cause was to enhance the company's image.[22] The image of a firm as self-serving was much greater than the image of a firm as a philanthropic partner.

The belief among consumers that firms are involved with causes only for revenue benefits is truly unfortunate. Firms involved in causes do, indeed, give or raise millions of dollars for worthy causes. Consumers shopping at Eddie Bauer outlets or ordering from catalogs are encouraged by salespeople to "Add a dollar, plant a tree." With this program, the clothing retailer is helping to raise money for American Forests Global ReLeaf Tree Project. So far, the program has raised more than $300,000, and Eddie Bauer has contributed another $75,000.[23]

Corporate advertising will never replace brand-specific advertising as the main thrust of corporate communication. But it can serve an important supportive role for brand advertising, and it can offer more depth and breadth to an integrated marketing communications program. One fundamental criticism corporate managers have with corporate advertising is the measurement of its specific effects on sales. If the sales effects of brand-specific advertising are difficult to measure, those for corporate advertising campaigns may be close to impossible to gauge.

22.   Geoffrey Smith and Ron Stodghill, "Are Good Causes Good Marketing?" *Business Week,* March 21, 1994, 64–65.
23.   Daniel Shannon, "Doing Well by Doing Good," *Promo,* February 1996, 29–33.

SUMMARY

1 Explain the role of public relations as part of an organization's overall IMC strategy and detail the objectives and tools of public relations.

Public relations represents another aspect of an organization's IMC programming that can play a key role in determining how the organization's many constituents view the organization and its products. An active public relations effort can serve many objectives, such as building goodwill and counteracting negative publicity. Public relations activities may also be orchestrated to support the launch of new products or communicate with employees on matters of interest to them. The public relations function may also be instrumental to the firm's lobbying efforts and in preparing executives to meet with the press. The primary tools of public relations experts are press releases, feature stories, corporate newsletters, interviews, press conferences, and participation in the firm's event sponsorship decisions and programs.

2 Describe two basic strategies for motivating an organization's public relations activities.

When companies perceive public relations as a source of opportunity for shaping public opinion, they are likely to pursue a proactive public relations strategy. With a proactive strategy, a firm strives to build goodwill with key constituents via aggressive programs. The foundation for these proactive programs is a rigorous public relations audit and a compre-

hensive public relations plan. The plan should include an explicit statement of objectives to guide the overall effort. In many instances, however, public relations activities take the form of damage control, and in these instances the firm is obviously in a reactive mode. While a reactive strategy may seem a contradiction in terms, it certainly is the case that organizations can be prepared to react to bad news. Organizations that understand their inherent vulnerabilities in the eyes of important constituents will be able to react quickly and effectively in the face of hostile publicity.

3 Discuss the applications and objectives of corporate advertising.

Corporate advertising is not undertaken to support an organization's specific brands, but rather to build the general reputation of the organization in the eyes of key constituents. This form of advertising uses various media and serves goals like image enhancement and building fundamental credibility for a firm's line of products. Corporate advertising may also serve diverse objectives, such as improving employee morale, building shareholder confidence, or denouncing foreign competitors. Corporate ad campaigns generally fall into one of three categories: image advertising, advocacy advertising, or cause-related advertising. Corporate advertising may also be orchestrated in such a way to be very newsworthy, and thus it needs to be carefully coordinated with the organization's ongoing public relations programs.

KEY TERMS

public relations (548)
publicity (552)
proactive public relations strategy (552)
reactive public relations strategy (553)
public relations audit (553)

public relations plan (553)
vulnerabilities (555)
corporate advertising (555)
advocacy advertising (558)
cause-related advertising (560)

QUESTIONS FOR REVIEW AND CRITICAL THINKING

1.   Describe the two basic strategies a firm can select in determining its approach to the public relations function. Which of these two strategies do you believe Intel operated under in the Pentium example discussed at the beginning of this chapter? (Be careful! This is a trick question.)

2.   Review the criteria presented in this chapter and in Chapter 16 regarding the selection of events to sponsor. Obviously, some events will have more potential for generating favorable publicity than others. What particular criteria should be emphasized in event selection when one has the goal of gaining publicity that will build goodwill via one's event sponsorship?

3.   Would it be appropriate to conclude that the entire point of public relations activity is to generate favorable publicity and stifle unfavorable publicity? What is it about publicity that makes it such an opportunity and threat?

4.   There is an old saying to the effect that "there is no such thing as bad publicity." Can you think of a situation in which bad publicity would actually be good publicity? Have another look at the Ethical Issues box in this chapter. What do Benetton's managers seem to believe about bad publicity? Can bad publicity be good for Benetton?

5.   Most organizations have vulnerabilities they should be aware of to help them anticipate and prepare for unfavorable publicity. What vulnerabilities would you associate with each of the following companies:

R. J. Reynolds—makers of Camel cigarettes
Procter & Gamble—makers of Pampers disposable
   diapers
Kellogg's—makers of Kellogg's Frosted Flakes
Exxon—worldwide oil and gasoline company
McDonald's—worldwide restaurateur

6.   Review the three basic types of corporate advertising and discuss how useful each would be as a device for generating publicity. What other forms of advertising or advertising tactics can be counted on to bring about publicity for its sponsor?

EXPERIENTIAL EXERCISE

This exercise involves an examination and assessment of corporate advertising. You will need recent issues of popular business magazines. Find and copy three examples of corporate image ads. Which ad do you think does the best job of building a positive corporate image? Explain why.

Find and copy one example of advocacy advertising. Describe the controversial issue and why you think the firm is taking a particular stance. Finally, find and copy a cause-related advertisement, and discuss how the firm can be certain it is sponsoring a good cause.

USING THE INTERNET

Often, the goal of public relations is to support a company's corporate image in the minds of consumers. Public relations departments need to keep abreast of what people are thinking and saying about the company and its products to take any necessary actions to maintain the intended corporate image. The Internet is a worldwide public forum in which people discuss their experiences and evaluations of products. Visit the following sites:

www.markwatch.com

www.ewatch.com

1.   What type of information is available to a corporate public relations department through subscribing to each site? Of what value is this information?

2.   How does the information available through each site compare to other information a public relations department can obtain, such as in news reports?

3.   Make an argument for why a public relations department should subscribe to these sites. Are there specific types of industries that should subscribe to these sites?

▲ Delta Air Lines

Placing and Coordinating Advertising and Supportive Communications

As we have now seen, advertisers have a vast and ever-expanding array of options for delivering messages to potential customers. From cable TV to virtual billboards to home pages on the World Wide Web, the diversity and capabilities of these options are daunting. Despite the growth of options and opportunities, advertising is still the dominant force for many organizations around the world. To be sure, Procter & Gamble, Philip Morris, and AT&T have set up Web sites and invested heavily in special promotions and public relations. But, it is also true that P&G, Philip Morris, and AT&T spend more than $7 billion collectively on advertising—an investment that dwarfs spending on all other communication tools.

A key to success then for firms that use multiple communications options is to coordinate the advertising effort with all other communication tools being used in an IMC program. To take the coordination challenge a step further, an additional goal is to manage these supportive communications in such a way that the advertising effort is enhanced—thus pursuing the goal of synergistic impact for an IMC effort.

Achieving such coordination is easier said than done. Many factors work against coordination. As communication choices have become more complex, advertisers have begun to rely on decision making by functional specialists. For example, a firm might have separate managers for advertising, direct marketing, and event sponsorship. A specialist will, by nature and motivation, focus on his or her specialty and may lose sight of overall communications goals.[1] Internal competition for limited promotional budgets can also create rivalries between communication specialists, thus working against the goal of coordination.

Coordination and integration are also complicated by the fact that few advertising agencies have personnel with all the skills necessary to fulfill clients' needs for integrated marketing communications.[2] For example, few agencies have developed the capability for securing and managing event sponsorships. Similarly, product placement is often handled by a specialist within the client's firm rather than within the agency. This lack of total IMC coverage creates a situation in which an agency may not even be aware of all aspects of the advertiser's IMC agenda. In addition, new media often require special skills that many agencies have not yet developed. Coors hired a completely separate agency to establish and upgrade its Zima home page on the World Wide Web.[3] Coors's general agency—Foote, Cone & Belding—was not involved in this project. With each new tool added to the IMC mix, the coordination process becomes more complicated. The basic challenge of coordinating multiple agency activities is hard enough, but this is only part of the job; an advertiser must also coordinate the messages these agencies produce.

The growing popularity of direct marketing programs is another factor that compounds the challenge of coordinating marketing communications. Often, direct-marketing programs come at the expense of conventional advertising campaigns that run in traditional mass media, like television and magazines.[4] Since direct marketing often takes dollars from those activities that have been the staple of traditional ad agency business, it is easy to see why some agencies view direct marketing with some resentment.[5] With this resentment can come a lack of sensitivity to the direct-marketing program—a near guarantee of lack of coordination in message development and message distribution.

There are no simple solutions for ensuring the coordination of advertising with supportive communications to achieve true integration across a firm's entire marketing communications program. One approach is the establishment of a marketing communications manager, or marcom, as they have come to be known.[6] The marcom manager is responsible for planning and coordinating an organization's overall communications program. Key to the coordination effort is that various functional specialists inside and outside the organization are monitored by the marcom manager to ensure that they are working together in developing and delivering a one-voice message to customers. Recall that one of the underpinnings of an effective integrated marketing communications effort is to appoint a single person to control and evaluate all communications with customers. The marcom position seems to be a workable solution for many firms.

Let's turn our attention now to Delta Air Lines and the way it coordinates communication efforts. In addition, we will conclude our examination of the promotional activities in the "Cincinnati Instead" integrated marketing communications campaign.

Delta Air Lines Coordination of Advertising and Supportive Communications

In Part 3, we learned that Delta's integrated marketing communications program takes advantage of a wide range of communications opportunities, from major broadcast campaigns to event sponsorships and a Web site. The process of coordinating these communications, and doing so in such a way that mainstream advertising is supported and enhanced, is a huge undertaking.

First, the Delta coordination effort takes place at several levels. Delta is a global brand with service in 41 countries around the world. Delta offices in London are responsible for all the communications in Europe and Asia. The office in Atlanta handles all U.S., Canadian, and Mexican programs. These different markets have different customers with different communication needs, and each market has different competitive challenges. Despite this diversity within markets, Delta's communication programs must remain tightly focused on core corporate objectives and strategies, and communications must be developed to support them.

With this context in mind, Delta coordinates and manages its integrated marketing communications in the following ways. At the national level, all communications are designed to establish a core brand presence. Whether the communication is a national television spot timed with the 1996 Atlanta Olympic Games or the ongoing development of the SkyMiles/American Express card partnership, the Delta name and its national presence are carefully nurtured. At the local level, the challenge is somewhat different, but all efforts must support the corporate agenda. Locally, the relevance of Delta is determined not only by consumers embracing the Delta brand (and all the inherent service and product attributes), but also by the schedule and special services Delta can offer consumers as a way of delivering value at the local level.

The coordination of programs and the support of advertising depend on a recognition that Delta can build a national presence but has to deliver (and communicate) value at the local level. To accomplish this feat administratively, cross-functional administrative teams are established to develop integrated marketing communications. (You may want to review the Delta organizational chart—Exhibit IMC 1.4 in Part 1.) For example, Advertising may work with Brand Management on in-flight entertainment. Similarly, the agency for interactive media, Modem Media, may work with Direct Marketing, Frequent Flyer Marketing, and Advertising on a Web selection. All in-house and agency communications are coordinated with other parts of the Marketing division, such as Field Sales and Travel Trade Sales, to ensure maximum impact. The main objective is that through the coordination effort, Delta communicates its competitive strengths and superior products and services to the core target groups in an efficient and effective manner. Now let's turn our attention to how the "Cincinnati Instead" campaign was coordinated.

Coordinating Advertising and Supportive Communications in the "Cincinnati Instead" Campaign

As we learned in the first three parts, the "Cincinnati Instead" campaign was conceived as a way to take advantage of Delta's strengths and competitors' weaknesses in midwestern airport hub service. Also recall that Delta used national advertising in newspapers and magazines, consumer and trade direct marketing, promotional events, and public relations to execute the campaign.

The advertising effort focused ad dollars in print media because these media provide the most effective way to target the "Cincinnati Instead" message to relevant segments. Placement in *USA Today* and the *Wall Street Journal* allowed the targeting of specific feeder markets. Further support came in the form of a national magazine campaign, with ads featured in publications such as *Fortune* and *Business Week*.

The direct-marketing effort targeted both consumers and travel agents, once again in feeder markets. The event promotion was focused primarily on a radio remote broadcast for two days from the new Cincinnati terminal.

Coordination of promotions and advertising for Delta's "Cincinnati Instead" campaign.

	CVG I	CVG II
Advertising		
Newspaper	May 95	Dec. 95
Magazine	May 95	Dec. 95–Jan. 96
Trade	Apr. 95	Dec. 95
Direct Mail		
Consumer	Apr. 95	Jan. 96
Trade	May 95	n/a
Promotions		
Local	Apr. 95–July 95	Oct.–Dec. 95
Remote	June 95	Dec. 95

The entire campaign with all its component communications was executed twice: in April through July 1995 and again in October 1995 through January 1996. Exhibit IMC 4.1 shows how the advertising, direct mail, and promotions were coordinated during the two executions of the "Cincinnati Instead" campaign. The main consideration here is that while advertising created a national presence for the brand and alerted customers to the value of the Cincinnati hub, other communications delivered the message at a more locally targeted level.

An important consideration is the tracking of the effects of these different communications. Delta estimates that the return on investment was extremely high for all three primary communications used in the campaigns. Using proprietary tracking methods, Delta estimates that the ratio of revenue to cost for the direct mail and promotions marketing was in the range of 15 to 1 across both executions. That means 15 dollars in revenue was generated for every 1 dollar invested in communications.

Delta and the World Wide Web

We would be remiss if we did not highlight Delta's venture into the World Wide Web. Delta was one of the first major corporations to establish a comprehensive Web site for its products and services. With the assistance of Modem Media, Delta's Distribution Planning department, and TransQuest (a wholly owned Delta subsidiary responsible for technical development), Delta Advertising created Delta Air Lines SkyLinks. The site as it appears on a computer screen is shown in Exhibit IMC 4.2.

The site allows visitors to view U.S. and world maps, check live flight schedules, view airport terminal configurations and aircraft seating charts, obtain real-time flight information, book domestic flights in all 50 states, enroll instantly in SkyMiles, check the status of SkyMiles accounts, and get the latest-breaking news. In addition, the site contains links, through the Travelogue icon, to other Web sites that contain details on hotels, restaurants, and attractions. The Gateways section helps travelers review weather and sports in cities throughout the world.

Notice how this site maintains an IMC perspective. The site name, SkyLinks, plays off the *SkyMiles* and *Sky Magazine* names, which are well established with the Delta Air Lines brand. The colors create a look and feel reminiscent of other Delta communication materials. It is no coincidence that the hue of the blue in this home page is matched to the "Delta blue" in the firm's brand mark and logo. And, of course, the Delta triangle logo itself is a way to integrate this communication with others.

Overall, Delta has kept its IMC focus with this new media option. The site contains information and has a look and feel consistent with other Delta communications. But the Web site extends the communications program as well. It provides types of information and an information format different from all the other communication options used by Delta. Senior executives at Delta are excited about the prospects for the site. They believe that the Web and other electronic media have tremendous communication potential. Again, in the context of a national brand that has to deliver a local, specialized service, the

IMC EXERCISES

Web provides Delta a two-way channel to communicate with its customers.

1. Visit the Web site of a major advertiser you are familiar with—Nike, Coca-Cola, the National Football League, your favorite clothing company. Compare the communications on the Web site with advertising you see for this company. Which is more effective? Why?

2. Why do you think some advertisers and their agencies have difficulty managing the coordination of communications tools? Is the large number of different communications being prepared disruptive? Are the new media options a threat to traditional agency turf?

3. Review the "Cincinnati Instead" creative materials highlighted in Part 3. How do the direct mail and promotional pieces fit with the advertising effort? What effect would lack of coordination have had on the advertising effort?

4. Visit the Delta Web site at www.delta-air .com. What features of the site are particularly appealing? Did you find the site provided information of general interest as well as Delta specific information? If you could add one additional section to the five included in the site, what would it be?

ENDNOTES

1. Don E. Schultz, Stanley I. Tannenbaum, and Robert F. Lauterborn, *Integrated Marketing Communications* (Lincolnwood, Ill.: NTC Business Books, 1993).

2. Don E. Schultz, "Why Ad Agencies Are Having So Much Trouble with IMC," *Marketing News,* April 26, 1993, 12.

3. For an in-depth description of the Zima Internet campaign, see Cathy Taylor, "Z Factor," *Adweek,* February 6, 1995, 14–16.

4. Scott Hample, "Fear of Commitment," *Marketing Tools,* January/February 1995, 6–10.

5. Jim Osterman, "This Changes Everything," *ADWEEK,* May 15, 1995, 44–45.

6. Schultz, Tannenbaum, and Lauterborn.

Appendix: Web Site Addresses

Company	Address
ABC News	www.realaudio.com/contentp/abc.html
Acer	www.acer.com/
Acura	www.acura.com/
Ad Kingdom	uts.cc.utexas.edu/~ccho/adworld.html
Ad Store, The	www.the-adstore.com/
Advertising Age	www.adage.com
Advertising Graveyard	www.zeldman.com/ad.html
Agfa	www.agfahome.com
AltaVista	www.altavista.digital.com/
Amazon.com Books	www.amazon.com
American Express	www.americanexpress.com/ www.americanexpress.com/student/
America Online	www.aol.com/
Ameritech	www.ameritech.com/
Andersen Consulting	www.ac.com/
Annie's All Natural Pasta	www.annies.com
Apple Computer	opendoc.apple.com/users/users.html product.info.apple.com/productinfo/tech/ www.apple.com/
Apple Mountain Software	www.apmtnsoft.com
Ariens	www.ariens.com
Army, U. S.	www.army.mil/

Company	Address
Audionet	www.audionet.com
Avis Rent a Car	www.avis.com/
Bacardi	www.bacardi.com
BBN Planet	www.near.net/
Beers Across America	www.beer.com
Ben & Jerry's Homemade Ice Cream	www.benjerry.com/
Birds Eye	www.birdseye.com
Black and Decker	www.blackanddecker.com/
Blue Marble	www.bluemarble.com/
BMW	www.bmwusa.com/
Boston Globe	www.boston.com
Bozell Worldwide	www.poppe.com
Breathe Right	www2.breathright.com/breatheright/html/breathel.html
Bristol-Myers-Squibb	www.bms.com/
Budweiser	www.budweiser.com/
Burlington Coat Factory	www.coat.com/
California State Automobile Association	www.csaa.com/
Campbell Soup Company	www.campbellsoups.com/
Cannondale	www.cannondale.com/
Carnival Cruise Line	firstct.com/carnival.html www.thetravelguide.com/carnival/
Casio	www.casio-usa.com/
Charles Schwab	www.schwab.com/
Chevrolet	www.chevrolet.com/
Chevron	www.chevron.com
Chiat/Day	www.chiatday.com/ www.chiatday.com/factory/
Chrysler	www.chryslercorp.com/
Clinique	www.clinique.com
Clio Awards	www.clioawards.com
Clorox	www.clorox.com/
CNN	www.cnn.com/
Coca-Cola	www.cocacola.com/
Comedy Channel	www.comcentral.com
Compaq Computer	www.compaq.com/
CompuServe	www.compuserve.com/
Coopers & Lybrand	www.colybrand.com/clwww0.html
Coupon Directory	www.couponsdirect.com
Crayola	www.crayola.com/
Cyclops	www.cyclops.com/

Company	Address
DD&B Needham Interactive Communications	www.ddbniac.com
DDB-Europe	www.globalnews.com/bmp
Dell Computer	www.dell.com/
Delta Air Lines	www.delta-air.com www.delta-air.com/index.html
Democratic Party	www.democrats.org
Dentsu Japan	www.dentsu.co.jp/DHP
Depo-Provera	www.pharmacia.se/
Detroit, Michigan	www.detroit.com
Digital	www.digital.com
Dilbert	www.unitedmedia.com/comics/dilbert/
Discovery Channel	www.discovery.com
DM Group	www.dml.com
Dodge	www.4adodge.com/neon/
Donna Karan	www.donnakaran.com/
Dow Chemical	www.dow.com
Dreamshop	www.dreamshop.com
Dun and Bradstreet	www.dnb.com
Eco Expo	ecoexpo.com
Edmund's Automobile Buyer's Guides	www.edmund.com
Elle	www.ellemag.com
Envirolink	envirolink.com
E*Trade	www.etrade.com/html/index.html
eWatch	www.ewatch.com
Excite	www.excite.com/
Express	express.style.com
Fallon McElligott	www.fallon.com/
FannieMae Foundation	www.fanniemae.com/
FedEx	www.fedex.com
Fingerhut	www.fingerhut.com
Ford	www.ford.com/
Fox	www.foxnetwork.com/
Fujifilm	www.fujifilm.co.jp/
G&D's Ice Cream and Cafe	www.gdhq.com/ice_cream.html
Gatorade	www.gatorade.com
General Electric	www.ge.com
General Motors	www.gm.com/edu_rul/
Geo	www.chevrolet.com/geo/a300.htm
Gitam International	www.gitam.co.za

Company	Address
Global Casino	www.gamblenet.com
GNN	gnn.com
Goodyear	www.goodyear.com/
Green Light Interactive	www.grnlt.com/
GreenMarket	greenmarket.com/GreenMarket
Guess	www.guess.com
Guinot	www.lotions.com/guinot.html
Harley-Davidson	www.harleydavidson.com
Hertz	www.singapore.com/companies/hertz/
Hewlett-Packard	www.hp.com
Holiday Inn	www.holiday-inn.com
Honda	www.honda.com/
HotWired	www.hotwired.com/
Hugo cologne	wordslam.hugo.com
Iams	www.iamsco.com/
IBM	www.ibm.com/
Infiniti	www.infinitimotors.com/
InfoWorld	www.infoworld.com
Inline Online	bird.taponline.com/inline/
Intel	www.intel.com/
Internet Mall	www.internet-mall.com/
Interse	www.interse.com/ourproducts/
Issaquah, Washington	www2.issaquah.com/iol/
Isuzu	www.isuzu.com www.isuzu.com//home.htm
iVillage	www.ivillage.com/
Jack Daniel's	www.jackdaniels.com/
Jaguar	www.jaguarcars.com/
jane's brain	maui.net/~jms/brainuse.html
J.C. Penney	www.jcpenney.com/
Jeep	www.jeepunpaved.com
Johnson & Johnson	www.jnj.com/
Jolt	www.joltcola.com
J. Walter Thompson	www.jwtworld.com/
JWT San Francisco	www.jwtsf.com
Kellogg's	www.kelloggs.com
Kellogg's Corn Pops	www.cornpops.com/granny/playpop.html
Kenwood	www.kenwoodcorp.com/
Ketchum	www.ketchum.com/catalyst.html
Kingdom Computers	www.kingdomcomputers.com/index.html
KVO-Portland	www.kvo.com

Company	Address
Lands' End	www.landsend.com/
Lang's Women's Web	www.womweb.com
L'eggs	www.leggs.com
Levi's	www.levi.com/menu
Lexus	www.lexususa.com/
Lincoln	www.lincolnvehicles.com/
Link Exchange	www.linkexchange.com
Lipton	www.lipton.com/
L. L. Bean	www.llbean.com:80/
Loopy	www.loopy.com
Lycos	home.netscape.com/escapes/search/ netsearch3.html www.lycos.com/
Magellan	home.netscape.com/escapes/search/ netsearch4.html
Markwatch	www.markwatch.com
Marriott	www.marriott.com/
McDonald's	www.mcdonalds.com/ www.mcdonalds.com/a_welcome
McGraw-Hill	www.mcgraw-hill.com
MCI	www.mci.com/
McMann and Tate	www.mcmann-tate.com/
Microsoft	www.microsoft.com/ www.microsoft.com/sitebuilder/
Miller Brewing Company	www.careermosaic.com/cm/miller/
Mitsubishi	www.mitsucars.com/
Molson Beer	www.molson.com
Mopar	www.chryslercars.com/
Motorola	www.mot.com/
Mountain Dew	www.dewbeep.com/
MTV	www.mtv.com
Nature's Course	www.purina.com
NBA	www.nba.com
Netscape	home.netscape.com/
New York Times	www.nytimes.com
Nielsen	www.nielsenmedia.com
Nike	www.nike.com
Nissan	www.nissan.com
Northwest Airlines	www.nwa.com/
Norwegian Cruise Line	www.ncl.com
Ogilvy & Mather	www.ogilvy.com www.ogilvy.com/english/index.html
Oldsmobile	www.oldsmobile.com/

Company	Address
Olestra	www.olean.com
Olivia Cruises & Resorts	www.oliviatravel.com/
Oneida	www.oneida.com/
O'Neill	www.oneill.jsi.nl
Oscar Mayer	www.oscar-mayer.com
Pathfinder	www.pathfinder.com
PBS	www.pbs.org
Pepsi	www.pepsi.com/
Pete Smith Advertising	www.winternet.com/~smithads/
Pillsbury	info.pillsbury.com/ www.pillsbury.com/
Piper-Heidsieck	www.piper.heidsieck.com/
Pizza Hut	www.pizzahut.com/
Plank Road Brewery	www.reddog.com:443
Playboy	www.playboy.com
Plymouth Voyager	www.rdc.nl/voyager
Polaroid	www.polaroid.com/
Pontiac	www.pontiac.com/ www.pontiac.com/index.html
Procter & Gamble	www.pg.com
Progresso	info.pillsbury.com/tpc/progresso.html
Project 2000	www2000ogsm.vanderbilt.edu/
Proxima	www.proxima.com
Prudential	www.prudential.com/
Pseudo Online Network	www.psuedo.com
Public Debt, Bureau of	www.publicdebt.treas.gov/sav/sav.htm
Publishers' Clearing House	www.pch.com
Purina	www.purina.com
Ragu	www.eat.com
Ray Ban	www.bushnell.com/bausch.htm
Rayovac	www.rayovac.com
RCA	www.nipper.com/
Red Dog	www.reddog.com:443
Reebok	planetreebok.com/ www.reebok.com
Republican Party	www.rnc.org
Royal Caribbean	www.royalcaribbean.com/
Rykä	www.ryka.com/
Saab	www.saabusa.com/
Saturn	www.saturncars.com/index.html
Savings Bonds, U.S.	www.publicdebt.treas.gov/sav/sav.htm
Schwinn Cycling & Fitness	www.schwinn.com

Company	Address
Sears	www.sears.com
Seymour Duncan	www.seymourduncan.com
Shareware	www.shareware.com
Sharper Image	www.sharperimage.com
Smirnoff	www.purethrill.com/
Snapple	www.snapple.com
Sony	www.sony.co.jp/
Southwest Airlines	www.iflyswa.com
Southwestern Bell	www.swbell.com/
Spiegel	www.spiegel.com
SportsLine	www.sportsline.com/
Sprint	www.sprint.com/ www.sprint.com/college/
State Farm	www.statefarm.com/
Stoli	www.stoli.com
Sun-Maid	www.sunmaid.com/
Sunny Delight	www.sunnyd.com
Svetlana	www.svetlana.com/
Tech Setter	www.techsetter.com/
Ted Bates-Dublin	www.ol.ie/resource/bates/index.html
Ticketmaster	www.ticketmaster.com
Timex	www.timex.com/
Toshiba	www.toshiba.com/
Toyota	www.toyota.com
Trilium Interactive	www.trilium.com
Trojan	www.linkmag.com/trojan
TV Food Network	www.foodtv.com
United Airlines	www.ual.com/
UPS	www.ups.com
USA Today	www.usatoday.com
U.S. News & World Report	www.usnews.com
Valvoline	www.valvoline.com
Virginia Power	www.vapower.com/
Virtual Vineyard	www.virtualvin.com
Virtual Yellow Pages	www.vyp.com/
VISA International	www.visa.com/
Volkswagen	www.vw.com/
Volvo	www.volvo.se/
Wall Street Journal	www.wsj.com
Warner-Lambert	www.warner-lambert.com/
WebStep	www.mmgco.com/webstep.html

Company	Address
Welinder-Stockholm	www.welinder.se/
Wendy's	www.wendys.com/
Wheelworks	dcn.davis.ca.us/bicycles
Winkler McManus	www.winklermcmanus.com/
Women's Link	www.womenslink.com/
Women's Web	www.womweb.com
Women's Wire	www.women.com
World Avenue Mall	www.worldavenue.com
X-Files, The	www.thex-files.com
Yahoo!	www.yahoo.com
Yellow Pages	www.bigyellow.com
Yoyodyne	www.yoyo.com

Glossary

A

Action for Children's Television (ACT) A group formed during the 1970s to lobby the government to limit the amount and content of advertising directed at children.

advertisement A specific message that an organization has placed to persuade an audience.

advertising A paid, mass-mediated attempt to persuade.

advertising agency An organization of professionals who provide creative and business services to clients related to planning, preparing, and placing advertisements.

advertising campaign A series of coordinated advertisements and other promotional efforts that communicate a single theme or idea.

advertising clutter An obstacle to advertising resulting from the large volume of similar ads for most products and services.

advertising plan A plan that specifies the thinking and tasks needed to conceive and implement an effective advertising effort.

advertising research A specialized form of marketing research that focuses on the planning, preparation, and placement of advertising; more simply stated, advertising research is any research conducted by an advertising agency.

advertising response function A mathematical relationship based on marginal analysis that associates dollars spent on advertising and sales generated; sometimes used to help establish an advertising budget.

advertising substantiation program An FTC program initiated in 1971 to ensure that advertisers make available to consumers supporting evidence for claims made in ads.

advertorial A special advertising section designed to look like the print publication in which it appears.

advocacy advertising Advertising that attempts to influence public opinion on important social, political, or environmental issues of concern to the sponsoring organization.

aerial advertising Advertising that involves airplanes (pulling signs or banners), skywriting, or blimps.

affirmative disclosure An FTC action requiring that important material determined to be absent from prior ads must be included in subsequent advertisements.

agency of record The advertising agency chosen by the advertiser to purchase media time and space.

animation The use of drawn figures and scenes (like cartoons) to produce a television commercial.

art Any graphics, photography, film, or video that offers visual information to the receiver of an advertisement.

aspirational groups Groups made up of people an individual admires or uses as role models but is unlikely to ever interact with in any meaningful way.

association tests A type of projective technique that asks consumers to express their feelings or thoughts after hearing a brand name or seeing a logo.

assorted media mix A media mix option that employs multiple media alternatives to reach target audiences.

attitude An overall evaluation of any object, person, or issue that varies along a continuum, like favorable to unfavorable or positive to negative.

attitude change study A type of advertising research that uses a before-and-after ad exposure design.

audience A group of individuals who may receive and interpret messages sent from advertisers through mass media.

average quarter-hour persons The average number of listeners tuned to a radio station during a specified 15-minute segment of a daypart.

average quarter-hour rating The radio audience during a quarter-hour daypart expressed as a percentage of the population of the measurement area.

average quarter-hour share The percentage of the total radio audience that was listening to a radio station during a specified quarter-hour daypart.

axis A line, real or imagined, that runs through an advertisement and from which the elements in the ad flare out.

B

balance An orderliness and compatibility of presentation in an advertisement.

bandwidth A measure of the computer resources used by a Web site on the Internet.

banner ads Advertisements placed on World Wide Web sites that contain editorial material.

barter syndication A form of television syndication that takes both off-network and first-run syndication shows and offers them free or at a reduced rate to local television stations, with some national advertising presold within the programs.

beliefs The knowledge and feelings a person has accumulated about an object or issue.

benefit positioning A positioning option that features a distinctive customer benefit.

benefit segmentation A type of market segmenting in which target segments are delineated by the various benefit packages that different consumers want from the same product category.

between-vehicle duplication Exposure to the same advertisement in different media.

big idea The creative concept behind an advertisement that attracts attention and creates a distinctive impression for the advertised brand in the mind of receivers.

bleed page A magazine page on which the background color of an ad runs to the edge of the page, replacing the standard white border.

border The space surrounding an advertisement; it keeps the ad elements from spilling over into other ads or into the printed matter next to the ad.

brand attitudes Summary evaluations that reflect preferences for various products and brands.

brand communities Groups of consumers who feel a commonality and a shared purpose grounded or attached to a consumer good or service.

branding The strategy of developing brand names so that manufacturers can focus consumer attention on a clearly identified item.

brand loyalty A decision-making mode in which consumers repeatedly buy the same brand of a product as their choice to fulfill a specific need.

brand-loyal users A market segment made up of consumers who repeatedly buy the same brand of a product.

build-up analysis A method of building up the expenditure levels of various tasks to help establish an advertising budget.

business markets The institutional buyers who purchase items to be used in other products and services or to be resold to other businesses or households.

C

cable television A type of television that transmits a wide range of programming to subscribers through wires rather than over airwaves.

caching The use of a kind of active memory to conserve computer system resources.

cause-related advertising Advertising that identifies corporate sponsorship of philanthropic activities.

cease and desist order An FTC action requiring an advertiser to stop running an ad within 30 days so a hearing can be held to determine whether the advertising in question is deceptive or unfair.

celebrity endorsements Advertisements that use an expert or celebrity as a spokesperson to endorse the use of a product or service.

channel grazing Using a television remote control to monitor programming on other channels while an advertisement is being broadcast.

circulation The number of newspapers distributed each day (for daily newspapers) or each week (for weekly publications).

classified advertising Newspaper advertising that appears as all-copy messages under categories such as sporting goods, employment, and automobiles.

client The company or organization that pays for advertising. Also called the *sponsor*.

closing date The date when production-ready advertising materials must be delivered to a publisher for an ad to make a newspaper or magazine issue.

cognitive consistency The maintenance of a system of beliefs and attitudes over time; consumers' desire for cognitive consistency is an obstacle to advertising.

cognitive dissonance The anxiety or regret that lingers after a difficult decision.

cognitive responses The thoughts that occur to individuals at that exact moment in time when their beliefs and attitudes are being challenged by some form of persuasive communication.

column inch A unit of advertising space in a newspaper, equal to one inch deep by one column wide.

combination produced-taped radio ad An ad created by sending a radio station a tape that includes background music or special sound effects and a script that is to be read by the announcer.

commission system A method of agency compensation based on the amount of money the advertiser spends on the media.

communications test A type of pretest message research that simply seeks to see if a message is communicating something close to what is desired.

community A group of people loosely joined by some common characteristic or interest.

comparison advertisements Advertisements in which an advertiser makes a comparison between the firm's brand and competitors' brands.

competitive field The companies that compete for a segment's business.

competitive positioning A positioning option that uses an explicit reference to an existing competitor to help define precisely what the advertised brand can do.

competitor analysis In an advertising plan, the section that discusses who the competitors are, discussing their strengths, weaknesses, tendencies, and any threats they pose.

comp layout A polished, drawn version of an ad.

computer print production A printing process whereby computerized typesetting combined with digitized art and fiber-optic communication replace traditional printing processes.

concentrated media mix A media mix option that focuses all the media placement dollars in one medium.

concept test A type of developmental research that seeks feedback designed to screen the quality of a new idea, using consumers as the final judge and jury.

consent order An FTC action asking an advertiser accused of running deceptive or unfair advertising to stop running the advertisement in question, without admitting guilt.

consideration set The subset of brands from a particular product category that becomes the focal point of a consumer's evaluation.

consumer behavior Those activities directly involved in obtaining, consuming, and disposing of products and services, including the decision processes that precede and follow these actions.

consumer culture A way of life centered around consumption.

consumerism The actions of individual consumers to exert power over the marketplace activities of organizations.

consumer markets The markets for products and services purchased by individuals or households to satisfy their specific needs.

consumer-market sales promotion A type of sales promotion designed to induce household consumers to purchase a firm's brand rather than a competitor's brand.

consumer satisfaction Satisfaction in a purchased product or service, deriving from a favorable postpurchase experience.

contest A sales promotion that has consumers compete for prizes based on skill or ability.

continuity The pattern of placement of advertisements in a media schedule.

continuous scheduling A pattern of placing ads at a steady rate over a period of time.

controlled circulation The number of copies of a newspaper that are given away free.

cookie A coded identifier that is downloaded to a Web site visitor's computer that allows an Internet server to keep track of, and collect data on, that visitor.

co-op advertising *See* **cooperative advertising**.

cooperative advertising The sharing of advertising expenses between national advertisers and local mer-

chants. Also called *co-op advertising*.

copy The verbal or written part of a message.

copywriting The process of expressing the value and benefits a brand has to offer, via written or verbal descriptions.

corporate advertising Advertising intended to establish a favorable attitude toward a company as a whole, not just toward a specific brand.

corporate home page A site on the World Wide Web that focuses on a corporation and its products.

corrective advertising An FTC action requiring an advertiser to run additional advertisements to dispel false beliefs created by deceptive advertising.

cost per inquiry (CPI) The number of inquiries generated by a direct-marketing program divided by that program's cost.

cost per order (CPO) The number of orders generated by a direct-marketing program divided by that program's cost.

cost per rating point (CPRP) The cost of a spot on television divided by the program's rating; the resulting dollar figure can be used to compare the efficiency of advertising on various programs.

cost per thousand (CPM) The dollar cost of reaching 1,000 members of an audience using a particular medium.

cost per thousand–target market (CPM–TM) The cost per thousand for a particular segment of an audience.

coupon A type of sales promotion that entitles a buyer to a designated reduction in price for a product or service.

cover date The date of publication appearing on a magazine.

creative boutique An advertising agency that emphasizes copywriting and artistic services to its clients.

creative concept The unique creative thought behind an advertising campaign.

creative plan A guideline used during the copywriting process to specify the message elements that must be coordinated during the preparation of copy.

creative revolution A revolution in the advertising industry during the 1960s, characterized by the "creatives" (art directors and copywriters) having a bigger say in the management of their agencies.

creative team The copywriters and art directors responsible for coming up with the creative concept for an advertising campaign.

culture What a people do—the way they eat, groom themselves, celebrate, mark their space and social position, and so forth.

cume The cumulative radio audience, which is the total number of different people who listen to a station for at least five minutes in a quarter-hour period within a specified daypart.

customer satisfaction Good feelings that derive from a favorable postpurchase experience.

D

dailies Newspapers published every weekday; also, in television ad production, the scenes shot during the previous day's production.

dayparts Segments of time during a television broadcast day.

deception Making false or misleading statements in an advertisement.

delayed response advertising Advertising that relies on imagery and message themes to emphasize the benefits and satisfying characteristics of a brand.

democracy of goods A distribution of goods in which products previously unavailable to the masses are now available across the social spectrum.

demographic segmentation Market segmenting based on basic descriptors like age, gender, race, marital status, income, education, and occupation.

design The structure (and the plan behind the structure) for the aesthetic and stylistic aspects of a print advertisement.

developmental copy research A type of copy research that helps copywriters at the early stages of copy development by providing audience interpretations and reactions to the proposed copy.

dialogue Advertising copy that delivers the selling points of a message to the audience through a character or characters in the ad.

dialogue balloons A type of projective technique that offers consumers the chance to fill in the dialogue of cartoonlike stories, as a way of indirectly gathering brand information.

direct broadcast satellite (DBS) A program delivery system whereby television (and radio) programs are sent directly from a satellite to homes equipped with small receiving dishes.

direct mail A direct-marketing medium that involves using the postal service to deliver marketing materials.

direct marketing According to the Direct Marketing Association, "An interactive system of marketing which uses one or more advertising media to effect a measurable response and/or transaction at any location."

direct-marketing firms Firms that maintain large databases of mailing lists; some of these firms can also design direct-marketing campaigns either through the mail or by telemarketing.

direct response advertising Advertising that asks the receiver of the message to act immediately.

direct response copy Advertising copy that highlights the urgency of acting immediately.

display advertising A newspaper ad that includes the standard components of a print ad—headline, body copy, and often an illustration—to set it off from the news content of the paper.

display type Larger-size copy in the headline and subhead of an advertisement.

door-to-door sampling A type of sampling in which samples are brought directly to the homes of a target segment in a well-defined geographic area.

double-page spreads Advertisements that bridge two facing pages.

dummy advertising vehicles A type of pretest message research that consists of mock-ups of magazines that contain editorial content and advertisements; the mock-ups are given to a test audience, whose responses to the test ads are assessed.

E

economies of scale The ability of a firm to lower the cost of each item produced because of high-volume production.

editing In television ad production, piecing together various scenes or shots of scenes to bring about the desired visual effect.

effective frequency The number of times a target audience needs to be exposed to a message before the objectives of the advertiser are met.

effective reach The number or percentage of consumers in the target audience that are exposed to an ad some minimum number of times.

electronic and inkjet printing A printing process that uses computers, electronics, electrostatics, and special toners and inks to produce images.

E-mail An Internet function that allows users to communicate much as they do using standard mail.

emergent consumers A market segment made up of the gradual but constant influx of first-time buyers.

emerging support media Support media that are relatively new and likely to grow in their importance to advertisers.

emotional benefits Those benefits not typically found in some tangible feature or objective characteristic of a product or service.

emphasis principle A principle of print ad design stating that effective design focuses attention on and emphasizes the key value or selling point of a brand.

environmental analysis A type of developmental advertising research that tries to assess the potential influence of social and cultural trends, economics, and politics on the consumer and the social environment into which the advertising will be injected.

ethics Moral standards and principles against which behavior is judged.

ethnocentrism The tendency to view and value things from the perspective of one's own culture.

evaluative copy research A type of copy research used to judge an advertisement after the fact—the audience expresses its approval or disapproval of the copy used in the ad.

evaluative criteria The product attributes or performance characteristics on which consumers base their product evaluations.

event sponsorship Providing financial support to help fund an event, in return for the right to display a brand name, logo, or advertising message on-site at the event.

extended problem solving A decision-making mode in which consumers are inexperienced in a particular consumption setting but find the setting highly involving.

external facilitators Organizations or individuals that provide specialized services to advertisers and agencies.

external lists Mailing lists purchased from a list compiler or rented from a list broker and used to help an organization cultivate new business.

external position The competitive niche a brand pursues.

external search A search for product information that

involves visiting retail stores to examine alternatives, seeking input from friends and relatives about their experiences with the products in question, or perusing professional product evaluations.

eye-tracking systems A type of physiological measure that monitors eye movements across print ads.

F

fact sheet radio ad A listing of important selling points that a radio announcer can use to ad-lib a radio spot.

Federal Trade Commission (FTC) The government regulatory agency that has the most power and is most directly involved in overseeing the advertising industry.

fee system A method of agency compensation whereby the advertiser and the agency agree on an hourly rate for different services provided.

film The most versatile and highest quality medium for television ad production.

first cover page The front cover of a magazine.

first-run syndication Television programs developed specifically for sale to individual stations.

flexography A printing technique similar to offset printing but that uses water-based ink, allowing printing to be done on any surface.

flighting A media-scheduling pattern of heavy advertising for a period of time, usually two weeks, followed by no advertising for a period, followed by another period of heavy advertising.

focus group A brainstorming session with a small group of target consumers and a professional moderator, used to gain new insights about consumer response to a brand.

formal balance A symmetrical presentation in an ad—every component on one side of an imaginary vertical line through the ad is repeated in approximate size and shape on the other side of the imaginary line.

fourth cover page The back cover of a magazine.

free premium A sales promotion that provides consumers with an item at no cost; the item is either included in the package of a purchased item or mailed to the consumer after proof of purchase is verified.

free-standing insert (FSI) A newspaper insert ad that contains cents-off coupons for a variety of products and is typically delivered with Sunday newspapers.

frequency The average number of times an individual or household within a target audience is exposed to a media vehicle in a given period of time.

frequency-marketing programs Direct-marketing programs that provide concrete rewards to frequent customers.

frequency programs A type of sales promotion that offers consumers discounts or free product rewards for repeat purchase or patronage of the same brand or company.

full position A basis of buying newspaper ad space, in which the ad is placed near the top of a page or in the middle of editorial material.

full-service agency An advertising agency that typically includes an array of advertising professionals to meet all the promotional needs of clients.

fully produced radio ad A radio ad produced, directed, and recorded for taped transmission.

functional benefits Those benefits that derive from the more objective performance characteristics of a product or service.

G

gatefold ads Advertisements that fold out of a magazine to display an extra-wide ad.

gender The social expression of sexual biology or choice.

geodemographic segmentation A form of market segmentation that identifies neighborhoods around the country that share common demographic characteristics.

geo-targeting The placement of ads in geographic regions where higher purchase tendencies for a brand are evident.

global advertising Developing and placing advertisements with a common theme and presentation in all markets around the world where the firm's brands are sold.

global agencies Advertising agencies with a worldwide presence.

globalized campaigns Advertising campaigns that use the same message and creative execution across all (or most) international markets.

government officials and employees One of the five types of audiences for advertising; includes employees of government organizations, such as schools and road maintenance operations, at the federal, state, and local levels.

gravure A print production method that uses a plate or mat; it is excellent for reproducing pictures.

gross domestic product (GDP) A measure of the total value of goods and services produced within an economic system.

gross impressions The sum of exposures to all the media placement in a media plan.

gross rating points (GRP) The product of reach times frequency.

guaranteed circulation A stated minimum number of copies of a particular issue of a magazine that will be delivered to readers.

H

habit A decision-making mode in which consumers buy a single brand repeatedly as a solution to a simple consumption problem.

handbill A small sheet printed on engraved wood or copper and distributed by hand.

headline The leading sentence or sentences, usually at the top or bottom of an ad, that attract attention, communicate a key selling point, or achieve brand identification.

heavy-up scheduling Placing advertising in media more heavily when consumers show buying tendencies.

heavy users Consumers who purchase a product or service much more frequently than others.

highly industrialized countries Countries with both a high GNP and a high standard of living.

hits The number of pages and graphical images requested from a Web site.

household consumers The most conspicuous of the five types of audiences for advertising; most mass media advertising is directed at them.

households using television (HUT) A measure of the number of households tuned to a television program during a particular time period.

I

illustration In the context of advertising, the drawing, painting, photography, or computer-generated art that forms the picture in an advertisement.

illustration format The way the product is displayed in a print advertisement.

Industrial Revolution A major change in Western society beginning in the mid-eighteenth century and marked by a rapid change from an agricultural to an industrial economy.

industry analysis In an advertising plan, the section that focuses on developments and trends within an industry and on any other factors that may make a difference in how an advertiser proceeds with an advertising plan.

inelasticity of demand Strong loyalty to a product, resulting in consumers being less sensitive to price increases.

infomercial A long advertisement that looks like a talk show or a half-hour product demonstration.

informal balance An asymmetrical presentation in an ad—nonsimilar sizes and shapes are optically weighed.

information intermediator An organization that collects customer purchase transaction histories, aggregates them across many firms that have sold merchandise to these customers, and then sells the customer names and addresses back to the firms that originally sold to these customers.

in-house agency The advertising department of a firm.

inquiry/direct response measures A type of posttest message tracking in which a print or broadcast advertisement offers the audience the opportunity to place an inquiry or respond directly through a reply card or toll-free number.

in-store sampling A type of sampling that occurs at the point of purchase and is popular for food products and cosmetics.

integrated marketing communications (IMC) The process of using promotional tools in a unified way so that a synergistic communications effect is created.

integrated programming Programming produced through the combined efforts of advertisers, entertainment companies, and media operators.

interactive agencies Advertising agencies that help advertisers prepare communications for new media like the Internet, interactive kiosks, CD-ROMs, and interactive television.

interactive media Media that allow consumers to call up games, entertainment, shopping opportunities, and educational programs on a subscription or pay-per-view basis.

internal lists An organization's records of its customers, subscribers, donors, and inquirers, used to develop better relationships with current customers.

internal position The niche a brand achieves with regard to the other similar brands a firm markets.

internal search A search for product information that draws on personal experience and prior knowledge.

international advertising The preparation and placement of advertising in different national and cultural markets.

international affiliates Foreign-market advertising agencies with which a local agency has established a relationship to handle clients' international advertising needs.

Internet A vast global network of scientific, military, and research computers that allows people inexpensive access to the largest storehouse of information in the world.

Internet relay chat (IRC) A component of the Internet that makes it possible for users to "talk" electronically with each other, despite their geographical separation.

involvement The degree of perceived relevance and personal importance accompanying the choice of a certain product or service within a particular context.

J, K, L

layout A drawing of a proposed print advertisement, showing where all the elements in the ad are positioned.

less-developed countries Countries whose economies lack almost all the resources necessary for development: capital, infrastructure, political stability, and trained workers.

letterpress The oldest and most versatile method of printing, in which text and images are printed from a plate or mat.

lifestyle segmentation A form of market segmenting that focuses on consumers' activities, interests, and opinions.

limited problem solving A decision-making mode in which consumers' experience and involvement are both low.

LISTSERVs Electronic mailing lists on the Internet.

live production The process of creating a live television commercial, which can result in realism and the capturing of spontaneous reactions and events but comes with a loss of control that can threaten the objectives of the commercial.

live script radio ad A detailed script read by an on-air radio personality.

local advertising Advertising directed at an audience in a single trading area, either a city or state.

local agency An advertising agency in a foreign market hired because of its knowledge of the culture and local market conditions.

localized campaigns Advertising campaigns that involve preparing different messages and creative executions for each foreign market a firm has entered.

local spot radio advertising Radio advertising placed directly with individual stations rather than with a network or syndicate.

local television Television programming other than the network broadcast that independent stations and network affiliates offer local audiences.

log analysis software Measurement software that allows a Web site to track hits, pages, visits, and users as well as audience traffic within the site.

M

mailing list A file of names and addresses that an organization might use for contacting prospective or prior customers.

mail sampling A type of sampling in which samples are delivered through the postal service.

marcom manager A marketing-communications manager who plans an organization's overall communications program and oversees the various functional specialists inside and outside the organization to ensure that they are working together to deliver the desired message to the customer.

market analysis In an advertising plan, the section that examines the factors that drive and determine the market for a firm's product or service.

marketing The process of conceiving, pricing, promoting, and distributing ideas, goods, and services to create exchanges that benefit consumers and organizations.

marketing database A mailing list that also includes information collected directly from individual customers.

marketing mix The blend of the four responsibilities of marketing—conception, pricing, promotion, and distribution—used for a particular idea, product, or service.

marketing research The systematic gathering, recording, and interpretation of information related to all marketing mix variables.

market niche A relatively small group of consumers who have a unique set of needs and who typically are willing to pay a premium price to a firm that specializes in meeting those needs.

market segmentation The breaking down of a large, heterogeneous market into submarkets or segments that are more homogeneous.

markup charge A method of agency compensation based on adding a percentage charge to a variety of services the agency purchases from outside suppliers.

meaningfulness In advertising research, a term used to describe the import of the information gathered.

mechanicals Carefully prepared pasteups of the exact components of an advertisement, prepared specifically for the printer.

media-buying service An independent organization that specializes in buying media time and space, particularly on radio and television, as a service to advertising agencies and advertisers.

media class A broad category of media, such as television, radio, or newspapers.

media mix The blend of different media that will be used to effectively reach the target audience.

media objectives The specific goals for a media placement: Reach the target audience, determine the geographic scope of placement, and identify the message weight, which determines the overall audience size.

media plan A plan specifying the media in which advertising messages will be placed to reach the desired target audience.

media-scheduling and -buying models Computerized media-planning models that allow media planners to develop and then evaluate alternative media schedules.

media strategy models Computerized media-planning models that compare media plans by focusing on the issues of reach, frequency, and efficiency.

media vehicle A particular option for placement within a media class (e.g., *Newsweek* is a media vehicle within the magazine media class).

medium The means by which an illustration in a print advertisement is rendered: either drawing, photography, or computer graphics.

membership groups Groups an individual interacts with in person on some regular basis.

members of business organizations One of the five types of audiences for advertising; the focus of advertising for firms that produce business and industrial goods and services.

members of a trade channel One of the five types of audiences for advertising; the retailers, wholesalers, and distributors targeted by producers of both household and business goods and services.

measured media Media that are closely measured to determine advertising costs and effectiveness: television, radio, newspapers, magazines, and outdoor media.

merchandise allowances A type of trade-market sales promotion in which free products are packed with regular shipments as payment to the trade for setting up and maintaining displays.

message What is said and/or shown in an advertisement or advertising campaign.

message strategy A component of an advertising strategy, it defines the goals of the advertiser and how those goals will be achieved.

message weight A sum of the total audience size of all the media specified in a media plan.

mobile sampling A type of sampling carried out by logo-emblazoned vehicles that dispense samples, coupons, and premiums to consumers at malls, shopping centers, fairgrounds, and recreational areas.

monopoly power The ability of a firm to make it impossible for rival firms to compete with the firm, either through advertising or in some other way.

multi-attribute attitude models (MAAMs) A framework and set of procedures for collecting information from consumers to assess their salient beliefs and attitudes about competitive brands.

N

narrowcasting The development and delivery of specialized television programming to well-defined audiences.

narrative Advertising copy that simply displays a series of statements about a brand.

national advertising Advertising that reaches all geographic areas of one nation.

National Advertising Review Board A body formed by the advertising industry to oversee its practice.

national spot radio advertising Radio advertising placed in nationally syndicated radio programming.

need state A psychological state arising when one's desired state of affairs differs from one's actual state of affairs.

network radio advertising Radio advertising placed within national network programs.

network television A type of television that broadcasts programming over airwaves to affiliate stations across the United States under a contract agreement.

newly industrialized countries Countries where traditional ways of life that have endured for centuries change into modern consumer cultures in a few short years.

nonusers A market segment made up of consumers who do not use a particular product or service.

O

objective-and-task approach A method of advertising budgeting that focuses on the relationship between spending and advertising objectives by identifying the specific tasks necessary to achieve different aspects of the advertising objectives.

off-network syndication Television programs that were previously run in network prime time.

offset lithography A printing process in which a flat, chemically treated surface attracts ink to the areas to be printed and repels ink from other areas; the inked image is then transferred to a rubber blanket on a roller, and from the roller the impression is carried to paper.

Old English A typeface with elaborate overlapping strokes.

online editing The transferring of the finalized rough cut of a television ad onto one-inch videotape, which is of on-air quality suitable for media transmission.

on-package sampling A type of sampling in which a sample item is attached to another product package.

on-sale date The date on which a magazine is issued to subscribers and for newsstand distribution.

out-of-home media The combination of transit and billboard advertising.

P

pages The particular pages sent from a Web site to a requesting site.

paid circulation The number of copies of a newspaper sold through subscriptions and newsstand distribution.

parallel layout structure A print ad design that employs art on the right-hand side of the page and repeats the art on the left-hand side.

participation A way of buying television advertising time in which several different advertisers buy commercial time during a specific television program.

pass-along readership An additional number of people, other than the original readers, who may see a magazine.

percentage-of-sales approach An advertising budgeting approach that calculates the advertising budget based on a percentage of the prior year's sales or the projected year's sales.

peripheral cues The features of an ad other than the actual arguments about the brand's performance.

physiological measures A type of pretest message research that uses physiological measurement devices to detect how consumers react to messages, based on physical responses.

pica A measure of the width of lines of type.

picturing Creating representations of things.

pilot testing A form of message evaluation consisting of experimentation in the marketplace.

point A measure of the size of type in height.

P-O-P advertising Advertising that appears at the point of purchase.

positioning The process of designing a product or service so that it can occupy a distinct and valued place in the target consumer's mind, and then communicating this distinctiveness through advertising.

positioning strategy The key themes or concepts an organization features for communicating the distinctiveness of its product or service to the target segment.

posttest message tracking Advertising research that assesses the performance of advertisements during or after the launch of an advertising campaign.

preferred position A basis of buying newspaper ad space, in which the ad is placed in a specific section of the paper.

premiums Items that feature the logo of a sponsor and that are offered free, or at a reduced price, with the purchase of another item.

preprinted insert An advertisement delivered to a newspaper fully printed and ready for insertion into the newspaper.

preproduction The stage in the television production process in which the advertiser and advertising agency (or in-house agency staff) carefully work out the precise details of how the creative planning behind an ad can best be brought to life with the opportunities offered by television.

price-off deal A type of sales promotion that offers a consumer cents or even dollars off merchandise at the point of purchase through specially marked packages.

primary demand stimulation Using advertising to create demand for a product category in general.

principle of limited liability An economic principle that allows an investor to risk only his or her shares of a corporation, rather than personal wealth, in business ventures.

principles of design General rules governing the elements within a print advertisement and the arrangement of and relationship between these elements.

private label brands Brands developed and marketed by members of a trade channel; they usually carry the retailer's name.

proactive public relations strategy A public relations strategy that is dictated by marketing objectives, seeks to publicize a company and its brands, and is offensive in spirit rather than defensive.

product differentiation The process of creating a perceived difference, in the mind of the consumer, between an organization's product or service and the competition's.

production stage The point at which the storyboard and script for a television ad come to life and are filmed. Also called the *shoot*.

production timetable A realistic schedule for all the preproduction, production, and postproduction activities involved with making a television commercial.

professionals One of the five types of audiences for advertising, defined as doctors, lawyers, accountants, teachers, or any other professionals who require special training or certification.

program rating The percentage of television households that are in a market and are tuned to a specific program during a specific time period.

projective techniques A type of developmental research designed to allow consumers to project thoughts and feelings (conscious or unconscious) in an indirect and unobtrusive way onto a theoretically neutral stimulus.

psychogalvanometer A type of physiological measure that detects galvanic skin response—minute changes in perspiration that suggest arousal related to some stimulus (such as an advertisement).

psychographics A form of market research that emphasizes the understanding of consumers' activities, interests, and opinions.

publicity Unpaid-for media exposure about a firm's activities or its products and services.

public relations A marketing and management function that focuses on communications that foster goodwill between a firm and its many constituent groups.

public relations audit An internal study that identifies the characteristics of a firm or the aspects of the firm's activities that are positive and newsworthy.

public relations firms Firms that handle the needs of organizations regarding relationships with the local community, competitors, industry associations, and government organizations.

public relations plan A plan that identifies the objectives and activities related to the public relations communications issued by a firm.

puffery The use of absolute superlatives like "Number One" and "Best in the World" in advertisements.

pulsing A media-scheduling strategy that combines elements from continuous and flighting techniques; advertisements are scheduled continuously in media over a period of time, but with periods of much heavier scheduling.

purchase intent A measure of whether or not a consumer intends to buy a product or service in the near future.

Pure Food and Drug Act A 1906 act of Congress requiring manufacturers to list the active ingredients of their products on their labels.

push strategy A sales promotion strategy in which marketers devise incentives to encourage purchases by members of the trade to help push a product into the distribution channel.

Q, R

radio networks A type of radio that delivers programming via satellite to affiliate stations across the United States.

radio syndication A type of radio that provides complete programs to stations on a contract basis.

rate card A form given to advertisers by a newspaper and containing information on costs, closing times, specifications for submitting an ad, and special pages or features available in the newspaper.

ratings point A measure indicating that 1 percent of all the television households in an area were tuned to the program measured.

reach The number of people or households in a target audience that will be exposed to a media vehicle or schedule at least one time during a given period of time. It is often expressed as a percentage.

reactive public relations strategy A public relations strategy that is dictated by influences outside the control of a company, focuses on problems to be solved rather than opportunities, and requires defensive rather than offensive measures.

readership A measure of a newspaper's circulation multiplied by the number of readers of a copy.

reference group Any configuration of other persons that a particular individual uses as a point of reference in making his or her own consumption decisions.

regional advertising Advertising carried out by producers, wholesalers, distributors, and retailers that concentrate their efforts in a particular geographic region.

reliability In advertising research, a term used to describe research that generates generally consistent findings over time.

repeat purchase A second purchase of a new product after trying it for the first time.

repositioning Returning to the process of segmenting, targeting, and positioning a product or service to arrive at a revised positioning strategy.

resonance test A type of message assessment in which the goal is to determine to what extent the message resonates or rings true with target audience members.

RFM analysis An analysis of how recently and how frequently a customer is buying from an organization, and of how much that customer is spending per order and over time.

riding the boards Assessing possible locations for billboard advertising.

rituals Repeated behaviors that affirm, express, and maintain cultural values.

roman The most popular category of type; it includes typefaces with serifs.

rough cut An assembly of the best scenes from a television ad shoot edited together using digital technology.

rough layout The second stage of the ad layout process, in which the headline is lettered in and the elements of the ad are further refined

run-of-paper (ROP) A basis of buying newspaper ad space, in which an ad may appear anywhere, on any page in the paper.

run-of-press A basis of buying magazine ad space, in which an ad may appear anywhere in the magazine, at the discretion of the publisher.

S

sales promotion The use of incentive techniques that create a perception of greater brand value among consumers or distributors.

sales promotion specialists Persons who design and then operate contests, sweepstakes, special displays, or couponing campaigns for advertisers.

salient beliefs A small number of beliefs that are the critical determinants of an attitude.

sampling A sales promotion technique designed to provide a consumer with a trial opportunity.

sans serif A category of type that includes typefaces with no small lines crossing the ends the main strokes.

scratch track A rough approximation of the musical score of a television ad, using only a piano and vocalists.

screen printing A printing process that employs a stencil produced on a screen. Also called *silk screening*.

script The written version of an ad; it specifies the coordination of the copy elements with the video scenes.

search engine A software tool used to find Web sites on the Internet by searching for keywords typed in by the user.

secondary data Information obtained from existing sources.

second cover page The inside front cover of a magazine.

selective attention The processing of only a few advertisements among the many encountered.

selective demand stimulation Using advertising to stimulate demand for a specific brand within a product category.

self-liquidating premium A sales promotion that requires a consumer to pay most of the cost of the item received as a premium.

self-reference criterion (SRC) The unconscious reference to one's own cultural values, experiences, and knowledge as a basis for decisions.

semicomp The third stage of the ad layout process, in which display type is lettered in; it is often used for preliminary presentations to the client.

sentence and picture completion A type of projective technique in which a researcher presents consumers with part of a picture or a sentence with words deleted and then asks that the stimulus be completed; the picture or sentence relates to one or several brands.

serifs The small lines that cross the ends of the main strokes in type.

share of audience A measure of the proportion of households that are using television during a specific time period and are tuned to a particular program.

share of voice A calculation of any advertiser's brand expenditures relative to the overall spending in a category.

shoot See **production stage**.

simulation models Computerized media-planning models that compare alternative media plans by computing the hypothetical effects of different plans on factors like reach, store traffic, information requests, and coupon redemption.

single-source tracking measures A type of posttest message tracking that provides information about brand purchases, coupon use, and television advertising exposure by combining grocery store scanner data and devices that monitor household television-viewing behavior.

single-source tracking services Research services that offer information not just on demographics but also on brands, purchase size, prices paid, and media exposure.

situation analysis In an advertising plan, the section in which the advertiser lays out the most important factors that define the situation, and then explains the importance of each factor.

slab serif A category of type that includes typefaces similar to sans serif typefaces but having serifs and employing varying thicknesses of letters.

slogan A short phrase in part used to help establish an image, identity, or position for a brand or an organization, but mostly used to increase memorability.

slotting fees A type of trade-market sales promotion in which manufacturers make direct cash payments to retailers to ensure shelf space.

social class A person's standing in the hierarchy resulting from the systematic inequalities in the social system.

social meaning What a product or service means in a societal context.

social tableau A representation of ordinary life used in an advertisement to suggest how to fit in with the smart crowd.

society A group of people living in a particular area who share a common culture and consider themselves a distinct and unified entity.

space contract A contract that establishes a rate for all advertising placed in a magazine by an advertiser over a specified period.

space order A commitment by an advertiser to advertising space in a particular issue of a magazine. Also called an *insertion order*.

spam To post messages to many unrelated newsgroups on Usenet.

specialty-advertising items Items used for advertising purposes and that have three defining elements: (1) they contain the sponsor's logo and perhaps a related promotional message; (2) this logo and message appear on a useful or decorative item; and (3) the item is given freely, as a gift from the sponsor.

split-cable transmission A type of pilot testing in which two different versions of an advertisement are transmitted to two separate samples of similar households within a single, well-defined market area; the ads are then compared on measures of exposure, recall, and persuasion.

split-list experiment A type of pilot testing in which multiple versions of a direct mail piece are prepared and sent to various segments of a mailing list; the version that pulls the best is deemed superior.

split-run distribution A type of pilot testing in which two different versions of an advertisement are placed in every other issue of a magazine; the ads are then compared on the basis of direct response.

sponsor See **client**.

sponsorship A way of buying television advertising time in which an advertiser agrees to pay for the production of a television program and for most (and often all) of the advertising that appears in the program.

spot advertising A way of buying television advertising time in which airtime is purchased through local television stations.

standard advertising unit (SAU) One of 57 defined sizes of newspaper advertisements.

still production A technique of television ad production whereby a series of photographs or slides is filmed and edited so that the resulting ad appears to have movement and action.

storyboard A frame-by-frame sketch or photo sequence depicting, in sequence, the visual scenes and copy that will be used in an advertisement.

story construction A type of projective technique that asks consumers to tell a story about people depicted in a scene or picture, as a way of gathering information about a brand.

straight-line copy Advertising copy that explains in straightforward terms why a reader will benefit from use of a product or service.

subhead In an advertisement, a few words or a short sentence that usually appears above or below the headline and includes important brand information not included in the headline.

subliminal advertising Advertising alleged to work on a subconscious level.

support media Media used to reinforce a message being delivered via some other media vehicle.

sweepstakes A sales promotion in which winners are determined purely by chance.

switchers A market segment made up of consumers who often buy what is on sale or choose brands that offer discount coupons or other price incentives. Also called *variety seekers.*

symbolic value What a product or service means to consumers in a nonliteral way.

T

target audience A particular group of consumers singled out for an advertisement or advertising campaign.

target segment The subgroup (of the larger market) chosen as the focal point for the marketing program and advertising campaign.

telemarketing A direct-marketing medium that involves using the telephone to deliver a spoken appeal.

television households An estimate of the number of households that are in a market and own a television.

testimonial An advertisement in which an advocacy position is taken by a spokesperson.

theater test A type of pretest message research in which advertisements are tested in small theaters; members of the theater audience have an electronic device through which they can express how much they like or dislike the advertisements shown.

third cover page The inside back cover of a magazine.

thought listing A type of pretest message research that tries to identify specific thoughts that may be generated by an advertisement.

three-point layout structure A print ad design that establishes three elements in an ad as dominant forces.

thumbnails, or thumbnail sketches The rough first drafts of an ad layout, roughly one-quarter the size of the finished ad.

top-of-the-mind awareness Keen consumer awareness of a certain brand, indicated by listing that brand first when asked to name a number of brands.

trade-market sales promotion A type of sales promotion designed to motivate distributors, wholesalers, and retailers to stock and feature a firm's brand in their merchandising programs.

trade shows Events where several related products from many manufacturers are displayed and demonstrated to members of the trade.

traditional support media Support media that have been around for years: outdoor billboard advertising, transit and aerial advertising, specialty advertising, point-of-purchase advertising, and directory advertising.

transit advertising Advertising that appears as both interior and exterior displays on mass transit vehicles and at terminal and station platforms.

trial offers A type of sales promotion in which expensive items are offered on a trial basis to induce consumer trial of a brand.

trustworthiness In advertising research, a term used to describe information that can be trusted.

type font A basic set of typeface letters.

U

unfair advertising Defined by Congress as "acts or practices that cause or are likely to cause substantial injury to consumers, which is not reasonably avoidable by consumers themselves and not outweighed by the countervailing benefits to consumers or competition."

unique selling proposition (USP) A promise contained in an advertisement in which the advertised brand offers a specific, unique, and relevant benefit to the consumer.

unit-of-sales approach An approach to advertising budgeting that allocates a specified dollar amount of advertising for each unit of a brand sold (or expected to be sold).

unmeasured media Media less-formally measured for advertising costs and effectiveness (as compared to the measured media): direct mail, catalogs, special events, and other ways to reach business and household consumers.

Usenet A collection of more than 13,000 discussion groups on the Internet.

user positioning A positioning option that focuses on a specific profile of the target user.

users The number of different people visiting X Web site during Y time.

V

validity In advertising research, a term used to describe information that is relevant to the research questions being investigated.

value A perception by consumers that a product or service provides satisfaction beyond the cost incurred to acquire the product or service.

value pricing The strategy of offering good-quality products at low prices to attract a high volume of customers.

values The defining expressions of culture, demonstrating in words and deeds what is important to a culture.

variety seekers *See* **switchers**.

variety seeking A decision-making mode in which consumers switch their selection among various brands in a given category in a random pattern.

vertical cooperative advertising An advertising technique whereby a manufacturer and dealer (either a wholesaler or retailer) share the expense of advertising.

videotape An option for television ad production that is less expensive than film but also of lower quality.

virtual mall A gateway to a group of Internet storefronts that provide access to mall sites by simply clicking on a storefront.

visits The number of occasions on which a user X looked up Y Web site during Z time.

vulnerabilities From a public relations standpoint, weaknesses in a firm's operations or products that can negatively affect its relationships with important constituents.

W

white space In a print advertisement, space not filled with a headline, subhead, body copy, or illustration.

within-vehicle duplication Exposure to the same advertisement in the same media at different times.

World Wide Web (WWW) A universal database of information available to most Internet users; its graphical environment makes navigation simple and exciting.

X, Y, Z

zapping The process of eliminating advertisements altogether from videotaped programs.

zipping The process of fast-forwarding through advertisements contained in videotaped programs.

Name/Brand/Company Index

Subject Index

Credits

23 Courtesy of Toshiba America Consumer Products, Inc. (top right).

23 Reprinted with the permission of General Motors Corporation (bottom).

24 ©1995 Lever Brothers Company "All" Laundry Detergent. Courtesy of Lever Brothers Company (left).

24 ©1995 Sears, Roebuck and Co. Reprinted with permission (right).

25 ©1993 American Plastics Council. Reprinted by permission.

28 Photo courtesy of Levi Strauss & Co. (top).

28 Ray-Ban sunglasses by Baush & Lomb. ©1995 Bausch & Lomb Incorporated. Reprinted by permission (bottom).

29 Courtesy of United Airlines (left).

29 ©1994 Waterford Wedgwood USA, Inc. Reprinted by permission (middle).

29 Courtesy of Gucci (right).

Chapter 2

32 ©1994-Sassaby Inc. Reprinted by permission.

34 Courtesy of The Coca-Cola Company.

43 Courtesy of the Pillsbury Company.

47 Courtesy of J. Walter Thompson Company (top).

47 Courtesy of Arian, Lowe & Travis Advertising-Chicago (bottom).

49 ©1994-Sassaby Inc. Reprinted by permission.

Chapter 3

54 Courtesy of Lever Brothers Company.

57 Courtesy of Lever Brothers Company.

62 Courtesy of Lever Brothers Company.

65 Courtesy of The Coca-Cola Company.

67 Courtesy of IBM Corporation (bottom left).

67 Courtesy of Chrysler Corporation (top).

67 Courtesy of Serta, Inc., Des Plaines, Illinois (bottom right).

68 ©Kellogg Company, ©1968 Kellogg Company; used with permission (top left).

68 Courtesy of Avis, Inc., Garden City, New York (top right).

68 Courtesy of Sears, Roebuck and Co. (bottom).

69 Reproduced with permission of PepsiCo, Inc., 1995 Purchase, New York (left).

69 Courtesy of Goodyear Tire & Rubber Company (right).

70 Photo courtesy of Polaroid Corporation; "Polaroid" and "One Step"® (left).

70 Courtesy of Nestle U.S.A., Inc. (middle).

70 Courtesy of Chrysler Corporation (right).

71 Courtesy of Kloster Cruise Line (left).

71 Courtesy of the Republican National Committee (right).

72 Reproduced with permission of PepsiCo, Inc., 1995, Purchase, New York.

Chapter 4

78 Courtesy of Partnership for a Drug-Free America.

81 ©1990 Anheuser-Busch, Inc., St. Louis, MO. Reprinted by permission (left).

81 The Facing HIV and AIDS campaign is a collaborative effort by the Asian Pacific AIDS Intervention Team and Pacific Asian Language Services of Special Service for Groups and Healthier Solutions, Inc., under a CARE grant from the County of Los Angeles Department of Health Services, AIDS Programs office (right).

83 Courtesy of Gianni Versace Home Signature.

84 Courtesy of Good Humor-Breyers Ice Cream (left).

84 Courtesy of Johnson & Johnson (right).

85 Courtesy of Lachman Imports.

88 ©1996 The Andy Warhol Foundation, Inc.

89 Courtesy of Partnership for a Drug-Free America.

Chapter 5

116 Ad reproduced with permission from Fox Broadcasting Company, 1995. Created and produced by Fox in-house print advertising. All rights reserved.

118 Courtesy of Lexus and Team One Advertising.

121 Courtesy Johnson & Johnson.

122 ©General Motor Corp.: used with permission.

123 Courtesy of Chrysler Corporation (top).

123 Courtesy of Acura Division, American Honda Motor Co., Inc. (bottom).

124 Courtesy of Campbell Soup Company.

125 Courtesy of Northwest Airlines.

127 Courtesy of American Isuzu Motors Inc.

128 Courtesy of Casio, Inc.

129 Courtesy of IAMS Food Company.

129 Courtesy of DeBeers Consolidated Mines, Ltd., and J. Walter Thompson (bottom).

130 Courtesy of Chrysler Corporation.

131 Courtesy Wendy's International.

134 Courtesy of Sears, Roebuck and Co.

136 Courtesy of Metropolitan Detroit Convention and Visitors Bureau.

139 Courtesy of Slater Hanft Martin (for Foster Grant). Raboy Stoner Advertising: Doug Raboy copywriter and Ken Ferris art director (left).

139 Courtesy of Mrs. Smith's Inc. (right).

141 Courtesy of Johnston & Murphy, Nashville, TN.

144 Reprinted by permission of Jaguar Cars Ltd. (left).

144 Courtesy of Wolverine Work Boots, Wolverine World Wide, Inc. (middle).

144 Courtesy Reebok, Inc. (right).

145 Ad reproduced with permission from Fox Broadcasting Company, 1995. Created and produced by Fox in-house print advertising. All rights reserved.

146 Courtesy of Fan Fair Store and BVK McDonald Advertising.

147 Bobby Holland, photographer, Holland Productions. Used with permission of General Mills (left).

147 Courtesy of United Airlines/Leo Burnett (middle).

147 Courtesy of Sprint Communications and Sosa, Bromley, Aguilar, Noble & Associates, 1996 (right).

148 Courtesy of Olivia Cruises & Resorts, Oakland, CA. Graphic design by Laura Parker Design, San Francisco, CA and photo by Helga Sigvaldadotir, San Francisco, CA (left).

148 Courtesy of Company Q (right).

150 Courtesy of Saturn Corporation.

151 Courtesy of Kingdom Computers (left).

151 Courtesy of The Upjohn Company (right).

Chapter 6

154 Courtesy of Rykä and Mullen Advertising.

156 Courtesy of Southland Corporation. Agency J. Walter Thompson, Chicago; creative director Matt Canzano; copy Steve Romenghi; director Tennay Fairchild.

158 ©1996 Olive Brumskill/Allsport (left).

158 ©1996 Chris Cole/Allsport (right).

161 ©1994 American Express Travel Related Services Company, Inc. Reprinted with permission.

163 Courtesy of JADO Bathroom and Hardware Manufacturing Corp.

165 Courtesy of Pillsbury Company; created by Foote, Cone & Belding (Chicago) (left).

165 Courtesy of Pillsbury Company; created by Leo Burnett (Chicago) (right).

167 Ad for Mitsubishi Motor Sales of America, Inc., created by G2 Advertising. Photography by Vic Huber. Reprinted by permission (top).

167 Copyright, Nissan 1995. Reproduced by permission (middle).

167 Courtesy of Volvo (bottom).

169 Reprinted by permission of Svetlana Electron Devices. Created in house by Svetlana Electron Devices. Creative Director: Terri Bates; Photographer: Jared Cassidy.

171 Courtesy of State Farm Insurance Companies.

172 ©General Motors Corp.; used with permission (left).

172 Courtesy of Apple Computer (right).

173 Courtesy of Rykä and Mullen Advertising.

174 Courtesy of Norwegian Cruise Line (left).

174 Property of Carnival Cruise Lines (right).

175 Courtesy of Volvo (left).

175 Reproduced with permission of PepsiCo, Inc., 1995, Purchase, New York (right).

177 Toshiba America Information Systems, Inc., Computer Systems Division.

179 Courtesy of Donna Karan (top left).

179 Courtesy of Saab Cars USA, Inc. (top middle and top right).

179 Courtesy of Virginia Power/Richmond, Virginia (bottom).

Chapter 7

182 JELL-O is a registered trademark of Kraft Foods, Inc.; used with permission.

184 Courtesy of the Goodyear Tire & Rubber Company

188 Courtesy of Harris Marketing Group.

190 JELL-O is a registered trademark of Kraft Foods, Inc.; used with permission.

192 Courtesy Sun-Maid Growers of California.

195 ©Jim Holland/Stock•Boston #JRH 1943C

200 Courtesy Campbell Soup Company.

201 Reprinted with permission of General Motors Corporation (top).

201 Courtesy of Ford Motor Company (bottom left).

201 Reprinted with permission of General Motors Corporation (bottom right).

202   Courtesy of E★Trade Securities.

Chapter 8

210   ©Anthony Suau/Gamma Liaison Network.

213   ©Anthony Suau/Gamma Liaison Network.

214   Screenshots reprinted with permission from Microsoft® Corporation.

215   Screen shots reprinted with permission from Microsoft® Corporation (top).

215   Courtesy Microsoft® Corporation (bottom).

217   ©1996 American Express Travel Related Services Company, Inc. Reprinted with permission.

218   ©American Express. All rights reserved. Reprinted with permission.

220   Courtesy of the Pillsbury Company.

Chapter 9

234   ©1994 Oneida Ltd.

237   ©Apple Computer, Inc. Used with permission. All rights reserved. Apple® and the Apple logo are registered trademarks of Apple Computer, Inc. (left)

237   Courtesy of McDonald's Corporation (right).

238   Courtesy of PepsiCo.

241   Courtesy of Tropicana Dole Beverages North America.

243   Courtesy of Schieffelin & Somerset Co., 2 Park Avenue, New York, NY 10016 (left).

243   Courtesy of International Business Machines Corporation (right).

245   Courtesy of Warner-Lambert Company. Lady Protector de Wilkinson is available in the French Market; it is a trademark of Wilkinson Sword GmbH (left).

245   Courtesy of Panzani-William Saurin (right).

247   Courtesy of Kenwood USA. Created by Citron, Haligman and Bedecarre, San Francisco, California, for Kenwood USA (top right).

247   ©1994 Oneida Ltd. (middle).

247   ©1995 Champagnes P. & C. Heidsieck, S.A. All rights reserved (bottom).

251   Courtesy SkyPort TV, CS Service Center Corporation, Yokohama, Japan.

254   Courtesy of Jack Daniel Distillery (left).

254   Courtesy of Jack Daniel Distillery (right).

257   Courtesy of Yokohama Rubber Company, Tokyo, Japan; advertising agency IDUE.

Chapter 10

270   Courtesy of The Coca-Cola Company.

273   ©Apple Computer, Inc. Used with permission. All rights reserved. Apple® and the Apple logo are registered trademarks of Apple Computer, Inc.

275   Courtesy of The Coca-Cola Company.

278   ©Heinz Pet Products.

280   Art director and headline: Ted R. Killian. Creative director and copywriter: Evan A. Skopp. Photos: Mary Temme, Robert John, and Kim Stephenson. ©1995 Seymour Duncan.

281   Courtesy of Schieffelin & Somerset Co., 2 Park Avenue, New York, NY 10016 (bottom).

281   Tabu by Dana Perfumes, 635 Madison Avenue, New York City. Courtesy of Corbin & Associates, Ltd. (top).

282   Courtesy of Portland General Electric.

285   Courtesy of Swisher International.

286   Courtesy CNS, Inc., manufacturer of Breathe Right nasal strips (left).

286   Courtesy of Putnam Investments (right).

287   Courtesy of Rayovac Corporation.

290   Courtesy of Young & Rubicam Agency. Creative director/writer Peter Angelos, art director Charlie McQuilkin, director Dan Barbieri, writer Keith Goldberg.

293   Courtesy of FannieMae.

Chapter 11

296   Courtesy of Intel Corporation.

299   Courtesy Richmond Technical Center (bottom left).

300   Courtesy of Avis Rent A Car System, Inc. (left).

300   Courtesy of C. F. Hathaway (right).

301   Reprinted with the permission of General Motors Corporation.

303   Courtesy Miller Brewing Company.

304   Courtesy MCI.

304   Courtesy of the U.S. Army (right).

305   Courtesy of Intel Corporation (top).

305   Courtesy of Goldsmith Jeffrey: Noam Murro, art director; Eddie Van Blaem, copy writer; Gary Goldsmith, creative director: Ilan Rubin, photographer (bottom).

306   Courtesy of Motorola, Inc. (left).

306   Courtesy of Unum Corporation and its advertising agency, Goodby, Silverstein & Partners, ©1996 Unum Corporation. Unum®, the lighthouse artwork, "We see farther," and "Here's to a long life" are service marks of Unum Corporation (top right).

306   Courtesy of The Pierre Smirnoff Company (bottom right).

307   Courtesy of The Clorox Company.

311   Courtesy of Toyota Motor Sales Australia, Ltd. (radio script).

Chapter 12

320   ©Apple Computer, Inc. Used with permission. All rights reserved. Apple® and the Apple logo and registered trademarks of Apple Computer, Inc.

323   Reprinted with permission of Thomson Consumer Electonics, Inc.

325   Reprinted with the permission of The Prudential Insurance Company of America. All rights reserved.

327   Courtesy of Barcardi Martini U.S.A., Inc. (top).

327   By Men's Journal Company, L.P. All rights reserved. Reprinted by permission (bottom).

328   Courtesy of Computer System Organization, Hewlett-Packard.

329   Courtesy of Cannondale Corporation (top).

329   Courtesy of Watkins Manufacturing Corporation, Vista, CA (bottom).

331   ©Apple Computer, Inc. Used with permission. All rights reserved. Apple® and the Apple logo are registered trademarks of Apple Computer, Inc. (top).

331   Courtesy of Digital Equipment Corporation (bottom).

333   Advertisement provided courtesy of Citibank (South Dakota) N.A. and Ford Motor Company (left).

333   Courtesy of Volkswagen and Arnold Fortuna Lawner & Cabot Inc., Advertising (right).

334   Copyright, Nissan 1994. Reproduced by permission. Infiniti is a registered trademark of Nissan.

339   Photography by Joe Higgins.

Chapter 13

344   Stephen Frisch/Stock Boston SUF3230R.

346   Courtesy of Warner-Lambert Company.

348   Reprinted with permission of PepsiCo. Inc., 1996, Purchase, New York.

349   Courtesy of Portland General Electric (bottom).

350   Reprinted with permission of Black & Decker Inc.

351   Courtesy Nation's Bank.

352   Courtesy Miller Brewing Company.

353   Courtesy Miller Brewing Company.

365   ©Stephen Frisch/Stock Boston SUF323OR.

Chapter 14

378   Excerpt reproduced with the permission of Binney & Smith Inc., maker of Crayola products.

380   Courtesy Inline/Online

389   Courtesy of Toyota and Saatchi & Saatchi DFS\Pacific; photos by Michael Raushe, David Lebon, and John Early.

391   Courtesy of The Quaker Oats Company.

399   Courtesy of CNN Airport Network.

402   Excerpt reproduced with the permission of Binney & Smith Inc., maker of Crayola products.

Chapter 15

406   Courtesy of Challenge Publications, Inc., and *Mountain Biking Magazine,* Canoga Park, CA 91304.

409   Courtesy of The Pierre Smirnoff Company.

412   Copyright, Nissan 1994. Reproduced by permission. Infiniti is a registered trademark of Nissan (left).

413   Courtesy of The Peoria Journal Star.

414   Photography by Joe Higgins.

415   Photography by Joe Higgins.

416   Photo Courtesy of Pizza Hut.

417   Courtesy of Leath Furniture Inc. Creative direction Sharron Hutto; art direction Sandia Chen.

418   Courtesy of Schwinn Corporation.

420   Courtesy of Challenge Publications, Inc., and *Mountain Biking Magazine,* Canoga Park, CA 91304 (left).

420   Courtesy of Ogilvy & Mather, Chicago (right).

421   Courtesy of Clarins Corporation.

423   Photography by Joe Higgins.

424– Courtesy of International Business Machines Corpo-
425   ration.

Chapter 16

440   Courtesy of the Museum of Flight, Seattle, Washington.

442   ©Bob Kramer/Stock Boston.